RETROSPECTIVE **ANDY WARHOL**

Heiner Bastian

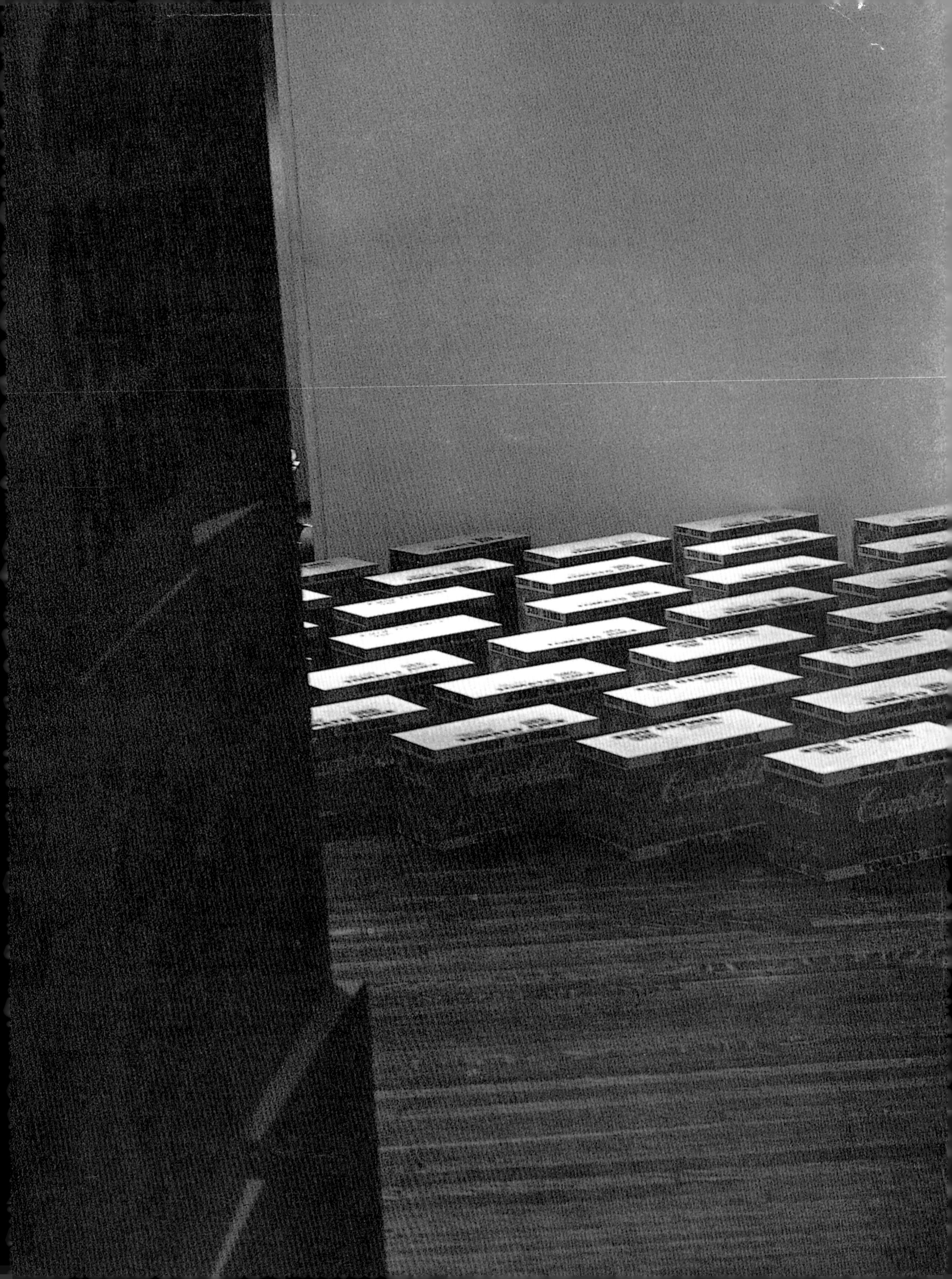

ANDY WARHOL

RETROSPECTIVE

Heiner Bastian

with essays by

Kirk Varnedoe

Donna De Salvo

Peter-Klaus Schuster

Antje Dallmann

Tate Publishing

The Museum of Contemporary Art
Los Angeles

IMPRINT

Andy Warhol Retrospective was organized by Heiner Bastian for the Neue Nationalgalerie, Berlin.

This exhibition is sponsored by Merrill Lynch. *Angeleno Magazine* is the exclusive magazine sponsor.

Generous support has been provided by The Broad Art Foundation; the City of Los Angeles; Lillian P. and Jon B. Lovelace; Jane and Marc Nathanson; Gilbert B. Friesen; Cynthia A. Miscikowski and Douglas Ring; Peter Morton; The Buehler Family Foundation; Maria and William Bell; E. Blake Byrne; Audrey M. Irmas; The Kwon Family; Lisa and T. Willem Mesdag; Paula and Allen Rudnick; Betye Monell Burton; Mandy and Cliff Einstein; Lenore S. and Bernard A. Greenberg; Susan Bay-Nimoy and Leonard Nimoy; Mark Siegel; Pamela and George Smith; the Wolff Family Foundation; Beatrice and Philip Gersh; The MOCA Projects Council; and the Frederick R. Weisman Art Foundation.

Significant promotional support has been provided by the Los Angeles Convention & Visitors Bureau.

ANDY WARHOL RETROSPECTIVE
Neue Nationalgalerie, Berlin, 2 October 2001 – 6 January 2002
Tate Modern, London, 7 February – 1 April 2002
The Museum of Contemporary Art, Los Angeles, 25 May – 18 August 2002

Exhibition and Catalogue: Heiner Bastian

EXHIBITION Exhibition assistants: Antje Dallmann, Nina Koidl · Members of team: Céline Bastian, Jens Kunath, Harriet Häußler, Katharina Hohenhörst, Laetitia von Baeyer · Conservation: Otto Hubacek · Project management for MOCA: Ann Goldstein

PUBLICATION Catalogue design: Heiner Bastian · Design assistants: Jens Kunath, Simone Aulenkamp · Layout of front matter and chronology: Polyform, Berlin · Photograph sources: see Photograph Credits · Lithographic work: K. H. Wächter, Bielefeld · Set and printed by: Druckerei Tiemann GmbH & Co. KG, Bielefeld · Bound by: RIB, Waldbüttelbrunn · The quotation on page 58 is taken from G. R. Swenson, "What Is Pop Art?: Answers from 8 Painters, Part I", *Art News* 62 (November 1963), p. 61. · · Photographic research: Christine Stotz, James Trainor, Elisa Primavera · The exhibition organisers would like to give special thanks to the staff at The Andy Warhol Museum, Pittsburgh, for their unstinting research assistance.

First published in German in 2001 by Neue Nationalgalerie, Berlin · The hardcover edition of the German publication is distributed by DuMont Buchverlag, Cologne. © 2001 Heiner Bastian and the authors.
First published in English in 2001 by order of the Tate Trustees by Tate Publishing, a division of Tate Enterprises Ltd, Millbank, London, SW1P 4RG. This revised edition published in English by Tate Publishing, London, 2002. Reprinted with permission by The Museum of Contemporary Art, Los Angeles, 2002.
English translation of Heiner Bastian's text Fiona Elliott; Peter-Klaus Schuster's text David Britt; Chronology and acknowledgments Helen Atkins · Copyright of English translations: © Tate, 2001.
A catalogue record for this book is available from the British Library ISBN 1 85437 410 9

CONTENTS

THE MUSEUM OF CONTEMPORARY ART, LOS ANGELES

LIST OF FUNDERS

The Broad Art Foundation · City of Los Angeles · Lillian P. and Jon B. Lovelace · Jane and Marc Nathanson · Gilbert B. Friesen · Cynthia A. Miscikowski and Douglas Ring · Peter Morton · The Buehler Family Foundation · Maria and William Bell · E. Blake Byrne · Audrey M. Irmas · The Kwon Family · Lisa and T. Willem Mesdag · Paula and Allen Rudnick · Betye Monell Burton · Mandy and Cliff Einstein · Lenore S. and Bernard A. Greenberg · Susan Bay-Nimoy and Leonard Nimoy · Mark Siegel · Pamela and George Smith · Wolff Family Foundation · Beatrice and Philip Gersh · The MOCA Projects Council · Frederick R. Weisman Art Foundation

The exhibition is sponsored by Merrill Lynch. *Angeleno Magazine* is the exclusive magazine sponsor.

Significant promotional support has been provided by the Los Angeles Convention & Visitors Bureau.

LENDERS

Private Lenders: Mr. and Mrs. Joseph Allen, New York · Doris Ammann, Zurich · Nicolas Berggruen, New York · Bruno Bischofberger, Zurich · Jacqueline and Irving Blum, Los Angeles · Stephanie and Peter Brant, Greenwich, CT · Eli and Edythe L. Broad, Santa Monica, CA · Anne and Anthony d'Offay, London · Anna and Josef W. Froehlich, Stuttgart · Larry Gagosian, New York · Stellan Holm, New York · Ivan Karp, New York · Uli Knecht, Stuttgart · Pamela and Richard Kramlich, San Francisco · Hubert Looser, Zurich · Erich Marx, Berlin · Ute and Reinhard Onnasch, Berlin · Gunter Sachs, Pully, Switzerland · Anders U. Schroeder, London · Ileana Sonnabend, New York · Mrs. John E. Steiner c/o The Andy Warhol Museum, Pittsburgh · Thea Westreich, New York · We would also like to thank those lenders who wish to remain anonymous.

Public Institutions: Ludwig Forum für Internationale Kunst, Aachen · Stedelijk Museum, Amsterdam · Öffentliche Kunstsammlung Basel, Kunstmuseum · Stiftung Sammlung Marx, Hamburger Bahnhof – Museum für Gegenwart, Berlin · Museum of Fine Arts, Boston · Albright-Knox Art Gallery, Buffalo · Kunstsammlung Nordrhein-Westfalen, Düsseldorf · Museum für Moderne Kunst, Frankfurt · The Brant Foundation, Greenwich, CT · The Menil Collection, Houston · Louisiana Museum of Modern Art, Humlebæk, Denmark · The Museum of Contemporary Art, Los Angeles · The Nelson-Atkins Museum of Art, Kansas City, MO · Kunstmuseen der Stadt Krefeld · Tate, London · Los Angeles County Museum of Art · Museum Ludwig, Cologne · Städtisches Museum Abteiberg Mönchengladbach · Bayerische Staatsgemäldesammlungen, Munich · Westdeutsche Spielbanken, Münster · The Metropolitan Museum of Art, New York · The Museum of Modern Art, New York · Norton Simon Museum, Pasadena · The Andy Warhol Museum, Pittsburgh · Carnegie Museum of Art, Pittsburgh · Museum of Contemporary Art, San Diego · Staatsgalerie Stuttgart · Art Gallery of Ontario, Toronto · Daros Collection, Zurich · Galerie Minerva, Zurich

DIRECTOR'S FOREWORD

Jeremy Strick

In 1962 the Ferus Gallery in Los Angeles mounted the now-legendary first solo show of paintings by Andy Warhol. It proved an immediate sensation and established Warhol's reputation as a compelling figure in contemporary art. A second show of Elvis portraits at Ferus the following year further cemented Warhol's renown and brought the artist into contact with members of Los Angeles's art and entertainment communities. In 1970, Los Angeles's landmark position in the history of Warhol's work was firmly fixed when the Pasadena Art Museum organized the first major American retrospective exhibition of his work. Despite his auspicious introduction to Los Angeles, Warhol has not been the subject of a major retrospective in this city for over thirty years.

Images of Hollywood glamour fired Warhol's imagination since childhood. Its icons – Marilyn, Liz, Elvis, and others – served as subjects for some of his greatest and most famous works. Although Warhol did not create the culture of celebrity, he recognized and represented this culture, and in doing so alluded to its importance within American culture at large.

Given the close association of Warhol's work to the city and culture of Los Angeles, it is fitting that MOCA should serve as the only North American venue for this Andy Warhol retrospective. Exhibition curator Heiner Bastian has chosen to concentrate on Warhol's work as a draftsman and painter, giving particular emphasis to the drawings of the 1950s and especially the paintings of the early 60s that effectively launched the artist's career. The effect is powerful, surprising, and stark. Through Bastian's emphasis on the Disaster paintings and Most Wanted Men series, Warhol emerges as an artist of high purpose, a chronicler of his time who uncompromisingly rendered the tragic qualities of contemporary life.

Many individuals played a role in bringing Warhol to MOCA, none so important as Heiner Bastian, who worked with exceptional commitment and diligence to extend the tour of the exhibition from the Neue Nationalgalerie, Berlin, and the Tate Modern, London, to our museum. We remain most deeply grateful to him for his extraordinary efforts and guidance, and to Céline Bastian for organizational assistance. As well, we thank our colleagues at the Tate Modern, especially Director Nicholas Serota and Senior Curator Donna De Salvo. Our thanks also go to the Neue Nationalgalerie, Berlin, where the exhibition started, and in particular to the Director General of the Staatliche Museen zu Berlin, Peter-Klaus Schuster, as well as to Peter Raue, Chairman of the Association of Friends of the Neue Nationalgalerie, for their support and cooperation.

We at MOCA are touched by the outpouring of support for this exhibition. The retrospective would not have been possible without the extraordinary generosity of the lenders who allowed their works to travel to Los Angeles with very little notice. MOCA's Founding Chairman Eli Broad, assisted by the Curator of The Broad Foundation Joanne Heyler, demonstrated his continuing commitment to this institution by initiating discussions with Berlin on MOCA's behalf. The Andy Warhol Foundation for the Visual Arts and its President, Joel Wachs, a longtime advocate of the museum, also played an essential role in bringing the exhibition to MOCA. Los Angeles Mayor James Hahn and the City of Los Angeles provided crucial financial support, which enabled us to mount this ambitious exhibition in such a short time. The Los Angeles Convention & Visitors Bureau lent tremendous promotional support, providing a unique opportunity for the community to become acquainted with Warhol's work.

The exceptional opportunity to bring Warhol to Los Angeles was secured through the visionary commitment of MOCA's Board of Trustees and through the leadership of Chairman Bob Tuttle, whose enthusiasm and commitment to this exhibition have proven inspirational. Numerous trustees came forward to assist, beginning with Jane and Marc Nathanson. This exhibition would not have been possible without the tremendous financial support of these trustees, as well as other individual donors listed elsewhere in this book. I would like to thank the Projects Council for organizing the spectacular gala event, and the UCLA Film and Television Archive and The Andy Warhol Museum, Pittsburgh, for their assistance with the film program, guest-curated by Bruce Hainley. Special thanks go to Thomas Sokolowski, Director of The Andy Warhol Museum, for his unwavering support of this presentation.

The realization of such a remarkable exhibition in just six month's time has been a museum-wide undertaking. I am grateful to everyone at MOCA for their exceptional collaborative efforts. As the exhibition's project director at MOCA, Senior Curator Ann Goldstein enriched the project with her leadership and insight. Chief Curator Paul Schimmel provided invaluable counsel and support. Curatorial Assistant Julia Langlotz worked tirelessly to coordinate all aspects of the MOCA presentation. Manager of Exhibitions and Curatorial Affairs Stacia Payne lent exceptional administrative support to the project. The organization of the MOCA edition of the exhibition catalogue was ably overseen by Senior Editor Lisa Mark. Educational programs offered in conjunction with the exhibition were thoughtfully developed by Director of Education Suzanne Isken and Adult Programs Coordinator Caroline Blackburn.

The stunning installation in MOCA's galleries reflects the excellent efforts of our exhibition team, including Director of Exhibitions Production Brian Gray, Chief Exhibition Technician Jang Park, Exhibitions Production Coordinator Zazu Faure, and Media Arts Technical Manager David Bradshaw. Chief Registrar Robert Hollister and Registrarial Assistant Melissa Altman expertly managed myriad details surrounding the loan and shipping of works.

The tremendous expertise and tireless efforts of Director of Development Paul Johnson and his staff secured crucial funding for the exhibition and organized an extraordinary series of events to celebrate it. The participation of Chief Financial Officer Jack Wiant in the planning of this project was absolutely indispensable. Executive Assistant to the Director Olga Gerrard and Special Assistant to the Director Ari Wiseman managed seemingly endless details with diligence and aplomb. Acting Communications Director Katherine Lee and the communications staff adeptly handled the exhibition's public promotion. I am grateful also to Director of Administration and Operations Randy Murphy, Associate Director of Operations Mimi McCormick, Associate Director of Facilities Gemma Beristain, and Director of Retail Operations Grant Breding.

With the Los Angeles presentation of "Andy Warhol Retrospective," we are invited to consider Warhol's vast achievements as an artist within the context of a city whose Hollywood "dream factory" became a model for Warhol's own Factory. Warhol's remarkable vision produced and continues to inspire a steady stream of works and images that offer a new synthesis of high and mass culture. With this exhibition, we are privileged to bring Andy Warhol back to Los Angeles and honor his extraordinary and lasting contributions to the art and culture of our time.

ACKNOWLEDGMENTS

Heiner Bastian

When I started to prepare for this exhibition of the work of Andy Warhol almost three years ago – it had long been a dream of mine to do so – I was fortunate enough to receive the enthusiastic support of a number of people whose generosity has made this exhibition possible. At the time I began to prepare for the exhibition in Berlin, I did not envision a second venue, much less a third. I am deeply grateful to all of those individuals whose early and sustaining commitment gave the exhibition a solid foundation – and a future life that I had not initially imagined.

Stephanie and Peter Brant of Greenwich, CT, not only spontaneously offered to lend important works when I first discussed the exhibition with them, but have continued to give the project their support throughout its course. I am further indebted to Peter for a number of valuable suggestions.

Kirk Varnedoe, former Director of the Department of Painting and Sculpture at The Museum of Modern Art, New York, has contributed throughout to my earnest endeavors in creating a notable exhibition, not least through the generous loan of works. In addition, his enlightening essay on Warhol's *Campbell's Soup Cans* significantly enriches the exhibition catalogue. At MOMA, I also extend my deepest gratitude and appreciation to Director Glenn Lowry, Senior Curator Kynaston McShine, and Chief Curator at Large John Elderfield. My thanks are also due to Director of The Andy Warhol Museum Thomas W. Sokolowski, who has loaned absolutely essential works to this retrospective. Without his commitment, the project could not have been realized in its present form. For his invaluable support and landmark role in the history of Warhol's work, I am especially indebted to Irving Blum. And for their special efforts on behalf of the Los Angeles venue, I extend my sincerest appreciation to Eli and Edythe L. Broad and Joanne Heyler, Curator of The Broad Art Foundation.

Key works were made available by Jacques Kaegi, President, and Eva Keller, Curator, of the magnificent Daros Collection in Zurich. From the outset they responded with generosity to our plan for an exhibition. I am sincerely grateful to them. In Germany I was able to count on the loan of works from the collection of Anna and Josef W. Froehlich, to whom I am deeply indebted. The exhibition has received support from Armin Zweite, Director of the Kunstsammlung Nordrhein-Westfalen, and Rolf Lauter of the Museum für Moderne Kunst, Frankfurt am Main. I wish to thank Anne and Anthony d'Offay in London, both of whom have given this exhibition every assistance, as have Doris Ammann, Bruno Bischofberger, and Kasper König, who generously agreed to lend a number of works. However the cornerstone of this retrospective is undoubtedly the body of works by Andy Warhol from the Marx Collection in Berlin.

While putting together this retrospective I often thought of my dear late friends Thomas Ammann and Frederick W. Hughes; both were profoundly dedicated to Warhol's work. I have had the good fortune to enjoy the trust and cooperation of a great number of lenders in Europe and North America. In an age when art is constantly on the move, lending important works is problematic, and I am all the more grateful for the magnanimity shown. I would particularly like to thank Jean-Christophe Ammann, Frankfurt am Main; Richard Armstrong, Pittsburgh; Wolfgang Becker, Aachen; Nicolas Berggruen, New York; Sandra Brant, New York; Sara Campbell, Pasadena; Winfried Drewer, Münster; Doris and Donald G. Fisher, San Francisco; Rudi H. Fuchs, Amsterdam; Larry Gagosian, New York; Martin Hentschel, Krefeld; Stellan Holm, New York; Christian von Holst, Stuttgart; Antonio Homem,

New York; William B. Jordan, Dallas; Ivan Karp, New York; James Kelly, Santa Fe; Uli Knecht, Stuttgart; Pamela and Richard Kramlich, San Francisco; Poul Erik Tøjner, Humlebæk; Veit Loers, Mönchengladbach; Hubert Looser, Zurich; Ute and Reinhard Onnasch, Berlin; Jost Prüm, Saarbrücken; Andrea L. Rich, Los Angeles; Ned Rifkin, Houston; Malcolm Rogers, Boston; Thaddaeus Ropac, Paris; Nan Rosenthal, New York; Gunter Sachs, Pully; Anders U. Schroeder, London; Douglas G. Schultz, Buffalo; Ileana Sonnabend, New York; Mrs. John E. Steiner, Pittsburgh; Matthew Teitelbaum, Toronto; and Marc F. Wilson, Kansas City.

Thanks are due to Director General of the Staatliche Museen zu Berlin Peter-Klaus Schuster, for the confidence he has placed in me in respect to the exhibition. My enthusiasm has been shared by the Freunde der Nationalgalerie, Berlin, whose support has been absolutely indispensable.

In the course of preparing the exhibition I received much appreciated, competent advice and comment, and I benefited from interesting and informative discussions. In this regard I am especially indebted to Victor Bockris, New York; Rainer Crone, Munich; Vincent Fremont, New York; Robert Pincus-Witten, New York; and Cy Twombly, Lexington. Gratias ago Céline and Aeneas Bastian, Berlin.

The responsibility for the administrative side of the initial organization of this project rested with Antje Dallmann. It has been her work above all – carried out with both style and calm efficiency – that has set the tone of the preparation for the exhibition. I am unable here to fully indicate the extent of her contribution. She has my most heartfelt appreciation. I am also grateful to her for providing the chronological outline of Andy Warhol's career for this catalogue. The successful accomplishment of the Los Angeles presentation could not have been possible without the tremendous dedication and tireless efforts of Nina Koidl, to whom I am truly indebted.

I wish to thank administrative staff members Katharina Hohenhörst and Harriet Häußler. The assistance of Jens Kunath in producing the catalogue has been especially valuable, and his many other contributions to the preparatory work for the exhibition cannot be adequately acknowledged here. He has my most sincere thanks for the commitment he has shown. I would also like to thank Simone Aulenkamp for her collaboration in the production of this publication. The realization of this project has been assisted in a variety of ways by Jean Bickley, Greenwich, CT, and Laura Ricketts, London. Thanks also go to the Chief Conservator of the Neue Nationalgalerie, my friend Otto Hubacek, for his many informed comments and suggestions. The printing of this catalogue has been undertaken by Hans-Dieter Henke in Bielefeld. As always I am indebted to him for his guidance and meticulous work.

Finally I wish to extend my deepest gratitude to Jeremy Strick, Director of The Museum of Contemporary Art, Los Angeles, for the unique and exceptional opportunity to present this exhibition in Los Angeles, and at this esteemed institution in particular. It has been a tremendous pleasure and honor to work with Jeremy and his superb staff. I wish to express my appreciation to Senior Curator Ann Goldstein for overseeing the Los Angeles presentation. I also extend my gratitude to Olga Gerrard, Brian Gray, Robert Hollister, Suzanne Isken, Paul Johnson, Julia Langlotz, Katherine Lee, Lisa Mark, Stacia Payne, Paul Schimmel, Jack Wiant, and Ari Wiseman – as well as to the entire MOCA staff for the remarkable commitment that has made this final venue possible.

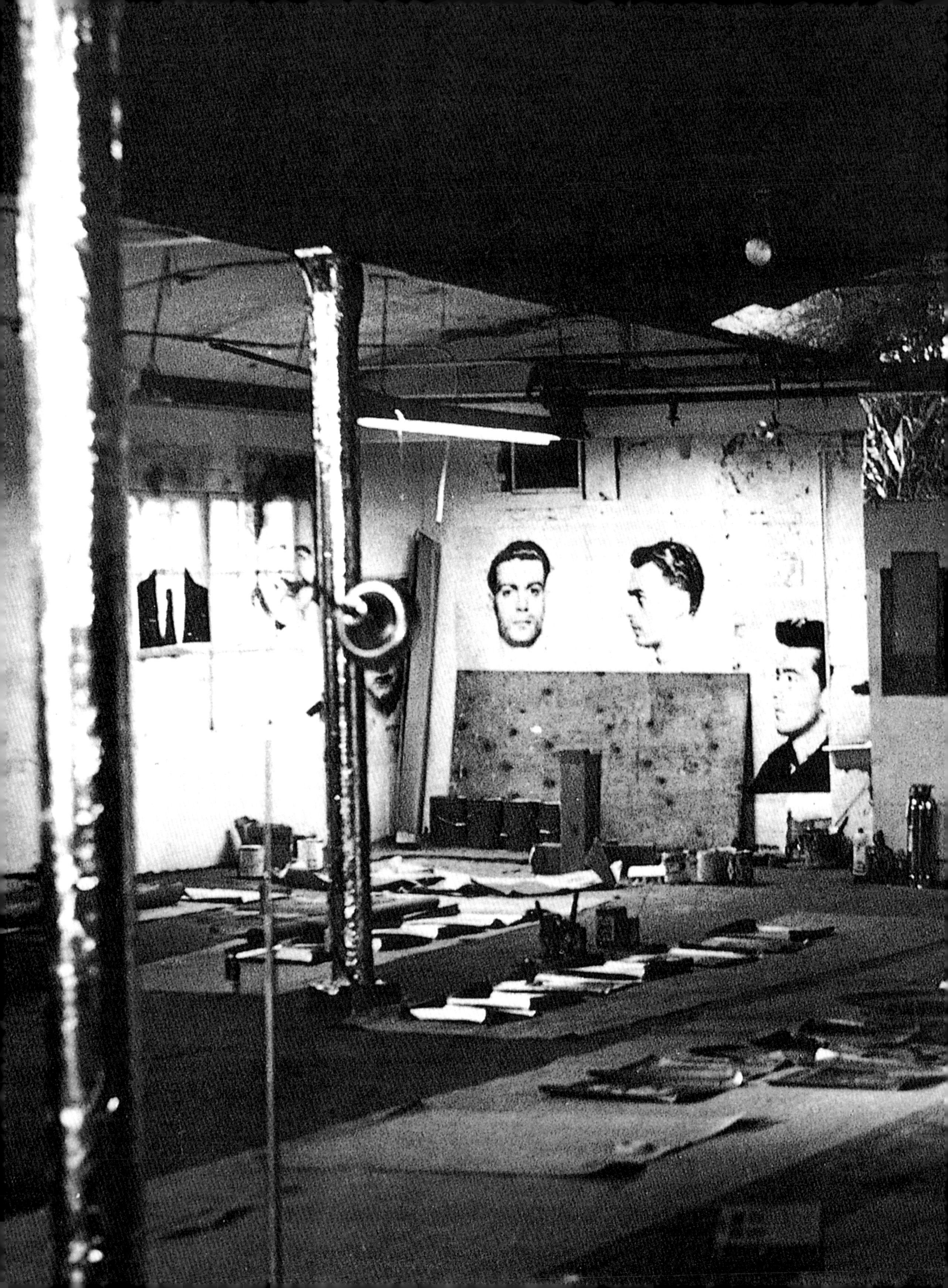

RITUALS OF UNFULFILLABLE INDIVIDUALITY – THE WHEREABOUTS OF EMOTIONS Part One

Heiner Bastian

The early drawings by Andy Warhol – made partly during his student days at the Art School of the Carnegie Institute of Technology in Pittsburgh but above all in the 1950s in New York – were scarcely known for many years. Apart from sporadic showings after 1953 in minor New York galleries, they were not exhibited at all. The decade when Warhol was working almost exclusively as a commercial graphic artist has been referred to as 'pre-Warhol' or 'pre-Pop', and the drawings Warhol produced then were assumed to be finished pieces from the world of advertising, graphics and commercial illustration. In fact, after 1960 when Warhol was setting out at last on his new existence as a purely autonomous artist, these early drawings seemed like an antagonistic body of work to him, discordant and contradictory. The early drawings were the diametric opposite of the new world of pictorial representation with its almost mythical fixation on the outside world: stylised phenomena whose playful iconography could scarcely have been more different from the new orientation towards 'the object' in painting.

Nearly two decades after they were made, it was Rainer Crone who, in his meticulous study of Andy Warhol's largely unknown early works, provided a proper critical appreciation of the work and demonstrated their significance within the development of the artist's œuvre as a whole.[1] Crone's observations laid the foundations for our understanding of Warhol's early works. He unlocked the iconography, the historical and contemporary references and paraphrases, and identified the axioms of Warhol's working processes. Not shying away from nomenclature, Crone delineates the artist's crucial notion of original and reproduction, of the transformation of the draughtsman's handwriting into an impersonal print process.

Nowadays the early drawings seem less distant to us. With our knowledge of the artist's biography and of his 'actual' œuvre, we draw conclusions, we see connections and correspondences. Leaving aside their 'isms' and inconspicuous iconography, as well as Warhol's particular notion of the original (yet to be fully defined), we see in these drawings the manifestation of an artistic language in the early days of an age that came to be dominated by mass media, an age of ever-accelerating experiences and news distribution: one might describe the early work, in all its formulations, as at once heterogeneous and affirmative. Among the arabesques and testimonies which strive towards a fantasy world, the 'news value' of the surface is the actual main essence of the work. Nothing in these works scales the dizzy heights beyond language, there is no need for existential explanations. Only in Warhol's commissioned works does the message escape into the immediacy of the relevant 'news', and into its lightness, even into its intent to please.

What we also read in the majority of the early drawings is the psychopathology of a young artist turning to unfulfillable romantic notions in an attempt to escape the poverty of his childhood, his experience of financial misery and the regulated constraints of a purely practical artistic training. Warhol undoubtedly did escape some of these, but only to replace them with the artificiality of surface or the real proximity of emotionlessness, which were to permeate his life and work as though both were reflected in the same mirror.

We will begin by examining and exploring the early graphic works, in their contours and changes, in their archetypal forms and constants, highlighting details. Many of these aspects will by definition touch on biographical circumstances that have been extensively described by several authors, including myself, and which will here simply appear as individual fixed beacons, providing a chronological framework for the text.[2]

In summer 1949 Andy Warhol was 21 years old. One afternoon in June, looking for new advertisement commissions, he hesitantly replied to a young New York editor: 'I can draw anything'.[3] If he had added to his reply, 'as long as you tell me what to draw', he would have perfectly described a quality that was to be evident throughout his life in his artistic praxis and as an underlying, dispassionate inner disposition. That afternoon in New York Warhol received his first commission. He made drawings of shoes for an advertising campaign and illustrations for a series of articles. Warhol drew the shoes during the night, corrected the drawings the next day, and drew them again until the editors were convinced that they would be an effective advertisement. He drew the shoes the way the art directors wanted them. Already the artist's hypersensitive notion of individuality that would never be fulfilled could take cover in the fiction inherent in the adjusted appearance of the shoes.

In June of that year Andy Warhol moved to New York having visited the city the previous autumn with his fellow students Philip Pearlstein and Arthur Elias. On that trip they had had their first sight of original works by Henri Matisse, Pablo Picasso and Paul Klee in the museums and galleries. At this time, as graduates of the Carnegie Institute of Technology in Pittsburgh, Warhol and Philip Pearlstein shared a friend's flat for some months in a dreary building on St. Mark's Place on the Lower East Side of New York. The meagre accommodation in this poor district must have reminded Warhol of his childhood and youth when poverty was as familiar to him as the eternally dark, smoke-laden sky above the workers' quarter in Pittsburgh, with its furnaces and coal works. He had first had to go out to work when he was just a schoolboy of thirteen following the death of his father, Andrej, who died in May 1942 at the age of forty-six. While his mother took on work cleaning and sewing, and sold home-made paper flowers in old tin cans which she called 'flower sculptures' and peddled door to door, Warhol worked from time to time in a dairy shop or helped his elder brother Paul, who worked as a street trader selling fruit and vegetables out of an open delivery van.[4] During these trips Warhol would be constantly sketching, offering to draw portraits for a dollar each. But on Saturday mornings, on the recommendation of his drawing teacher, he attended the art lessons for gifted children held in the Carnegie Museum. Here, in the company of children of his own age from a completely different social milieu, he at last found himself in a situation where he was not an outsider.

A slight, quietly withdrawn, perpetually pale student who was anxious about his appearance, at school Andy Warhol had always kept out of things. He had tried to find his own world in comics and Shirley Temple films, and had discovered the isolation and self-imposed seclusion that went with his constant drawing, painting, cutting out and collecting – all of which his strictly Catholic mother understood and approved of. But after the first few semesters at the Carnegie Institute, he started to overcome the trauma of exclusion during his dismal schooldays. Warhol had already evolved his own distinctive, independent 'style' and, according to one of his teachers, he only paid attention in class to the things that really interested him. His works rarely had much to do with fulfilling a particular task. But the drawings and the self-portrait that he showed in his first 'exhibition' in the faculty in 1948, and which won a prize, created a great deal of interest amongst his fellow students. Unlike most of the staff, they regarded him as unusually talented. In summer 1948 Warhol and a group of friends took over a habitable barn near the campus as a shared studio space. He drew portraits at the Pittsburgh Arts and Crafts Center for five dollars each, and worked as an assistant in the window display section of a department store.[5] He was interested in modern dance and experimental theatre, and was involved with producing the university's literary journal. Warhol was one of a group of students who were picturing their future as artists together in New York. In this circle his friends accepted his somewhat ethereal being and took his curiously withdrawn behaviour as a form of elfin eccentricity.

At the end of the spring semester of 1949 Andy Warhol submitted an autobiographical picture as his final piece of work: this met with a mixed reception from the panel of judges, who included George Grosz amongst their number. While Grosz and some others regarded *The Broad Gave Me My Face, But I Can Pick My Own Nose* [cat. no. 3] as a significant work, the majority of the panel rejected it as a scandal and an outrage.[6] With its naive, caricature-like style this picture, as do so many, has an affinity with folkloric depiction, but at the same time it also points to the proximity of the art of George Grosz. Above all, as a provocative, ironic and melancholic self-portrait, this picture is also a contemporary interpretation of grotesque realism as it had been practised in the painting of *objets désagréables*. In an exhibition of rejected works, Warhol's picture ultimately became a notoriously admired spectacle.

A number of authors have already pointed out that towards the end of his studies and during the first years in New York, Warhol felt drawn in his attitudes and beliefs to Henri Matisse and Jean Cocteau, to Grosz and Ben Shahn, and that he clearly also studied the work of Paul Klee which was exhibited in New York in the early 1950s.

Benjamin Buchloh rightly makes mention of the illustrations Saul Steinberg was doing in the late 1940s.[7] But Andy Warhol's development was, in effect, a matter of selecting and rejecting different artistic possibilities; during this time the pure line contour and consistently solid, planar colouration of internal spaces came ever more noticeably to the fore. It may be that with his vulnerable naiveté and his tendency to idolisation, he also absorbed the aura of the fame of Greta Garbo, James Dean and Truman Capote as a necessary therapy against being cast as an outsider. Yet, in the things that he accepted, there was already a manifest rejection of any kind of affect: the psychic immanence of gestural drawing would always remain foreign to him.

During his last two semesters at the Carnegie Institute Warhol had started experimenting with a way to give the lines in his drawings an instantly recognisable improvised look.[8] Some have claimed that at that time Warhol admired the effect of the so-called 'variable' or 'broken' lines in Ben Shahn's drawings and that he had tried to achieve similar results in his own work. In the few published drawings from his Pittsburgh days, there would appear to be many different influences; in addition there was his own experimentation with the rhythm of jagged cross-hatchings. As it is driven forwards, the graphite creates sharp, intricate contours which imitate spontaneity in their improvised 'continuance', exaggerating what any predecessors had done: with its unsettling rhythm, Warhol's staccato line seemed uncommonly succinct and, with its illusory volume, no doubt also intentionally naively contrived. Dieter Koepplin very aptly calls this characteristic line an 'artificial language', 'a stylistic translation of the overall outline'.[9] The parallels to Klee's work, which Warhol knew, are unmistakable in this graphic mode, in the sense that Klee would lend a dynamic note to his lineation by adding very fine, playful, variable contours around a clear line.[10] Warhol's own experiments seem to be directed towards achieving a similar dynamic [cat. no. 2]. Nevertheless these drawings were only the preliminary stage of a lineation which, as a 'blotted line', created a contour that intentionally looked reproduced (printed). This suited Warhol's spirit and ultimately pervaded all his early work. Years later, looking back at this stage, Warhol himself said: 'I always wanted to see how my work would look if it was printed.'[11]

Philip Pearlstein, one of the most reliable sources of information on those days, remembers that around 1948 Andy Warhol was 'interested in variations', that he arrived at this idiosyncratic line of his own accord, and that he then explored it and took it further. The fact that this new technique also opened up the different possibilities of multi-layered work processes, and in itself laid the foundations for the notion of the repetition of partial and whole motifs even in the first making of a work, may have further encouraged the artist to pursue this course.

After all, 'blotted-line' drawings meant possible reproduction and further use: a projection of efficient production. Warhol thus first drew the motif in pencil on water-resistant or heavily saturated paper. Next he retraced the contours with a pen and drawing ink or Indian ink; the ink would sit on the surface of the paper without sinking in. At the same time the surface tension of the ink through adhesion on the water-repellent ground would cause the liquid to contract. The ink line would break up into pearls and dots, and into a whole variety of fragments of a line. The resulting contour thus became the first 'original'; then absorbent watercolour paper would be laid on this to make a print of the original [cat. nos. 26, 38, 39]. The drawing, made by this copying process, was the first sign Warhol gave of having consciously chosen a particular path whereby the copy indirectly takes precedence over the original: the print becomes the original.

By repeatedly starting anew with pen and ink, the strength and intensity, and hence also the presence of the ink line, were constantly changing: a supremely manipulable procedure which, however, only acquired the intended 'printed quality' in the copying process through the absorbency of the paper used. The effects of chance thus further increased the distance to the individual handwriting of the copyist. The *accidentia* that ensued through this translation simply served to strengthen the alienating, passionless copying process. Some of these drawings reject any notion of form or of subjective emotion and convey the impression of an anonymously illusory event that has been arrested for a moment: nothing happens, everything is down to the mood, as in a film still. The reality conveyed through the image has already entered that category of pictures that are defined by pure outline. Individuality can become a platonic manifestation; on closer examination, in Warhol's many portrait 'drawings', in the act of seeing, emotion always becomes distance, the scope of one's own vision – and this vision itself becomes the correlate.

It may be that Warhol welcomed the discovery of the printed original and its astonishing reproducibility as a synonym for emotional distance: no doubt ideal for an artist who only a few years later was on the way to revolutionising traditional easel painting and who was to endow virtuosic screen-print techniques with an authenticity all of their own. For Warhol this print process proved to be the most suitable aid and the best method for what he wanted to do. It was possible to combine photographic originals and found images from magazines and books as if in a raw collage; they could virtually be altered and reproduced however he might choose. An image could now logically be created by a third party and the work involved in producing a 'Warhol picture' could be delegated.

Warhol's early works show a readiness to use mechanical production processes. At the same time there is also already a tendency towards simplification, to find the most immediate solution, which turns ever more energetically to the factual and the mundane in its idiomatic graphic expression. The art directors of the magazines that Warhol was working for admired the ephemeral character of his fragmentary, broken line. While this gave his visual language (in the context of the advertising of the time) a wished-for singular, innocently suggestive effect, Warhol was aware that the effectiveness of his work had its roots in the graphic code of a mode of representation whose calculated improvisation heightened the impact of the factual qualities of the subject. His images create their own room for visual manoeuvre quietly and unemphatically; they come up with variations of stylistic modalities, but the main focus of the drawing is always on both facets and syntheses.

Within two years of moving to New York, Warhol had secured so many commissions from the advertising industry that his financial situation improved markedly. As Victor Bockris writes in his biography *The Life and Death of Andy Warhol*,[12] Andrew Warhola gradually metamorphosed into Andy Warhol, the artist, who lived in a state of isolation that he compensated for with his work. Behind the façade of one who was seeking sympathy and attention, whose external cipher was the boyish, helpless demeanour he had devised for the purpose, was the truth of his life as a loner which in fact caused him considerable suffering. Bockris describes him on a stroll through the campus, suddenly crying out 'Entertain me' to his then fellow student, Arthur Elias.[13] Years later he was to turn to Henry Geldzahler with the words 'Say something', having asked Geldzahler to come out at night for an unpostponable meeting.[14] His loneliness in the presence of others had by then clearly already become for him the major, paradoxical metaphor of his life; it increasingly took hold of him in the 1960s, like an invisible, never-ending withdrawal from any emotional ties.

Commissioned graphic work by Warhol was now regularly to be seen in the magazines *Glamour, Vogue, Harper's Bazaar* and *Interiors*; he worked for the Sunday supplements of the *New York Times*; he had made illustrations for pieces by the French dramatist Jean Giraudoux; he designed record sleeves and book jackets; he drew shoes the like of which had never been seen before. For the radio programme 'The Nation's Nightmare' he had designed a startling image for a record sleeve which then appeared on 13 September 1951 as a full-page advertisement in the *New York Times*. Warhol's drawing shows a young sailor injecting drugs [see the study: cat. no. 11]. In the confrontation between two men the drawing symbolises very vividly the social and psychological dependencies of the violent, criminal drug-dealing milieu. With his increasing commercial success, Warhol could now devote more time to his own work; he entrusted entire commissions to his assistant Nathan Gluck. The ever greater distance from original, unique production meant that with this teamwork, Warhol could step back yet further: the cult dimension of uniqueness is already giving way at this stage to the collective subject.

Well into the late 1950s Warhol's 'blotted-line' process, which he and his assistants carried out with virtuosic skill, was also his trade mark. It was only when he turned to offset prints that he was able to enter into a new typographical discourse. Reproduction as a depiction of reality became a mania. For his large arsenal of ironic pictograms Warhol made stamps from balsa wood, stencils and soft erasers, which he then also used for schematic cross-hatching to accentuate figurative and spatial anatomies [cat. nos. 12, 40, 41]. The use of the stamp facilitated additive procedures and series; paradigmatic first steps towards a later, advanced use of templates for an emotionally cleansed register of life.

When we look at Warhol's early non-commercial, 'private' works made before and during the early 1960s, we cannot help but be struck by the way that the antinomy between attribute-free stylisation and subjective evocation takes on a strangely synthetic insistence. The portrayed world becomes the context of these works, and it appears as an amalgam of different, recurring pictorial themes. Warhol never resolved the discrepancy between denied and desirable sensuality on the one hand and calculated conception on the other; there can be no doubt that in the early years of his artistic development he was more deeply aware than any of his contemporaries of the shared affinities between commercial art and free composition, although he no longer wanted to make a difference between the two. Thirty years later he was to say: 'I'm still a commercial artist. I was always a commercial artist.'[15] But he was also to say: 'I'd do anything they told me to do, correct it and do it right. I'd have to invent and now I don't; after all that "correction", those commercial drawings would have feelings, they would have style. The attitude of those who hired me had feeling or something to it; they knew what they wanted, they insisted; sometimes they got very emotional. The process of doing work in commercial studios was machine-like, but the attitude had feeling to it.'[16]

Frequently the light touch of his drawings in fact conceals a certain alienation which resonates right from the outset as a form of existential failure, in the sense that – in the spirit of Bertolt Brecht – he 'leaves out all orientating motivations'. Even the many portrait drawings, which are no more than ballpoint-pen outlines with an almost classical lineation, are dominated by stylisation [cat. nos. 15-17]. It is in these works that Warhol undoubtedly comes the closest he ever does to Matisse, whom he admired, even if the emotional content of his drawings does not speak the same lyrical language of affect as do Matisse's works. What we read in Matisse's line drawings of human figures as a psycho-graphic statement is present in Warhol's drawings without the same existential foundation: less enigmatic because in their reduction to outline alone, these portraits avoid the slightest hint of metaphor.

The persistently empty inner areas, abandoning light modulations, tonality, half-tones and often without corporeality of any kind, are the only aspect of these drawings which would appear to derive from Matisse and perhaps from the classical drawings that Picasso was making in the early 1920s. But while Matisse used the abbreviation of pure contours as a metaphor for mysterious associations and Picasso saw his own drawings as a dialogue with forms found in Mediterranean antiquity, the type of reduction found in Warhol's drawings is not a psychogram, but simply a projected distillation of his relationship to the motif. And yet Warhol's portraits of men have the charm of erotic allusion because they admit their hidden or open associations. These drawings can also be seen as a mirror of Warhol's life at the time; they are perhaps amongst the most poetic examples of his work during the 1950s. In these images we can read the real autobiography behind the artistic one. The portrait studies of Ralph Thomas Ward, Alfred Carlton Williams, John Butler and later Charles Lisanby, reveal their platonic significance, in the sense that the artist only romanticises his 'model'. The viewer realises that the allusion to and fantasy of appropriation are always intended in one and the same paradigmatic sense, because the artist's passionate confession can only exist in the actual physis of the reproduction. There are no doubt many reasons why, in Warhol's case, friendships if anything increased the distance between himself and others – because they could not be lived out, or out of a fear of close ties. In some of these captured moments, the drawing has an affinity to portraits by Jean Cocteau; to studies that Cocteau made in the early 1920s of his friend Raymond Radiguet: displaying the statuesque and at the same time almost weightless poetry of a succinct outline drawing. Warhol's drawings, predominantly line drawings executed in ballpoint pen on rough printing paper, are spellbinding in their equally weightless contours, yet they say nothing about the sitter's salient features or innermost aspects, nothing about passion. They 'reproduce' a classical style. The authority of Warhol's mise-en-scènes is astonishing for its realistic lineation and precise proportionality; but it is the authority of a meta-language which Warhol favours like a model that is somehow superior to reality. The sight of these drawings again raises questions: why do these pure contours not lead to yet more possible solutions, exploring shading, tonality, light values and corporeal modelling with light and shade; why is no new vocabulary sought using cross-hatchings, washes and colour? Even today it is still surprising to see the hermeneutics of Warhol's stylistic anthology; it will change later, but it will never really be any different.

In June 1952 Warhol had an exhibition at Alexandre Iolas' Hugo Gallery, New York, of large-format, coloured works which he had made after reading texts by Truman Capote. Not a single piece from the exhibition was sold, and one critic at least could only see in Warhol's pictures references and affinities to Toulouse-Lautrec, Aubrey Beardsley, Charles Demuth and Cocteau: '…the air of carefully studied perversity'.[17] Nevertheless the exhibition was a success as far as Warhol was concerned because Truman Capote – the stunningly good-looking young author, the idol of unattainable celebrity – had seen the work.

The following year Warhol started to have books of offset prints of his works published in small private editions. One of the first of these 'presentation books' was called *A Is an Alphabet*.[18] It was made in collaboration with the poet and artist Ralph Thomas Ward, whom Warhol had met in late 1951. Warhol made drawings to go with Ward's short, hand-written, aphoristic texts, composed in a light-hearted language of fairy tales and fables. In a playful, often only two-dimensional and extremely tender style which hinted at portraiture, we see silhouettes of children, schematically ephemeral faces, distanced and detached from any context. The pellucid, almost dematerialised lineation seems like a game with the transparency of the space in which these equally transparent faces appear. This book was followed by further bound albums that Warhol produced as presents for art directors, publishers and influential editors. The type of drawing he used in these books in fact always takes the form of reduced, linear contours which often parody the whimsical nonsense-fantasy of the texts and take on the capricious quality of masquerades or stage acts. Warhol persuaded his friends to colour the offset prints, and his mother wrote out the texts in her awkward calligraphy and uncertain spelling.

While the art world and the worlds of film and of modern dance were changing dramatically in New York, and artists like Robert Rauschenberg, Cy Twombly and Jasper Johns were showing work at the Stable Gallery as well as at Betty Parsons and Charles Eagan; while many young artists were organising their own shows, and in their best moments devising a wholly rejuvenated language in which a whole number of original, even contradictory movements and trends were competing with each other,[19] Warhol had become one of the best paid and, no doubt, best known commercial artists in New York. He continued to fulfil lucrative commissions for the advertising industry, above all for the exclusive shoe shop I. Miller, and his drawings of shoes appeared each week in the *New York Times*. They made him so well-known that he decided to exhibit the unpublished drawings of shoes at the Serendipity coffee shop. In the iconography of his early works the shoes became objects that seem to have attracted him as magically as the naked feet of the friends and acquaintances that he frequently sketched [cat. nos. 19, 25]. Warhol drew the shoes in ever new variations in a positive mania of discursive rhetoric. He tried them out in every imaginable style and formal variant. He accentuated their effect in pseudo-historical, ironic exaggeration: the shoes became an obsessively repeated motif. In forms that are strict and naive, subtle and subversive, in forms that are symbolic, he operated with the syntax of fetishism. In 1955 he devoted a portfolio with fourteen offset prints to shoe drawings, for which he adapts Proust's title, calling it *A la Recherche du Shoe Perdu*.[20] In December 1956, after returning from a trip round the world with his friend Charles Lisanby, Warhol showed the most remarkable of his shoe drawings in the Bodley Gallery. He coloured the body of the shoes with applied (imitation) gold leaf and added fanciful gold and silver decorations, as in children's poetry albums. He invented imaginary characters for the different shoe types and dedicated the sheets to famous movie actors, fashion icons, and later even artists [cat. no. 34]. As Rainer Crone has pointed out, the unspoken connotations of the motif was the 'erotic metaphor' that Warhol saw in every shoe. Nevertheless, in all these whimsical motifs, the suggestive language of these objects always turned into the same mannered or banal irony. It can only have been disturbing for Warhol when the magazine *Life* described his works as '… imaginary footwear as a hobby … ornamented with candy-box decorations'.[21] His exhibition of erotic drawings of young men in February 1956 had been similarly spurned by critics [cat. nos. 33, 35]. These drawings were seen as narcissistic images of a wayward sensuality, which failed to live up to the pictorial discourse in the work of Matisse and Cocteau. The response to both of these exhibitions made Warhol only too aware of the dilemma between 'high art' and commercial artwork.

Nevertheless Warhol was still prepared to use the same style of gold collages of the shoe drawings for the romantically stylised imagery in a set of illustrations for *In the Bottom of My Garden*, an utterly sensual sequence of erotic allusions which almost exactly followed a series of etchings published in the seventeenth century by Jacques Stella.[22] What had started as androgynous, childish innuendo turns into a frozen pantomime in an empty space. Even in the context of the drawings that Warhol was by now making as a 'free' artist, these twenty-one sheets – pseudo-sensitive and playing with an artificial representationalism – seem like no more than a naive panorama of artful vignettes. In these compositions the pure contour of the line takes on an almost unparalleled level of empty abstraction.

And yet, the illustrations for this book reflect the paradoxical circumstances in which Warhol was living and working in the 1950s. The phenomenology of his works at the time was geared towards the aesthetic of the trivial – invariably the same as the aesthetic of deceptive appearances – and the dictates of appealing product promotion. The thread running through this period was the ever-new paraphrases he found for an already unconstrained, incongruous world of improvised forms. Warhol was travelling along a path that he had not really looked at with open eyes; but his works showed all too clearly that he could not escape from this self-imposed situation.

It was not until his third exhibition in the Bodley Gallery in December 1957 that Warhol showed pen and ink drawings on a gold ground along with additional sheets intended for a new book entitled *A Gold Book by Andy Warhol.*[23] The cover of the book shows James Dean in a scene from the film *Rebel Without a Cause*. The pure outline drawings had been transferred in ink directly onto the gold ground of the paper. There is an entirely new virtuosity in the stenographic reduction of Warhol's studies and portraits of these 'street kids' from such a variety of angles and perspectives. With his known preference for two-dimensional originals, Warhol created a pictorial language based on photographs of a friend that is as free from determinants as if it were the precise outcome of exhaustive experiments with preparatory studies. The lines are uncommonly sure and succinct, free of imitative signs and they attain a rare, contemplative intensity. These images are indubitably amongst the most outstanding works of Warhol's early career, because in them the visual level as it were also takes on a truly sensual dimension. More clearly than ever before they exploit the potential of a powerful, self-confident lyricism and a capacity for symbiosis. These drawings also have to be seen as the first steps in a critical dialogue with an age when the prevalent thought patterns and critical apparatus accommodated an artificially cool rationalism, an age when the spirit of Abstract Expressionism would ultimately be overcome. During the course of this year at the latest, Warhol became much more urgently aware of his ambivalent situation. The prize-winning illustrator who was recognised in the world of fashion and advertising as an outstanding graphic artist found himself marginalised in the world of contemporary art. The paradigms of a new pictorial language were starting to emerge – particularly in the work of Rauschenberg and Johns – responding to Dada, to Kurt Schwitters and Marcel Duchamp's aporias, self-confidently reacting to the subtle everyday myths and the banal ambiguity of the media world.

By the following year, these artists' work was already being discussed more heatedly than that of Willem de Kooning, Franz Kline or Jackson Pollock. At the heart of the debate were Johns' encaustic paintings and the provocative combine paintings by Rauschenberg, who had in effect laid down a programmatic challenge to innovation by developing these works from the purification of monochrome paintings. For Warhol, the astonishing reception that met these works could only show him all the more clearly that, as yet, he personally had no answer. While he was now a regular visitor to Leo Castelli's gallery and observed with incredulous amazement the surprising appreciation that greeted the work of Rauschenberg and Johns in the famous exhibition *Sixteen Americans* at The Museum of Modern Art, he was himself working with Suzie Frankfurt on one of his 'presentation books'.[24] They called it *Wild Raspberries.*[25] It was to be Warhol's last portfolio. It contained recipes invented by Frankfurt, written out by Warhol's mother in her best handwriting, and drawings by Warhol and his assistants, coloured in Dr. Martin's dye watercolours and extravagantly decorated. The single sheets were exhibited in 1959 in the Bodley Gallery. Once again the 'disarming naiveté' (Crone) of a whole decade of drawings comes alive and is summed up in the positively prismatic glow of the coloured offset lithographs. And this work too, with its innocently subversive stance, touches on the realms of travesty, creating the fiction of a childhood which never could be. Warhol invented a whole number of subsidiary gestures for that childhood, in whose reflection memory is the invisible yet perhaps most important feature. Memory is not meant to be read, although it tells the story of a whole decade. Others will identify as axioms in these works the artist's psychological disposition, his active practice of Catholicism, his past poverty and persistent fear of poverty. On the path to that new, still elusive reality of 'serious artist', of being purely a painter, the portfolio *Wild Raspberries* seems like a last, or provisionally last, detour – for it was to be a long time yet before Warhol gave up commercial art. One day he will call a halt, only to return to it years later and even to redefine it.

Part Two

In all probability, around 1959 Andy Warhol saw the radicalism of the new painting not so much as a specific artistic praxis that derived a precise symbolic codification from using images from ordinary life, but simply as everyone saw it: in terms of the compelling effectiveness of a banal, everyday motif. Jasper Johns' *Flag* fascinated many as a painted object that provoked renewed debate about the relationship between perception and representation of the object, above all by using the language of objectivity. This was a language that Warhol was just as fluent in, although in a different way, and as yet he was unable to apply it with such radical concentration to a singular motif. He must have seen that Rauschenberg's works operated according to a hierarchy-free maxim which regarded the physical, extra-aesthetic object and the painterly gesture as the 'only subject', and that in Rauschenberg's works the material of the everyday urban world was a suitable vehicle for unadulterated, free communication. Warhol had long since recognised that the new painting needed clear messages and physical entities from the outside world for its motifs and forms, which – in the pictures of Johns and Rauschenberg – became enigmatic, isolated phenomena, even though the identity of the everyday items did not change.

Sometime in late autumn 1960, at a time when Warhol was almost despairing in his search for an iconography that would establish his place in the ranks of those painters causing a stir in galleries and museums as Pop artists, he suddenly started work on a group of pictures in which the subject of painting, without comment, upheld trivial pictorial representation against aesthetic strategies of whatever kind.[26] Without further ado these pictures abandon the thematic potential of his output so far, although not the idea of projection and reproduction for which he had found the perfect mechanisms in his early work. Warhol's new 'black-and-white' pictures expose the reality of banal objects. His works address the question of ordinariness on the level of the least remarkable, insignificant mass products very differently from the ways favoured by Johns and Rauschenberg. His first pictures show items of the kind listed under 'Miscellaneous' in the classified advertisements in a daily paper: refrigerators and wigs, household goods and cosmetic correctives, television sets and crossword puzzles or imitation jewellery. Having made a small slide picture of the item, Warhol would project the enlarged image onto a grounded canvas, trace the outline with a pencil and fill in the internal planes with black casein colour. The shocking banality of these objects which Warhol chose from trivial advertising – far-removed from his own advertising images with their allusive, seductive language – would appear to bear witness to the artist's efforts to stake his claim as an exponent of new painting.

The distance between the explosively colourful, often garish opulence of his last book *Wild Raspberries*, and these new works in terse greys and blacks which he called 'no-comment' paintings, demonstrates not only the break he was seeking to make with his own artistic past, but also the lengths he would go to emulate the nature of vulgarity through shock-tactics and provocation. In the half-tone grey of the monochrome ground of these pictures there is no doubt also a conscious mirroring of the grid structured backgrounds of the offset reproductions that he used – a specifically intentional production that simply negates the pictorial space and turns it into an empty reproduced plane.

In these first pictures we already see Warhol's dialogue with the outside world, recreating a template-like correspondence with the surface of the object. As he began to distance himself from his past as a commercial artist, these pictures seemed like an angry postulation which even in its choice of motif is perplexingly only using the language of rejected conventions: the object that Warhol is searching for is the meaning of the object which resembles the nothingness and emptiness of its consumption. In the works *Advertisement* [cat. no. 46 – Warhol's first such picture?],[27] *Where Is Your Rupture* [cat. no. 51], *Crossword* [cat. no. 61], *Pipe* [cat. no. 60] or *Before and After* [cat. no. 50], Warhol finds the formula of the self-perpetuating existence of contemporary depiction: the pre-formulated citations of an already stylised, trivialised language of forms. Where Warhol, more out of indecision and doubt, turns in his representation of the motif to graphic marks, 'formal graphic alienation effects' (Crone) or outlines the motif in a pseudo-expressive manner, fragmenting it or depicting it in an exaggeratedly casual, incomplete way, the expressive gesture can only appear as intentional coincidence. It is as though Warhol wanted deliberately to tell us how aware he is of the falseness of these gestures, how superfluous they are, and that anyone could have made these pictures.

Even in the works that are derived from originals in cartoons and comics which Warhol had known since childhood and which he was now making concurrently with the black-and-white pictures, he retains the language of their former function, keeping to the rhetoric of the originals and their stylised vocabulary. The very essence of Pop art is contained in the connotations of these images. In contrast to the black-and-grey pictures, here the 'artificiality' of the motif or the figure that serves as a source image is linked to the narrative structure of the original – the world as experienced by the protagonist of a cartoon. In the paintings *Superman* [cat. no. 48], *Dick Tracy* [cat. no.53] or the recently rediscovered *Little King* [cat. no. 47], the message conveyed by the work is linked to the mentality that we associate with the character of the 'hero' it depicts, the places in which he operates and the way he talks and acts. The paths of the illusion of reproduced real life cross in the reality of the picture. In the words of Roland Barthes: 'Comment le sens propre peut-il être le sens "naturel" et le sens figuré "originel"?'[28]

One day in winter 1960, or in the following spring, Warhol overcame the last remnant of the in fact unliberated, arbitrary artistic expression which lingered on in his pictures as a false context of aesthetic convention. He did this by depicting a single Coca-Cola bottle in black casein paint on canvas, cool and sober, mechanically executed. The utter isolation of the much-enlarged object and its alien lack of compromise which can only be seen as futurist, puts this motif in a class of its own. When Warhol's new friend Emile de Antonio saw this picture, he encouraged Warhol to continue down this route, with clearly defined subjects, perfectly proportioned and authentic in every detail of their form. De Antonio, Ivan Karp, who worked at the Castelli Gallery, and Henry Geldzahler, at the time curator for contemporary art at the Metropolitan Museum, advised Warhol to avoid subjective, relational signs in his pictures.[29] They already saw the *sujet* of a powerful prophecy of the future of American art in the cold reproduction of the Coca-Cola bottle. The anti-metaphorical style of this painting marks an important step Warhol had taken in the direction of new painting, where the subject comprises the unaltered reproduction of an original on canvas.

Without doubt this decision by Warhol changed the paradigms of easel painting in the second half of the twentieth century more fundamentally than the aporias of the avant-garde with their notion of convergence that was variously open to interpretation. The accepted and transitional categories of aesthetics, ethics and integrity were now not only questioned; in fact their very foundations had been shattered, firstly in the metaphysical correspondence of the picture and secondly in its transcendental fulfilment.

While Karp sought in vain to interest collectors in Warhol's paintings, and the New York galleries showing Rauschenberg, Johns, James Rosenquist, Frank Stella and Robert Indiana similarly rejected Warhol's works, the artist was making pictures that again replicated, unaltered, the diction and graphic mode of its source images: *Say Pepsi Please, Close Cover Before Striking* [cat. no. 67] and also the five paraphrases of the *Do-It-Yourself* series [cat. nos. 69, 70, 71], the *Dance Diagram* pictures [cat. nos. 72, 73] and *A Boy for Meg*. Warhol had stopped registering the particularities of his contemporaries: he no longer even rejected them, either because he was indifferent or because they really did not affect him any longer. His pictures were entities which, having themselves the character of objects, gave the mimesis of the object a status all of its own. Expressive content became pure communication. The difficult-to-grasp idea that there is nothing behind the surface was now exclusively a matter of interpretation for the viewer, who was henceforth responsible for the mystery of the picture's possibilities and meanings.

In the *Do-It-Yourself* pictures Warhol, just one last time, ironically imitated the credo of the inter-subjective complicity of step-by-step renewal as an outmoded aesthetic position. Using a painting-by-numbers set for amateurs or children with a key for the colours to be used in different parts of the composition (which Warhol does not keep to), he made five pictures which document his conjunction of mechanical production and pictorial idea as a provocation heralding the end of the painted picture. And so that everyone understands that the painting process used here is untouched by any of the usual modalities of painting, Warhol ironically left the colour-key numbers visibly live on in the colour fields, although they are supposed to be out of sight. In this parody the artist is telling us that these paintings have only been 'fabricated' because they have been 'pre-fabricated' by someone else. Nowadays these *Do-It-Yourself* pictures seem like a last, logical farewell to neo-Dada comment and to the criteria of the principles of the readymade, paraphrased in Warhol's works.

After Leo Castelli had also rejected Warhol's pictures because of their thematic and iconographic similarity to the work of Roy Lichtenstein, Warhol still had not found a gallerist who would take him on. In April 1961 he installed the pictures *Advertisement, Little King, Superman, Before and After* and *Saturday's Popeye* [cat. nos. 46-50] in the display window of the department store Bonwit Teller. However, this first exhibition by Warhol received as little attention as Johns' first version of his *White Flag*, which the latter had shown under a pseudonym five years earlier in the same department store window.

Among the works that no-one wanted to show in New York at that time were *A Boy for Meg* as well as, importantly, *Daily News* [cat. no. 90] and *129 Die in Jet (Plane Crash)* [cat. no. 109], which directly demonstrate Warhol's allegiance to the uncompromising typography of reproduction. To this day one cannot help but be amazed that the fundamental changes in the code of painting in these works were not perceived straight away. The pictures constitute meticulously exact copies of the front pages of daily papers, in so far as they can be summarily 'transposed' using the graphic mode of Warhol's method of transposition. On closer examination they are of course less painted than 'drawn' in a schematic manner. However these pictures may be designated, the term 'Pop art' is hardly applicable to these silhouette pictures and, indeed, in the burgeoning 'colourful' world of the media, these black-and-white pictures are almost archaic. It is not the redundant exactitude of the likeness which takes the *trompe-l'œil* debate *ad absurdum*, that is so astonishing in these pictures, but the message apparently caught in a mirror that does not distinguish between fiction and reality. The message is the sole issue here – the message that Warhol reproduces, which declares its own alienation; the emptiness, the insufficiency of language that excludes the mystical. In a metaphorical sense, these pictures stand alone; they form a kind of concluding sentence which, as it seems to me, more powerfully shatters the fundamentals of the sense of the work than do the strategies and rituals of a form of painting that was in any case attempting to get by without the magical, immaterial formulas that we live by. A year later, after discovering and 'taking possession' of the silkscreen, Warhol created a new schema for the technical production of his pictures, and in the veracity of the reproduction renewed the break with semiotic convention.

Anyone who views this series with a critical eye invariably singles out the painting *129 Die in Jet*. It is Warhol's first so-called disaster painting, and would be followed a year later by an important sequence of related paintings which show death and the anonymity of death as complementary existential messages. When Warhol was working on silkscreens of these images some months later, he remarked: 'I guess it was the big plane crash picture, the front page of a newspaper: *129 DIE*. I was also painting the Marilyns. I realized that everything I was doing must have been Death. It was Christmas or Labor Day – a holiday – and every time you turned on the radio they said something like "4 million are going to die". That started it. But when you see a gruesome picture over and over again, it doesn't really have any effect.'[30]

Mythological, ethical or methodological problems were never the focus of the artist's interest. What did constantly occupy him was the search for hyper-resonant motifs, for a distinct object of representation already publicly interpreted in the media, already beyond aestheticisation. In December 1961, in response to his insistent demand to know what he could paint, Muriel Latow replied: 'You should paint pictures of money … You should paint something that everybody sees every day, that everybody recognises like a can of soup.'[31] At which point Warhol did in fact start his thirty-two *Campbell's Soup Can* pictures [cat. no. 76], which were to have a lasting effect on his future pictorial motifs from the iconography of the prefabricated world of things.

For this series Warhol chose a relatively small format (which he later repeatedly used for series of all kinds of subjects), no doubt in order that in its mimetic stylisation and size, the picture should correspond to the identity of its subject matter (the soup can). For the first time he used templates and stencils, because it was the empirical 'fact' of the object – which he neither wants to evaluate nor to describe – that is being depicted by means of its mode of 'production'. Warhol's soup cans do not seek to be pictures about something, but the picture of a picture; they choose purely to affirm the object. Warhol's repetition of the motif can no doubt also be seen as the meta-level of an illustration of consumer-goods advertising, a kind of unbiased litany for the optical formulas of everyday myths that have lost their appeal. (One is tempted to claim that it is only Warhol's repetition of the motif that raises it out of its litany of a now dulled myth.)

When the art dealer Irving Blum presented the complete series of thirty-two *Campbell's Soup Cans* in the Ferus Gallery in Los Angeles in July 1962 – when no gallerists in New York wanted to show them – Warhol was greeted with muted scorn rather than critical attention.[32] The pictures were presented on narrow white ledges on the wall at regular intervals like an obvious range of consumer goods types. Viewers took them for no more than a harmless provocation; they did not understand them. The identity of the iconography multiplied in Warhol's series in the unmistakable outlines of the consumer item. In the eyes of the visitors these pictures probably had no dignity, they were evidently lacking in any reference to artistic norms. Warhol himself adopted a very clear standpoint. In reply to a friend in New York who asked him why he had painted the soup cans, he said: 'I wanted to paint nothing. I was looking for something that was the essence of nothing, and that was it.'[33]

It is clear that Warhol had both heightened the signal effect of the 'given' object through the impact of the series and, at the same time, returned it for the viewer to its existence outside the gallery as a simple consumer item.

As Duchamp's factory-made objects had done in the past, in the moment of their presentation as works of art, Warhol's thirty-two *Campbell's Soup Cans* (which were not conceived as a single body of work) reopened the epistemological discourse on the objective function and associated mode of reflection of the artwork that is defined as such by artist's decision alone.

Then, as now, this very remarkable series speaks of the multiple levels of reality in a work of art which, on the one hand, innocently yet cruelly betrays all its moral and artistic forerunners and, on the other hand, constitutes a wholly free, futuristic optical illusion, which in the first instance abandons all transhistorical typologies. As a strangely persistent constant, the return of the eternally same has social implications, perhaps unwittingly, yet it is unmistakably present. One might perhaps best describe the *Campbell's Soup Cans* as sublime and vital, with no need of a rhetorical net: a modern Grimm's fairy tale, that tells of one who went out into the world to learn about fear, and to teach others to fear.

During the summer exhibition in Los Angeles in 1962 Warhol, still working in one room of his house on Lexington Avenue, turned his attention to making several completely different variations on a number of themes. Multiplication of motifs in serially structured sequences was henceforth to form the basis of his pictorial production. In the case of *S&H Green Stamps* [cat. no. 84] and *192 One Dollar Bills* [cat. no. 86] Warhol did not use templates; instead he took rubberised stamps. The print quality of these stamps was suited to relatively small, limited sections of Warhol's motifs; above all they facilitated the process of repetition. In these pictures the strict, additive procedure of repetition gives the viewer the impression of a single plane that excludes notions of pictorial space, instead suggesting the endlessness of the emblematic character of the image. In this sense, colour is simply a medium that stands for the accuracy of the replication and for the over-arching immanence of the subject matter. For Warhol these works established once and for all that he wanted to make works with surfaces that could stand alone in semantic terms and hence hermetically reproduce the object without transitional features.

At about the same time as Rauschenberg, in July 1962, Warhol discovered the advantages of screen printing, as a form of pure reproduction which can produce pictures more efficiently and neutrally. The process by which it is possible to transfer a photographed motif directly onto the screen is in keeping with Warhol's credo, as one who 'sees' the replication of reality in the reality of the picture (at least he appears to see this). Warhol had now found the ideal medium to depersonalise production: the print reflects the actual commensurability of the sheer facticity of the depicted object. Pictures of the human face and images of tragedies from the real world seemed predestined to become the subject for works that Warhol planned to make over the following months and years: paradoxically both of these topics of necessity induce an element of subjectivity that Warhol was prepared to exclude in all his experiments without ever really excluding it.

The very first works that Andy Warhol made using silkscreen techniques were portraits of Troy Donahue and Warren Beatty. For another picture, made at the same time as these portraits, he used the press photograph of a scene from a game with the famous baseball player Roger Maris.[34] Using this new technique Warhol makes 'photographically' exact pictures which are formed solely and exclusively by the silkscreen colour on the surface of the canvas. In the picture *Baseball* [cat. no. 97], Warhol places the screens into a horizontal grid, superimposes them and varies the light-dark rhythm by exactly determining the amount of silkscreen ink used as though he wanted to imbue the scene from the game with dynamic, imaginary movement. But, aside from their precision, all these reproductions are overlaid with a certain alienating effect and by a discontinuity that interrupts any emotion-led reading. Relics of easel painting! For, despite their apparent stereotypical making and extinguished subjectivity, the impersonal automatism of their production nevertheless results in semantics of a kind, in which the viewer will read claims and appeals, will find 'mimicry', will seek to find the real meaning.

When the actress Marilyn Monroe took her own life on 4 August 1962, Warhol spontaneously decided to make a portrait of her. He based a series of silkscreens on a now famous photograph that shows her as a film star, as an icon: a distinctly mythical figure.[35] Particularly the silkscreens on a connotative gold ground that imply emptiness, the distant past, and the after life – but also the antinomy between saintly relic and fallen woman – articulate 'the high and the utterly base' that are always simultaneously perceptible in Warhol's work and preclude any hint of nobility. In the *Liz* (Taylor) and the *Marilyn* portraits [cat. nos. 91-96, 102, 102a], and in the *Elvis* silkscreens [cat. nos. 107, 108], the aura of utterly affirmative idolisation already stands as a stereotype of a 'consumer-goods style' expression of an American way of life and of the mass-media culture of a nation, which, in the early 1960s, were creating dreams and hegemonies (according to wholly technical and material premises), in which goods and messages were beholden to mechanisms of consumerism that applied to both alike. In these works the hyper-icons of Pop turn into icons of demonic emptiness; Warhol's notion of 'beauty' cannot be imagined without tragedy.

What Warhol subjected to the magic ritual in his pictures was the tradable consciousness of the world of things, which he progressively inscribed into all his motifs. It existed as a truth that was not of his invention. In the end, for all its closeness to life, Warhol's art became what it had never wanted to be: now it was no longer to be surpassed by life. Pointing to his work which depicts the outside world, the artist said: 'If you want to know all about Andy Warhol, just look at the surface: of my paintings and films and me, and there I am. There's nothing behind it.'[36] But this 'surface' was not of his invention either.

Even today the pictures that Warhol made up until his first exhibition in early November 1962 in Eleanor Ward's New York Stable Gallery are still the epitome of what we call Pop art: they demonstrate the inevitability of a banal reality which, like an abrupt change of direction, maps out in the 1960s the first terrifying, virtual glimpses of future life forms. Warhol's production methods used the same typologies for the reproductions of *Campbell's Soup Cans* in different variations and formats, as for the dollar notes and the paraphrases of Coca-Cola and of Marilyn in ever different colours. Thus even the schematically melancholy, hand-done retouches in the *Marilyn* portraits seem as distanced as the inevitable, cosmetic products without which no-one can be deemed beautiful. The sphinx of nothingness, like a first foretaste of social phenomenology, made its way into Warhol's studio and, while not yet really tangible in his pictures, is now legible, or at least can be sensed in the erotic statement of belief that everything is equally beautiful.

In the midst of the general mood of affirmation in this Pop production which had already found its prototypical subjects, it is probably in autumn 1962 that Warhol produced his first disaster picture, *Suicide*, solely using a silkscreen technique [see also *Suicide (Silver Jumping Man)* cat. no. 111]. The original for this was a photograph showing a man leaping to his death.[37] Warhol enlarged the shot, which has been cropped at the edges, and reproduced it as a photo-silkscreen on vertical-format paper. Aside from the conventions and archetypes of his age which Warhol is constantly using, in this picture the sense of individual humanity returns all too painfully. The harsh nature of the black-and-white print, its bald statement of fact, heightens the enigmatic quality of the picture. The man who takes on the physiognomy of death here, brightly back-lit against the 'façade of the world' also reveals – in philosophical terms – the dereliction of life, its confused, accidentally tragic contradiction.

Whatever the many different conclusions arrived at in art-historical observations on the significance of Warhol's work in the context of his time and his contemporaries, it is in the images of disaster and death that he started to make in 1963 that Warhol the chronicler gains his credibility and Warhol the artist explains the world. It is of no consequence that what these pictures express most clearly is the manic idea of only ever duplicating things that have already 'signified' something. Indiscriminate death – that most incredible devaluation of life, as we know it in Albert Camus and in the Sisyphus dictum, in the work of Francis Bacon, very differently in that of Joseph Beuys and differently again in the monologues laden with auras of the memento mori of a whole century – is Warhol's weighty theme. Only this theme brings with it the return of painting – that knows no subject – as an anonymous, speechless emotion.

The exhibition in the renowned Stable Gallery in late 1962 had propelled Warhol overnight into the group of artists whose work was heatedly debated in New York at the time. For a few months in late spring of 1963 he had a studio in the second storey of an empty inner-city fire station on the east side of 87th Street. The young New York poet Gerard Malanga helped him with the large-format silkscreens. Concurrently with the first Elvis Presley works, the Liz Taylor portraits, which include the picture *Blue Liz as Cleopatra* [cat. no. 103], Warhol also dedicated a number of portraits to Rauschenberg [cat. no. 98]. During this period he also produced his *Statue of Liberty* [cat. no. 104], an attempt to use intentionally blurred lines and superimposition to create the effect of a three-dimensional image (made using silkscreen techniques), like the illusionistic effect of three-dimensionality on postcards of the World Trade Center. The tautological procession of motifs seems like clips from a movie or the endless return of rhythmic syntagms. It is the grid of reproduction that so insistently conveys instability and strangeness, for it is as though it takes the factual content of the source photograph and virtually revokes it through the language of production.

The works Warhol was now producing centred on images of disasters and catastrophes, pictures of racial unrest, victims of traffic accidents and, in one, the execution device used in the United States: the electric chair. It is impossible to escape the effect of these pictures in which death, and forms of death mythologised by language, echo in terrifying scenarios. *Suicide (Silver Jumping Man)* [cat. no. 111], *Woman Suicide* [cat. no. 110] and *Suicide (Fallen Body)* [cat. no. 113] have such an identity of their own that an epic reading or interpretation of them become irrelevant. For most of these pictures Warhol uses mercilessly hard-hitting press photographs and archive material – some of these agency photographs were never published in the press because of their sheer brutality.

In all these pictures of death it is the sharply outlined multiplication of the motif, the clearly defined edges, that paradoxically strengthen the hermeneutics of the ex-centric image. It seems that in this tautological role-play of repetition, the physis of the image stands out all the more convincingly in the viewer's mind. The unpredictable moment of reality conveyed through the pictures is also the heterogeneous alienness that strikes out at us, the viewers, from the reality of the picture. In the large-format painting *Foot and Tire* [cat. no. 118], misfortune is potentiated in a supreme polarisation: monumental car tires and a tiny shoe. The picture engages with the unresolved dissonance of nothingness and silence. The absence of the body is its evidence. Death, which – supposedly because of its anonymity in these disaster pictures – cannot be conveyed as 'tragic' or metaphysical, manifests itself in the assumption of unmistakably overturned values. If these pictures reveal anything, then it is the absurdity and statuesque loneliness of life that they point to. Warhol's disaster pictures are almost entirely dominated by the original photographs, which are in themselves a reconstitution of concrete physical events, that in fact, remarkably cruelly, banish death itself. The paintings made using these originals replicate the language of the photographs of scenes of death, and nothing else; they are the unaltered given image. In the series *Tunafish Disaster* [cat. no. 122] this prototypical principle is reversed. When Warhol read a report in *Newsweek* in April 1963 about two women who had died from an unusual tuna fish toxin, he extracted the illustration from the article: a photograph showing the victims with a tin of tuna fish.[38] Warhol's *Tunafish Disasters* point to the event, they convey what has happened purely through a language of analogies. And since death itself is not depicted, death in these works is an inflection of death, for it is only the echo of the news that stages the invisible drama.

In the pictures showing the electric chair in the execution room, Warhol again operates solely with the tension of allusion, with those connotations that refer to something else, something unspoken, and which, like a magnetic pull, point to the event that is hidden from sight and only ever implied. On the wall of the execution chamber the word 'Silence' is illuminated, but it is the emptiness in the *Electric Chair* pictures [cat. nos. 123-127] that alludes to modes of perception that imbue the stasis of this fearfully mystified sight of the death machine with the horror of moral retribution. Warhol added empty panels to some of the disaster scenarios [cat. nos. 117, 125]. In these diptychs the monochrome canvases are juxtaposed – almost like demiurges – to the depictions of horrific reports. These pictures are like thought-provoking *sopraporte*, and intended as such, creating myths and casting the depiction of death on the neighbouring picture in a metaphorical light: panels that may be red and orange, lilac, black and silver, but secretly they are ciphers for the gold which has been metaphysically exhausted over the centuries and which can never be axiomatic.

Warhol's *Disaster Pictures* show death one last time, at the end, when all is said and done, in the museum and as a late show when no-one asks how these pictures could ever have become art objects. And perhaps one only needs to erase the word 'art' to see their morbidity.

Particular mention should be made of *Thirty Are Better Than One* [cat. no. 101], a large-format painting made in 1963, notably in the context of the images of death and disaster.[39] With its additive ornamental pictorial grid it is neither a pure portrait nor a metonym of the historic model it is based on, namely Leonardo da Vinci's *Mona Lisa*. The mythology of the historic original, and the connotations of the endless interpretations of one of the most famous works in art history, recedes entirely into the background in Warhol's paraphrase. It in fact frees the meaning of the original. Having been reduced in so many ways to an allegory that forever has to be read into Leonardo's work, in Warhol's picture the Mona Lisa is filled with a quite different mystery that illuminates these non-individualised portraits with a passionless aura of surprising strangeness and immediacy. It is wholly inexplicable.

Much has been said about Andy Warhol's *Thirty Are Better Than One*. It has become one of those works of art that seem predestined to kindle philosophical argument. No doubt our knowledge of the preconditioning of the art historical motif it is based on is at the forefront of all our discussions. At the same time this work is frequently cited in the persistent debate that has been conducted ever since Walter Benjamin described the lost aura of the work of art in the age of its mechanical reproduction. And yet it seems to me today that there is another, very significant aspect of this work: Warhol's reprographic images (and this one above all) exist by virtue of the conversion of the subjectivity of the distant aura of the original. The extreme reduction that results from its mode of production, registered by us as a loss of uniqueness, nevertheless constitutes an extremely hard to describe, defensive 'yet': the sensual reinstatement of an aura, however that aura may be defined, within which the sadness of loss resonates. Even in its reification through social appropriation this picture resists, and retains its 'alien' quality.

In its unapproachable perfection this picture withstands every attempt to decode it and to interpret it, but it precisely identifies the intended laconicism of its own time and shadow which we read but which remain concealed from us. The simple logic of the structure of the work already evokes the hypothetical quality of later conceptual art, which will exist only as an ideal or pure idea. But above all *Thirty Are Better Than One* is an audacious painting that does not shroud itself in mystery, a black-and-white metaphor that lays its claim to absolute existence at the moment of interpretation.

Among the *Disaster* paintings made in 1965, there is one picture – *Atomic Bomb* [cat. no. 128] – that expresses, with relentless consequentiality, the complementary messages of absoluteness and absurdity. In this picture the time of an entire century is arrested, painfully, as in almost no other work. This painting tells of the dichotomy that Anselm Kiefer once referred to as *Lebenszeit* ('life time') and *Weltenzeit* ('world time'); it tells of the overwhelming, destructive impulse felt by human beings who, in possession of a monstrous weapon, 'superior to nature', threaten our very planet. Warhol's picture, which addresses extinction, the unimaginable 'afterwards' of the fires of purgatory, is one of the most remarkable images produced by this chronicler of his own time. Aesthetic terminology is defeated by this painting. All the more astonishing is the artist who did not fear *sancta simplicitas* as he worked on this piece.

In summer 1963 Warhol bought his first movie camera, and almost in passing produced the film *Sleep*, which was followed a few weeks later by the films *Kiss, Tarzan and Jane Regained, Haircut* and *Blow Job. Sleep* is a silent, black-and-white film, in which the camera passively shoots long passages showing a man sleeping, passages that Warhol edits into repeating sequences. Nothing happens, was the widespread comment on these scenes, their subject was a demonic silence, whose meaning touched on a form of totality as well as on complete nothingness. Nothing happens, and if one were to stop the film, one would be where one had started. This notion of time was one of Warhol's guiding principles, hard for anyone else to comprehend. And yet this extreme reduction of life 'so close you could reach out and touch it' – of life 'as it is' – is arrested in a moment of unfalsified truth and the viewer learns to see anew beyond the event itself, beyond the high points and the drama, because Warhol manages to get back behind any kind of gesture or formalism. By avoiding any incorporation of cinematic strategies, these films uphold their idea of pure perception. I think it was Jonas Mekas who said that 'it is hard to bear the unveiled gaze with which Warhol's camera stares at life like a new-born child.'

In early October 1963 Warhol travelled with friends to Los Angeles for the opening of his second exhibition in the Ferus Gallery. Years later he wrote in *POPism*: 'The farther west we drove, the more Pop everything looked on the highways. Suddenly we all felt like insiders because even though

Pop was everywhere – that was the thing about it, most people still took it for granted, whereas we were dazzled by it – to us, it was the new Art. Once you "got" Pop, you could never see a sign the same way again. And once you thought Pop, you could never see America the same way again.'[40]

In November that year Warhol had to leave his studio in the fire station on 79th Street. He moved into a large space in an industrial building on 47th Street, which became his first 'Factory'; his friend Billy Linich wallpapered it, turning it into a silver-foil loft.

When John F. Kennedy was murdered on 22 November 1963 in Dallas, Warhol recognised the press photographs of the grieving widow, Jackie Kennedy, as the portrait that mirrored the whole of the double-edged trauma that had struck the United States. The originals that he used for his silkscreen paintings are the memorable 'face object', in which the inexplicable nature of the event itself and the sense of being damned take on the qualities of a myth, since for a brief moment in time the whole world only 'sees' sadness in this face. It is the same moment of social convention that was once depicted in the cipher of the mysterious face of Greta Garbo in printed letters. In these portraits Warhol once again and for the last time, expressed the violence of the United States that is also present in the language of the blatant exhibitionism of American emotions, before continuing in the *Brillo, Heinz* and *Del Monte* boxes [cat. nos. 159-162] with his monologic discourse on the replication of 'sculptures' from everyday American life.

Within a few short years the artist Andy Warhol is himself part of the myth of a contemporary culture that euphemistically formulated innocent notions of so-called freedom, and demonstrated how one might lead such a subjective existence. But only an illusion! Yet the 1960s were also that decade in the century just passed that invented individuality as programmatic individuality with all its affirmative traits. 'Freedom' was only an illusion, in truth it was its own progressive annihilation. Warhol, who certainly had a decisive influence on that decade, must have been aware of this process of transformation in his own person and in the way he related to his own time. In 1964, when he used a photo of himself from a photo-booth as an exhibition poster and, shortly afterwards, as the image for his first series of *Self-Portraits* [cat. nos. 147-149], he in effect included himself in the images of stylised iconic objects. 'Star Icons' was and still is the term usually applied to these works, although that did more to obscure than to reveal the social phenomenology that underlies them. At the height of his fame Warhol's loneliness in the company of others was in direct proportion to the distance he maintained from his admirers. The same thing that attracted him to new acquaintances also frightened him away and deepened his loneliness; despite this the Factory on 47th Street had long since become an 'open studio', a kind of rehearsal room and salvation army station, where artists and drug addicts, filmmakers and those seeking refuge, poets, drop-outs and whores, met day and night. Warhol looked on curiously like a voyeur who was at the centre of it all, but at the same time he saw ever more clearly through the hysterical compulsion of social determinants, without ever being able to escape them. For some years Warhol's Factory was the centre of gravity that was responsible for all the extreme attacks on convention. The Factory became the department store for new lifestyles.

In early 1964, when the architect Philip Johnson asked Warhol to create a work for the façade of the New York State Pavilion at the World's Fair just outside Manhattan, the artist chose to use

FBI posters of the thirteen most wanted criminals for his project. But just before the opening in April the silkscreen caused a political scandal and the mural was censored: Warhol was asked either to remove or to paint over the panels.[41] He decided to obliterate them, thereby changing the pictures' 'existence' into a kind of 'nothingness'. For the first time he experienced how an aesthetically provocative strategy outside the museum could indeed lead to hypocritical political debate. We reject out of hand the notion that Warhol's provocative 'mural' wanted to question the convergence of the cult-like conventions of Pop art.

While the World's Fair was still running Warhol decided to re-make the series *Thirteen Most Wanted Men* [cat. nos. 129-142] as photo-silkscreens on canvas. Clearly these 'portraits' are different from all the other portraits Warhol had made because they render unaltered the original police photos as a literal fact, as an extra-aesthetic category per se. So the life damned in these wanted posters becomes devalued as never before. And in these paintings the morphology of the face becomes the absence of the individuality of the person depicted. Warhol simply vastly enlarged his offset originals without any intermediate steps, and in the process the faces – with their features schematically broken down into black dots – once again became the 'original' devalued, discriminated-against object. In the series *Thirteen Most Wanted Men*, behind the surface of nothingness, a form of senseless affliction is exemplified which, like an invisible morpheme, points to the whole œuvre.

November 1964 at last saw the fulfilment of Warhol's prophecy of an exhibition of his works in the Leo Castelli Gallery that had been rejected two years previously. The reproduction of a colour photograph of hibiscus flowers that Warhol found in a magazine became the starting point for an extensive series of *Flowers* [cat. nos. 164-168], silkscreens on canvas in a whole variety of sizes.[42] The sharply outlined blossoms glow against a green-and-black background, creating a virtual, painful stillness. Since they seemingly only live on the surface, in the stasis of their colouration, they also initiate only the one metamorphosis which is a fundamental tenet of Warhol's work: moments in a notion of transience. The flower pictures were for Everyman, they embodied Warhol's power of concretisation, the shortest possible route to stylisation, both open to psychological interpretation and an ephemeral symbol. But the flowers with their black-and-white or black-and-green backgrounds, were also to be read as metaphors for the flowers of death. 'It is the flash of beauty', wrote John Coplans, 'that suddenly becomes tragic under the viewer's gaze. The garish and brilliantly coloured flowers always gravitate towards the surrounding blackness and finally end up in a sea of morbidity. No matter how much one wishes these flowers to remain beautiful they perish under one's gaze, as if haunted by death.'[43] Warhol's *Flowers* resist every philosophical transfiguration as effectively as the pictures of disasters and catastrophes which they now seem ever closer to.

After the *Flowers* had sold out in New York, Warhol created new images of flowers which were shown in May 1965 in his second exhibition in Europe, at the Galerie Ileana Sonnabend in Paris. While European critics saw in Warhol the most important, most 'modern' Pop artist, the artist himself responded in Paris by proclaiming the end of his own painting, and the end of Pop art. The positive 'coherence' of the Pop movement may have unsettled him; he may have been bothered to find himself part of a widely accepted 'ism'; nevertheless, even now Warhol was not able to resolve this possible contradiction. His announcement that he only wanted to make films in future rested on the fact that he had long since emotionlessly connected 'actual' reality and 'virtual' reality as the legitimation of his work. 'People sometimes say that the way things happen in the movies is unreal, but actually it's the way things happen to you in life that's unreal. The movies make emotions look so strong and real, whereas when things really do happen to you, it's like watching television – you don't feel anything.'[44] Years later in his book, *The Philosophy of Andy Warhol*, he once again questioned what he saw as the bizarre distance between reality and his own life: 'I think, people forget what emotions were supposed to be. And I don't think they've ever remembered. I think that once you see emotions from a certain angle you can never think of them as real again. That's what more or less happened to me.'[45]

In the years to come the Factory served both as a film studio and as a workshop, turning out countless commissioned portraits. The portraits, for which Warhol now made his own polaroids, were produced in a rapid silkscreen process, their surfaces retouched in a cursory, painterly manner and almost always in the same square format. In all of these portraits the language of artificial ideality is repeated, emerging as an aesthetic dimension. In truth, however, it is a standardised aesthetic dedicated to one class alone which, as ceremony and ritual, enacts the anthology of illusions of *Zeitgeist* for that same bourgeois class. Free from any notions of psychology and the metamorphosis of the person portrayed in the work, in each of these paintings Warhol only pursues his own concept of cosmetic pathos, free of psychological traits. If anything, these are rather light commissioned works, bowing to an obsessive mania for repetitive sameness.

For some years Warhol's life was inseparably bound up with his films. Edie Sedgwick, Gerard Malanga, Chuck Wein, International Velvet, René Ricard and various unknowns from amongst the stream of visitors to the Factory become the 'superstars' in his underground films: *Harlot, Suicide, Vinyl, Kitchen, Beauty No. 2* and *My Hustler*. After the cool voyeurism with which he had presented moments in the lives of others as scenes in these films, where he only had people act out what he already considered to be reality, in the end his own emotions, his cult of distance, provided the material for a film. Nothing in these scenes from life looks produced. And perhaps that is why the ordinariness and emptiness, the idleness and the hysterically concealed boredom became one of the most accurate mirrors of a whole generation. Warhol's epigrammatic precision in his films had also found a metaphor in the 'uniqueness' of the everyday which stood for truth and lies alike.

In April 1966 Warhol had a room in the Castelli Gallery papered with *Cow Wallpaper* [ill. p.233] – rows of silkscreened yellow and red cows' heads. *Silver Clouds* [ill. p.231] floated in another room – foil cushions filled with helium gas. There was an astonishing irony in the way that Warhol seemingly exposed this exhibition to the excessive fiction of a cult and to the unscrupulousness of the mise-en-scène. And yet Warhol was in fact attacking the last archetypal identity of the picture – by affixing senselessness and its alliance with susceptibility to the walls. Four years later, during an exhibition in the Whitney Museum in 1970, Warhol once again took the dimensionless parable of the identity of the picture as his discourse. On walls papered with his bright, cheerful cow paper, he hung the cruel images of the *Electric Chair*. He did not reconcile this two-faced affirmation and alienation, as the museum readily appropriated both.

A year before the assassination attempt in June 1968, which Warhol survived despite being severely injured and which was to change his life and his relations with others, he produced his important series of *Self-Portraits* [cat. nos. 152-155], again in various different formats. With these paintings Warhol himself became a distinct, myth-like icon. With the largest of them being more than life-size, these portraits radiate a pensive self-confidence, but also a certain distance between himself and his own image, denoted in the veiling shadow that blanks out the expressivity of one half of the face. It was not until five years later that Warhol was to start on his series of *Mao* paintings [cat. nos. 170-174], thereby continuing to turn motifs into icons. The mass-effective aura of the Mao portrait puts it in the same category as idealised types of hypostatised reality which always provided the most suitable source material for his work. The painterly treatment of these pictures relies both on the cool, lucid self-image of the subject and – later when the series is extended in the most diverse of formats – on expressive, gestural dialogues between the surface of the silkscreen and the layers of paint applied to it. The painterly gestures of these pictures recur henceforth in other themes. Their often astonishing, paradoxical patterns already point towards the postulates of postmodernism which account for every style and its historical references according to their own time. The ensemble of *Skull* paintings [cat. nos. 175-182], which Warhol made in 1976, are amongst the later important recollections of the disaster pictures of 1963, as well as citing many-faceted memento mori allegories from art history.

The Mao pictures and the *Skull* series were followed in the late 1970s and early 1980s by cycles in which Warhol again took motifs from art history, but at the same time still intentionally reflected on his own work. Some of these later images adhere almost stoically to a meaning that was already part of history. The *Retrospective* paintings [cat. no. 215] seem to associate the motifs of the 1960s to conjunctions like in a stop motion effect. They are pure, undetermined dictions which only transfix Warhol's own earlier subjects: oversized panels without contemporary critical reflection that look back without looking at the present. Basically they show that the artist was prepared for the first time to take fragments of his own pictures and join them together in a synthesis of their disparate messages. The *Reversal* series [cat. nos. 214, 218] also obeys a similar structure. The once positive depiction of the images becomes its own alchemical negative and is thereby, as it were, manically demystified and tamed. There is no over-arching thought, no questioning gaze of transformation from the present back to the vitality of the originals from a decade earlier. And yet here, too, extinction, disappearance and the rupture of the motif in the rupture of time, are reflected.

On a footing with this retrospective work there are also the *Shadow* paintings [cat. nos. 206-210] which were first shown in an impressive installation in 1979 in the exhibition space of the Dia Art Foundation. With these works Warhol returns to panels of mystical allusion, of the kind that had distinguished the material he had used years before. In the emptiness of these paintings – landscapes of the inner self – which some did not even want to recognise as 'paintings', we see the extent of Warhol's sense of distance and his view of the reality of life that touches the world in its entirety, as though in a Zen message. And Julian Schnabel was not wrong when he wrote twelve years ago: 'All of the images of Andy's paintings have passed through the shadow and light of these paintings, bolstering up and heralding in this vision of the existential.'[46] It would not even be odd to read the obvious allegory of open interpretations in the purity of a glass bead game: life is meant and, once again, the chance dereliction that is expressed in a new quality of contemplation, represented in these paintings by the mysterious shadow – in itself a highly abstract reflection.

Andy Warhol's *Shadow* paintings, particularly the large-format panels, have never really been appreciated. Their significance went unnoticed in the early 1980s in the midst of ever new attempts by the artist to make abstraction iconic, working in collaboration with other artists and revitalising his own themes, which then, unrecognised, disappeared in the lightness of the motif.

Between 1985 and 1987 Warhol produced an important, comprehensive series of paintings: his transformations of Leonardo da Vinci's *Last Supper*, suggested in 1984 by Alexandre Iolas, the artist's first gallerist.[47] This commission on the subject of Leonardo's mural in the refectory of Santa Maria delle Grazie (1495-97) became a requiem for Andy Warhol, who died during the exhibition of the works in the Palazzo delle Stelline in Milan in February 1987.

In view of the short time between its making and Andy Warhol's death, this work has been open to more speculation than any of his other works. Leonardo's depiction in the *Last Supper* of the prophetic reference by Christ to his imminent crucifixion and the Christian belief in transubstantiation inevitably induced contradictory interpretations of Warhol's works.

What Warhol was certainly concerned with was the everyday of the interpretation of the historic original he was dealing with: the paradoxical task Leonardo faced when he had to portray the heavenly vision of a human Christ who knows of the depths of human betrayal that exist in one of his disciples. In some of Warhol's large-format silkscreens, which heighten the shadowy, restored figure of the original as an unspoilt replica [cat. no. 239], we still sense the sacrosanct image of a metaphysical space. But what is the space we are looking at: is it Leonardo's fresco or is it the aura of a picture that the era of Leonardo's work induced? The profane depiction of Christ in Warhol's pictures daringly contrasts with the possibility of a Christian, existential interpretation. Above all in the hand-painted pictures, as paraphrases of non-central and other wayward themes, the presence of the Last Supper is relativised in contradictory versions. These provocative paraphrases that combine the image of Christ with gaudy aspects of the *Zeitgeist* chosen by the artist, reflect what Joseph Beuys once said about the state of society: 'Mysteries happen in the main station.'

Andy Warhol, the most important chronicler of the second half of the twentieth century, symbolises in his work all the seeds of alienation that appeared in that century of fragmentation. The bright flash of beauty as a tragic moment; the recognition of a reality that can be abstracted to particular, virtual reality – these were experiences that Warhol also shared, as an artist who more than anyone before him took the idea of the work and the work itself and plunged them into confusingly circling reality, because he saw his own time in the images of reproduced objectivity. In his works the explicit communicates with the implicit, even if the artist himself was only dealing with the visible and referred his viewers to others for individuality. Warhol transposed the ritual of the painting process into his own time and doubtless the history of the term as well. He did not give up the ritual, but turned the process into the ritual: his pictorial world, derived from other media, itself becomes the medium. The work leaves behind it questions about questions which in their nature supersede mere painting.

Almost forty years have now passed since Andy Warhol made his first most striking paintings in the early 1960s. His works have moved from the popular, ideographic context of Pop art into a different realm of memory. The layers of meaning that they once alluded to have also changed. The notion of Pop art hardly explains these works any more; today it leads only to dissent. But what is the phenomenon that has made these pictures different, more puritanical? Behind the closed surface of the ascetics of their reproduction, with time their psychological uniqueness has taken on an alien quality. A voice that makes no appeal, without pathos, without didactic zeal, that – behind the mask of distance (and of existential uncertainty), behind the supposed emptiness – in reality has morals and faith (Psyche). Warhol's Catholicism, for 'that is what he at heart remained',[48] had in fact already lodged itself forever in the surface of his works. They are unceasingly moral. When Warhol's supposedly metaphor-free extremes emotionlessly document the unbearable, then it is above all the metaphor of Catholicism that is the hidden element in these extremes, like a void suppressed in panic. The paradox of mental distance on the one hand and a moral dimension on the other is part of the mode of expression of Warhol's paintings – a 'union of opposites'. It is legible not as harmony but as a shadow that wants to remain alien to the world.

Neither the panels of the *Last Supper*, which retain some of their secrets, nor the *Skull* paintings, can entirely escape the embrace of terror and of monotonous visions of bitter premises. In Warhol's work it is always the two together that prevent an aura of heresy from emerging: in the *Shadow* paintings it is the loneliness of an individual that speaks, who evidently, without having any choice, over several decades, preferred his own loneliness to our epidemic loneliness. The artist's conception of the world of unattainable emotionlessness and the unfulfillable desire to be like a machine is only countered by the notion that the world is already a machine.

ENDNOTES

1 Rainer Crone, *Andy Warhol, Das zeichnerische Werk 1942-1975*, exh. cat., Württembergischer Kunstverein, Stuttgart 1976.

2 Rainer Crone, *Das bildnerische Werk Andy Warhols* (dissertation), Berlin 1976; Jesse Kornbluth, *Pre-Pop Warhol*, New York 1988; Nan Rosenthal, 'Let Us Now Praise Famous Men: Warhol as Art Director', *The Work of Andy Warhol*, ed. Gary Garrels, Seattle 1989; Heiner Bastian, *Andy Warhol. Frühe Zeichnungen [Sammlung Marx]*, exh. cat., Museum für Gegenwart – Hamburger Bahnhof, Berlin, 1996; Patrick S. Smith, *Andy Warhol's Art and Films*, Ann Arbor, Michigan 1986; Mark Francis and Dieter Koepplin, *Andy Warhol. Zeichnungen 1942-1987*, exh. cat., The Andy Warhol Museum, Pittsburgh/Öffentliche Kunstsammlung, Basel 1998.

3 Tina S. Fredericks, 'Remembering Andy', Kornbluth, 1988, p.12.

4 Victor Bockris, *The Life and Death of Andy Warhol*, New York 1989, p.38. I am most grateful to Victor Bockris for the wealth of information that I was able to access in his archive.

5 Andy Warhol and Pat Hackett, *The Philosophy of Andy Warhol. From A to B and Back Again*, New York 1975, p.22. cf. Bockris, 1989, pp.43f.

6 Smith, 1986, p.14. Warhol used the title *The Broad ...* for two works. See Crone, 1976, cat. no. 92, p.109 (colour reproduction of one version). See also Kynaston McShine, *Andy Warhol. A Retrospective*, exh. cat., The Museum of Modern Art, New York 1989, p.14 (reproduction of the second version, p.403). In 'The Education of Andy Warhol', *The Andy Warhol Museum*, Pittsburgh 1994, p.164, Bennard P. Perlman recounts that when *The Broad Gave Me My Face But I Can Pick My Own Nose* had not been accepted, Warhol gave it a new title alluding to the rejection: *Why Pick on Me*. The painting was later shown in the group exhibition Arts and Crafts Center in Pittsburgh under this title.

7 Benjamin Buchloh, 'The Andy Warhol Line', Garrels, 1989, pp.52f.

8 Philip Pearlstein was the slightly older fellow-student and friend of Warhol's during the last two years at the Carnegie Institute in Pittsburgh. He is the most reliable source on the artistic development of Warhol during that time. See the interview between Rainer Crone and Philip Pearlstein in Crone, 1976, pp.253-71. See also Philip Pearlstein, in McShine, 1989, p.419. See also Bockris, 1989, pp.39ff. For more on Warhol's artistic development and work in the 1950s see also Donna De Salvo, *Success Is A Job in New York – The Early Art and Business of Andy Warhol*, exh. cat., Grey Art Gallery and Study Center, New York University, New York 1989.

9 Dieter Koepplin, 'Andy Warhol's Zeichnungen nach der Photonatur', Francis and Koepplin, 1998, p.21.

10 Mark Francis, 'Einfache Schönheit. Andy Warhols Zeichnungen', Francis and Koepplin, 1998, p.10; see also Bockris, 1989, p.40.

11 Kornbluth, 1988, p.48; Smith, 1986, p.15; see also Crone, 'Form and Ideology: Warhol's Techniques from Blotted Line to Film', Garrels, 1989, p.74.

12 Bockris, 1989, p.42.

13 Ibid.

14 Henry Geldzahler, 'Andy Warhol: Erinnerungen', Crone, Stuttgart 1976, p.26.

15 Koepplin, 1998, p.19.

16 Gene R. Swenson, 'What Is Pop Art? Answers from 8 Painters', *Artnews*, vol. 62, no. 7, November 1963, p.26.

17 James Fitzsimmons, 'Irving Sherman, Andy Warhol', *Art Digest*, vol. 26, July 1952, p.19.

18 The first of the so-called presentation books, *A Is an Alphabet* (1953), was followed by *There Was Snow on the Street and Rain in the Sky* (1953), *Love Is A Pink Cake* (1953), *25 Cats Name(d) Sam and One Blue Pussy* (1954), *A la Recherche du Shoe Perdu* (1955), *In the Bottom of My Garden* (1956), *A Gold Book by Andy Warhol* (1957) and *Wild Raspberries* (1959).

19 See Walter Hopps, *Robert Rauschenberg. The Early 1950s*, exh. cat., The Menil Collection, Houston 1991, p.231.

20 In 1955 Warhol produced the portfolio *A la Recherche du Shoe Perdu* with fourteen offset lithographs, variously water-coloured by himself and his friends. The texts were composed by Ralph Pomery, and Andy Warhol's mother wrote them out.

21 'Andy Warhol. Crazy Golden Slippers', *Life*, vol. 42, 21 January, 1957, pp.12f.; see also Kornbluth, 1988, pp.106f.

22 Crone, 1976, pp.80ff.

23 *A Gold Book by Andy Warhol* was published privately in 1957. The bound book contains eighteen, partly hand-coloured offset lithographs in an edition of 100. The book was designed by Georgie Duffee.

24 Besides Abstract Expressionist works, the exhibition at The Museum of Modern Art, *Sixteen Americans* [16 December 1959-14 February 1960] also presented works by Jasper Johns, Robert Rauschenberg, Frank Stella, Ellsworth Kelly and other artists whose new pictorial language had a cool rationality that was distinctly different from the gestures and the psychic expression of the works of Jackson Pollock, Franz Kline and Robert Motherwell.

25 *Wild Raspberries*, a fantasy cookery book, is the last of Warhol's 'presentation books'. It was produced jointly by Warhol and Suzie Frankfurt and put on sale in Bloomingdale's department store. *Wild Raspberries* consists of twenty sheets with offset lithographs, which were coloured by Warhol and friends. The sheets were individually displayed in December 1959 in the Bodley Gallery.

26 Information from the artist in conversations with the author in 1982 in Berlin and in 1983 in New York.

27 Information from the artist in a conversation with the author in 1985 in New York after the purchase of *Advertisement* for the Marx Collection. As far as Warhol could remember, *Advertisement* was the first of his so-called 'no comment paintings'.

28 Roland Barthes, *L'aventure sémiologique*, Paris 1985, p.160 [How can the actual meaning be the 'natural' meaning and the metaphorical meaning the 'original' meaning?].

29 Andy Warhol met Emile de Antonio through Tina S. Fredericks, who gave him his first commission in New York, Kornbluth, 1988. Ivan Karp was on the staff at the Leo Castelli Gallery. Warhol met him one afternoon in the gallery and asked him to look at the pictures he was working on. See also Warhol's account of the meeting in Andy Warhol and Pat Hackett, *POPism. The Warhol 60s*, New York 1980, pp.7ff. Ivan Karp introduced Warhol to Henry Geldzahler, who was curator of contemporary art at the Metropolitan Museum in New York at the time, and was to become one of Warhol's most influential friends.

30 Swenson, 1963, p.60.

31 Smith, 1986, p.130; see also Bockris, 1989, p.105.

32 In a lengthy conversation in East Hampton in August 2000, Irving Blum described to me his encounters and exhibitions with Warhol.

33 Bockris, 1989, p.115.

34 See the source photograph used by Warhol in: *Andy Warhol Photography*, Pittsburgh 1999, p.130.

35 Ibid., ill. p.299. The photograph used by Warhol, reproduced here, shows Marilyn Monroe in a shot from the film *Niagara* (1953).

36 Gretchen Berg, 'Andy: My True Story', *Los Angeles Free Press*, 17 March 1967, p.3.

37 Neil Printz, 'Painting Death in America', *Andy Warhol Death and Disasters*, exh. cat., The Menil Collection, Houston 1988, p.46.

38 Warhol must presumably have chanced on the report about the fatal poisoning on p.76 of *Newsweek*, published on 1 April 1963. On p.80 of the same issue there is a reproduction of Warhol's painting *Dick Tracy*, as part of a review of the exhibition *6 Painters and the Object* at the Solomon R. Guggenheim Museum, organised by Lawrence Alloway.

39 The making of *Thirty Are Better Than One* was connected to the exhibition in the USA of Leonardo da Vinci's *Mona Lisa*, on loan from the Louvre on the request of President John F. Kennedy.

40 Warhol and Hackett, 1975, p.39.

41 In a conversation in New York in 1983, Warhol told me that the paintings were not wanted. Initially Warhol was told that not all the most-wanted criminals were still on the wanted list; not long afterwards it was pointed out that the pictures could cause problems since the majority of the wanted criminals were of Italian extraction. The fact was that the authorities wanted to have Warhol's murals stopped at all costs.

42 See the colour photograph used by Warhol, in Dallmann, ill. p.296 of this publication.

43 John Coplans, *Andy Warhol*, Greenwich, Connecticut 1970, p.52.

44 Warhol and Hackett, 1975, p.91.

45 Ibid., p.27.

46 Julian Schnabel in, *Andy Warhol. Shadow Paintings*, exh. cat., Gagosian Gallery, New York 1989, p.7.

47 In the early 1950s Alexandre Iolas owned the Hugo Gallery, which showed Warhol's first exhibition of drawings in June 1952, with works made after reading Truman Capote's writings.

48 John Richardson, 'Eulogy for Andy Warhol', in McShine, 1989, p.454.

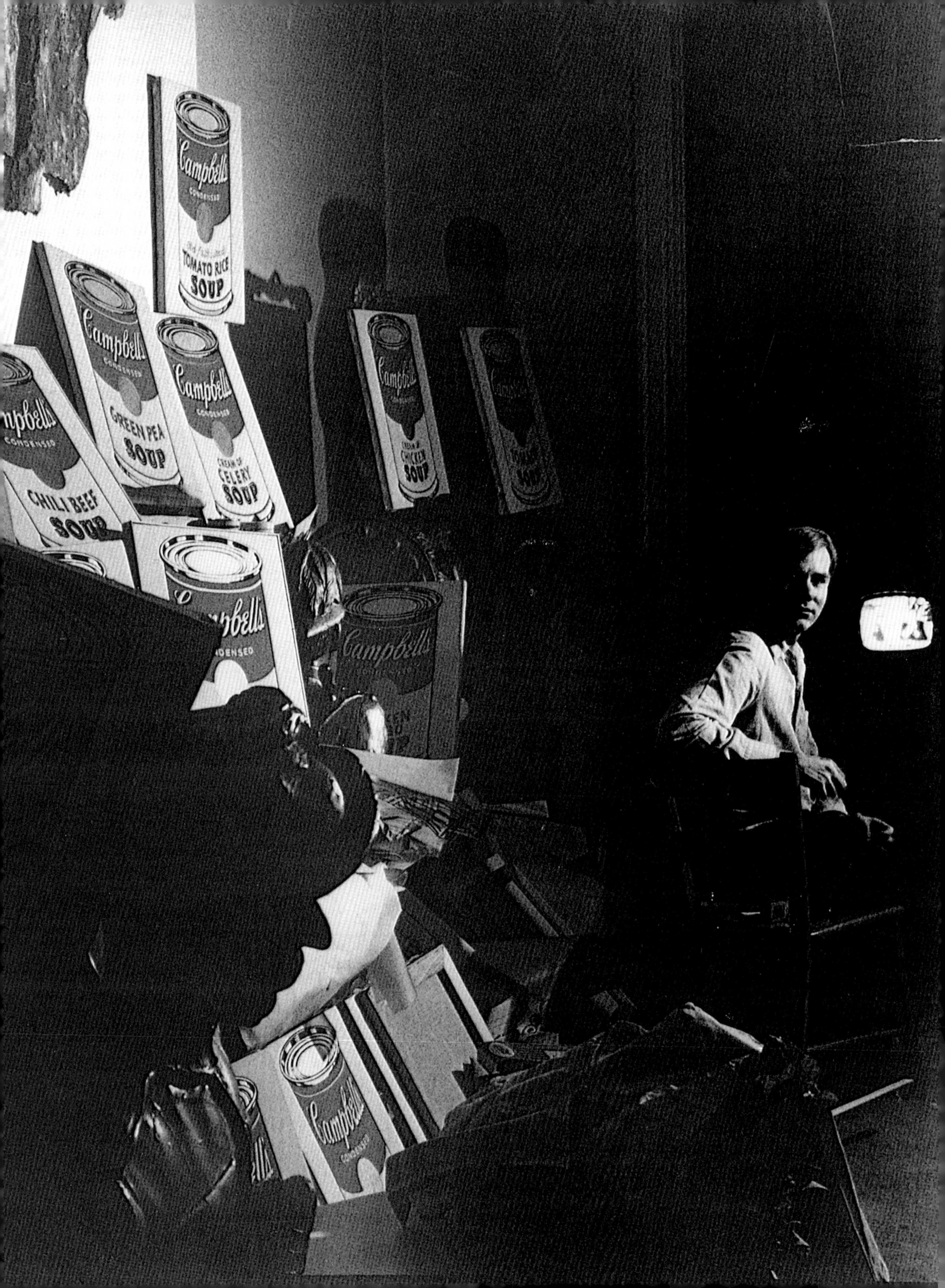
Campbell's
CONDENSED
TOMATO RICE
SOUP
Campbell's
CONDENSED
GREEN PEA
SOUP
Campbell's
CONDENSED
CREAM OF
CELERY
SOUP
Campbell's
CONDENSED
CHILI BEEF
SOUP
Campbell's
CREAM OF
CHICKEN
SOUP
Campbell's
CONDENSED
Campbell's
Campbell's

CAMPBELL'S SOUP CANS, 1962

Kirk Varnedoe

How They Came to Be. Andy Warhol's first solo exhibition happened, as important things often do, through a quilt of intent and accident, forward planning and spur-of-the-moment hunches.[1] Irving Blum, then running the Ferus Gallery in Los Angeles, usually came to New York once a year, to make the rounds of artists' studios. In the latter part of 1961, Blum visited Warhol, on the recommendation of David Herbert, who worked for the Betty Parsons Gallery. While he took a quick liking to the artist (who peppered him with questions about Hollywood, movie stars, and so on), Blum was at a loss to understand the paintings he was shown – big canvases with comic-book images, recently returned to the studio from a display in the windows at Bonwit Teller. Befuddled by these pictures, he opted for a wait-and-see attitude, and returned to Los Angeles. There the matter might have remained, save for the serendipity of his unexpected return to New York five months later, via a ticket offered by the Los Angeles collector Ed Janss. Seeking counsel on a Giacometti painting he was considering (and in fact subsequently purchased) at the Klaus Perls Gallery, Janss brought Blum with him to New York, leaving him with a second chance, within the same year, to catch up on new art in the city.

The first stop this time was Leo Castelli's gallery, where Ivan Karp brought out transparencies of paintings with comic-book images – not Warhol's, but those of Roy Lichtenstein. Prepared by months of thinking about what he had seen at Warhol's, Blum now took an immediate interest in Lichtenstein's work (in which he sensed some connection to Léger), and made a fast commitment to an exhibition. The encounter also primed him for a return visit to Warhol. Here there were no longer any comic-book pictures. Warhol told Blum that he, too, had seen the Lichtensteins, and had decided to abandon that field to someone who was doing better work in it. There were, however, six new canvases, each showing a single can of Campbell's Soup. Asked what he was up to, Warhol explained that he was going to paint a whole series, one for each of the soup flavours in the manufacturer's catalogue. Blum asked if there were any commitment for a show of the group, and finding there was none, offered a summer exhibition. Warhol eagerly accepted.

When the pictures arrived in Los Angeles, Blum came up with the idea of installing the entire series over a 'shelf', in the form of a moulding applied to the wall. This seemed a pretty obvious joke on the supermarket-commodity subject, and besides, it provided a quick and easy way to hang everything on the same level. The shelf gambit was proposed to Warhol on the phone, and he embraced it. The show ran from 9 July to 4 August, and despite the summer season, when visitors were predictably scarce, it caused some furor in the local art world. Several Los Angeles artists were, in Blum's words, 'tortured by it'. David Stewart, a dealer in Pre-Columbian art a few doors down from Ferus, teased Blum by buying about fifty cans of Campbell's Soup at a nearby market and displaying them stacked in his shop window, with a notice to the effect of 'Buy Them Cheaper Here'.

As the exhibition drew to a close, Blum had grown strangely attached to the pictures. Seeing them day after day, he had found that they had a collective resonance, and gave rise to 'all sorts of funny thoughts and ideas'. He came to feel that the group should not be broken up, and that he should own them all. However, by that time there were five commitments to purchase individual canvases at $100.00 each. No money had yet changed hands, and the paintings were all still in the gallery, when Blum called the five collectors – Ed Janss, Robert Rowan, Monte Factor, Dennis Hopper and Betty Asher – and asked them to relinquish their claims. With varying degrees of difficulty (Hopper being the toughest to persuade), he 'got back' the pictures. Meanwhile, he also called Warhol, who warmed to Blum's proposal to keep the group together, and agreed to offer a discount price for the whole lot: $1,000.00 for all 32, payable in installments. The deal was sealed, and finalized over ten monthly payments of $100.00 (for comparison, the monthly rent on the gallery was then $60.00).

What They Are and What They Are Not. One caveat we can glean from the story of their first display is that the initial logic of the *Campbell's Soup Cans* did not involve the grid array in which they have typically been shown since. Hanging them in this fashion – in, say, four rows of eight cans – pushes the work further into the territory of Minimalism, and suggests a rationale akin to that of Carl Andre's modular floor sculptures of the same period. Of course, Warhol did include multiple repeated units in other single works – *S&H Green Stamps*, later soup cans, and countless photo-silkscreened images from portraits to electric chairs and beyond. But those arrays are typically crowded into rows of abutments and overlaps that express a run-on, stuttering profusion, distinctly separate from the cool of the evenly-spaced grid. Thinking of the cans as a continuous one-line stream brings us closer, at least, to the first display. Still, we cannot know what idea, if any, Warhol originally had for the installation (he had of course never seen the gallery space). The basic practice of hanging at a common level, with even spacing, would by itself have been perfectly suited to emphasize the standardized nature of the same-subject, same-size pieces. Blum's ironic and pragmatic shelf-moulding literally underlined that standardized quality, and made the mocking conflation inherent in the pictures – between supermarket and gallery, unique artwork and staple commodity – still more blatant.

The other, most important truth imposed by the story of their initial exhibition is that the 32 canvases were not conceived as a single work of art. They were meant to be shown together, but then sold separately. The gallery was a showroom or shopping point, stocked with the full gamut of choices from which purchasers would select and take home individual units – with the field of their discrimination reduced to that of the consumer who chooses only a flavour from a line of routine alternatives. The exhibition was a special event, where the whole was something more than the sum of its parts. Blum was right to see that event – the big stunt, the wholesale advertisement for the retail sales – as a superior creation, with meaning in its mass effect that would be lost when the pieces were dispersed for domestic consumption. By keeping all 32 works together, and then by hanging them so they could be seen all in one view (his home was the first place such an installation was made), Blum forced to the fore the interlock between multiplied 'variety' and monotonous conformity that would have been tacit if the canvases had been scattered into separate collections. Much more impressively and memorably than the individual cans could be, the array uses art to make vivid a symptomatic system of commercial society, and mimes that commercial system to impose a purposefully provocative and problematic idea of art. The wry irony is that, both in the little joke of the shelf and in his shrewdly acquisitive itch to keep the group intact, Blum – the very model of an arch-capitalist and happy merchant/entrepreneur – should have been the key 'collaborator' who set these canvases on the way to enshrinement, in many a text, as one of Warhol's most biting indictments of American consumer society.

Old, Slow, and Archaic. When Warhol was a successful commercial artist in the 1950s, his style in advertising was personal, fey, and trendily of-the-moment. In order to become an artist he strangled all that, by moving backward and downward in the world of commercial imagery, to find crudely anonymous, out-of-date, tasteless trash. His initial choices – the nose job as in *Before and After*, the wig and rupture images – were dregs pulled up from the sludge of cheap commerce that filled the small-notice sections of low-end newspapers and magazines. This taste for the retrograde cliché was consistent with a strain apparent in modern art since Picasso began using newspaper clippings in 1912, whereby the hot new art style of the moment exploited the deadest and most shopworn elements of the commercial culture around it.[2] Even the early Warhol paintings of tabloid front pages that seem, in promotional terms, 'torn from today's headlines!' have this outmoded quality, when one sees them in the context of the colour television news that was the hot new medium of the day.

The phenomenon is still broadly evident in more fully developed Pop art. Often celebrated for boosting the flashy, here-today-gone-tomorrow sensationalism of contemporary consumer culture, Pop is actually soaked with nostalgia for outmoded things (Oldenburg's clothespins and icebags, or Rosenquist's painted billboard ads) and dotes on faded sheen (Warhol's off-new movie stars, characteristically dragging a tarnished glamour from the tail-fin era into the space age). In choosing the Campbell's Soup cans in particular, Warhol moved out of the expressionist grunge of tabloid vulgarity towards the commonplace banality of middle-class commodities, and into a zone of commerce where time stood still.

Campbell's Soup proudly presented itself, in the early 1960s, as a model of enduring stability. The label design had not changed in over fifty years, and the price of a can had held steady for almost forty.[3] Put otherwise, when Warhol painted these cans, in the second year of John F. Kennedy's presidency, he was featuring an item that had looked the same under William Howard Taft and cost the same under Calvin Coolidge. Like the Coca-Cola bottle that both Rauschenberg and Warhol used, or the black high-top sneakers and comic strips Lichtenstein featured, this product was, if not quite an anachronism, then certainly an enduring testament to the large sector of American life where buying patterns and choices seemed glacially unvarying. As Warhol's later comments about Coca-Cola make clear, such consumables seemed to provide a steady common denominator of experience across every age and class – and thus to be wrapped up with the constrictions and the consolations of mass democracy itself.[4] It is important to the meaning and impact of *Campbell's Soup Cans* that the industrial, same-damned-thing-again-and-again repetition of the units be paired, for the viewer, with this sense of stagnant stability across decades and generations. Without that, some of the fullness of Warhol's jibes at the ongoing ambivalencies of modern city life – the marriages of ample abundance and stultifying narrowness, comfort and numbness, security and monotony – would be denied.

Yet just as with the Coca-Cola bottle (which Rauschenberg and Warhol selected at the last moment before canned Coke became the rising norm), the Campbell's can was singled out at the very moment when changes in marketing strategies, sweeping through all consumer commerce in the 1960s, had started their tentative inroads into even this bastion of constancy. The lone variant in the array of all the labels, the two-part banner on the can of Cheddar Cheese Soup ('New!', 'Great As a

Sauce, Too!'), is the fatal first index of swifter change – the *Et in arcadia ego* of the commercial imperatives of accelerated innovation and obsolescence – on this otherwise placidly implacable landscape.

The 32 paintings are similarly transitional – and also old-fashioned in their way – in terms of Warhol's style as a painter. At this moment, he was on the move from the cruder, beat-generation world of raw black-and-white into the bright colours and crisper edges of mature Pop. The pre-primed off-white canvas for the ground and label, plus red and black with accents of silver and gold, all constituted an upbeat 'found' palette – still entirely naturalistic and unexaggerated, not yet marked by the space-age, day-glo transpositions of hue he would shortly start exploiting. The 'machine style' of the pictures was also still artisanal. He had his assistants invest considerable labour in miming a mechanical look, without yet adopting the techniques or technologies that might have given him the real thing. The appearance of breezy ease was doggedly laboured, as lots of rough ingenuity and tedious sweat went into making these images play the ragged masquerade of mindless, effortless products. The basic pencil schemas for the cans, still visible throughout the series, followed a template, either through stencilling or transfer drawing. After that the images were wholly hand-painted, with the exception of the fleur-de-lis motifs along each label's bottom edge (which were each individually printed, with varying degrees of completeness and clarity, via hand-made gum-rubber stamps). Only the vertical sides of the cans, with their slightly feathered edges, seem to have profited from masking tape or other methods. Elsewhere, there are painstaking freehand efforts at slavish naturalism, especially in the clumsy attempts to make the lettering on each can, in varying typefaces and sizes, conform to the implied curvature of the surface. And there are equally intent but always imprecise efforts at repetitive conventions, as in the rendering of the black reflections on the can tops. In contrast, Warhol added one central, repeated note of expediently pure abstraction in the solid gold disk that utterly ignores the fine black printing actually found on this area of the real label. Everywhere, inconsistency and approximation reign. The 'white' canvases vary in greyed brightness; the reds range from near-orange to Indian; the band encircling the label's top, patchily filled-in with mottled gold on 31 canvases, is left unpainted in 'Tomato Rice'; most cans have 11 fleurs-de-lis, but 'Bean with Bacon' has 12; and so on.

And on. But of course none of this uneven quirkiness concerns those who value the work principally for what they see as its conceptual agenda. Indeed, for many who esteem it as a radical assault on traditional notions of art, any attention to the canvases' sensual existence seems not just embarrassingly beside the point, but treacherous and reactionary to the point of fetishism. In this way, some of the most professedly materialist interpretations of the *Campbell's Soup Cans* often evince a contradictory, thoroughgoing idealism, which would set up a false dichotomy between the work of art itself and the ideal, less muddied meaning said to lie beneath or above its imperfections. Yet the stylistic and physical peculiarities of these 32 canvases are neither apart from nor less than the art's meanings, but integral to them. As surely as the structure of repetition or the strategy of appropriation, the slurs and gaps and mottlings and tics constitute the particular artist and the particular cultural moment at issue. There is a huge, complex difference between seeing these 32 canvases and the experience of seeing that many labels or cans or printed reproductions, in natural size, in this size, or in larger sizes. Any of those arrays, displayed, could synchronize with numerous interpretations of what Warhol intended. None would be, or be near, this work of art. Over time, its specific realities will resist, annoy and ultimately subvert any reductive reading that shuns them.

In person, the singular presence of the 32-canvas array, different in kind from any of Warhol's other commodity-label works, then or later,[5] depends absolutely on the interplay between the regular and the irregular, the almost-machine-like impact and the almost-subliminal handmade feel. Experiencing this ensemble first-hand, it now has something of the character of Muybridge's first sequential frames of equine motion, or the earliest NASA photographs of the moon surface. The feel is of a modern 'archaic' rigour, of a moment of genesis that embodies – in an as yet un-slicked-up rawness, with peculiar encrusted variegations – a new way of seeing, mapping, and giving form to an unlimned or neglected part of the world; and that implicitly lays the rougher foundation stones of a whole new sensibility. Seen against later Pop works, or especially against brasher appropriations from commercial imagery in the age of Koons or Hirst, the *Campbell's Soup Cans* of 1962 can seem – even with their 32-part jackhammer insistence – almost reticent or even (perversely) intimate, in their relatively small scale and the delicate particularity of their naturalistic detail. In such contexts, they can be at least temporarily disadvantaged by some of the same qualities of quieter, homespun aggression and laconically deadpan audacity that ensure their palpable freshness across the decades.

A Smart Dumb Thing. After the 1962 show, the can of Campbell's Soup swiftly became something like Warhol's own house brand, a logo for everything that was outrageous about him. Along with enlarged comic-book Ben Day dots, it is now something of a visual sound bite for all Pop art, if not for a whole post-1960 attitude of hip irony. This iconic status has subsumed, and by the mechanisms of celebrity marketing, made almost invisible the most basic questions the 32 paintings of cans first raised. Was there then, for example, any art, or any worthy meaning, in the act of painting a series of canvases of every flavour from a commercial soup catalogue? Certainly the gesture was intended to provoke just that anxiety. It was in Warhol's nature as an artist – in his particular combination of money-grubbing hunger for celebrity and painful, self-flagellating shyness, stammering dyslexia and sharp social radar, pliant, inarticulate passivity and stubborn intuitive insistence – to irritate this sensitive nerve of misgiving again and again, and re-animate an important genealogy of such doubt.

The *Campbell's Soup Cans* are preceded by a long tradition of modern art's engagement with the artifacts and designs of commercial and consumer culture, and by a narrower lineage – leading from Duchamp's readymade objects through an immediate precedent such as Jasper Johns' sculptures of beer cans – of bald and direct appropriation of found commercial images or objects. Great advantages of that inheritance – indeed, of the sum of permissions and arguments we could refer to as the modern tradition in art – are that it allowed for a more direct engagement with some of the most powerful social forces and visual experiences in modern life, and hugely expanded in art the range of gestures, activities, motifs and means that could spark argument, spawn emulation, force fresh thought, and generally hold worthwhile meaning for an expanding community of people. A trade-off for that gain, however, is a lingering and often-renewed necessity to deal with worries about the emperor's new clothes, and with the even unhappier question of bad faith. Permanent discomfort about being duped, and unshakeable suspicions about maliciously nihilist hoaxes, haunt all but the most blinkered and credulous followers of innovation in modern art. This uncertainty is in fact its own tradition.[6] And on this sophisticated level, the knowing observer of modern art asks a more complexly loaded version of the same question that the naive first-timer puts more bluntly: 'Is this a joke?'

The answers are 'Yes, of course,' and 'No, not entirely.' The lasting worth of the work is interwoven with its origin as a cheap stunt, and its ongoing intelligence is tied just as tightly to its blatant dumbness. Go one way or the other – make it only a stupid prank or only a trenchant social statement – and one reduces the power of the achievement. Many on the right would like to dismiss Warhol as a charlatan of mindless ambition, and just as many on the left would like to extoll him as a prophet of radical critique. The latter may be just as condescending as the former in its failure to allow art a different kind of intelligence from that of manifestos (including their own). If the *Campbell's Soup Cans* of 1962 prove anything – and they have been asked to prove a great many things – it must be that art does not need to be deep to be profound. A large part of intellectual life, and especially critical writing, seems dedicated to the notion that such work is worthy only to the degree that it can be abstracted into a fixed idea. In a case like Warhol's, the further imperative seems to hold that bald ideas that are widely evident gain stature by translation into difficult ideas intelligible to far fewer people. Yet, for all that elaboration, these same approaches tend almost fatally to reduce to a 'message' or moralizing little sermon, the work's slippery, hydra-headed meanings.

Like a great many other key pieces of modern art, *Campbell's Soup Cans* has a polyvalence that is completely at one with its drop-dead simplicity. The art in it has already been reduced so hard and so far that it is virtually impossible to split it any further into more convenient categories such as happy or sad, energetic or enervated, complacent or critical. That is part of why it is such a pleasure – a pleasure of exacerbated and lingering uncertainties – to keep looking at and thinking about this array four decades later. No summation or paraphrase anyone will ever write of it, nor any theoretical web to be spun around it, is ever even remotely likely to be anything like the panoply of things it effortlessly is all at once: hot, cold, heartless, funny, lively, boring, sad, outrageous, economical, memorable, vicious, stupid, sophisticated, crass and more.

ENDNOTES

1 The account of Warhol's show at the Ferus Gallery in 1962 is drawn from a recent conversation between the author and Irving Blum.

2 See K. Varnedoe and A. Gopnik, *High and Low: Modern Art and Popular Culture*, exh. cat., The Museum of Modern Art, New York 1990, especially the chapters on 'Words' and on 'Advertising', for numerous examples of this tendency.

3 Ibid., pp. 344-5.

4 Andy Warhol and Pat Hackett, *The Philosophy of Andy Warhol: From A to B and Back Again*, New York 1975. Warhol wrote: 'What's great about this country is that America started the tradition where the richest consumers buy essentially the same things as the poorest. You can be watching TV and see Coca-Cola, and you can know that the President drinks Coke, Liz Taylor drinks Coke, and just think, you can drink Coke, too. A Coke is a Coke and no amount of money can get you a better Coke than the one the bum on the corner is drinking. All the Cokes are the same and all the Cokes are good ... The idea of America is so wonderful because the more equal something is, the more American it is.'

5 To choose one obvious comparison, set these 32 units in juxtaposition with the single-canvas *200 Campbell's Soup Cans* (John and Kimiko Powers Collection) of the same year, and one can see how quickly Warhol began streamlining the task of replicating these labels, by eliminating the subheads, using only selected flavours, and resorting to stencils. Neither the (still crude) handling of this latter canvas, though, nor the more crisply standardised silkscreen cans Warhol would soon start making, have the impact of the 32-unit array, with its particular combination of diligently detailed handwork, rough approximation and serial replication.

6 For a ground-breaking treatment of the origins of this modern tradition of bad faith, see Jeffrey Weiss, *The Popular Culture of Modern Art: Picasso, Duchamp, and Avant-Gardism*, New Haven and London 1994, especially the chapter, '"Marcel Duchamp qui est inquiétant": Avant-gardism and the culture of mystification and *blague*.'

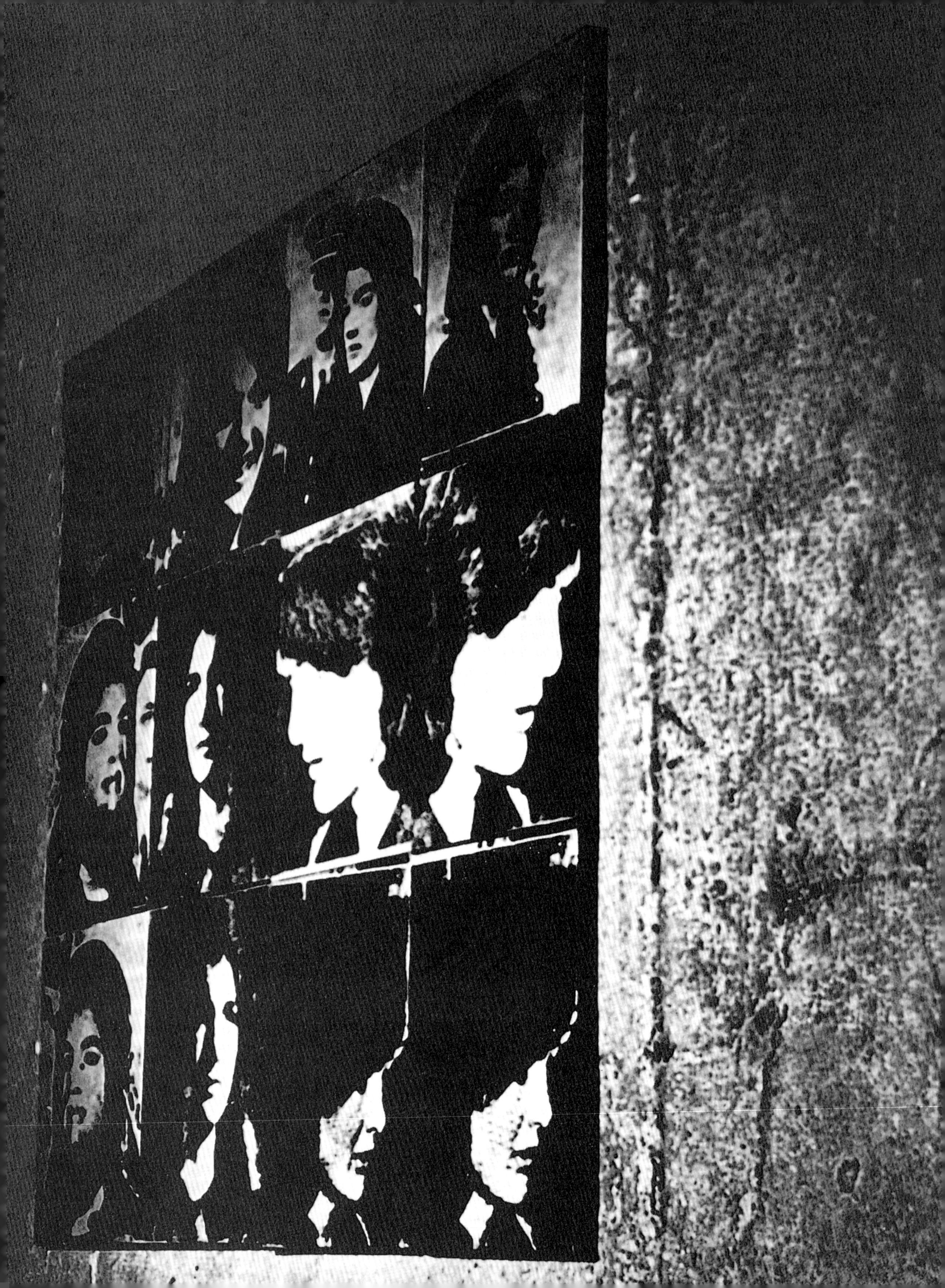

AFTERIMAGE

Donna De Salvo

A sheet of S&H Green Stamps, each a picture within a picture, pulsate red and green as they cling to the surface of an easel-size canvas. Produced by Andy Warhol in 1962, the work was 'painted' using a stencil repeatedly hand-stamped onto canvas. The combination of colours, the grid produced by the repeated stamps, the flattening of forms and unevenness of inks make for an 'all-over', painterly field; but nothing would seem to be further from a painting like Barnett Newman's *Vir Heroicus Sublimas* than Warhol's *S&H Green Stamps* [cat. no. 84]. Warhol's painting refers to another abstraction, a kind of fake money, and the trading stamps consumers saved to purchase a much desired toaster or blender. Yet Warhol's painting could be described using words offered by Newman and his fellow painters, Adolph Gottlieb and Mark Rothko, who proclaimed in 1943, 'We favour the simple expression of the complex thought. We are for the large shape because it has the impact of the unequivocal. We wish to reassert the picture plane. We are for flat forms because they destroy illusion and reveal truth'.[1] Warhol's painting also reveals a truth, but unlike his predecessors, a truth without any promise of the absolute.

Among the first generation of Pop artists, the criticism has focused on 'subject matter' at the expense of attention to the painting itself. Warhol of course did open up his painting to referential content and he was not alone in doing so. (The obvious artists that come to mind are his Pop contemporaries – James Rosenquist and Roy Lichtenstein, for instance – but the process began even earlier. During the early 1950s, Larry Rivers, Robert Rauschenberg, Grace Hartigan, and Jasper Johns, among others, expanded the field of painting to include references drawn from the world.)[2] Part of the problem was the critical split fomented by Clement Greenberg's efforts to limit painting to its constituent elements; faced with the graphic content offered up by a Warhol or Lichtenstein, many critics were unable to see the painting. One exception was Donald Judd, who in his insightful review of Warhol's first exhibition at the Stable Gallery observed, 'it is easy to imagine Warhol's painting without any subject matter, simply as "overall" paintings of repeated elements. The best thing about Warhol's work is the color.'[3]

This essay considers Warhol as a painter and focuses on an aspect of his painterly strategy – the creation of what can be called an afterimage, which Warhol developed in the early 1960s and pursued through the late 1970s and into the 1980s in his *Shadow* and *Camouflage* paintings. It was because of Warhol's intuitive understanding of the parallels between contemporary strategies in print advertising and high-art painting in the late 1950s and early 1960s, I believe, that he was able to produce a painting such as *S&H Green Stamps*.

Asked what his work was about, Warhol often replied, 'Look at the surface of my paintings, film and me, and there I am.'[4] This comment is usually read as an evasion; in fact it was a reply. There is a lot to be discovered if one takes Warhol at his word and looks closely at the surfaces of his paintings. More importantly, Warhol himself understood the implications of surface in contemporary culture. Consider, for example, Vance Packard's recounting of a mid-1950s executive in his famous analysis of post-war marketing, *The Hidden Persuaders*: 'Some colors such as red and yellow are helpful in creating hypnotic effects. Just putting the name and maker on the product of the box is old-fashioned and, he says, has absolutely no effect on the mid-century woman. She can't read anything, really, until she has picked the box up in her hands. To get the woman to reach and get the package in her hands, designers, he explained, are now using "symbols that have dreamlike quality". To cite examples of dreamlike quality, he mentioned the mouth-watering frosted cakes that decorate the packages of cake mixes, sizzling steaks, and mushrooms frying in butter. The idea is to sell the sizzle rather than the meat.'[5]

One can say that what Warhol painted was not the thing itself, but the feeling that it evoked; not the image, but the afterimage. The means toward that end, however, depended crucially on subject matter that functioned formally and provoked a response.

Warhol's 1962 *Close Cover Before Striking* [cat. no. 67] is an uninflected red field punctuated by a horizontal black band. As with his *S&H Green Stamps*, this is an abstract painting that self-consciously acknowledges the contemporary discourse around pure painting. It is also a painting of a matchbook. The red is Coca-Cola red, the black is the matchbook's flint and the text reminds us that this is not simply an abstract painting. One could say it both mocks and reveres a Newman 'zip' and Ellsworth Kelly's *Brooklyn Bridge VII* (1962), which despite its inspiration, the artist's own drawing of a sneaker, was shown with no reference to its actual source. Like the matchbook cover, the sheets of S&H Green Stamps that Warhol appropriated for his 1962 painting were already optical fields. In choosing the matchbook cover or the S&H Green Stamps, Warhol strategically selected a readymade that operated as painterly field and cultural artifact. Unlike Duchamp, however, Warhol tampered with his readymades. In some ways Warhol's *S&H Green Stamps*, with its complementary red and green, achieved what Michael Fried found in the painting Frank Stella was doing at the time. 'The literalness of the picture surface is not denied; but one's experience of that literalness is an experience of the properties of different pigments, of foreign substances applied to the surface of the painting, of the weave of the canvas, above all of color – but not, or not in particular, of the flatness of the support.'[6] Neither Warhol nor Stella were limiting themselves to Greenberg's narrow definition of painting. But, where Stella had used his commercial paints directly from the can in order to keep the colour 'as good as [it] was in the can', Warhol achieved a different effect with his silkscreen painting.[7] The unevenness of the hand-applied stencils, the off-registration, the vibrating colours – all conspire to create a shimmering field of hypnotic effect that functions purely optically but stays in the mind.

When he moved from stamps to photo-silkscreens, Warhol was able to extend the effect of the afterimage, combining the pulsating red and green of the *S&H Green Stamps* with an implied narrative. In *Optical Car Crash* (1962) and *Statue of Liberty* (1963) [cat. no. 104], Warhol screened the image twice, once in green and then again in red, to achieve a 3-D effect.[8] He repeats the image of the car crash (or Statue of Liberty) to create an off-register grid. One would expect that the repeated image tends to de-sensitise us to its content. In fact, it complicates the painting because we believe that so much information should lead us to know what is going on. Initially, our eye believes each image to be identical, yet the blurred image produced by varying the pressure of inks accomplishes something different – its painterly gesture renders the content ambiguous and abstract.

In another repeated image of Warhol's, the projected film of the Empire State Building – made with a stationary camera over a twenty-four-hour period – the moving image is made still. Staring at this film, the image becomes an afterimage as it is burned into the viewer's mind. Warhol began making films in 1963, a development that inevitably affected his painting.[9] In 1963, a blank canvas began appearing in some of Warhol's paintings functioning as what might be understood as a projection screen. In these paintings [cat. nos. 117,125], the afterimage becomes quite literal. As one's eye moves from the repeated images that Warhol screened on the left panel to the blank panel on its right, we see a mirage. Trevor Fairbrother describes Warhol's use of the formal device of the blank panel in terms of its content. 'With chilling, minimal matter-of-factness, this formal device allowed him to articulate the antagonism of life and death, the idea of death as the nothingness of a blank afterimage, and the perception of that bare figment of color as escape from a society that commits electrocution.'[10] The blank screen is also an optical device.

Warhol's understanding of the commercial uses of what can be described as afterimage were gained during his fourteen-year career as a commercial illustrator in New York. Throughout the 1950s, he had worked with award-winning art directors and graphic designers, many of whom – Alexey Brodovitch and Will Burtin, for instance – had been trained in the sophisticated visual strategies of the

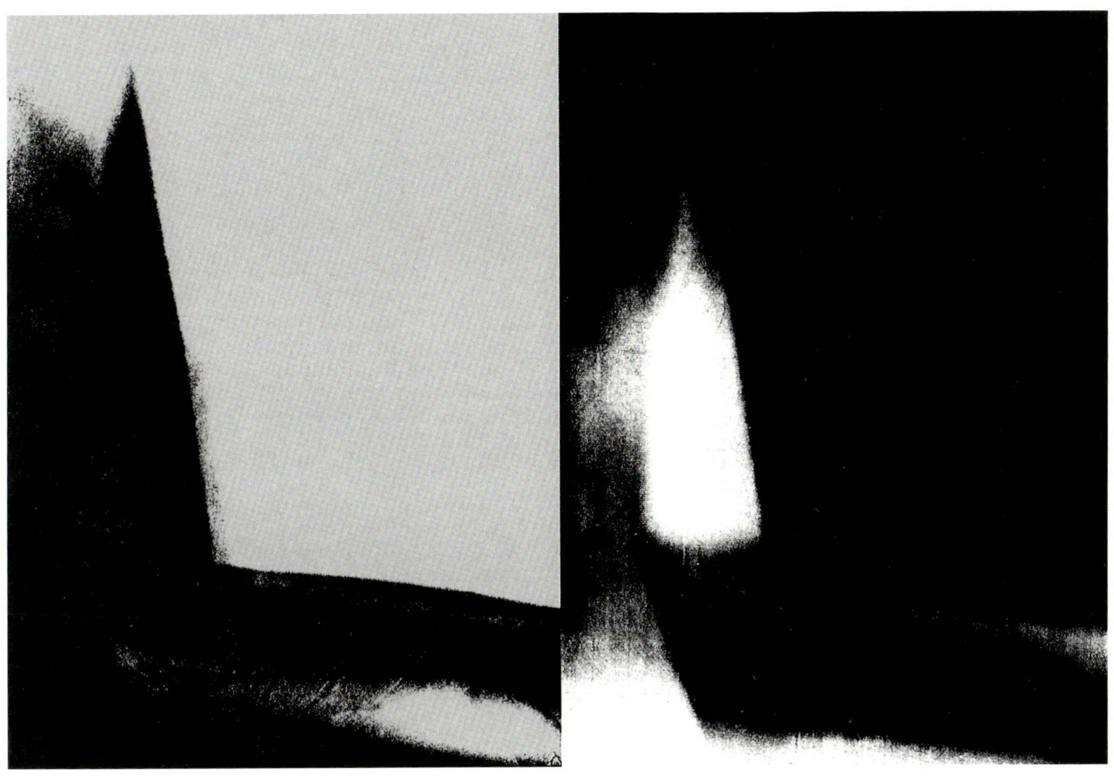

Andy Warhol
***Shadows*, 1979**
[Detail]

Bauhaus. While Warhol produced a variety of illustrations for hire, it was his two-year stint as the sole illustrator for I. Miller Shoes that brought him the greatest attention. Art-directed by Peter Palazzo along with fashion editor Geraldine Stutz, from 1955-57 the campaign won several awards for its revamped image of what had once been a rather sedate line of women's shoes. Using line drawings, they consolidated their advertising strategy, nearly always placing ads at the bottom of the page, only on Sundays and only in the society pages of the *New York Times* and *Herald Tribune*. The hope was that the repeated I. Miller image would be imprinted on the mind of the consumer, who would then subconsciously associate the product with its upscale surroundings. As the campaign gained momentum, the team even felt confident enough to occasionally run ads that illustrated no shoes at all. Stutz, who was the company's vice-president at the time, remembered that the campaign 'was meant to give the impression of a fresh and modern Miller rather than a stodgy, old-fashioned Miller … it was the beginning of an era when one … sold the sizzle and not the steak.'[11]

In his 1965 *Atomic Bomb* [cat. no. 128], Warhol paints what may be the most iconic after-image of the twentieth century. He offers us something other than the twisted bodies and cars to be found in his other disaster paintings. Instead he presents us with one aspect of the bomb's effect, the cloud it produced. The first two rows of the painting record a sinister image, but this time, as he varies the pressure of the inks for each of the images, the atomic cloud becomes increasingly abstract, even dream-like. In fact, in the bottom row of the canvas, the edge of the cloud appears to have meta-morphosed into something resembling a rather romantic quarter moon on a dark night.

Just a few years later, the circular outline of the bomb was replaced by what might be seen as a post-atomic sunset. Originally commissioned by architects Johnson & Burgee for the Marquette Hotel in Minneapolis, the 632 unique silkscreen prints comprising *Sunset* are notable for their complete abandon of the photographic silkscreen. Image here is created purely through the juxtaposition of flat colour. Warhol's sunsets are highly reductive, unified, and overtly abstract, the kind of pure effect that presages that of the *Shadow* paintings some six years later.

First shown at the Lone Star Foundation in New York, Warhol conceived the *Shadows* as one painting with eighty-three parts (102 were originally created but did not fit the space). 'I called them "*Shadows*"', says Warhol, 'because they are based on a photo of a shadow in my office'.[12] Warhol's studio assistant at the time, Ronnie Cutrone, recalls that Warhol had asked him to take photographs of the shadows generated by some abstract maquettes. But there are several contradictory stories about the sources for the *Shadows*. They began making an appearance in the early 1970s in Warhol's prints and drawings and are critical components in his still-lifes, including those of hammer and sickles, as well as skulls. Very little attention was paid to the *Shadow* paintings when they were exhibited in 1979, the same year that an exhibition of his portraits of the 1970s was held at the Whitney Museum of American Art in New York.[13] For an artist who at the time was identified with his paintings of celebrities, and who had so successfully exploited provocative, referential content, the *Shadows* must have appeared as an anomaly. The *Shadows* have been discussed as existential statements, as everything and nothing, as something fleeting, changeable and as intangible as real shadows. They have also been characterised as commentary on the very act of painting. But invariably, they have been positioned, along with the *Rorschachs, Camouflage* [cat. no. 238] and *Oxidation* paintings [cat. no. 211], as a late career development. It is true that Warhol seemed to be taking stock of his painterly output in the late 1970s. Anticipating the negative reaction to the *Shadows*, he commented, 'This show will be like all the others. The review will be bad – my reviews always are. But the reviews of the party will be terrific.'[14]

I would like to suggest another interpretation of these paintings as pure effect, nothing but an afterimage. In the *Shadow* paintings, the subject has become afterimage. Julian Schnabel has written about the *Shadows*, 'There is a lot in them, all of the images of Andy's paintings have passed through the light and shadow of these paintings, bolstering up and heralding in this vision of the existential.'[15] Each of the visual strategies operative in these paintings is the same as those used some seventeen years before. As with the earlier silkscreen paintings, although we at first believe each canvas to be the same

– a belief emphasised here by the repeated pattern of the shadow – they are not. Our eye moves instinctively from canvas to canvas searching for additional information. Difference is created through colour and the bravura brushwork made with a mop and silkscreen. The combinations of colour, and the changing arc of the shadow, conspire to create a mesmerising and hypnotic field. There is a sense of sheer transcendent beauty. Installed one after another, they envelop the viewer in what Warhol once described as 'disco décor'. They can only be experienced by walking their length, as one might do with Barnett Newman's *Stations of the Cross*, an ironic comparison given Warhol's determination to make light of his *Shadows*. Despite the deeply abstract quality of the *Shadows*, their connection to the world can never be erased, if only because they are so inextricable from Warhol's entire project. Whereas in the 1960s, Warhol could paint the afterimage of an atomic bomb – an image people could still identify – by the late 1970s, all that was left was the 'disco décor', the 'sizzle without the steak'.[16]

Warhol's decision to paint his *Camouflage* series in 1986, seems a next step in this direction. The biomorphic colour forms undulate over a staggering thirty feet. As in the *Shadows*, no essence is revealed, no single truth asserts itself. The experience is one of a late-twentieth-century simulated landscape, everything is surface and nothing but surface. Warhol has led us into another hypnotic pasture, one in which he intimates he is hiding, as in his *Camouflage Self-Portrait*. If we want to know all about Andy Warhol and his painting and his films, and perhaps even ourselves, all we have to do is look really hard at that surface.

ENDNOTES

My thanks to Katherine Rose, Emma Neill, Mark Francis, and Thomas Middlemost for their assistance in the preparation of this essay. I would especially like to acknowledge Linda Norden, whose incisive comments and spirited reading of the text cleared the path.

1 Statement by Mark Rothko, Adolf Gottlieb, Barnett Newman, 7 June 1943.

2 Donna De Salvo and Paul Schimmel (eds.), *Hand-Painted Pop: American Art in Transition 1955-1962*, exh. cat., The Museum of Contemporary Art, Los Angeles 1992.

3 Donald Judd, *Donald Judd: Complete Writings 1959-1975*, New York and Halifax 1975, p.70.

4 Gretchen Berg, 'Andy: My True Story', *Los Angeles Free Press*, 17 March 1967, p.3.

5 Vance Packard, *The Hidden Persuaders*, New York 1957, p.108.

6 Michael Fried, *Art and Objecthood: Essays and Reviews*, Chicago 1998, pp.404f.

7 See Charles E. Stuckey, 'Warhol in Context', Gary Garrels (ed.), *The Work of Andy Warhol*, Seattle 1989. Stuckey authors an in-depth discussion and analysis of Warhol's work within the climate of painting and sculpture in New York, especially during the 1960s. For his insightful discussion of Warhol's later work, see his 'Heaven and Hell are just one breath away!' in: *Andy Warhol, Heaven and Hell are just one breath away! Late paintings and related works, 1984-86*, exh. cat., Gagosian Gallery, New York 1992.

8 It is not known whether Warhol intended viewers to experience these paintings through 3-D glasses; however, it is difficult to imagine that the effect was purely accidental. In 1952, Hollywood had begun producing films in 3-D and, during the 1960s, structuralist filmmakers such as Ken Jacobs were experimenting with the optical effects to be achieved through stereoscopic techniques. A few years later, Warhol made a painting using fluorescent inks to be viewed under black light.

9 For a discussion of the American avant-garde film activity of this period see P. Adams Sitney, *The Visionary Film: The American Avant-Garde 1943-1978*, Oxford 1979.

10 Trevor Fairbrother, 'Skulls', in Garrels, 1989, p.104.

11 Donna De Salvo, *'Success is a Job in New York': The Early Art and Business of Andy Warhol*, exh. cat., Grey Art and Study Center, New York 1989, p.9. As a student at the Carnegie Institute, Warhol had developed a blotted-line technique that art directors found appealing, especially as its distinctive look lent itself to reproduction. 'During the 1950s', note design historians Ellen Lupton and J. Abbott Miller, 'line drawing became an aesthetically *and* technically economical solution to the twin demands of reproduction and artistic singularity; it served as a "signature" or records of the artist's personality, and it also gave the printer "camera-ready" material.' (De Salvo, 1989, p.29.)

12 Andy Warhol, 'Painter Hangs Own Paintings', February 1979. Repr. in: *Warhol Shadows*, The Menil Collection, Houston 1987, n.p.

13 One reviewer noted, 'Still, this passive attitude toward *Shadows* – prevalent also among some curators, artists and critics who should know better – is disappointing.' *ARTnews*, vol. 78, 1979, p.172.

14 Warhol, Houston 1987, n.p.

15 Julian Schnabel, preface to *Andy Warhol: Shadow Paintings*, exh. cat., Gagosian Gallery, New York 1989, p.7.

16 Brenda Richardson has discussed the *Camouflage* series in 'Hiding in Plain Sight: Warhol's Camouflage', *Andy Warhol: Camouflage*, exh. cat., Gagosian Gallery, New York 1998, pp.11-31.

WARHOL AND GOYA

Peter-Klaus
Schuster

I. New Perspectives. It was Kirk Varnedoe who, in one of the discussions that led up to this exhibition, likened Warhol to Goya. He delivered himself of this startling analogy against the provocatively deadpan background of the comfortable-looking townhouses that overlook the sculpture garden of The Museum of Modern Art. The explosive force of Varnedoe's remark is obvious: to see Warhol as the Goya of our time lends unsuspected and alarming depths to an art of surface perfection. It is as if someone were to redefine the surface of America itself.

There in the heart of New York, this evocation of the most radical exponent of European art *c.*1800 was all the more surprising because it was Heiner Bastian's declared intention as curator of the exhibition to show Warhol for the first time purely and exclusively as one of the great artists of Classic Modernism. All contextualisation, as seen recently at the Whitney Museum of American Art under the title *The Warhol Look – Glamour, Style, Fashion,* was to be eschewed. As majestic as a Matisse retrospective, this particular Warhol exhibition sets out to show nothing but art. The Matisse reference stands for beauty and perfection; although anyone who saw Warhol's *Last Supper* cycle of paintings at the Guggenheim SoHo recently was more likely to think of an American Raphael. Warhol's monumental variations on popular reproductions of Leonardo's *Last Supper* – the Christian devotional painting *par excellence* – with their, at times, positively Nazarene colour and their sweetness of linear flow, are not so much Leonardo as 'Raphael in America'. Every external perspective drawn from art history thus tends to show us a different Warhol. All, however, reveal him as unquestionably a great master in his own right; and the claims made for Warhol in terms of one perspective turn out to confirm those made in terms of another. Euphony, beauty and perfection, *à la* Matisse, with the added dimension of an immaculate technique of image production that has reproduced itself in unbroken succession from the 'Divine Raphael' to the religious kitsch of today: all this makes us receptive to Goya's disillusioned insight that beauty is only the mask that society assumes to disguise its true nature. All these external perspectives combine to show how, by pushing to an extreme the identity of art itself, Warhol brings into the open the prescriptions and proscriptions that modern society imposes on its members.

II. American Beauty. Warhol the social critic is hard to pin down. A child of European immigrants, an outsider who devoted his life to the pursuit of recognition and success, Warhol loved and celebrated the egalitarian structures of American society, whereby everyone is equal and therefore democratic. The President drinks the same Coca-Cola as any other American citizen. Mass production thus guarantees democratic happiness.

Accordingly, Warhol sets out to pay homage to the perfection of mechanical production; and this he combines with a love of the perfect surfaces that make anything look beautiful. In the service of this collective longing for immaculate beauty, for fame and for eternity, Warhol produces images in which the presiding aesthetic ideal is the perfection of the machine. Accordingly, the studio transforms itself into a 'Factory' in which the artist does no more than give instructions, leaving the execution to others. In Warhol's immaculate images, quasi-mechanically generated from existing reproductions, the cult figures and banal myths of mass society seem to find their way onto the flawless surface of the support as emanations from higher beings, entirely divorced from their artistic creator. The image is anonymous and mass-produced; only the selection and cropping of the motif, the variations in its proportions, the choice of colour and the irregularities of printing or paint-application confirm the presence of an artist's hand behind it all. By employing powerful strategies in and through the image to confer the aura of art on the implied eternal recurrence of sameness, this seemingly impersonal hand metamorphoses back into the hand of an Artist God. In this commodified mass society, he alone, the master of media, can introduce visual eternity into the deluge of images. As the aseptically neutral chronicler of the everyday myths and cult figures of modern life, Warhol becomes a cult figure and a myth in his own right: the Demiurge who creates immaculately evident phenomenal surfaces. In the democratic equality of media transience, everything on those surfaces becomes a purchasable icon of eternity.

Warhol well knew that beneath the perfect surface of images – if not his own, certainly those of the society that he appreciated on so many different levels – something else lies concealed. Assuming the guise of a detached observer, he elected to respond to this with wonderment. In his last book, *America*, he wrote of the American suburban idyll: 'You see the houses everywhere, the green lawns with the sprinklers, the jungle gyms in the backyards, the kids riding their bikes to school, the mailman coming by with a smile, a woman unloading bags of groceries from her station wagon, and you can't help but think, "This is the real America". You imagine that everyone around who you haven't seen in a long time is living this very regular, humdrum life that's peaceful ... But then you start learning the details. You find out the nice man who always had an extra piece of gum to give you has gone completely off his rocker and killed his wife, that the ex-minister of the church you grew up in is now a big drunk who's totalled three cars. You learn that your best friend's parents who were always so great are getting a divorce, that the woman who you always thought was the most ordinary housewife ran off with another man to Canada. You find out that the girl you had a crush on in elementary school is now a religious fanatic living in India with a bald head ... Nobody in America has an ordinary life.'[1]

It was just such an idyllic view – that of the pleasant town houses overlooking the sculpture garden of The Museum of Modern Art – that lent such power to the critic's definition of Warhol as the Goya of our time.

III. Goya's Footsteps. The analogy between Warhol and Goya has rarely been drawn. Surprisingly, it is not to be found where one would most have expected it, in Robert Rosenblum's writing on Warhol.[2] Though an expert in early nineteenth-century art, Rosenblum finds his precedent for the reportage element in Warhol's art – with its equal attention to the beauty and to the horror of his age – in the work of Manet. For him, Manet exemplifies Baudelaire's ideal of *le peintre de la vie moderne* – an ideal that would have been inconceivable without the example of Goya – and he rediscovers that ideal in Warhol's dispassionate, observant, encyclopaedic involvement with contemporary life and all its sensations and fashions. It therefore comes as no surprise that Rosenblum cites a succession of fashionable society painters – Blanche, Boldini, Whistler, Sickert – as links in a chain that leads from Manet in the nineteenth century to Warhol in the twentieth. Rosenblum's point here is to identify a conceptual derivation for the elegant portraits of rich, beautiful and famous people that Warhol produced in the 1970s. However, as an 'artist-dandy' and successor to Manet, the portraitist Warhol has in Rosenblum's view only one significant counterpart in the Aestheticism of the *fin de siècle*: this is Whistler. Rosenblum's brilliant account of Warhol as 'Court Painter to the 70s' is subtly complemented by Philip Core's references to Marcel Proust and to Warhol's own youthful Proustian parodies. *'A la Recherche du Shoe Perdu'* was the title of a study of Edwardian footwear that Warhol published in his early days in New York, when he was working as a commercial artist for magazines and department stores. According to Core, the notion of the snobbery and decadence of a metropolitan elite of pure aesthetes had a defining effect on Warhol's life as well as his art. It was, says Core, Warhol's dual existence as a socialite and as an artist that defined the dual social function of his enormous output of images – the prototype here being Proust's twofold role as both the elegant arbiter of fashion and the archival memory of his age.[3]

The Warhol-Goya analogy makes its appearance in the writing of Barbara Rose, again in relation to the jet-set portraits of the 1970s. She likens those works, some of which were commissioned, to Goya's portraits of members of the Spanish nobility, which surprise us today with the sheer ugliness of the sitters, evidently unperceived by them as paying customers. Perhaps, Rose suggests, something similar might be said of the presentation or rather self-presentation of Warhol's clients.[4]

In his own journal, Warhol mentions Goya only once. On 31 December 1976, he goes to Kitty Miller's New Year's Eve party on Park Avenue: 'And after dinner, I sat underneath Goya's *Red Boy*. Kitty has this most famous painting right there in her house, it's unbelievable.'[5]

IV. Disasters. This is by no means Warhol's only allusion to Goya. In the memoir *POPism*, he mentions that the subject of his first disaster picture, *129 Die in Jet* [cat. no. 109], came from Henry Geldzahler. No one in Warhol's world at that time knew so much about art history as Geldzahler. It is no surprise, therefore, to find that, in recalling Geldzahler's momentous suggestion, Warhol repeatedly cites Goya's famous suite of etchings, *Los desastres de la guerra (The Disasters of War)*. What is more, he uses the word 'disasters' to create an intimate link between his own work and life: 'It was Henry who gave me the idea to start the *Death* and *Disaster* series ... he laid the *Daily News* out on the table. The headline was "129 DIE IN JET". And that's what started me on the death series – the Car Crashes, the Disasters, the Electric Chairs ... Whenever I look back at that front page, I'm struck by the date – June 4, 1962. Six years – to the date – later, my own disaster was the front-page headline: "ARTIST SHOT".'[6]

Coincidentally or not, Warhol's use of the word 'disaster' to describe his own near-fatal shooting takes us straight back to Goya's title page for *Los desastres*. This shows a kneeling figure with outstretched arms, a secularized Christ in Gethsemane, who laments his own impending death by firing-squad amid the apocalypse of war. His fate stands for all those French atrocities in Spain that Goya himself depicted in *Los desastres de la guerra*.[7] In Warhol's *Death* and *Disaster* sequences, however, his theme is not *los desastres de la guerra* but *los desastres de la paz*: Marilyn Monroe, radiant before her suicide; Jackie Kennedy, mourning the assassination of the President; plane crashes; road fatalities; suicides leaping from skyscrapers; victims of polluted tuna; America's most wanted criminals; the electric chair; the atom bomb; earthquakes; volcanic eruptions; skulls; pistols and knives – a ritualistic procession of unending catastrophe, murder and mayhem [cat. nos. 110ff., 212, 223].

There is in Warhol's work a deep and indissoluble affinity with death; and yet, remarkably, he never interpreted this in terms of social criticism. Indeed, he did his utmost to make death into a taboo subject. In the 'Death' chapter of *The Philosophy of Andy Warhol* he remarks only that it is a sad topic, concluding with this lapidary statement: 'I can't say anything about it because I'm not prepared for it.'[8] In the preceding chapter, 'Time', Warhol wonders: 'What makes a person spend time being sad when they could be happy?'[9] His idea of a perfect American death is just to disappear in some purpose-built machine; all alternatives are repellent. 'That could be a really American invention, the best American invention – to be able to disappear. I mean, that way they couldn't say you died, they couldn't say you were murdered, they couldn't say you committed suicide over somebody.'[10]

Despite the irony and cynicism with which he dismissed the subjects of death and suffering, Warhol saw quite clearly 'that everything I was doing must have been Death'.[11] Beyond this awareness of the inevitability and omnipotence of death, as expressed by Goya in the motto that sums up his *Caprichos*, 'All will fall', Warhol – the same Warhol who would have liked to turn death into a discreet vanishing act – detected a blind spot in the consciousness of the media society. Constantly assailed by news reports of catastrophes, society was losing all feeling for the unhappiness in the world. In the wake of Goya's atrocity images, Warhol's *Disasters* can thus be seen not as a critique of a callous, unjust society but as a critique of the media message, and of the attendant desensitisation and dehumanisation of public consciousness. Warhol told his interviewer Gretchen Berg: 'The *Death* series I painted was in two parts: the first part was about dead celebrities, the second about individuals no one had ever heard of. I thought people ought to think about them: the girl who jumped off the Empire State Building, the women who ate poisoned tuna fish, the car crash victims. I wasn't sorry for them exactly, but people go on their way and they don't really care if some stranger just got killed. So I thought it would be nice for those unknowns to be thought about by people who would never normally do that.'[12]

Warhol, who appeared to set so little store by the omnipotence of death, nevertheless allowed it to maintain a subversive presence even in his icons of consumerism. Kirk Varnedoe is right when he discusses the adaptations made to the labels of Warhol's soup cans in terms of the elegiac motto that speaks of the ineluctable passage of time and the inevitability of death: *'Et in Arcadia ego'*.[13] Death holds court at the very heart of the consumer paradise; consumerism is the modern Vanitas, with the sanction of the market economy. That is also the message of Warhol's crushed, empty Campbell's soup cans. Warhol transforms the myths of American life into a panorama of the macabre and the depressive, in which Uncle Sam is an aged spectre escorted by Dracula and witches.[14] By way of antithesis to the dynamism of Superman, Warhol the artist here assumes responsibility for the darker, shadow side of life. He had first reflected America's propensity for violence in his series of *Most Wanted Men*, and again in the *Guns* and *Knives*. The venality of this society – as expressed in its key ingredient, money – is illustrated by Warhol's *Dollar Bills* and *Dollar Signs*. Finally, the *Skulls* and *Shadows* sequences point to the presence of death, to transience, and to the dark shadow that hangs over a success-ridden society that is haunted – amid the stardust of Warhol's pictures, as elsewhere – by glitz and glamour.

V. The Dream of Reason Produces Monsters. On the strength of these multiple sequences of *Death* and *Disasters*, it is tempting to define Warhol exclusively as a critic of a deeply corrupt, superficial or unhappy society; but this does not work. Warhol himself crisply rejected any interpretation of the *Last Supper* series as compensatory images of Christian redemption for a sinful society, and also any parallel between Christ, surrounded by his disciples, and Warhol's own role at the Factory: 'That's negative, to me it's negative. I don't want to talk about negative things.'[15] After the attempt on his life, however, Warhol unhesitatingly assumed the messianic role that is played by the secularized Christ on the title leaf of Goya's *Desastres*. He did this by having Richard Avedon take photographs of the wounds left by his own 'disaster'. By thus exhibiting his pain, the artist turned himself into the Man of Sorrows. At the same time, Warhol confessed that he himself had experienced the shooting like something in a TV movie: 'Right when I was being shot and ever since, I knew that I was watching television.'[16] Warhol's life and his art are reproductions of pictures of life and art. Through his own indifference – whether this be callous or innocent – he elicits our own reactions of wonder or horror at the state of the world. It is on a similar multiplicity of levels – the artist as sacrificial victim, superstar and messianic redeemer – that Warhol confronts us in his late self-portraits [cat. nos. 235-37]. His face a mask of makeup beneath a coruscating silver wig, Warhol looks like a will-o'-the-wisp against a black background. What we see exists on many levels: it is the *vera icon* of a superstar, or the portrait of a severed head with eyes still open; it is a puckish dream-vision at dead of night, or a resurrected, spiritual being who – in some versions – fixes us with a yet more piercing stare through the endless ornamental pattern of military camouflage. In these final self-portraits, commissioned by the London art dealer Anthony d'Offay, Warhol shows the artist as a disturbing monstrosity.

When Goya depicted himself in the celebrated etching *Capricho 43* (1797–98), he became the first to show the artist in the dual role of creator and victim of a monstrous world. We see him as a melancholic dreamer who has fallen asleep at his workbench and is beset by the figments of his own imagination. In the initial drawing, these are represented by an explosion of faces and animal forms. The second drawing and the final etching reduce this to a swarm of bats, owls and cats: creatures of the night that haunt the sleeping artist like evil spirits, though their origins lie in his own teeming brain. The artist is both perpetrator and victim. The legend reads as follows: 'The dream of reason produces monsters' *(El sueño de la razón produce monstruos)*. Since *sueño* can mean either 'dream' or 'sleep', Goya is not telling us whether reason is absent (in sleep) or present (in a dream). With him, there is also every likelihood that this is a critique of the Enlightenment and its overweening pride: reason dreams of its own omnipotence and accordingly produces monsters of reason.[17]

Warhol, too, presents himself as melancholic, in a pensive pose, with his face in shadow [cat. nos. 152-55]. In *Electric Chair* and *Atom Bomb*, he appears as the recorder of the excesses of rationalism – and thus as a clear successor to Goya. The 'dream of reason' also encompasses Warhol's images of consumerism and mass entertainment: the idols of beauty and fame, and the endless repetition that transforms them into the media nightmare. The nightmares of reason also include Warhol's *Death* and *Disaster* series, which unmask modern civilization as a public stage for the enactment of countless fatalities, crimes, executions, accidents, and suicides.

Goya's programmatic inscription, 'The dream of reason produces monsters', is ambiguous in a further sense. It warns us against the monsters that society is capable of bringing forth, either through the absence of reason or through its presence; and, at the same time, it invites our admiration for the artistic imagination that can capture such monsters in an image. Goya's own commentary on *Capricho 43* and its title, runs as follows: 'Imagination, divorced from reason, brings forth monsters.

United with reason, imagination is the mother of arts and the source of wonders.'[18]

In reference to the artist's special gift of using the force of imagination to make visible the madhouse that is the world and the follies of humanity, Goya defined the imaginative images of his *Caprichos* with the phrase *'Ydioma universal'*, universal language. The implication here is that this universal language, the product of the artist's exceptional imagination, is there for all to read without difficulty. Its messages are addressed to everyone and have something to teach everyone.[19] It was in this vein that Goya advertised his *Caprichos* in the *Diario de Madrid* in February 1799. This was an art that was meant to be affordable and popular; hence Goya's chosen sales outlet, a perfume and liquor store in Calle del Desengaño, Disillusion Street.

Goya's *Caprichos*, the graphically reproduced 'dreams of reason', are thus just as much 'business art' as Warhol's mass-produced silkscreens. The images that Warhol has derived from often-reproduced photographs represent an *Ydioma universal* of their own: a pictorial language that all can read. However, there is more to Warhol's universal language than instant comprehensibility. These are the reproduced messages not of the Enlightenment but of the mass media – clichés, symbols and myths included – and stand for the subliminal normative impulse inherent in those media. In itself, Warhol's artistic method of image-production is a reproduction of a critical truth about society: the truth, as Heiner Bastian describes it here, of an alienated society that denies the individuality of its members.[20] Through a calculated recourse to collective archetypes, Warhol's universal language of multiple images reflects and intensifies the image-oriented media society's dream of identical, predictable consumers. The artistic monster of this same image-oriented media society is Warhol. At the same time, he creates its visual wonders. Warhol thus offers the artwork of an aesthete and a dandy as a source of moral authority.

ENDNOTES

1 Andy Warhol, *America*, New York 1985, p.176.

2 Robert Rosenblum, 'Andy Warhol. Court Painter to the 70s', *Andy Warhol: Portraits of the 70s*, exh. cat., Whitney Museum of American Art, New York 1979, p.9ff., and Robert Rosenblum, 'Warhol as Art History', *Andy Warhol. A Retrospective*, exh. cat., The Museum of Modern Art, New York 1989, p.25ff.

3 Philip Core, 'Andy Warhol', *Independent*, 23 February 1987.

4 On Warhol and Goya as seen by Barbara Rose, see Karl-Egon Vester, 'Wiederholung und Distanz. Zur Bildkonzeption von Andy Warhol', *Warhol. 'Ich erkannte, daß alles, was ich tue, mit dem Tod zusammenhängt'*, exh. cat., Kunstverein in Hamburg 1987, p.9.

5 Andy Warhol, *The Andy Warhol Diaries*, ed. Pat Hackett, New York 1989, p.12.

6 Andy Warhol and Pat Hackett, *POPism. The Warhol '60s*, New York/London 1989, p.17.

7 *Goya. Das Zeitalter der Revolution 1789–1830*, exh. cat., Hamburger Kunsthalle 1980, p.125f., cat. no. 69.

8 Andy Warhol, *The Philosophy of Andy Warhol*, New York 1975, p.123.

9 Ibid., p.112.

10 Ibid., p.113.

11 *Warhol. 'Ich erkannte'*, 1987, p.61ff.

12 Quoted (and translated) from Enno Patalas, *Andy Warhol und seine Filme*, Munich 1971, p.18.

13 See Kirk Varnedoe's essay in the present catalogue.

14 See Laszlo Glozer, 'Die müden Mythen. Andy Warhol im Münchener Lenbachhaus', *Süddeutsche Zeitung*, 9 January 1982, p.81.

15 Carla Schulz-Hoffmann, '"Are you serious or delirious." Vom Last Supper und anderen Dingen', *Andy Warhol: The Last Supper*, exh. cat., Staatsgalerie Moderner Kunst, Munich 1998, p.17.

16 Warhol, 1975, p.91.

17 For an account of Goya's *Capricho 43*, with reproductions of all the sketches, see Werner Hofmann, 'Der Traum der Vernunft oder: Täter und Opfer', *Goya. Das Zeitalter*, 1980, p.50ff., and Werner Hofmann, 'Goya's negative Morphologie', Werner Hofmann, Edith Helmann, Martin Warnke, *Goya – 'Alle werden fallen'*, exh. cat., Frankfurt am Main 1981, p.15ff.

18 Ibid., p.26.

19 Ibid., p.21, and Martin Warnke, 'Goya's Gesten', Hofmann et al., 1981, p.120ff.

20 See Heiner Bastian's essay in this catalogue and Michael Lüthy, *Andy Warhol. Thirty Are Better Than One*, Frankfurt/M. 1995, p.105ff.

«It doesn't matter what you do.
Everybody just goes on thinking the same thing,
and every year it gets more and more alike.
Those who talk about individuality the most
are the ones who most object to deviation,
and in a few years it may be the other way around.
Some day everybody will think just
what they want to think, and then
everybody will probably be thinking alike;
that seems to be what is happening.»

ANDY WARHOL

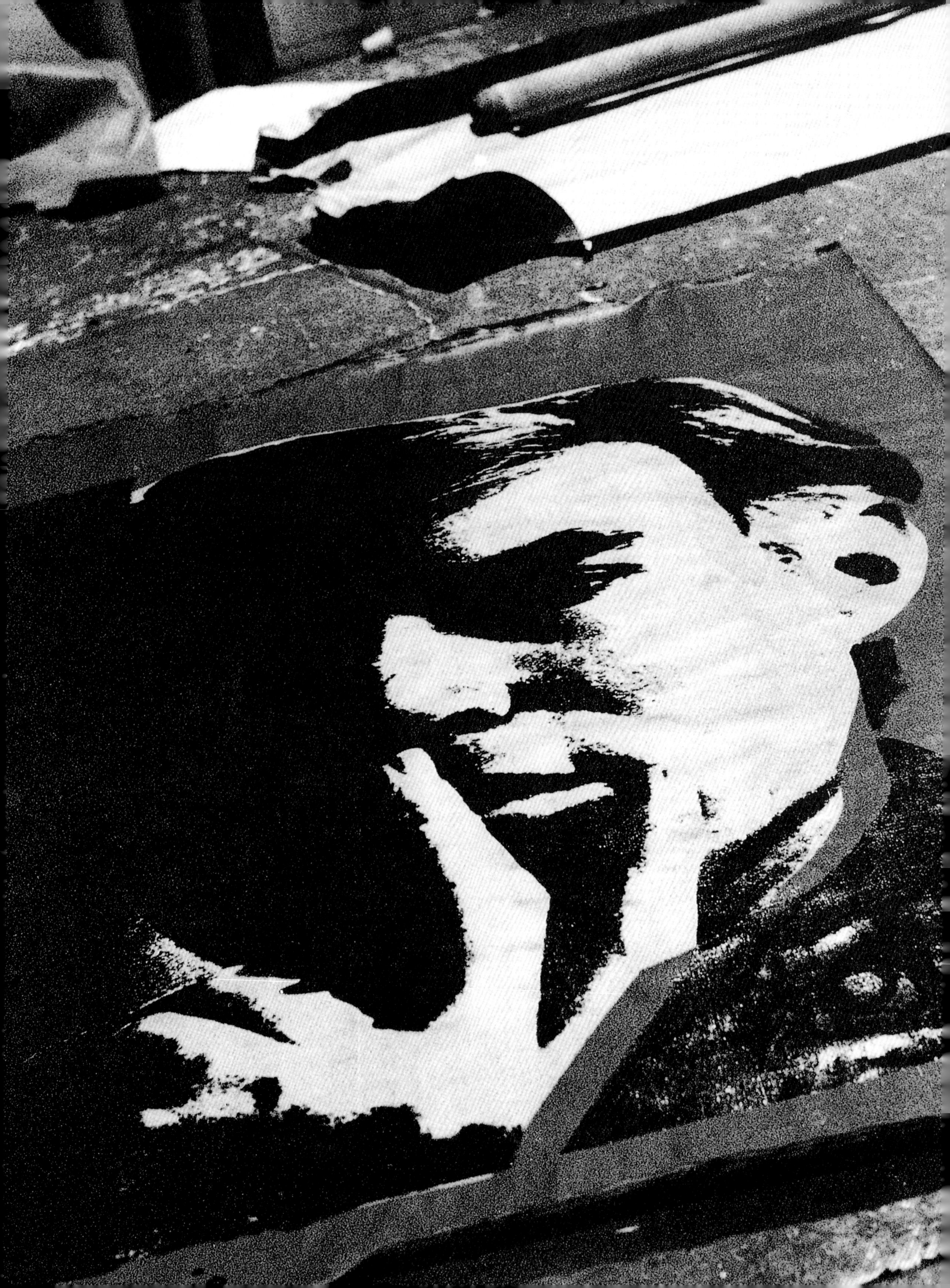

EARLY DRAWINGS

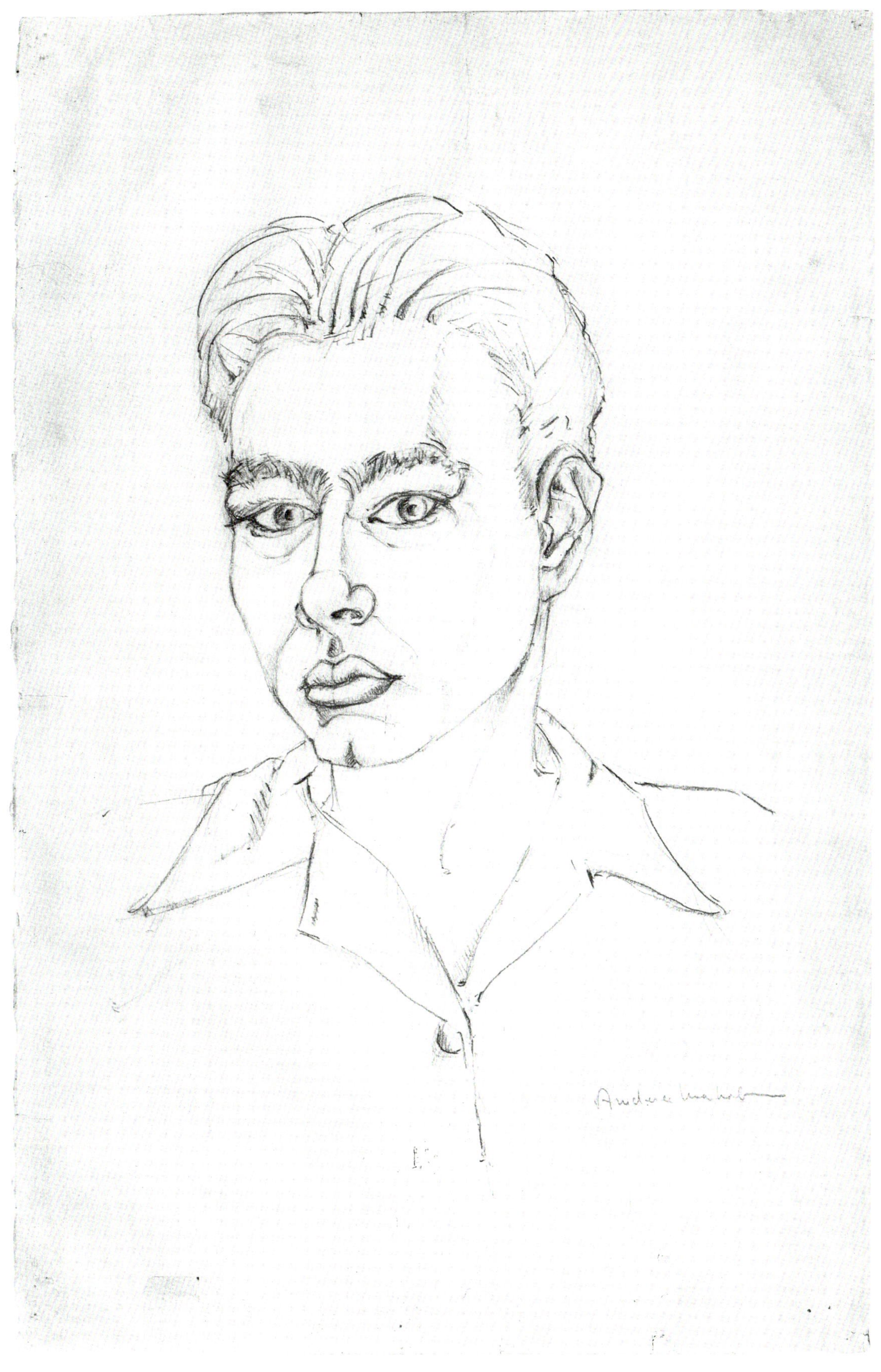

1 **Self-Portrait 1942** Collection Mrs. John F. Steiner • On loan to The Andy Warhol Museum, Pittsburgh

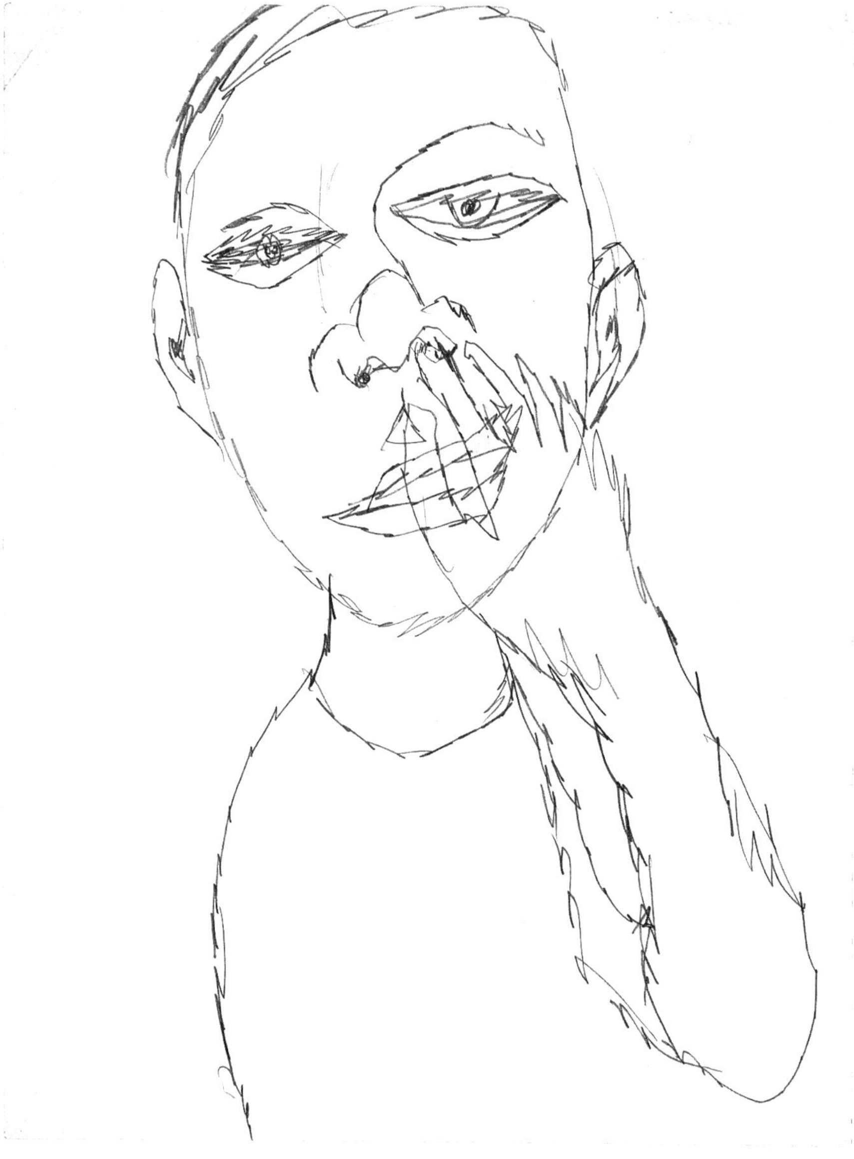

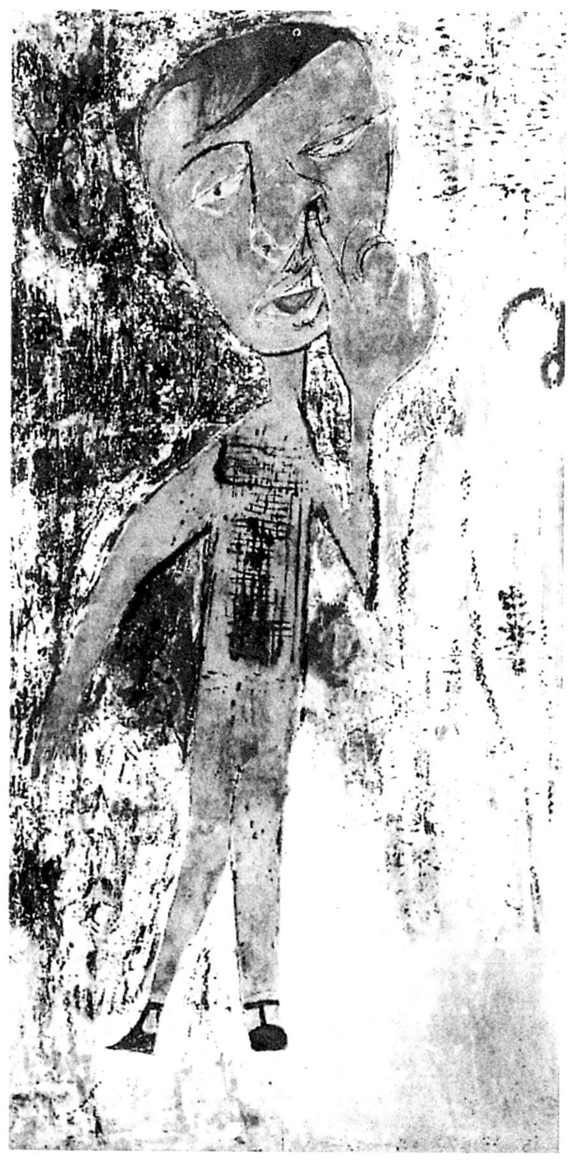

2 **Boy Picking His Nose 1948/49**
The Andy Warhol Museum, Pittsburgh
Founding Collection, Contribution
The Andy Warhol Foundation
for the Visual Arts, Inc.

3 **The Broad Gave Me My Face, But I Can Pick My Own Nose 1948/49**
Collection Ethel and Leonard Kessler*

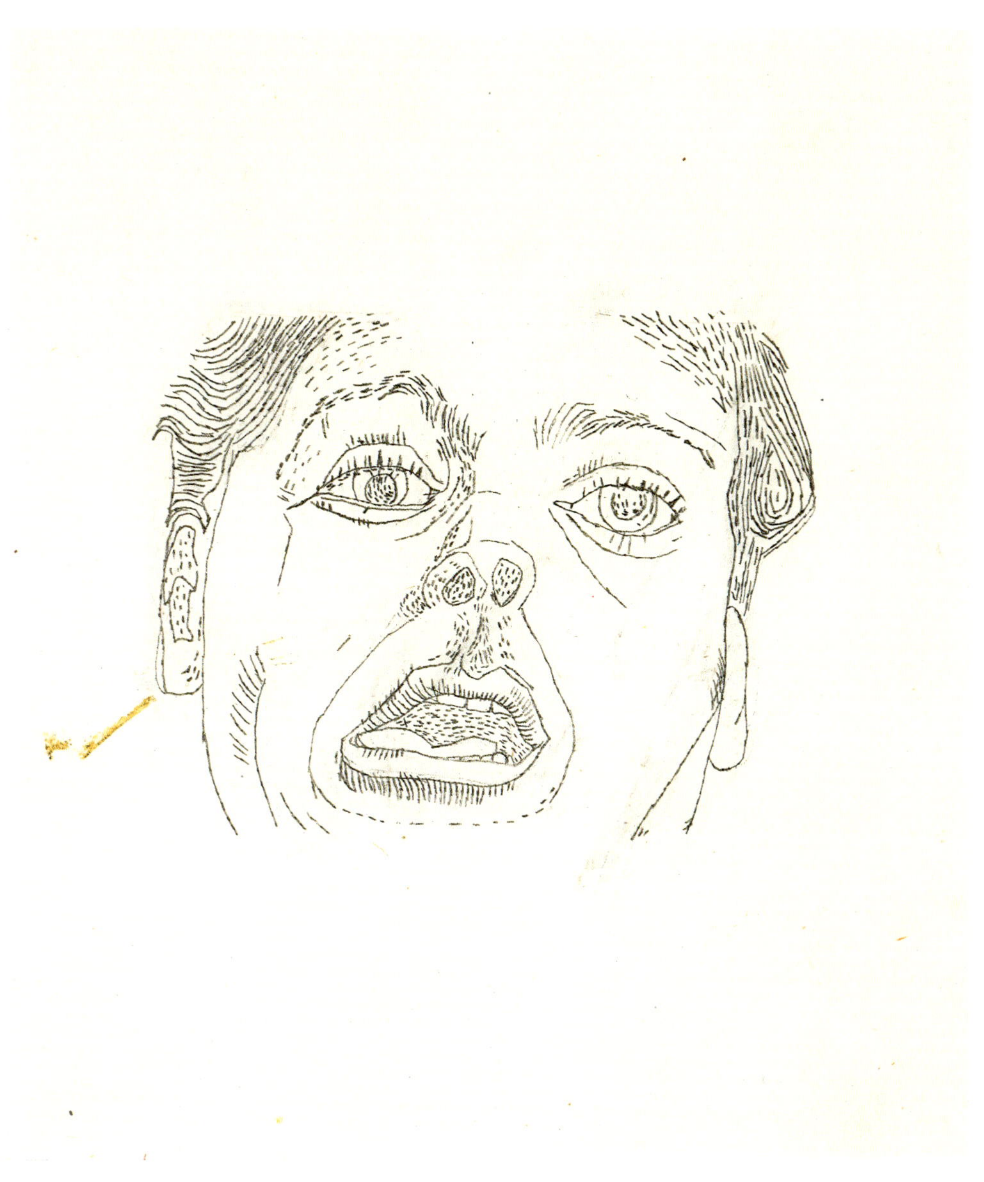

4 **Male Head c. 1950**
Private collection

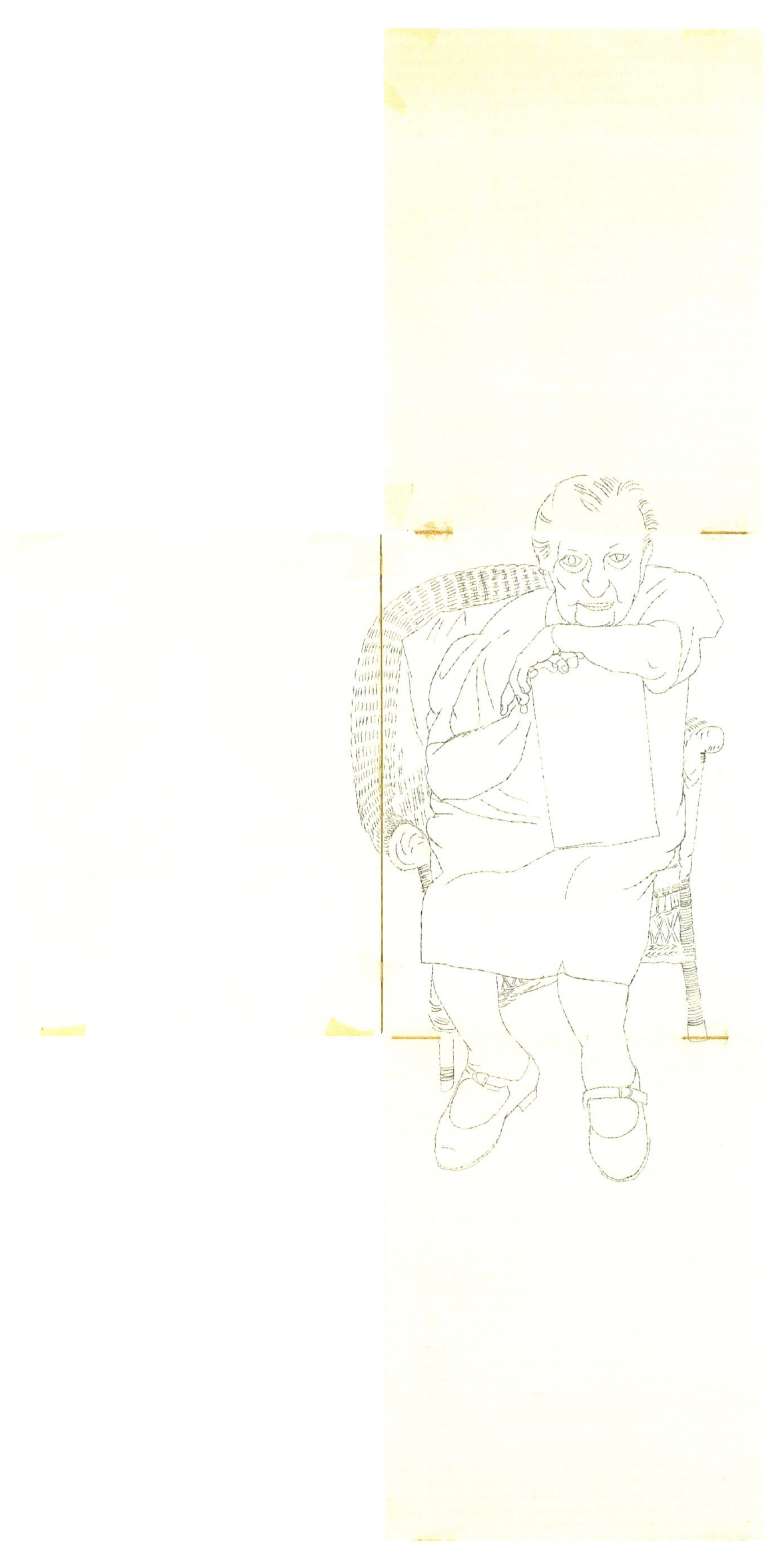

5 **Seated Aging Female c. 1948** Courtesy Anthony d'Offay Gallery, London

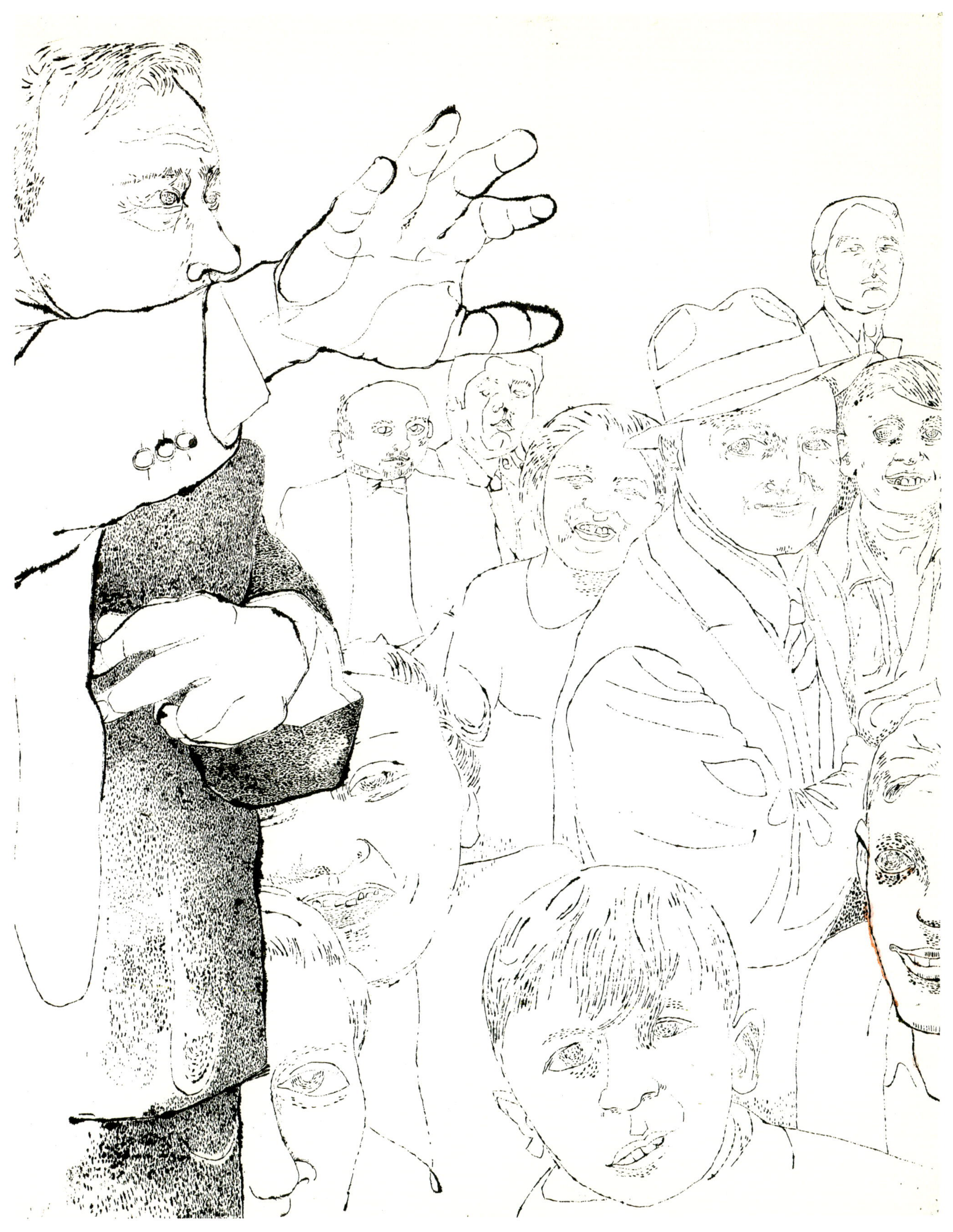

6 **Untitled (Hucy Long)** **1948/49** Carnegie Museum of Art, Pittsburgh, Gift of Russel G. Twiggs

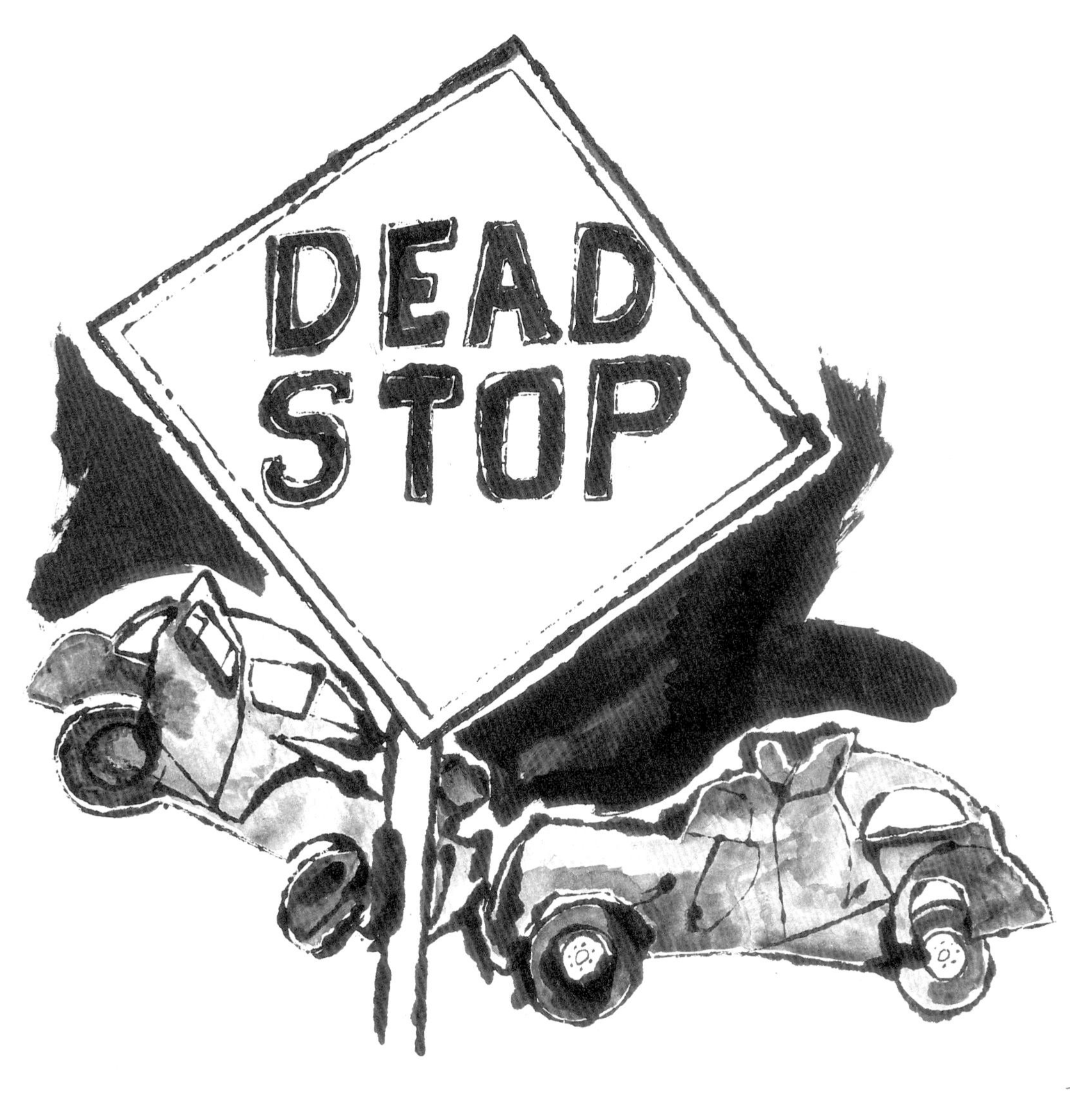

7 **Dead Stop 1954** Private collection, New York

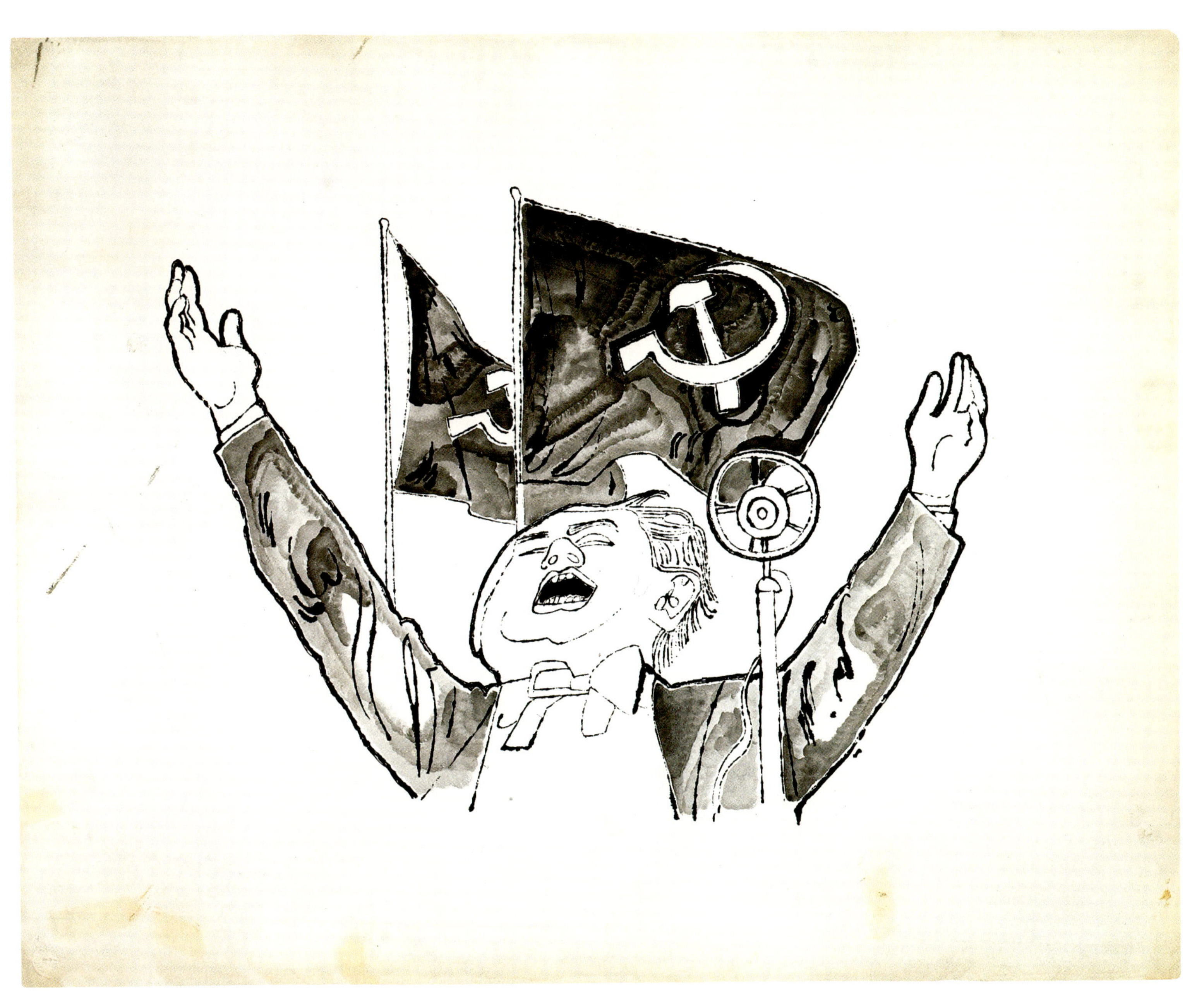

8 **Communist Speaker** **c. 1950** The Andy Warhol Museum, Pittsburgh • Founding Collection, Contribution The Andy Warhol Foundation for the Visual Arts, Inc.

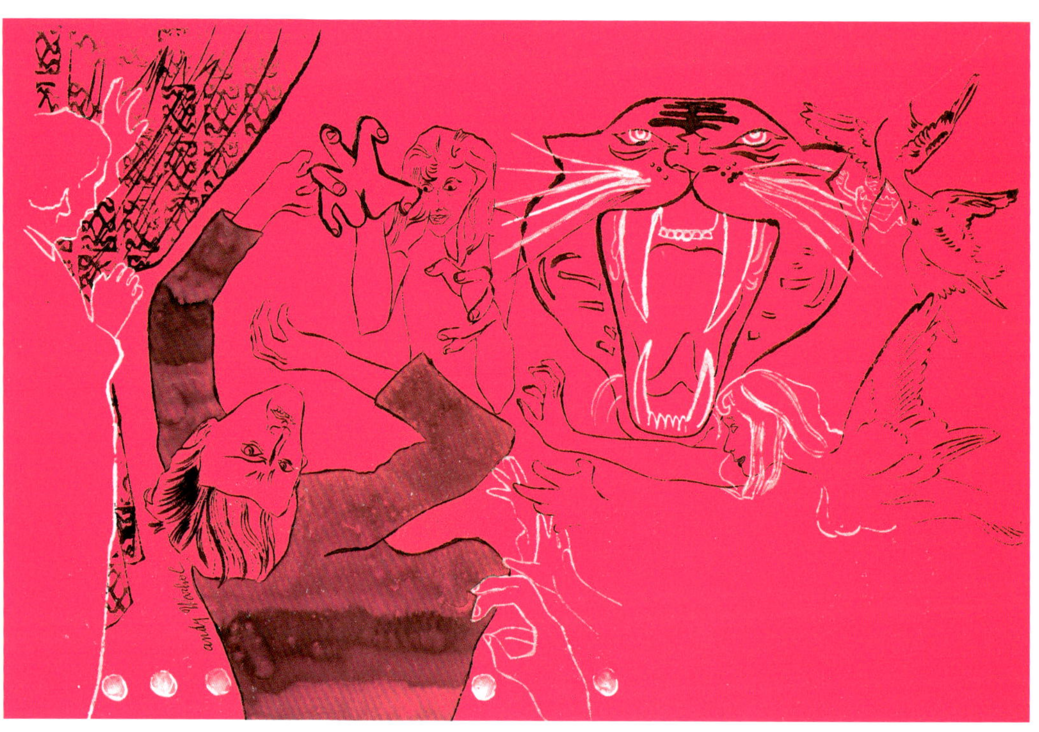

9 **Grasping Figures With Tiger Head 1956**
Private collection, New York

10 **Chess Player 1954**
Private collection

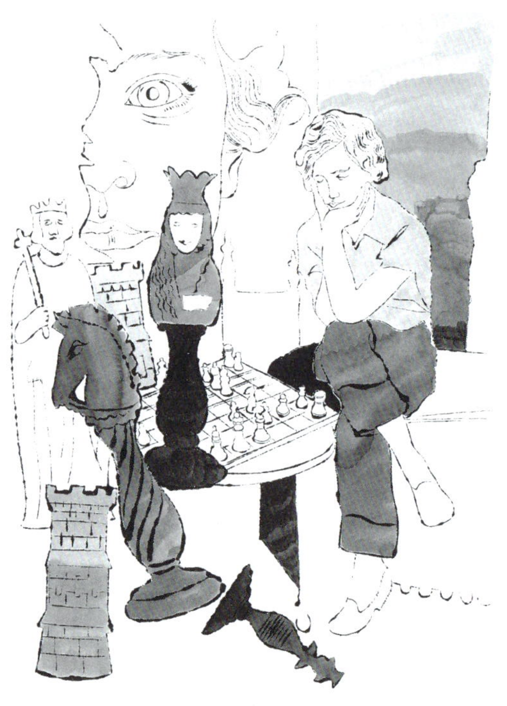

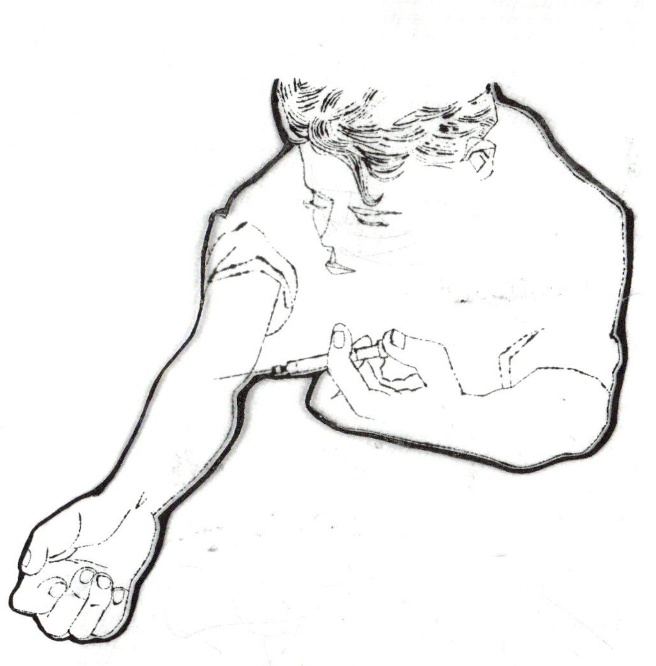

11 **Untitled (»The Nation's Nightmare«) 1951**
Private collection, London

12 **Male Seated at Automat Counter 1958**
Courtesy Anthony d'Offay Gallery, London

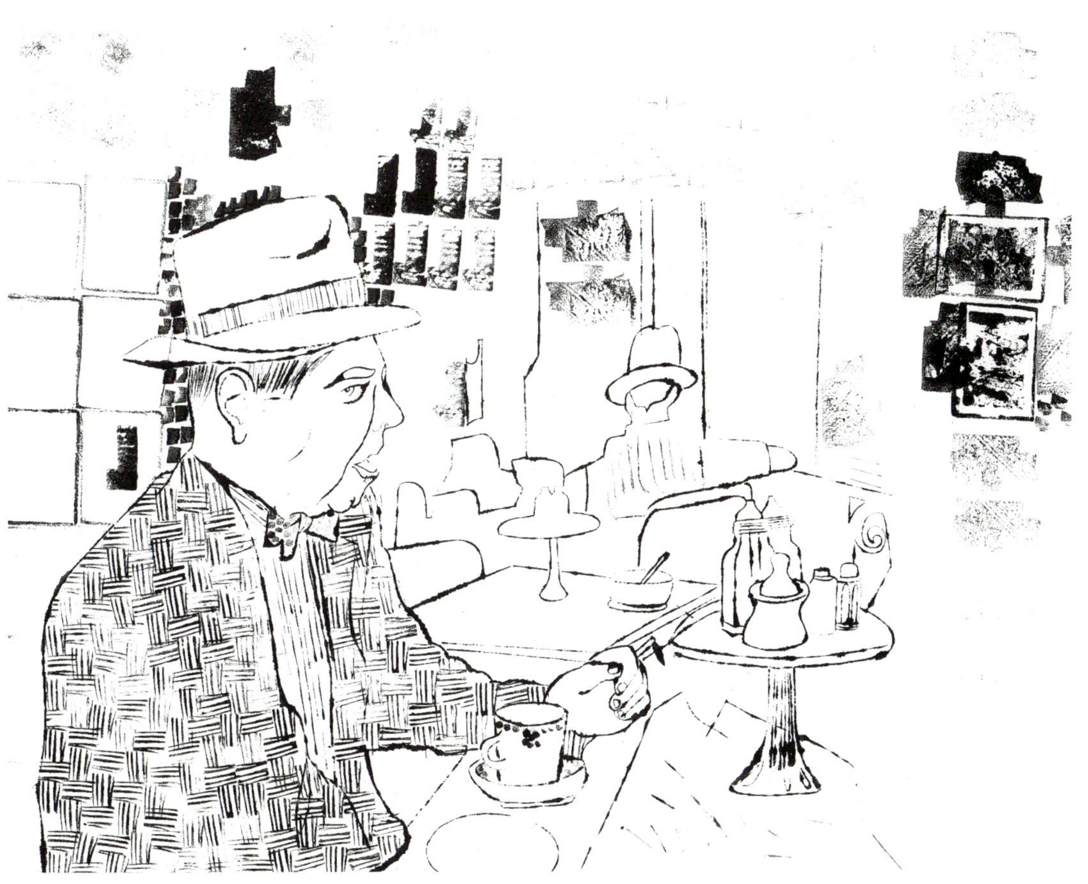

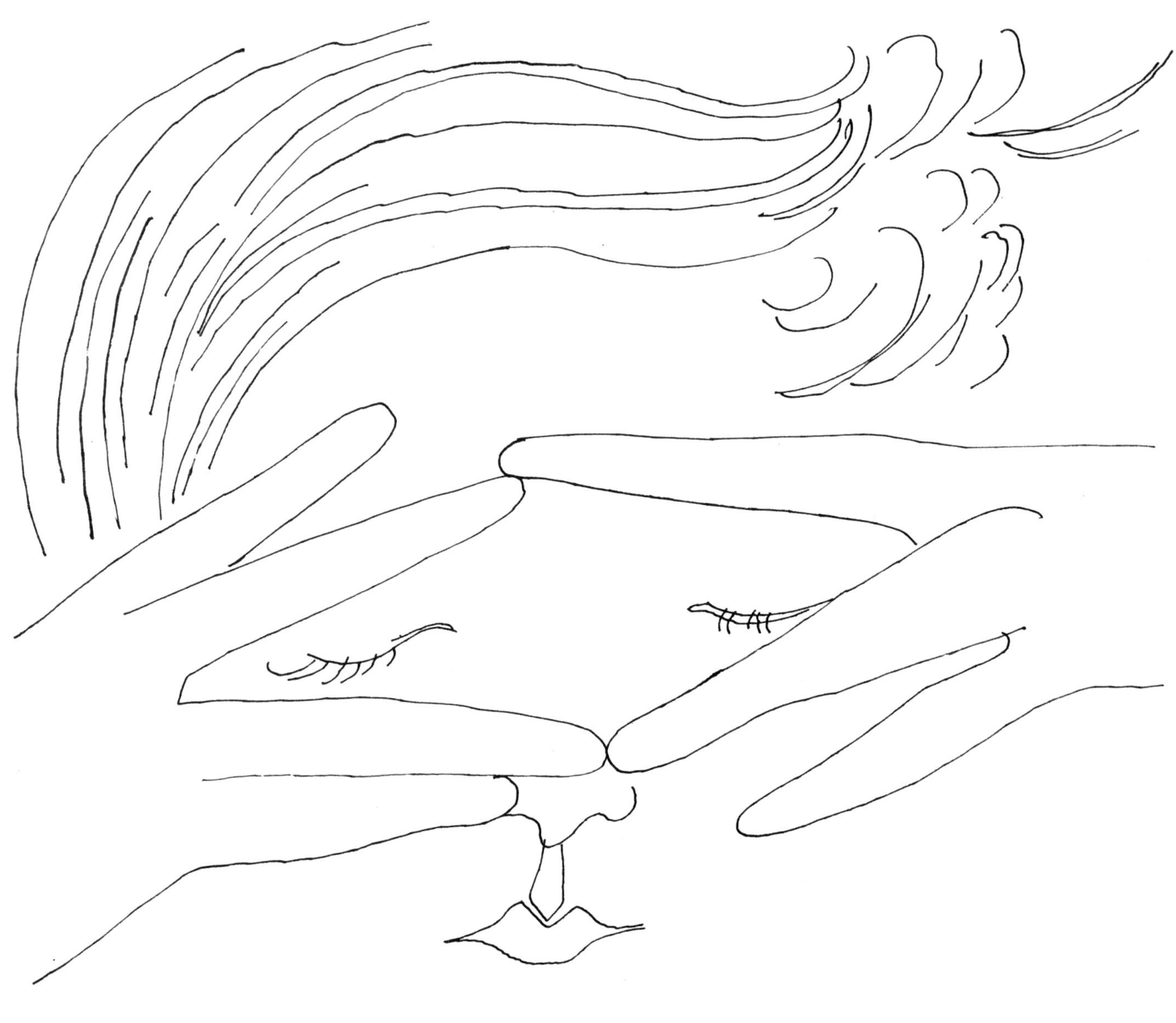

13 Truman Capote c. 1954 Stiftung Sammlung Marx, Hamburger Bahnhof – Museum für Gegenwart, Berlin

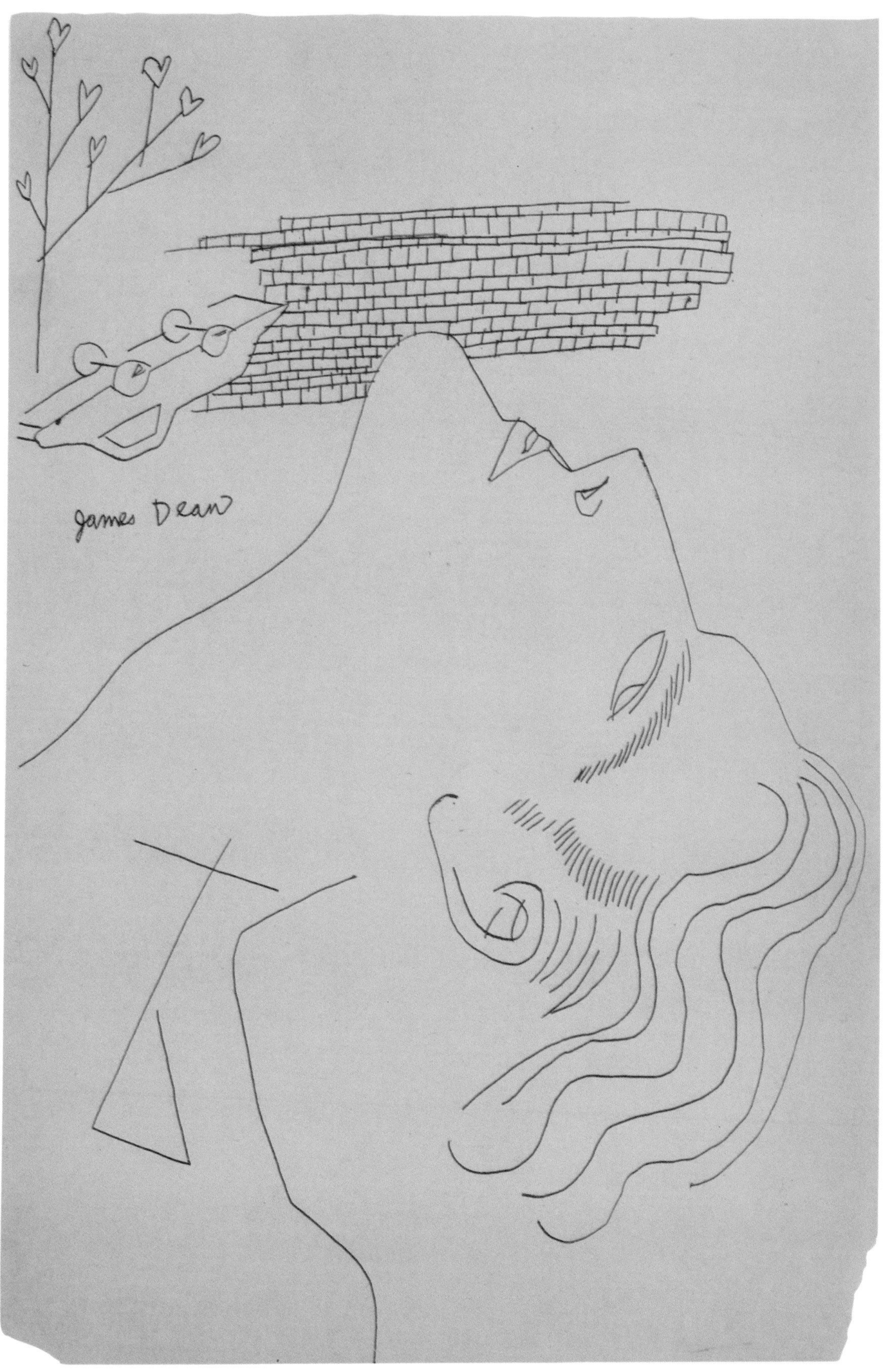

14 James Dean 1955 Courtesy The Brant Foundation, Greenwich, CT

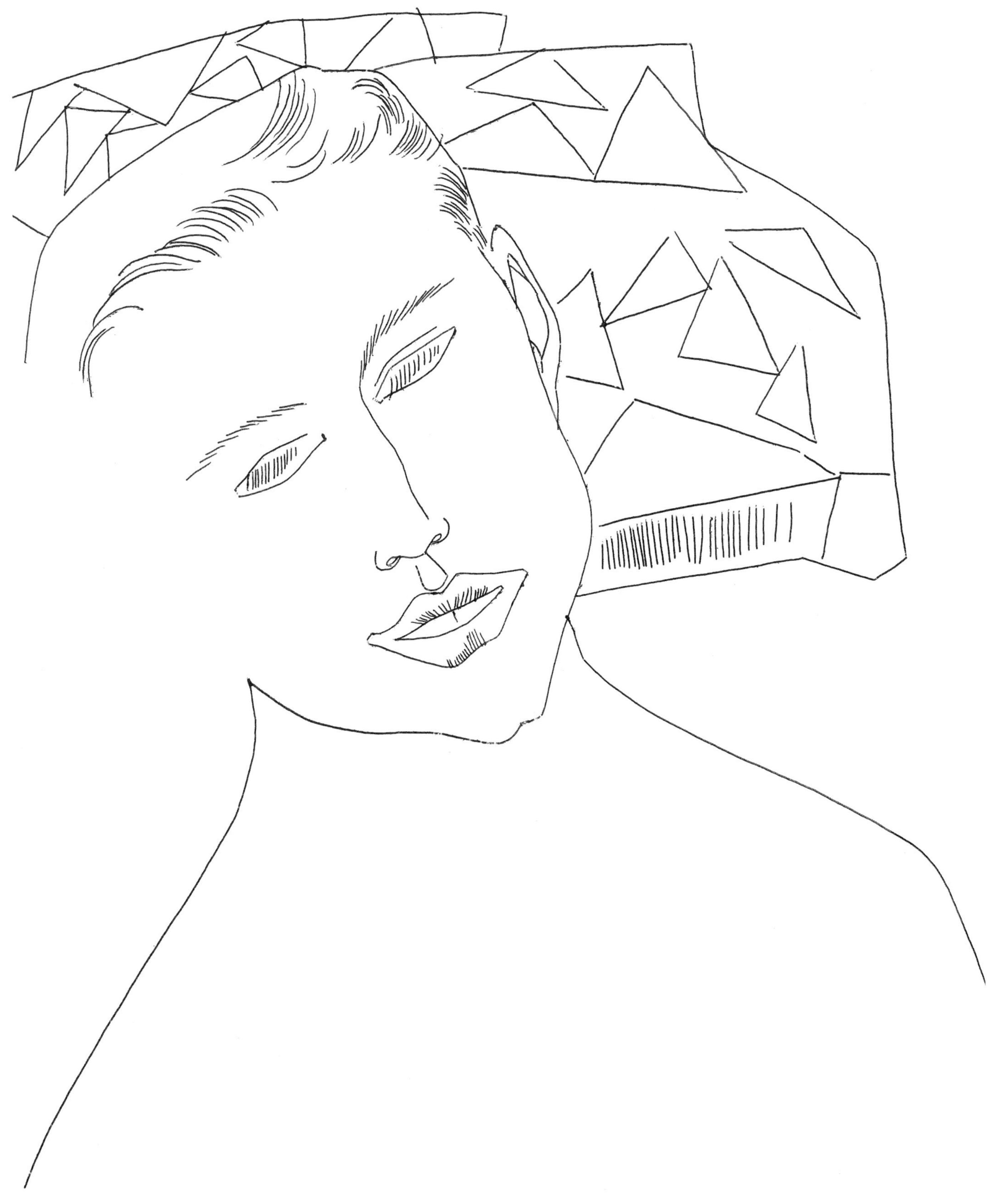

15 Untitled c. 1955/57 Private collection

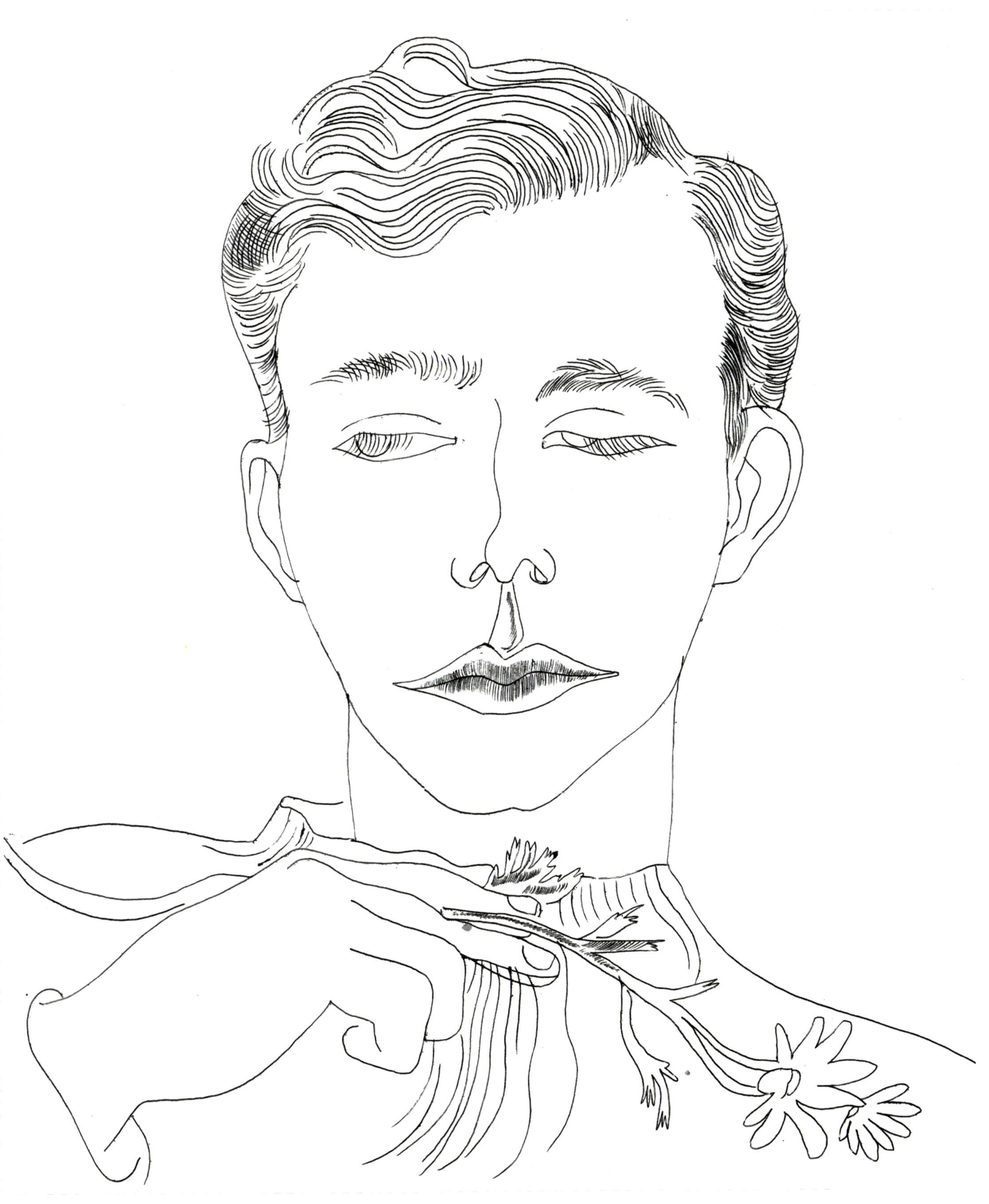

16 Untitled c. 1957 Stiftung Sammlung Marx, Hamburger Bahnhof – Museum für Gegenwart, Berlin

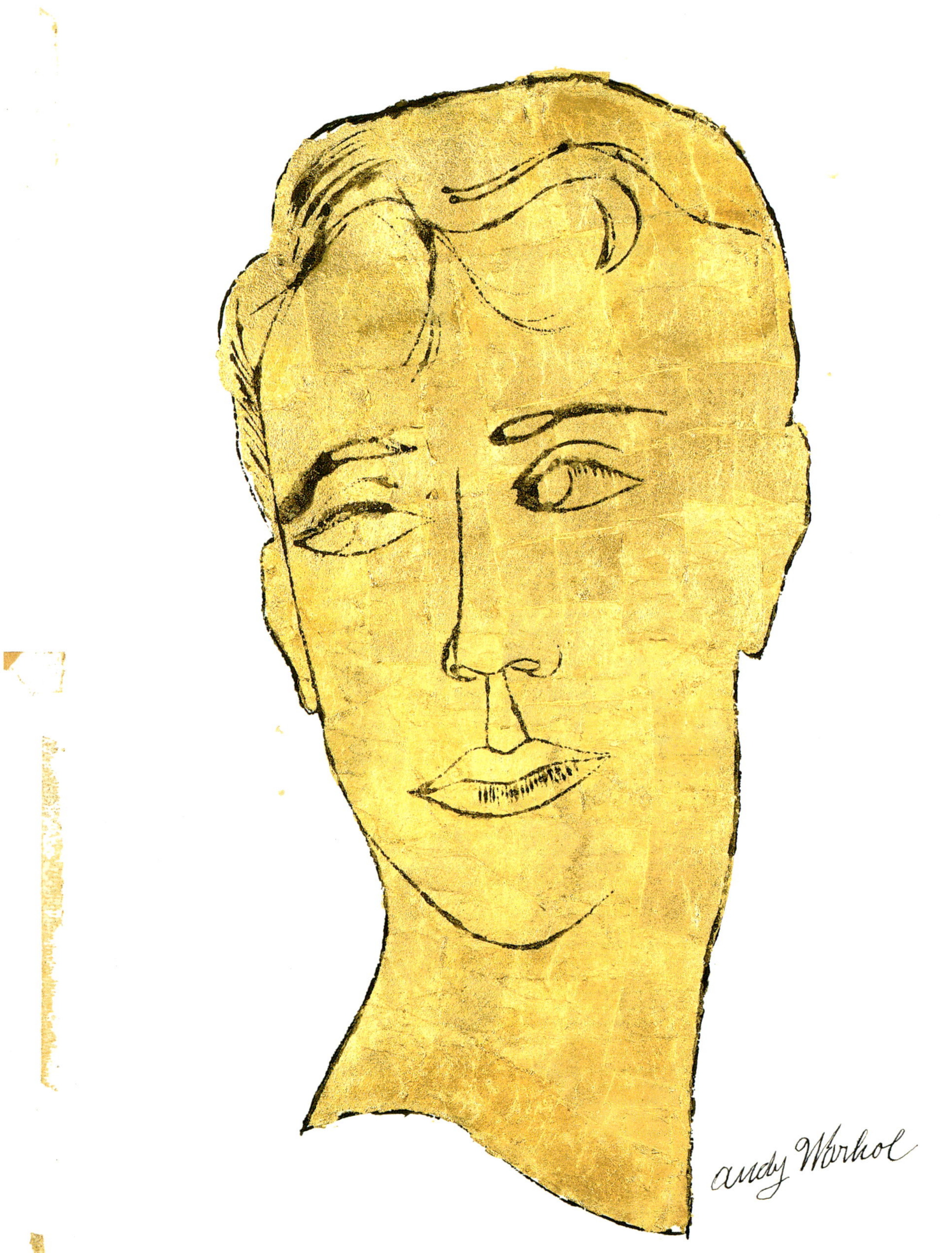
Andy Warhol

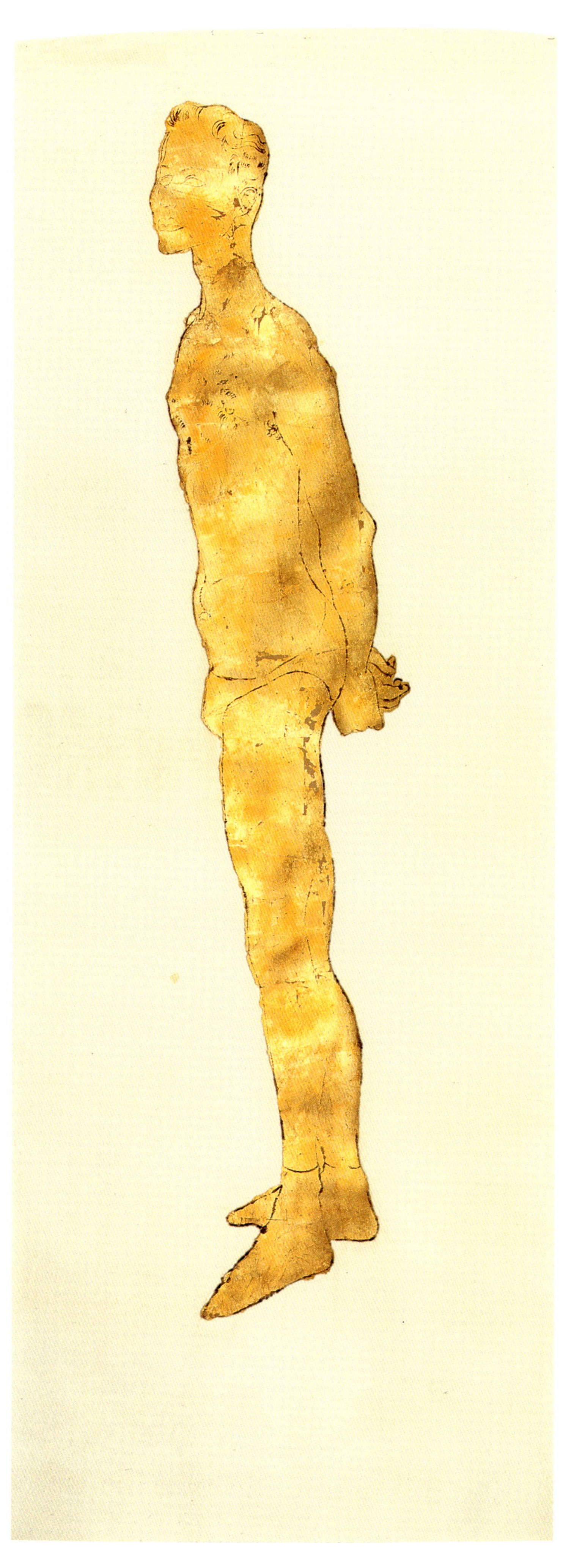

17 **Untitled 1955**
Stiftung Sammlung Marx,
Hamburger Bahnhof –
Museum für Gegenwart, Berlin

18 **Untitled (Golden Boy) 1957**
Stiftung Sammlung Marx,
Hamburger Bahnhof –
Museum für Gegenwart, Berlin

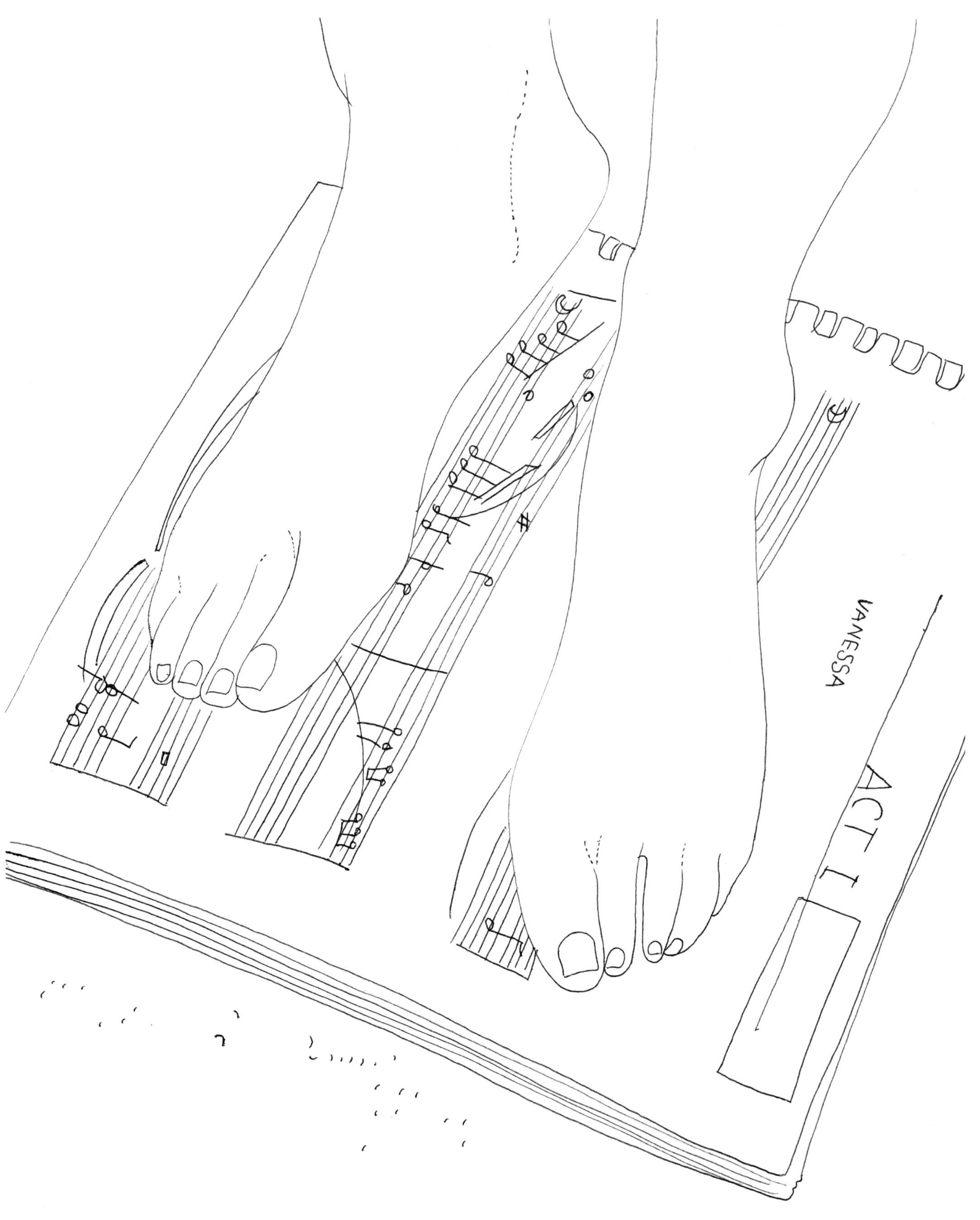

19 **Untitled** **c. 1960** Private collection

20 **Golden Portrait with Cat** **1957** Stiftung Sammlung Marx, Hamburger Bahnhof – Museum für Gegenwart, Berlin

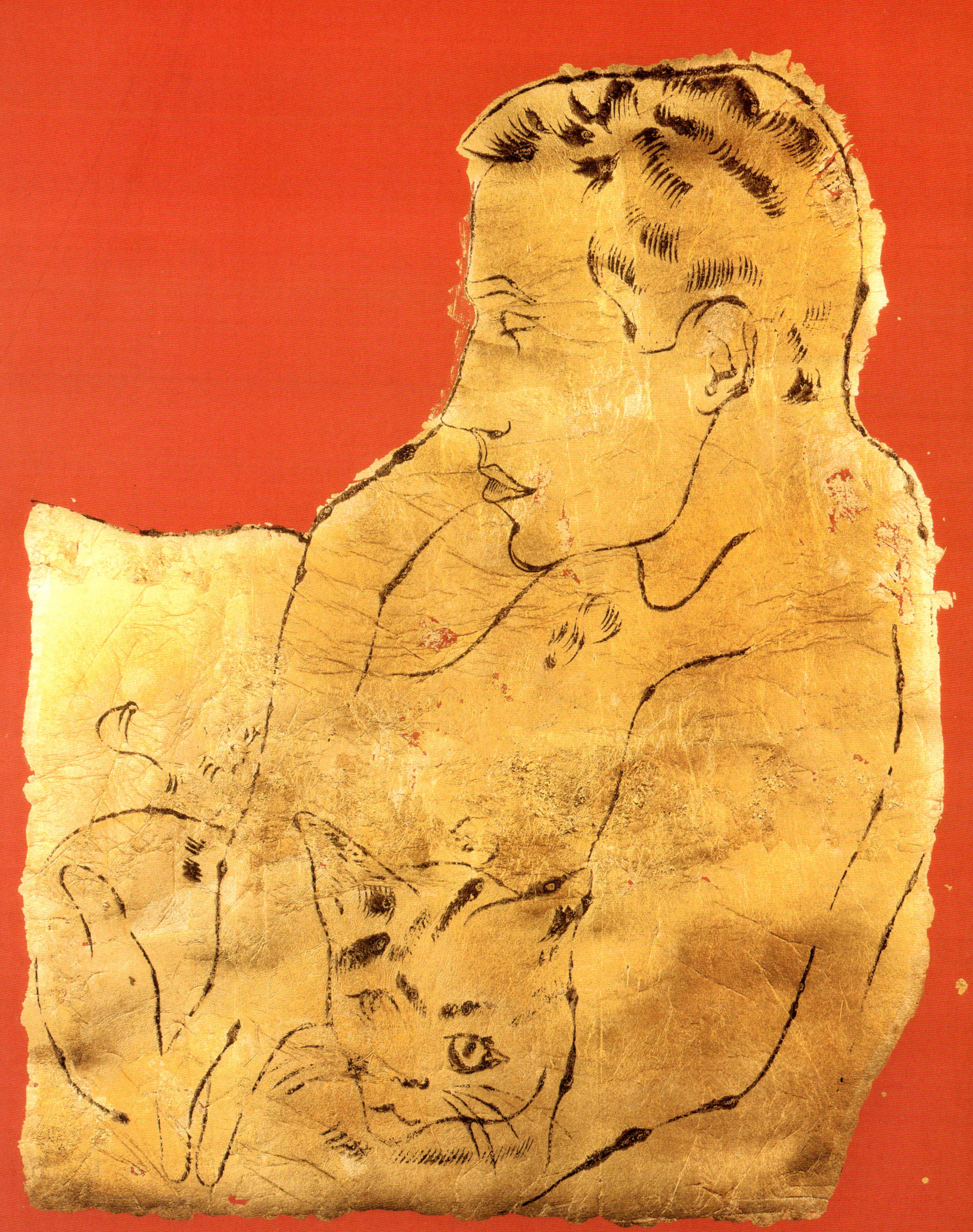

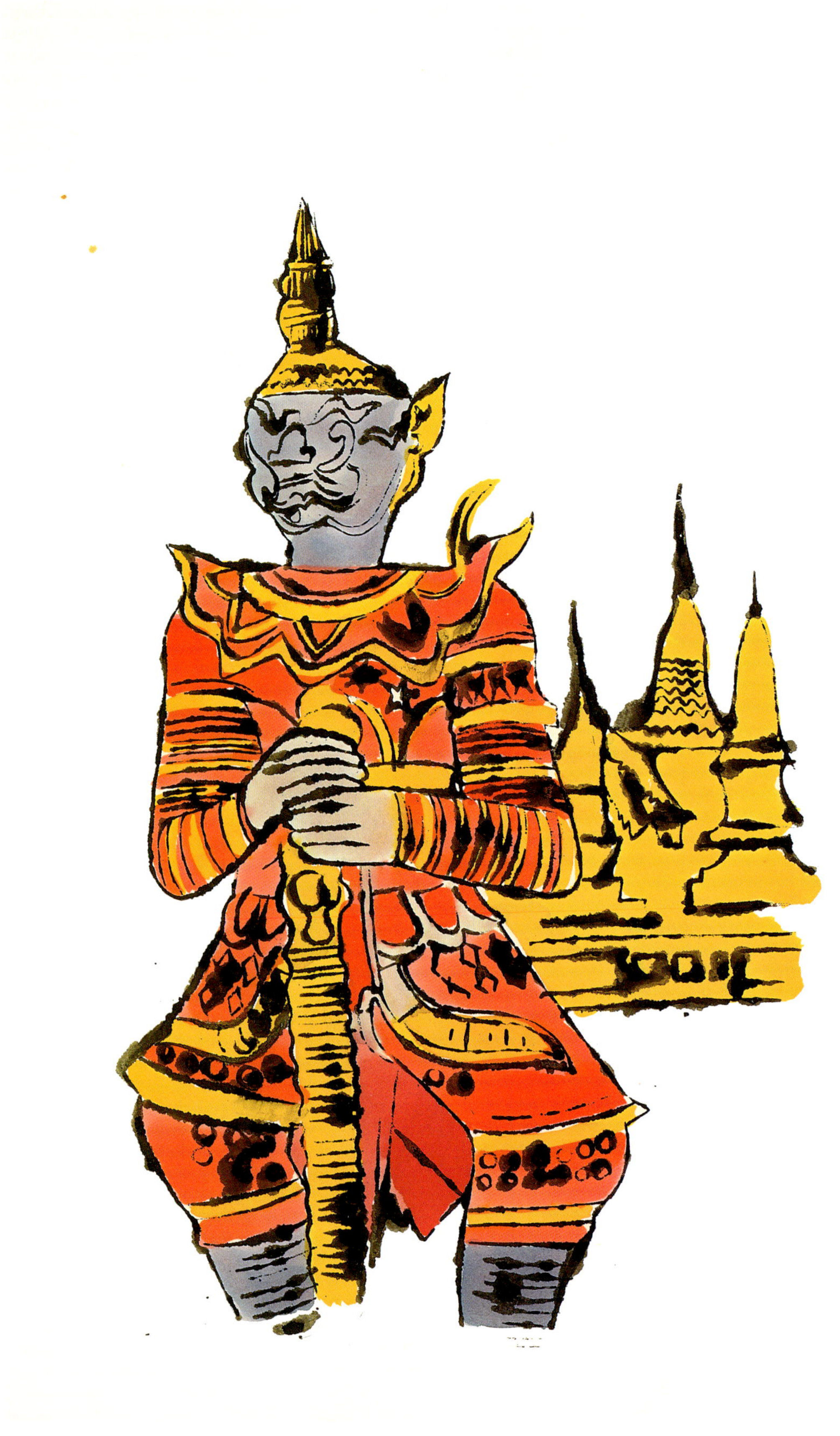

21 **Angkor Wat, Cambodia 1956** Private collection

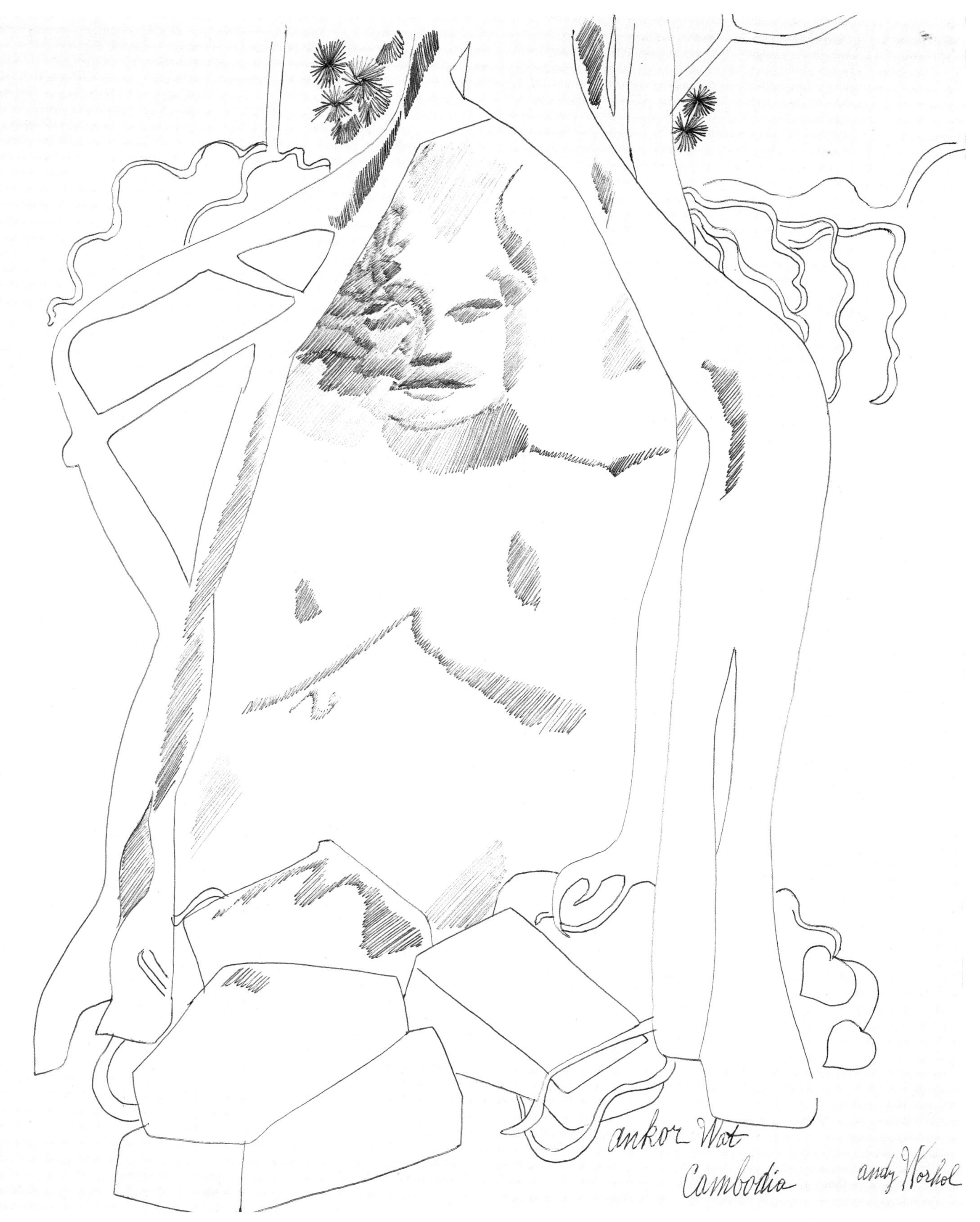

22 **Angkor Wat, Cambodia** **1956** Private collection

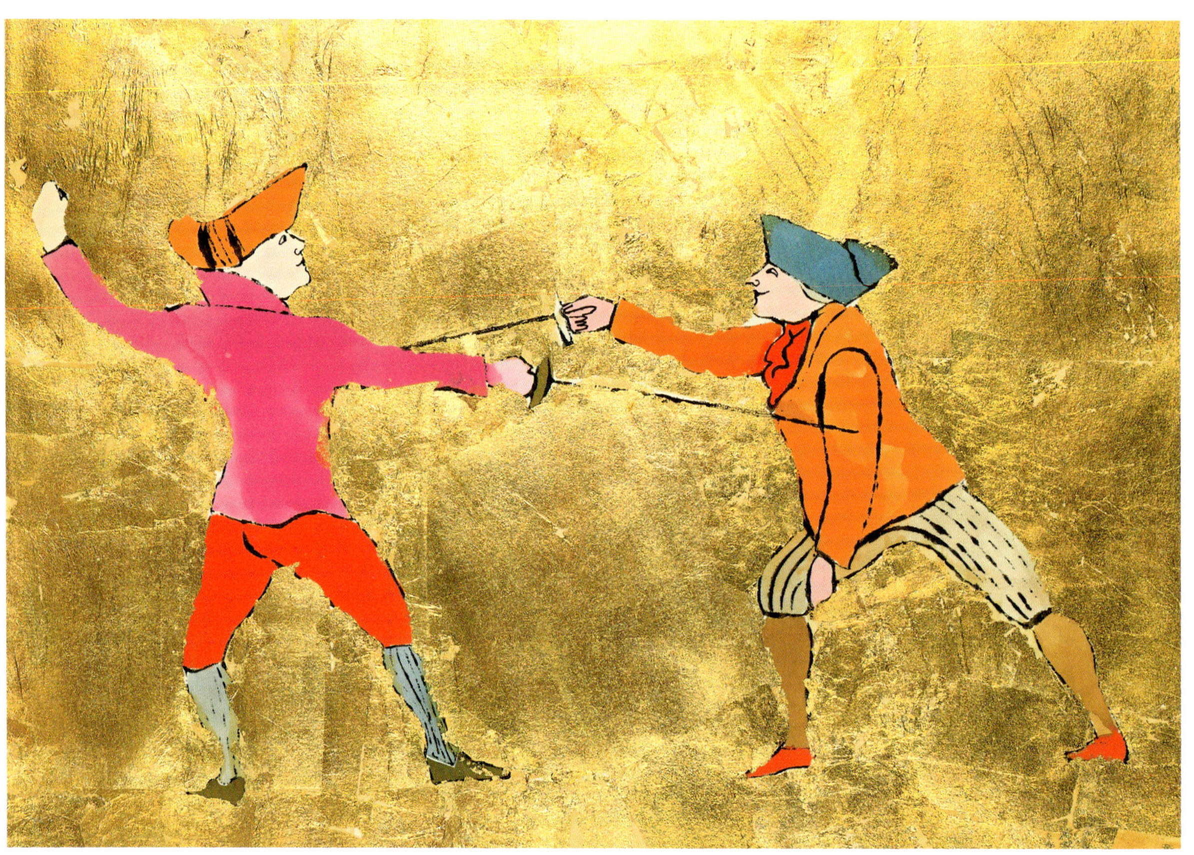

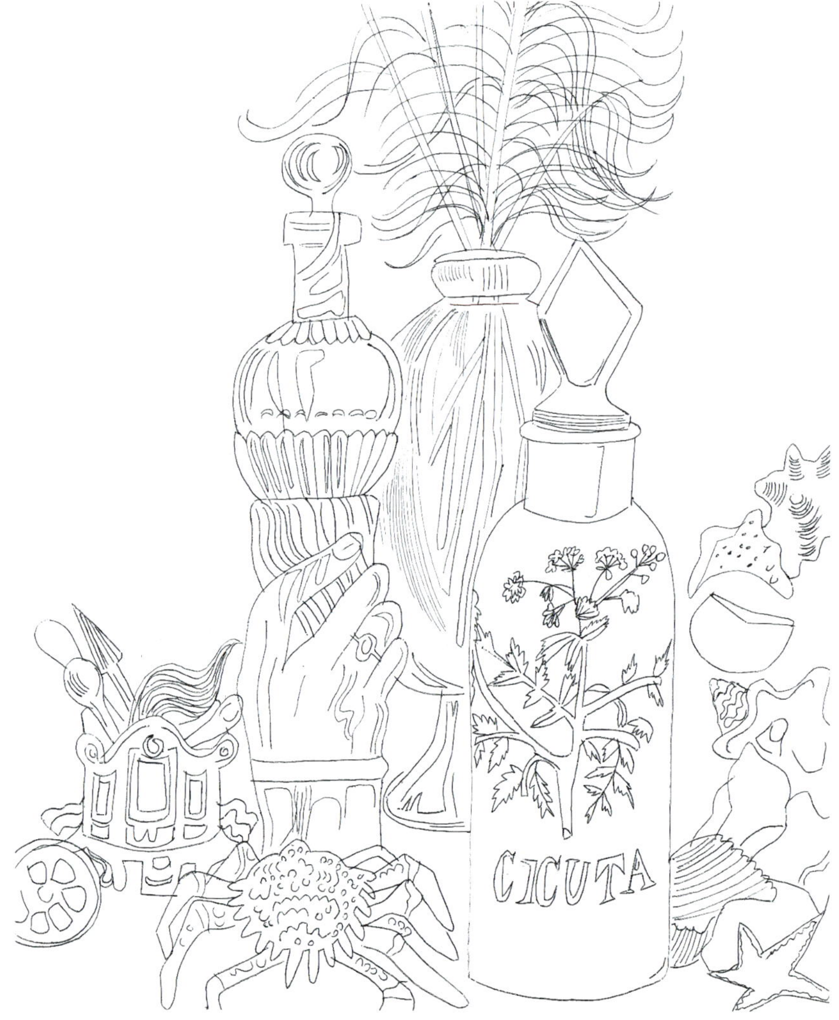

23 **Two Fencing Men c. 1957**
Private collection

24 **Still-Life (Flacon) c. 1957**
Private collection

25 **Untitled c. 1955**
Stiftung Sammlung Marx,
Hamburger Bahnhof –
Museum für Gegenwart, Berlin

26 **Untitled c. 1957**
Stiftung Sammlung Marx,
Hamburger Bahnhof –
Museum für Gegenwart, Berlin

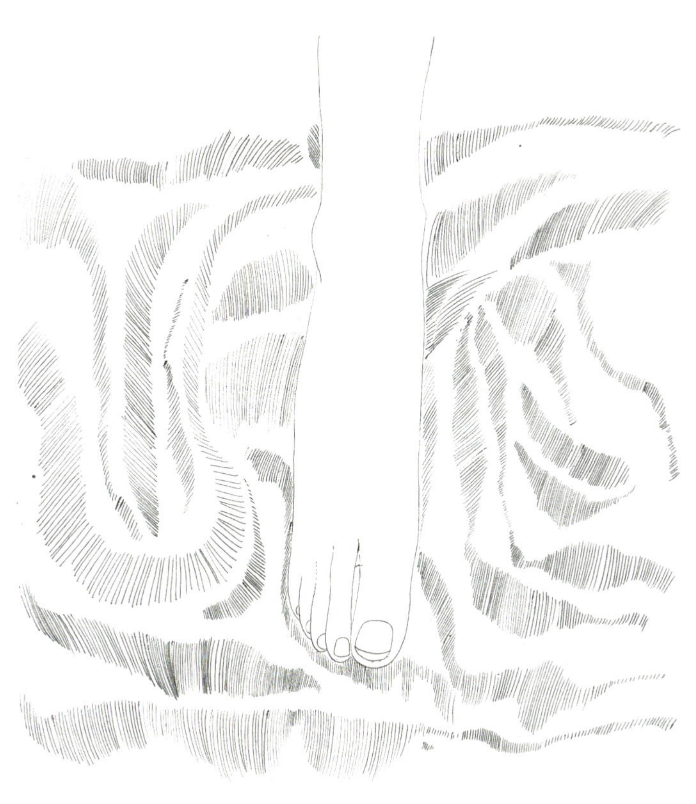

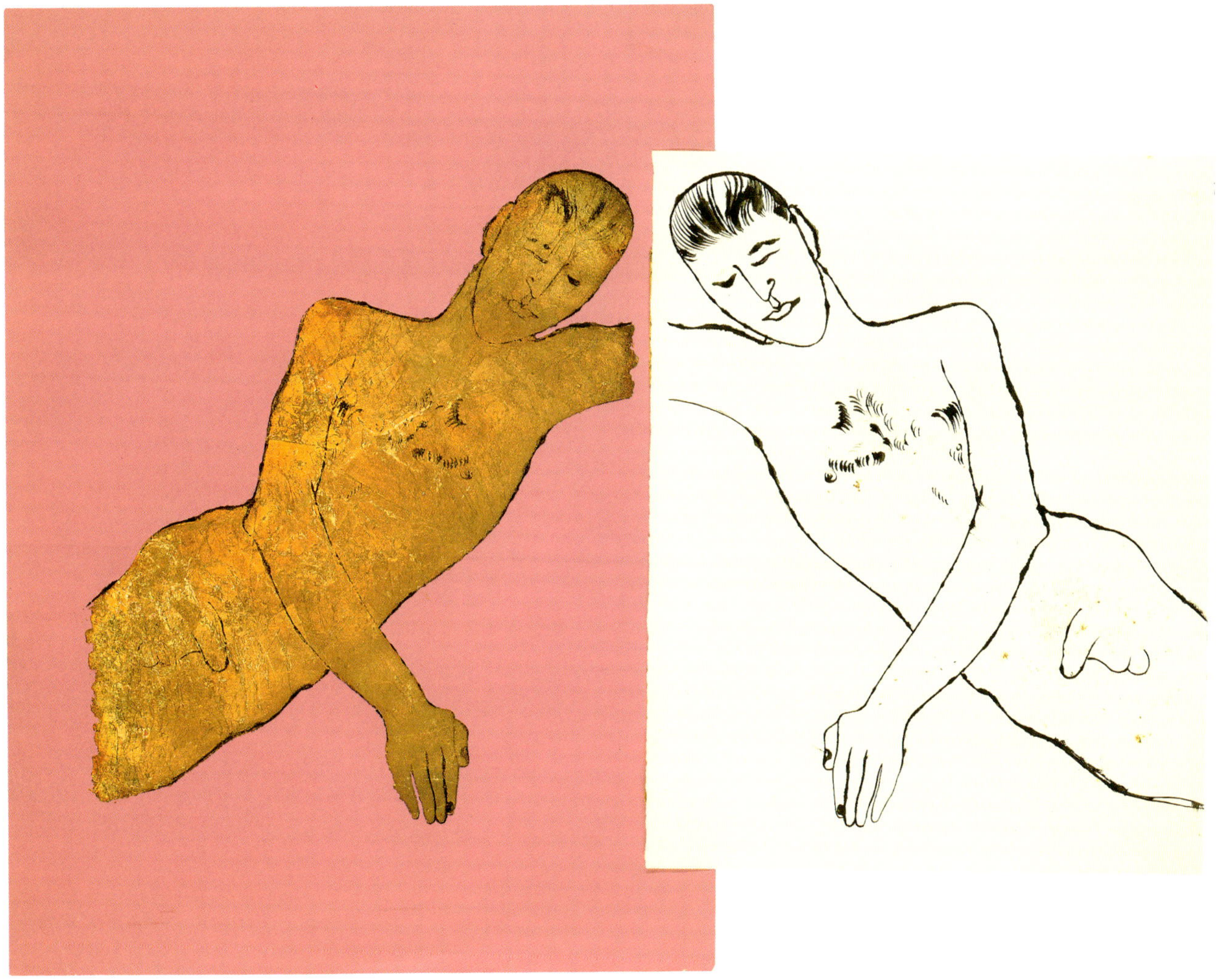

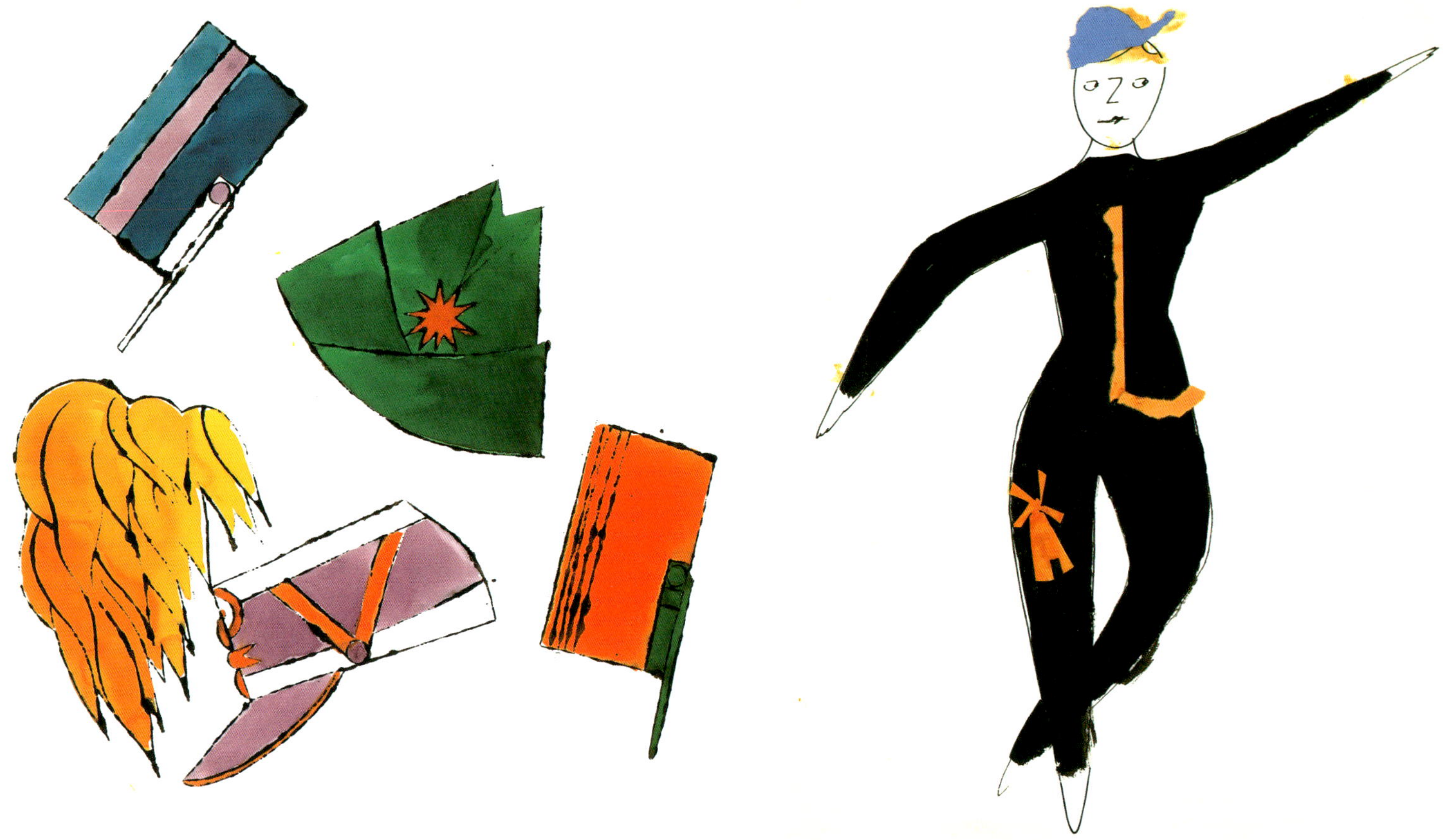

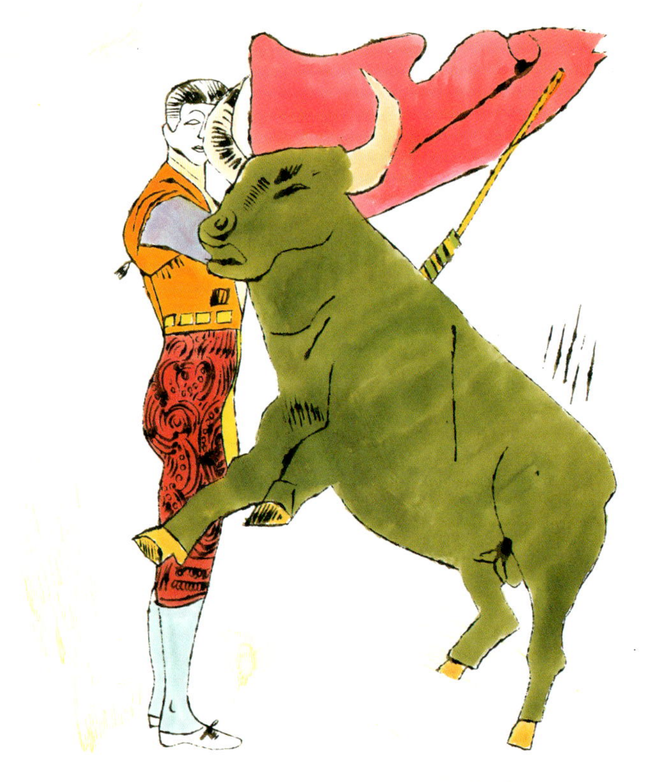

27 **Hats c. 1958**
Private collection

28 **Dancer c. 1955**
Private collection

29 **Bullfighter c. 1955**
Private collection

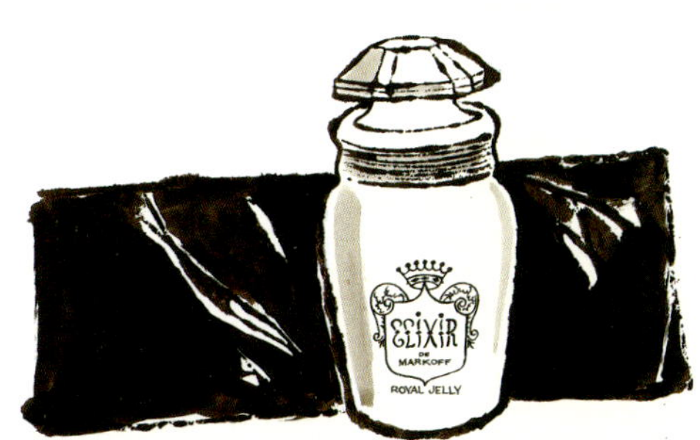

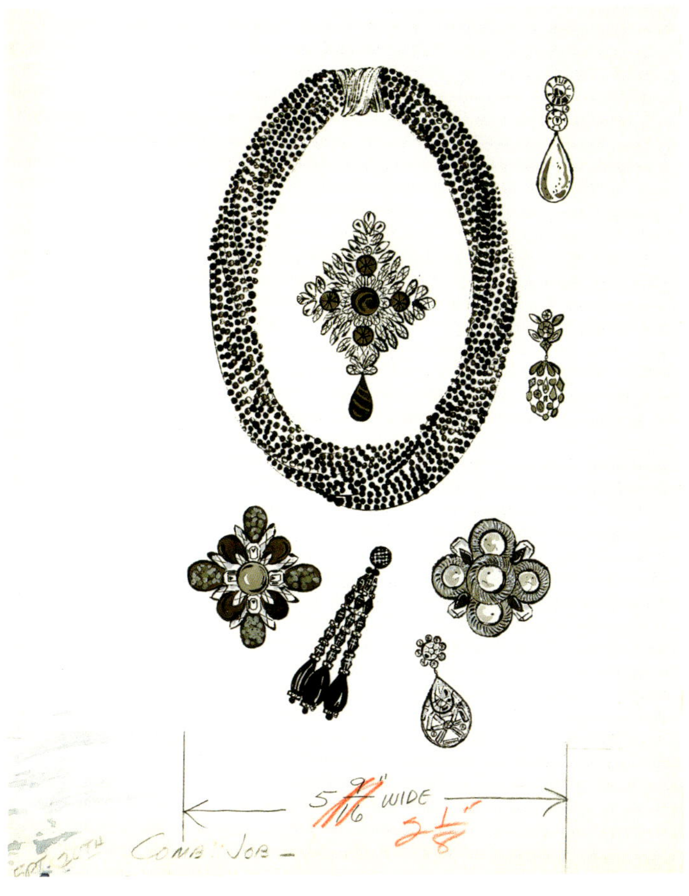

30 **Elixir de Markoff (Royal Jelly)** **c. 1960**
Courtesy Anthony d'Offay Gallery, London

31 **Jewelry (Necklace)** **c. 1960**
Courtesy Anthony d'Offay Gallery, London

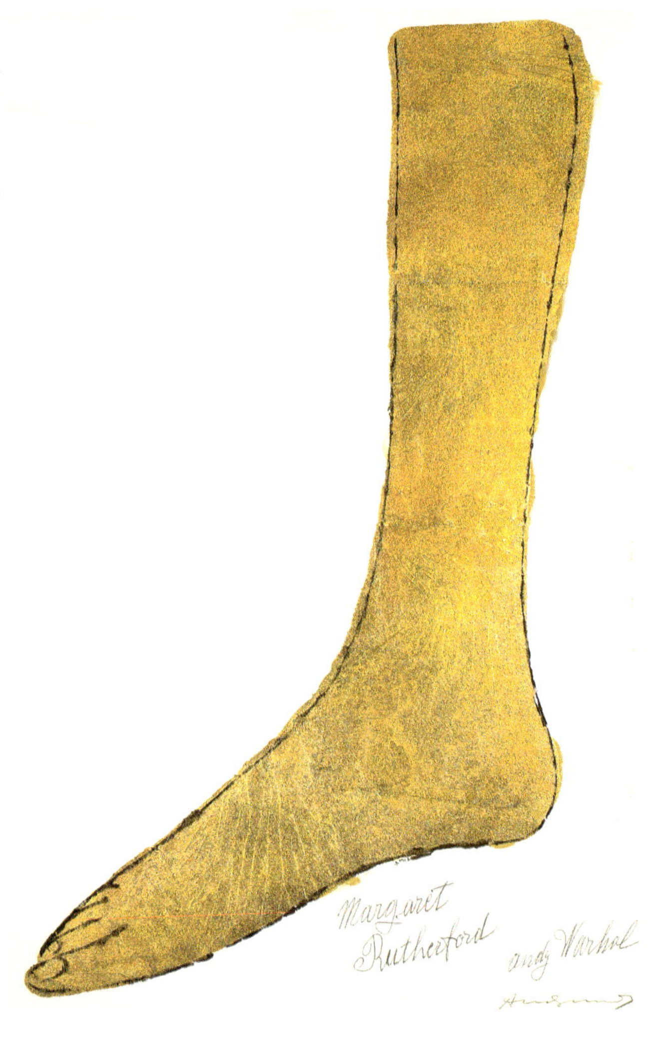
Margaret
Rutherford
andy Warhol

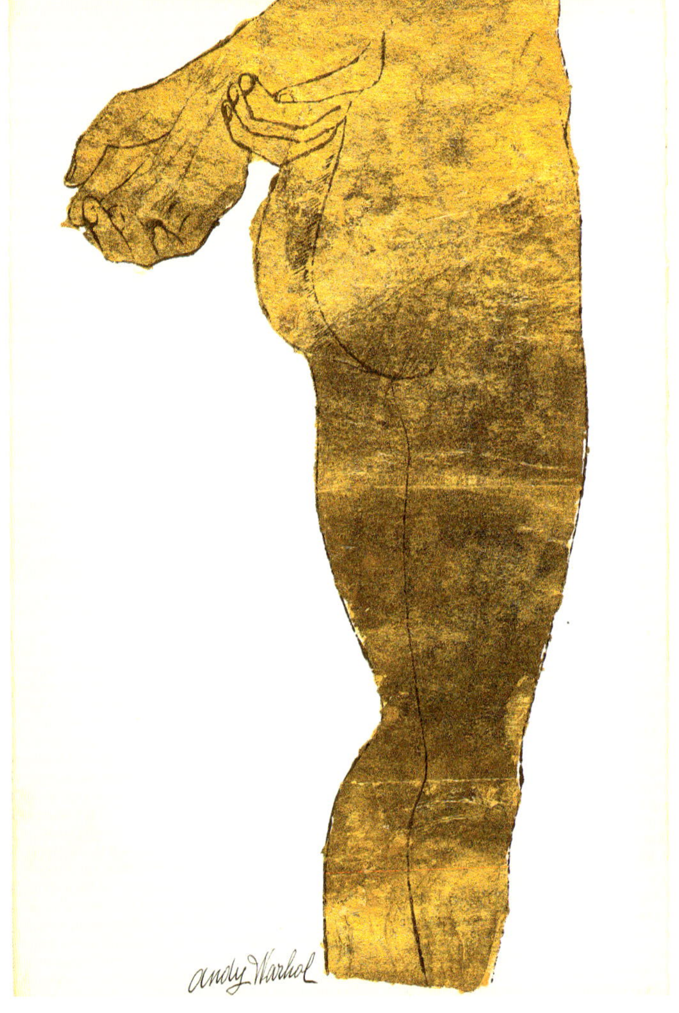
andy Warhol

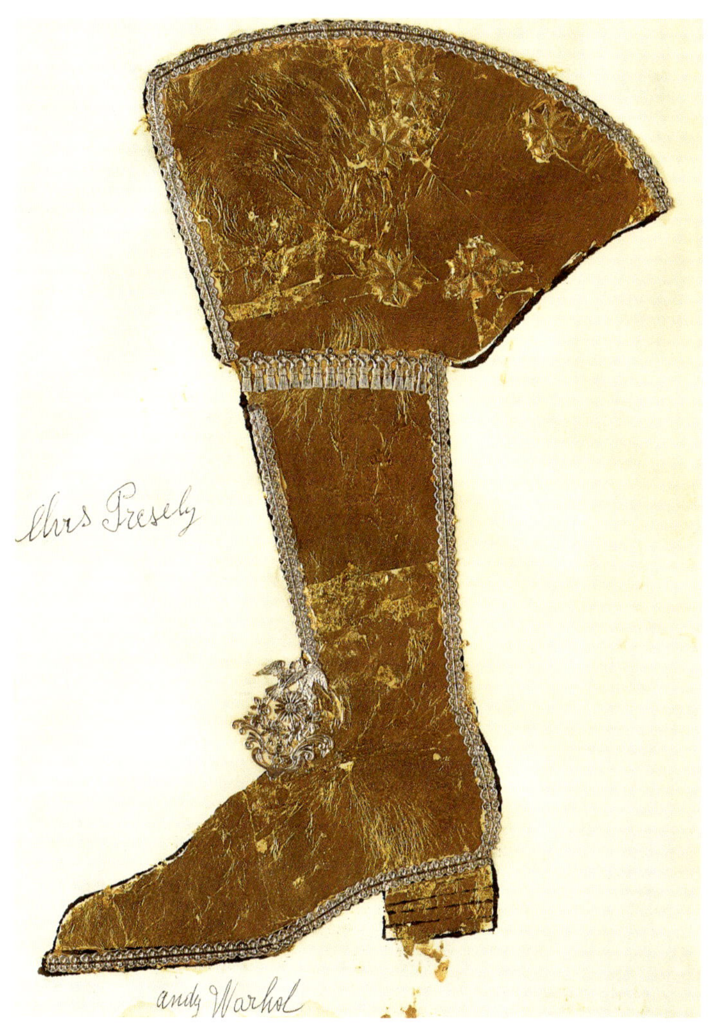

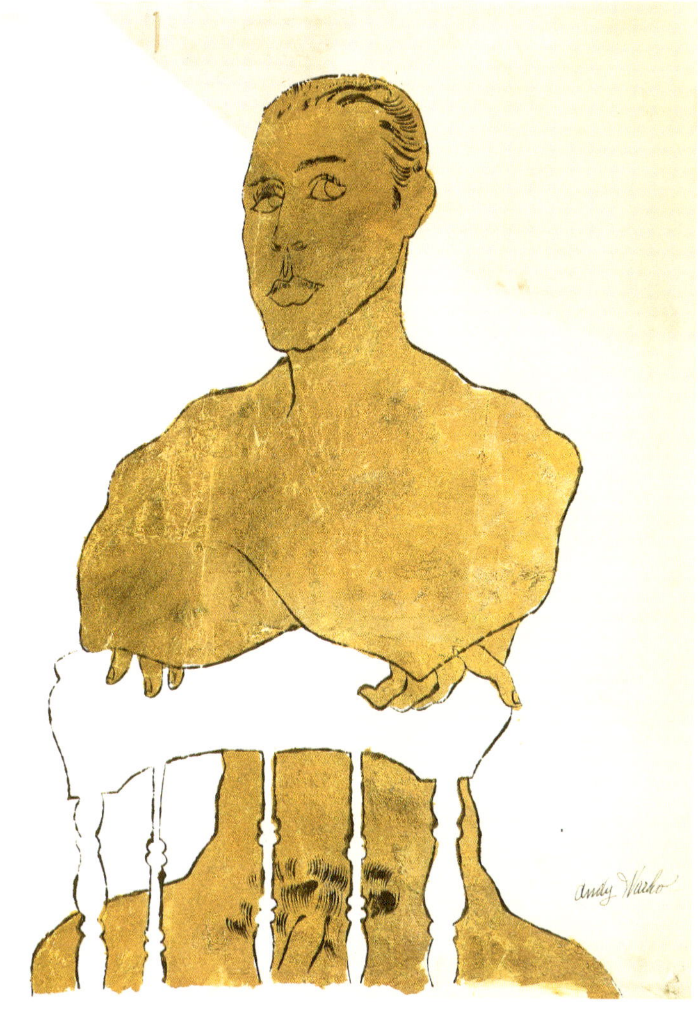

32 **Margaret Rutherford 1957**
Stiftung Sammlung Marx,
Hamburger Bahnhof –
Museum für Gegenwart, Berlin

33 **Golden Nude 1957**
Collection Froehlich, Stuttgart

34 **Elvis Presley (Gold Boot) 1956**
Courtesy The Brant Foundation,
Greenwich, CT

35 **Seated Male c. 1957**
Collection Froehlich, Stuttgart

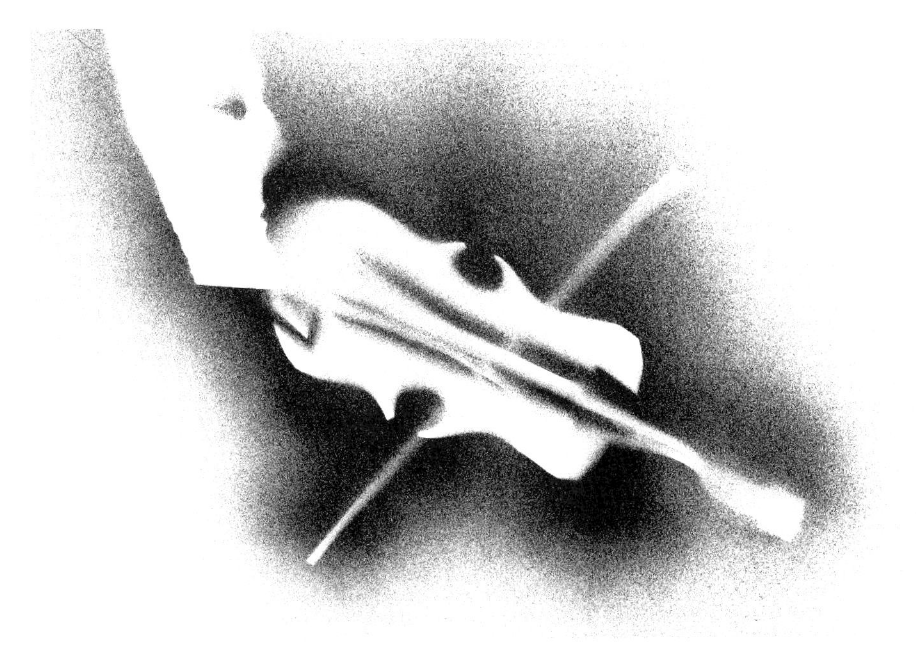

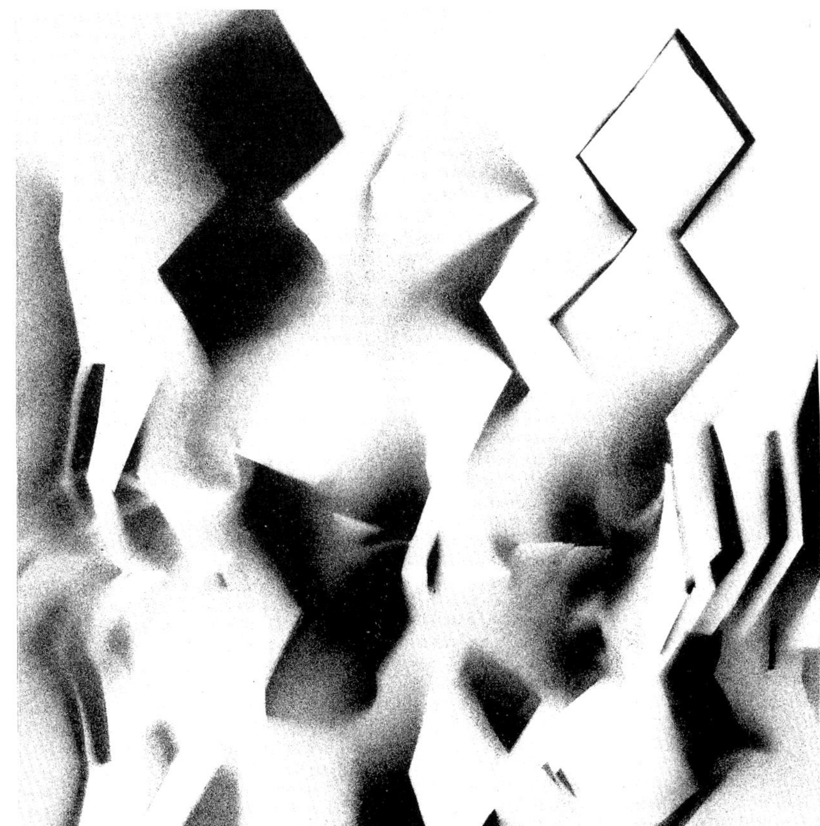

36 **(Stenciled) Violin and Bow c. 1958**
Private collection

37 **Abstract Stenciled Images c. 1958**
Private collection

38 **Bird on Branch of Leaves c. 1957**
Private collection

39 **Untitled (Baboon) c. 1957**
Private collection

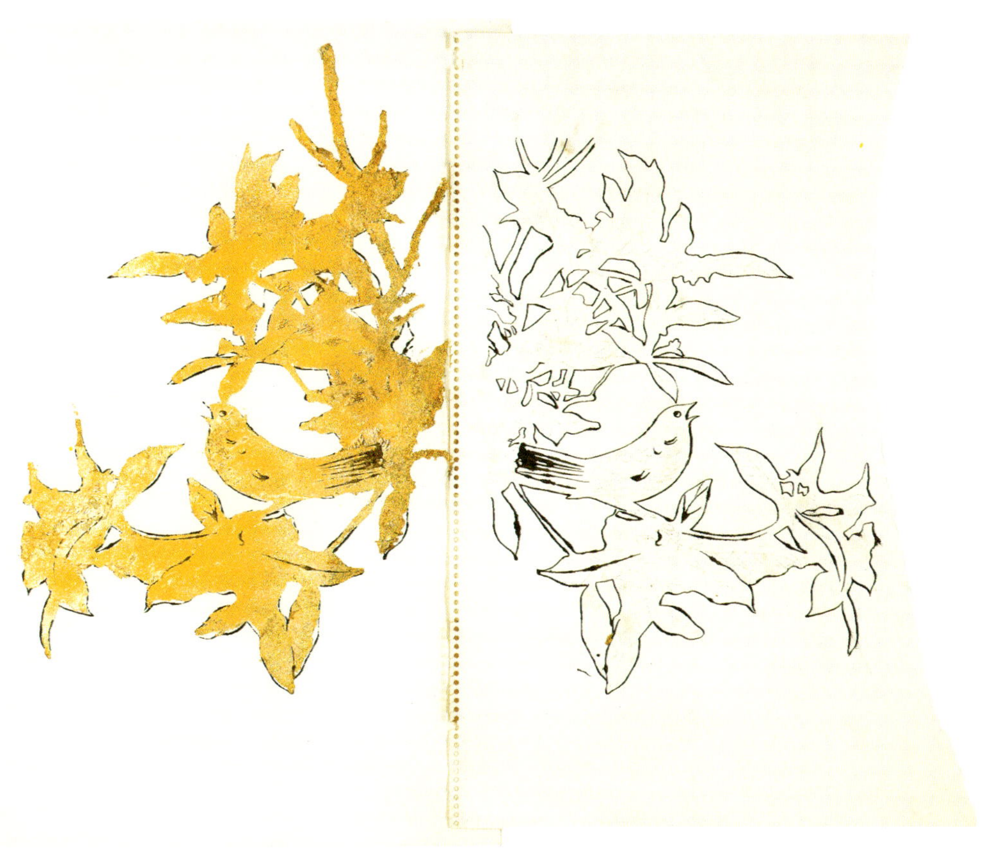

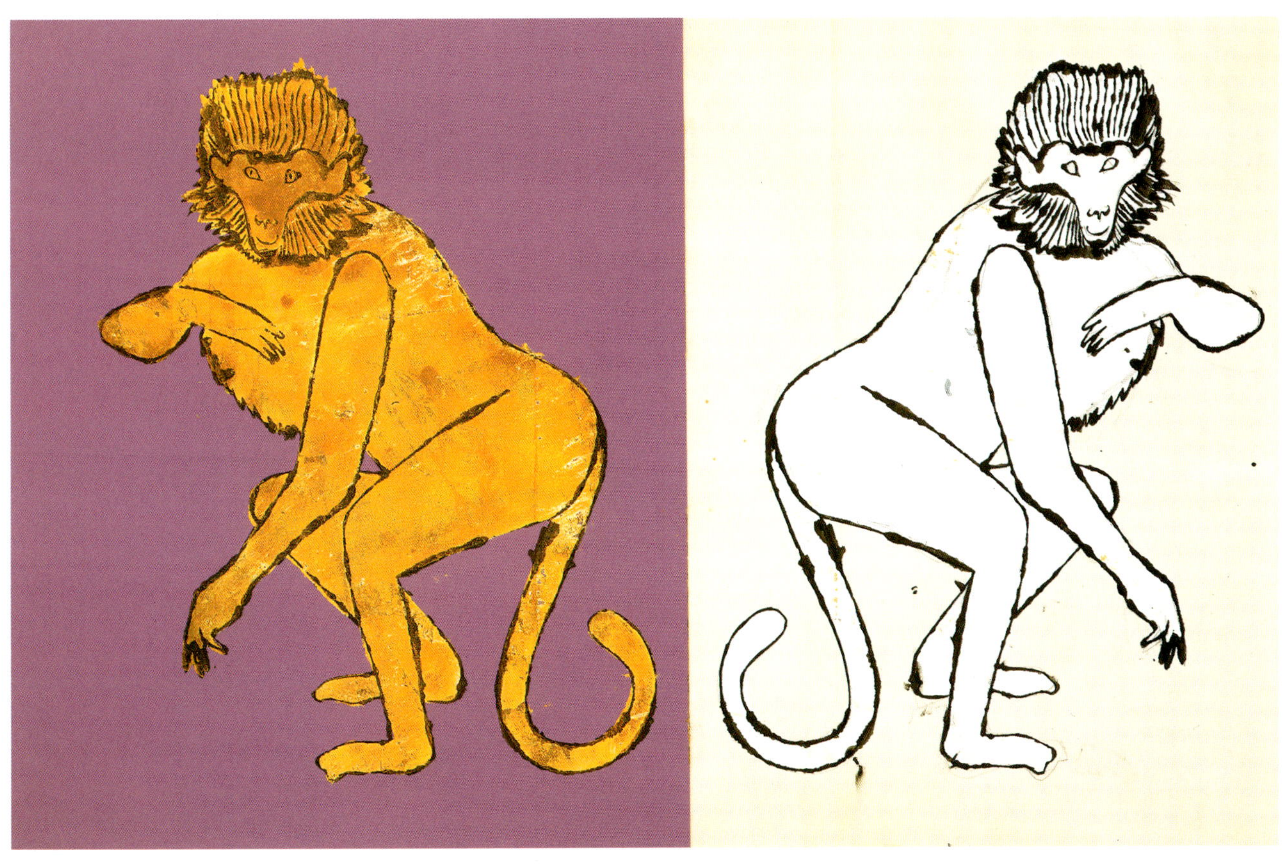

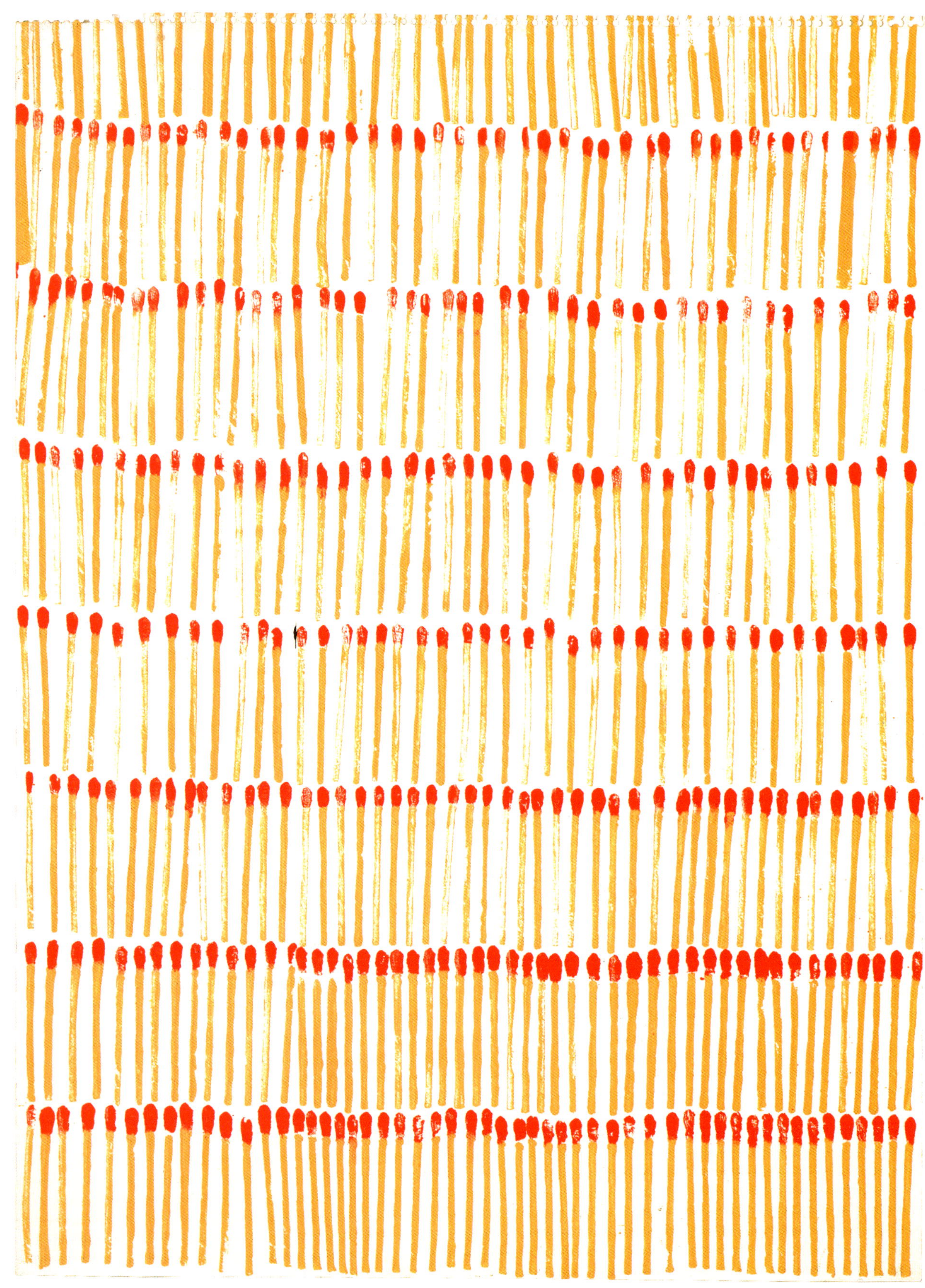

40 **Matches** **c. 1957** Stiftung Sammlung Marx, Hamburger Bahnhof – Museum für Gegenwart, Berlin

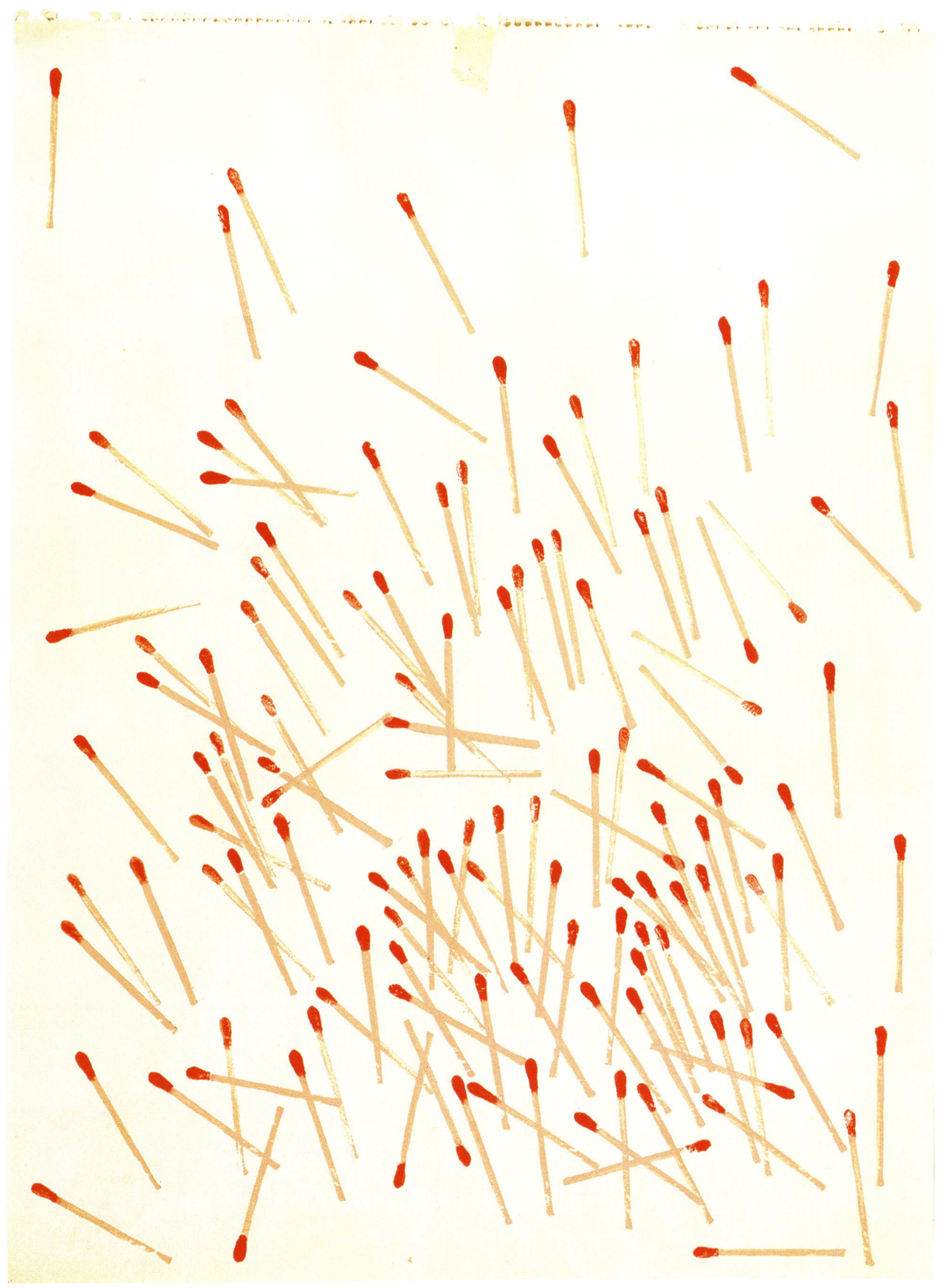

41 Matchsticks c. 1962 Courtesy The Brant Foundation, Greenwich, CT

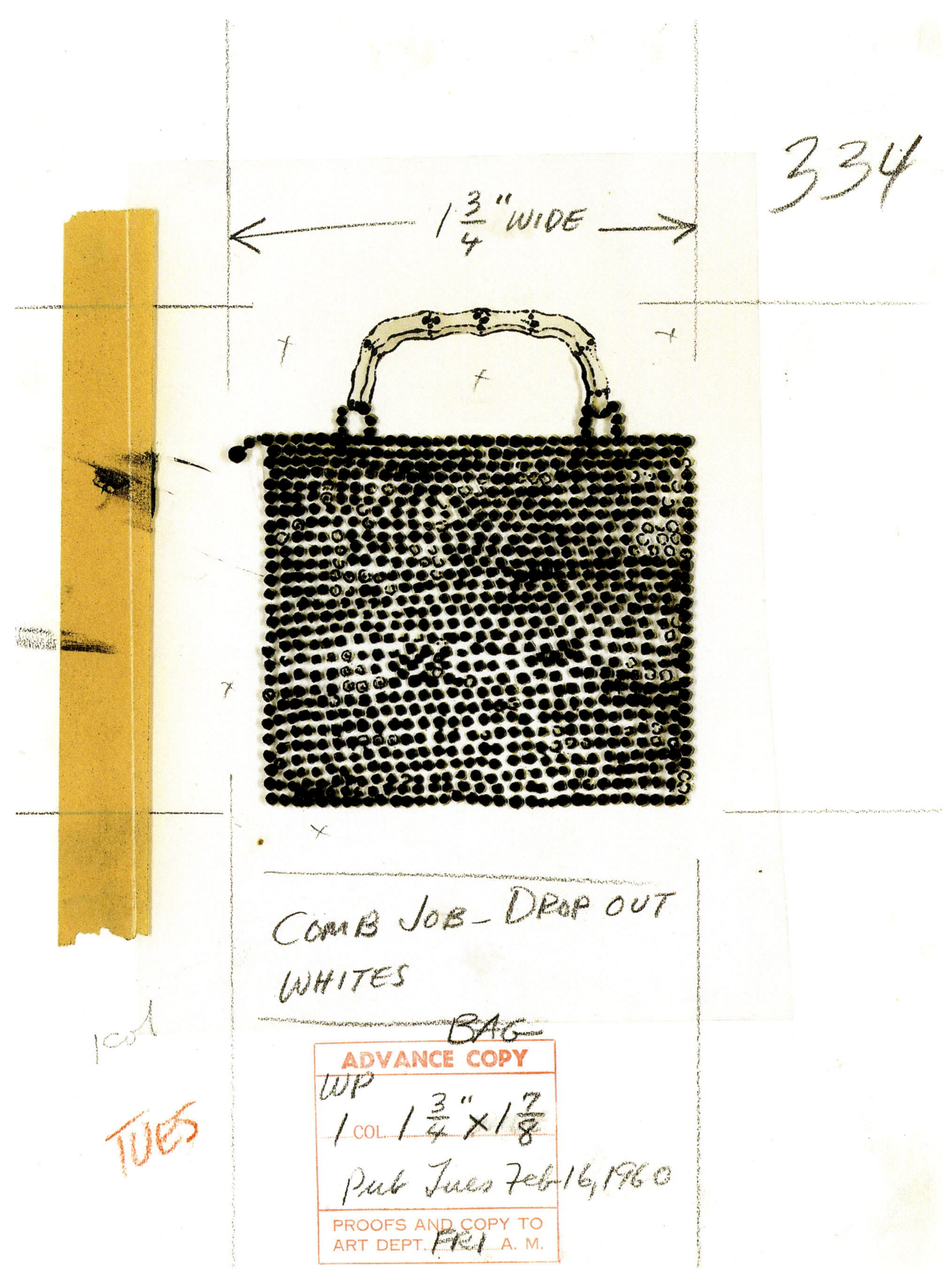

42 Purse c. 1960 Courtesy Anthony d'Offay Gallery, London

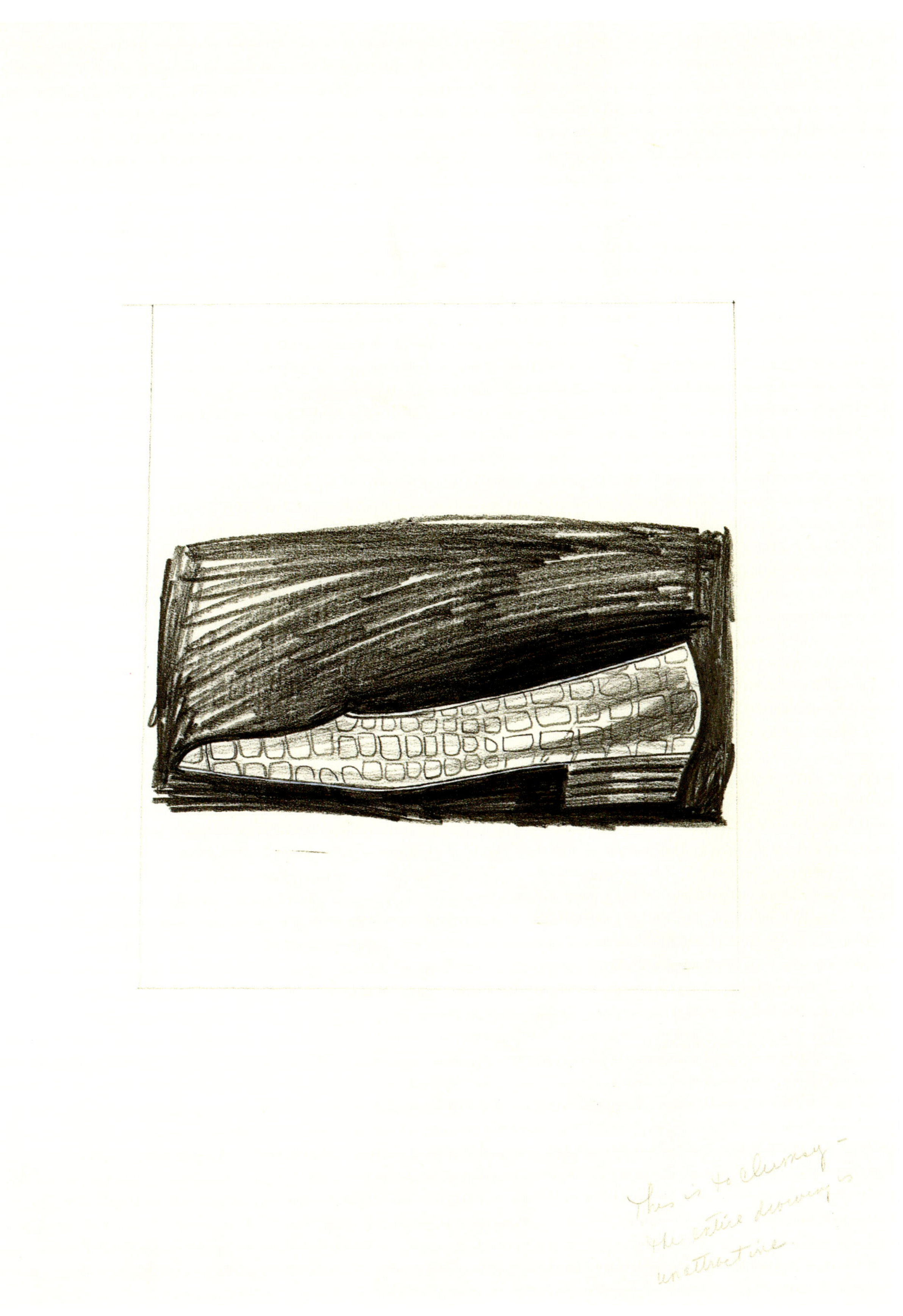

43 **Shoe** **c. 1960** Courtesy Anthony d'Offay Gallery, London

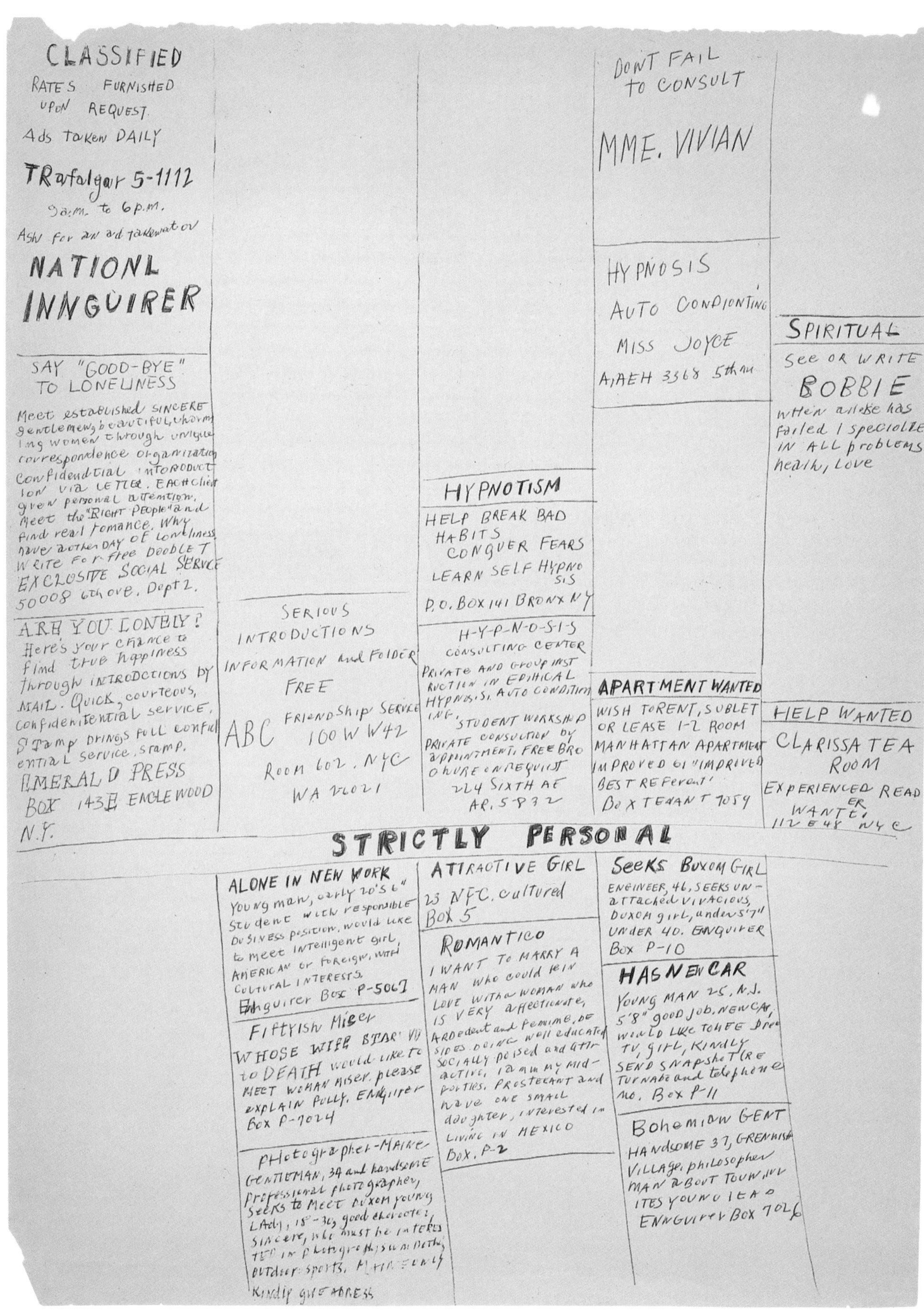

44 **Strictly Personal** **1956** Private collection, New York

Introducing the New Jackie Gleason

START THIS SERIES TODAY ON PAGE 16

Find the Name $75,000 contest turn to Page 18

NEW YORK Journal American

SUNDAY FINAL Todays Weather: RAIN. Temp. near 70

NO 25727 SUNDAY SEPTEMBER 21, 1958 10 CENTS

Woman Stabs Rev. King in Harlem

Ike Blasts 'Abusive' Soviet Note

He Returns It Stamped 'Rejected'

NEWPORT, R.I. Sept 20 (AP). — The United States Threw Soviet Russias latest letter back in Premier Nikata Khrushchevs face today. The U.S. called the note too false, abusive and threatening to be acceptable under international standards.

The Summer White House announcing this on behalf of President Eisenhower, said it believed such a rejection of a note has no precent in the history of U.S. -Soviet relations,

Eisenhower's action meant. This country will ignore Khrushchev's demand that this country pull its forces out of Formosa and the Summary area — a much -

Columbia Outsails Sceptre

PRESIDENT EISENHOWER AND MAMIE ATOLL RACES sun gets in their eyes as they watch start off

Special to N.Y. Times.

NEWPORT, R.I., Sept. 20 — The defending Columbia ran away from Great Britain's sceptre yest in their first America's Cup race and dealt a heavy blow to Englands hope of winning back the prized yachting trophy.

When the white-hulled American sloop shot across the finish of the Brisuled challenger was just visible on the horizon. It was the most lop-sided race in the history of international yacting clash.

Cheered by the unexpectedly easy triumph, American yachtsmen were predicting there the Columbia would win the present competition in four straight races

AVE JOINS DESAPIO IN UNITY MOVE

BY SANFORD STATON

Gov. HARRIMAN and tammany hall leader CARMINE De Sapio joined yesterday in declarations that the

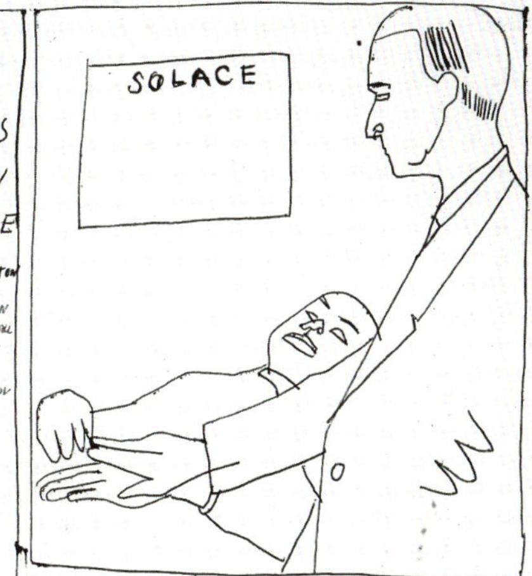

MBA Approves Union Merger

Accused Attacker Called Demented

Defer Test Firing OF Atomic Device

Atomic Test site, NEV. Firing of an atomic device in a 500-foot vertical shaft has been postponed. The Atomic Energy Commission

Police Say Dying Dr. Nimer Called Killer 'Different Color'

Investigation into the double slaying of Dr. and Mrs Melvin Nimer took a new turn yesterday with the disclosure

Editor's Report:

AUTO PACTS BOON to EC

BY WILLIAM RANDOLPH HEARST JR

10 days Chrysler and

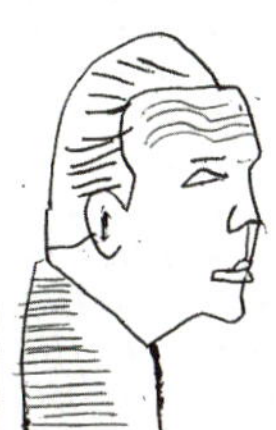

W. R. HEARST JR

On the Inside...

RUSSIA AND the ATOM Thomas E Murrays Revealing on Geneva Science Parley

FOOTBALL'S HUMAN MISSILE read about Oliveing Fullback

SPECIAL FALL TV PREVIEW Jack O'Brian eyes the New Season in Pictorial Magazine TV

Read every page of New York's most interesting Sunday newspaper for top news coverage photos and features.

Chief and 6 to Die

LAGOS, Nigeria. Sept 20 (UPI). — A British court today sentenced an eastern Nigerian tribal chief and six other men to death

THE WEATHER (US. Weather Bureau)

TODAY'S INDEX

Andy Warhol 60

45 **Journal American c. 1958/60** The Andy Warhol Museum, Pittsburgh • Founding Collection, Contribution Dia Center for the Arts

WORKS 1960-1986

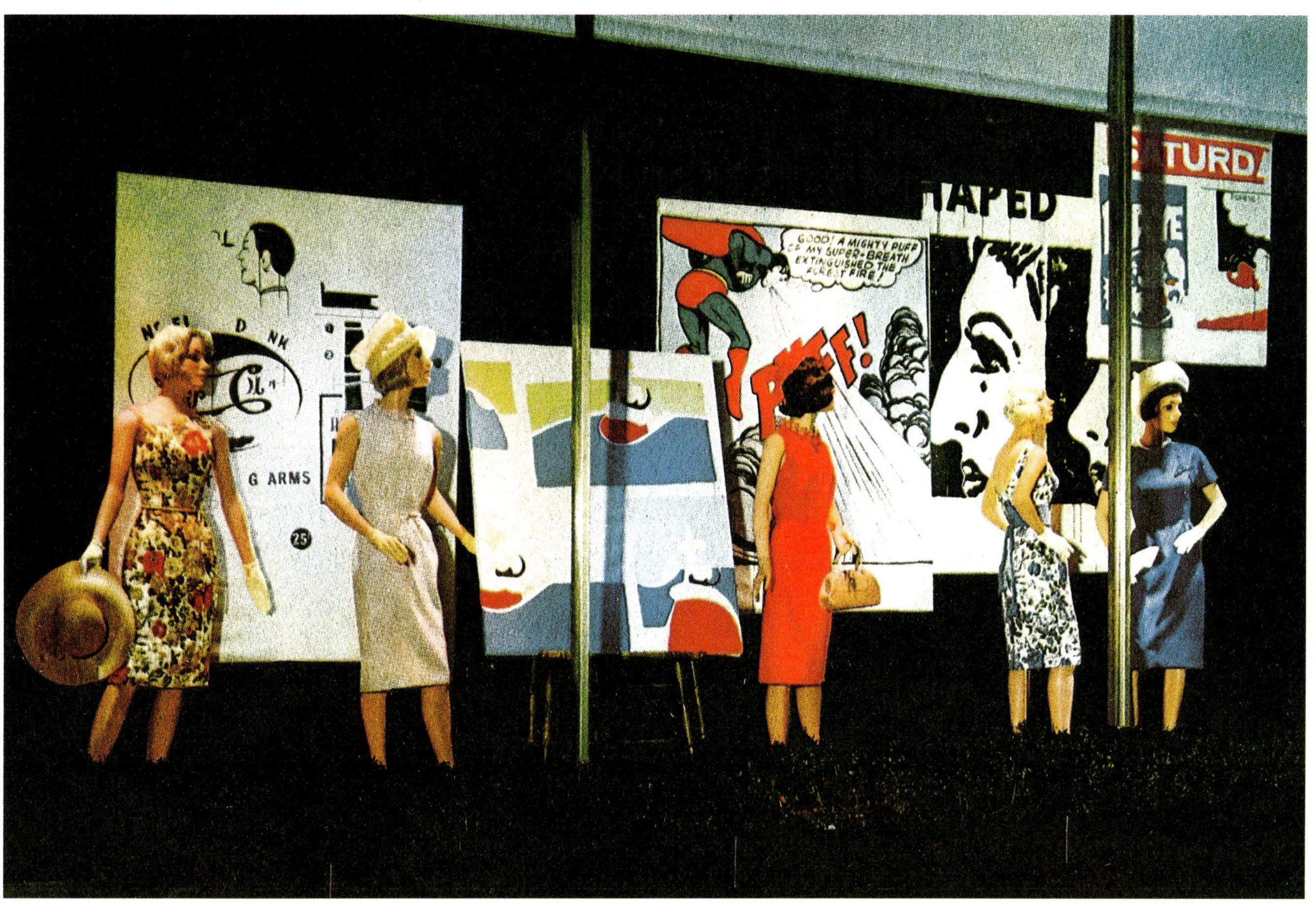

First ›exhibition‹ of the paintings *Advertisement, Little King, Superman, Before and After* and *Saturday's Popeye*, window display, Bonwit Teller, New York, April 1961.

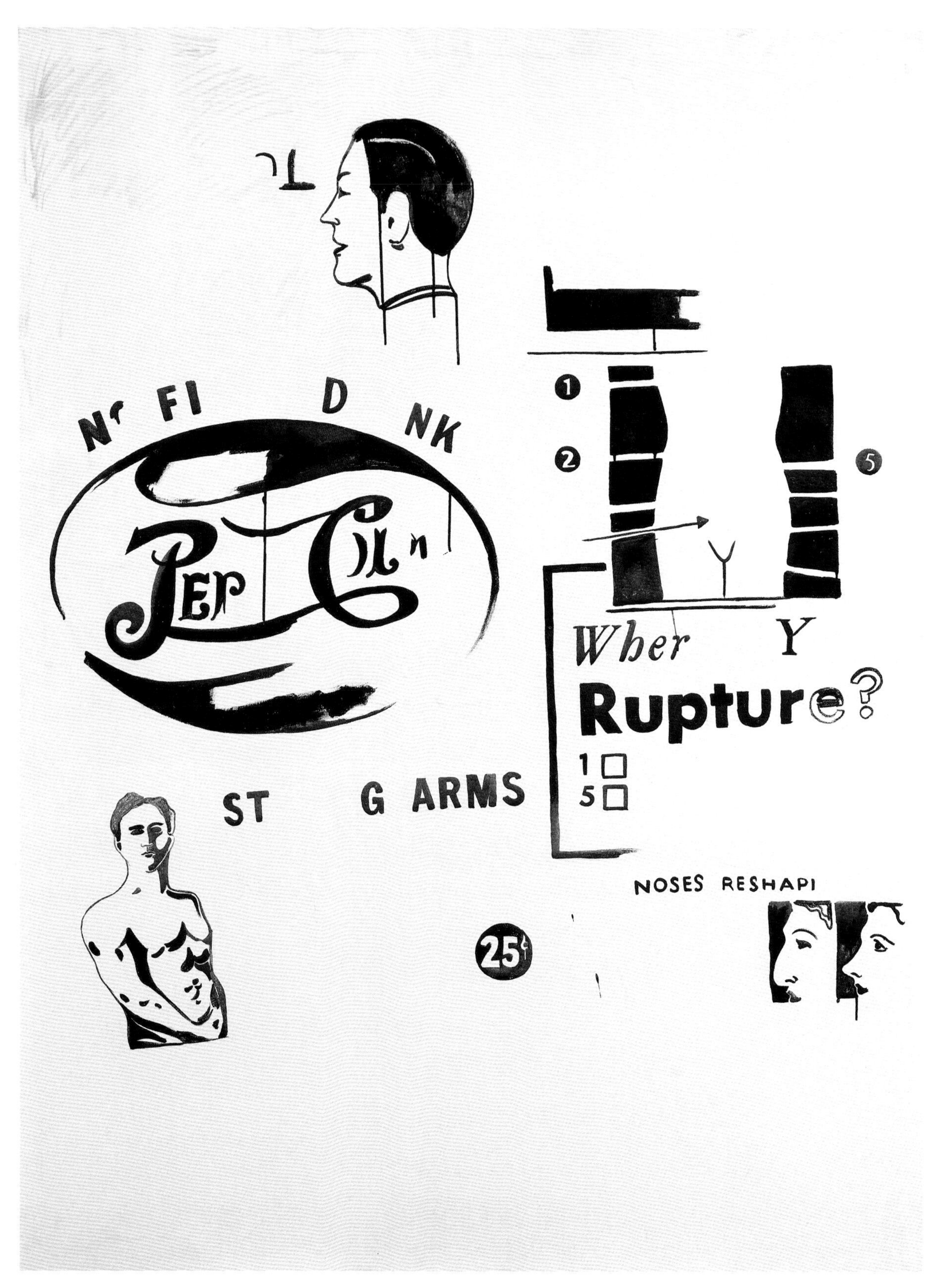

46 Advertisement 1960 Stiftung Sammlung Marx, Hamburger Bahnhof – Museum für Gegenwart, Berlin

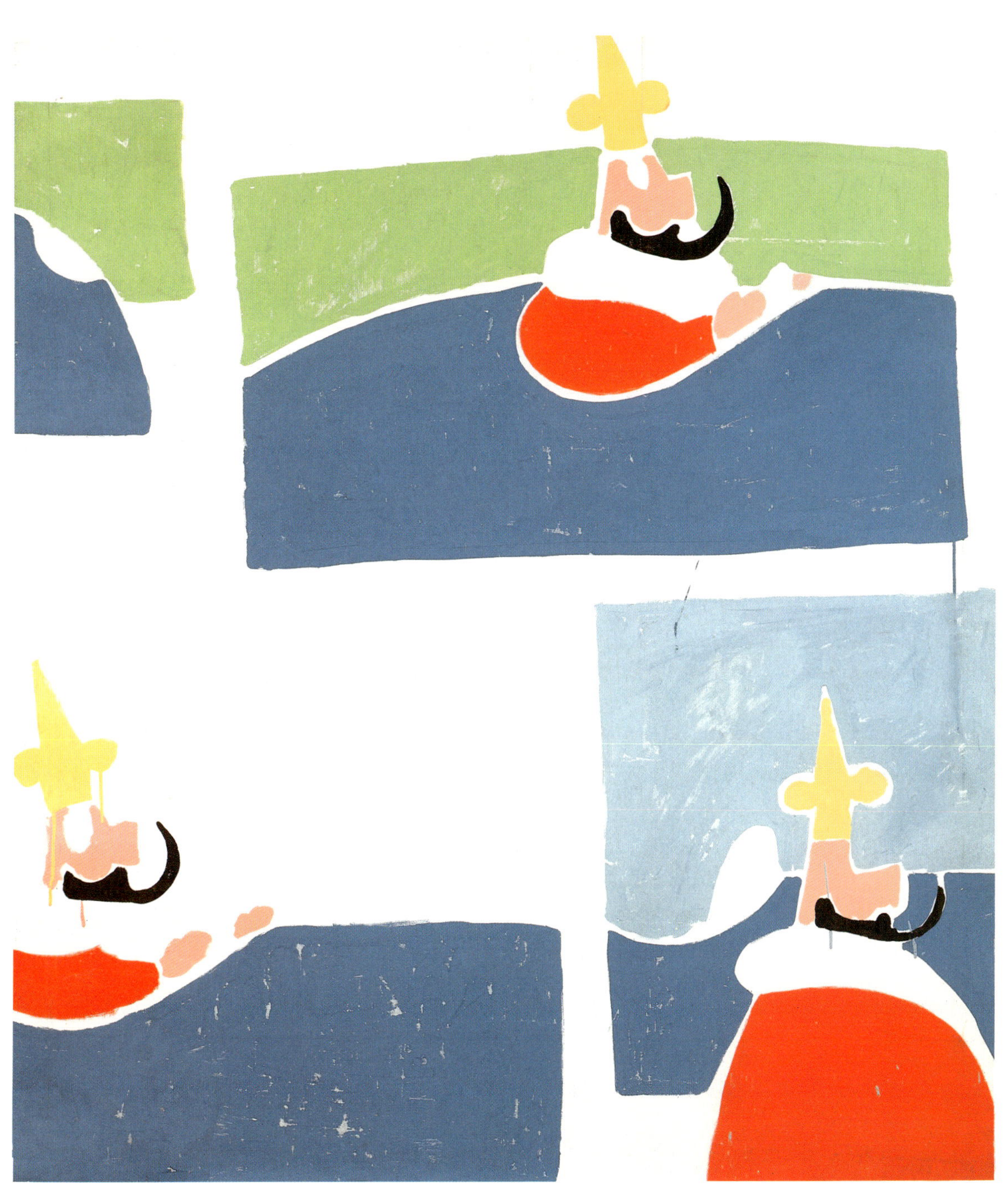

47 **Little King 1961** Private collection

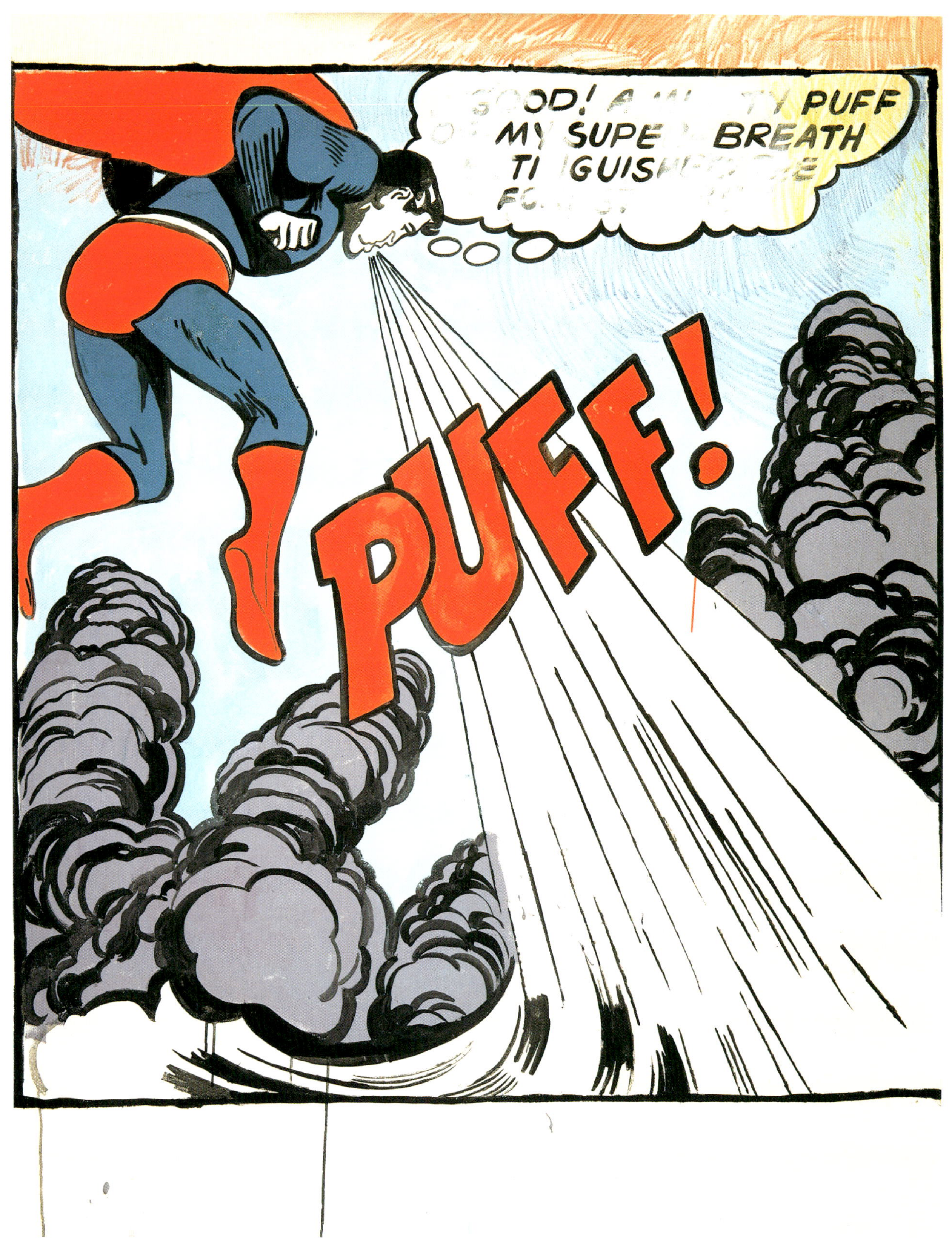

48 Superman 1961 Collection Gunter Sachs

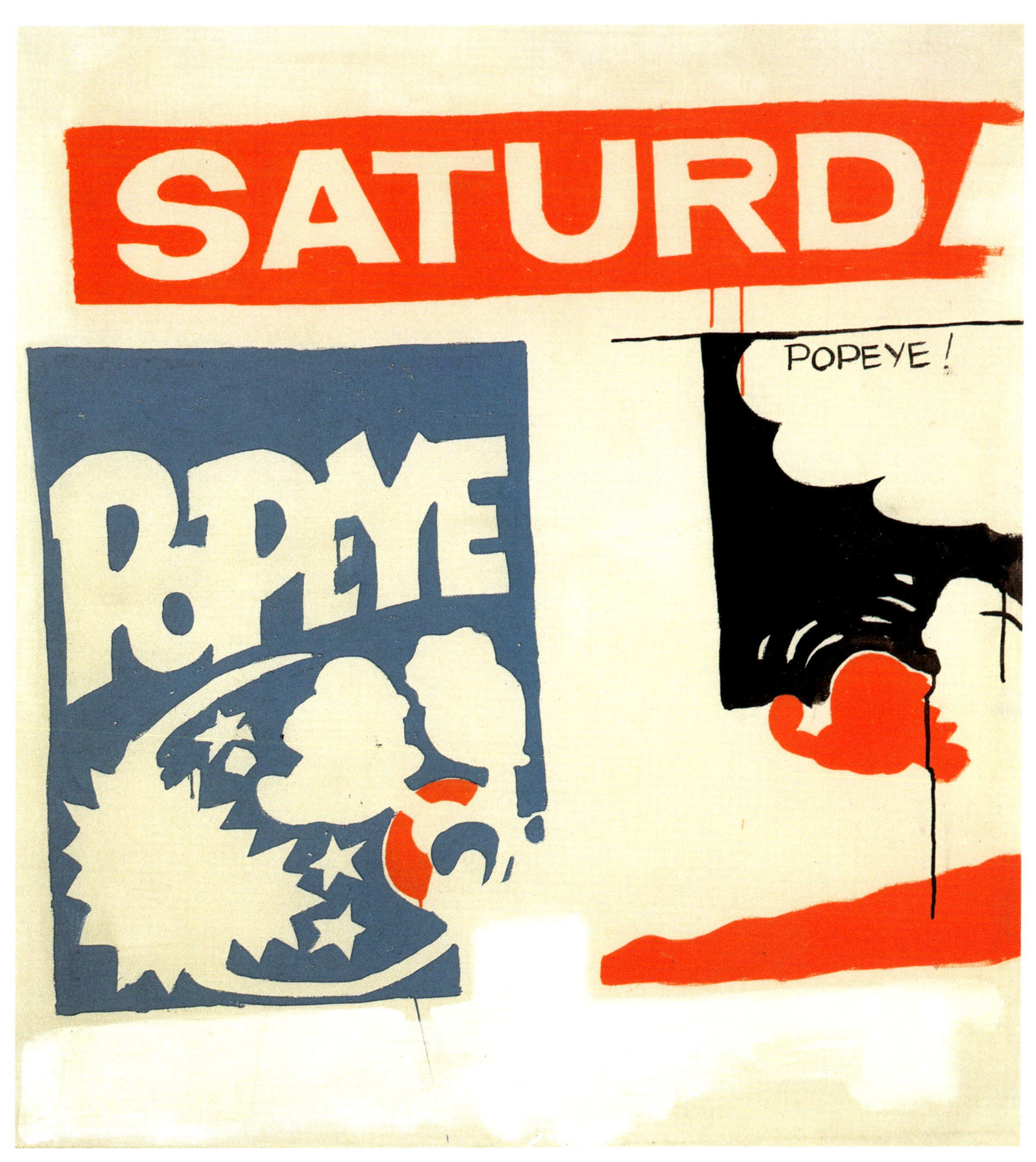

49 Saturday's Popeye 1961 Ludwig Forum für Internationale Kunst, Aachen – Collection Ludwig

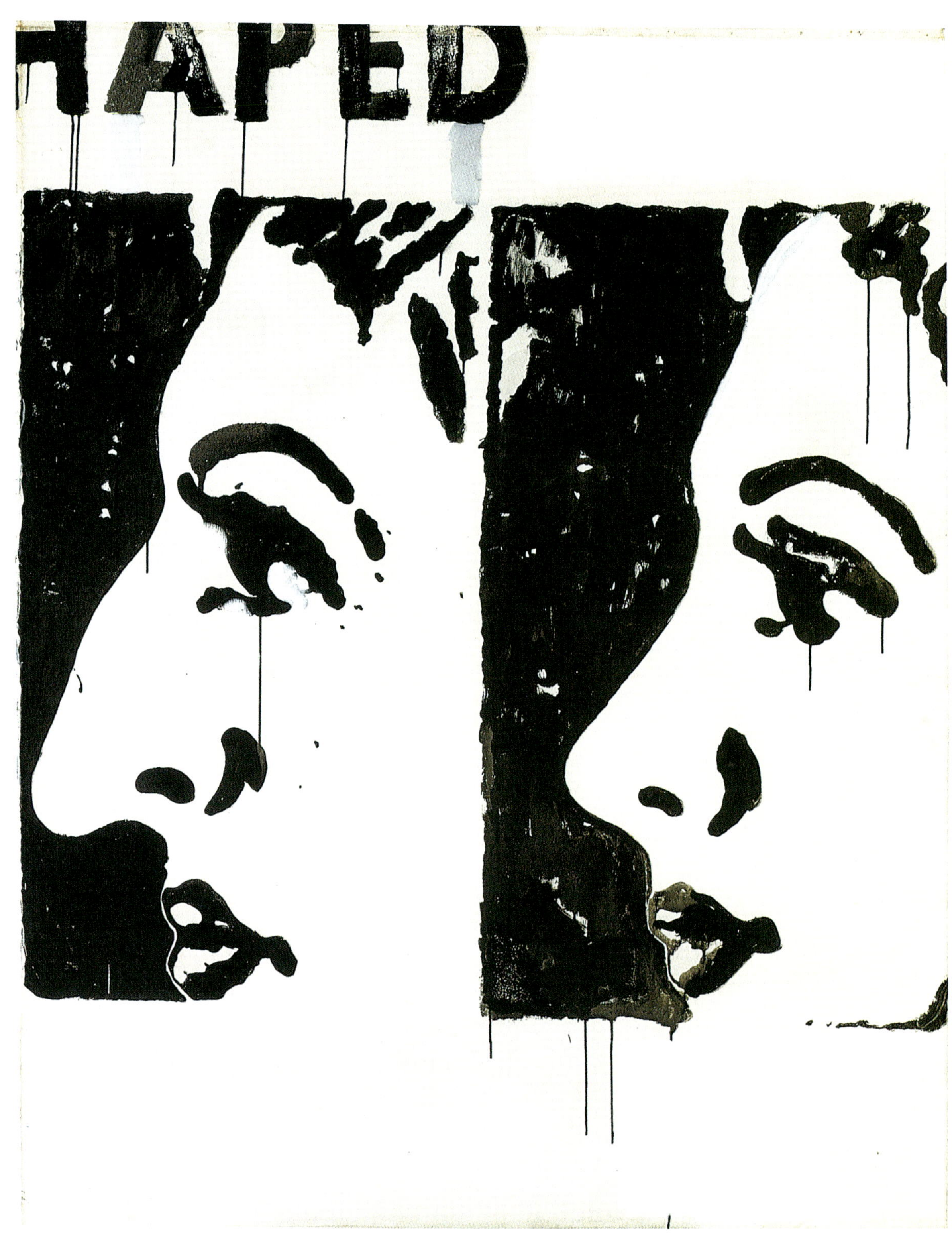

50 Before and After [1] 1961 The Metropolitan Museum of Art, New York • Gift of Halston, 1981

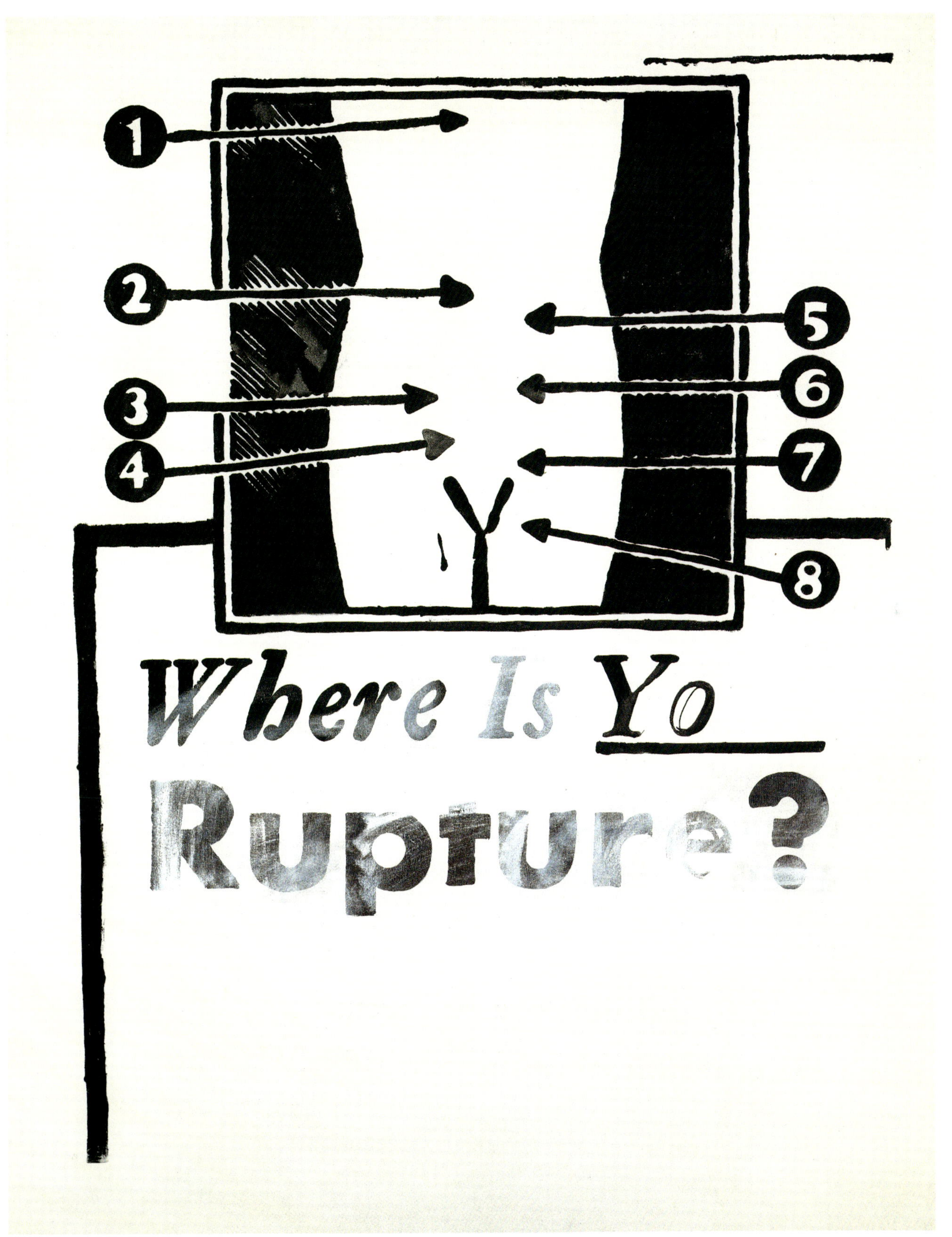

51 **Where Is Your Rupture? 1960** Private collection

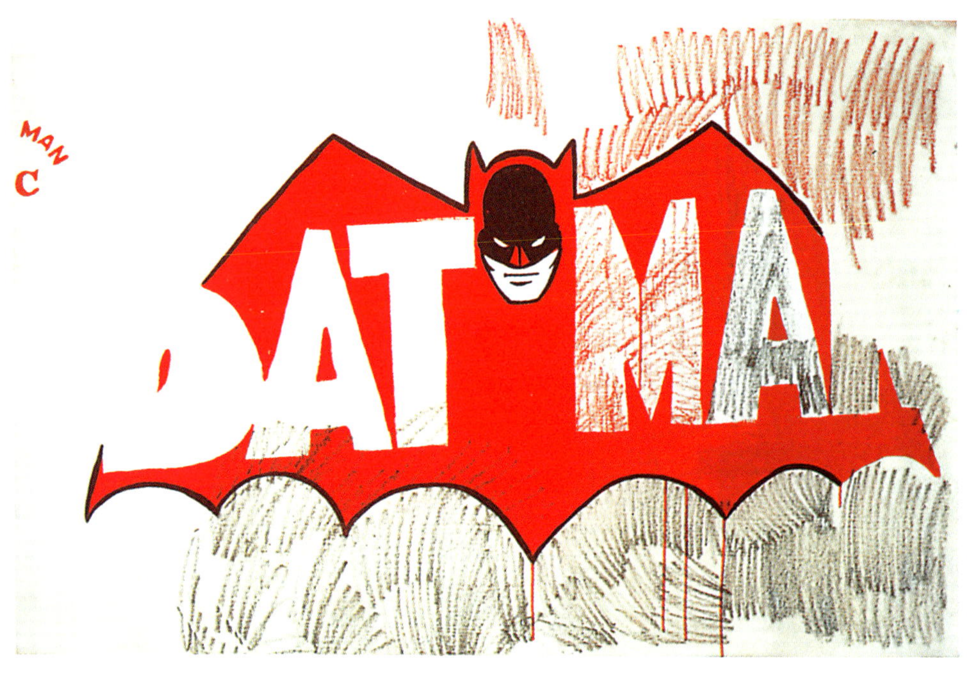

52 **Batman 1961** Private collection

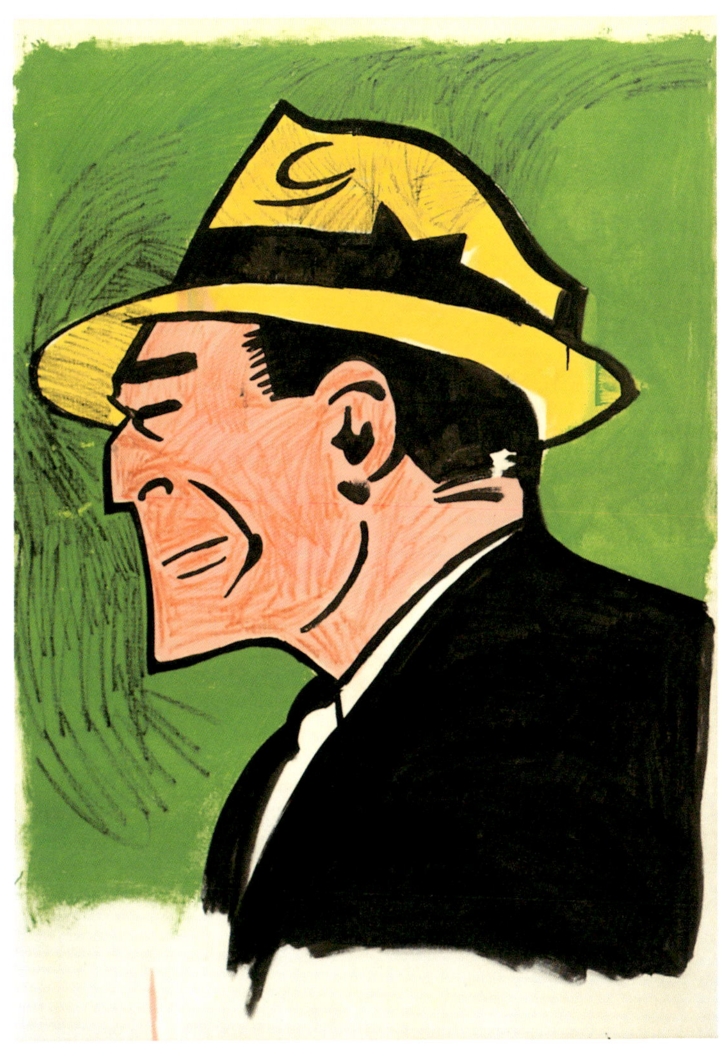

53 Dick Tracy 1961 Courtesy The Brant Foundation, Greenwich, CT

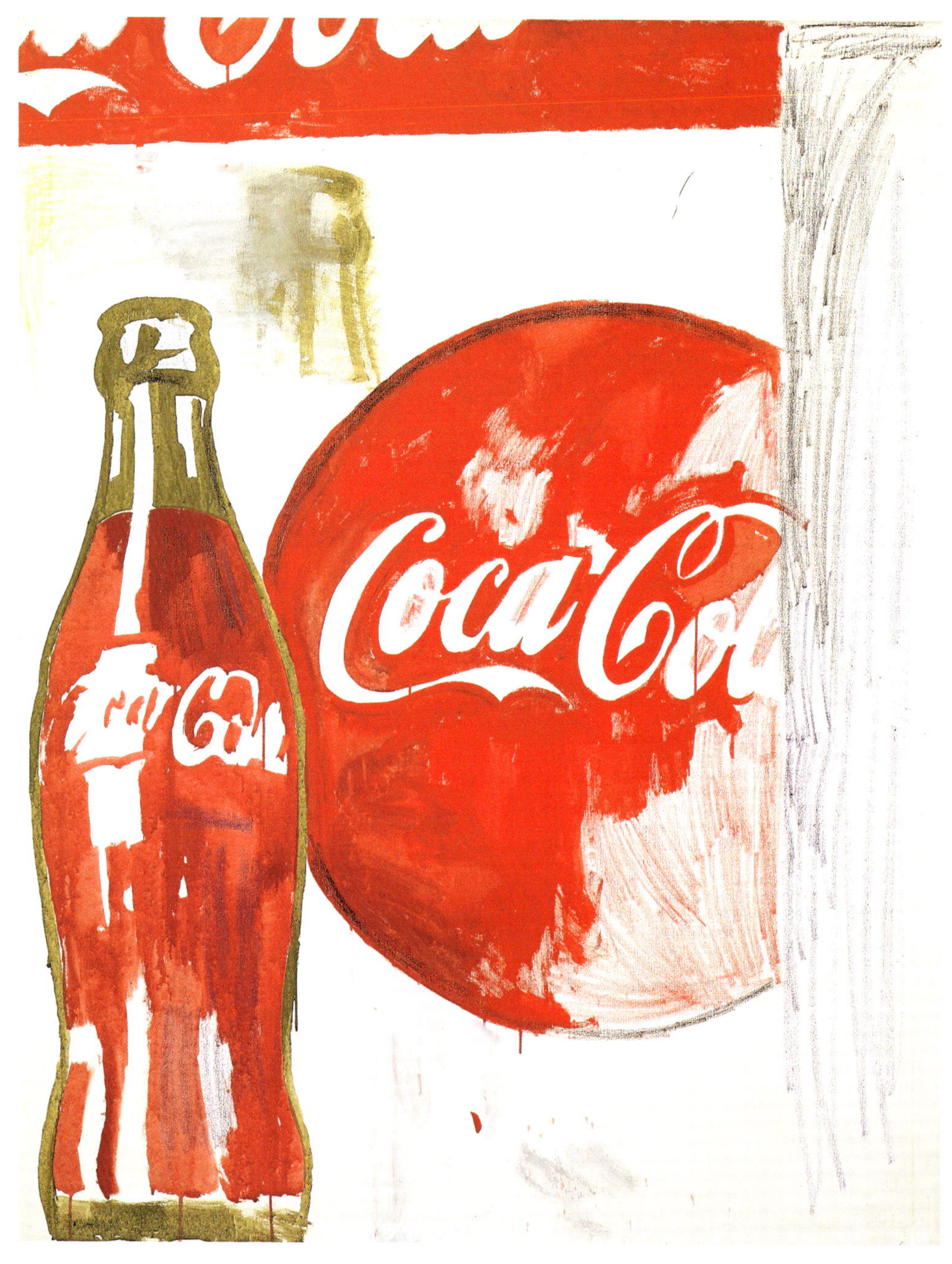

54 **Coca-Cola** **1960** Private collection

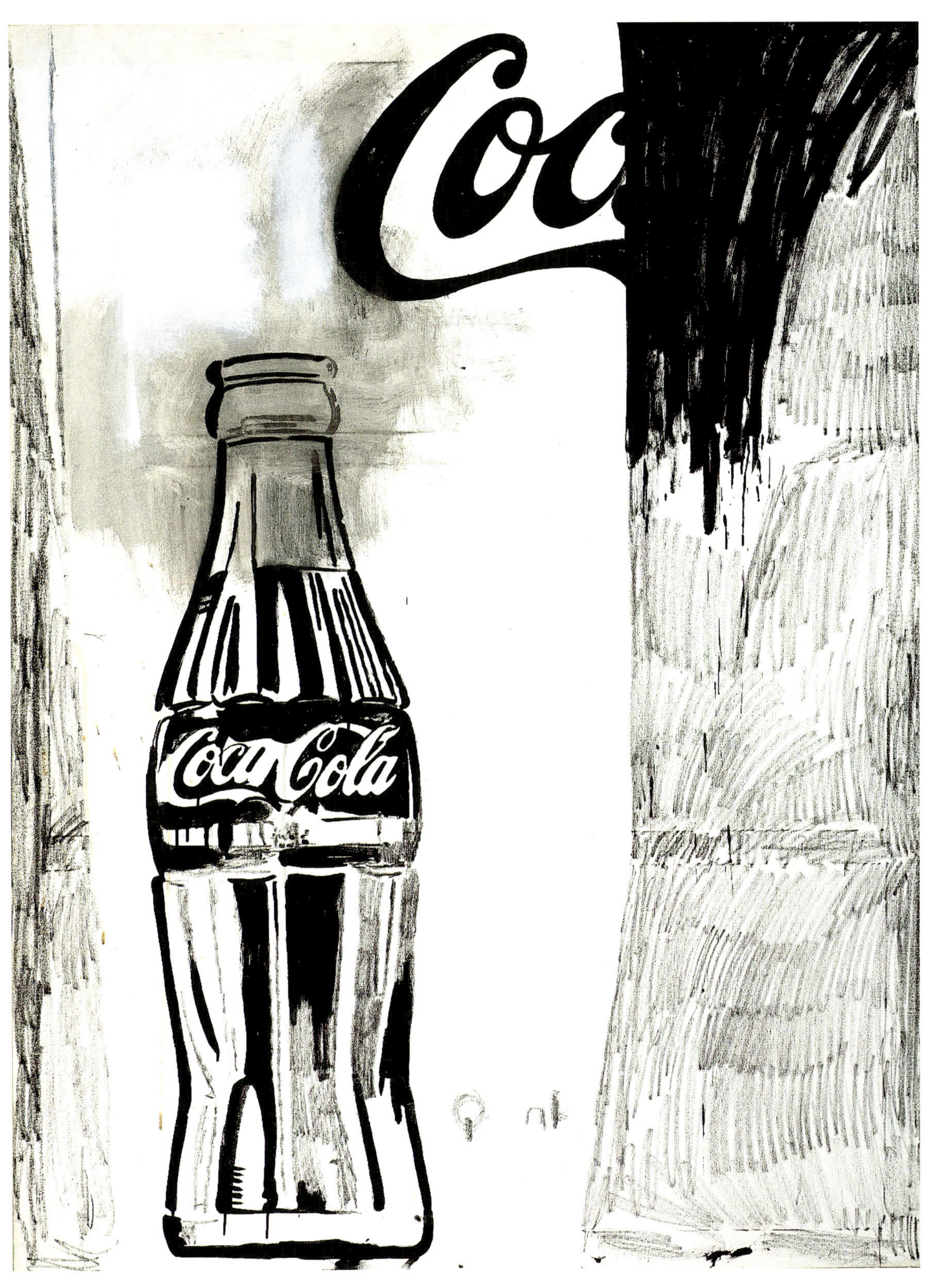

55 Coca-Cola 1960 The Andy Warhol Museum, Pittsburgh
Founding Collection, Contribution Dia Center for the Arts

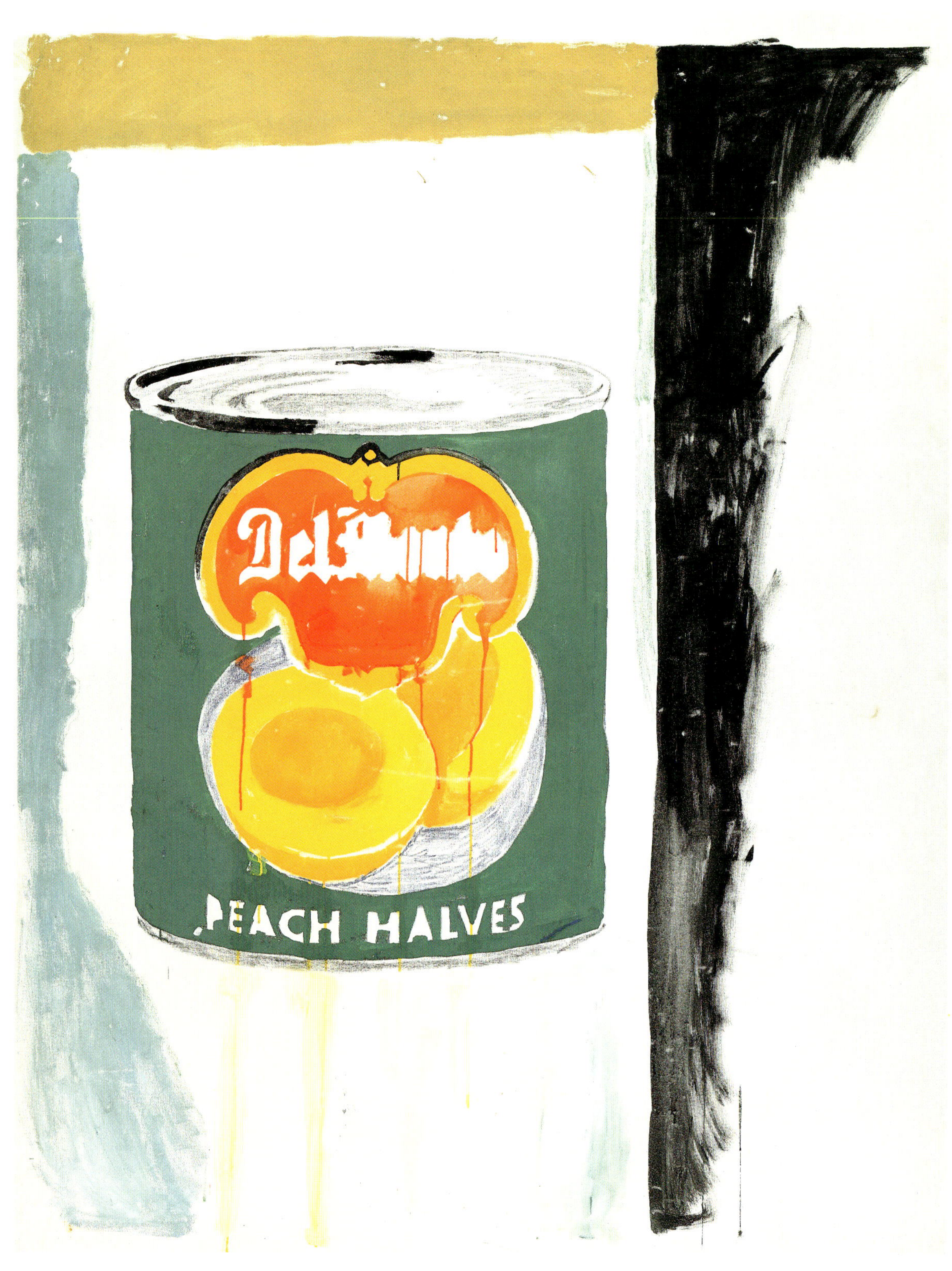

56 Peach Halves 1962 Staatsgalerie Stuttgart*

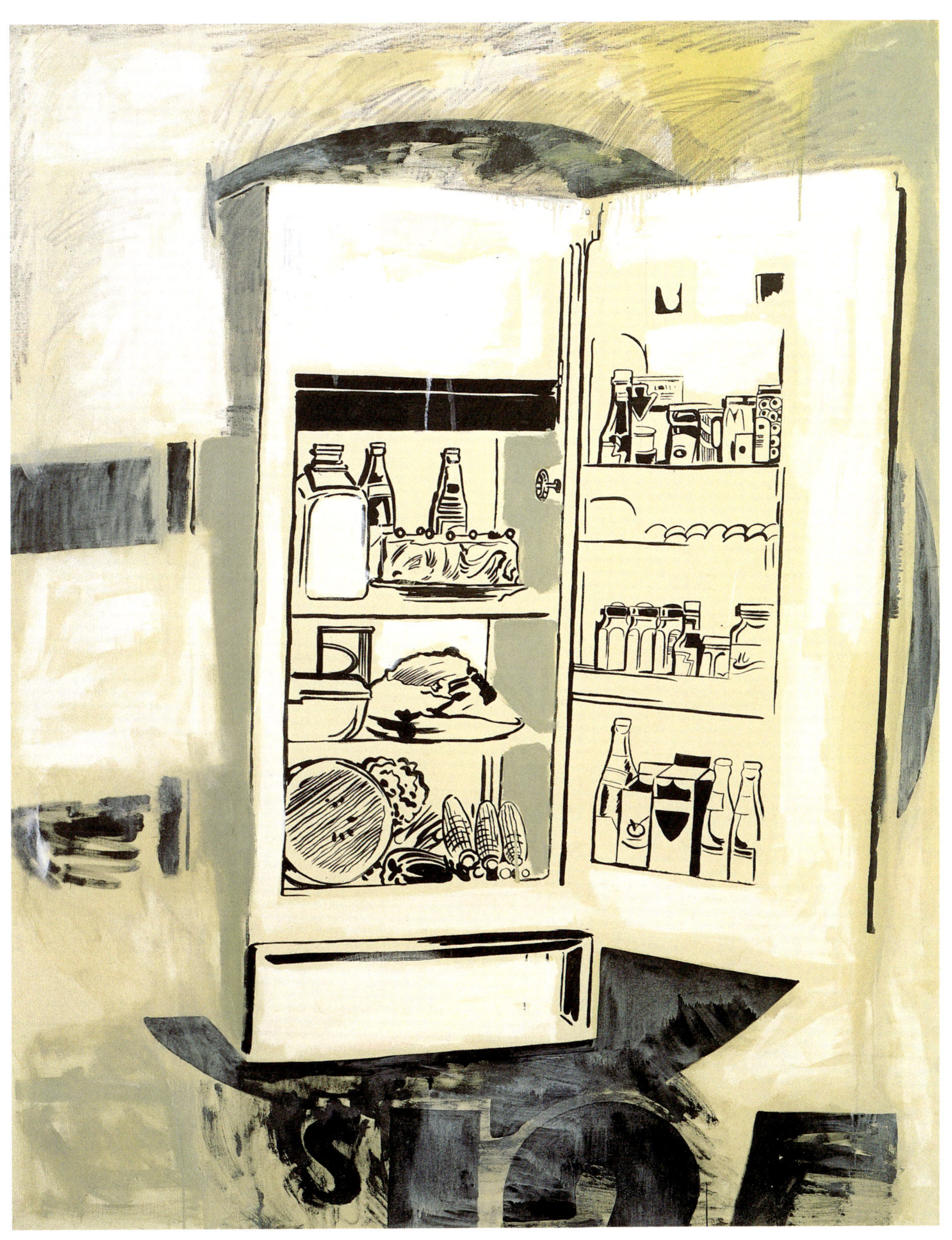

57 **Icebox 1960** The Menil Collection, Houston

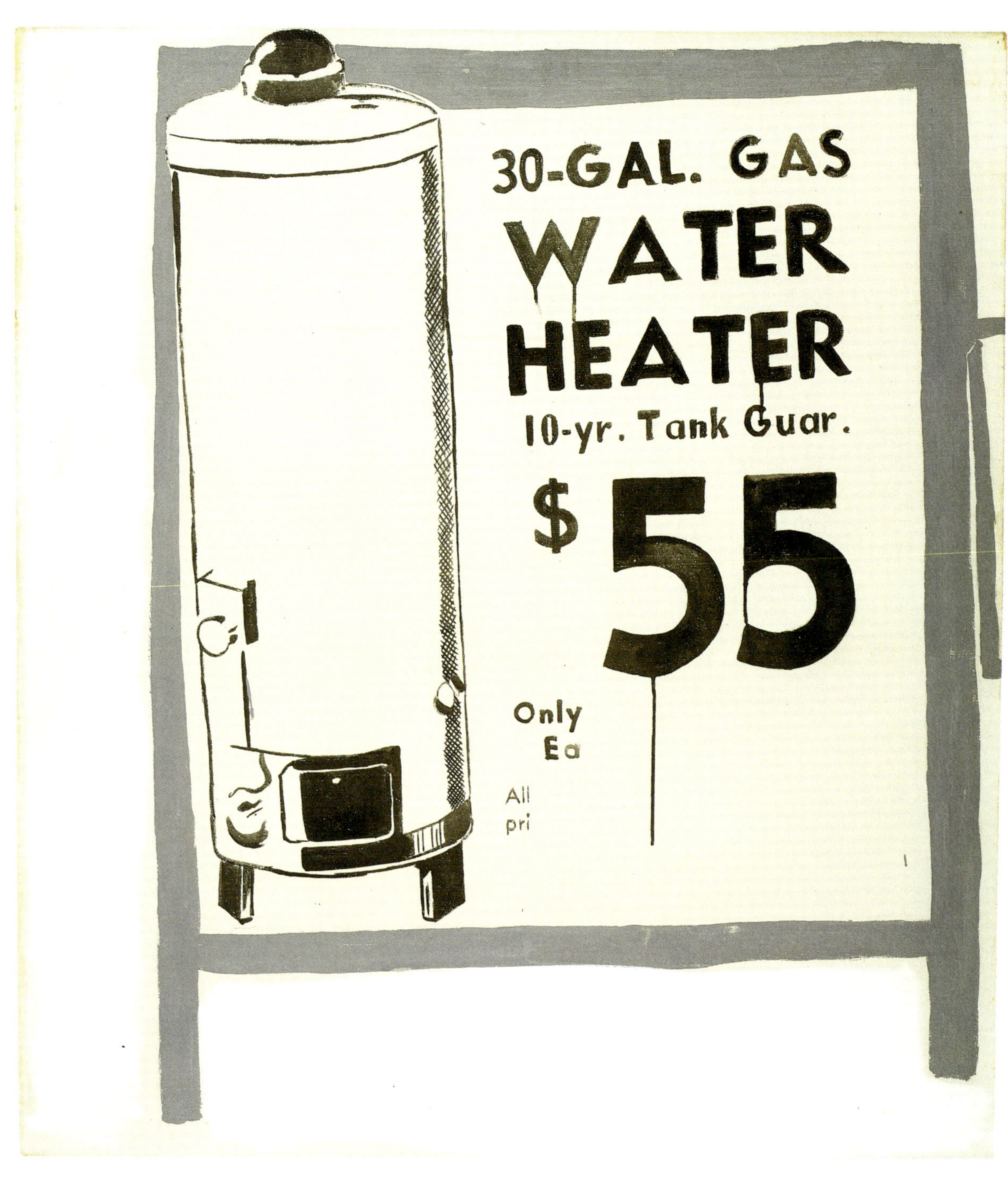

58 **Water Heater** **1960** The Museum of Modern Art, New York • Gift of Roy Lichtenstein

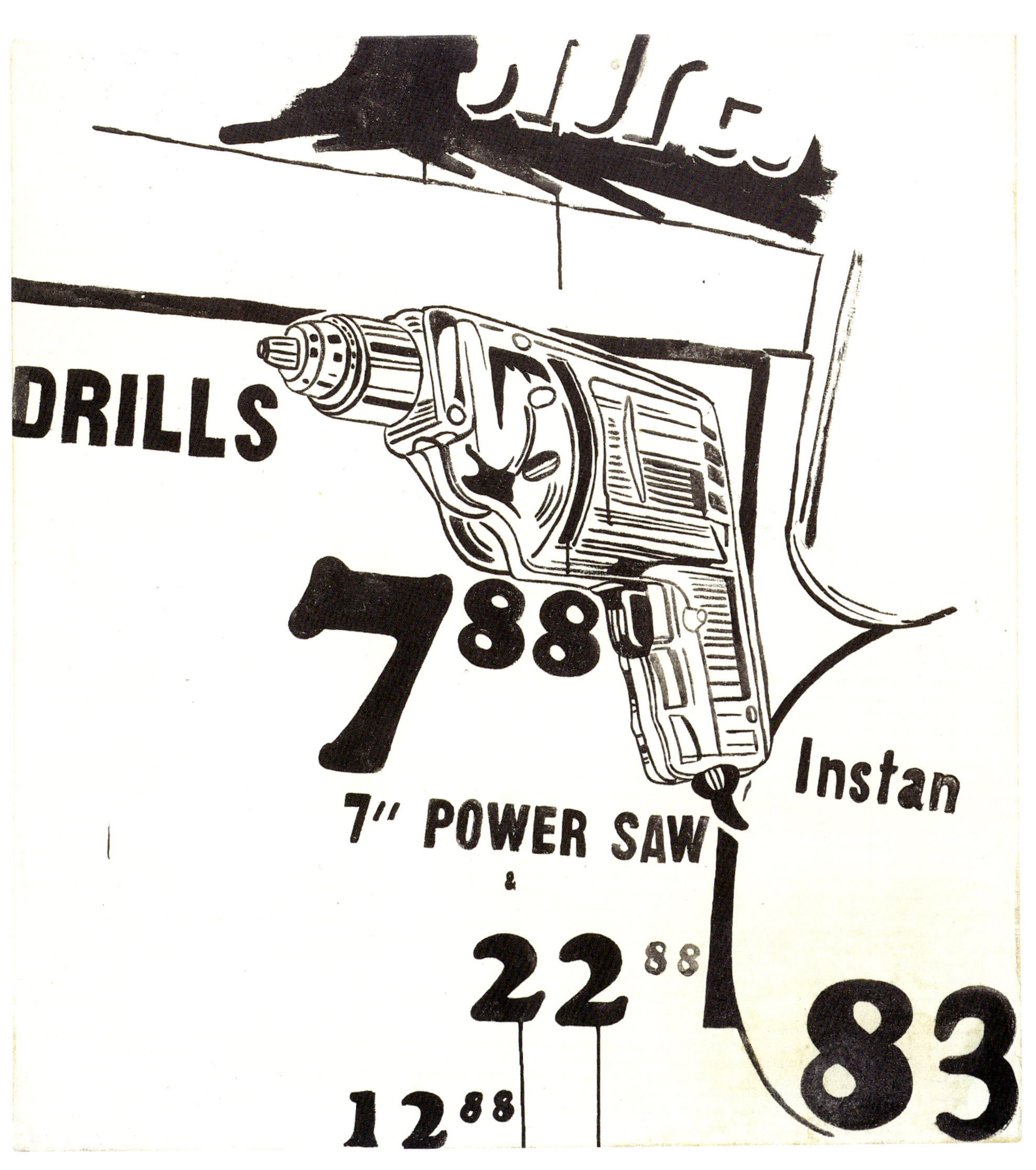

59 **Drills 7.88** **1960** Private collection

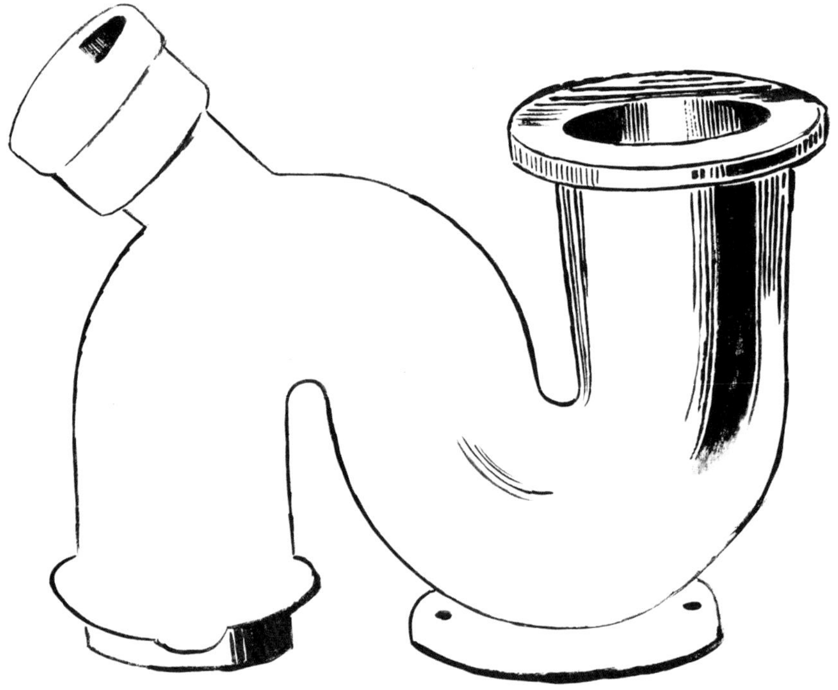

60 **Pipe** **1961** Private collection

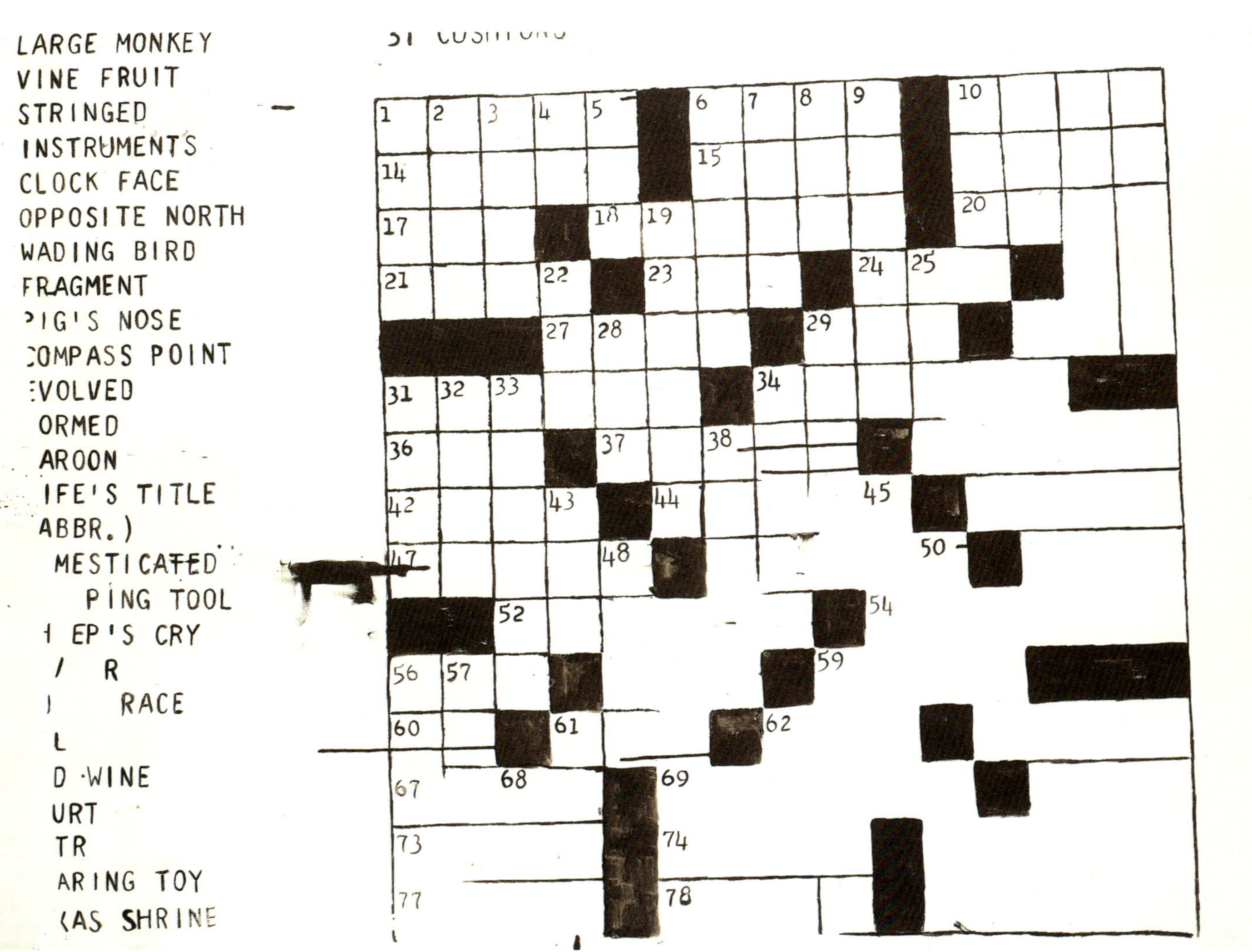

61 **Crossword** **1960** Private collection

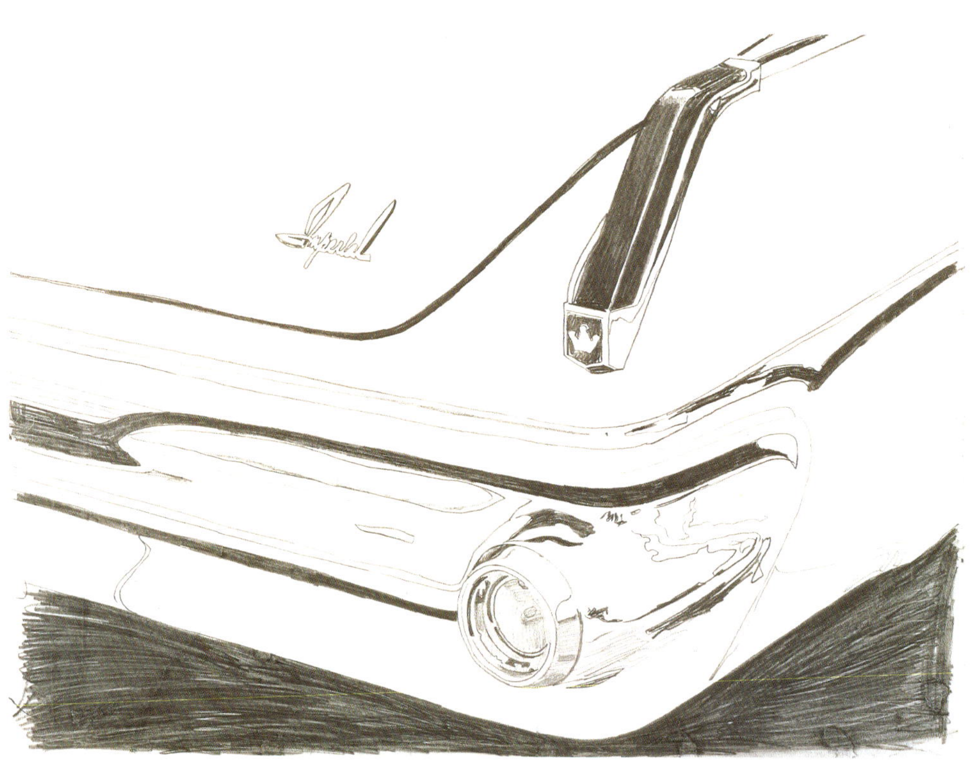

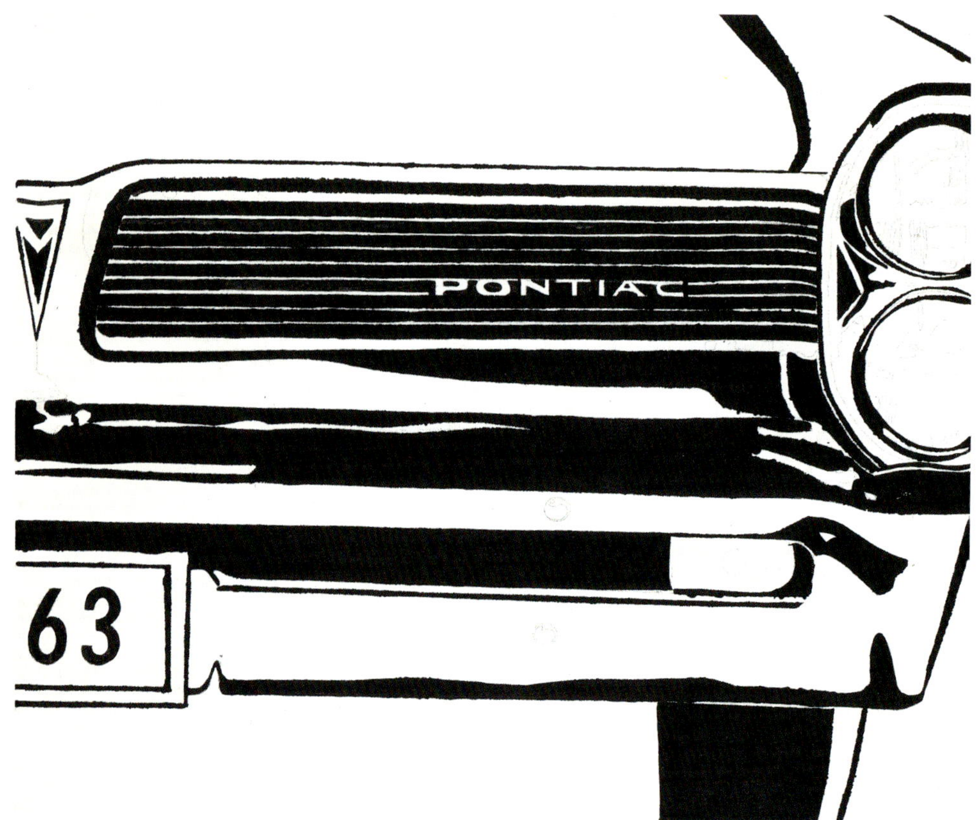

62 Imperial Car Detail 1962
Private collection

63 Pontiac c. 1961
Private collection

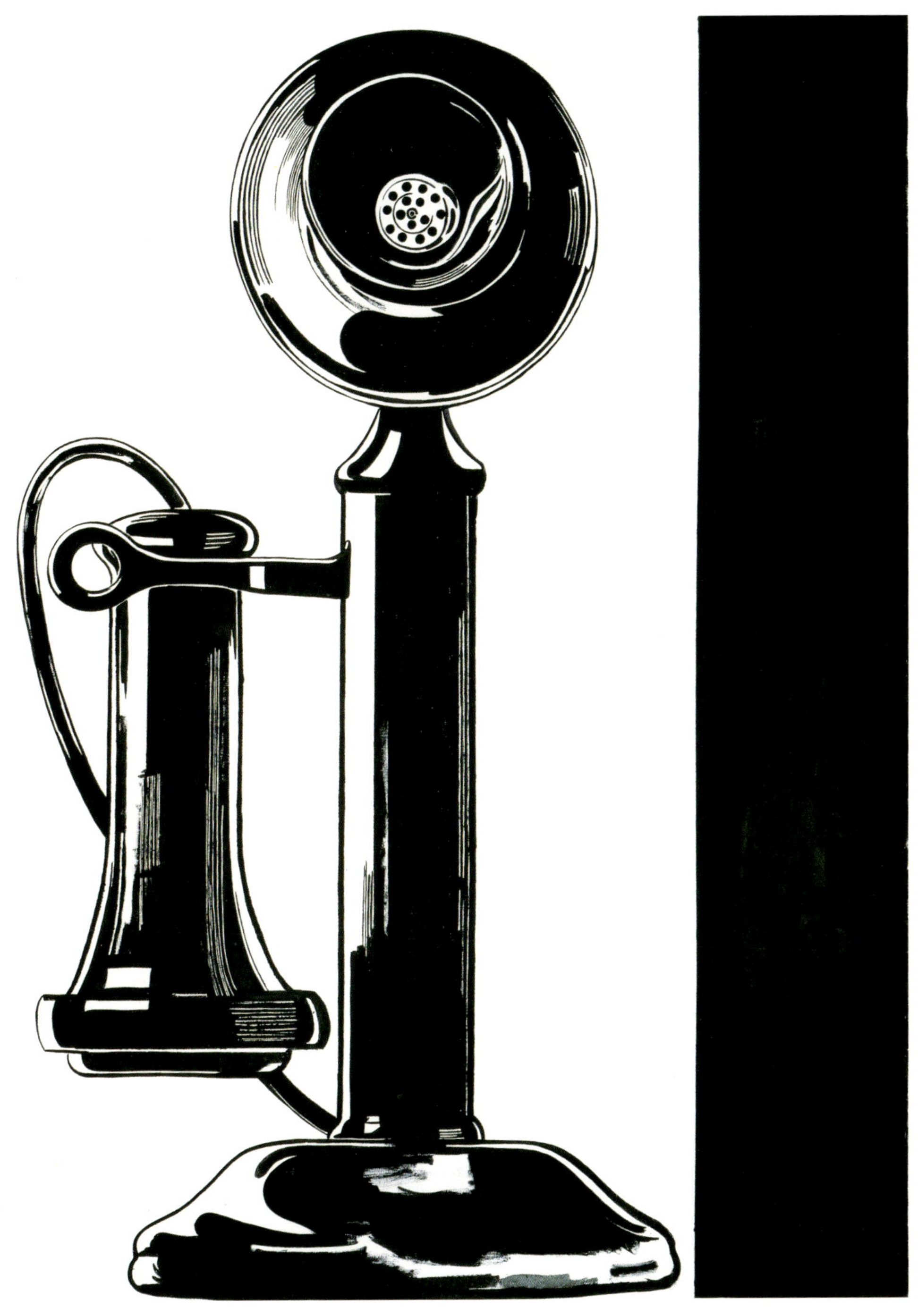

64 Telephone 1961 The Museum of Contemporary Art, Los Angeles
Purchased with funds provided by an Anonymous Donor

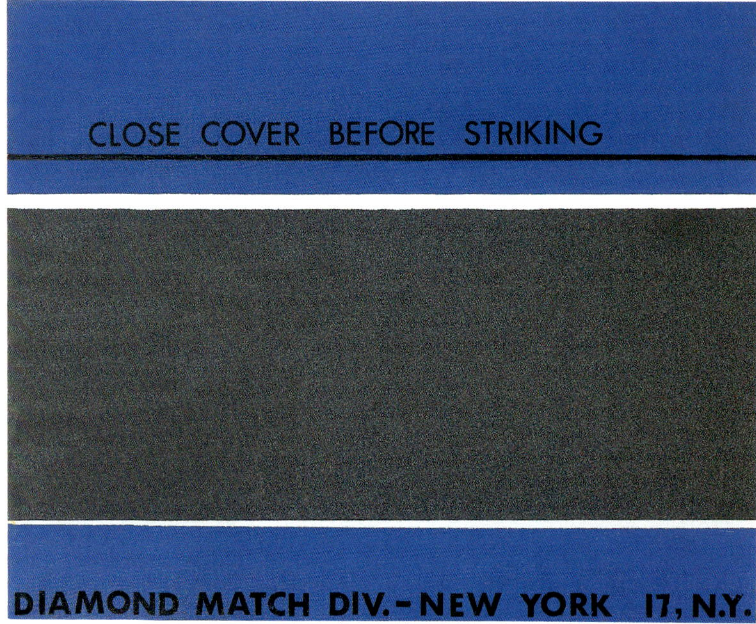

65 Close Cover Before Striking 1962
The Andy Warhol Museum, Pittsburgh
Founding Collection, Contribution
The Andy Warhol Foundation
for the Visual Arts, Inc.
Given in celebration of the first anniversary
of the directorship of Thomas Sokolowski

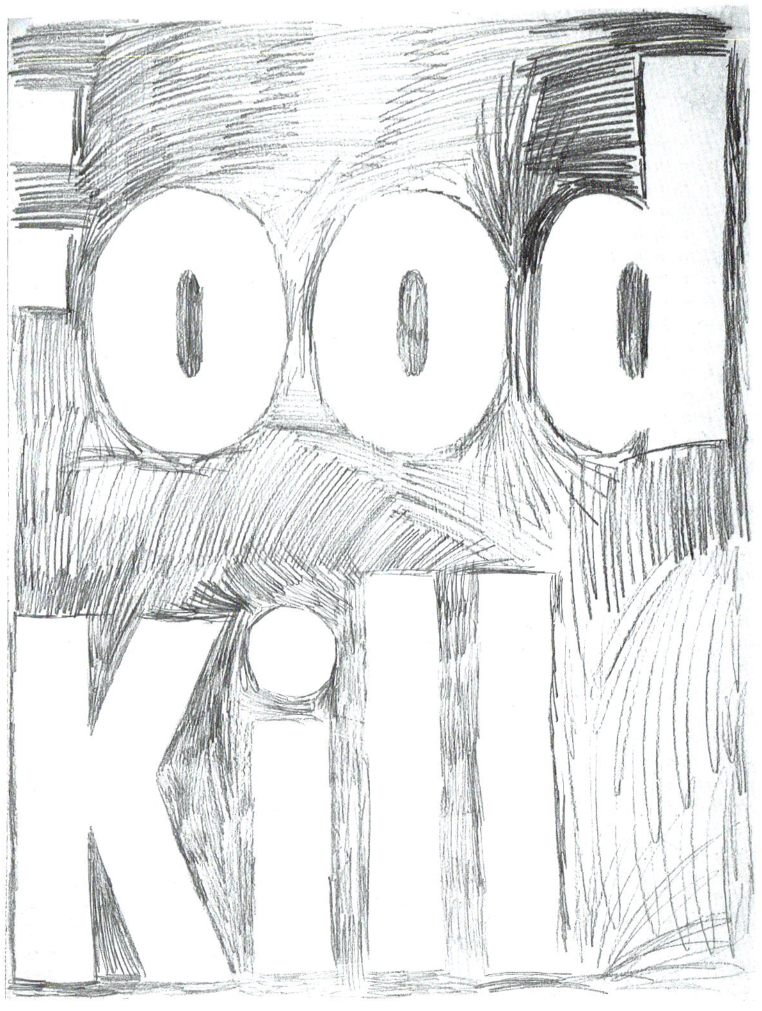

66 Food Kill 1962
Private collection

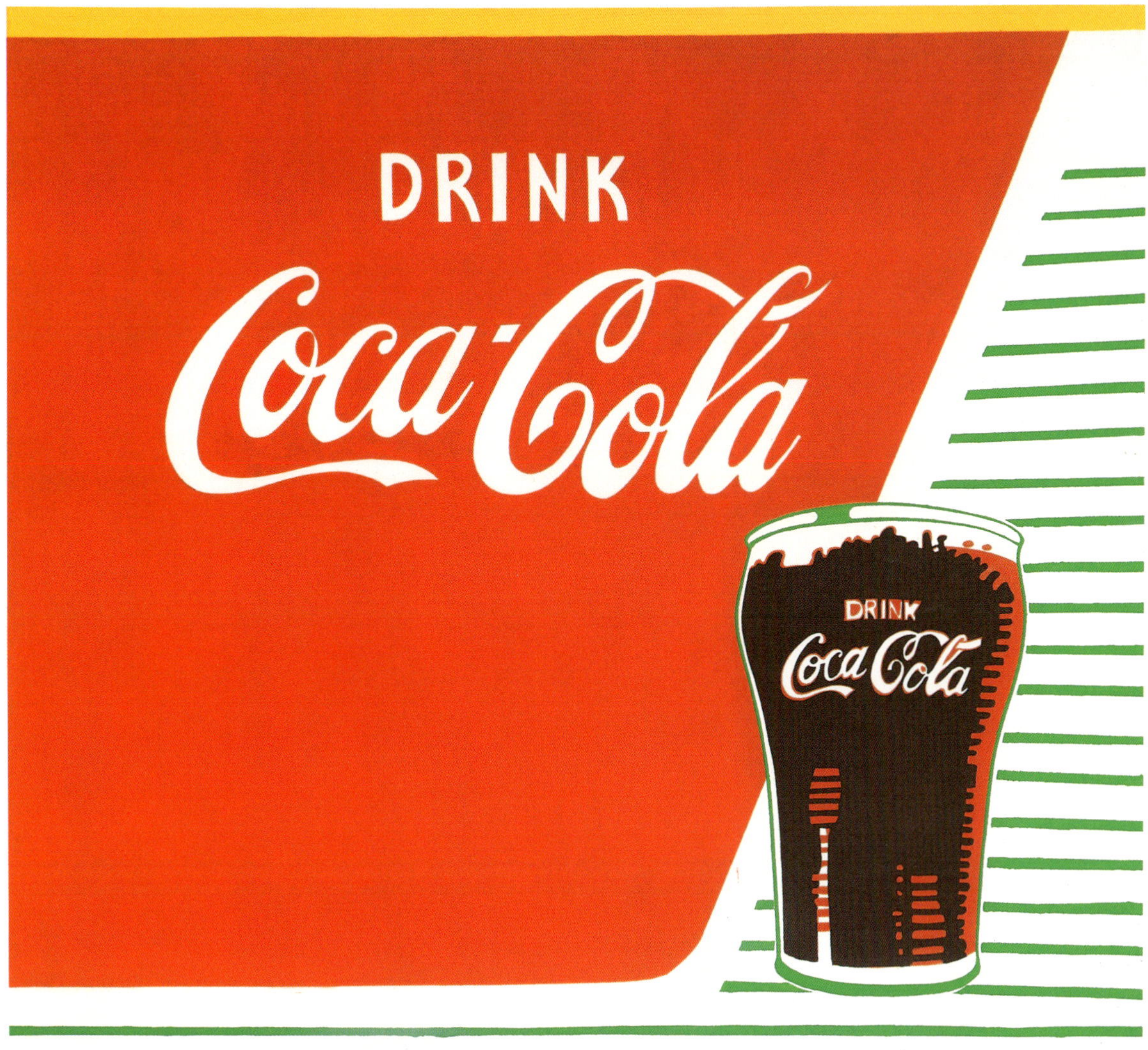

67 **Close Cover Before Striking 1962** Louisiana Museum of Modern Art, Humlebæk, Denmark

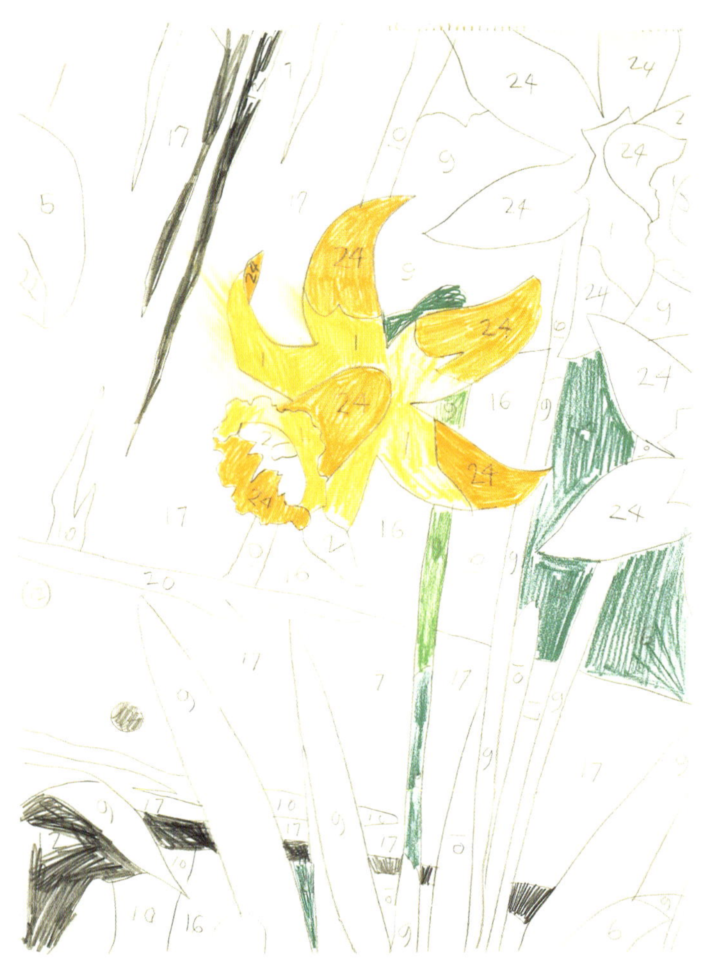

68 Do It Yourself (Narcissus) 1962
Öffentliche Kunstsammlung Basel,
Kupferstichkabinett
K. A. Burckhardt-Koechlin-Fonds

69 Do It Yourself (Landscape) 1962
Museum Ludwig, Köln

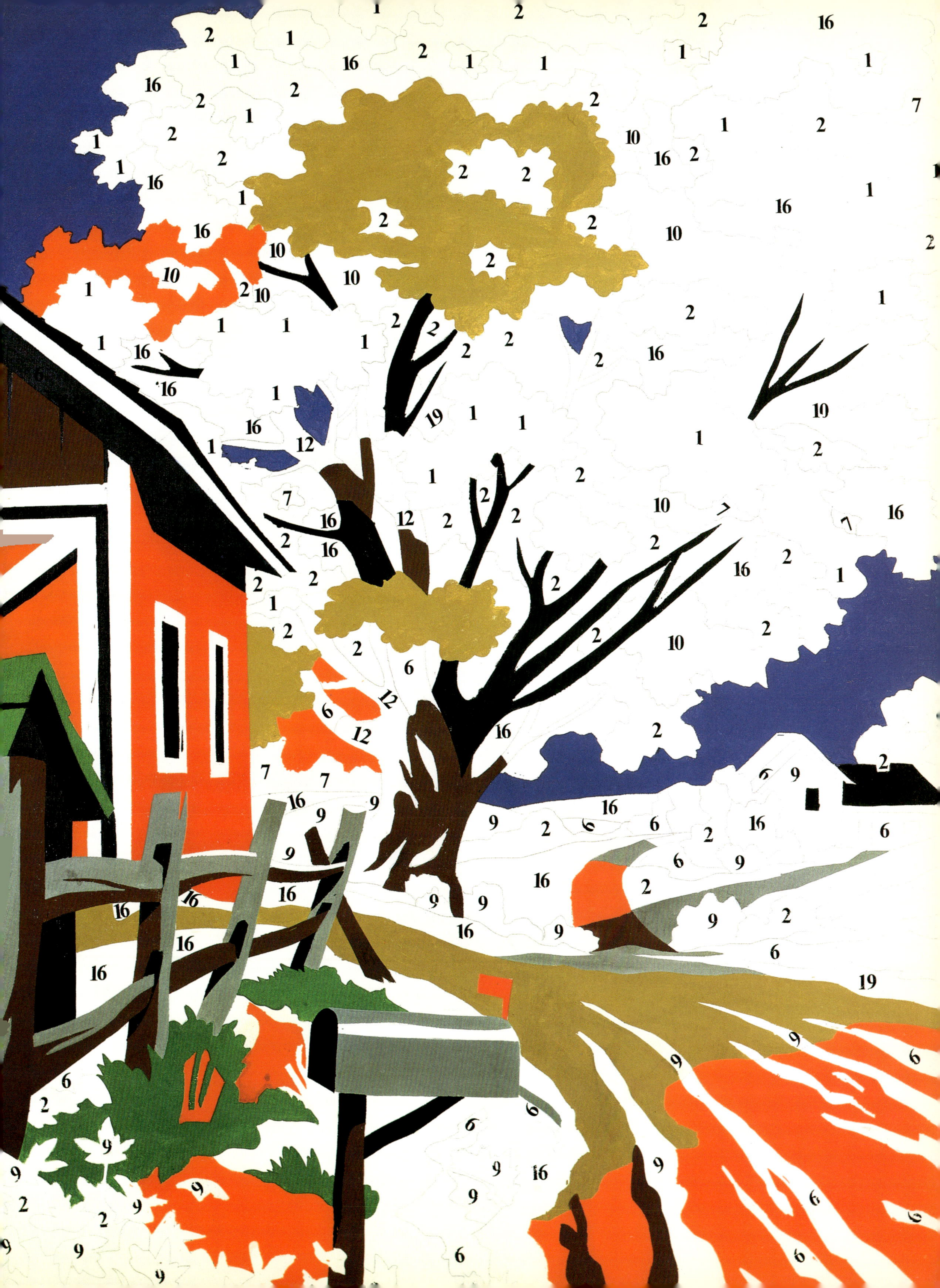

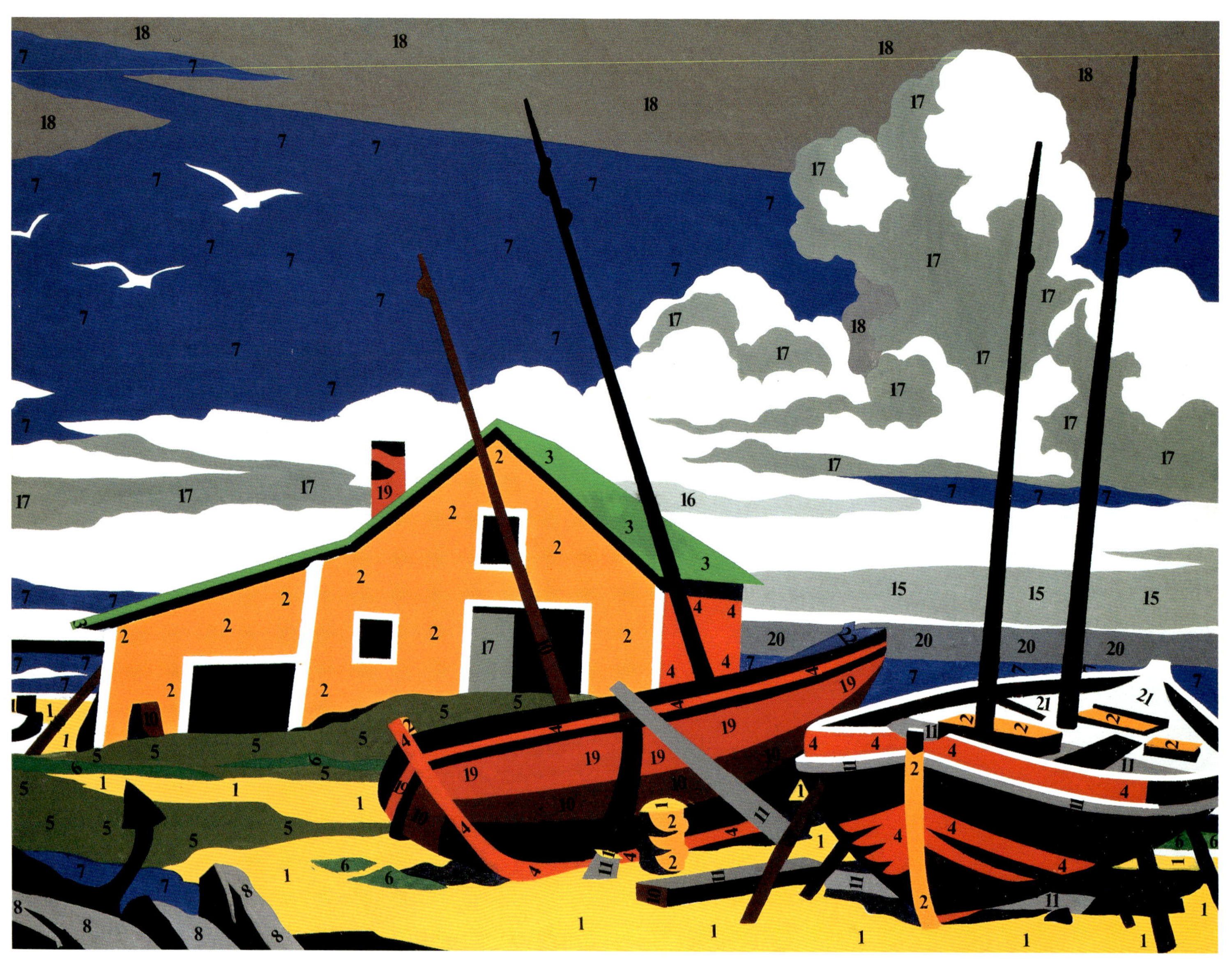

70 **Do It Yourself (Seascape)** **1962** Stiftung Sammlung Marx, Hamburger Bahnhof – Museum für Gegenwart, Berlin

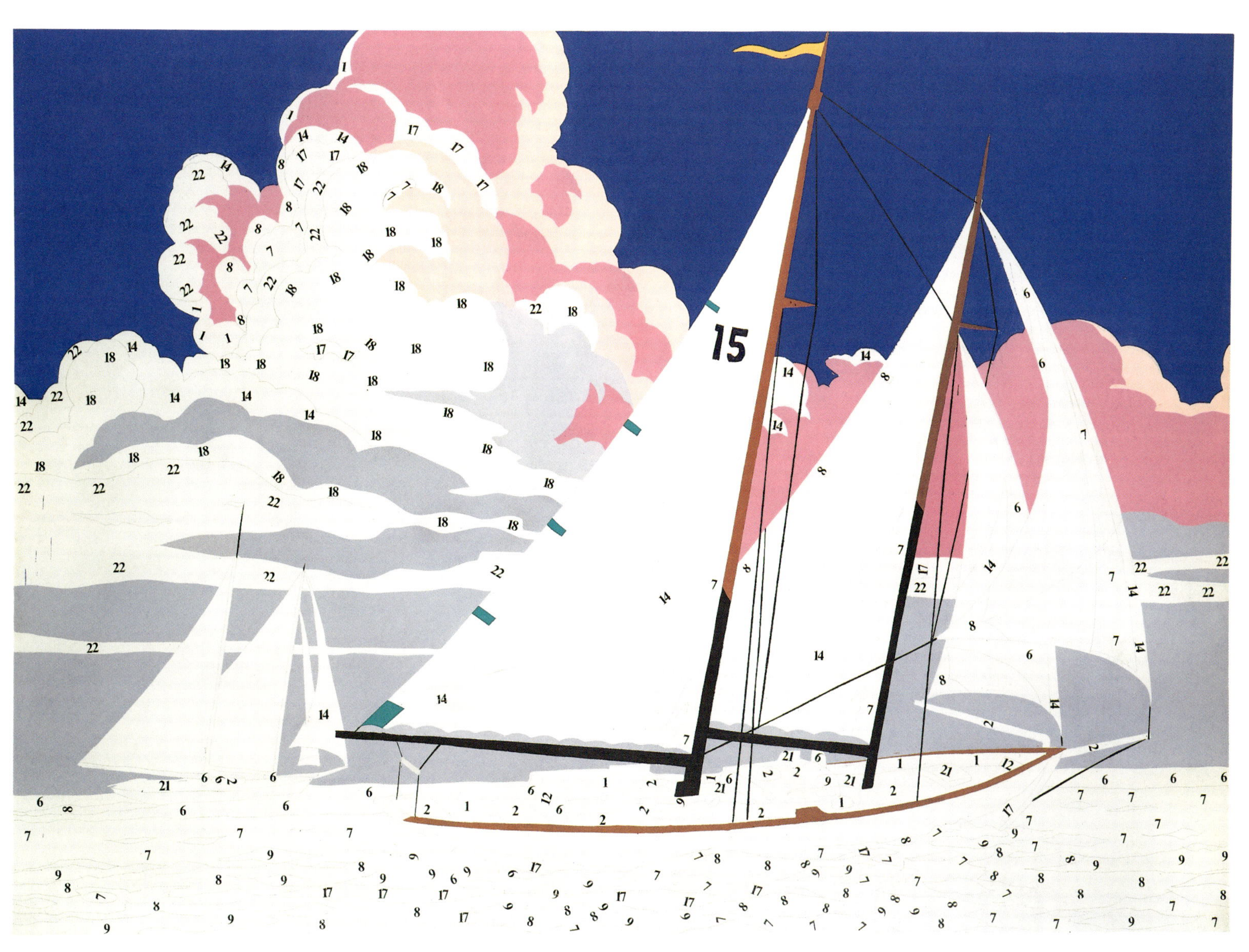

71 **Do It Yourself (Sailboats) 1962** Daros Collection, Switzerland

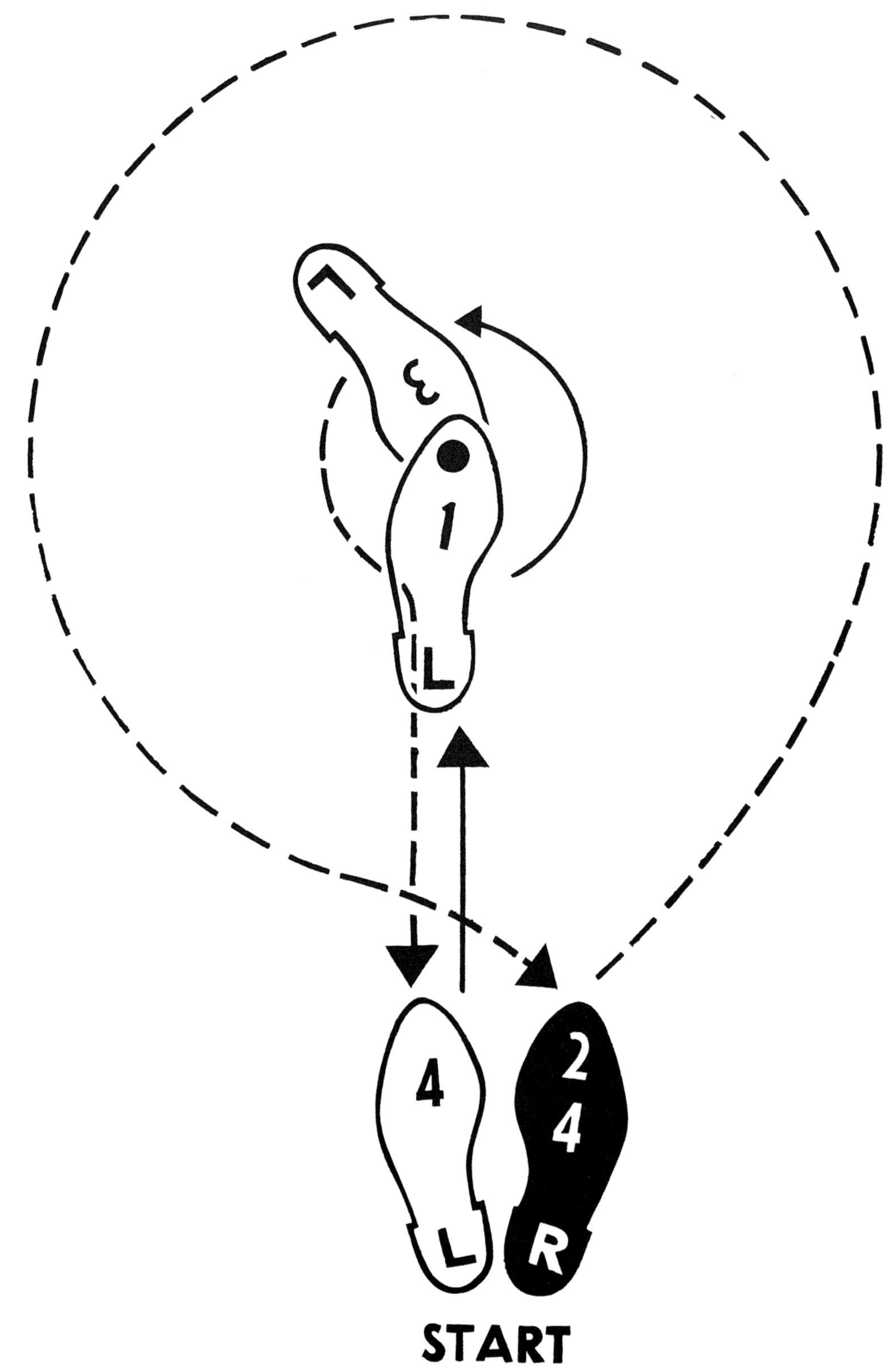

72 **Dance Diagram (Fox Trot) 1962** Collection Onnasch

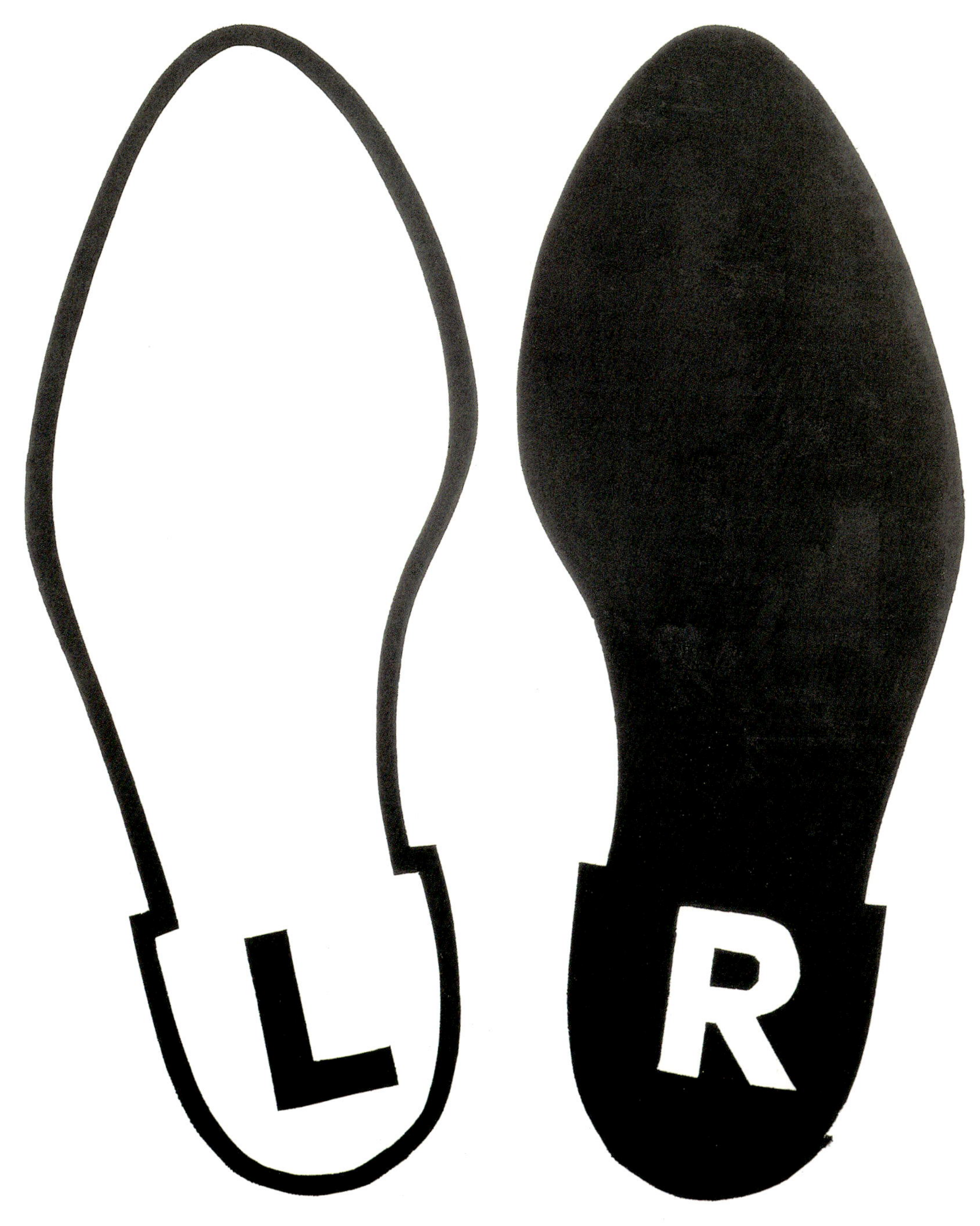

73 **Dancestep (Two Feet) 1962** Courtesy The Brant Foundation, Greenwich, CT

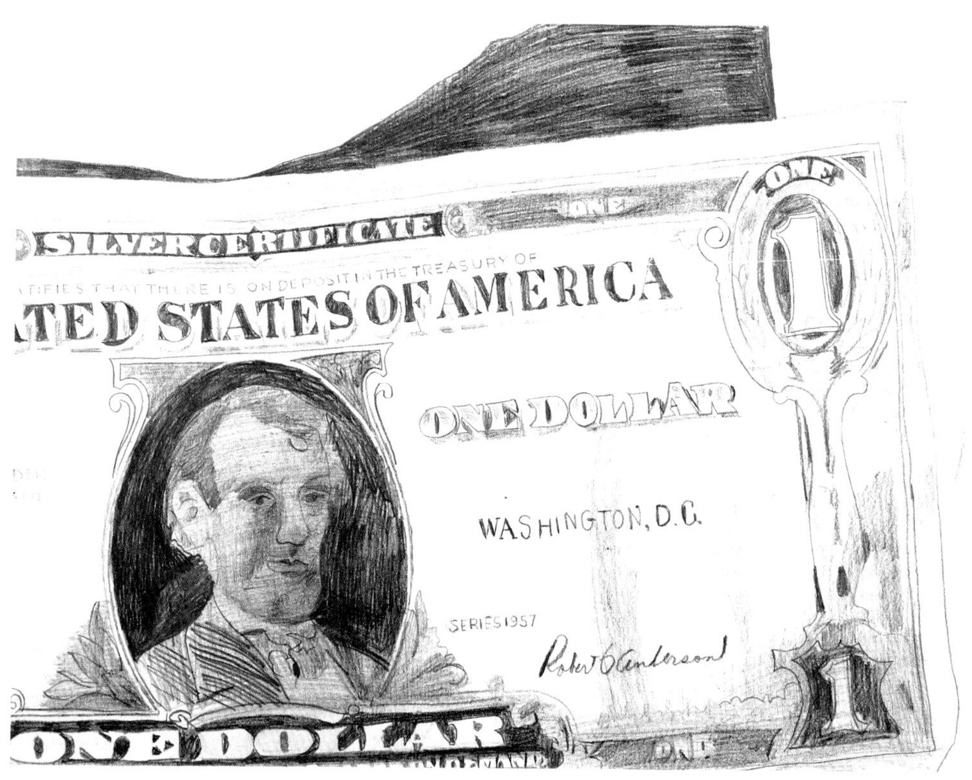

74 **One Dollar Bill with Lincoln's Portrait 1962** Private collection

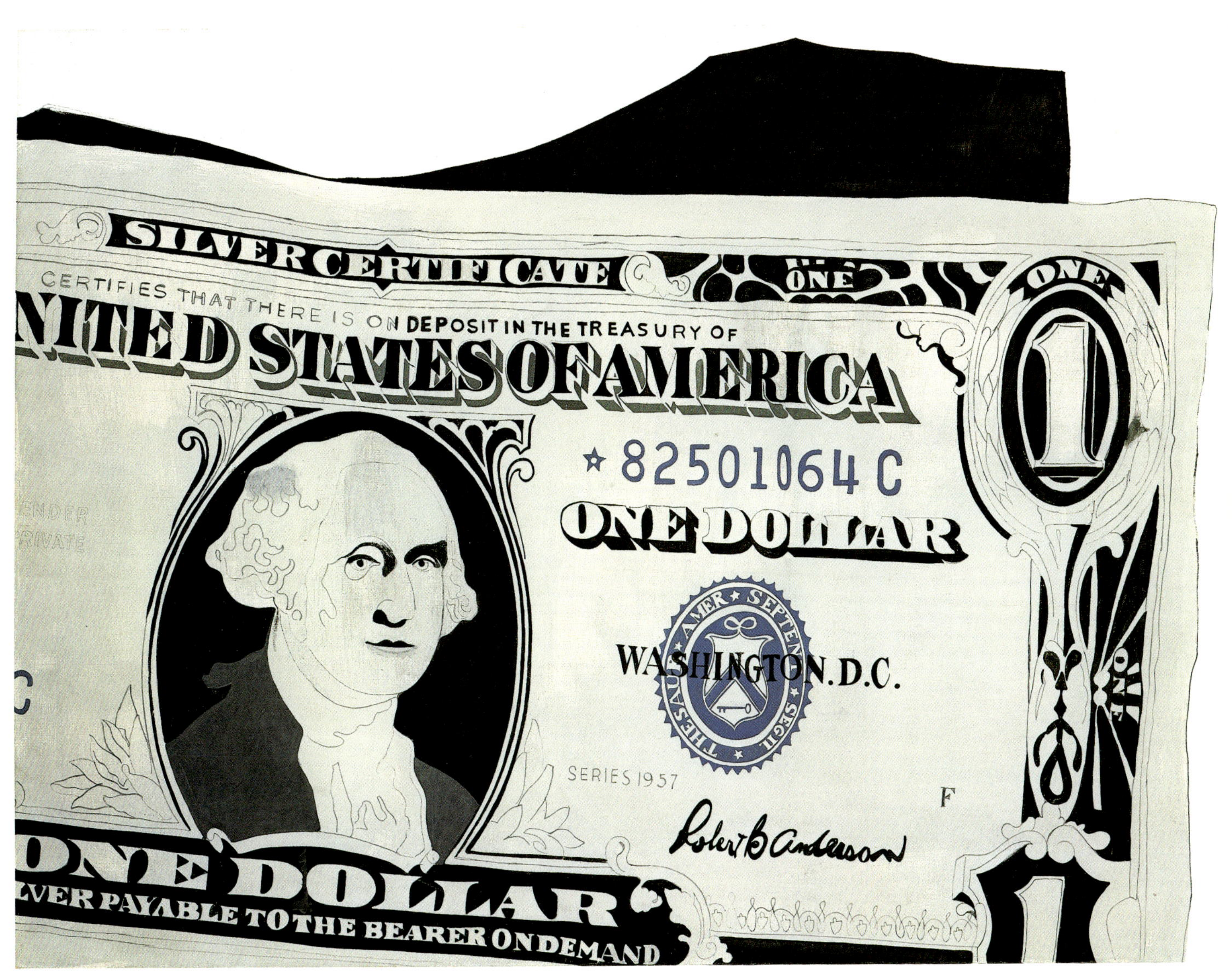

75 **Silver Certificate 1962** Private collection, Switzerland

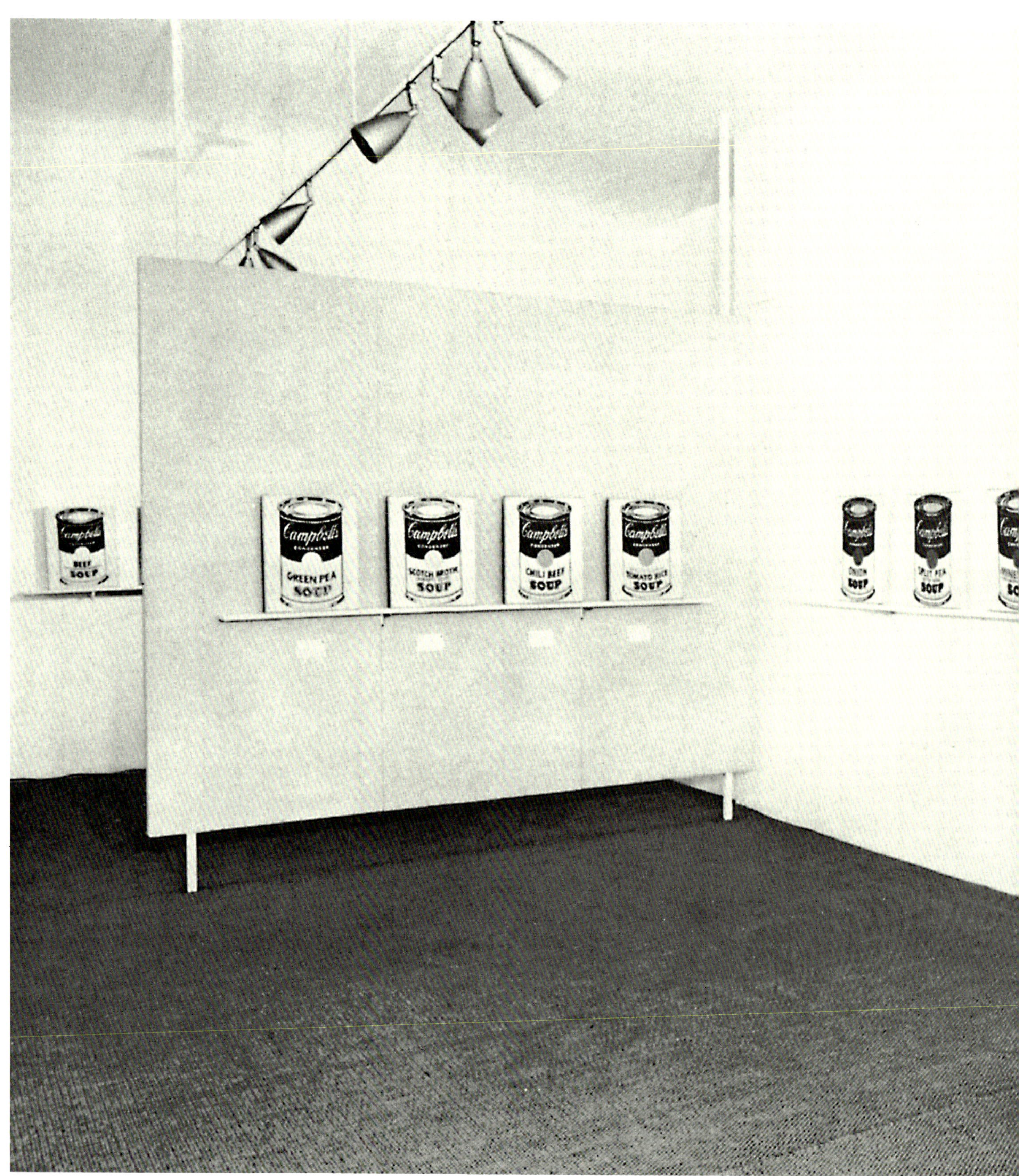
Campbell's
BEEF
SOUP
Campbell's
GREEN PEA
SOUP
Campbell's
SCOTCH BROTH
SOUP
Campbell's
CHILI BEEF
SOUP
Campbell's
TOMATO RICE
SOUP

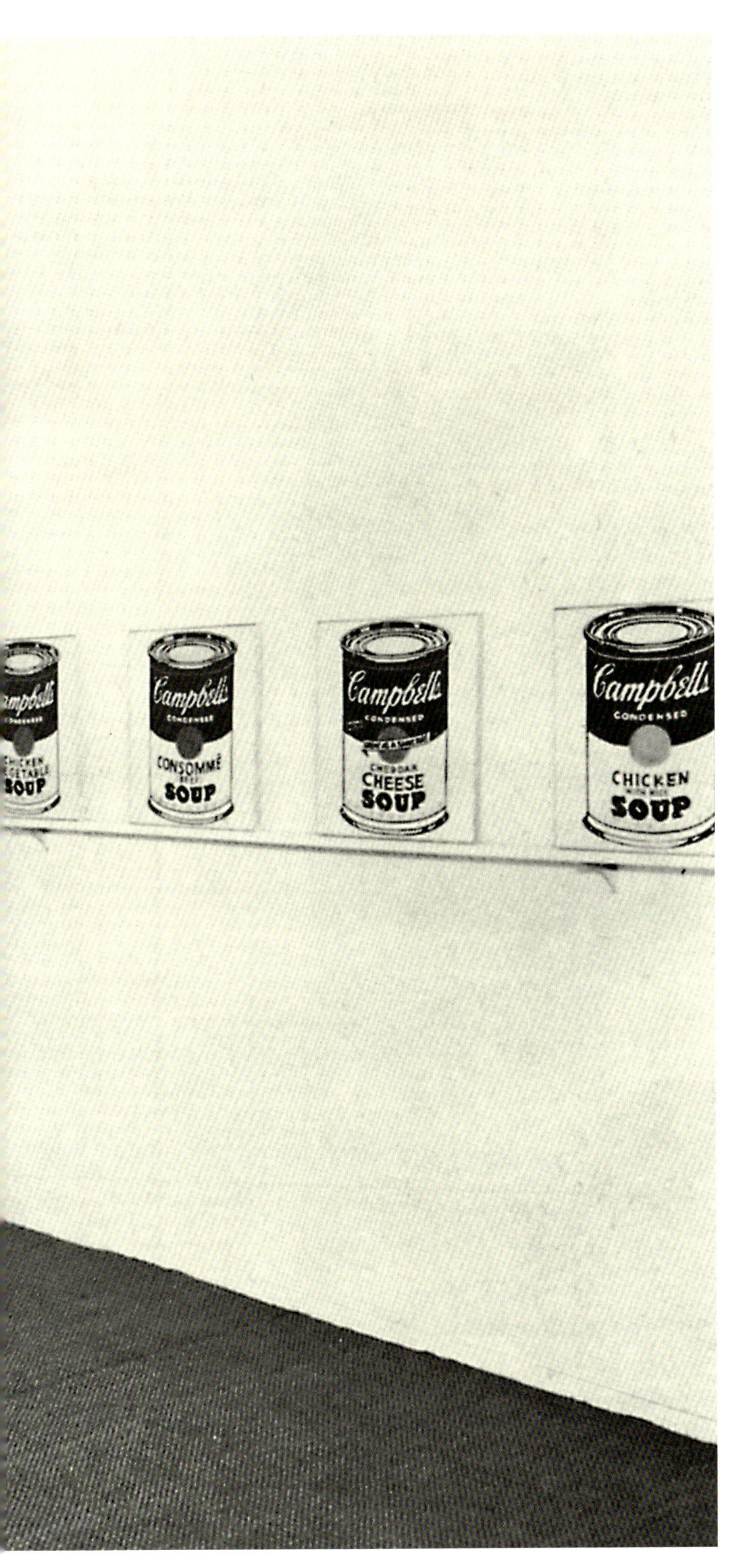

First exhibition of *Campbell's Soup Cans*,
Ferus Gallery, Los Angeles, July 1962

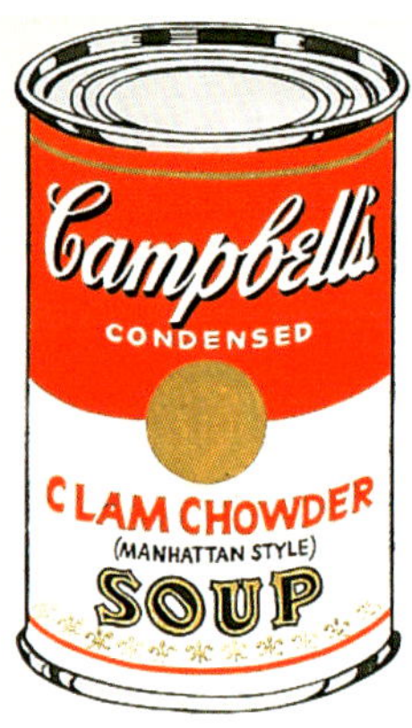
Campbell's
CONDENSED
CLAM CHOWDER
(MANHATTAN STYLE)
SOUP
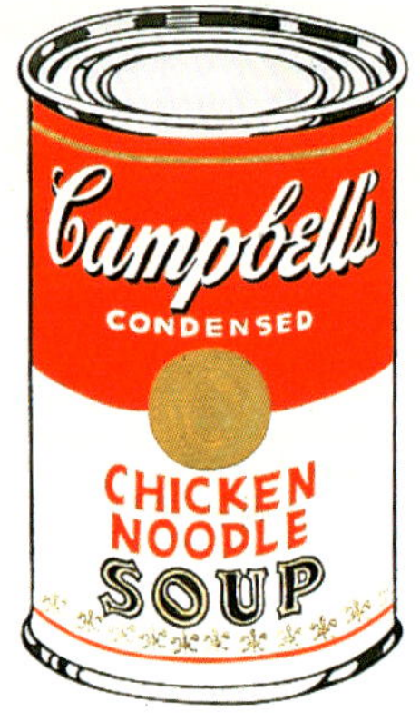
Campbell's
CONDENSED
CHICKEN NOODLE
SOUP
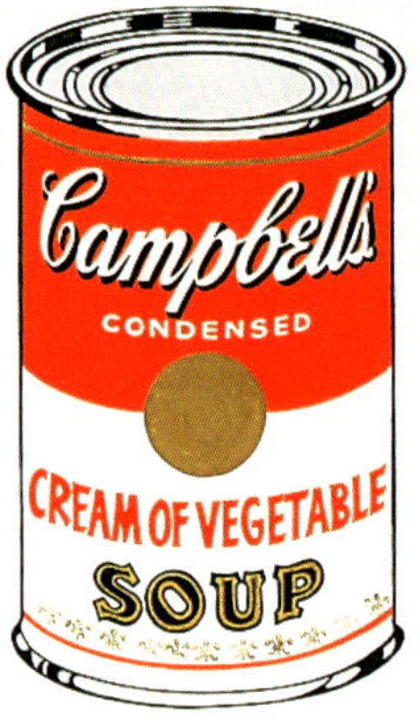
Campbell's
CONDENSED
CREAM OF VEGETABLE
SOUP
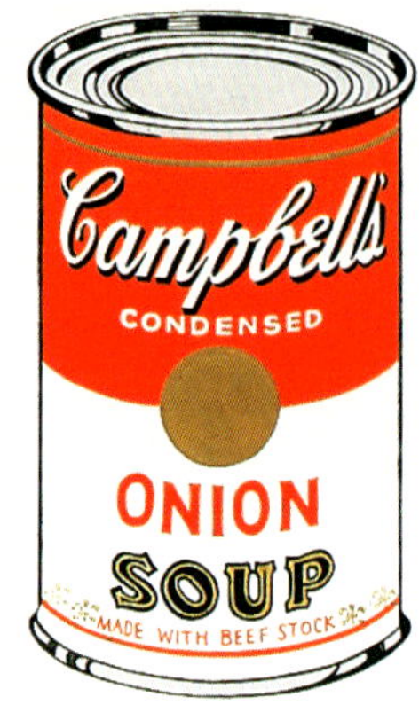
Campbell's
CONDENSED
ONION
SOUP
MADE WITH BEEF STOCK
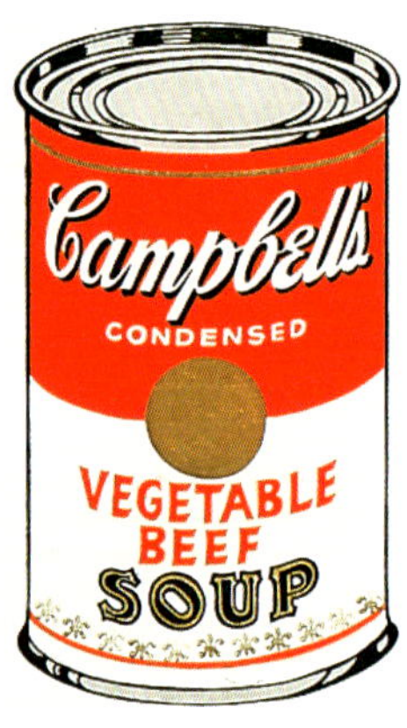
Campbell's
CONDENSED
VEGETABLE BEEF
SOUP
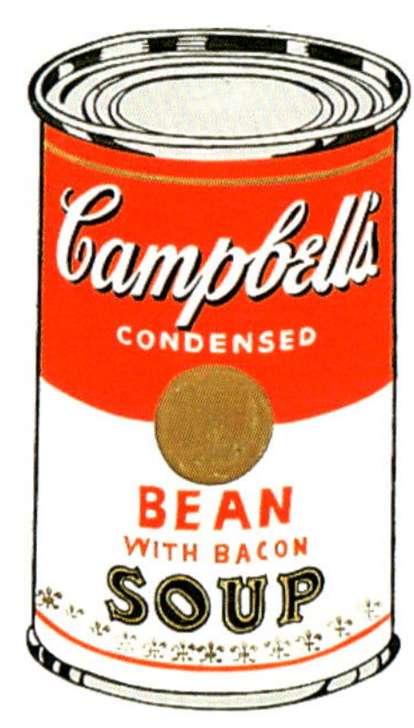
Campbell's
CONDENSED
BEAN
WITH BACON
SOUP
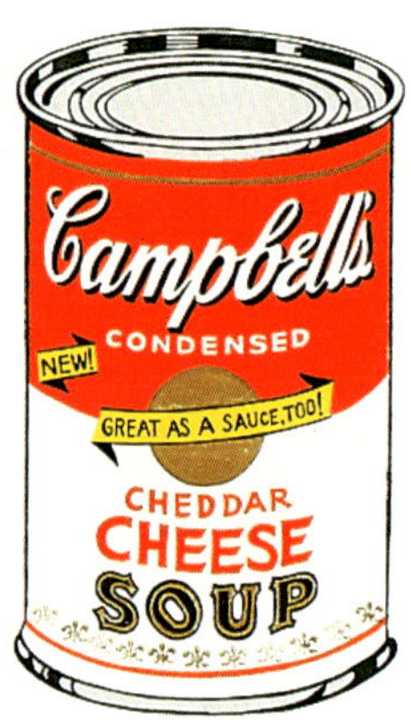
Campbell's
NEW!
CONDENSED
GREAT AS A SAUCE, TOO!
CHEDDAR CHEESE
SOUP
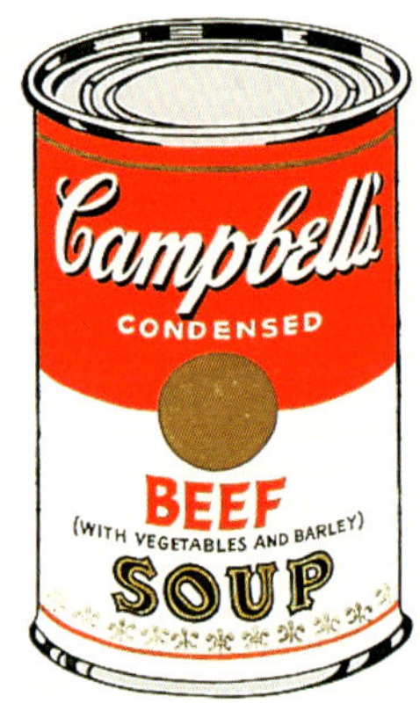
Campbell's
CONDENSED
BEEF
(WITH VEGETABLES AND BARLEY)
SOUP
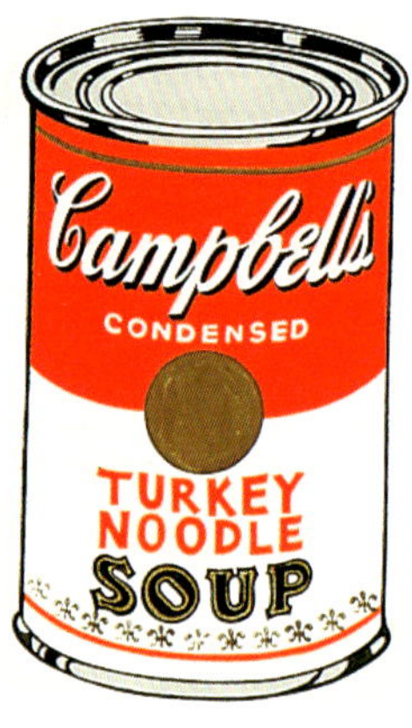
Campbell's
CONDENSED
TURKEY NOODLE
SOUP
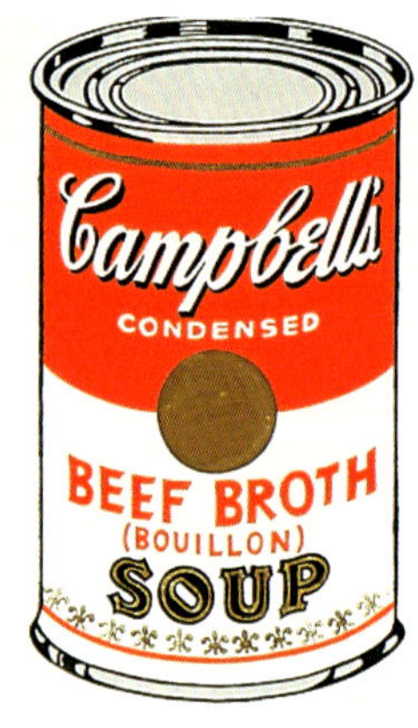
Campbell's
CONDENSED
BEEF BROTH
(BOUILLON)
SOUP
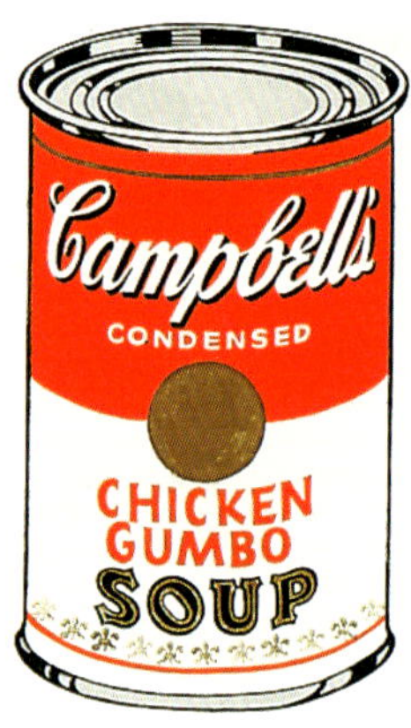
Campbell's
CONDENSED
CHICKEN GUMBO
SOUP
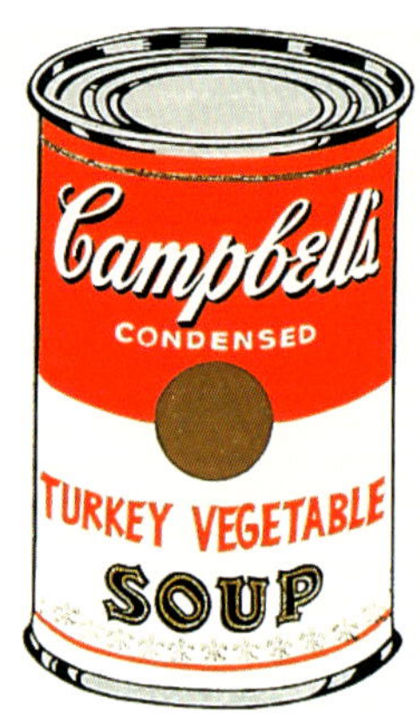
Campbell's
CONDENSED
TURKEY VEGETABLE
SOUP
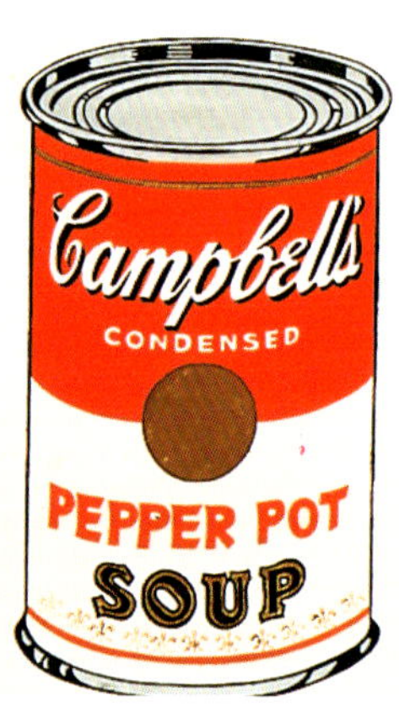
Campbell's
CONDENSED
PEPPER POT
SOUP
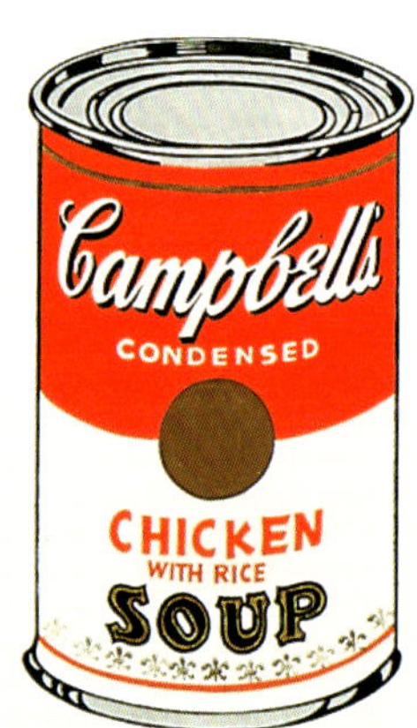
Campbell's
CONDENSED
CHICKEN
WITH RICE
SOUP
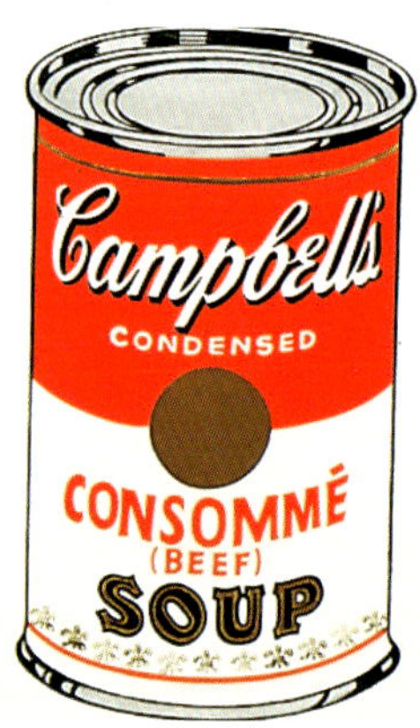
Campbell's
CONDENSED
CONSOMMÉ
(BEEF)
SOUP
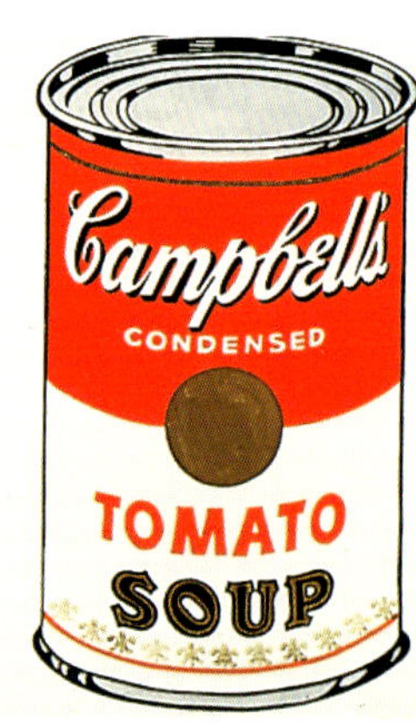
Campbell's
CONDENSED
TOMATO
SOUP

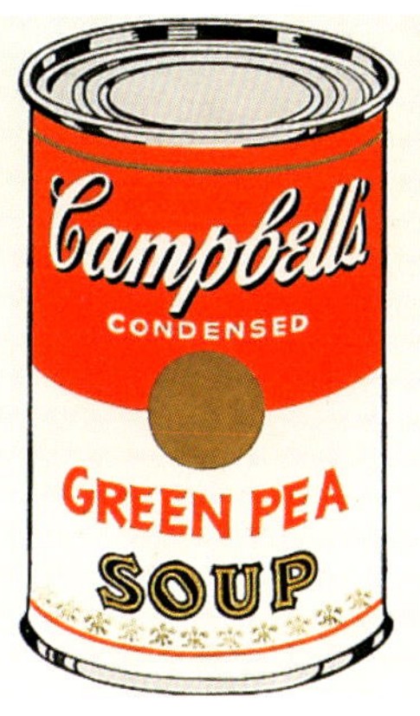

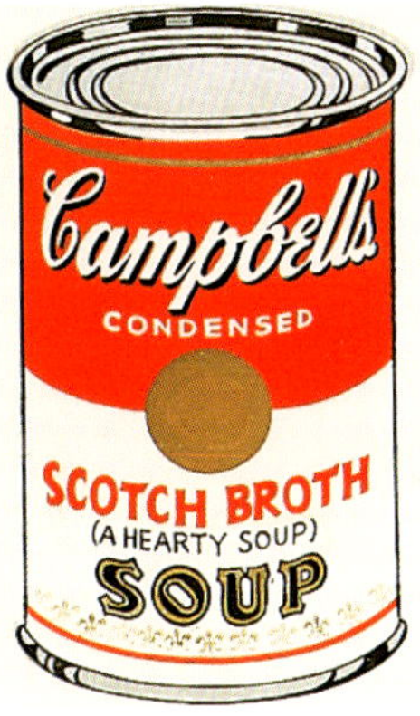

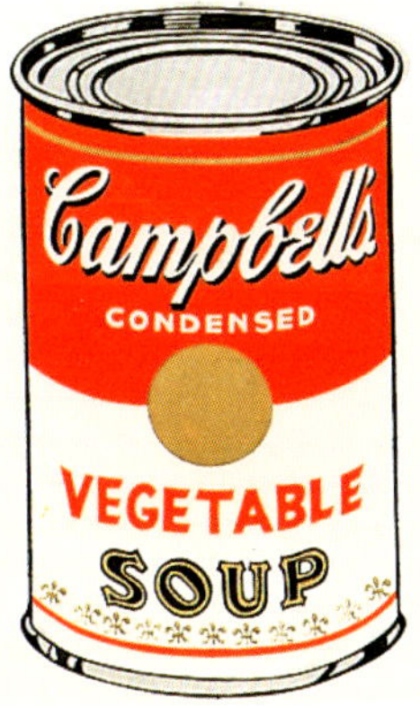

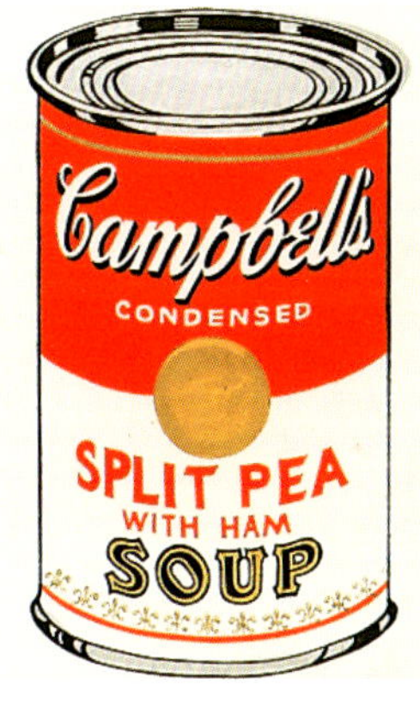

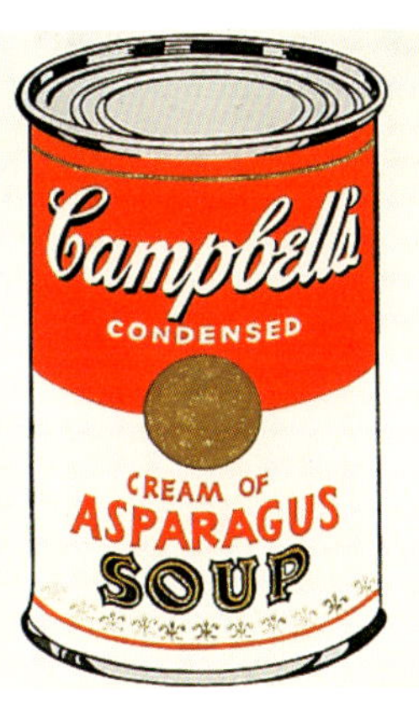

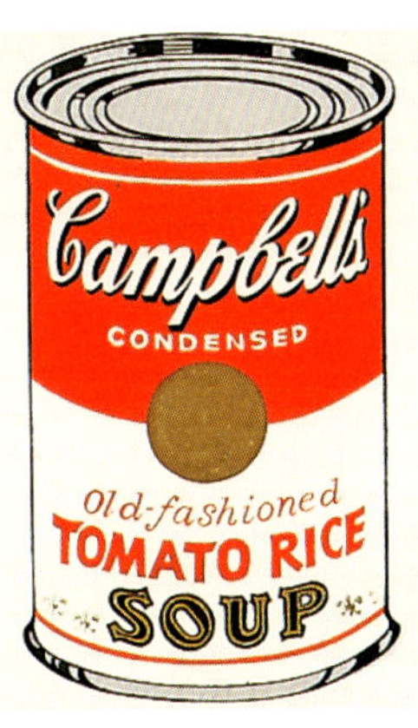

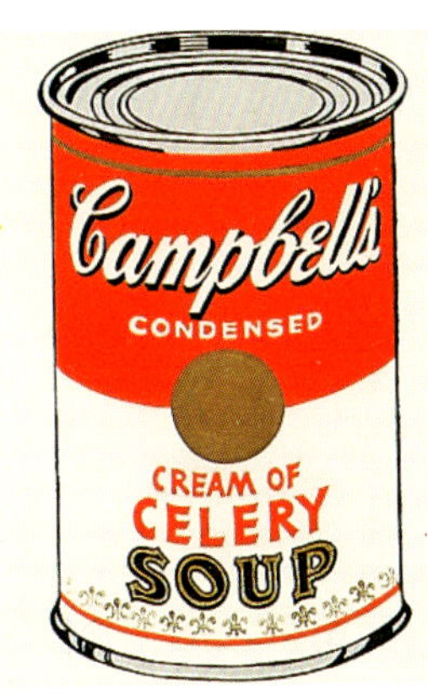

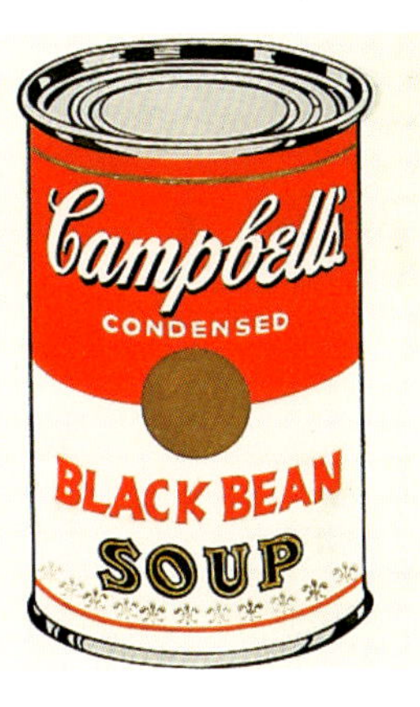

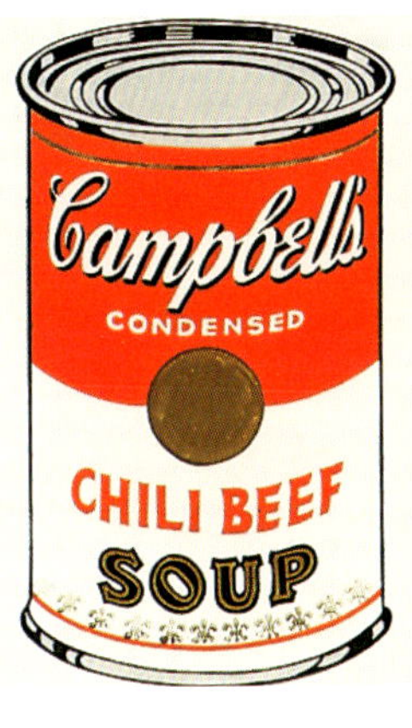

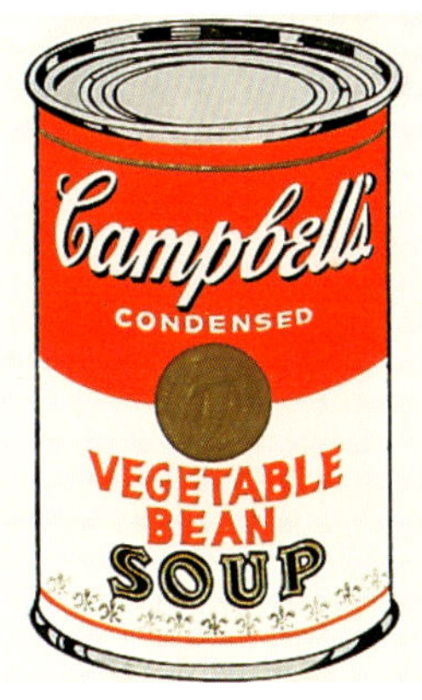

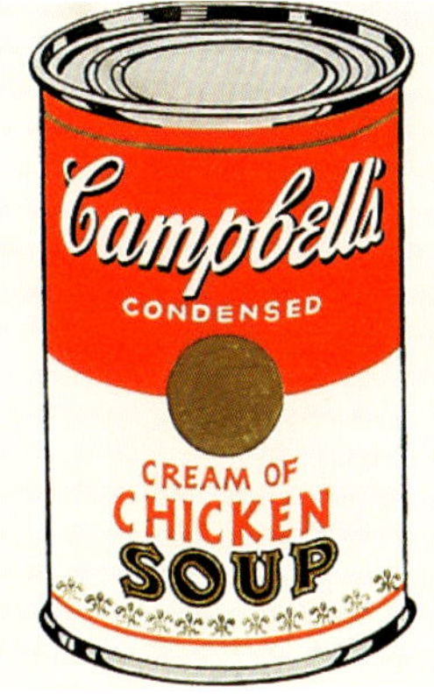

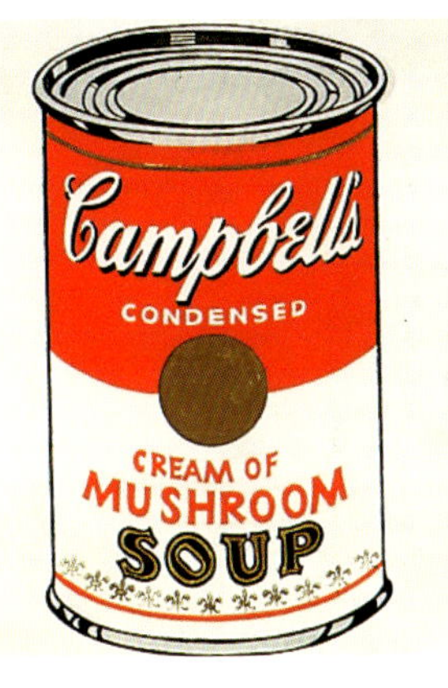

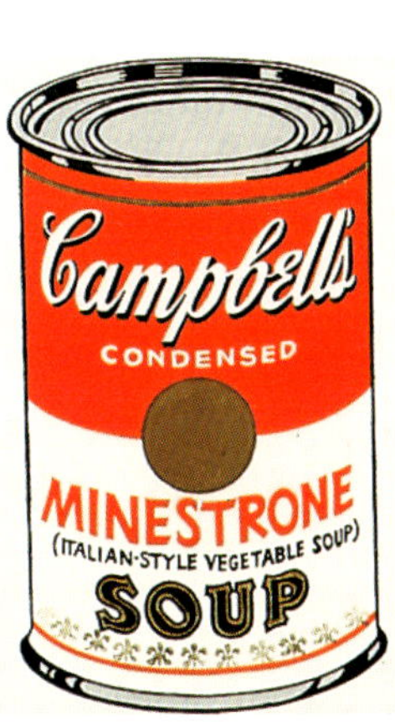

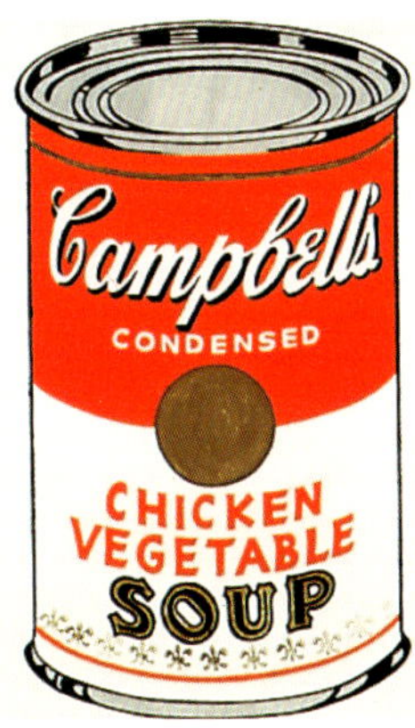

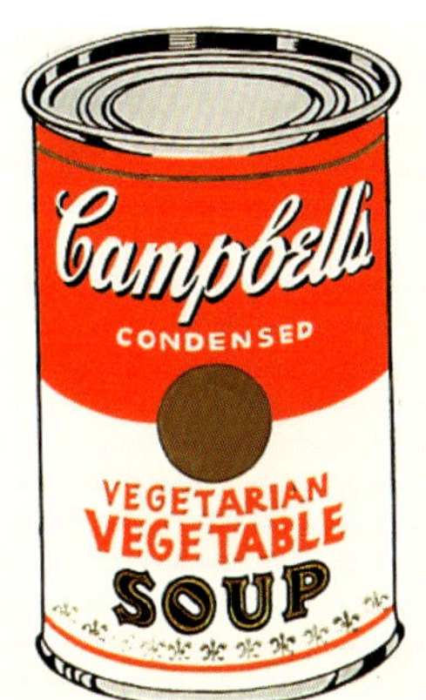

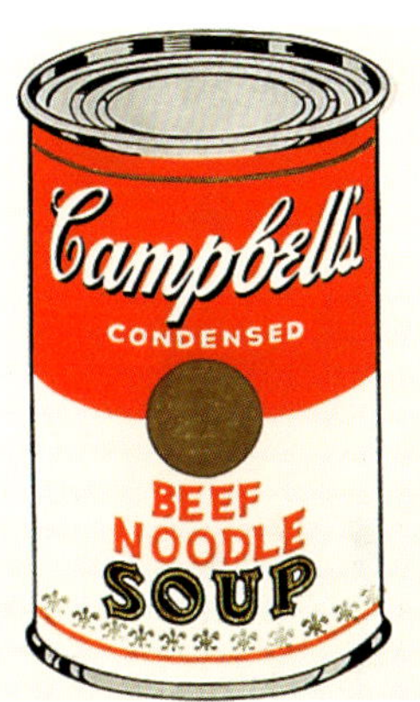

76 **Campbell's Soup Cans 1962** The Museum of Modern Art, New York • Purchase and partial gift of Irving Blum

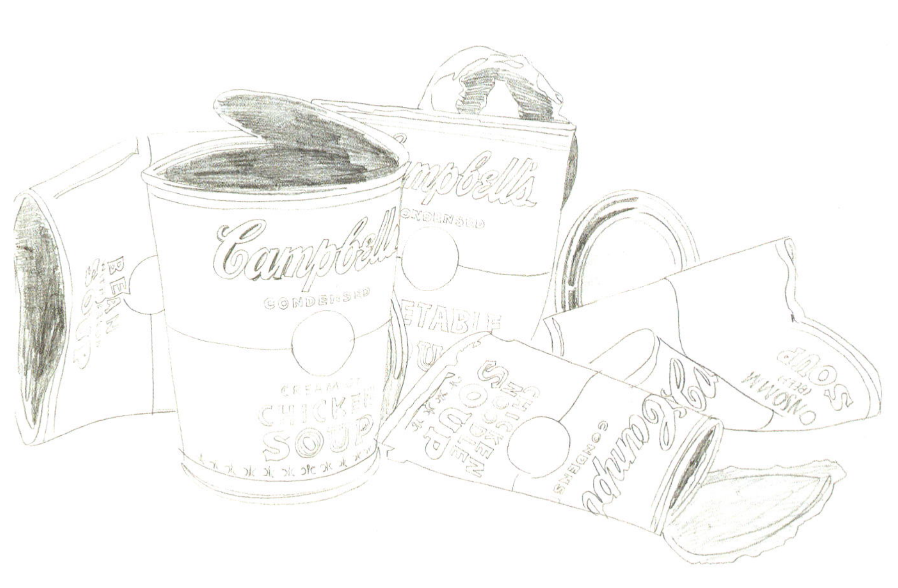

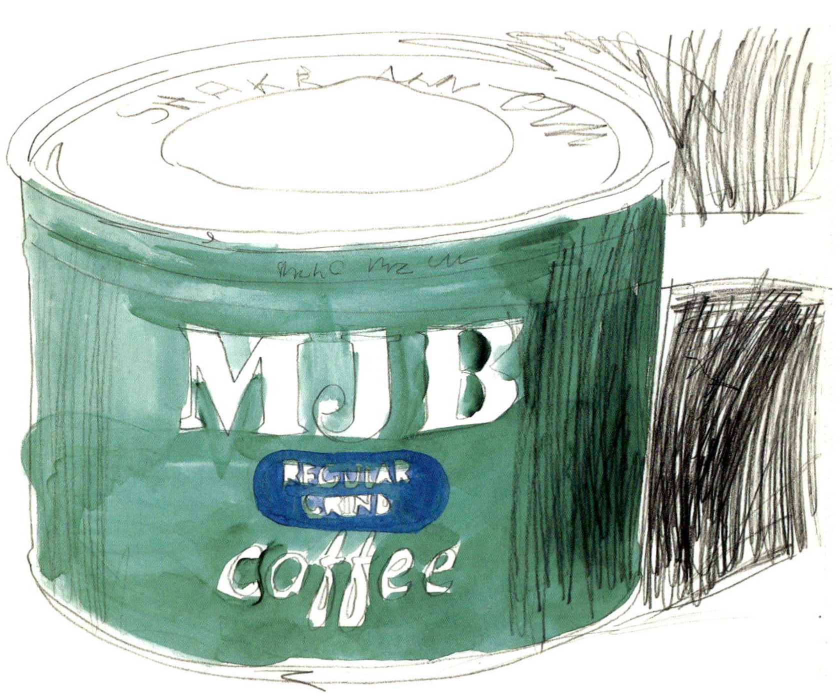

77 **Five Campbell's Soup Cans 1962** Courtesy Sonnabend Collection

78 **Big Coffee-Tin 1962** Öffentliche Kunstsammlung Basel, Kupferstichkabinett K. A. Burckhardt-Koechlin-Fonds

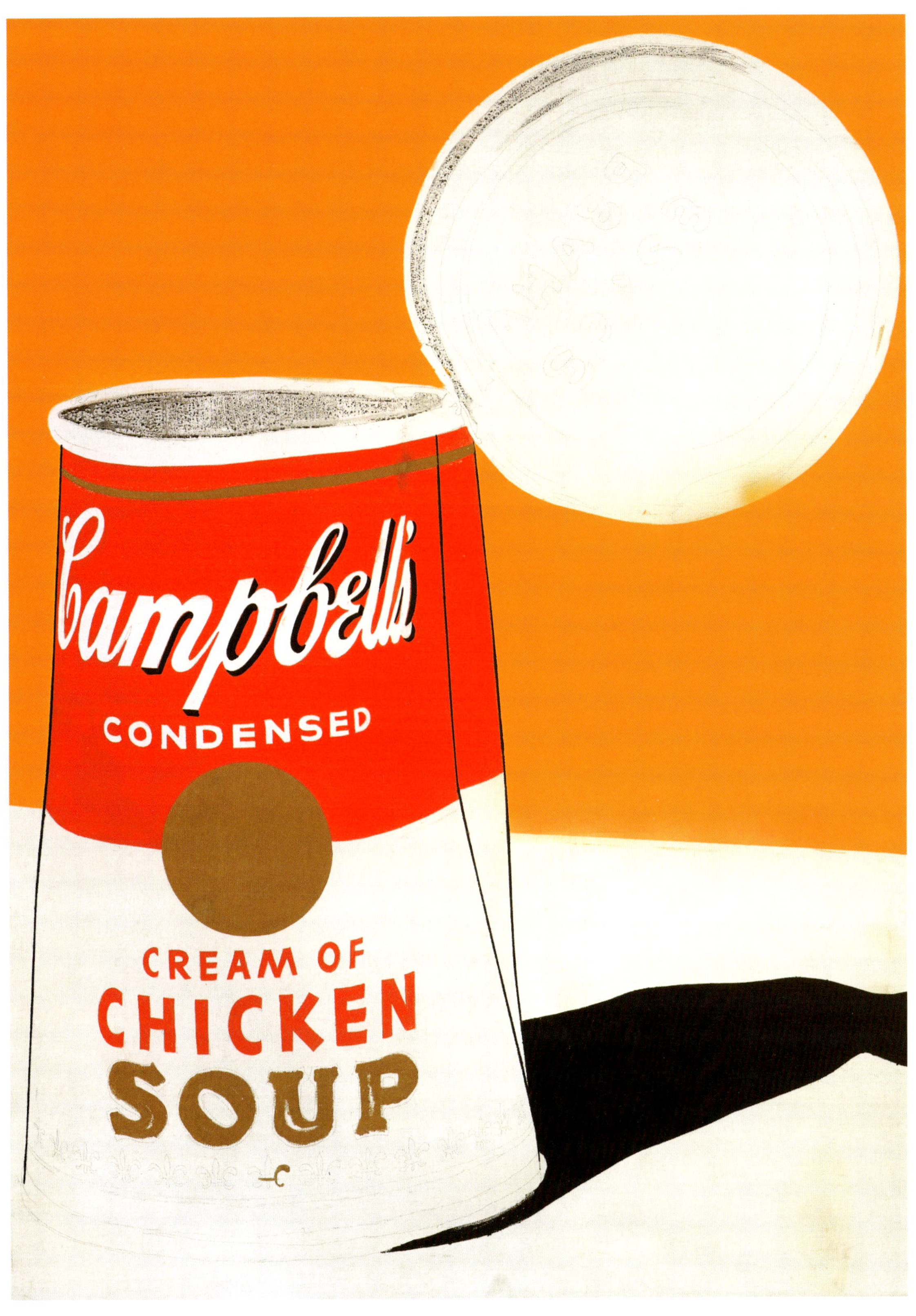

79 **Campbell's Soup Can (Cream of Chicken) 1962** Courtesy Gagosian Gallery

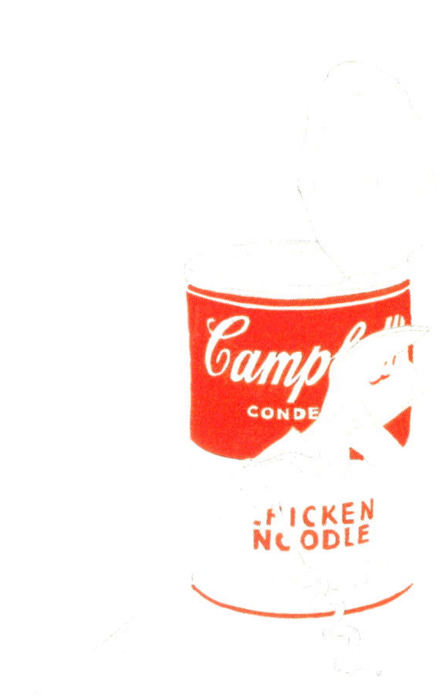

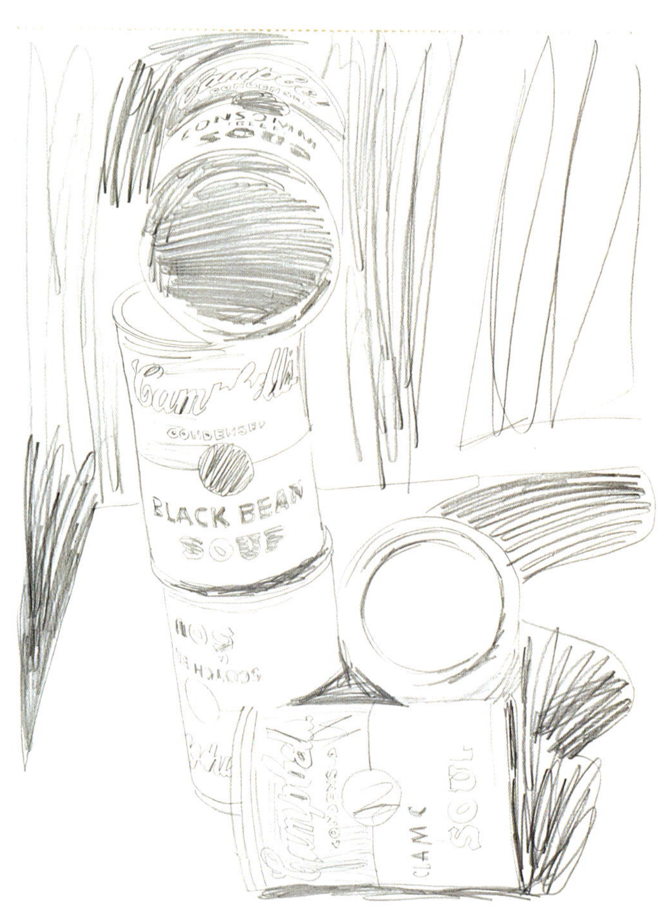

80 **Campbell's Soup Can (Chicken Noodle)** **1962**
Courtesy Sonnabend Collection

81 **Campbell's Soup Cans (Black Bean Soup)** **1962**
Courtesy The Brant Foundation, Greenwich, CT

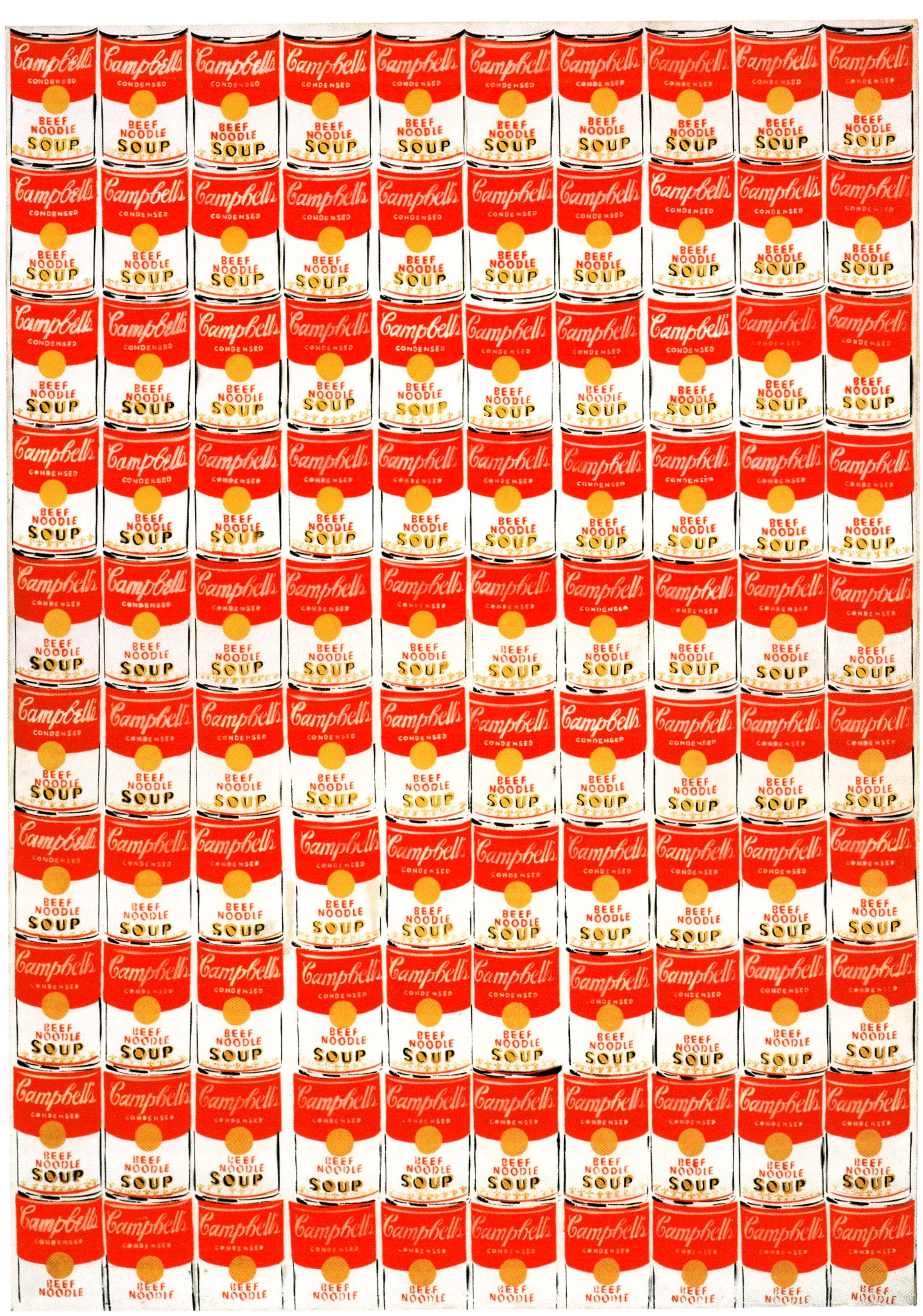

82 **100 Cans 1962** Albright-Knox Art Gallery, Buffalo, NY • Gift of Seymour H. Knox, Jr., 1963

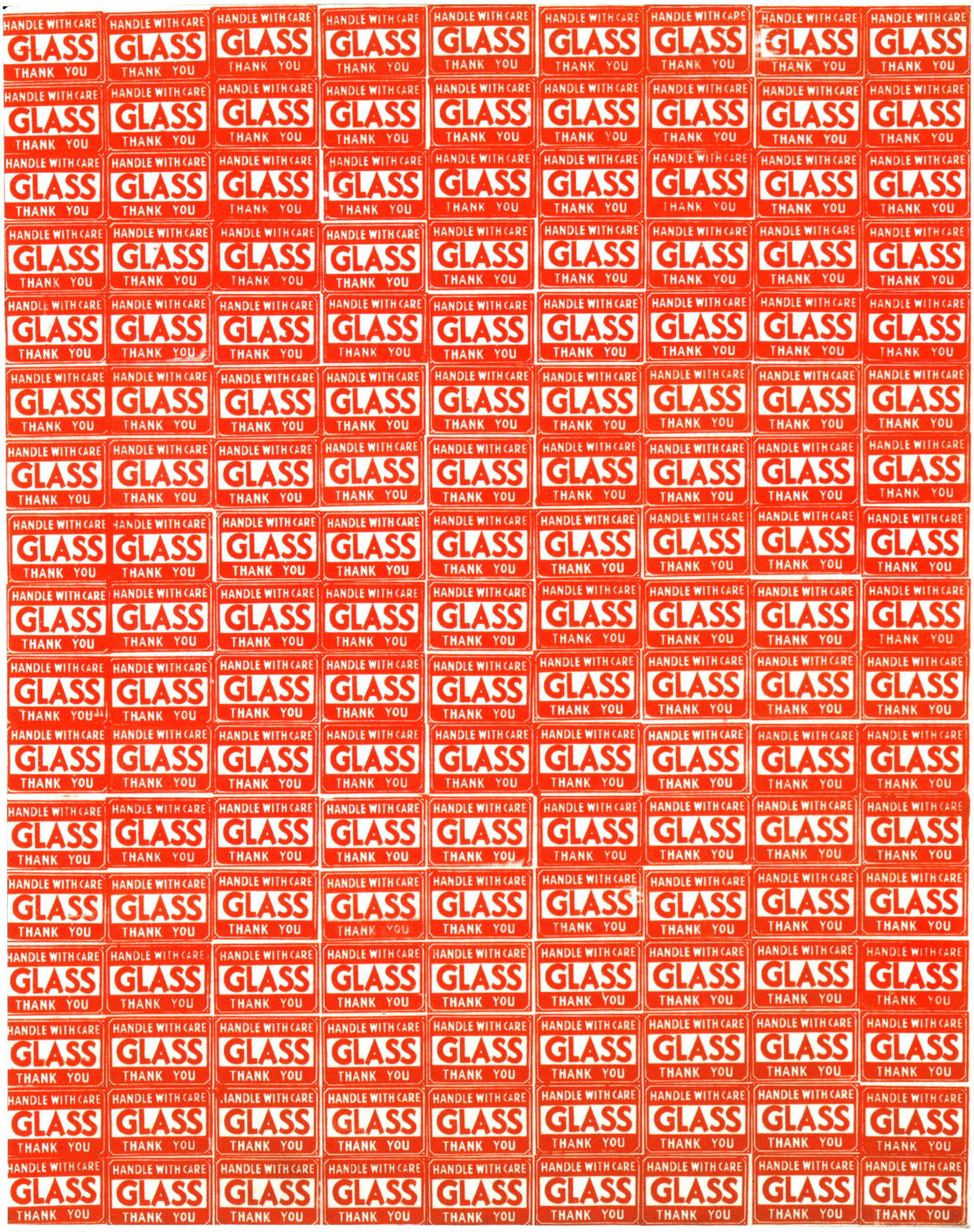

83 Handle with Care – Glass – Thank You 1962 Daros Collection, Switzerland

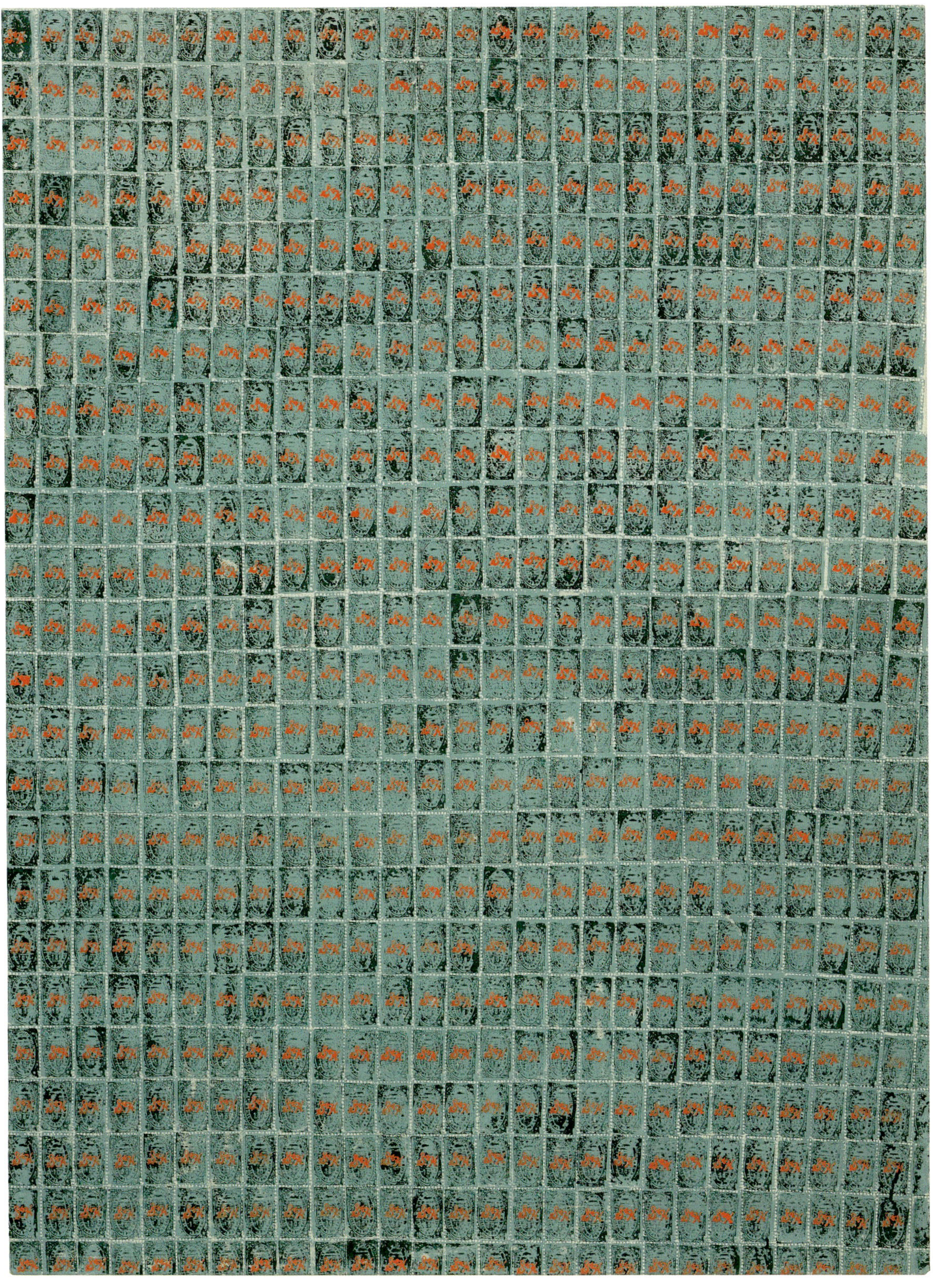

84 S & H Green Stamps 1962 The Museum of Modern Art, New York • Gift of Philip Johnson, 1998

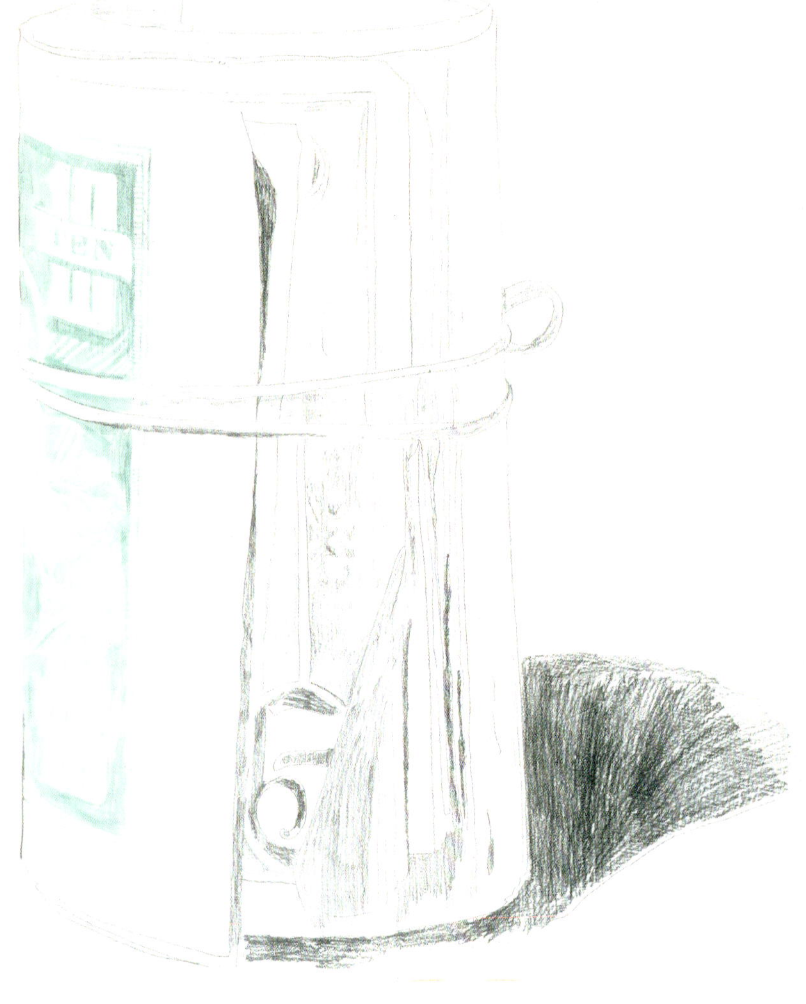

85 **Untitled (Roll of Bills) 1962**
Courtesy The Brant Foundation, Greenwich, CT

86 **192 One Dollar Bills 1962**
Stiftung Sammlung Marx, Hamburger Bahnhof – Museum für Gegenwart, Berlin

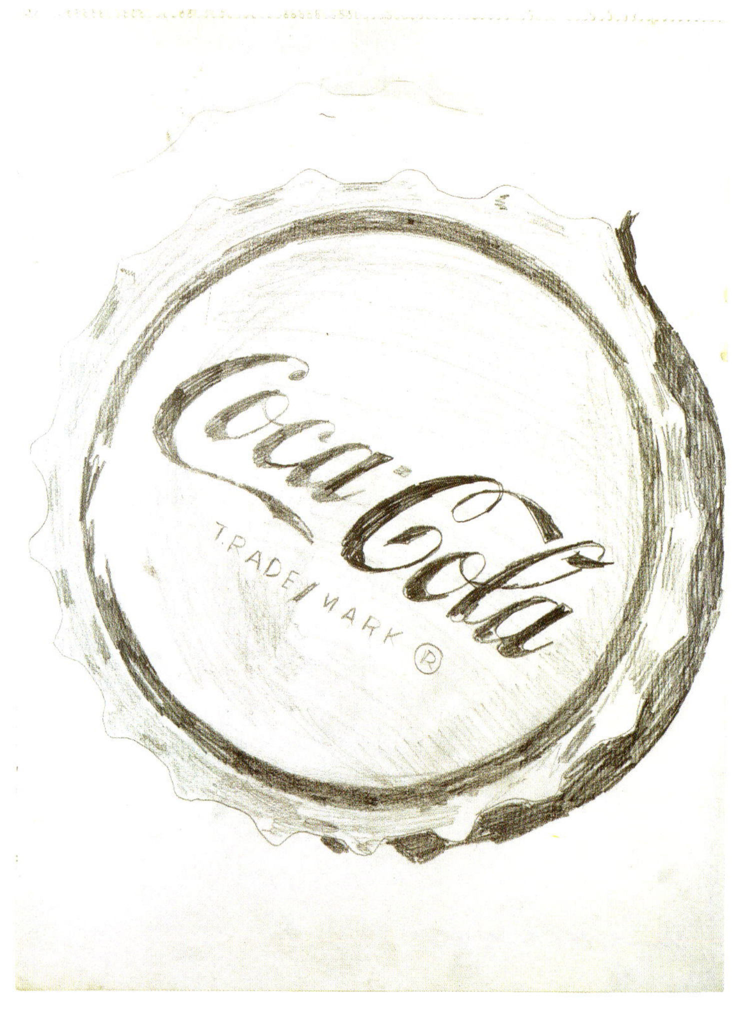

87 Coca-Cola 1962
Sonnabend Collection

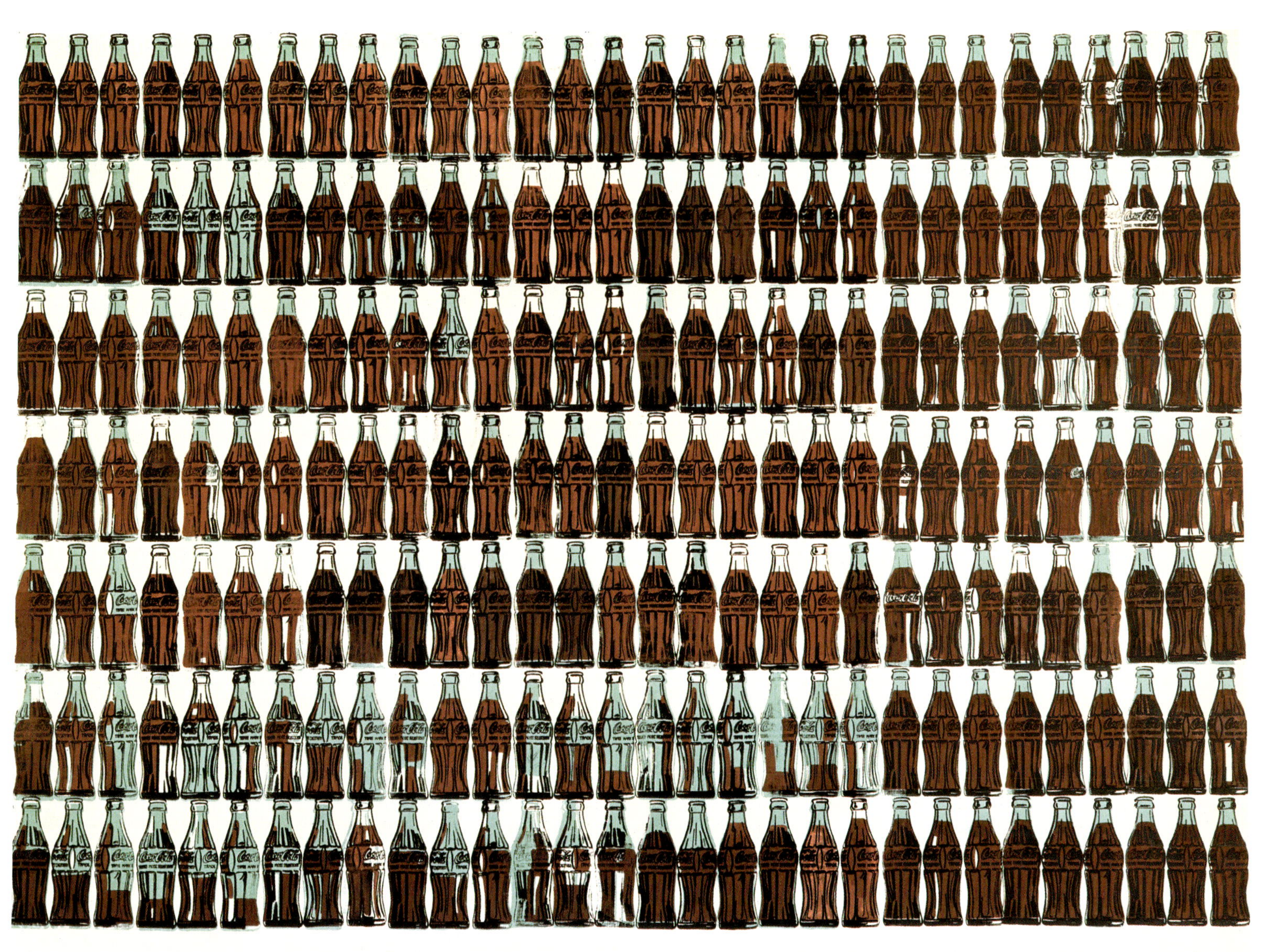

88 **210 Coca-Cola Bottles 1962** Daros Collection, Switzerland

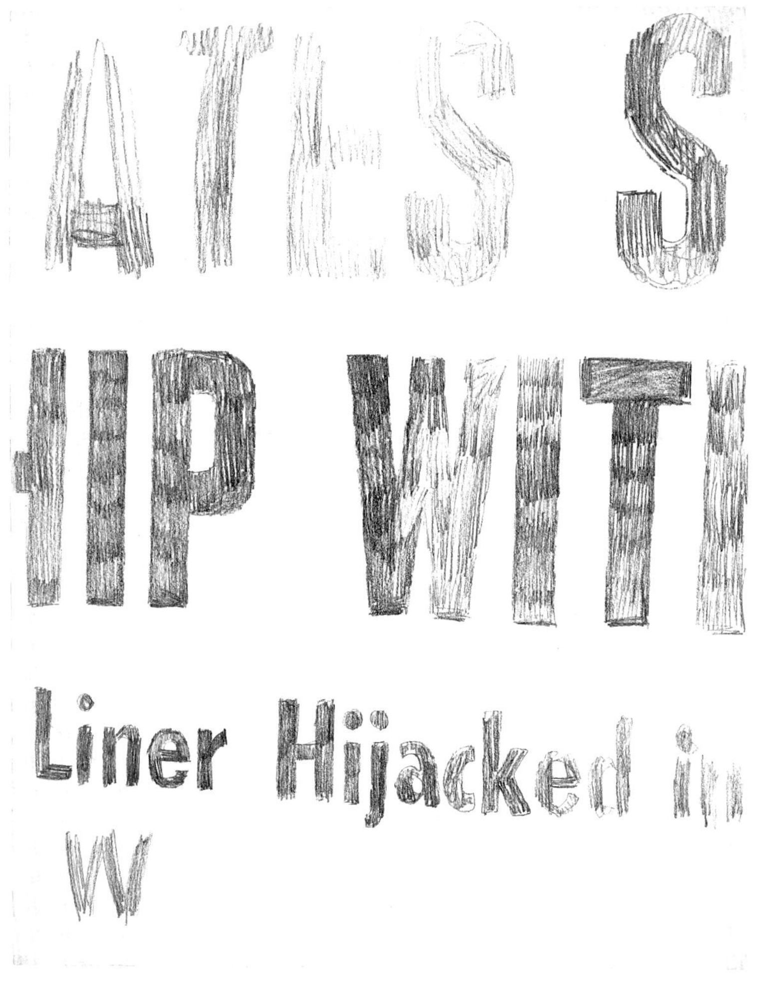

89 **Liner Hijacked** **1961** The Andy Warhol Museum, Pittsburgh Founding Collection, Contribution The Andy Warhol Foundation for the Visual Arts, Inc.

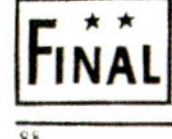

DAILY NEWS
NEW YORK'S PICTURE NEWSPAPER

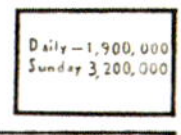

88 New York 17, N.Y., Thursday, March 29, 1962 5 CENTS

MET RALLY EDGES LA, 4-3
YANKS CURB CARDS, 4-1

Stories on Page 78

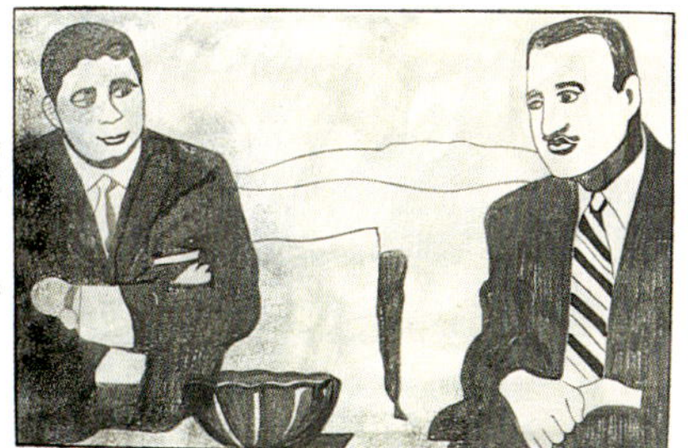

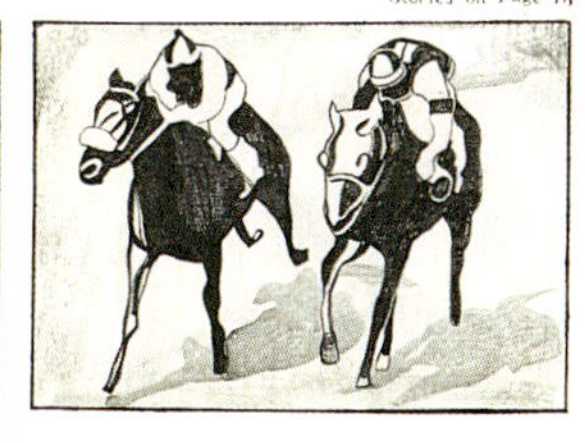

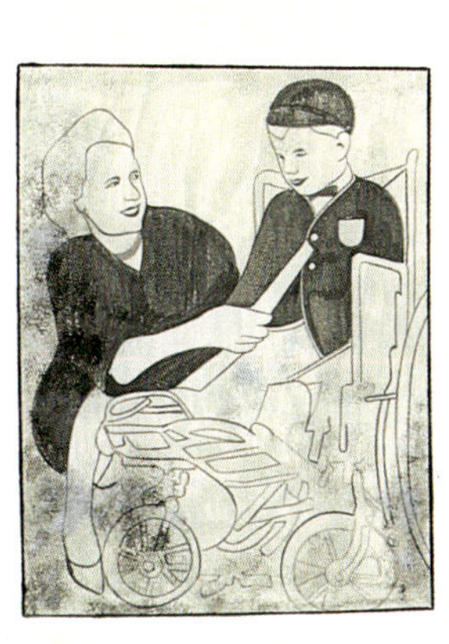

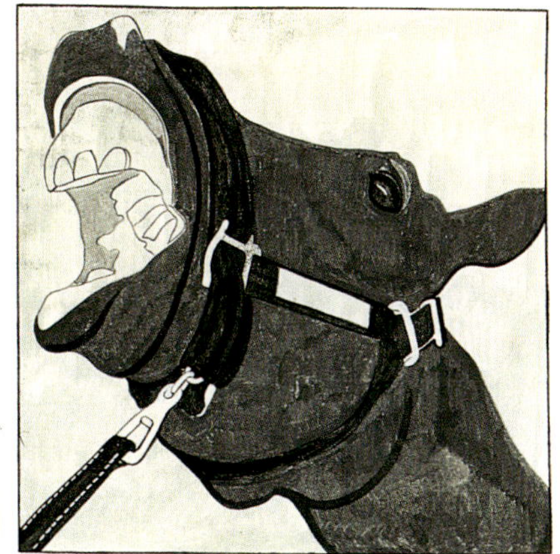

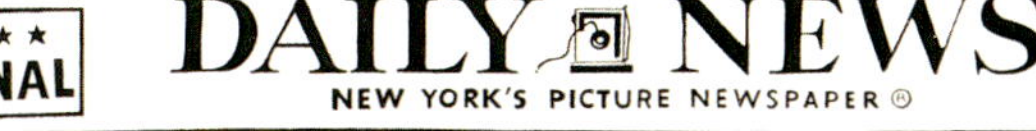

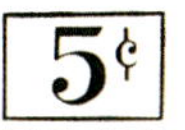

Vol. 43. No. 238 New York 17, N.Y., Thursday, March 29, 1962

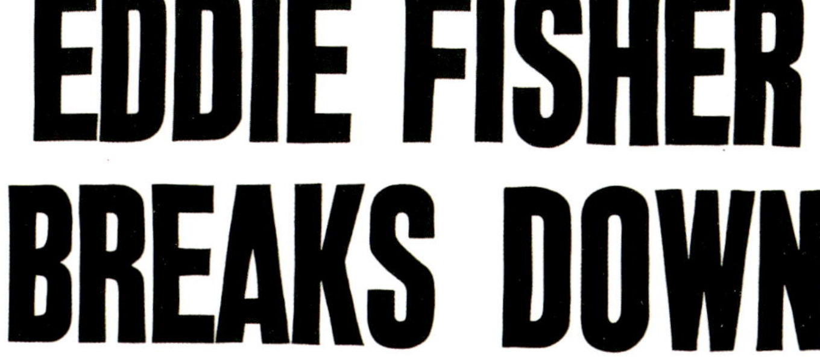

In Hospital Here; Liz in Rome

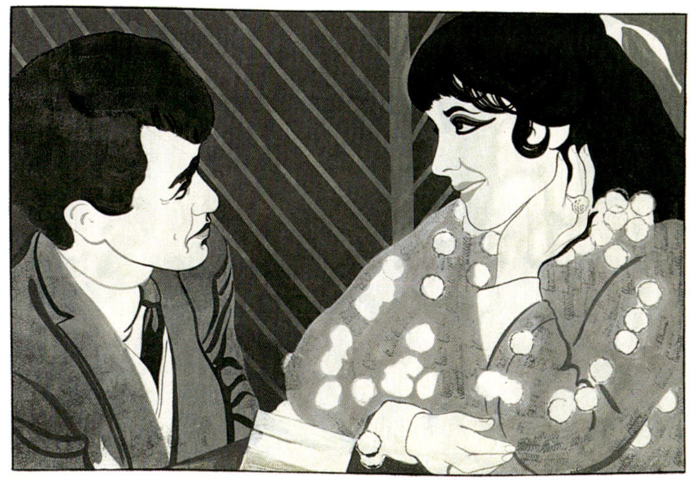

90 Daily News 1962 Museum für Moderne Kunst, Frankfurt am Main [Former Ströher Collection]

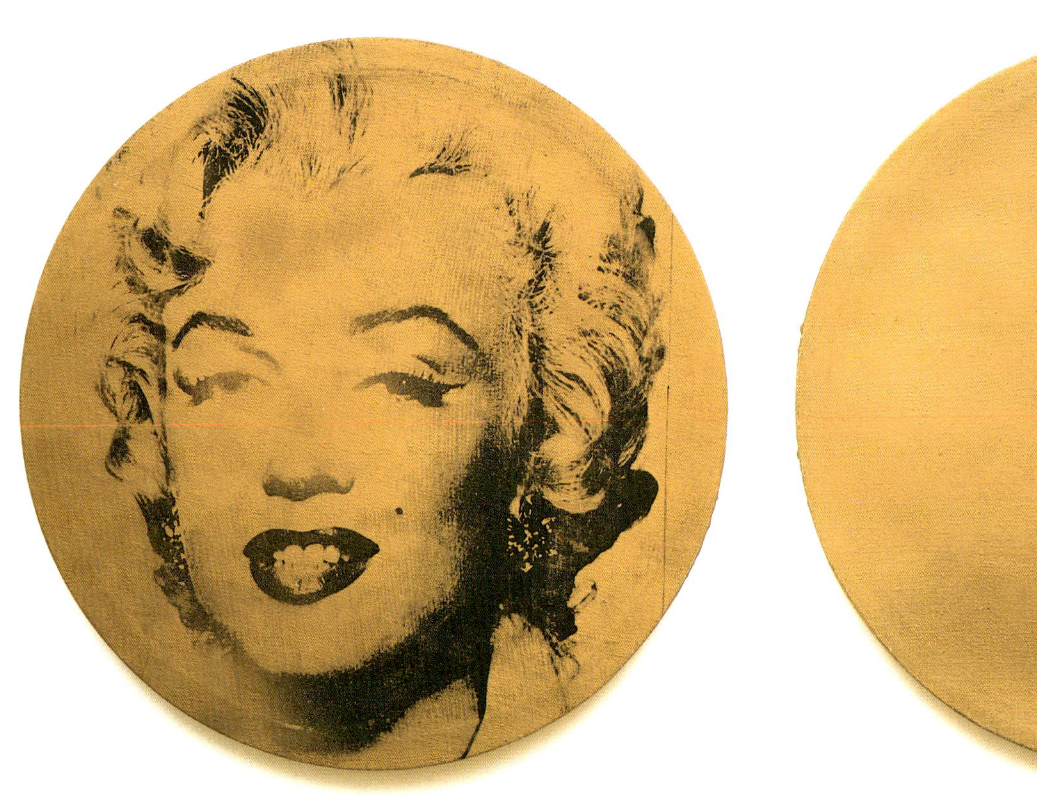

91 Gold Marilyn 1962
Collection Froehlich, Stuttgart

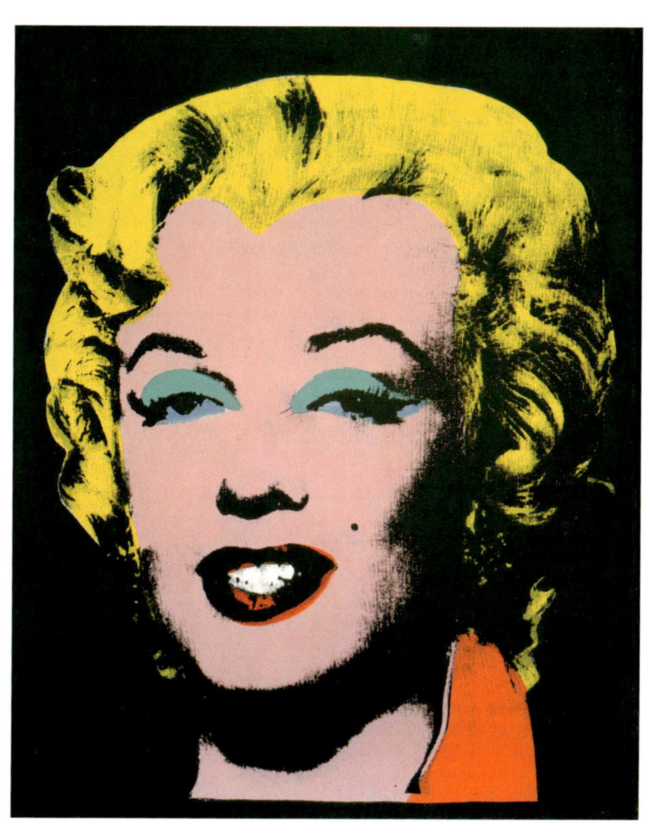

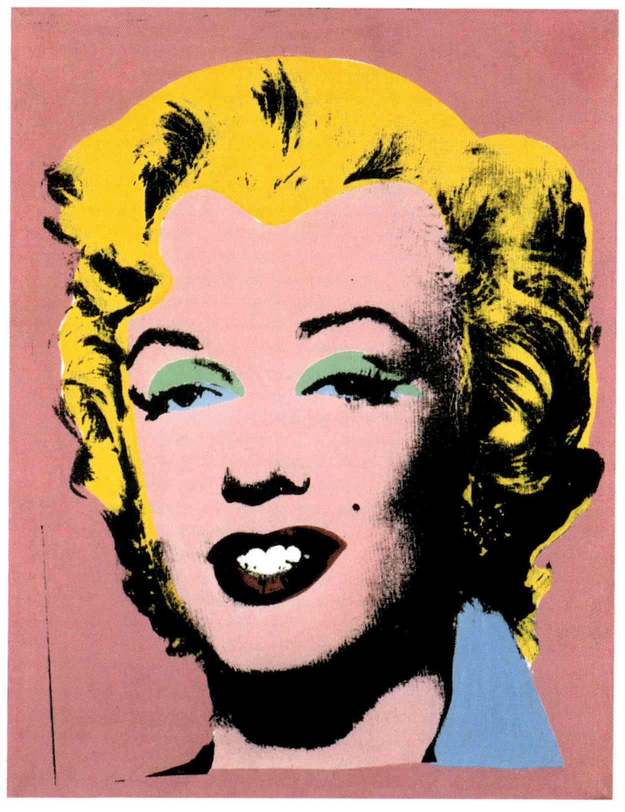

92 **Liquorice Marilyn 1962**
Courtesy The Brant Foundation, Greenwich, CT

93 **Lavender Marilyn 1962**
Collection Uli Knecht

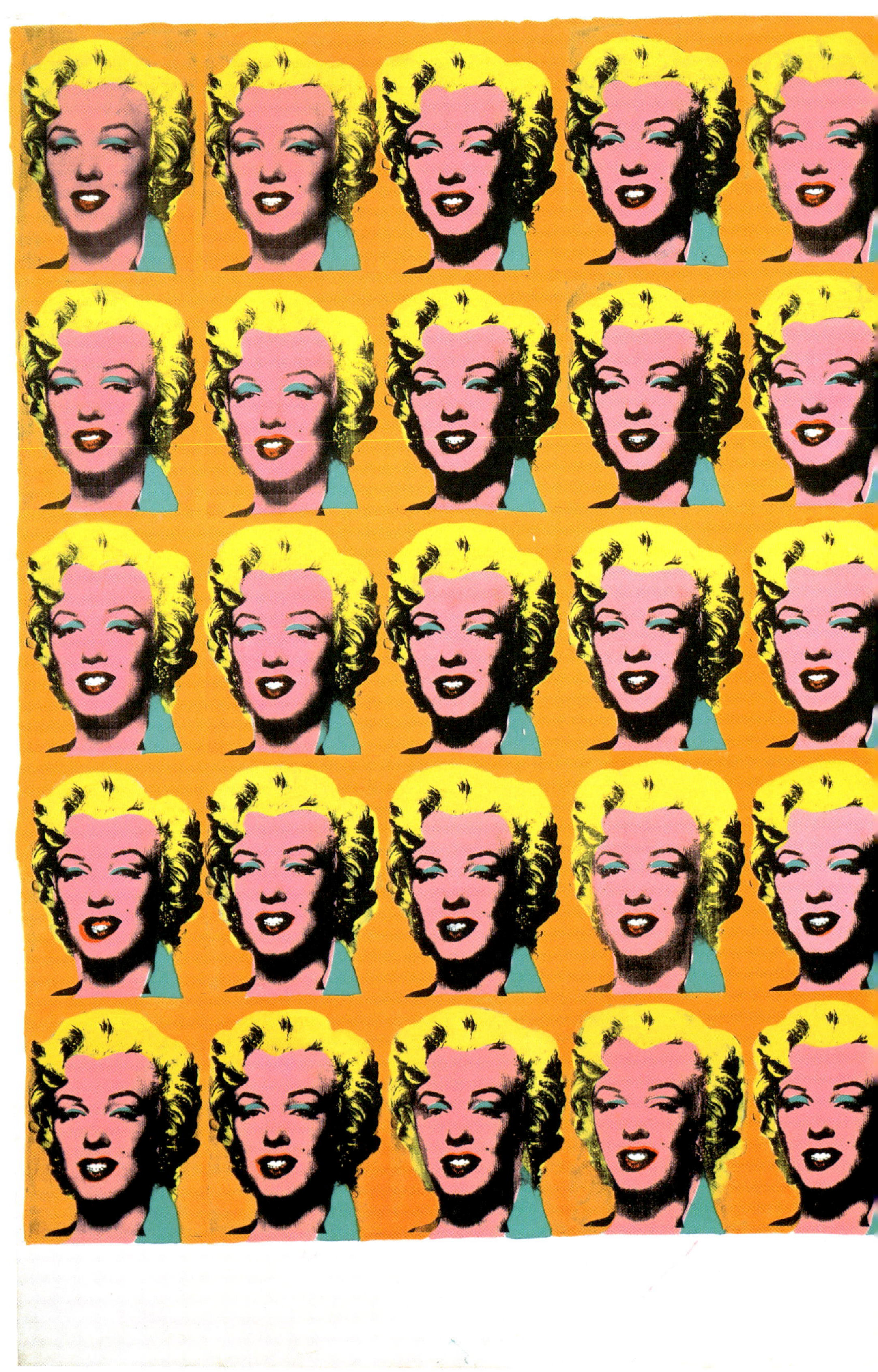

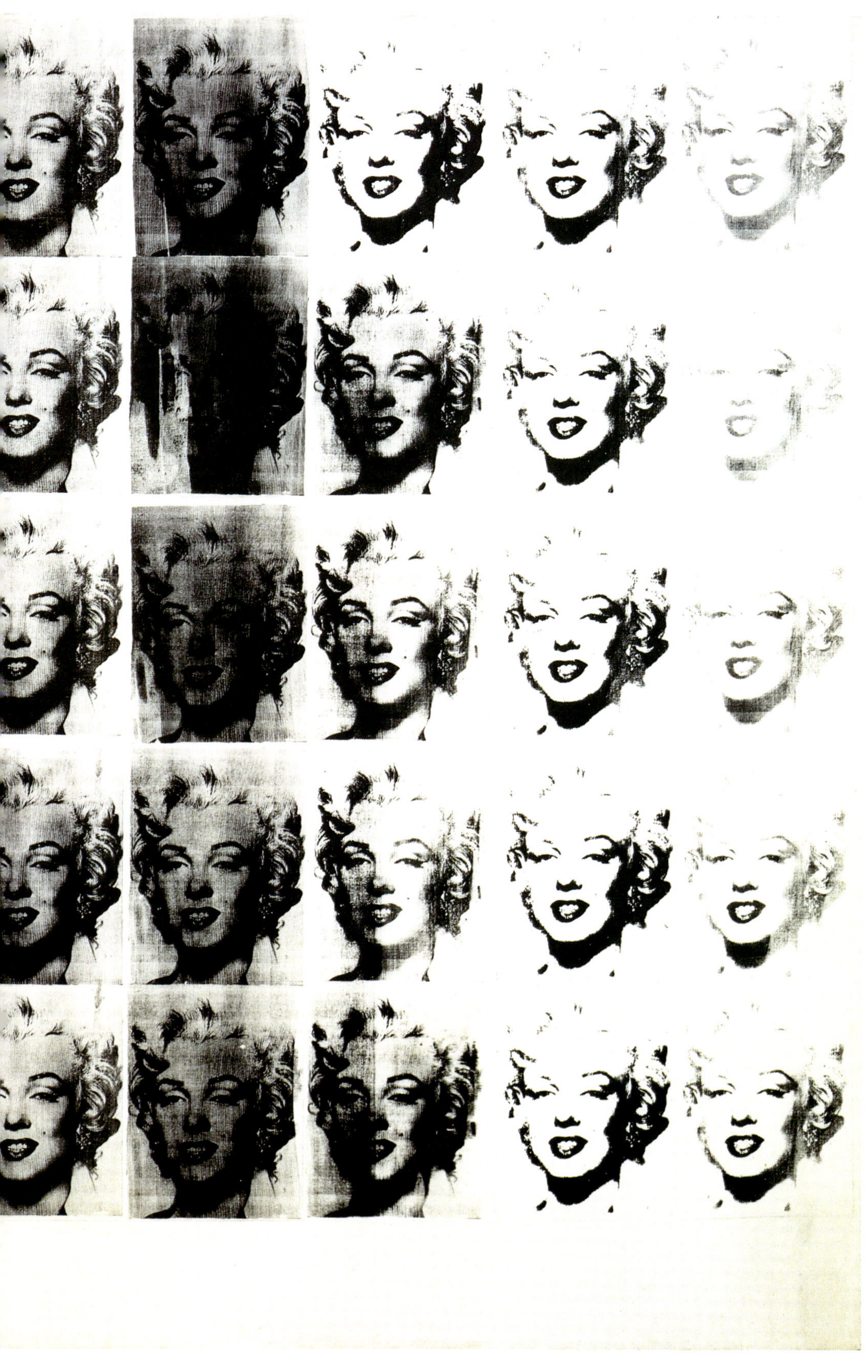

94 **Marilyn Diptych 1962** The Trustees of the Tate Gallery

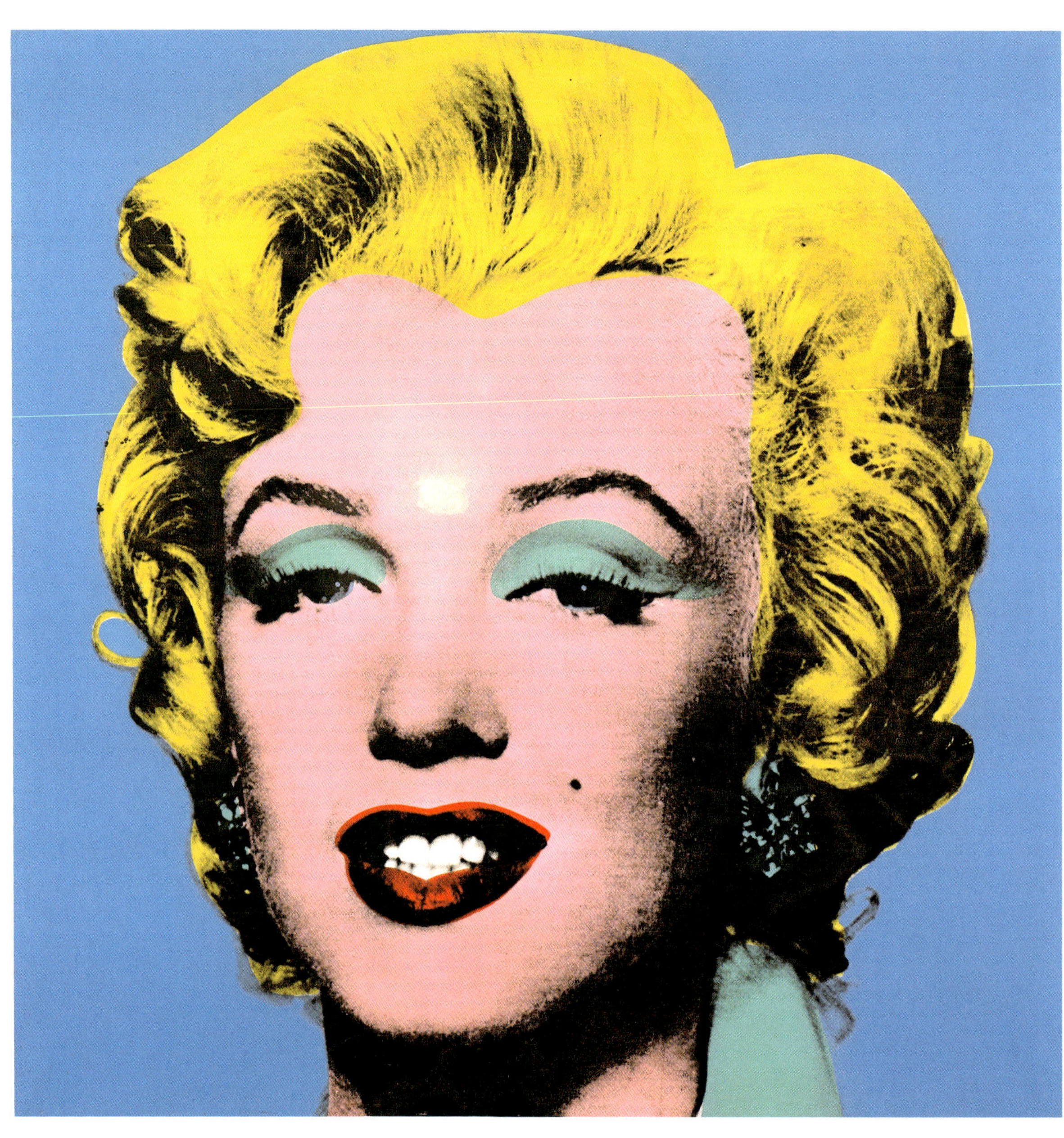

95 Shot Blue Marilyn 1964 Courtesy The Brant Foundation, Greenwich, CT

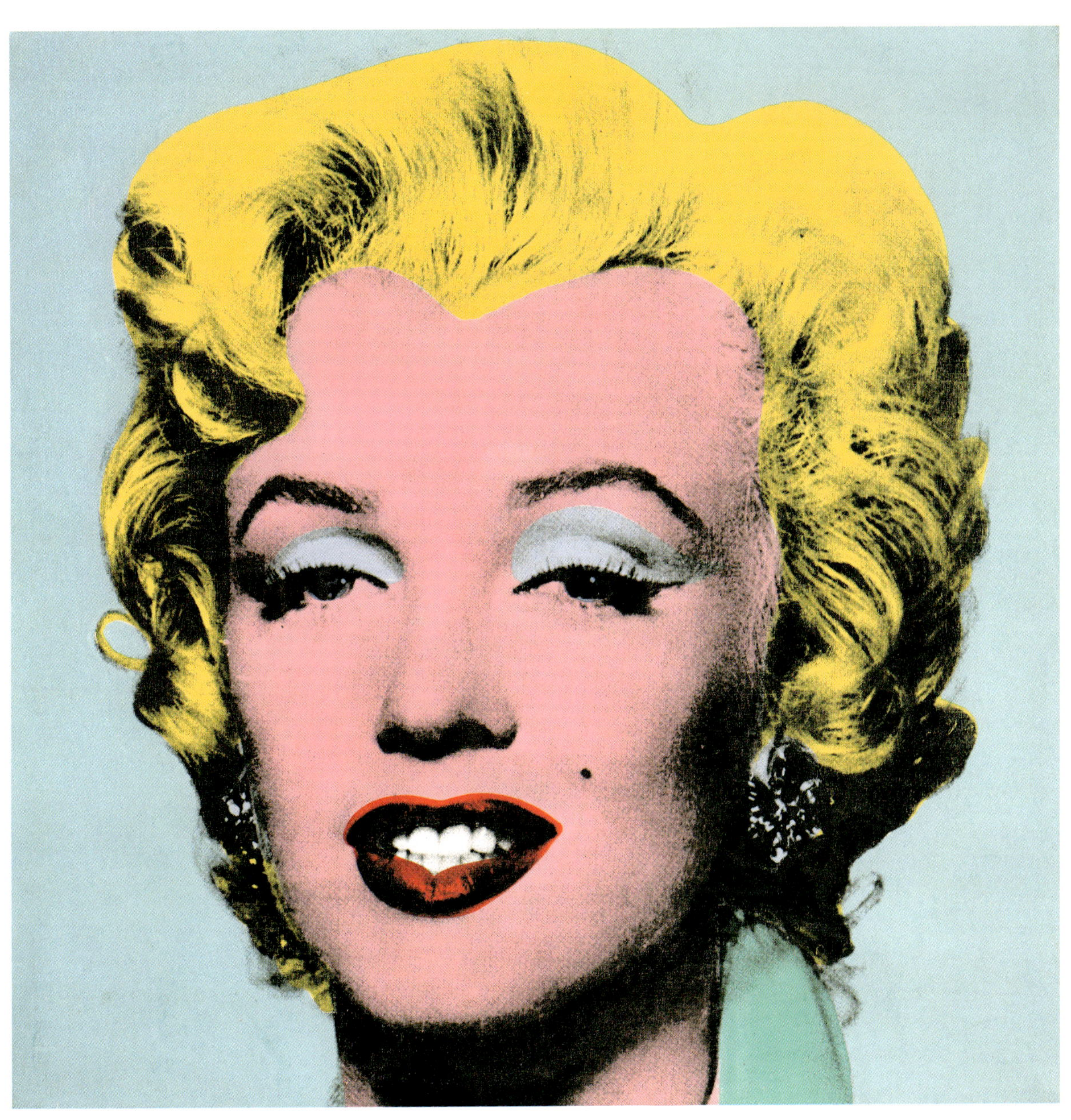

96 **Shot Sage Blue Marilyn 1964** Private collection; Courtesy Doris Ammann

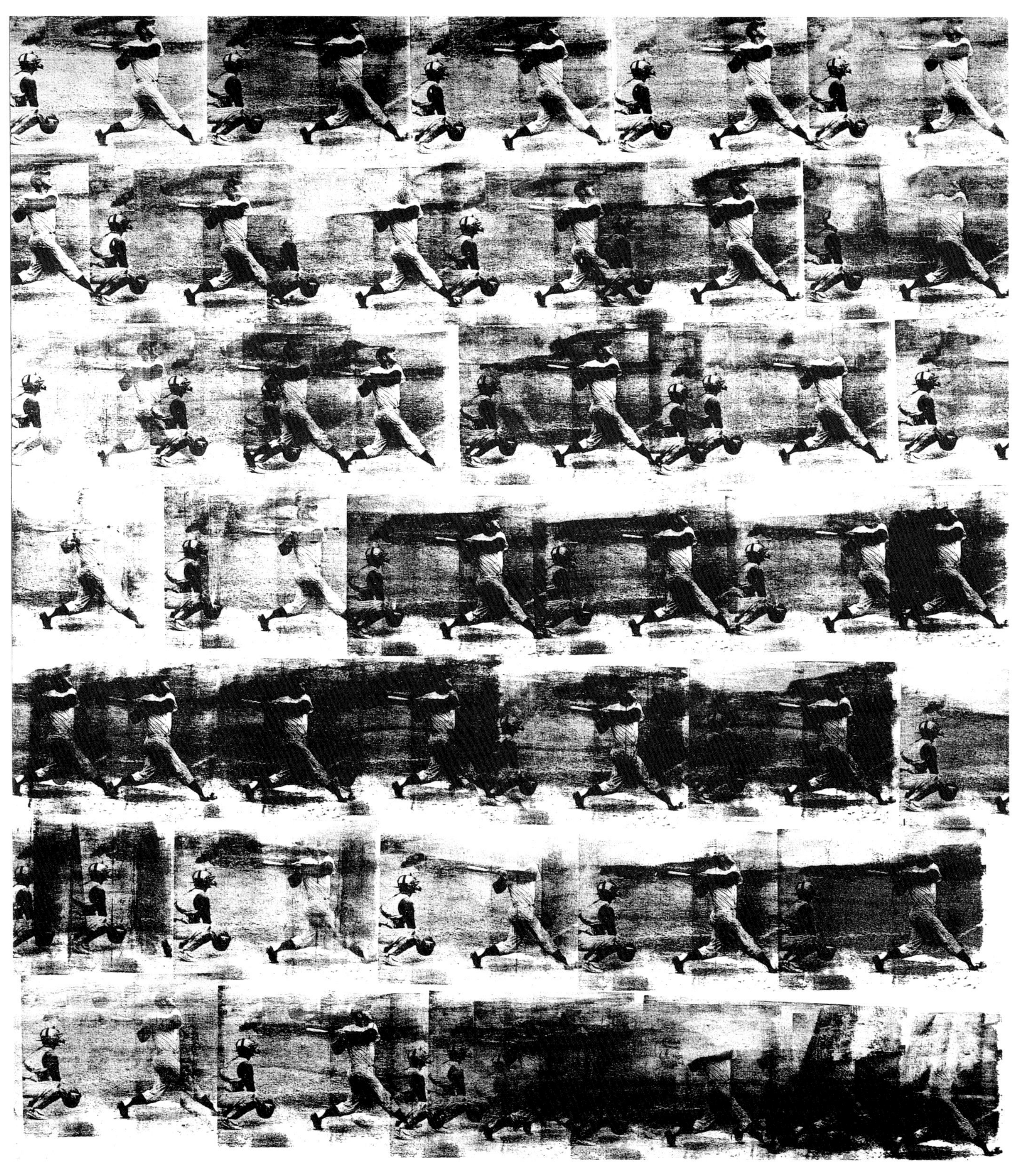

97 **Baseball 1962** Collection of The Nelson-Atkins Museum of Art, Kansas City, MO. Gift of the Guild of the Friends of Art and other Friends of the Museum

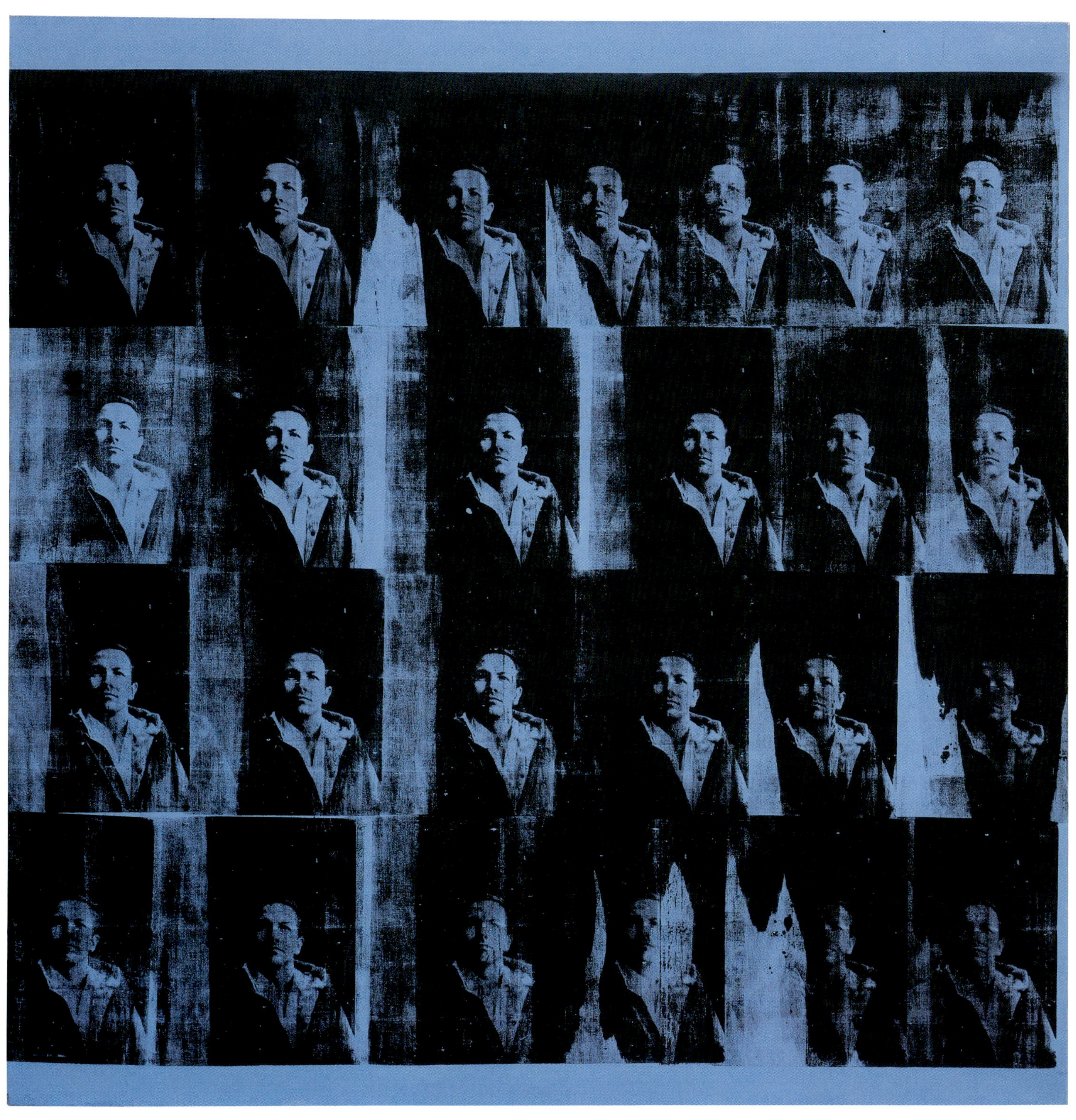

98 **Texan (Portrait Robert Rauschenberg)** **1963** Museum Ludwig, Köln

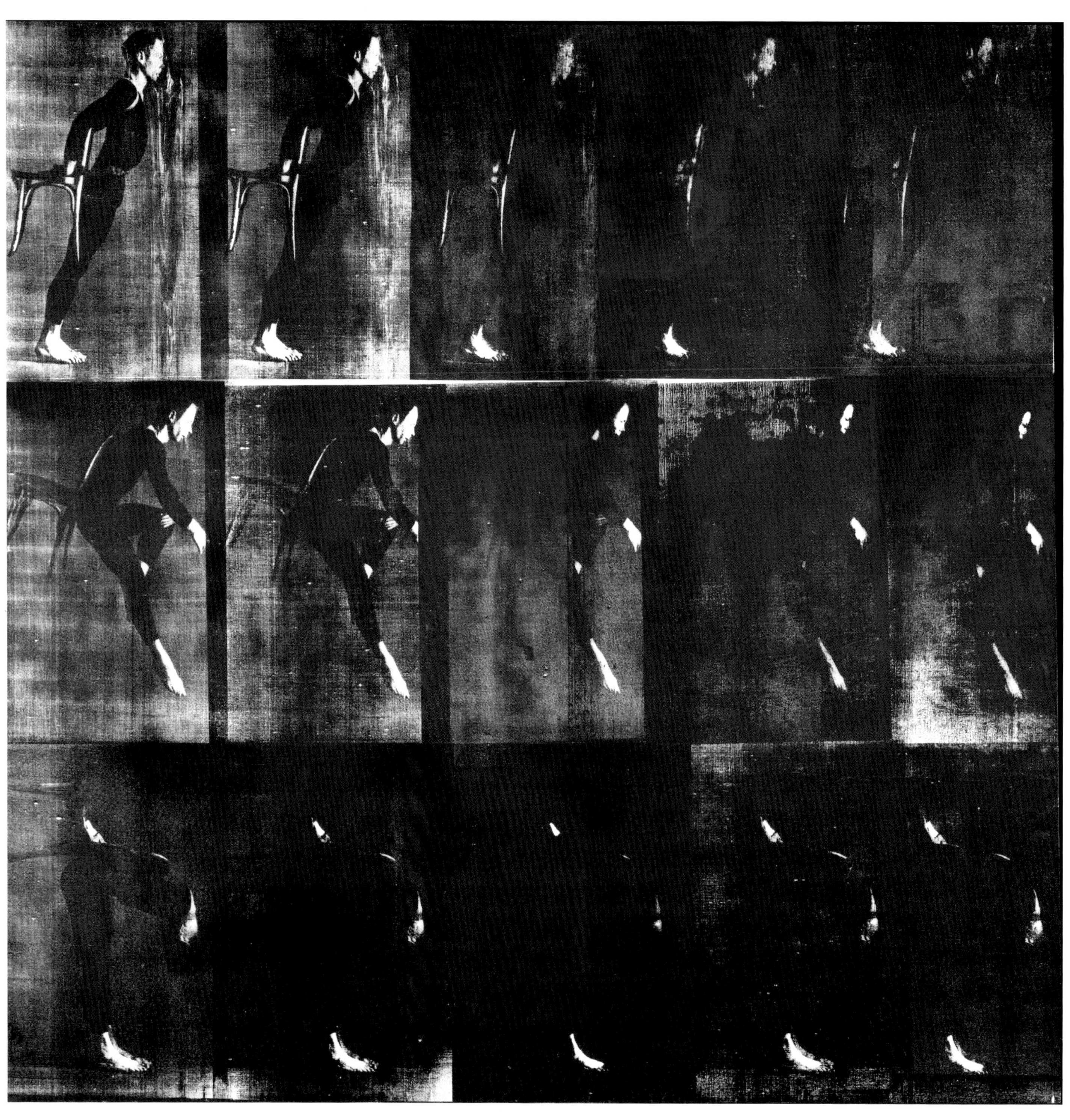

99 Merce 1963 Daros Collection, Switzerland

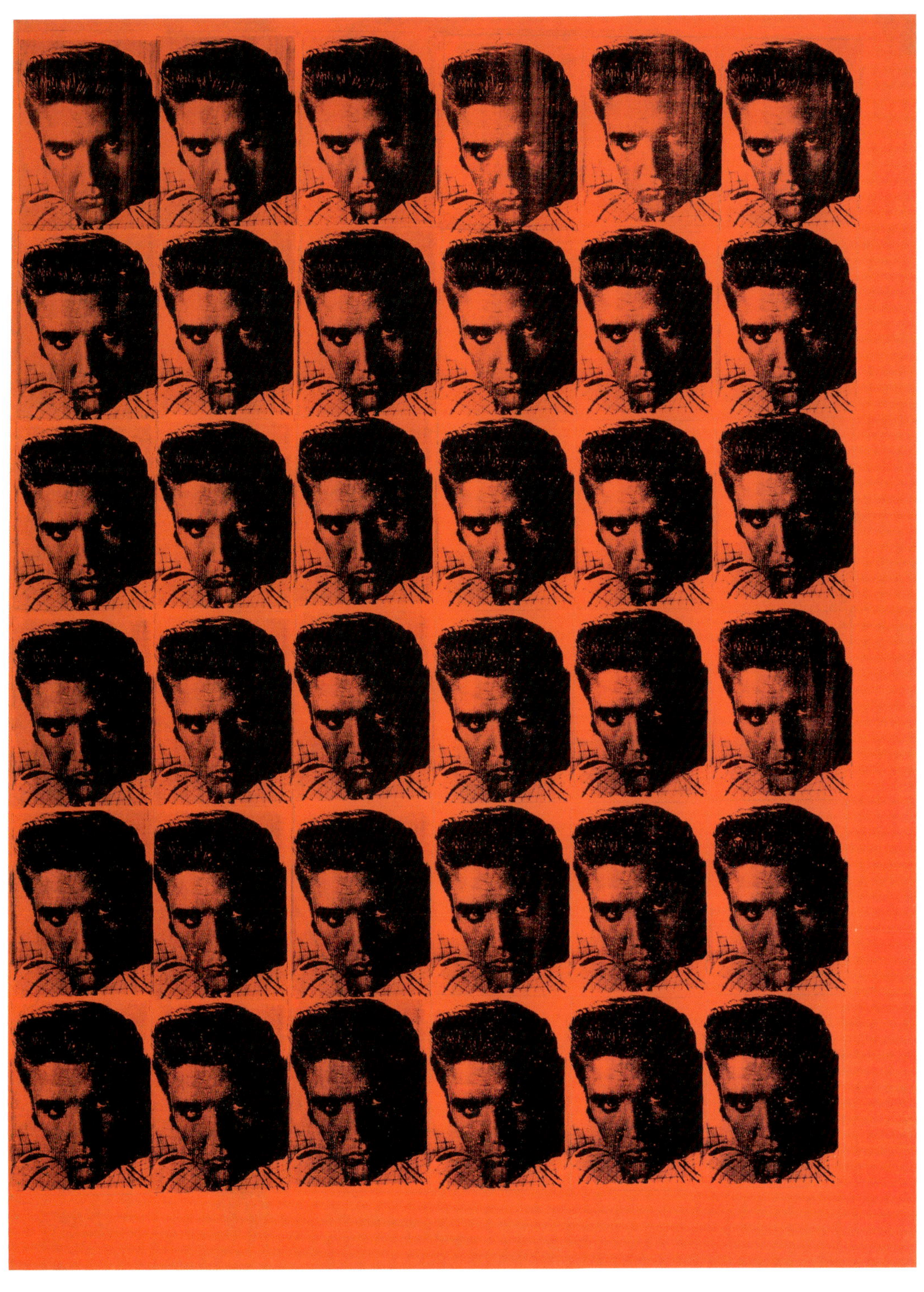

100 Red Elvis 1962 Courtesy The Brant Foundation, Greenwich, CT

101 Thirty Are Better Than One 1963
Courtesy The Brant Foundation,
Greenwich, CT

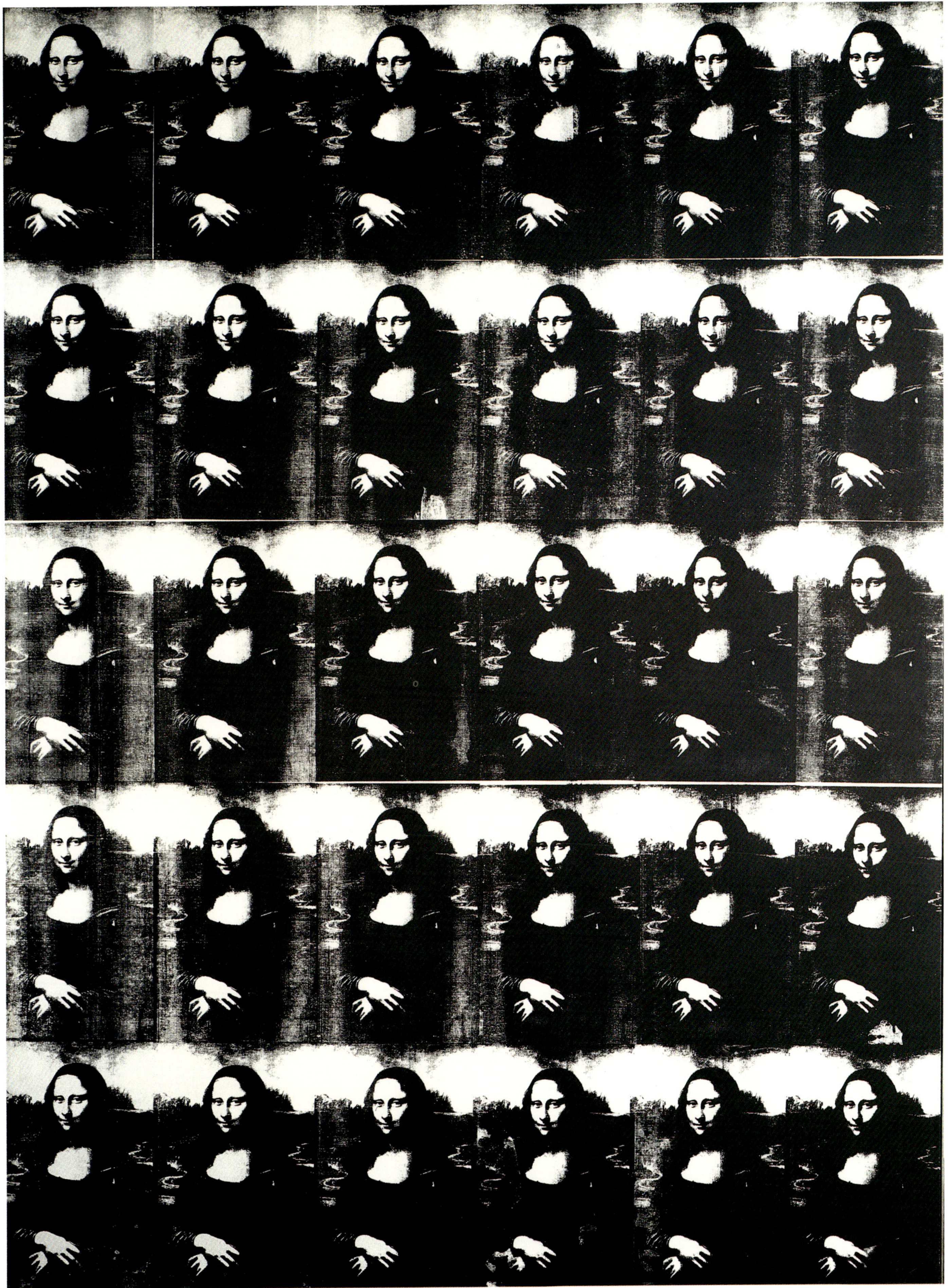

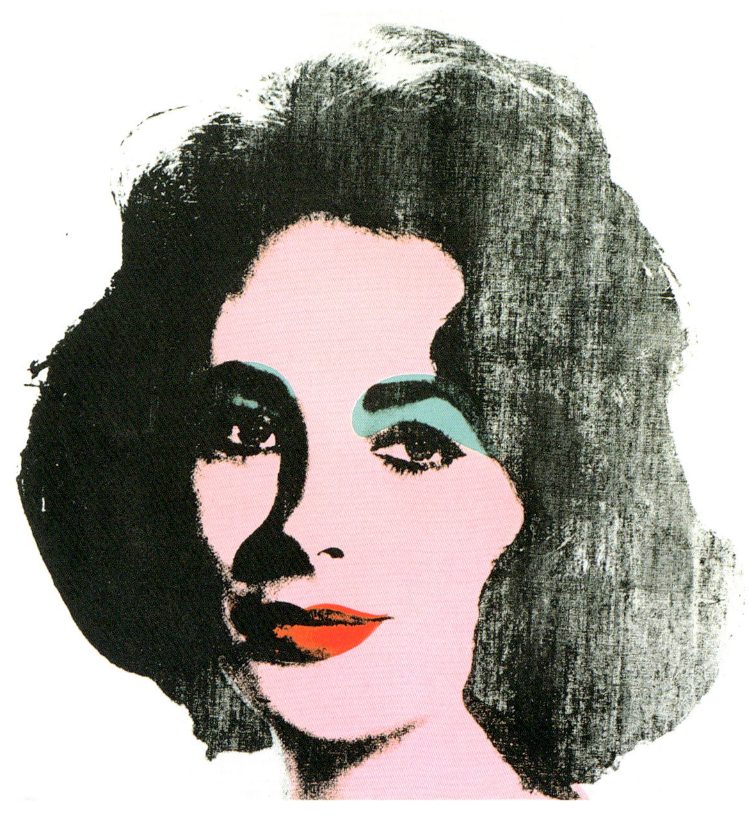

102 **Liz 1963** Collection Froehlich, Stuttgart

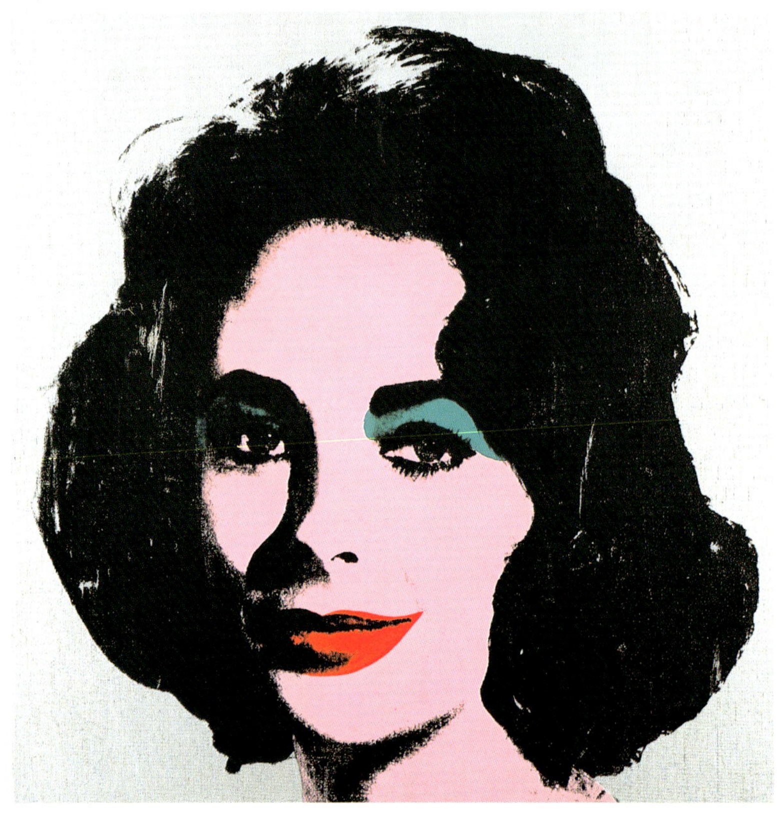

102 a **Silver Liz 1963**
Courtesy The Brant Foundation, Greenwich, CT

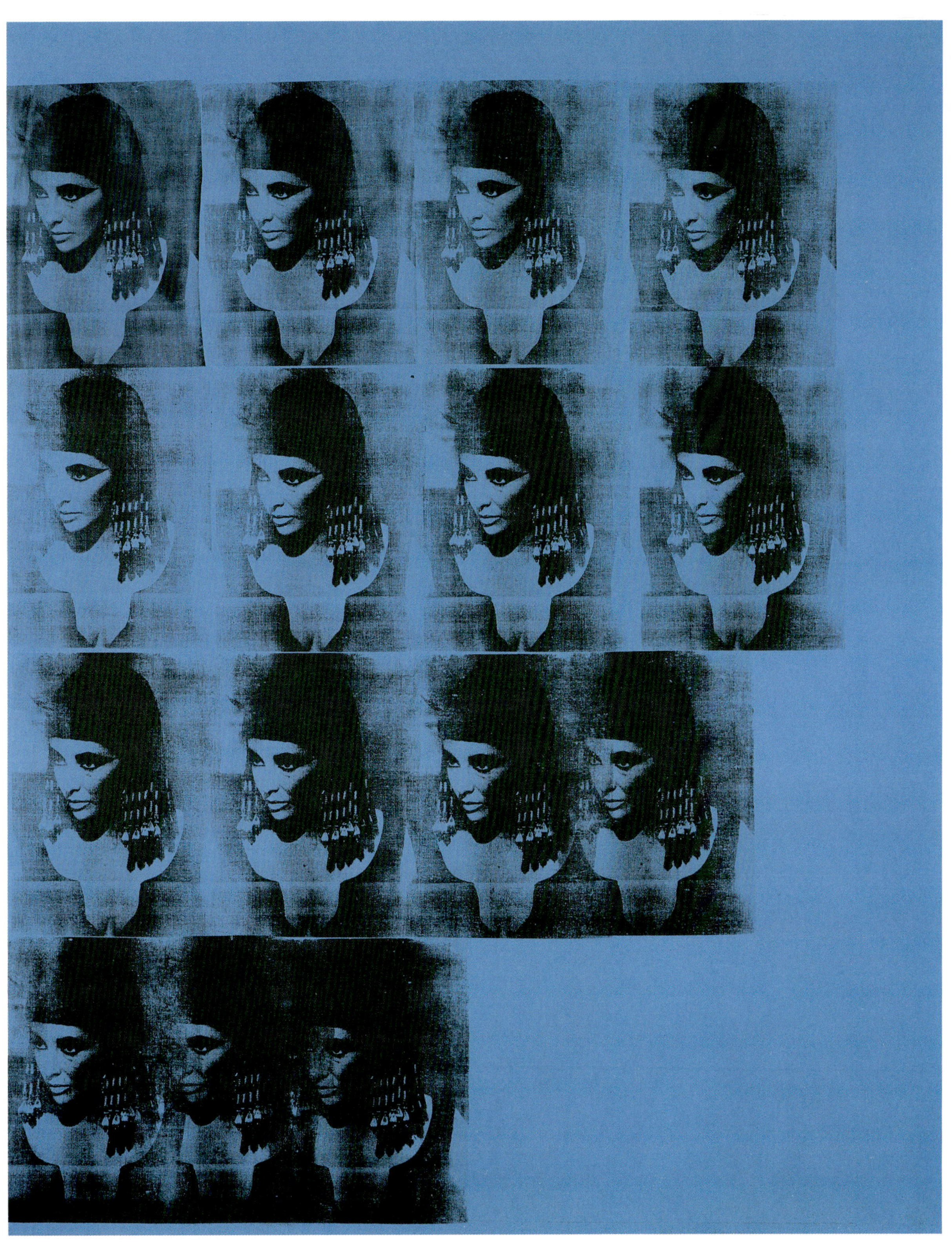

103 **Blue Liz as Cleopatra 1963** Daros Collection, Switzerland

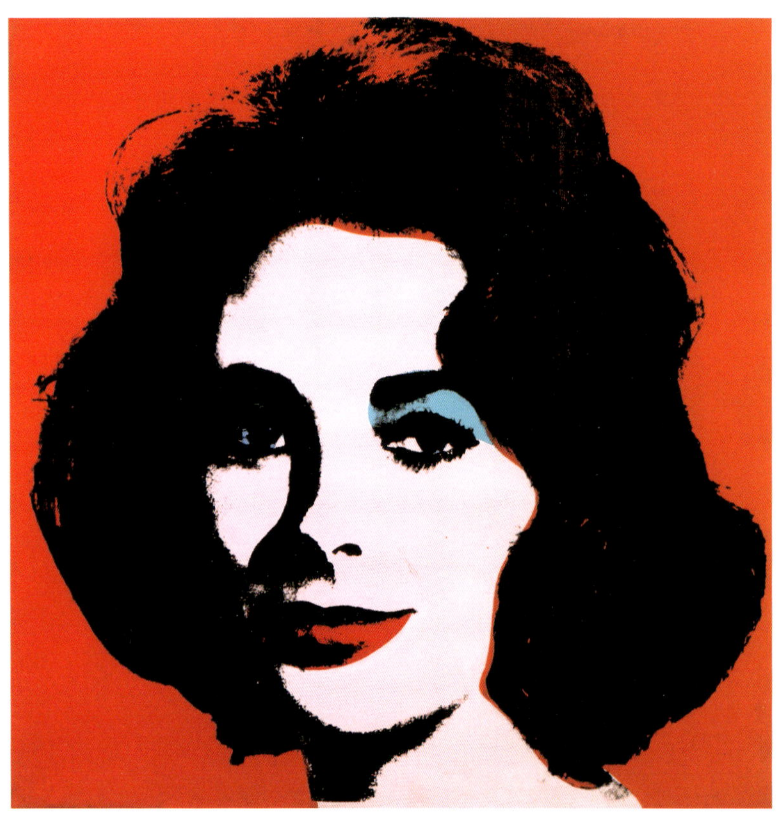

103a **Liz** **1963** Mrs. and Mr. Irving Blum

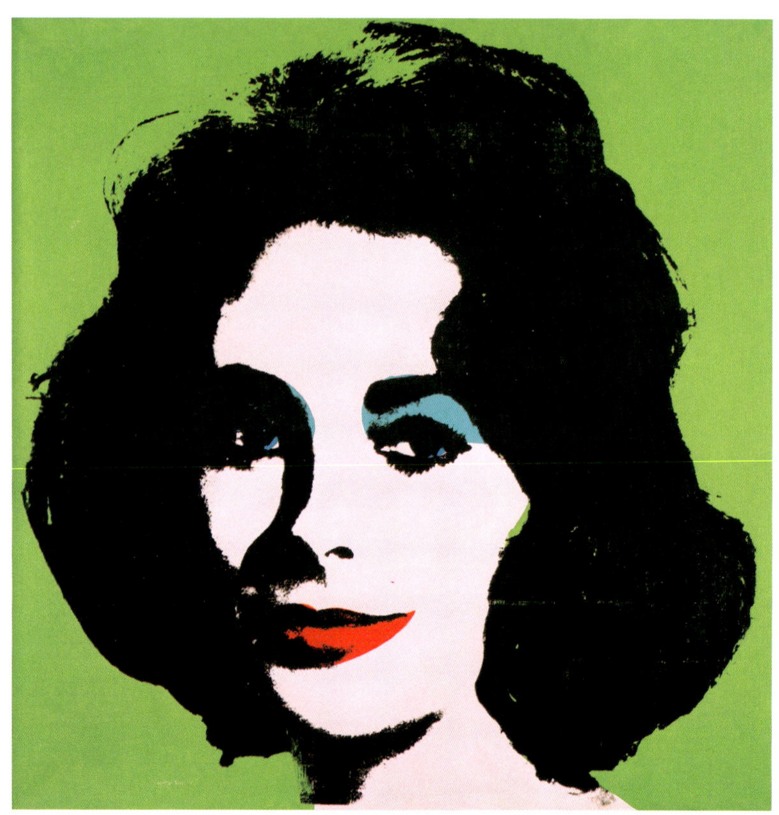

103b **Liz** **1963** Mrs. and Mr. Irving Blum

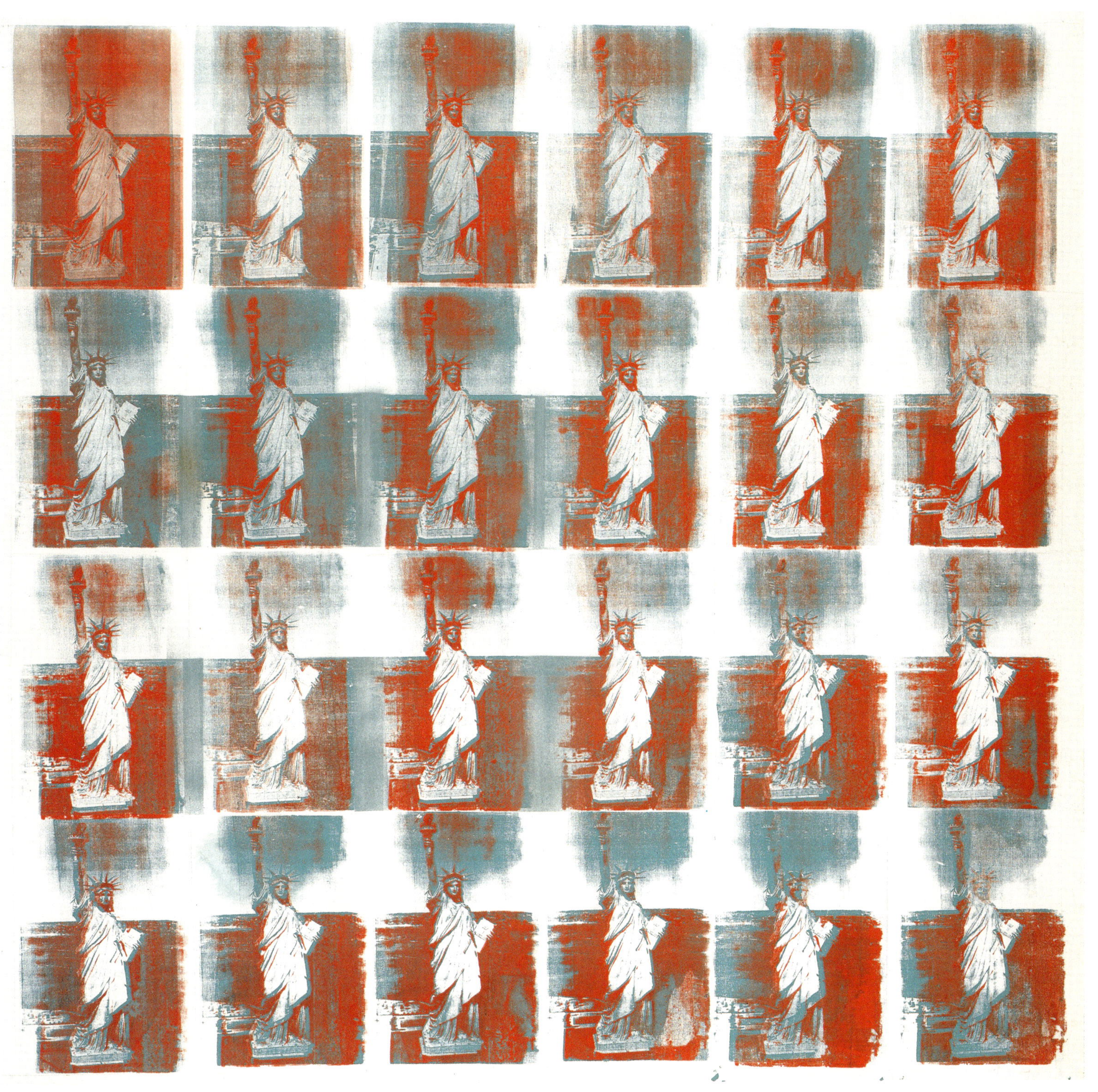

104 Statue of Liberty 1963 Daros Collection, Switzerland

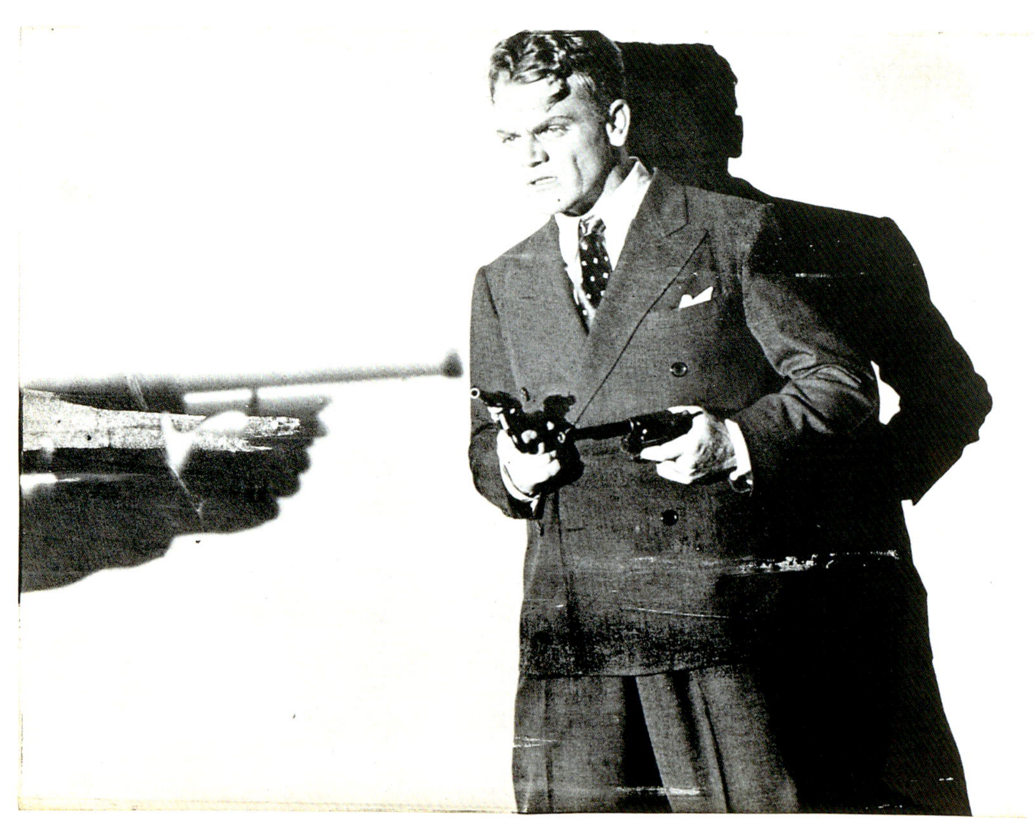

105 **Cagney** **1964** Collection Froehlich, Stuttgart

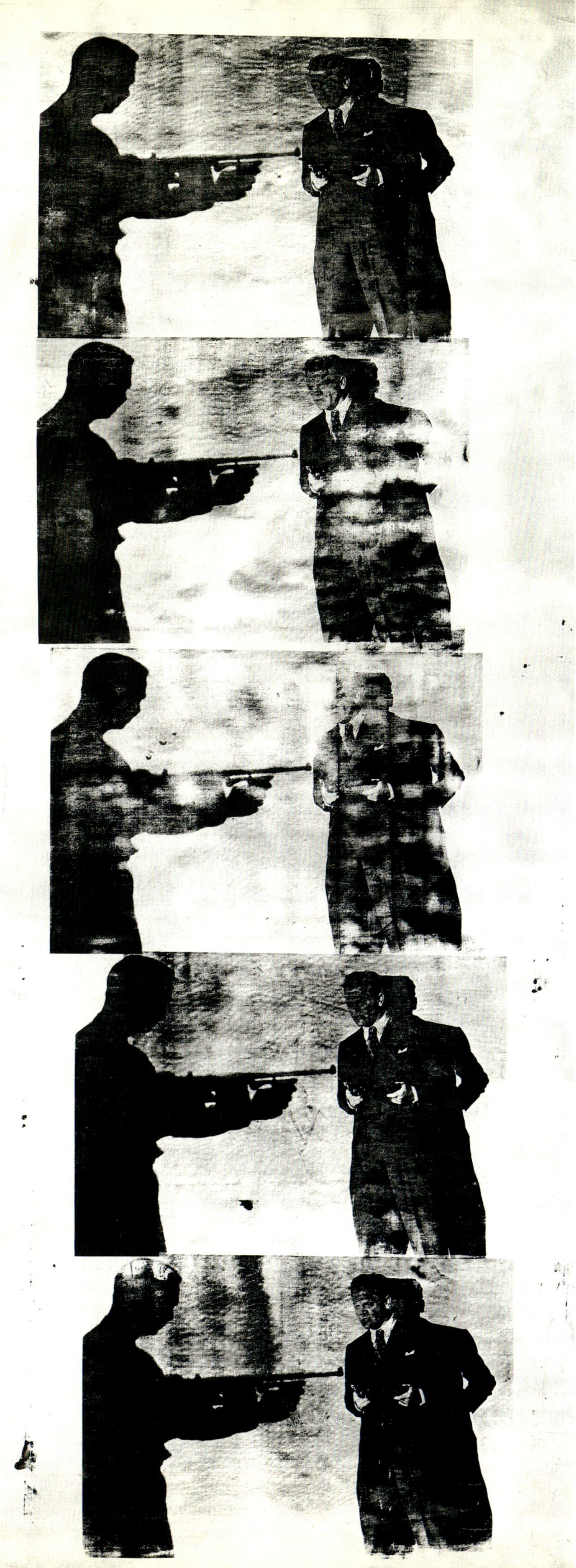

106 **Cagney 1962**
Stiftung Sammlung Marx,
Hamburger Bahnhof –
Museum für Gegenwart, Berlin

First exhibition of *Elvis* paintings, Ferus Gallery, Los Angeles, September 1963

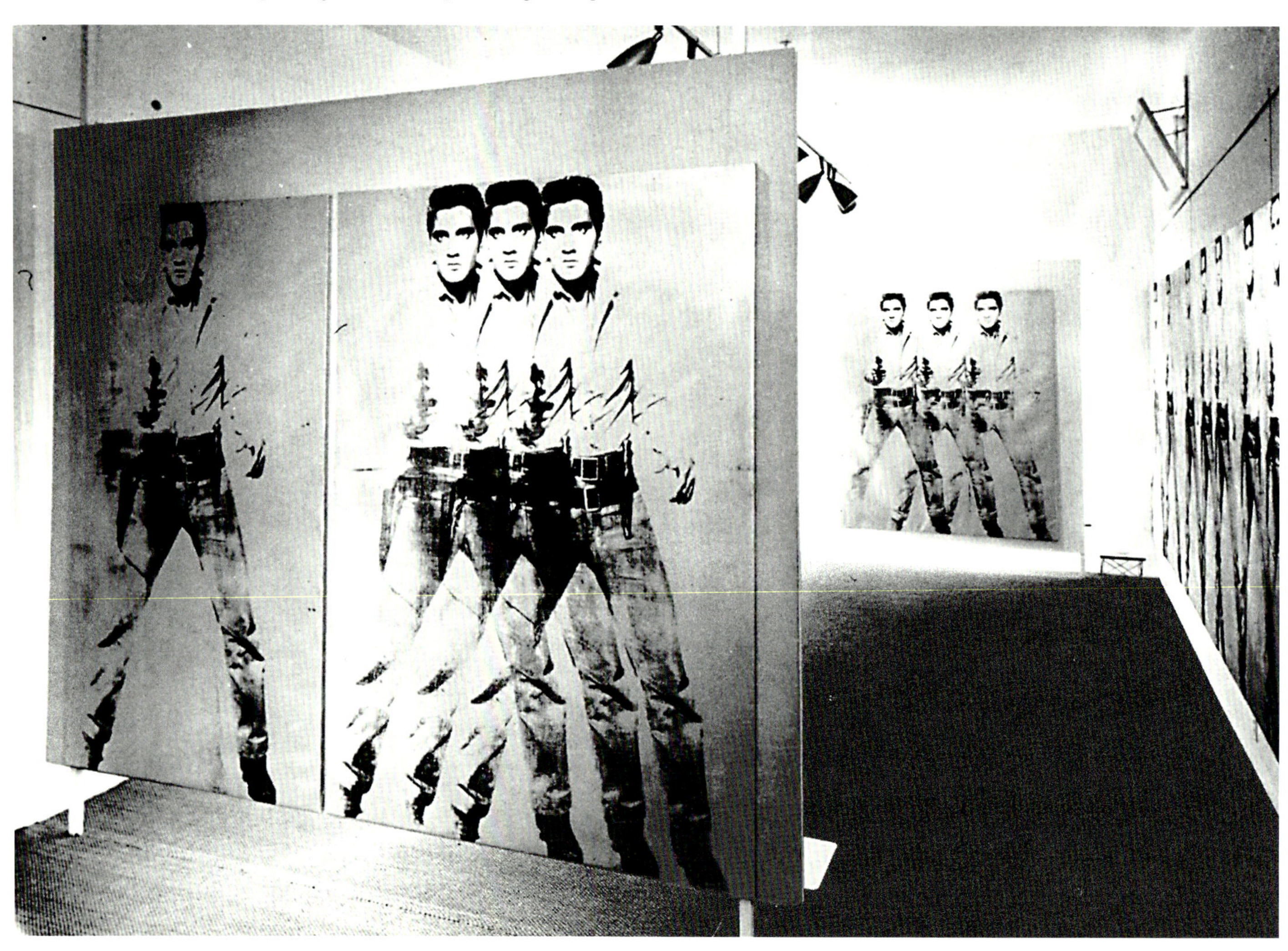

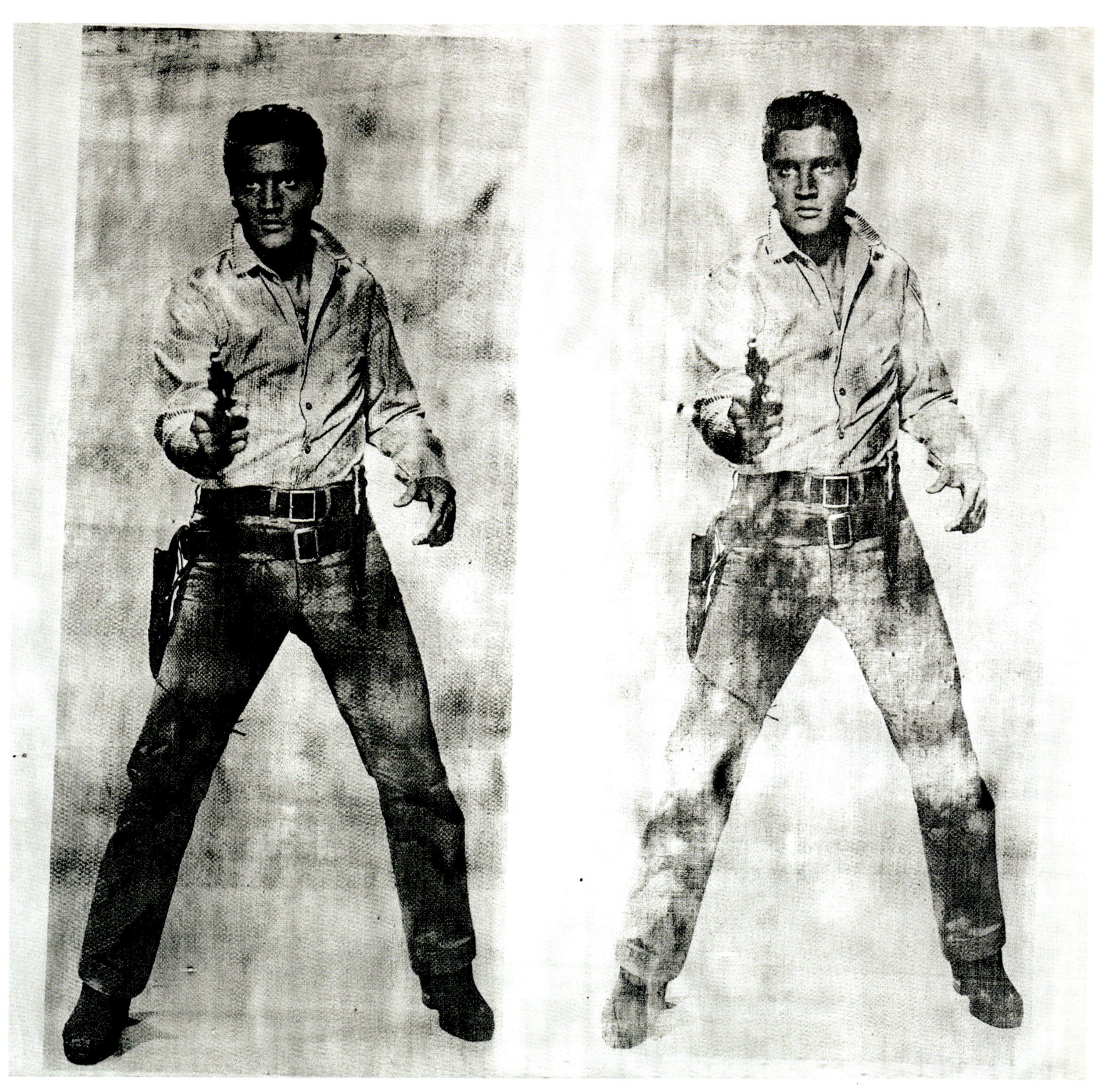

107 **Double Elvis** **1963** Stiftung Sammlung Marx, Hamburger Bahnhof – Museum für Gegenwart, Berlin

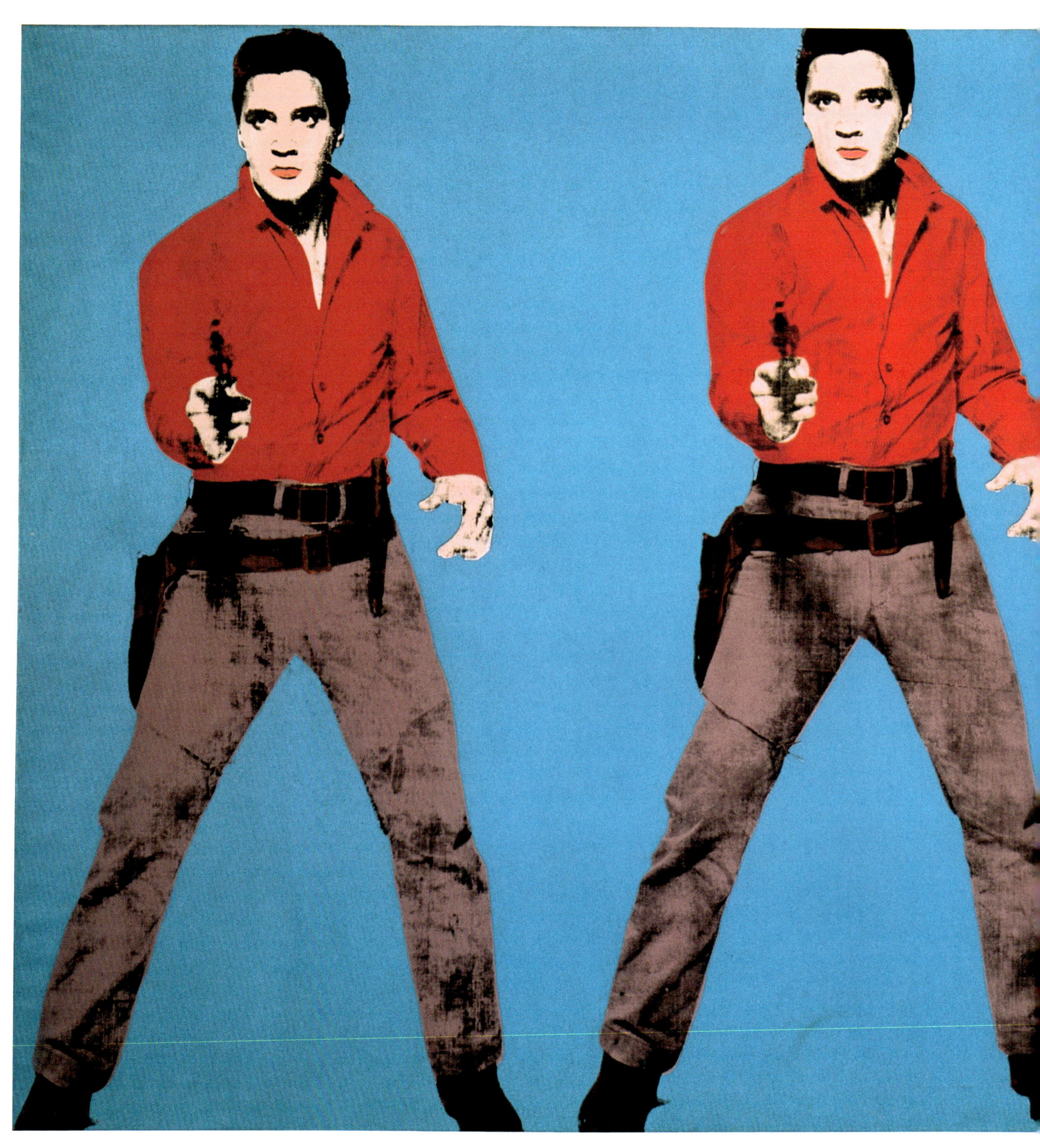

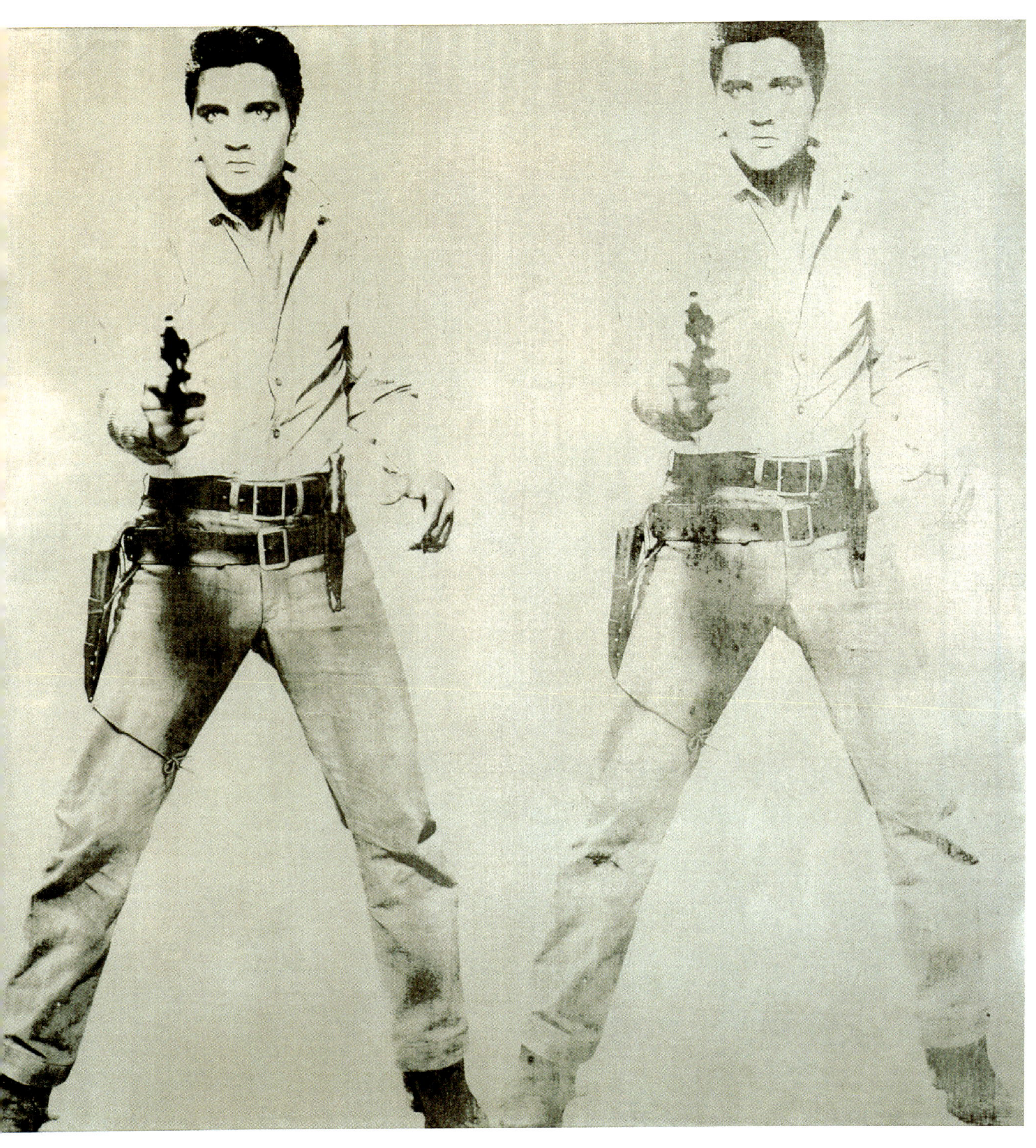

108 Elvis I and II 1964 Art Gallery of Ontario, Toronto • Gift from the Women's Committee Fund, 1966

109 129 Die in Jet (Plane Crash) 1962
Museum Ludwig, Köln*

FINAL★★ 5¢ **New York Mirror** 

WEATHER: Fair with little change in temperature.

Vol. 37, No 296 MONDAY, JUNE 4, 1962 C

129 DIE

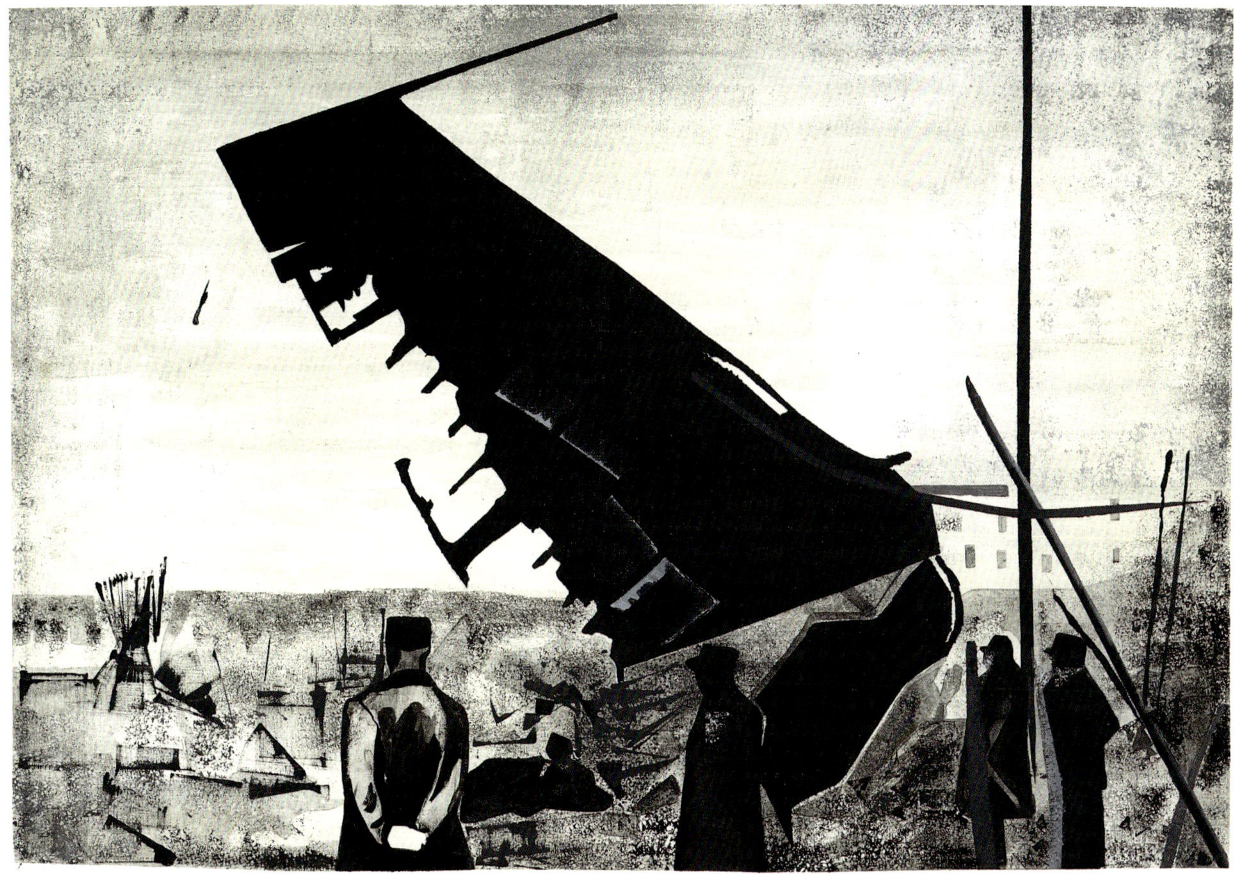

(UPI RADIOTELEphoto)

IN JET!

110 Woman Suicide 1963
Kunstsammlung Nordrhein-Westfalen, Düsseldorf

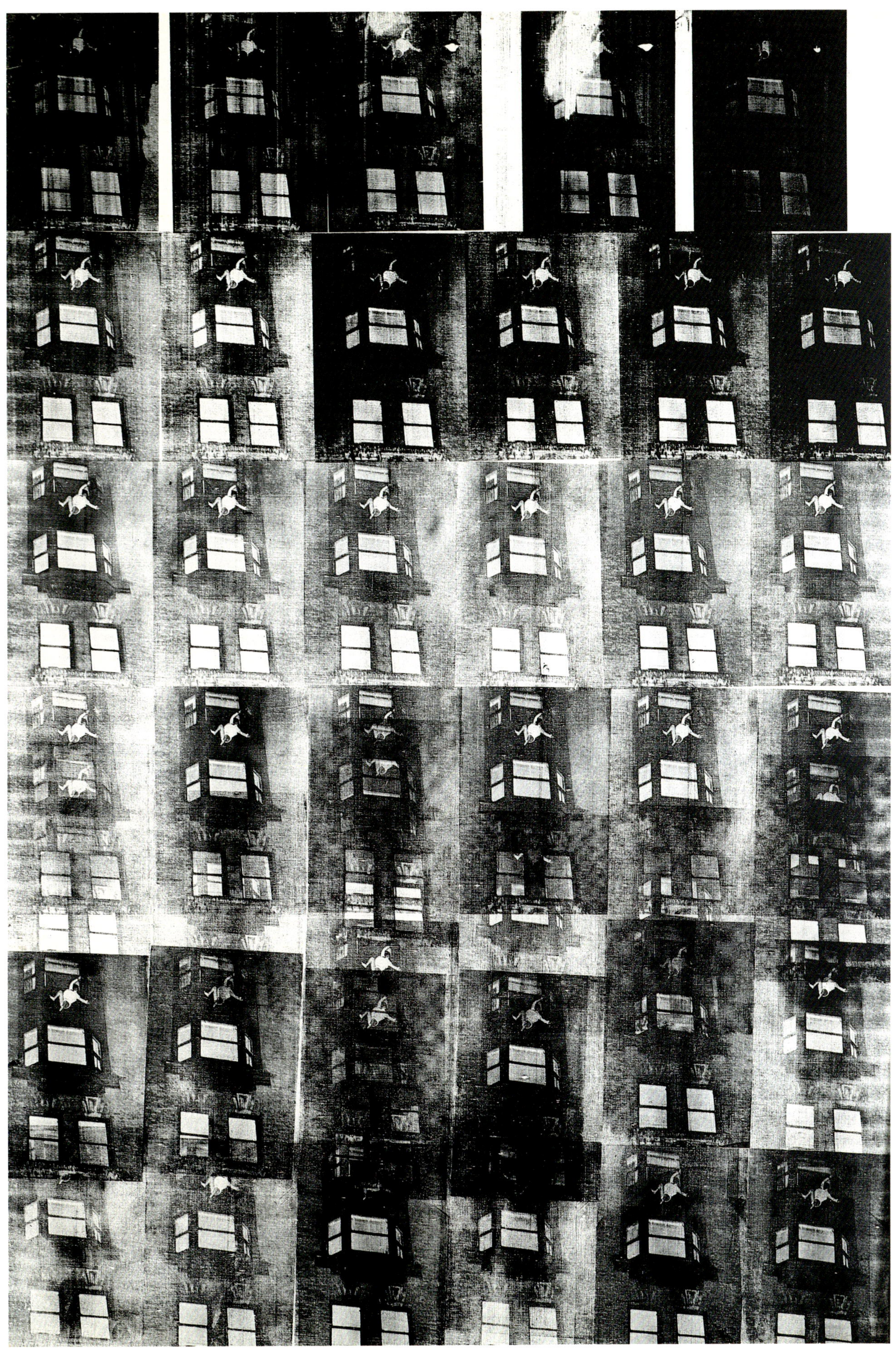

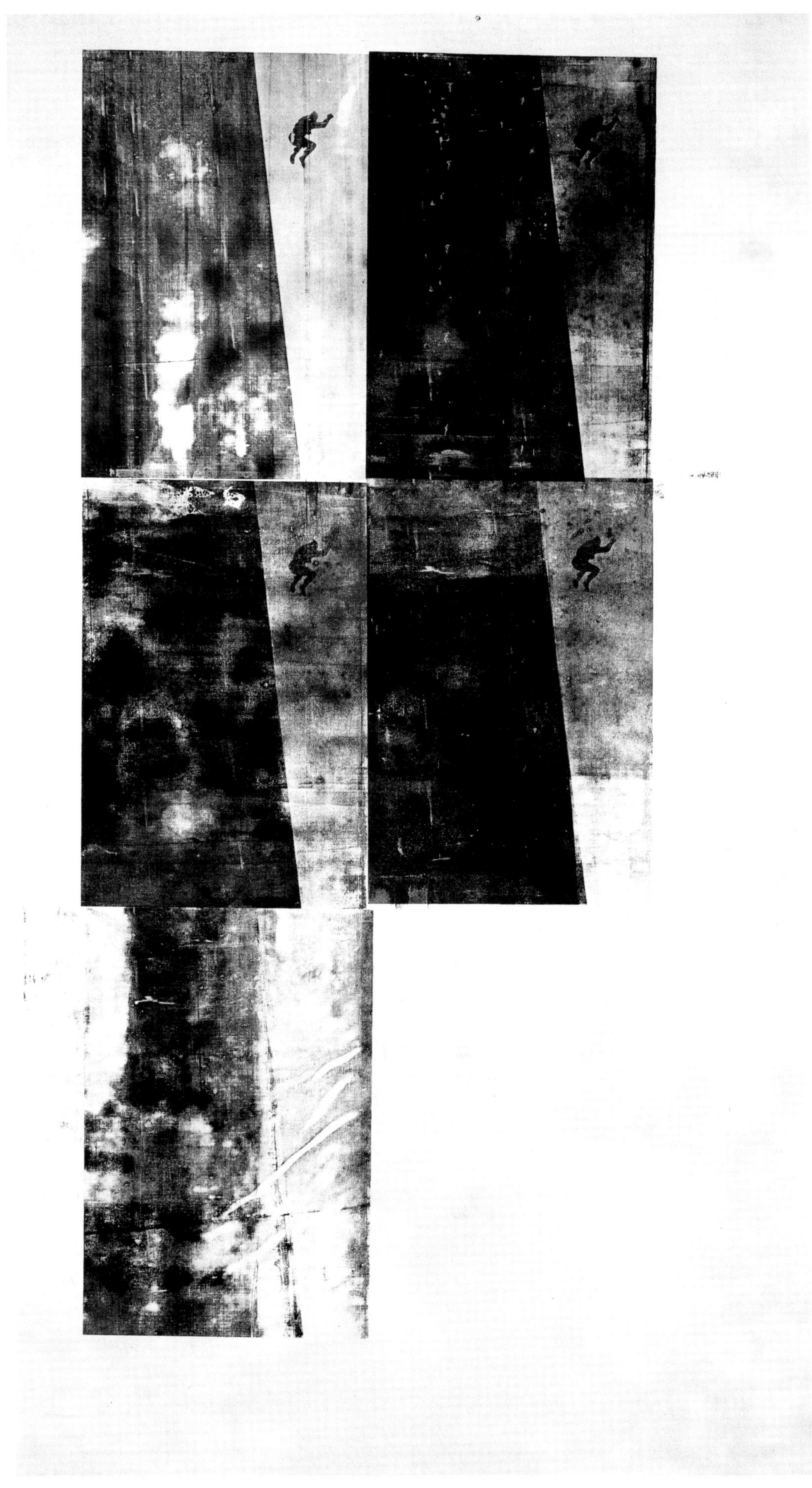

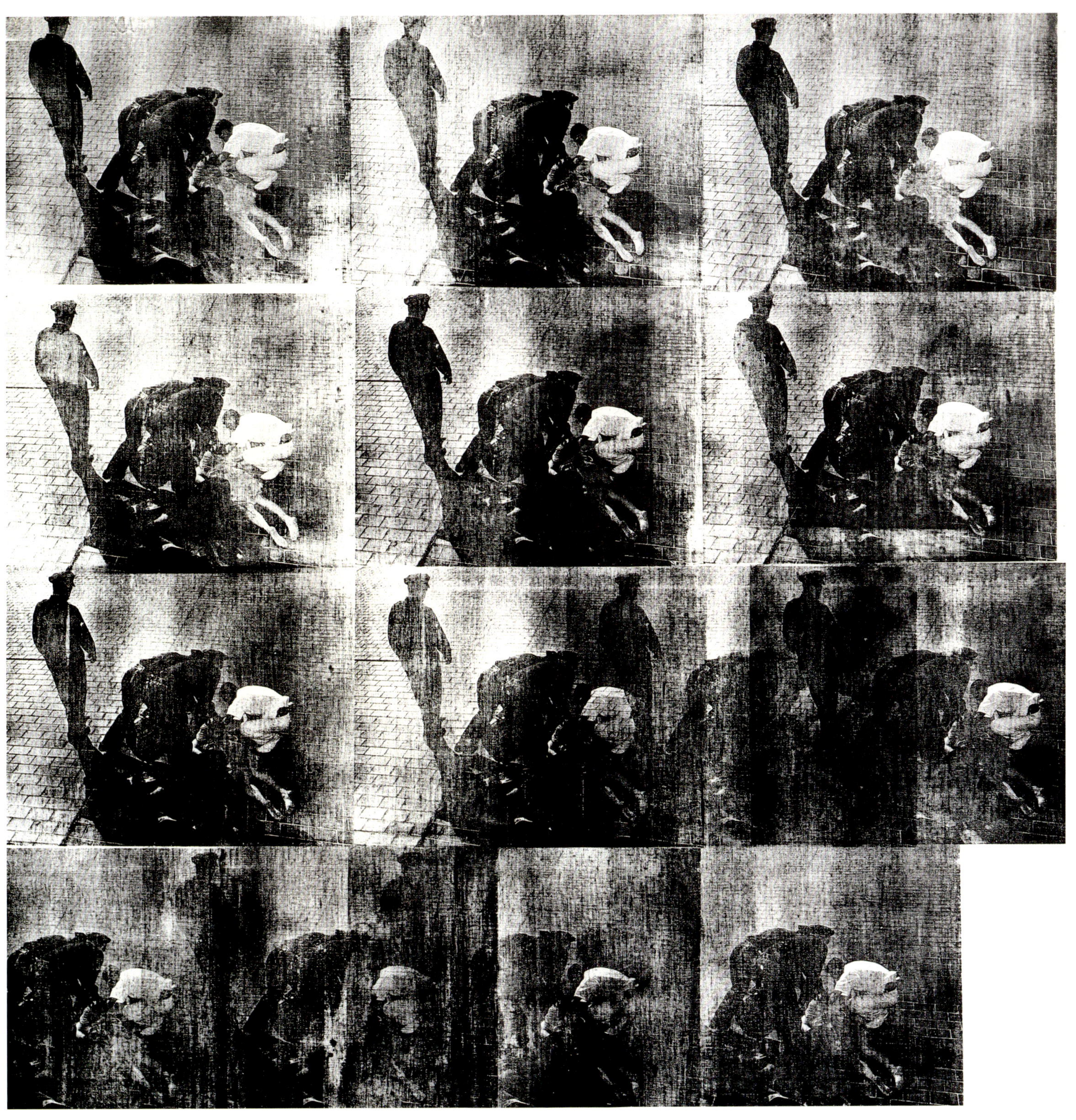

◂ 111 **Suicide (Silver Jumping Man) 1963**
Daros Collection, Switzerland

112 **Bellevue II 1963** Stedelijk Museum, Amsterdam

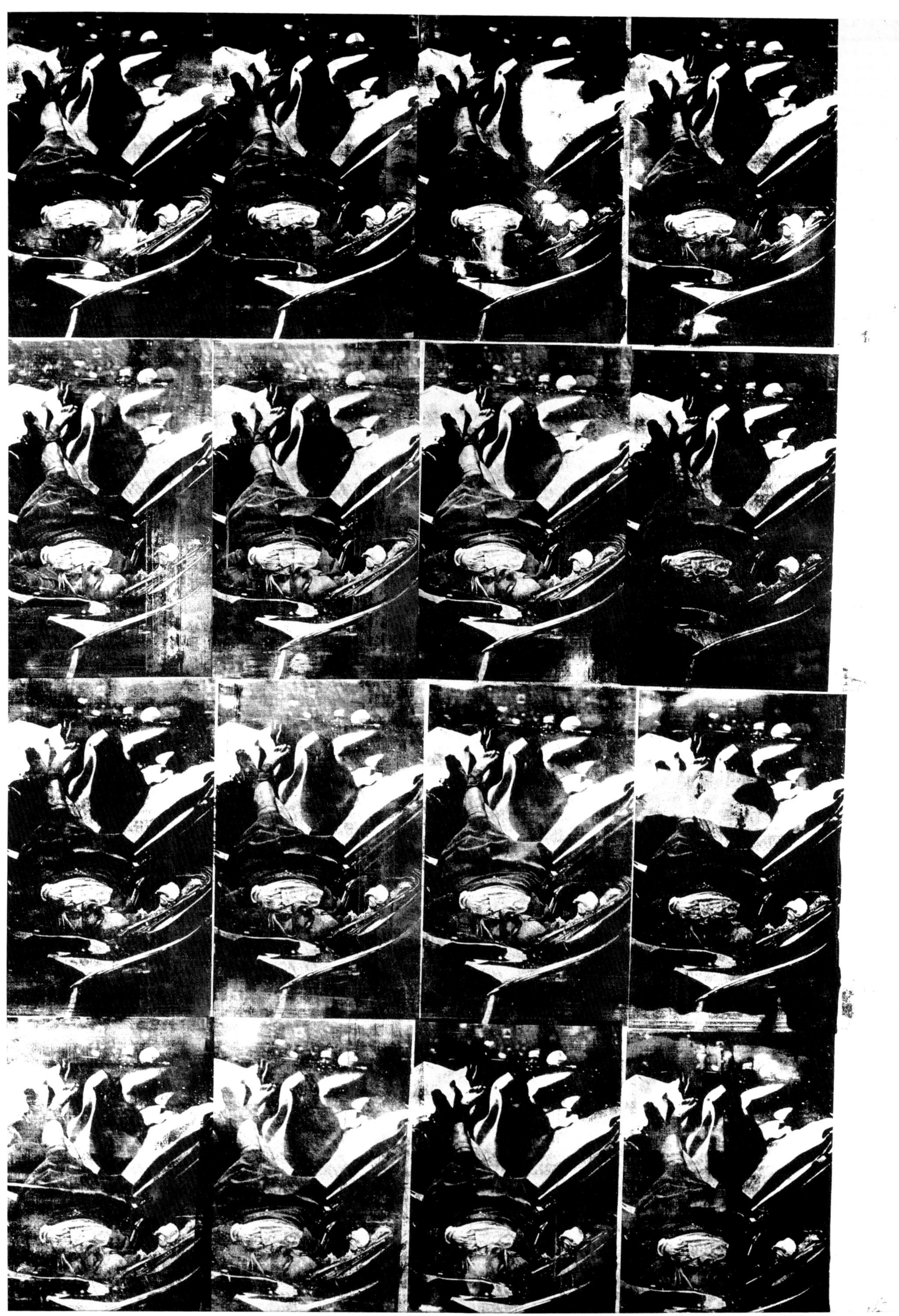

113 Suicide (Fallen Body) 1963 Private collection; Courtesy Doris Ammann

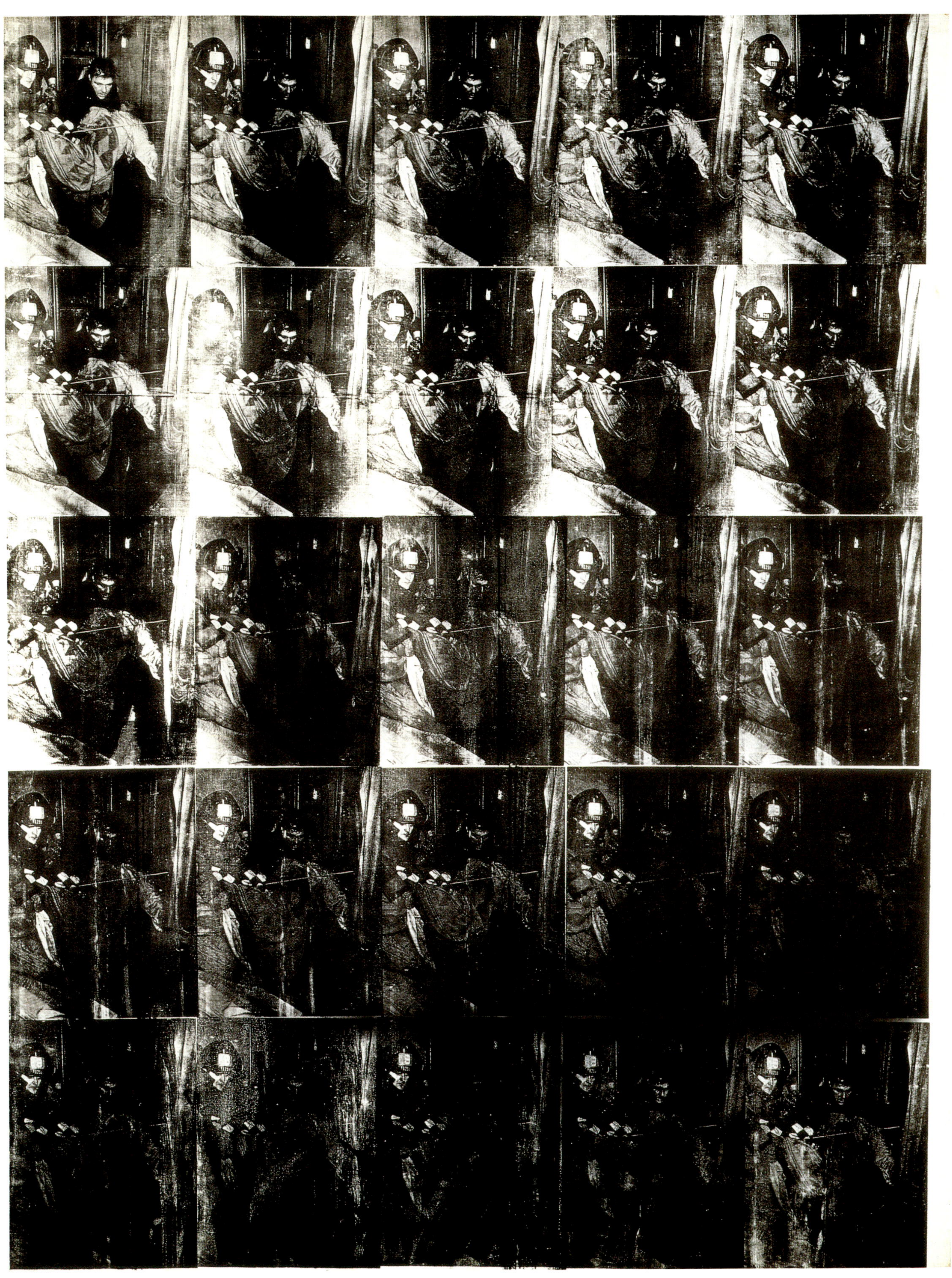

114 Black and White Disaster 1962 Los Angeles County Museum of Art • Gift of Castelli & Ferus galleries through the Contemporary Art Council

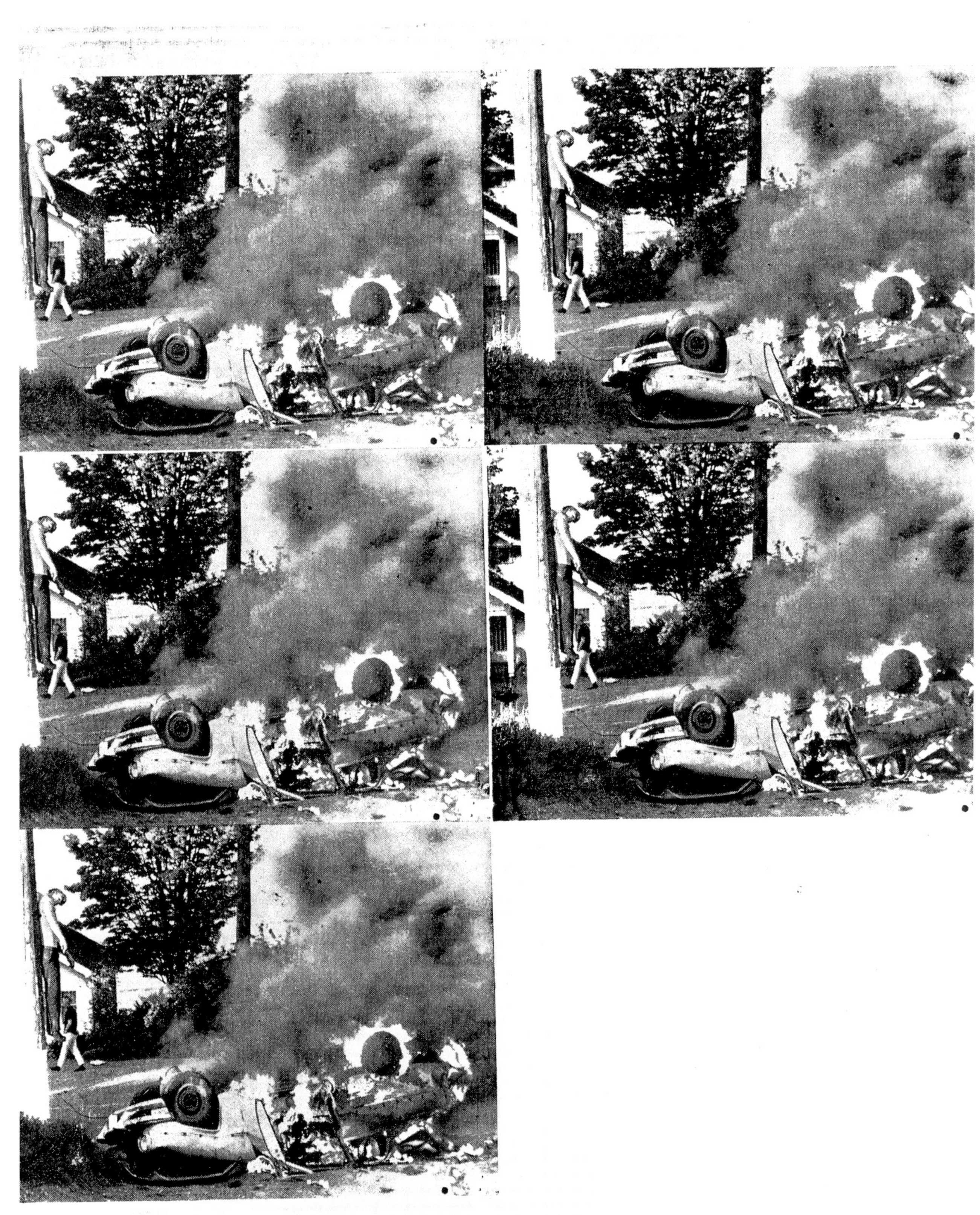

115 White Burning Car III 1963 The Andy Warhol Museum, Pittsburgh
Founding Collection, Contribution Dia Center for the Arts

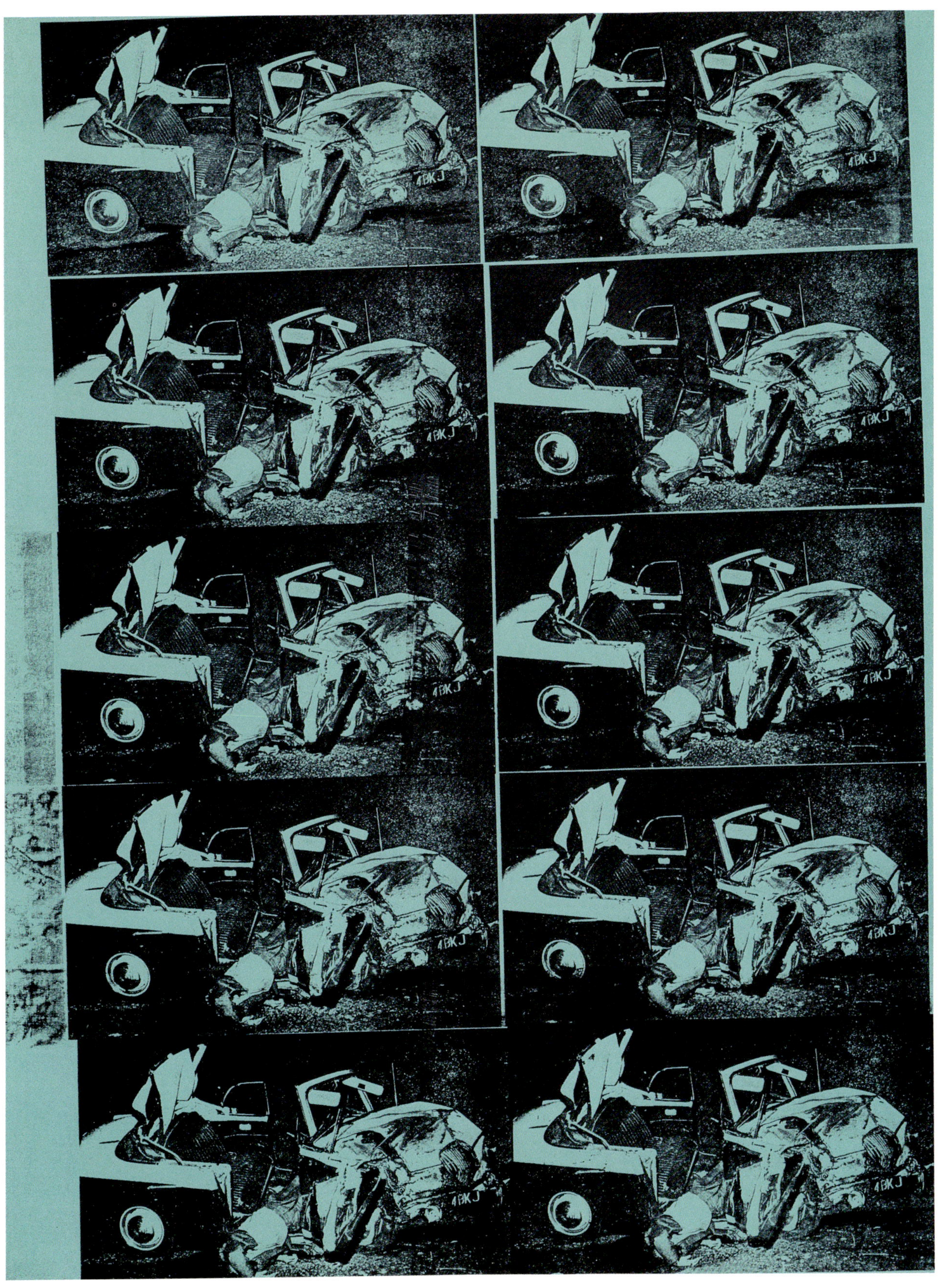

116 **Green Disaster 10 Times** **1963** Museum für Moderne Kunst, Frankfurt am Main [Former Ströher Collection]

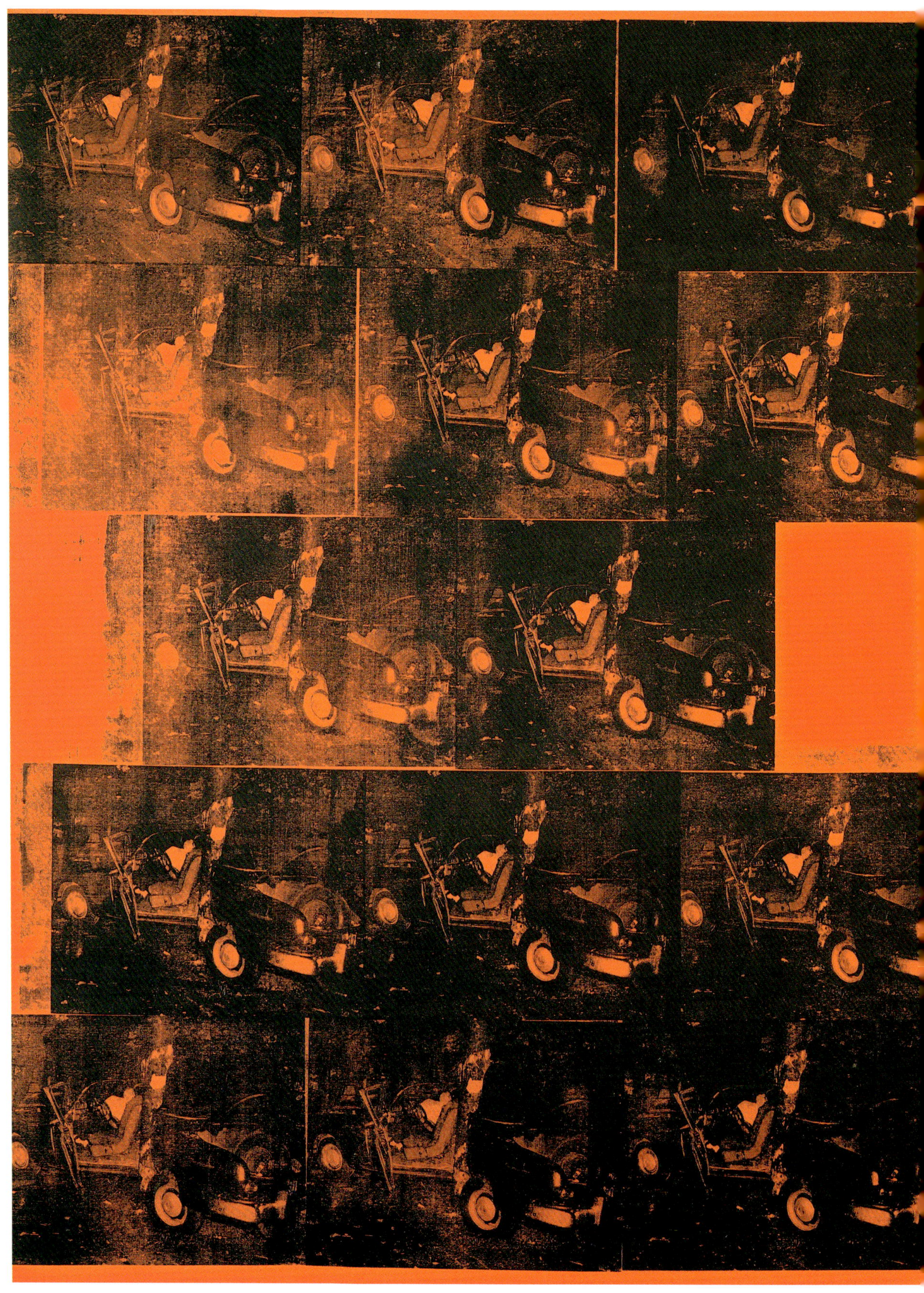

117 **Orange Car Crash Fourteen Times 1963** The Museum of Modern Art, New York • Gift of Philip Johnson, 1991

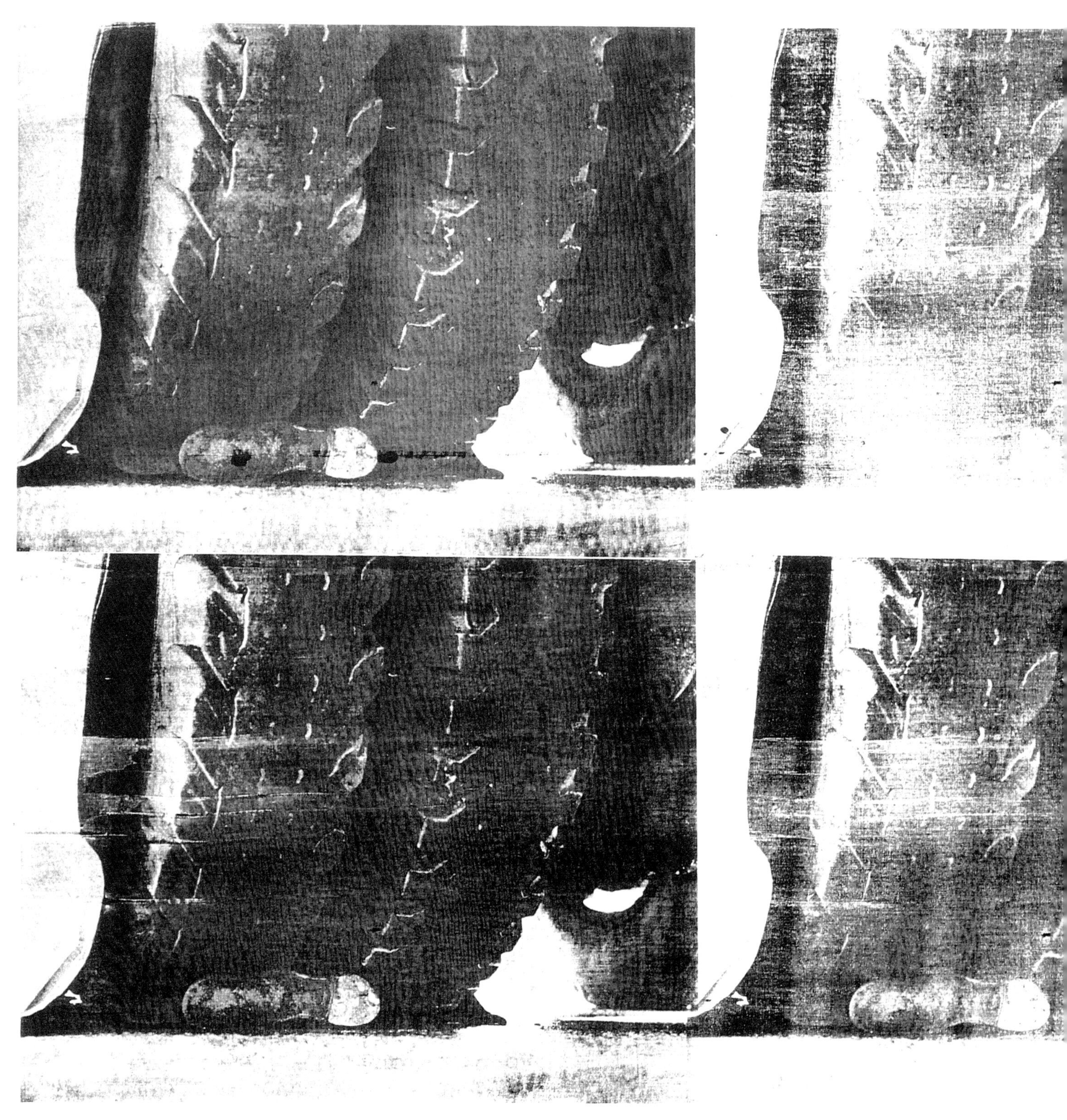

118 Foot and Tire 1963 The Andy Warhol Museum, Pittsburgh • Founding Collection, Contribution Dia Center for the Arts

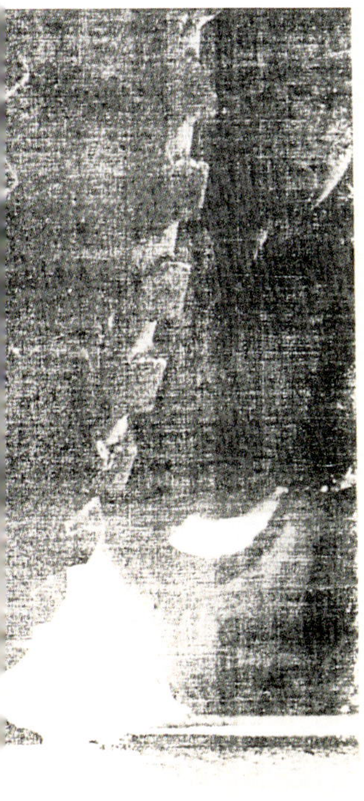

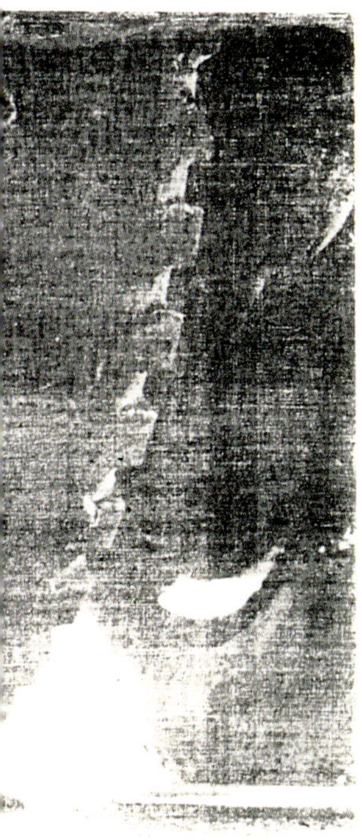

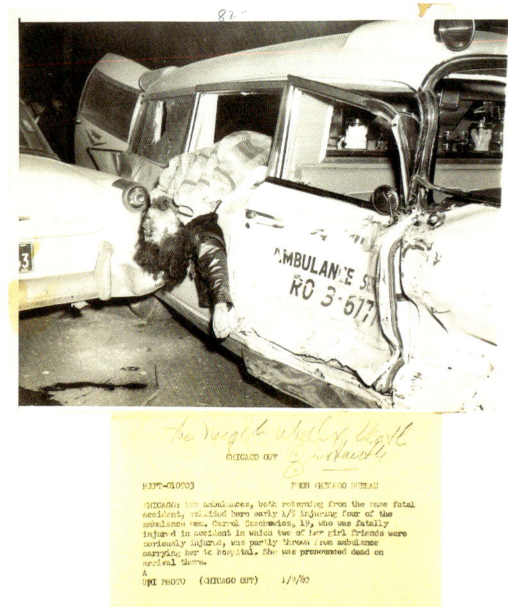

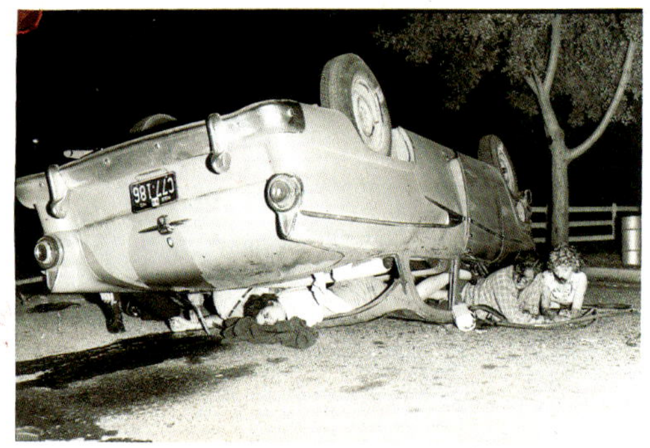

CHICAGO OUT

HXPT-010903 FROM CHICAGO BUREAU

CHICAGO: [illegible] ambulances, both returning from the same fatal accident, collided here early 1/9 injuring four of the ambulance men. Carrol Czechowicz, 19, who was fatally injured in accident in which two of her girl friends were seriously injured, was partly thrown from ambulance carrying her to hospital. She was pronounced dead on arrival there.

A

UPI PHOTO (CHICAGO OUT) 1/9/60

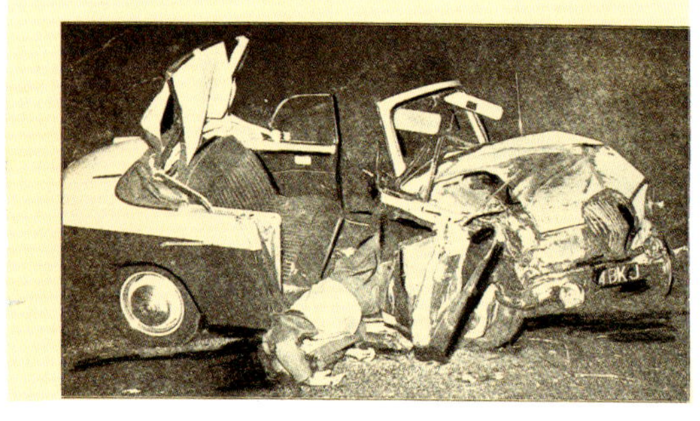

Examples of Andy Warhol's source material for three different images of *Car Crash* silkscreens.

119 Ambulance Disaster 1963
Stiftung Sammlung Marx,
Hamburger Bahnhof –
Museum für Gegenwart, Berlin

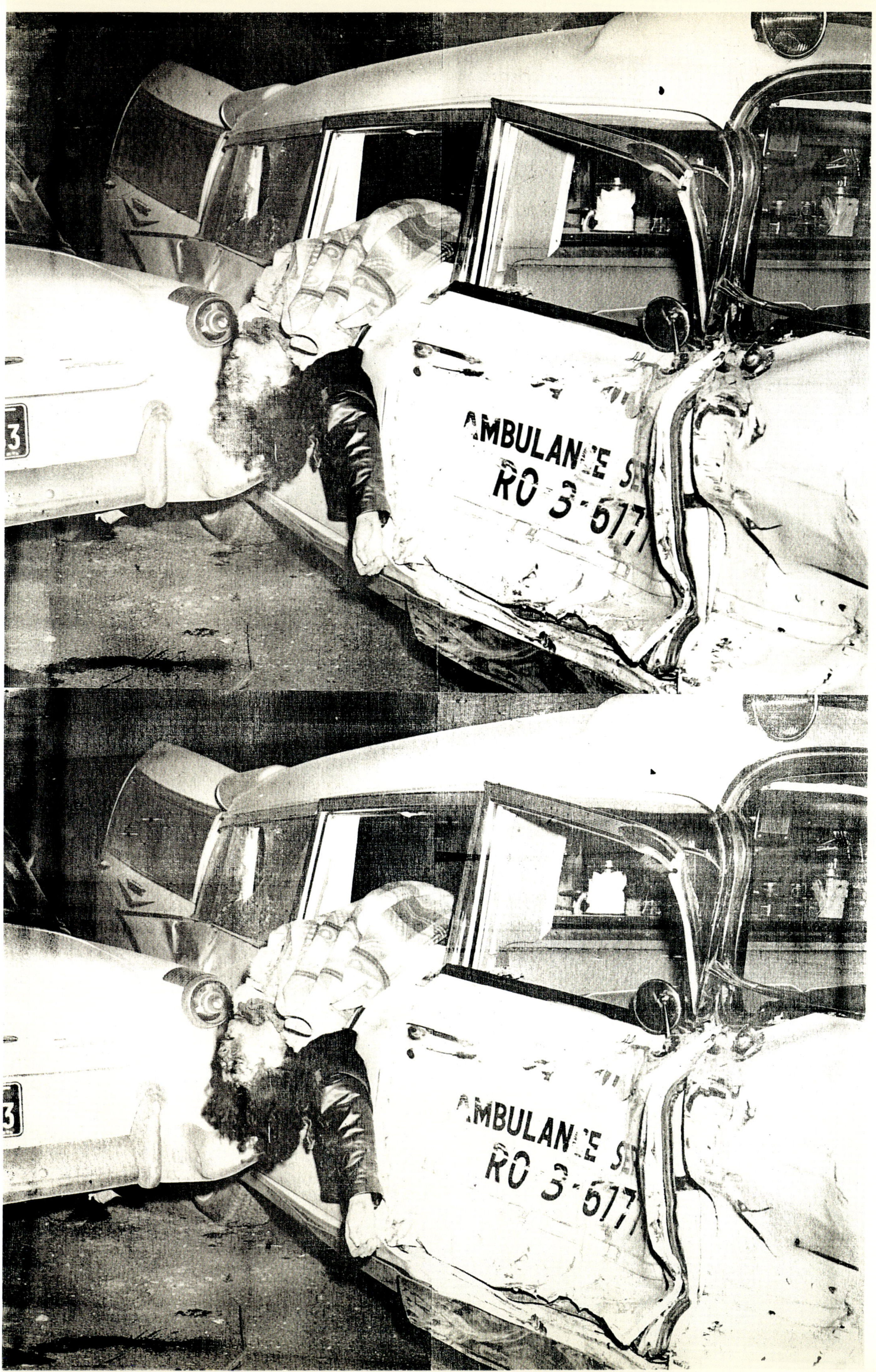

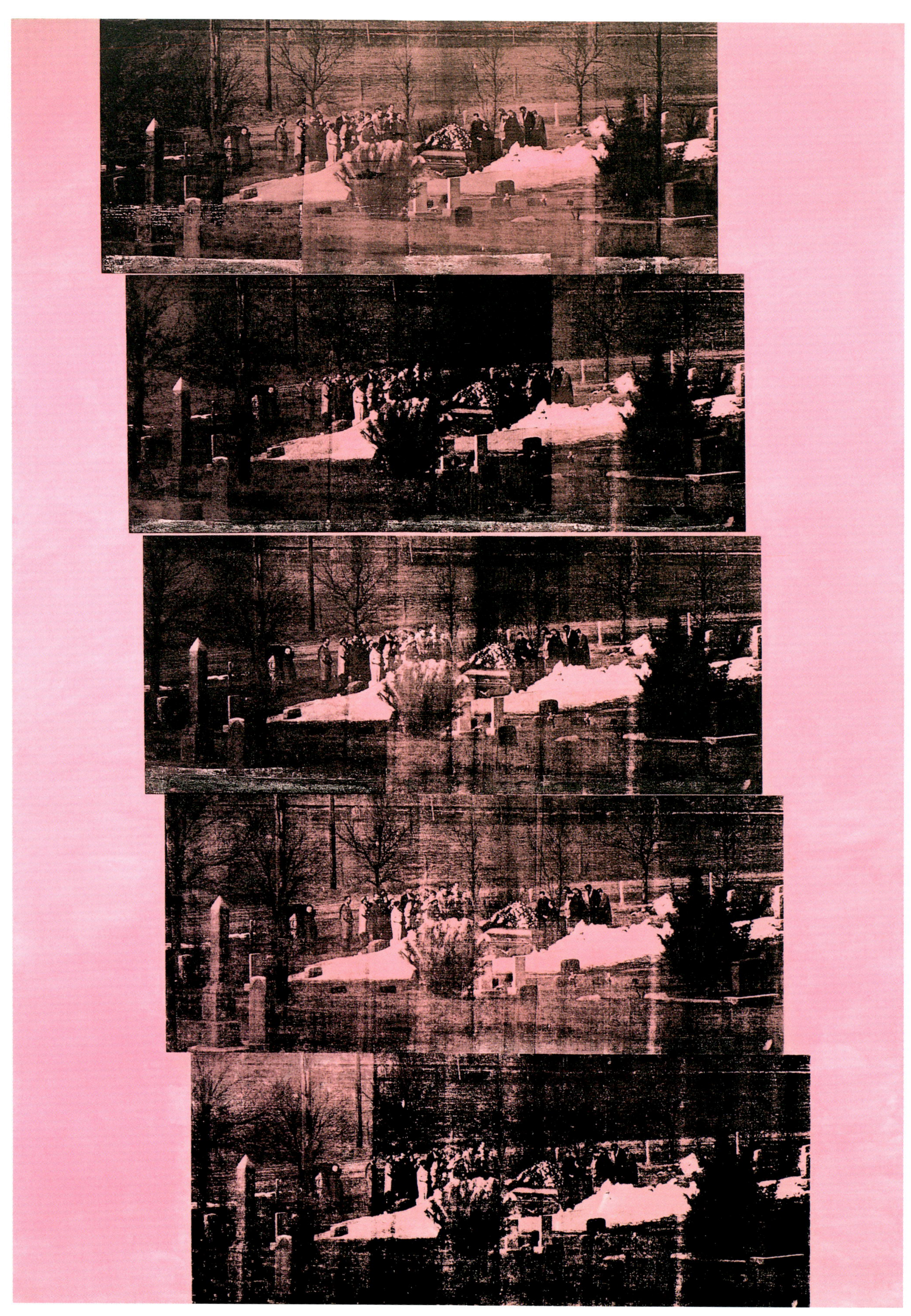

120 **Gangster Funeral** **1963** The Andy Warhol Museum, Pittsburgh • Founding Collection, Contribution Dia Center for the Arts

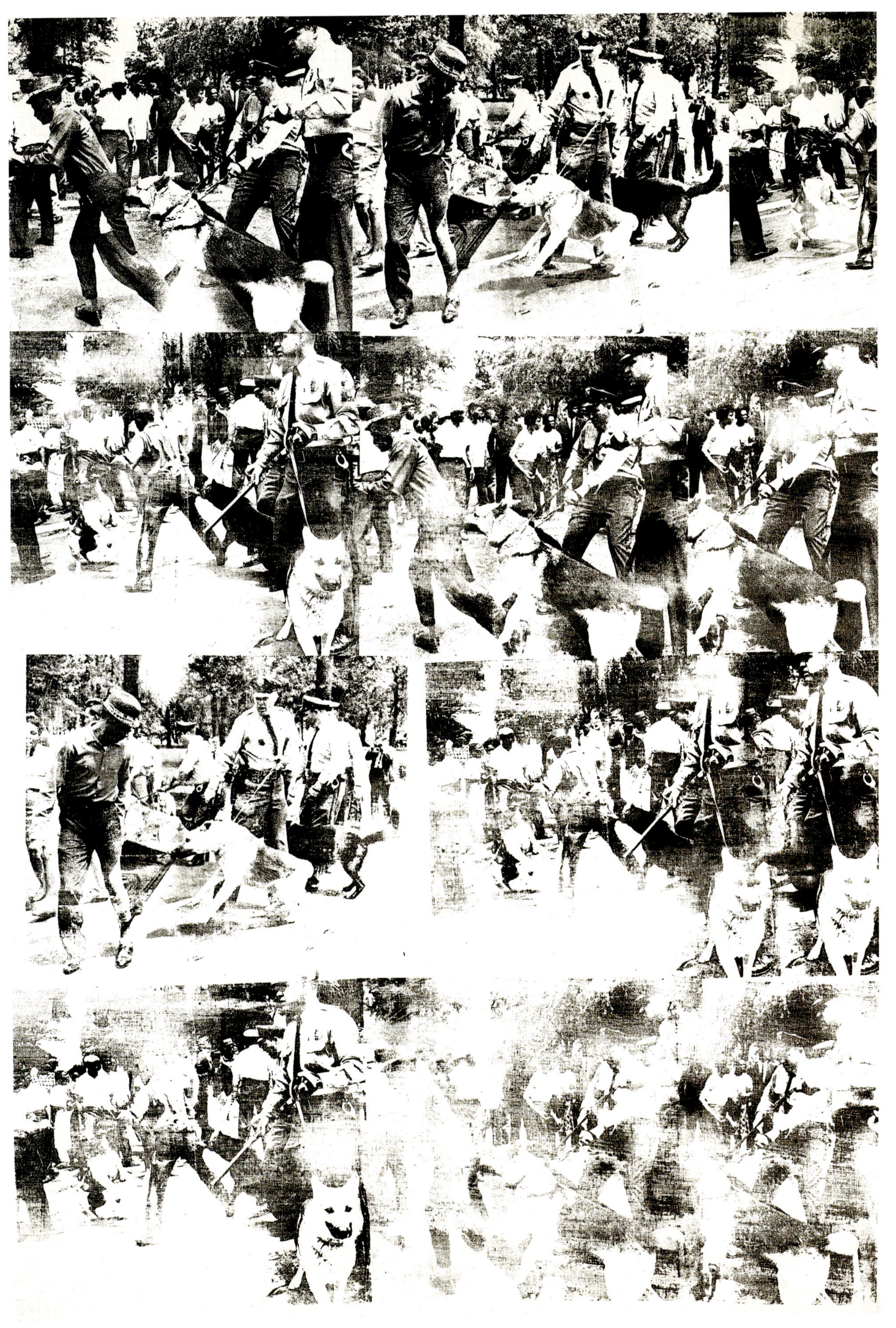

121 **Race Riot** **1963** Daros Collection, Switzerland

122 Tunafish Disaster 1963
Daros Collection, Switzerland

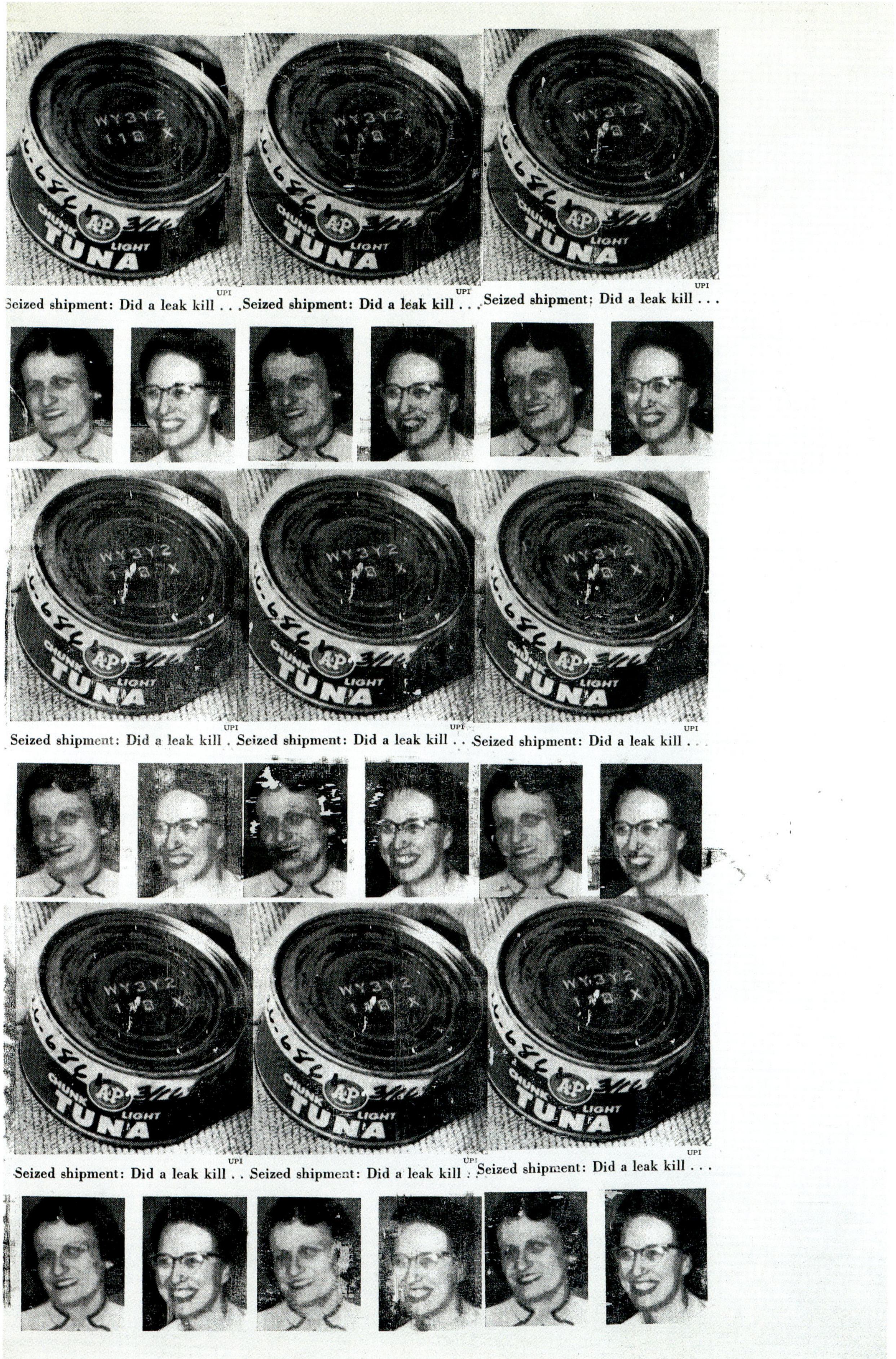

UPI
Seized shipment: Did a leak kill . . .
UPI
Seized shipment: Did a leak kill . . .
UPI
Seized shipment: Did a leak kill . . .

UPI
Seized shipment: Did a leak kill . . .
UPI
Seized shipment: Did a leak kill . . .
UPI
Seized shipment: Did a leak kill . . .

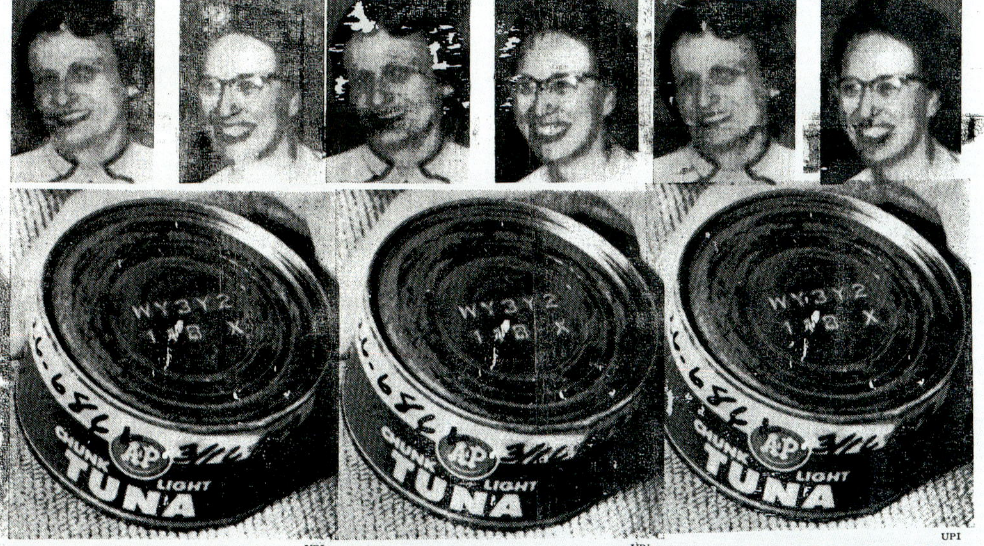

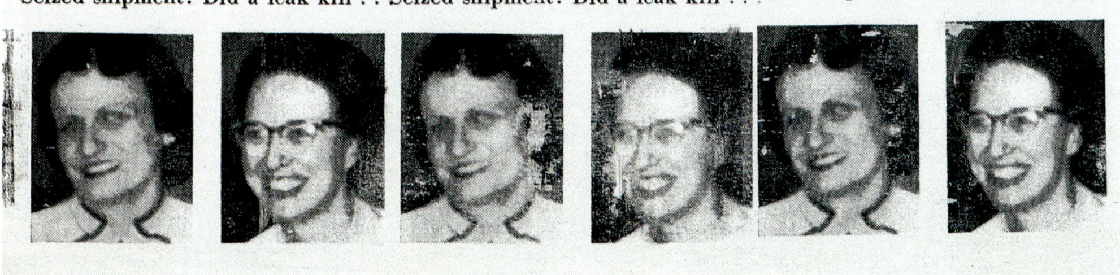

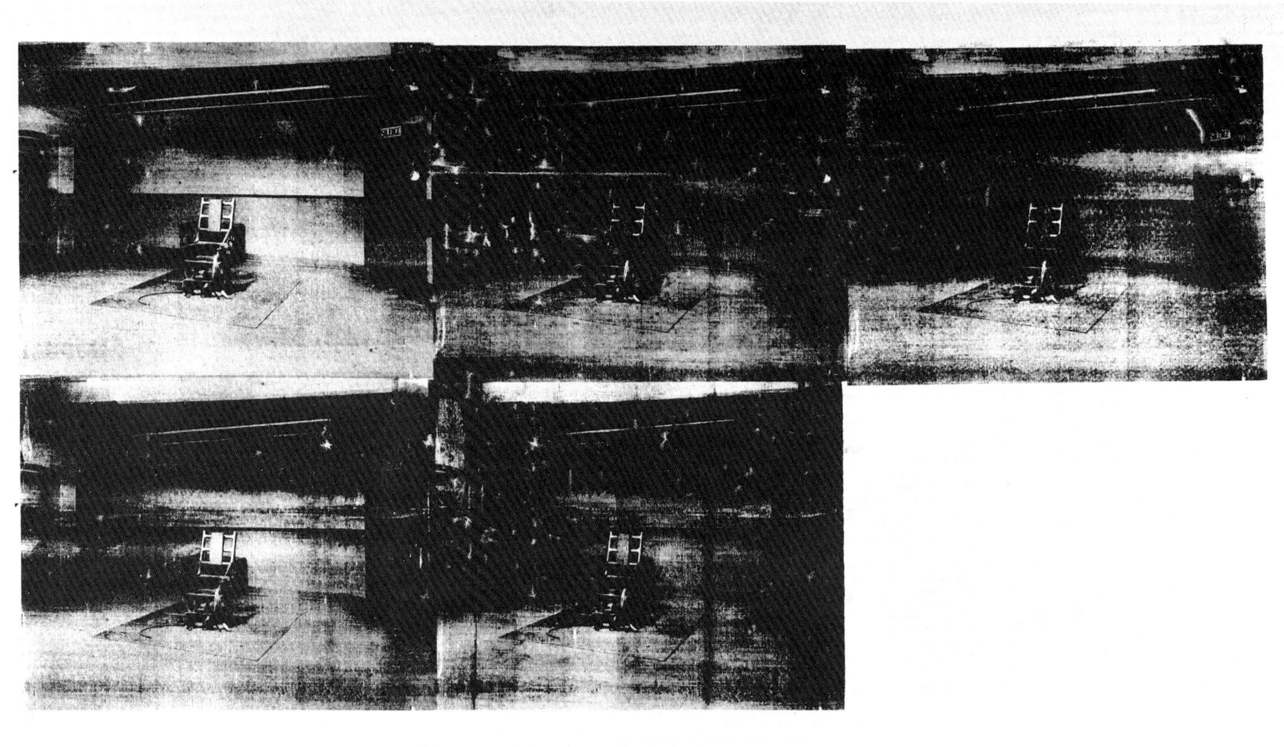

123 Silver Disaster 1964
Collection Bruno Bischofberger, Zürich

124 Twelve Electric Chairs 1964/65
Courtesy The Brant Foundation,
Greenwich, CT

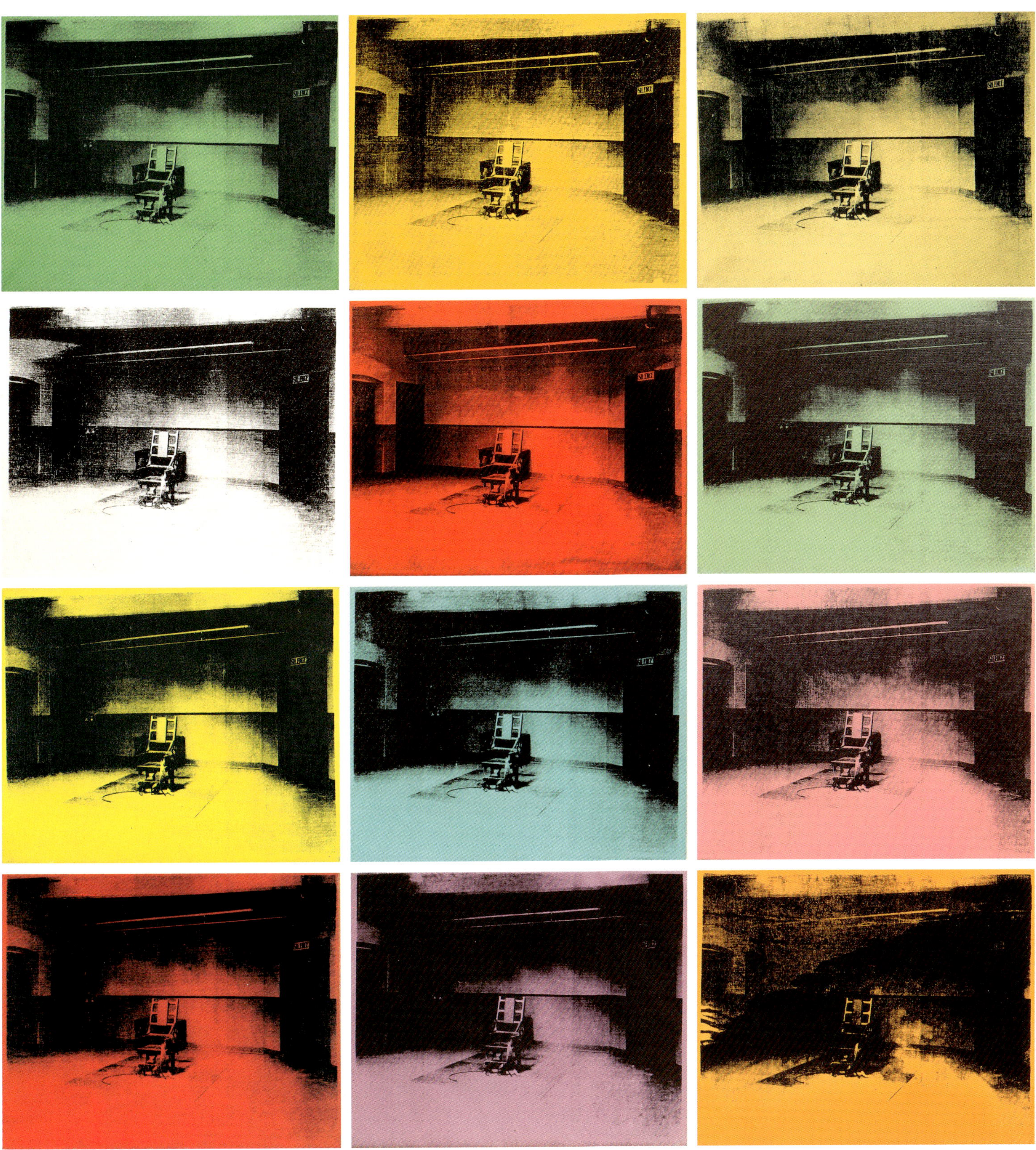

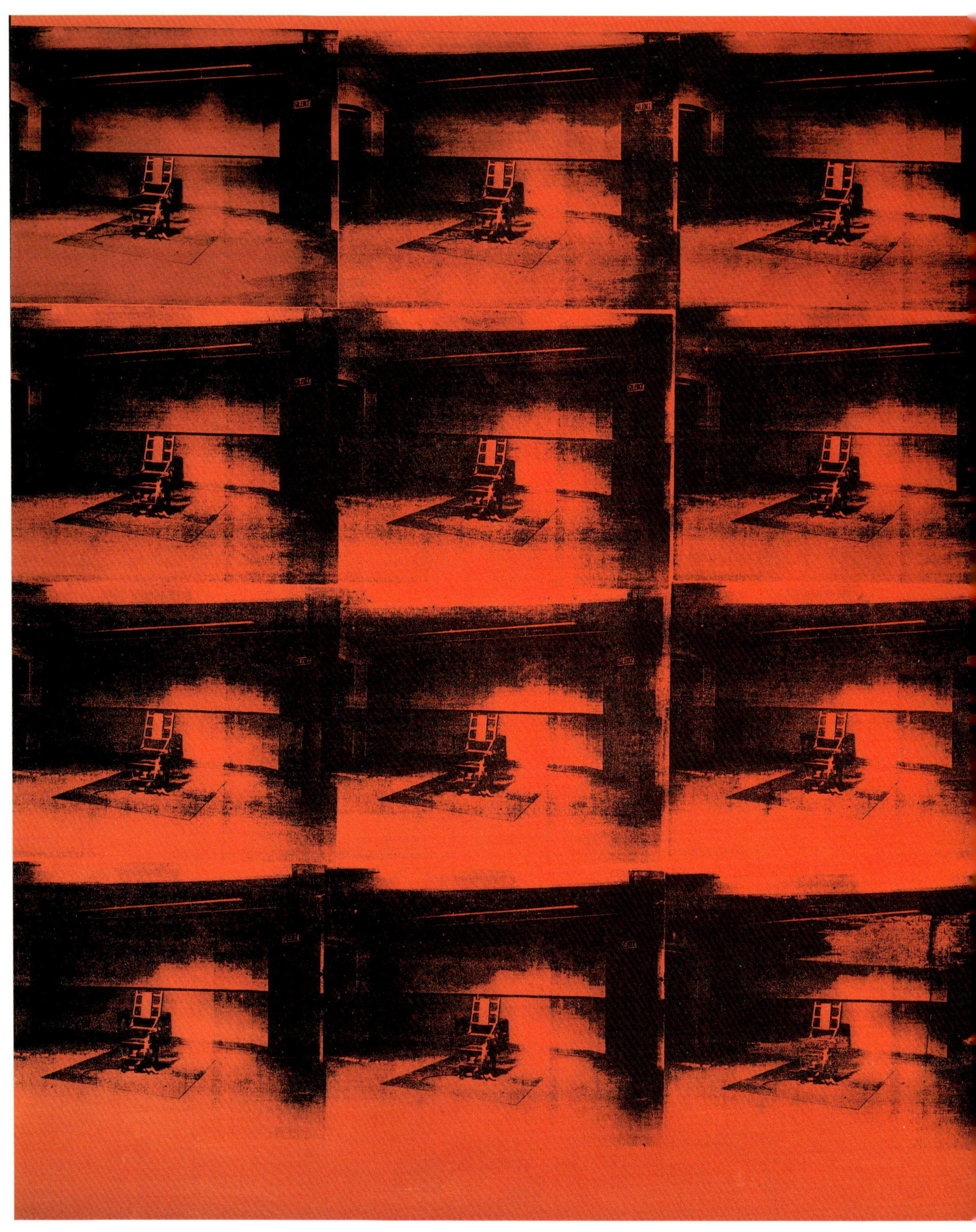

125 Red Disaster 1963, 1985 Museum of Fine Arts, Boston • Charles H. Bayley Picture and Painting Fund, 1986

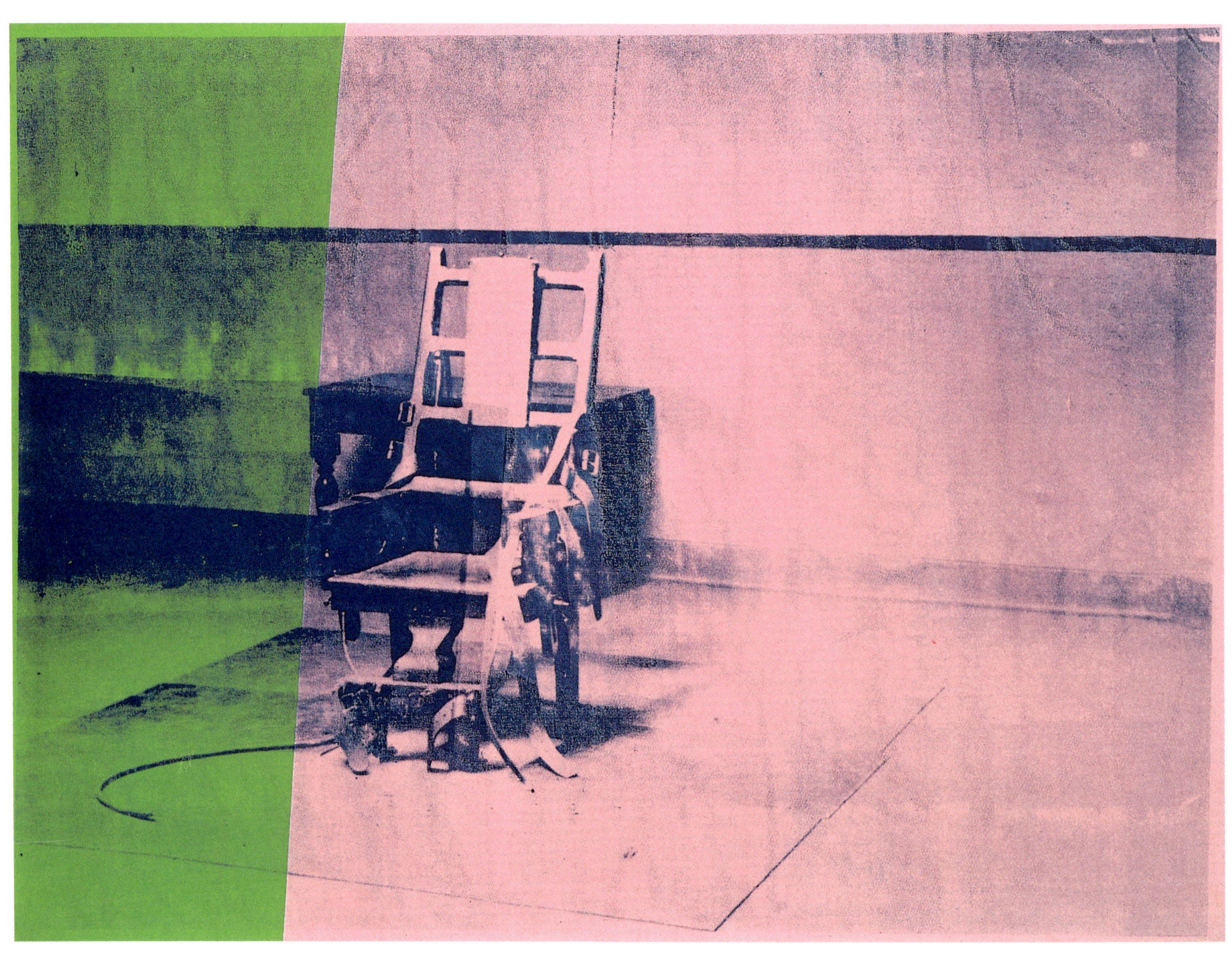

126 Big Electric Chair 1967 Collection Froehlich, Stuttgart

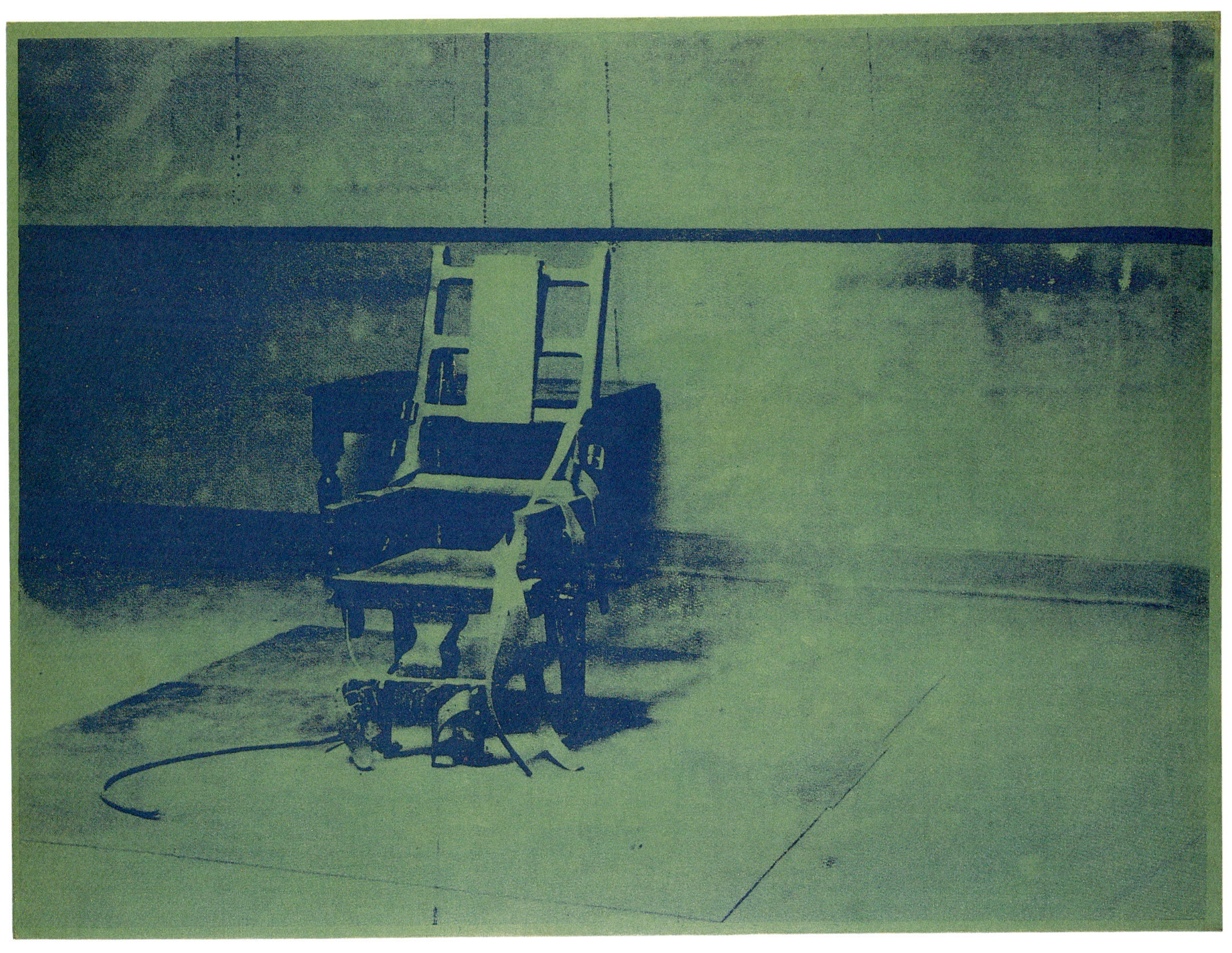

127 **Big Electric Chair 1967** Stiftung Sammlung Marx, Hamburger Bahnhof - Museum für Gegenwart, Berlin

128 Atomic Bomb 1965
Daros Collection, Switzerland

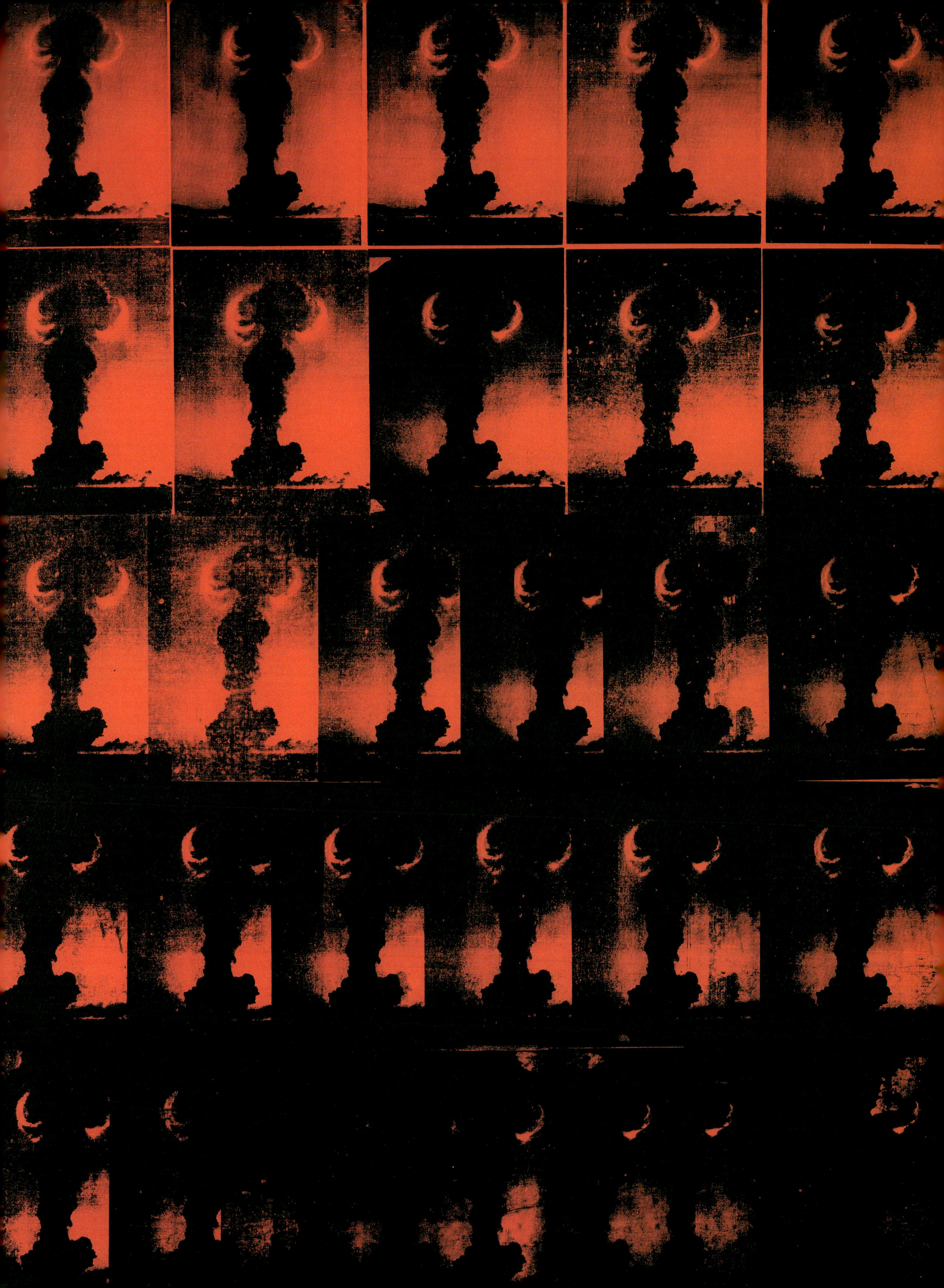

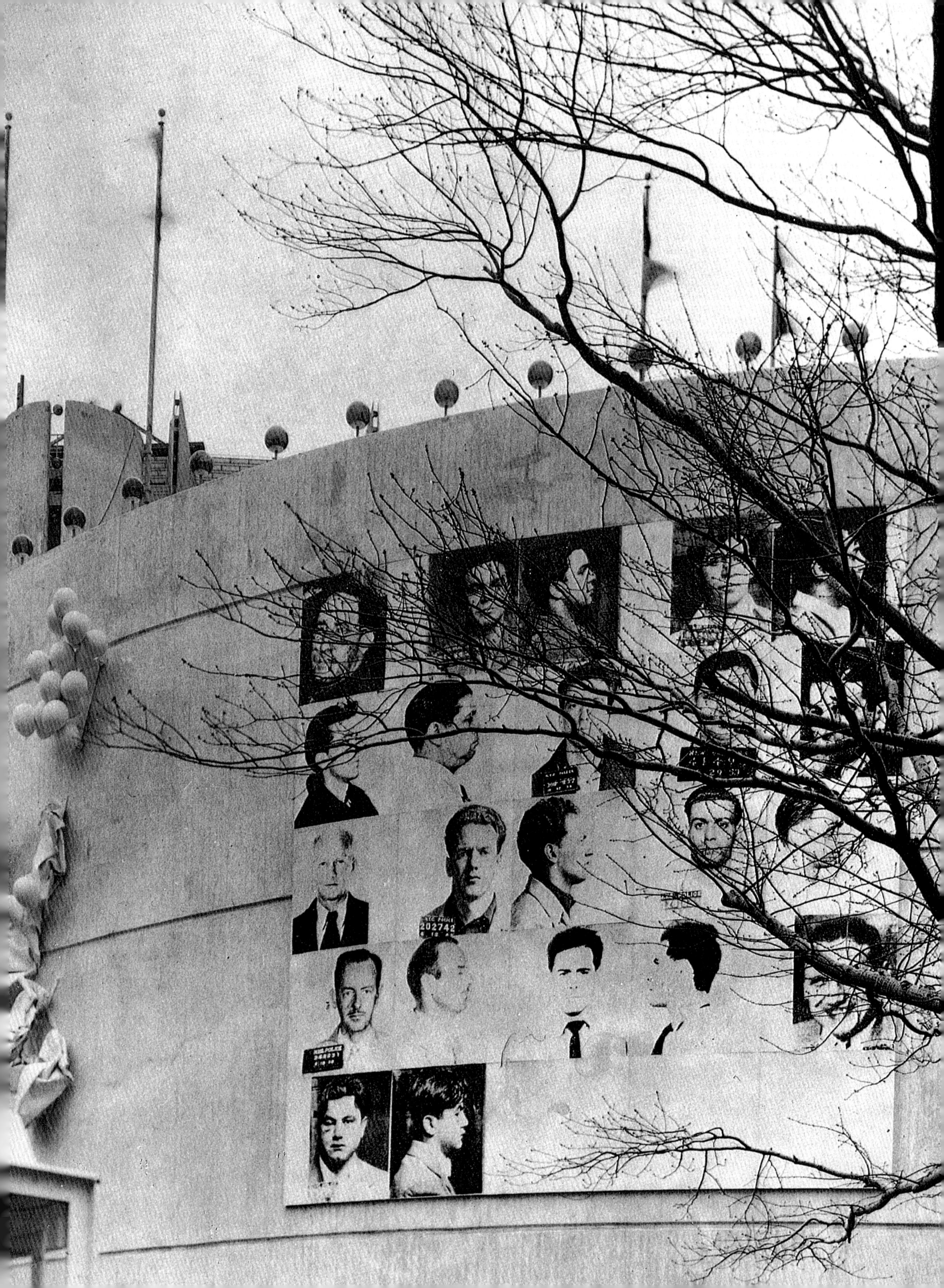
202742

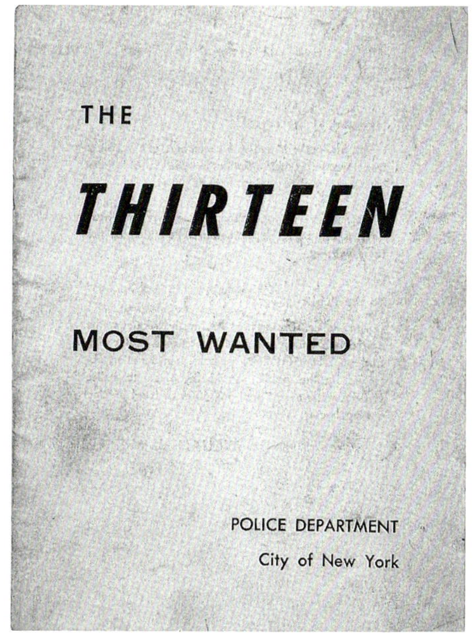

THE

THIRTEEN

MOST WANTED

POLICE DEPARTMENT
City of New York

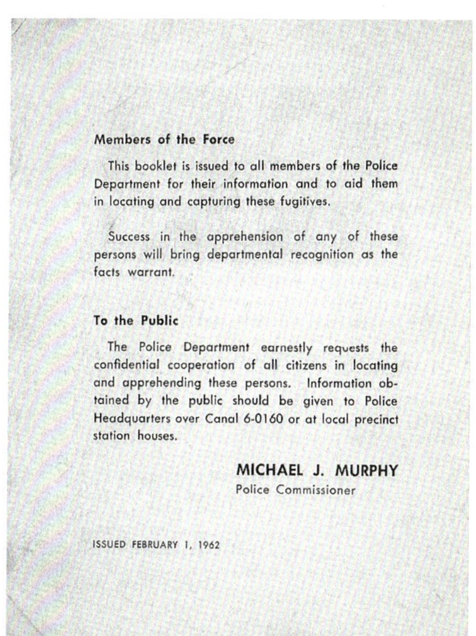

Members of the Force

This booklet is issued to all members of the Police Department for their information and to aid them in locating and capturing these fugitives.

Success in the apprehension of any of these persons will bring departmental recognition as the facts warrant.

To the Public

The Police Department earnestly requests the confidential cooperation of all citizens in locating and apprehending these persons. Information obtained by the public should be given to Police Headquarters over Canal 6-0160 or at local precinct station houses.

MICHAEL J. MURPHY
Police Commissioner

ISSUED FEBRUARY 1, 1962

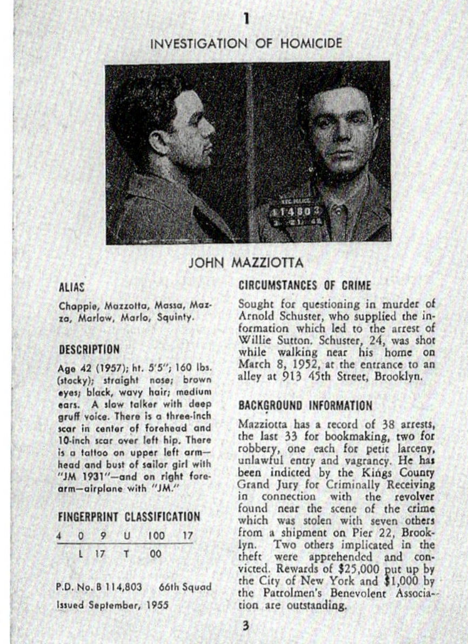

1
INVESTIGATION OF HOMICIDE

JOHN MAZZIOTTA

ALIAS

Chappie, Mazzotta, Massa, Mazza, Marlow, Marlo, Squinty.

DESCRIPTION

Age 42 (1957); ht. 5'5"; 160 lbs. (stocky); straight nose; brown eyes; black, wavy hair; medium ears. A slow talker with deep gruff voice. There is a three-inch scar in center of forehead and 10-inch scar over left hip. There is a tattoo on upper left arm—head and bust of sailor girl with "JM 1931"—and on right forearm—airplane with "JM."

FINGERPRINT CLASSIFICATION

4 0 9 U 100 17
L 17 T 00

P.D. No. B 114,803 66th Squad
Issued September, 1955

CIRCUMSTANCES OF CRIME

Sought for questioning in murder of Arnold Schuster, who supplied the information which led to the arrest of Willie Sutton. Schuster, 24, was shot while walking near his home on March 8, 1952, at the entrance to an alley at 913 45th Street, Brooklyn.

BACKGROUND INFORMATION

Mazziotta has a record of 38 arrests, the last 33 for bookmaking, two for robbery, one each for petit larceny, unlawful entry and vagrancy. He has been indicted by the Kings County Grand Jury for Criminally Receiving in connection with the revolver found near the scene of the crime which was stolen with seven others from a shipment on Pier 22, Brooklyn. Two others implicated in the theft were apprehended and convicted. Rewards of $25,000 put up by the City of New York and $1,000 by the Patrolmen's Benevolent Association are outstanding.

3

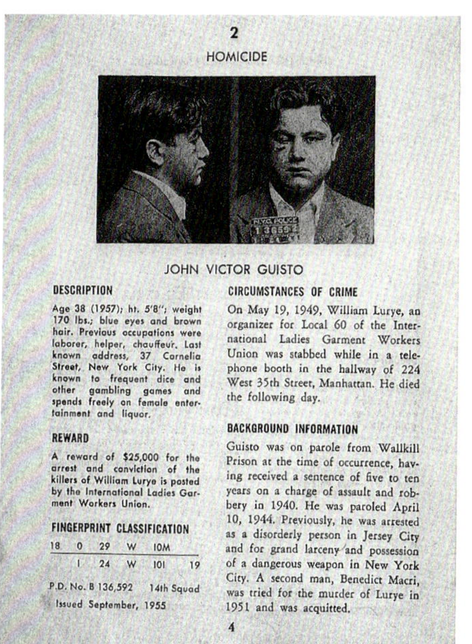

2
HOMICIDE

JOHN VICTOR GUISTO

DESCRIPTION

Age 38 (1957); ht. 5'8"; weight 170 lbs.; blue eyes and brown hair. Previous occupations were laborer, helper, chauffeur. Last known address, 37 Cornelia Street, New York City. He is known to frequent dice and other gambling games and spends freely on female entertainment and liquor.

REWARD

A reward of $25,000 for the arrest and conviction of the killers of William Lurye is posted by the International Ladies Garment Workers Union.

FINGERPRINT CLASSIFICATION

18 0 29 W 10M
1 24 W 101 19

P.D. No. B 136,592 14th Squad
Issued September, 1955

CIRCUMSTANCES OF CRIME

On May 19, 1949, William Lurye, an organizer for Local 60 of the International Ladies Garment Workers Union was stabbed while in a telephone booth in the hallway of 224 West 35th Street, Manhattan. He died the following day.

BACKGROUND INFORMATION

Guisto was on parole from Wallkill Prison at the time of occurrence, having received a sentence of five to ten years on a charge of assault and robbery in 1940. He was paroled April 10, 1944. Previously, he was arrested as a disorderly person in Jersey City and for grand larceny and possession of a dangerous weapon in New York City. A second man, Benedict Macri, was tried for the murder of Lurye in 1951 and was acquitted.

4

Cover and the first three pages of a booklet with warrants for the 13 most wanted criminals issued by the police department of the City of New York in February 1962. The booklet was Andy Warhol's source material for the *Thirteen Most Wanted Men* series.

◂ Andy Warhol's commissioned mural, the portraits of the *Thirteen Most Wanted Men* on the facade of the New York State Pavilion, shortly before the opening of the World's Fair in April 1964.

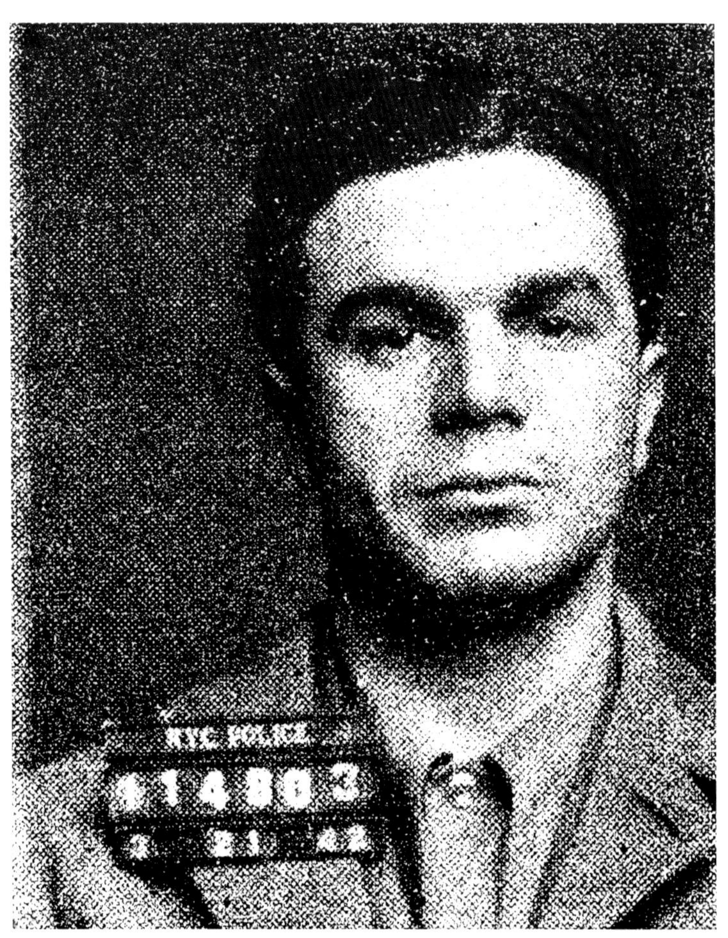

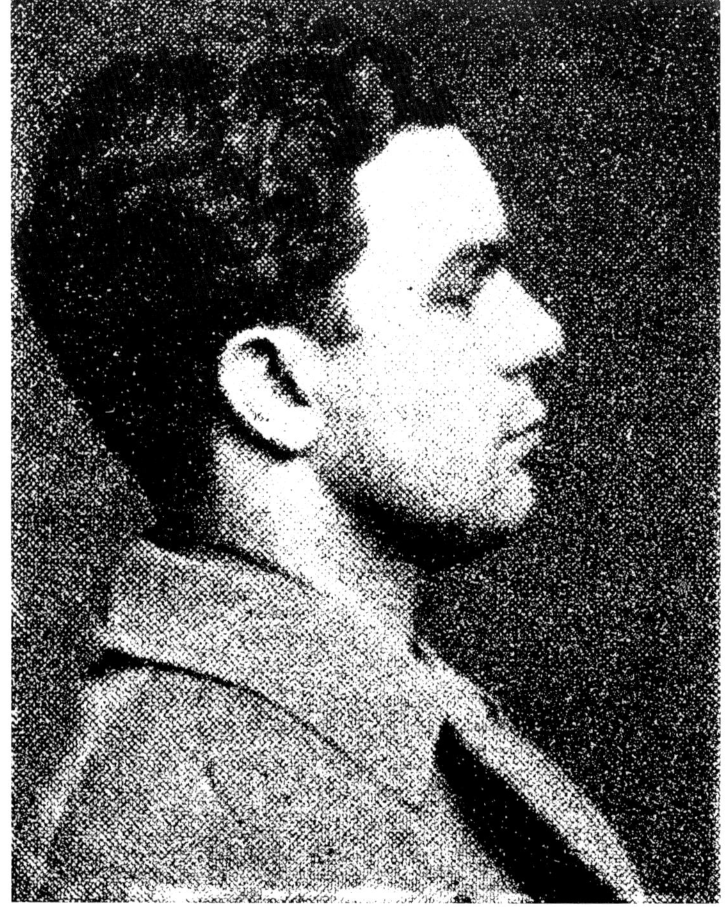

129 **Most Wanted Men No. 1, John M. 1964**
Kaiser Wilhelm Museum Krefeld

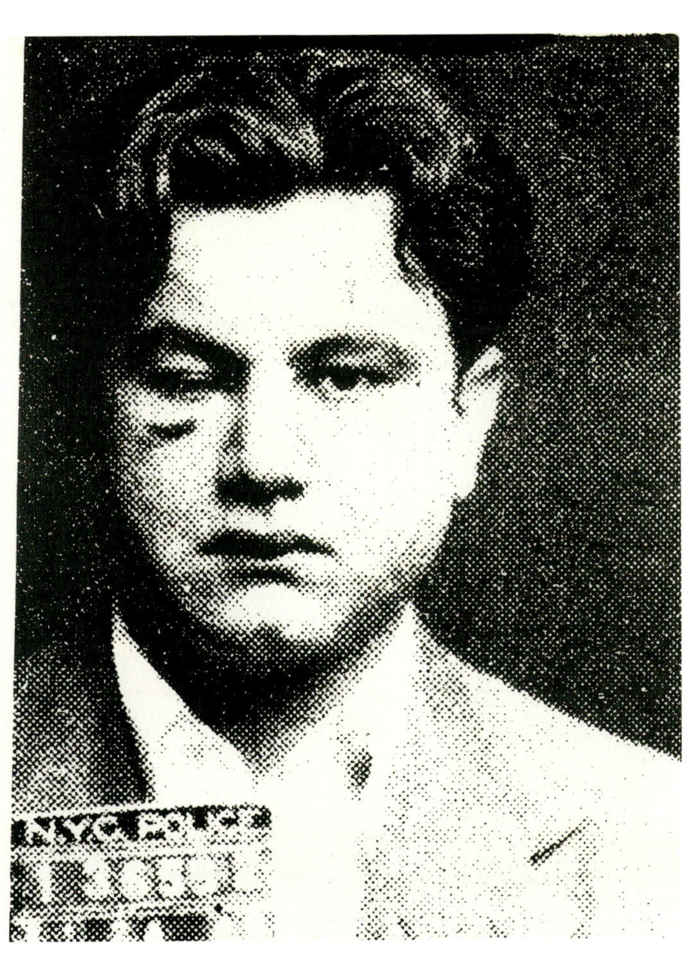

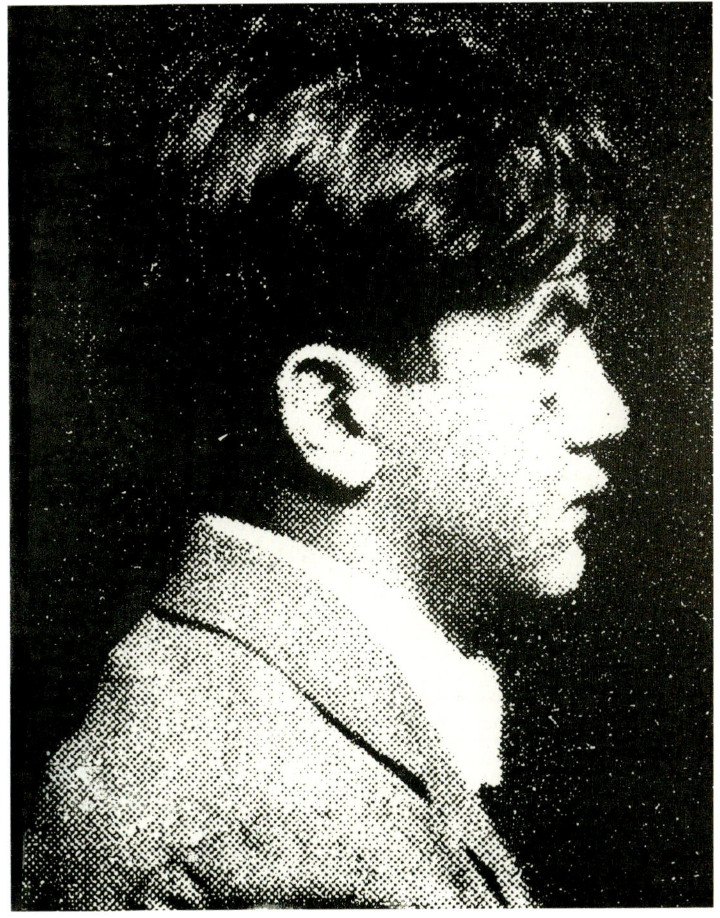

130 **Most Wanted Men No. 2, John Victor G. 1964**
Daros Collection, Switzerland

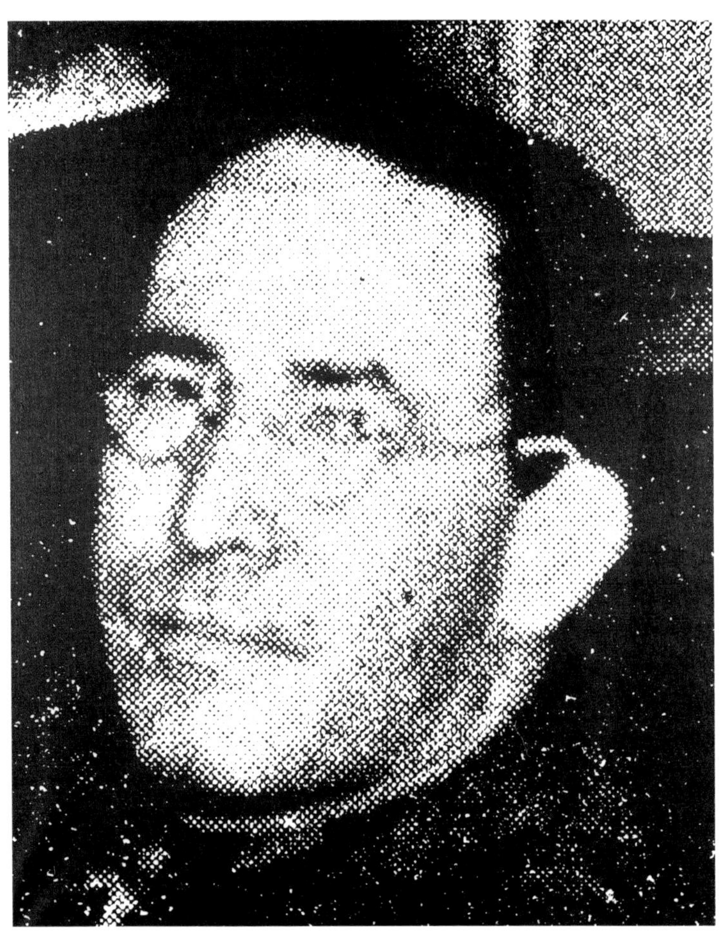

131 **Most Wanted Men No. 3, Ellis Ruez B. 1964**
Daros Collection, Switzerland

132 **Most Wanted Men No. 4, Redmond C. 1964**
Private collection, San Francisco

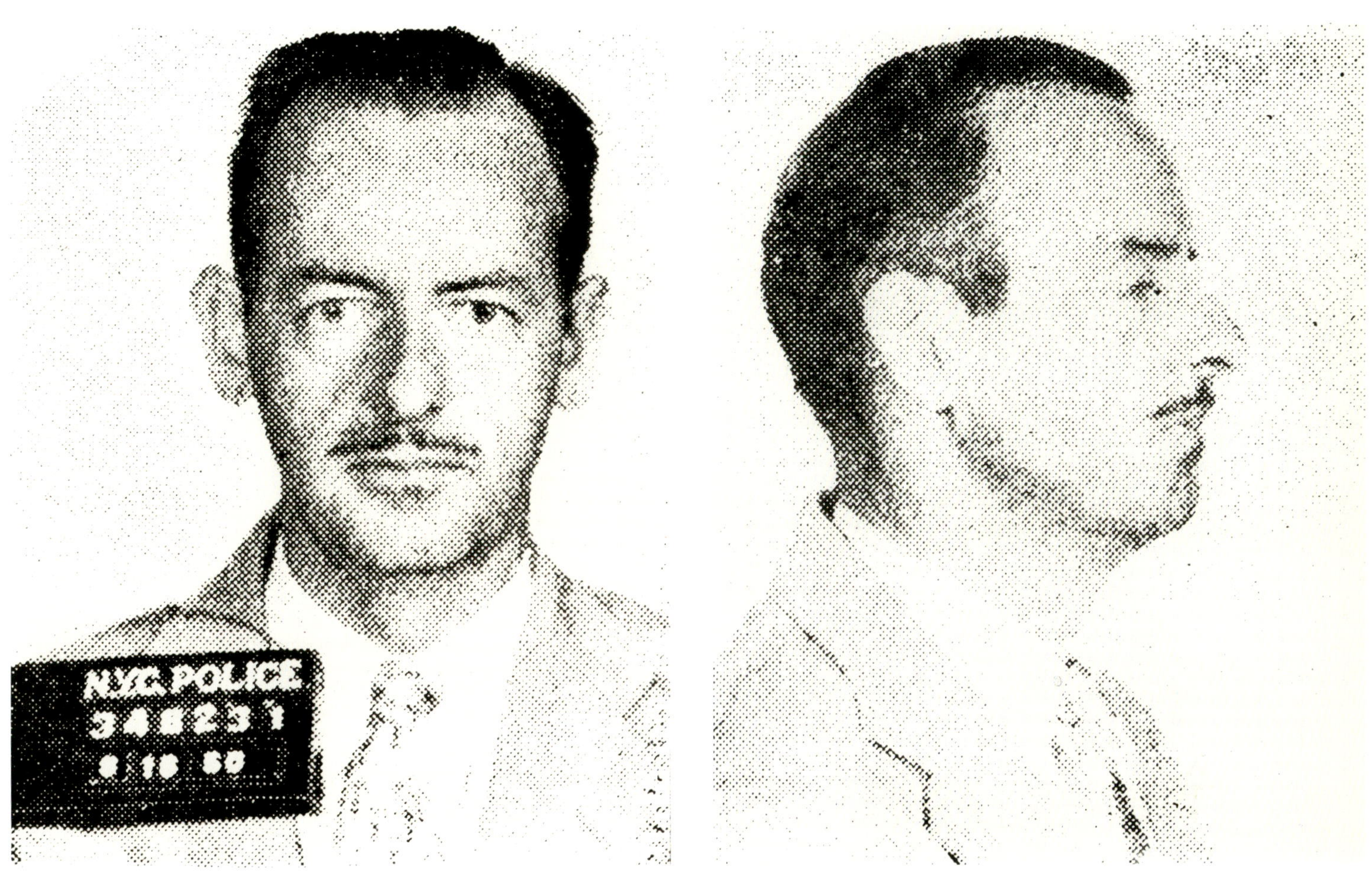

133 Most Wanted Men No. 5, Arthur Alvin M. 1964
Courtesy The Brant Foundation, Greenwich, CT

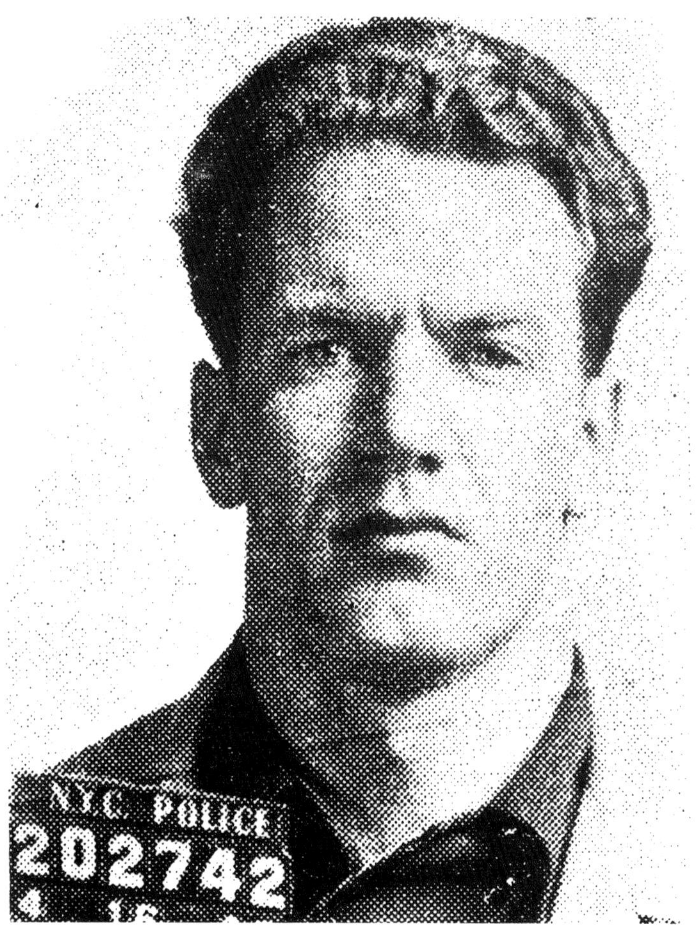

134 **Most Wanted Men No. 6, Thomas Francis C. 1964**
The Eli and Edythe L. Broad Collection, Los Angeles

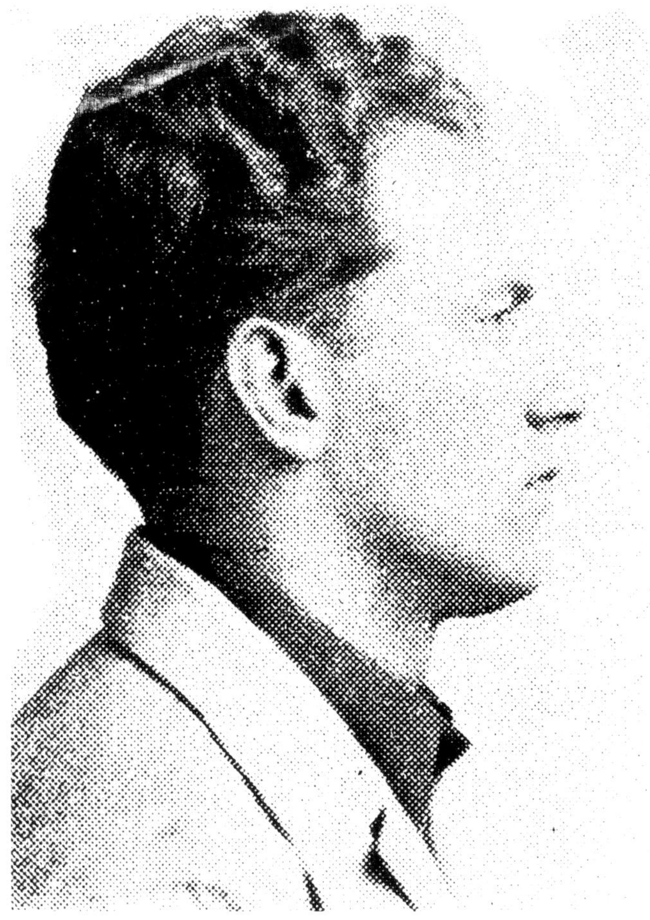

135 **Most Wanted Men No. 6, Thomas Francis C. 1964**
The Eli and Edythe L. Broad Collection, Los Angeles

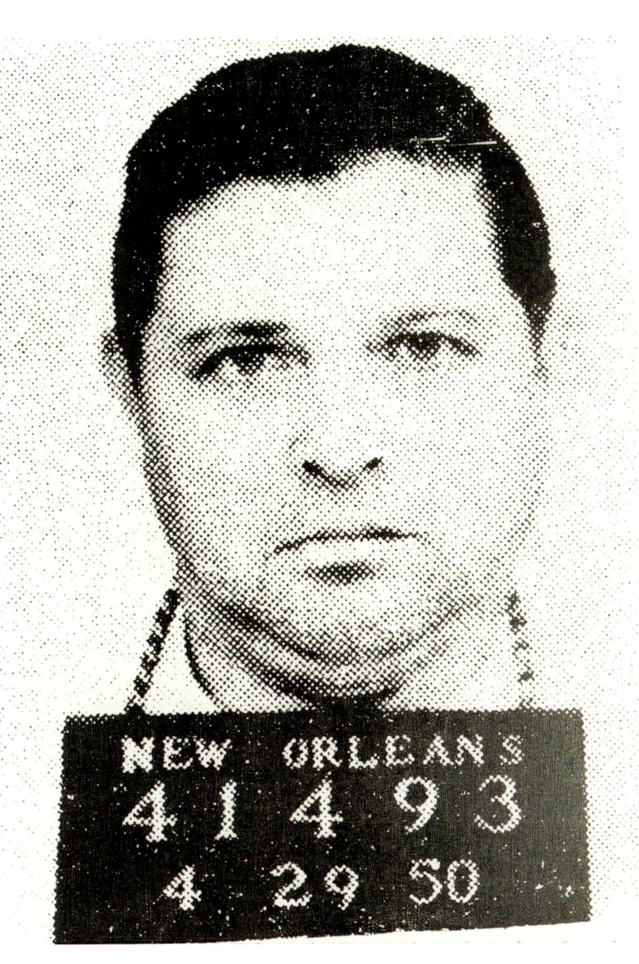

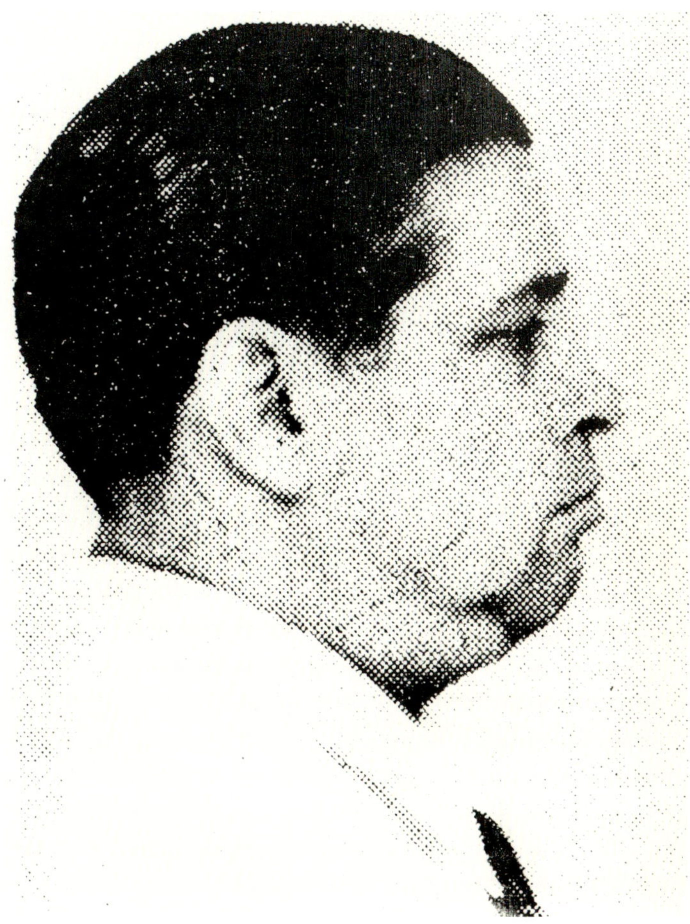

136 Most Wanted Men No. 7, Salvatore V. 1964
Museum Ludwig, Köln

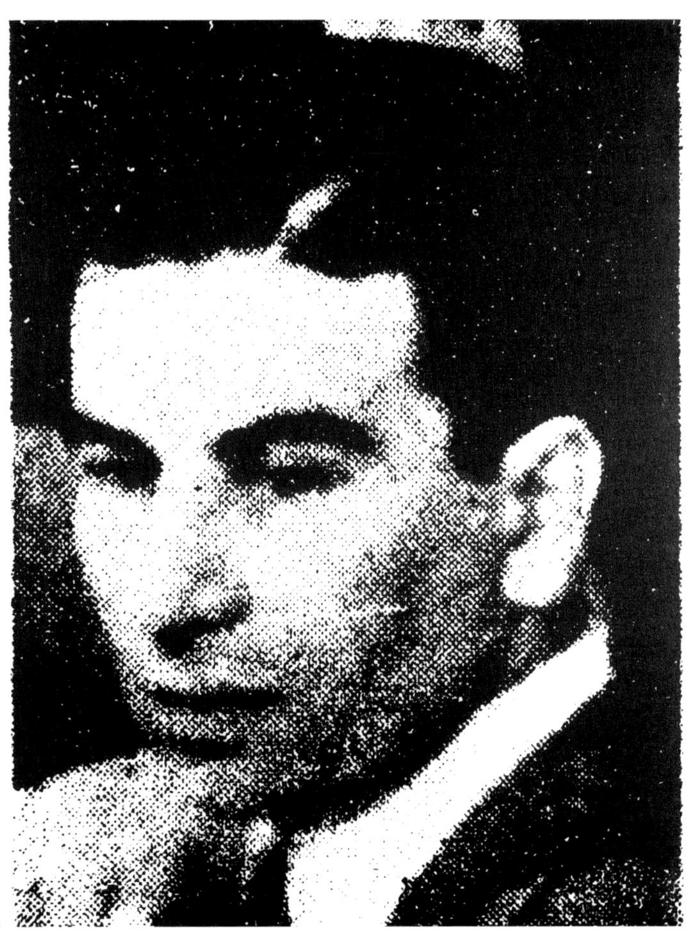

137 **Most Wanted Men No. 8, Andrew F. 1964**
Daros Collection, Switzerland

138 **Most Wanted Men No. 9, John S. 1964**
Daros Collection, Switzerland

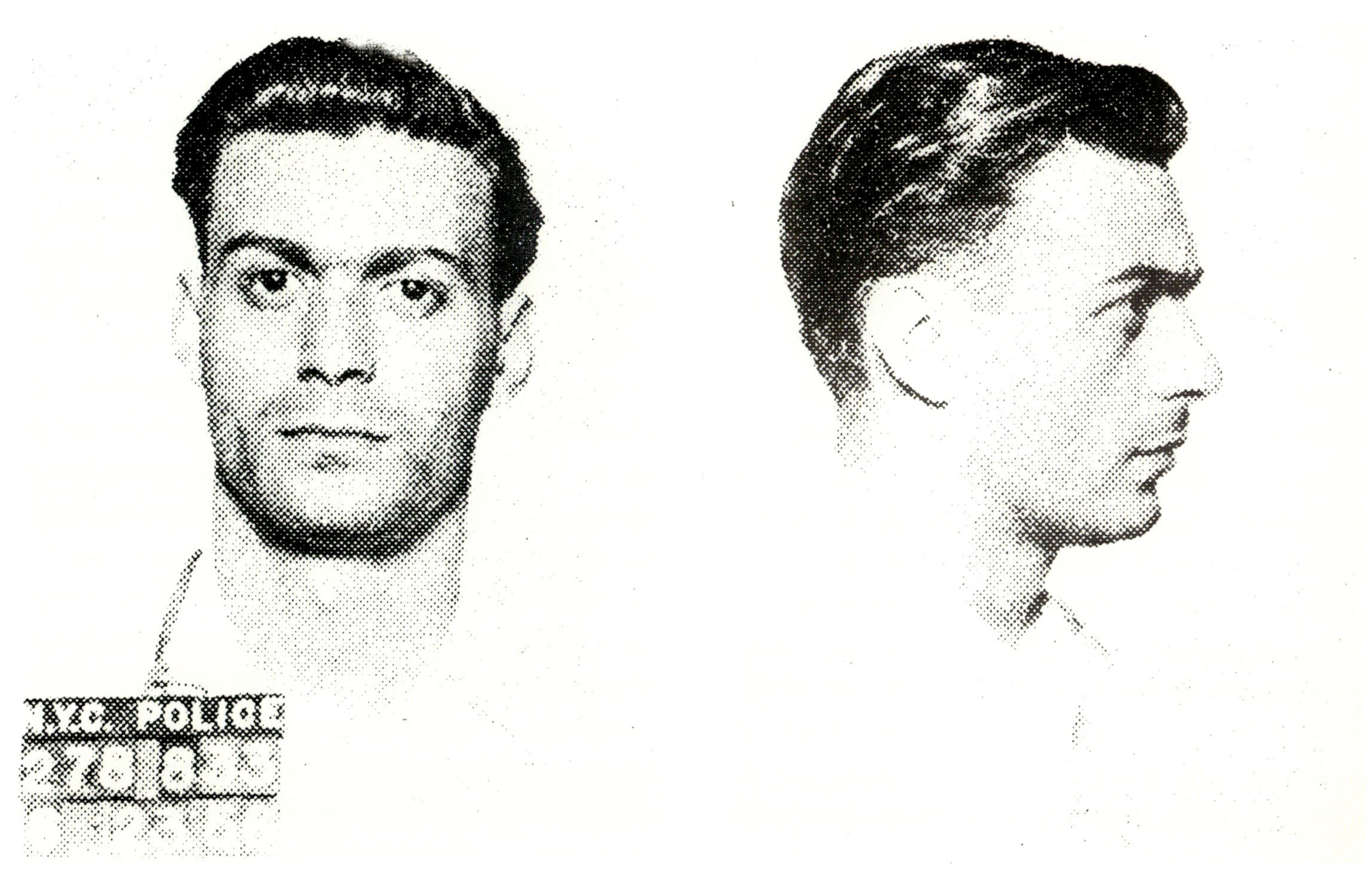

139 **Most Wanted Men No. 10, Louis Joseph M. 1964**
Städtisches Museum Abteiberg Mönchengladbach

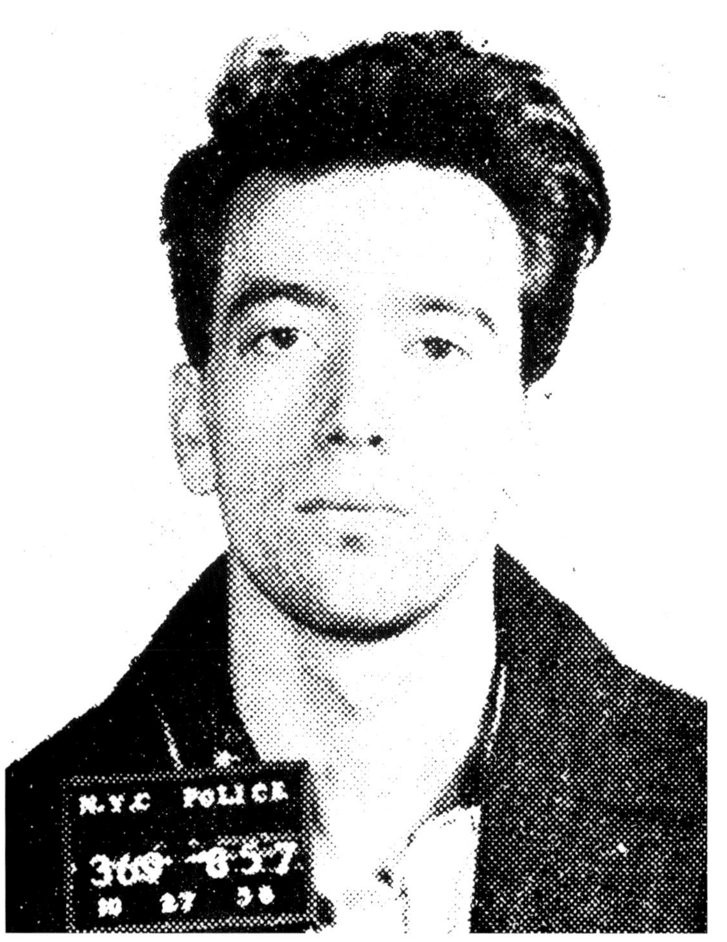

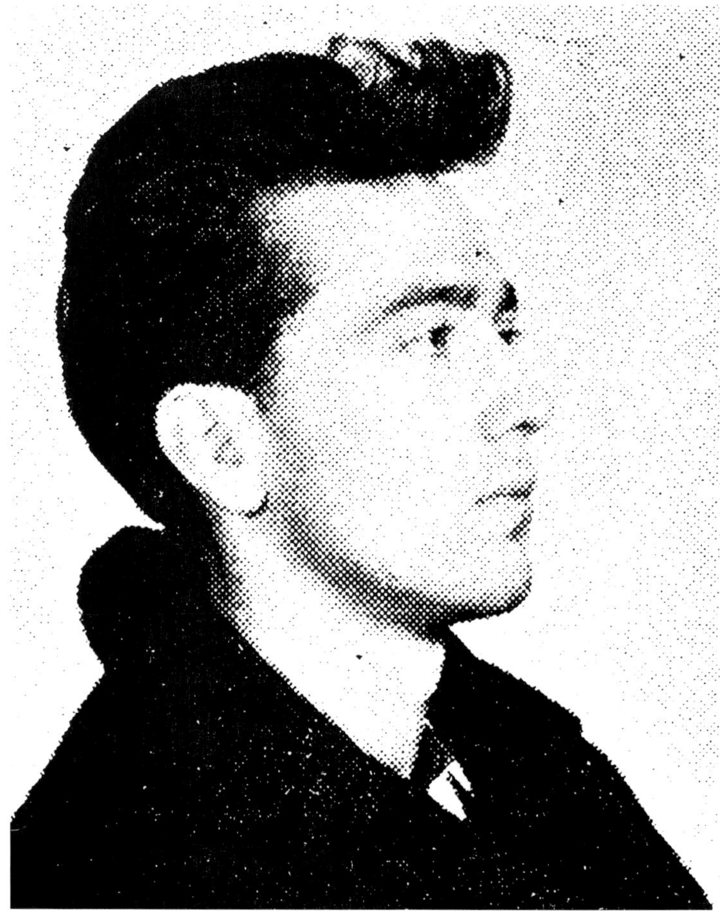

140 Most Wanted Men No. 11, John Joseph H. 1964
Museum für Moderne Kunst, Frankfurt am Main
[Former Ströher Collection]

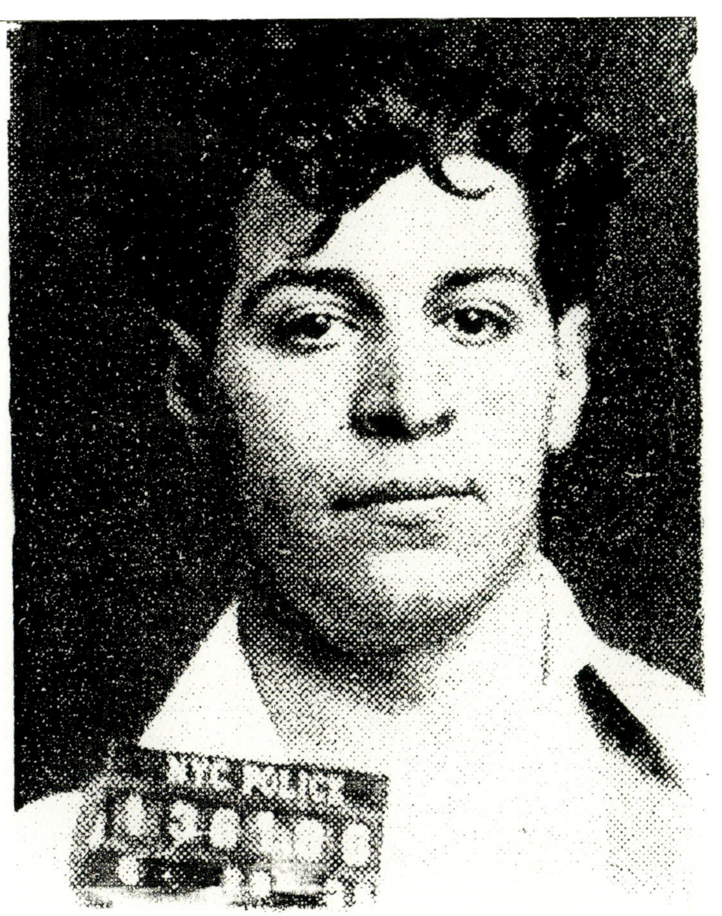

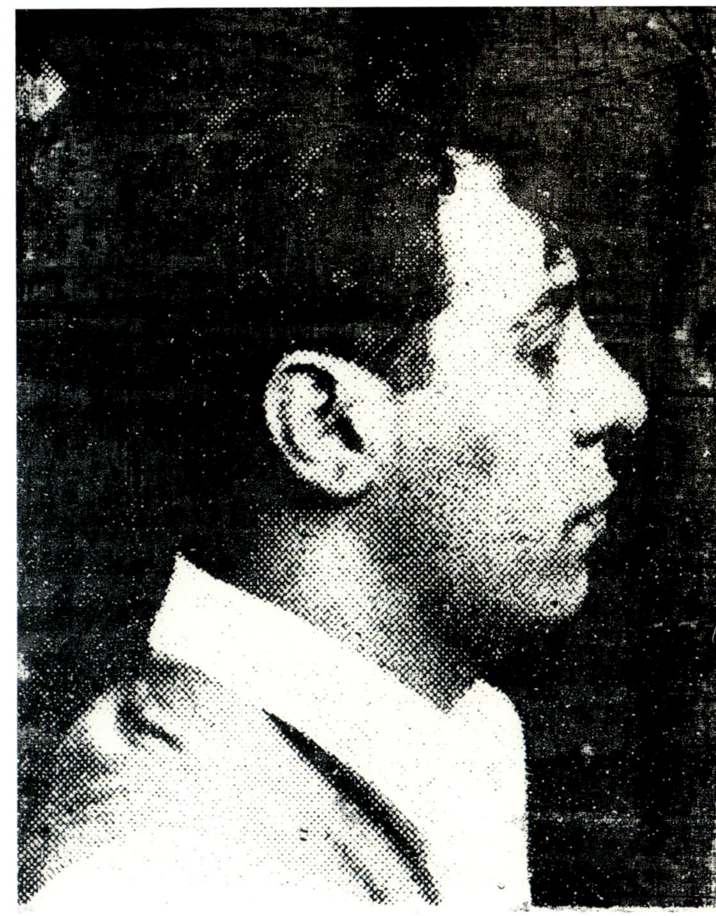

141 **Most Wanted Men No. 12, Frank B. 1964**
The Andy Warhol Museum, Pittsburgh
Founding Collection, Contribution
The Andy Warhol Foundation
for the Visual Arts, Inc.

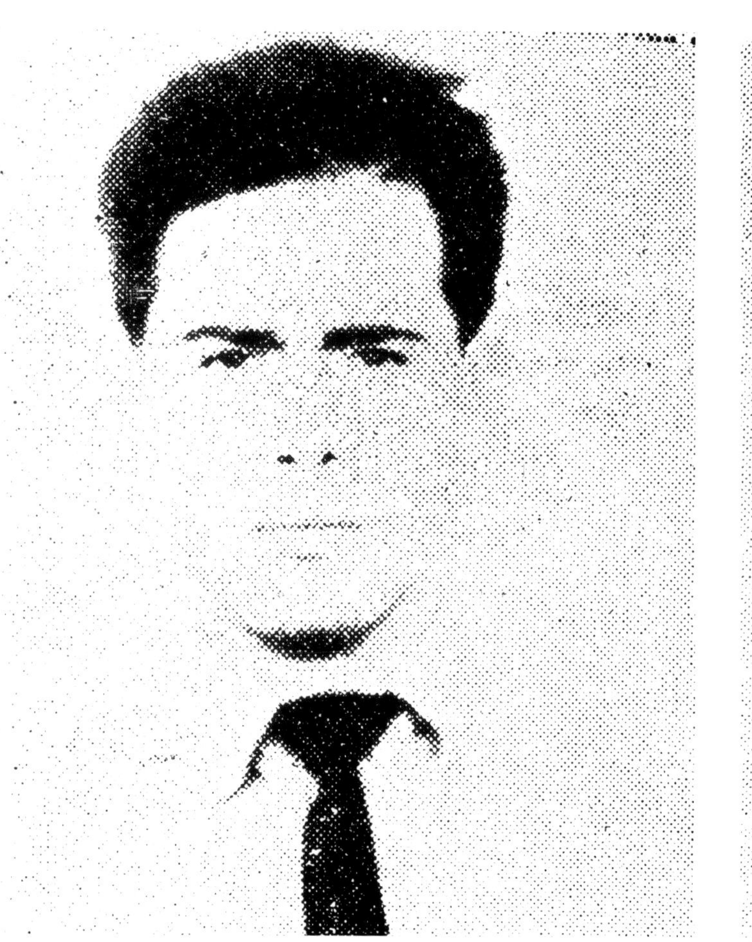

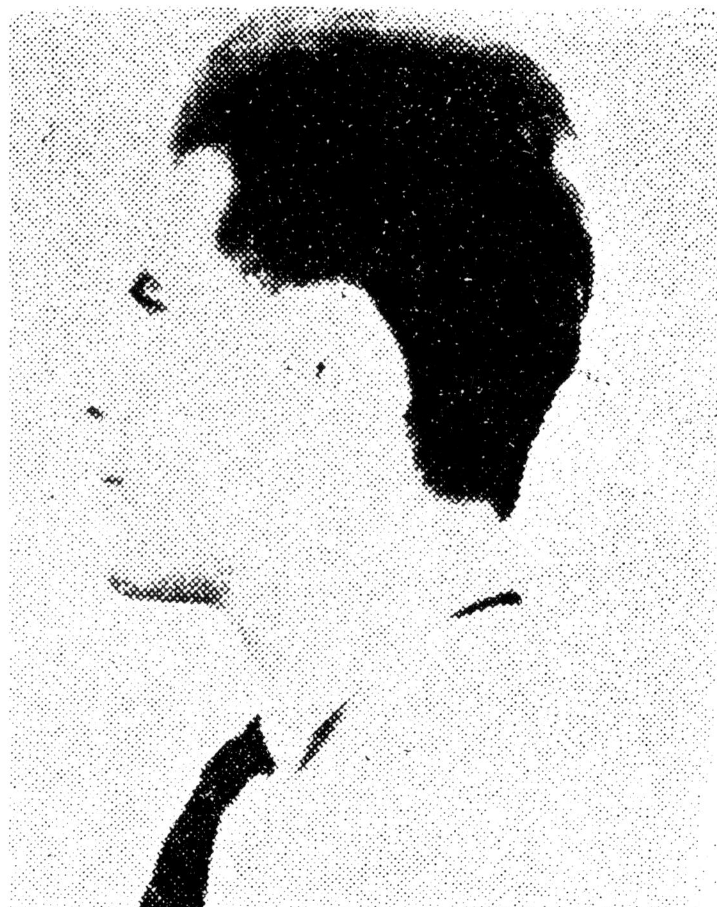

142 Most Wanted Men No. 13, Joseph F. 1964
Sonnabend Collection

After the political éclat: the ›effaced‹ mural of the *Thirteen Most Wanted Men*, painted out with aluminum paint shortly before the opening of the World's Fair, April 1964.

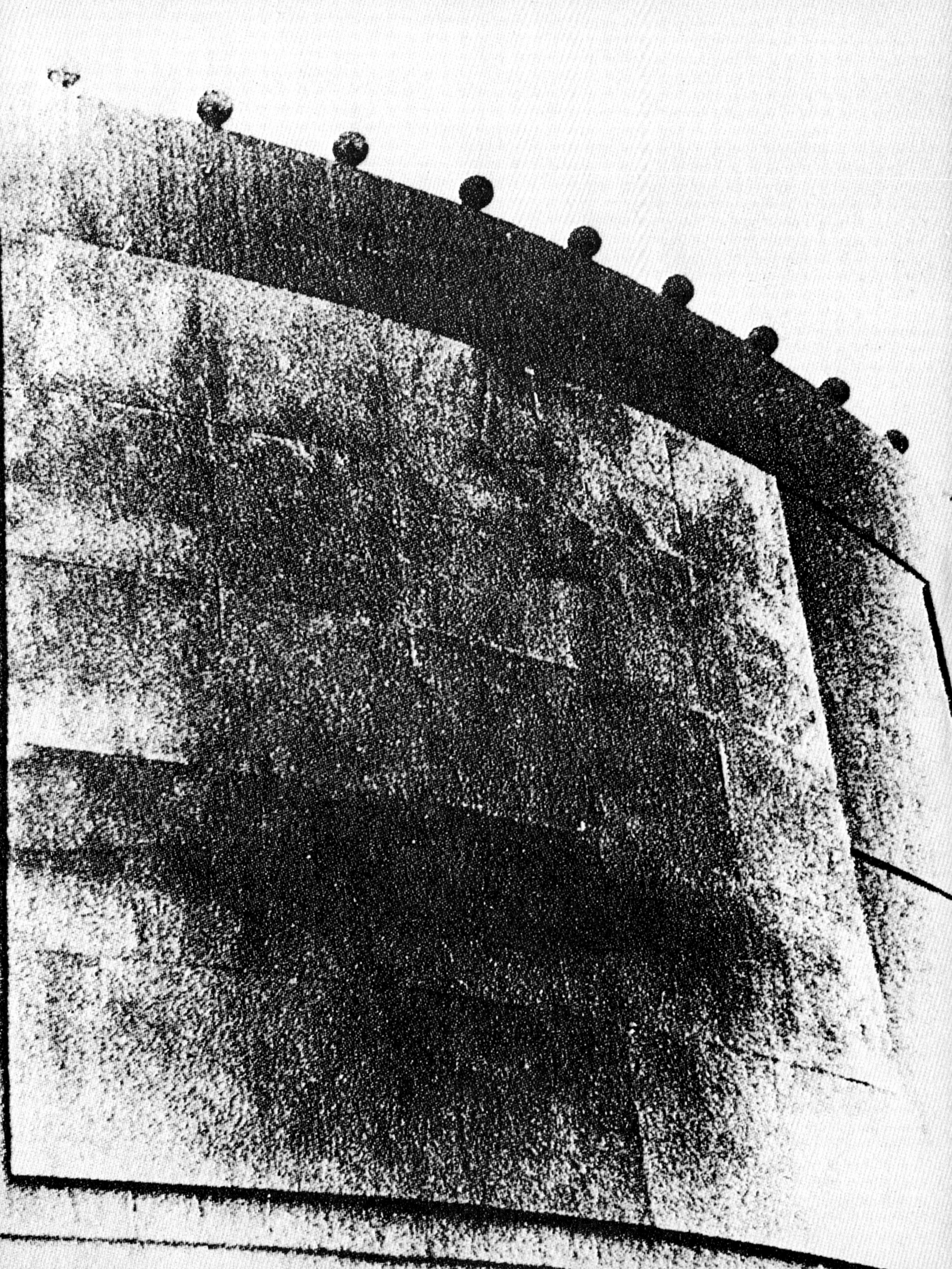

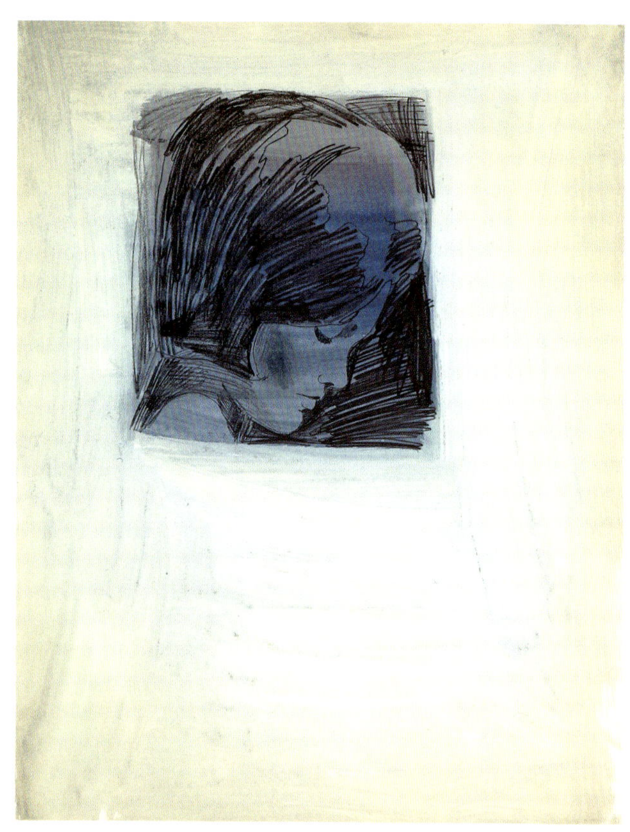

143 Profile of a Woman (Jackie Kennedy) 1964
Courtesy The Brant Foundation, Greenwich, CT

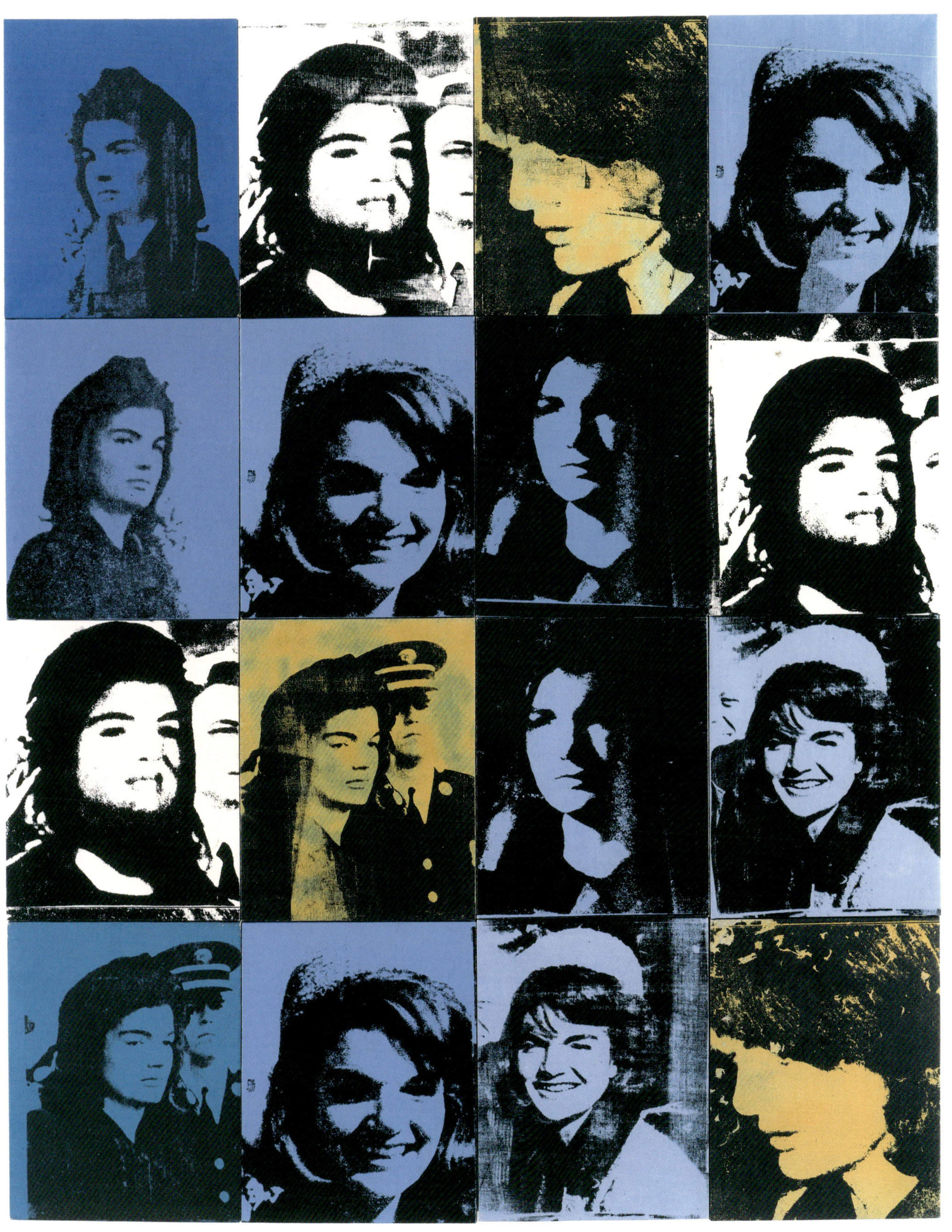

144 **16 Jackies** **1964** Courtesy The Brant Foundation, Greenwich, CT

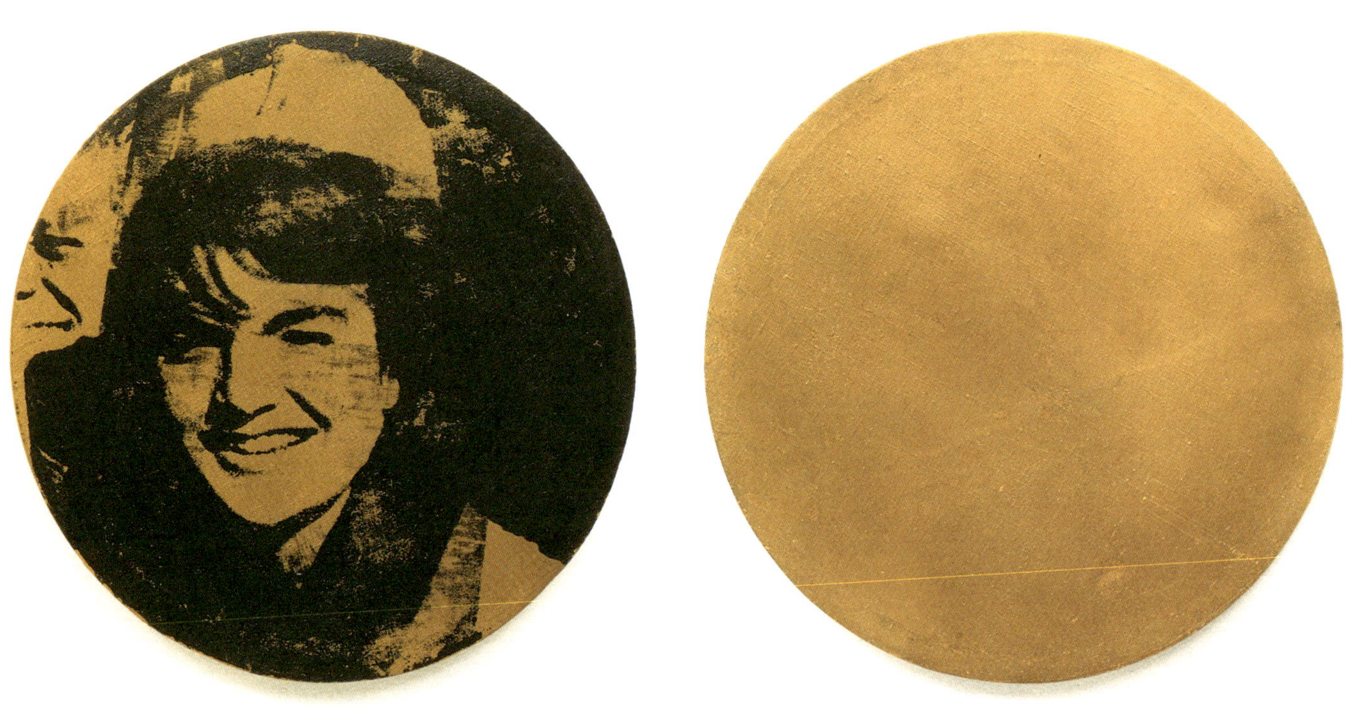

145 Gold Jackie 1964 Collection Froehlich, Stuttgart

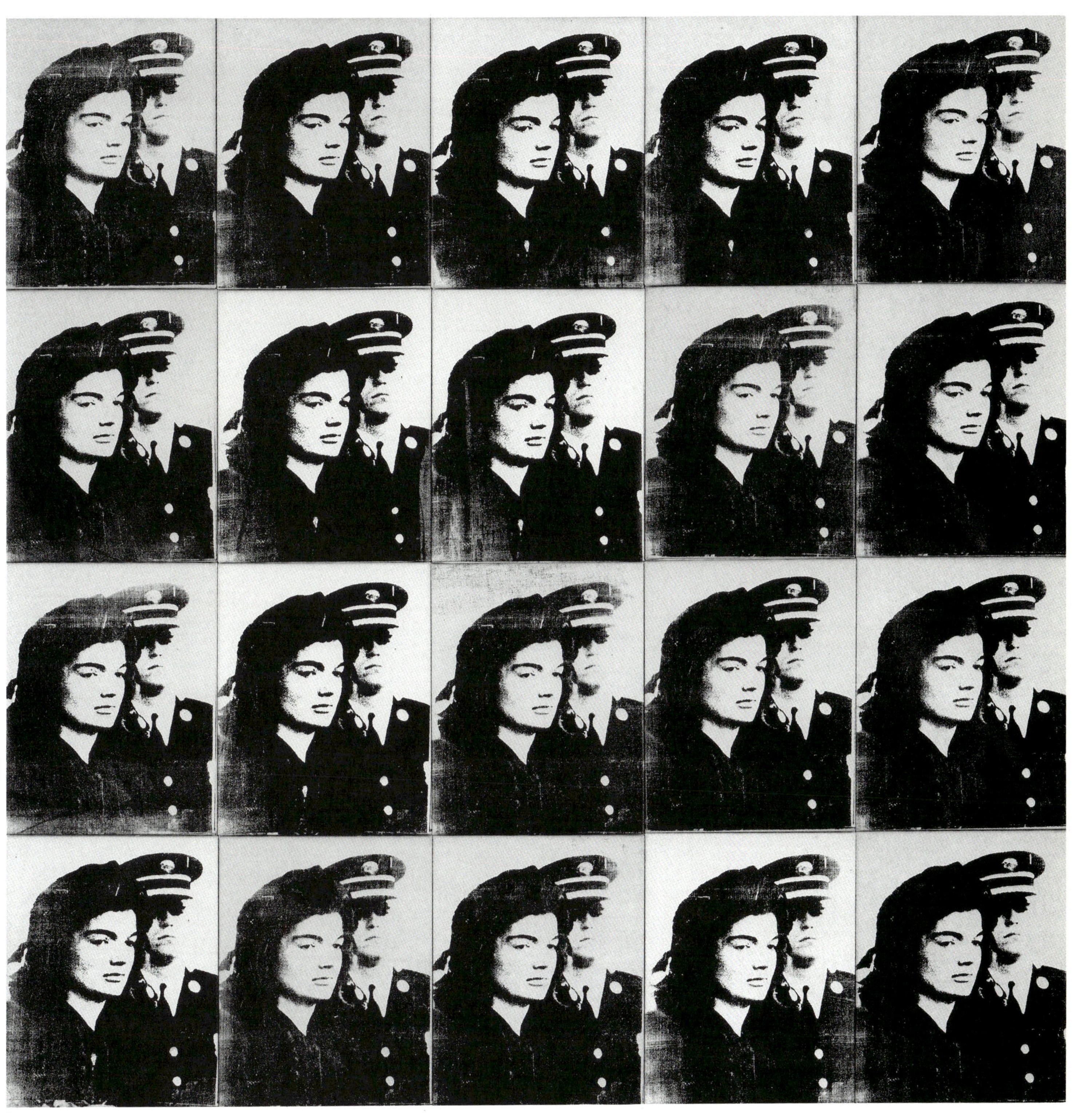

146 Twenty Jackies 1964 Stiftung Sammlung Marx, Hamburger Bahnhof - Museum für Gegenwart, Berlin

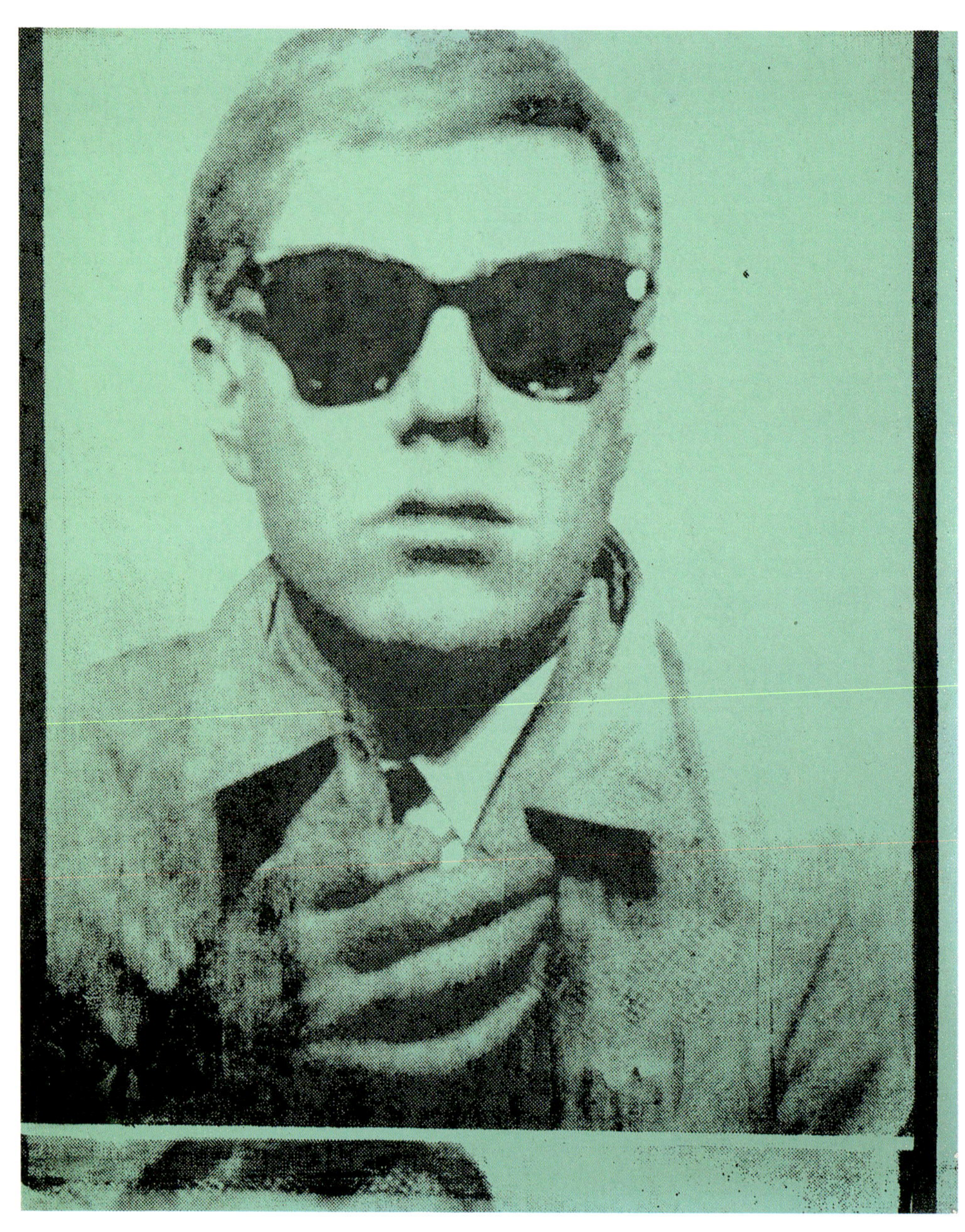

147 **Self-Portrait** **1964** Private collection

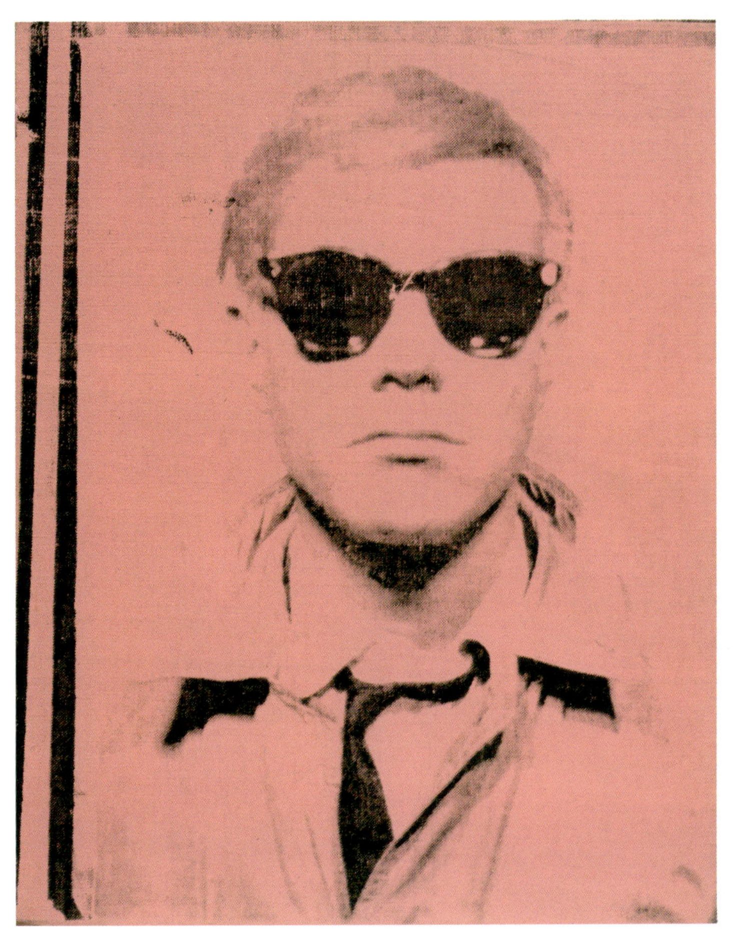

148 **Self-Portrait** **1964** Courtesy The Brant Foundation, Greenwich, CT

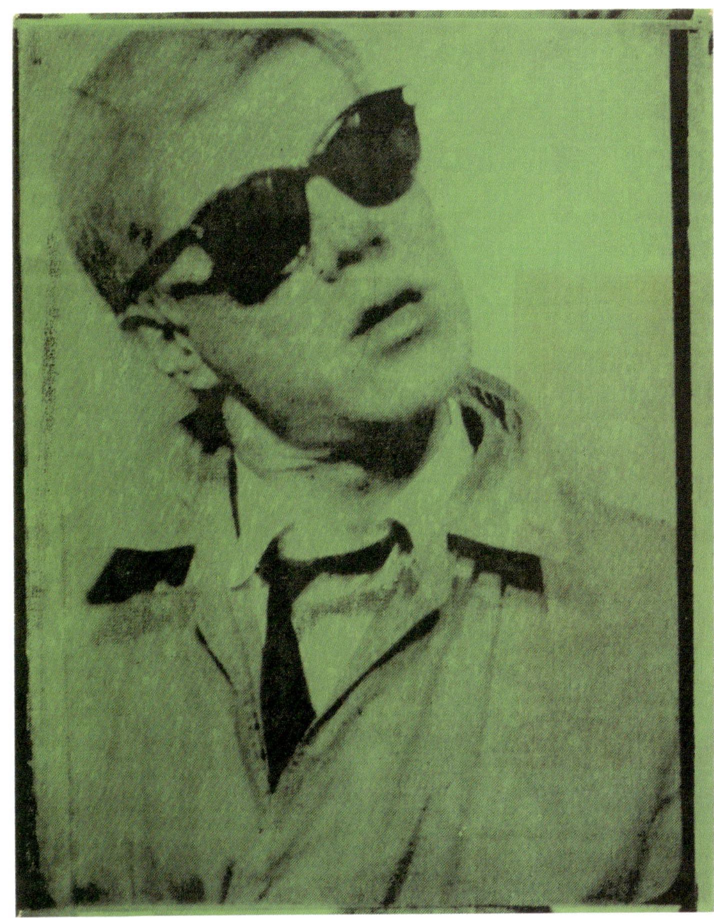

149 **Self-Portrait** **1964** Courtesy The Brant Foundation Greenwich, CT

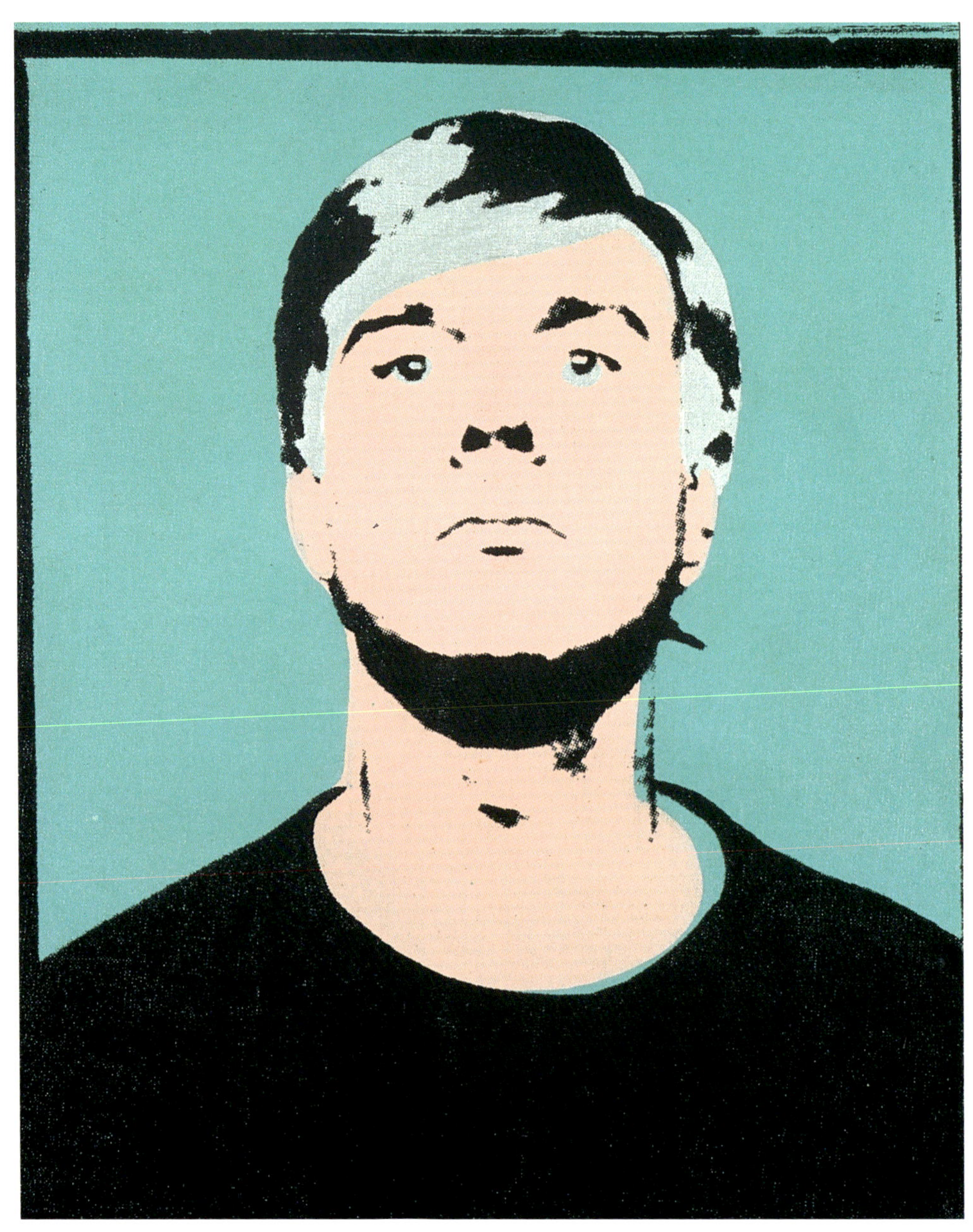

150 Self-Portrait 1964
The Andy Warhol Museum, Pittsburgh
Founding Collection, Contribution
Dia Center for the Arts

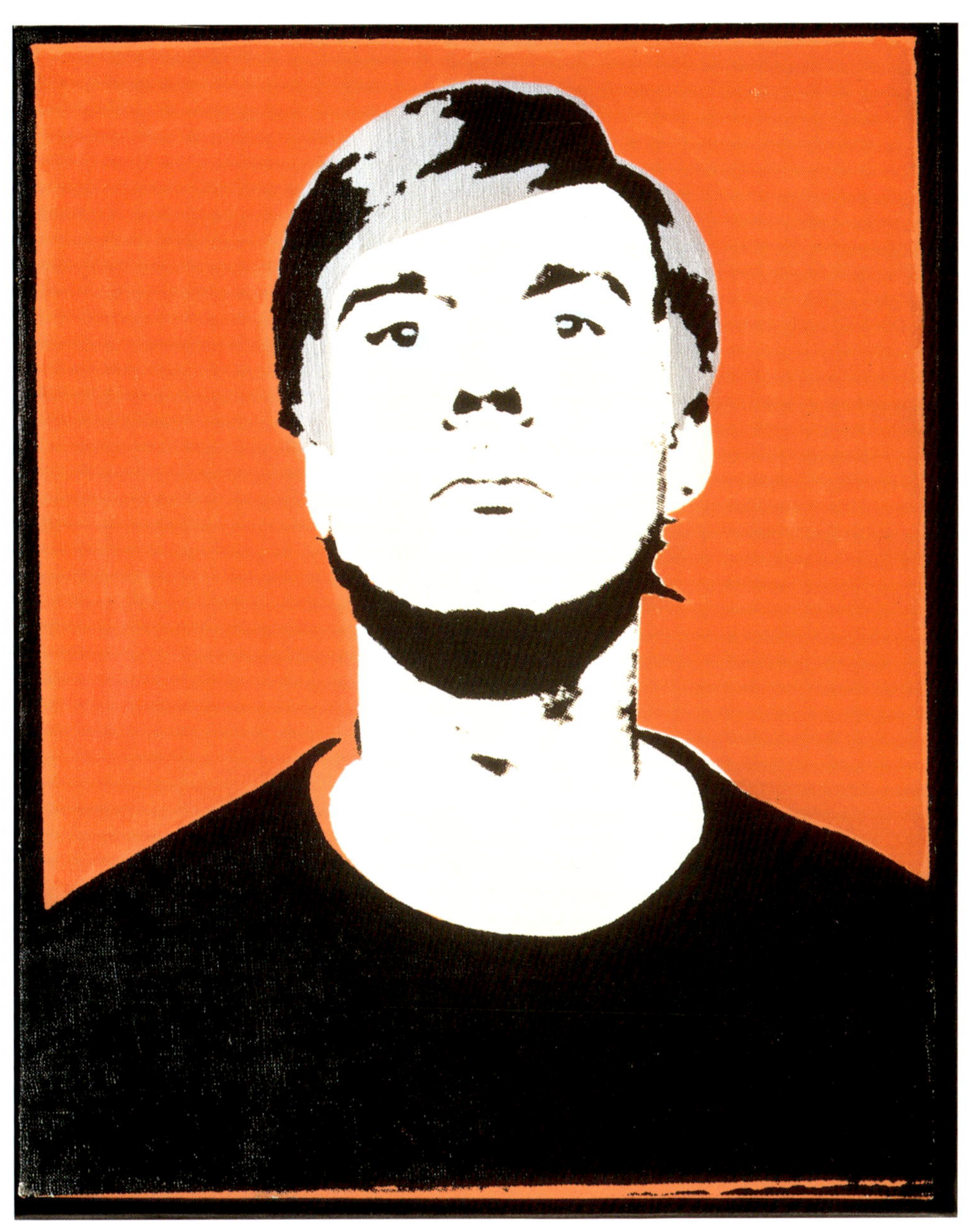

151 **Self-Portrait 1964**
Collection Froehlich,
Stuttgart

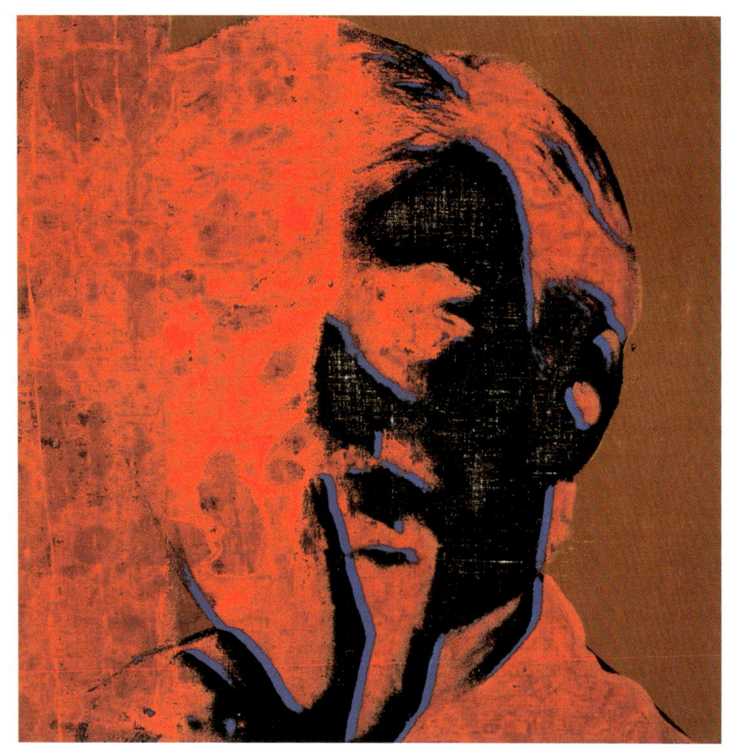

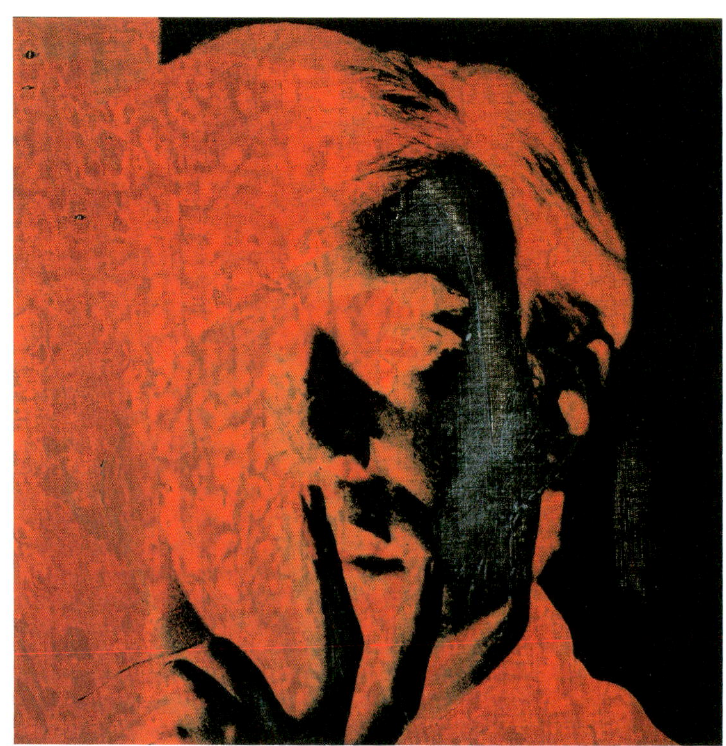

152 Self-Portraits 1966/67 Courtesy The Brant Foundation, Greenwich, CT

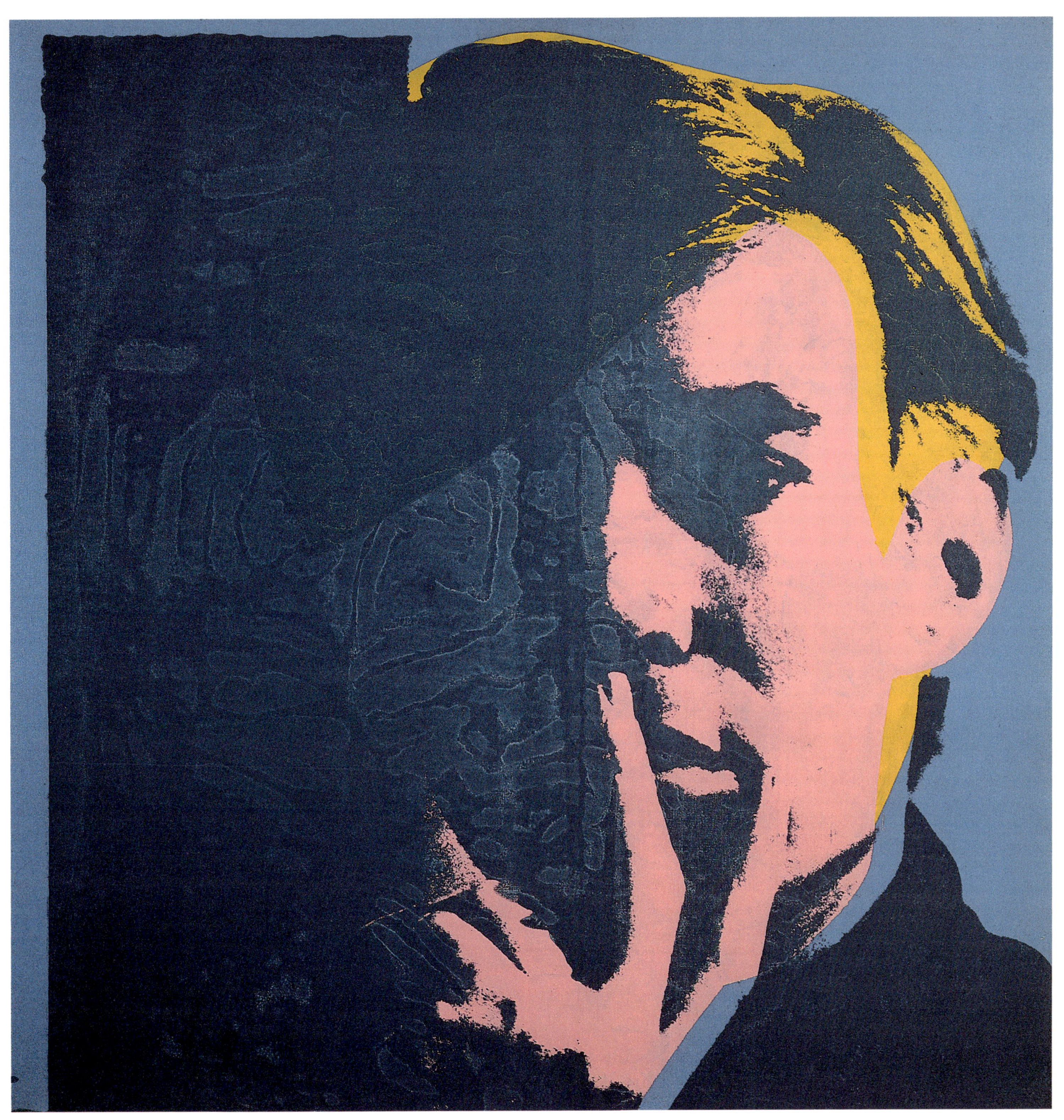

153 Self-Portrait 1967 Collection Froehlich, Stuttgart

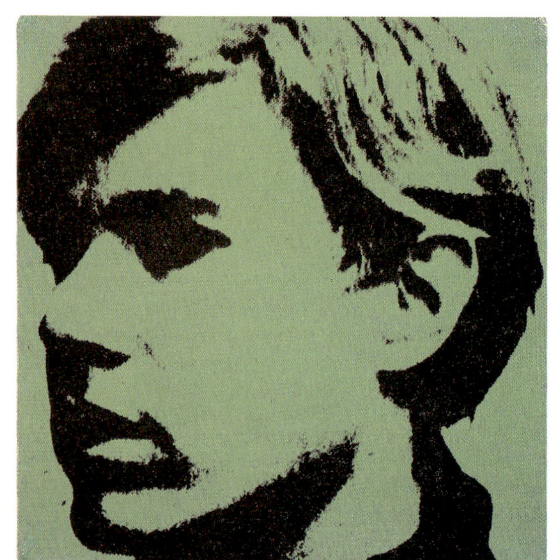

154 **Green Self-Portrait** 1967
Private collection, Houston

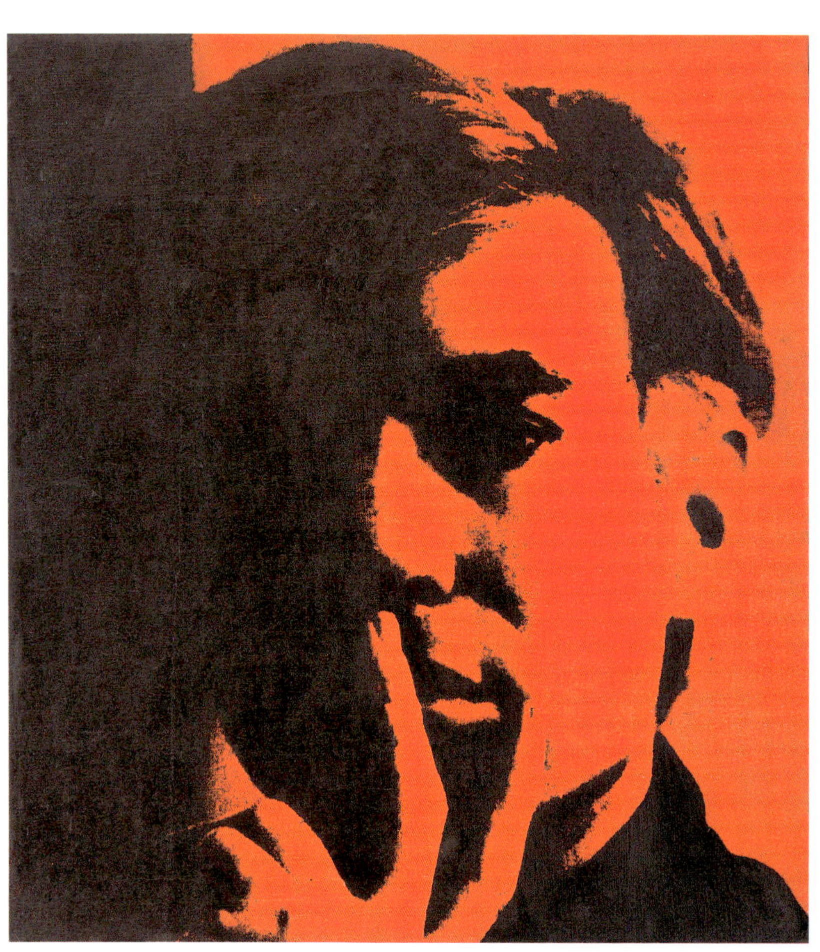

155 **Self-Portrait** 1967
Aaron I. Fleischman

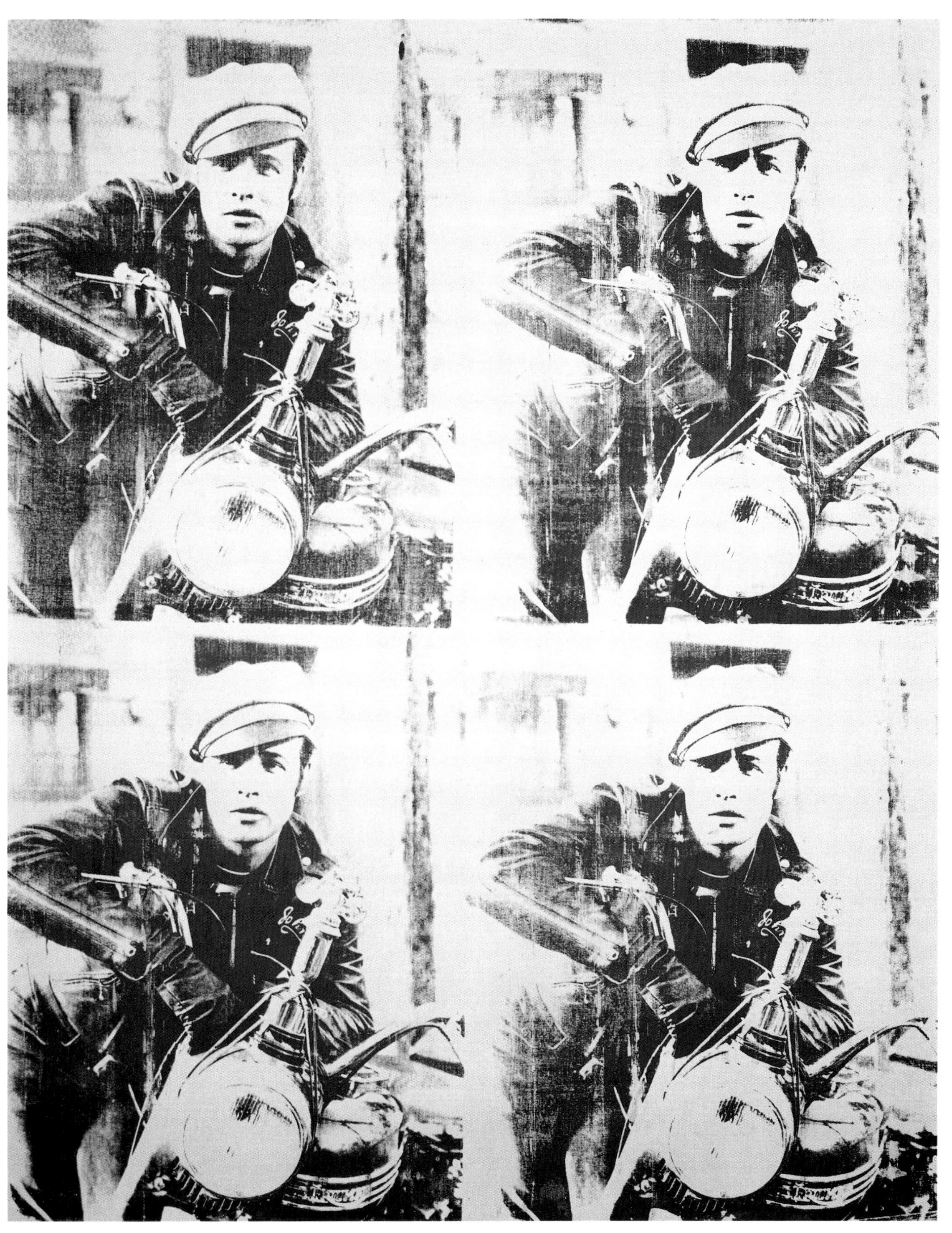

156 **Marlon** **1966** Westdeutsche Spielbanken, Münster

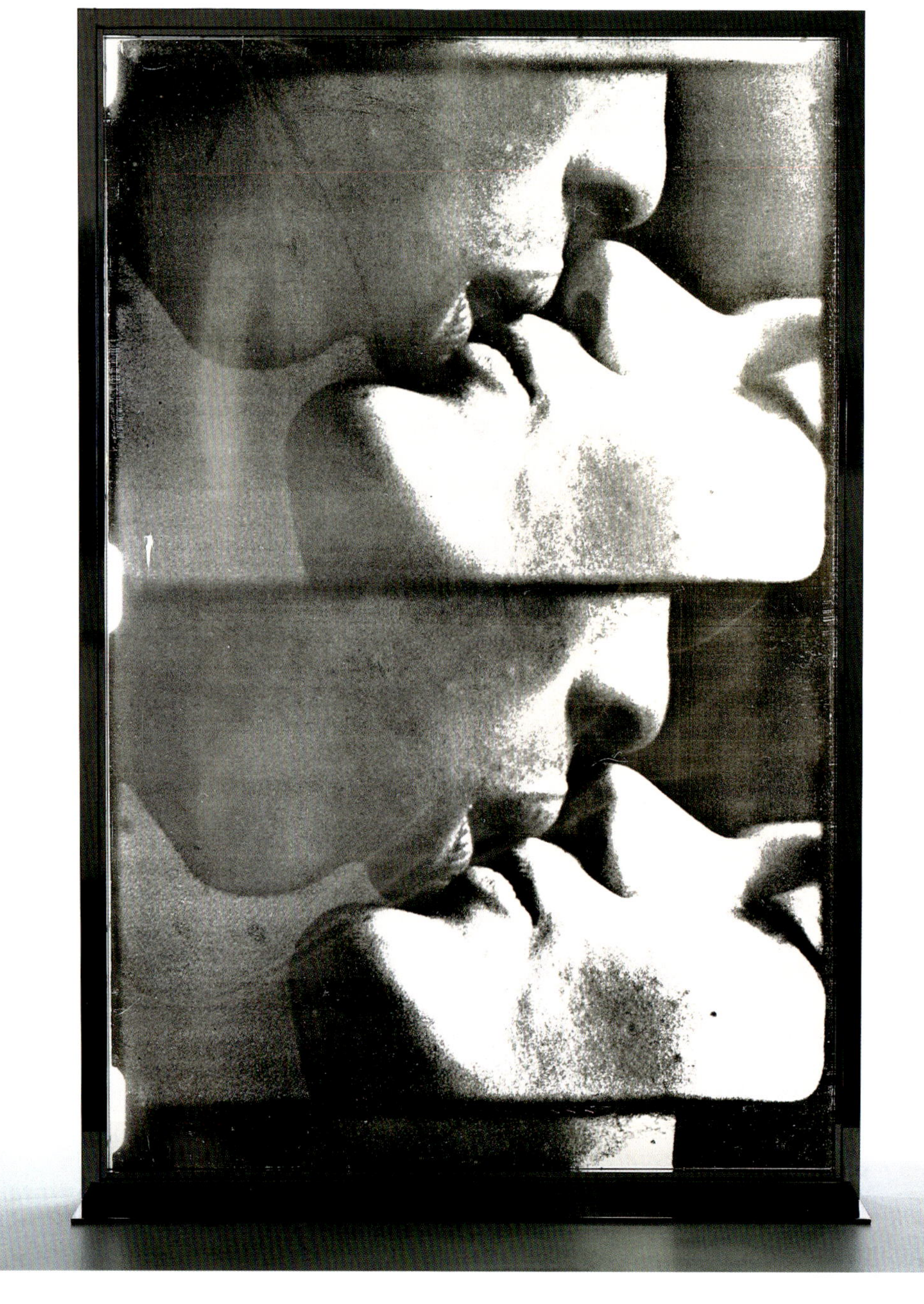

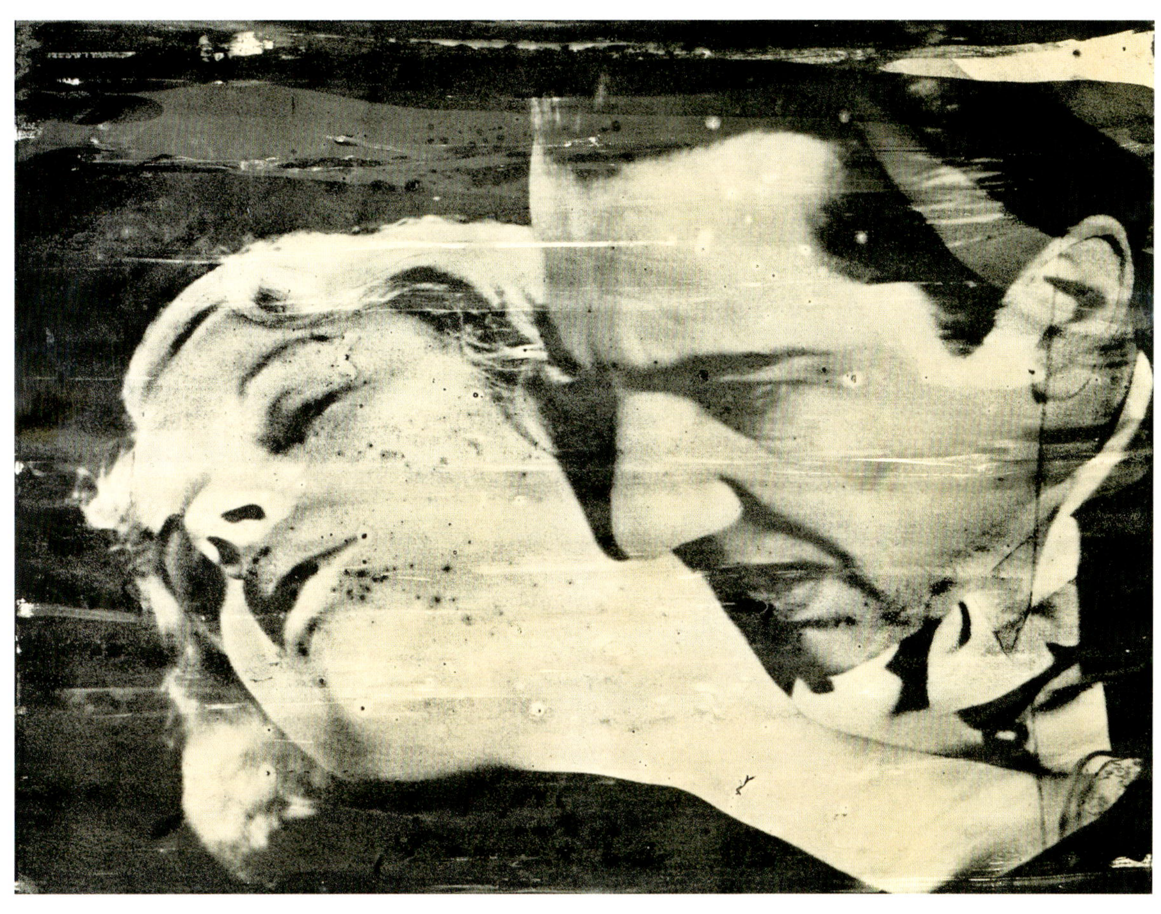

◂ 157 **Kiss 1965**
The Andy Warhol Museum, Pittsburgh
Founding Collection, Contribution
The Andy Warhol Foundation
for the Visual Arts, Inc.

158 **The Kiss (Bela Lugosi) 1964**
Collection Sylvio Perlstein, Antwerp

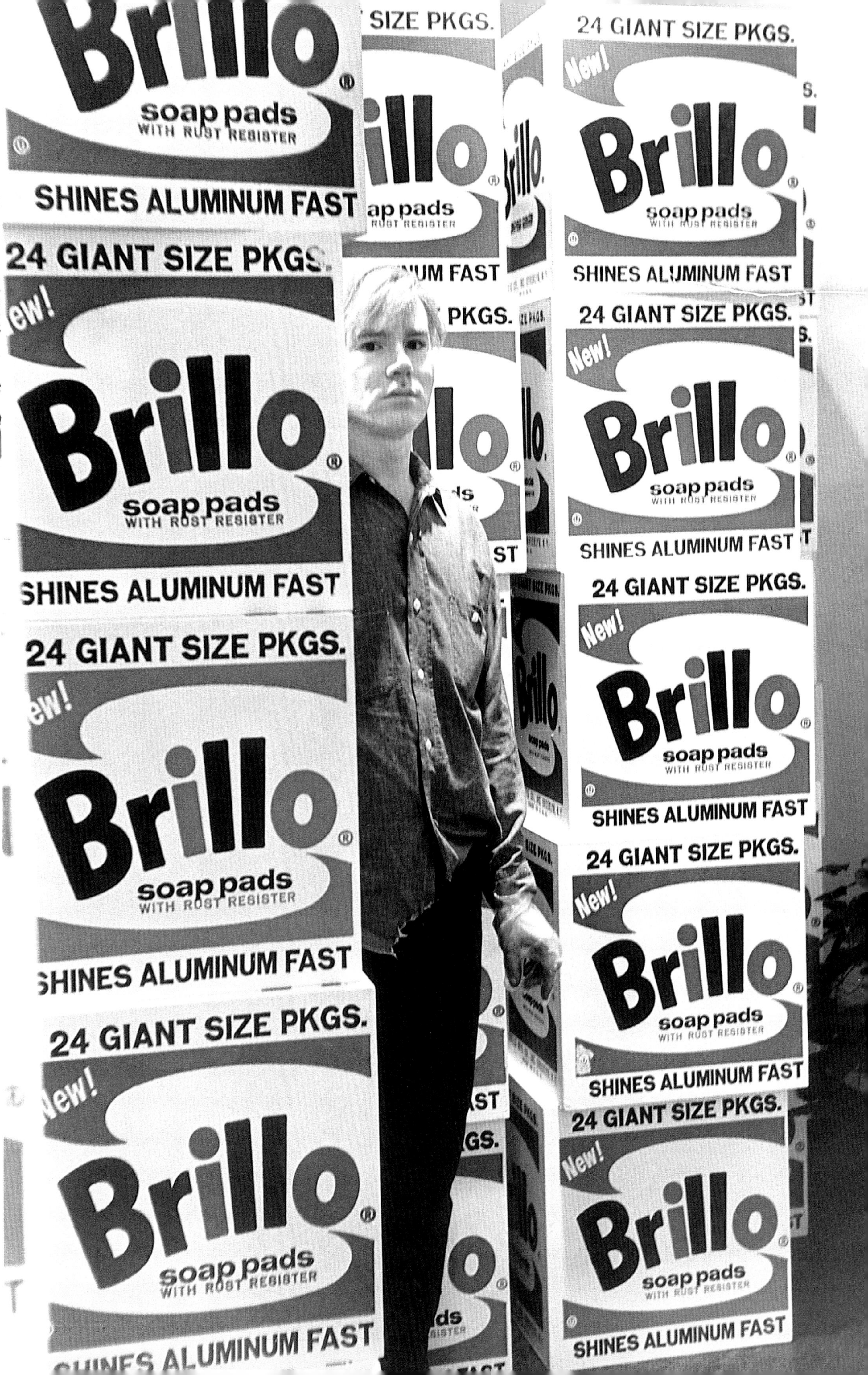

24 GIANT SIZE PKGS.
New!
Brillo®
soap pads
WITH RUST RESISTER
SHINES ALUMINUM FAST

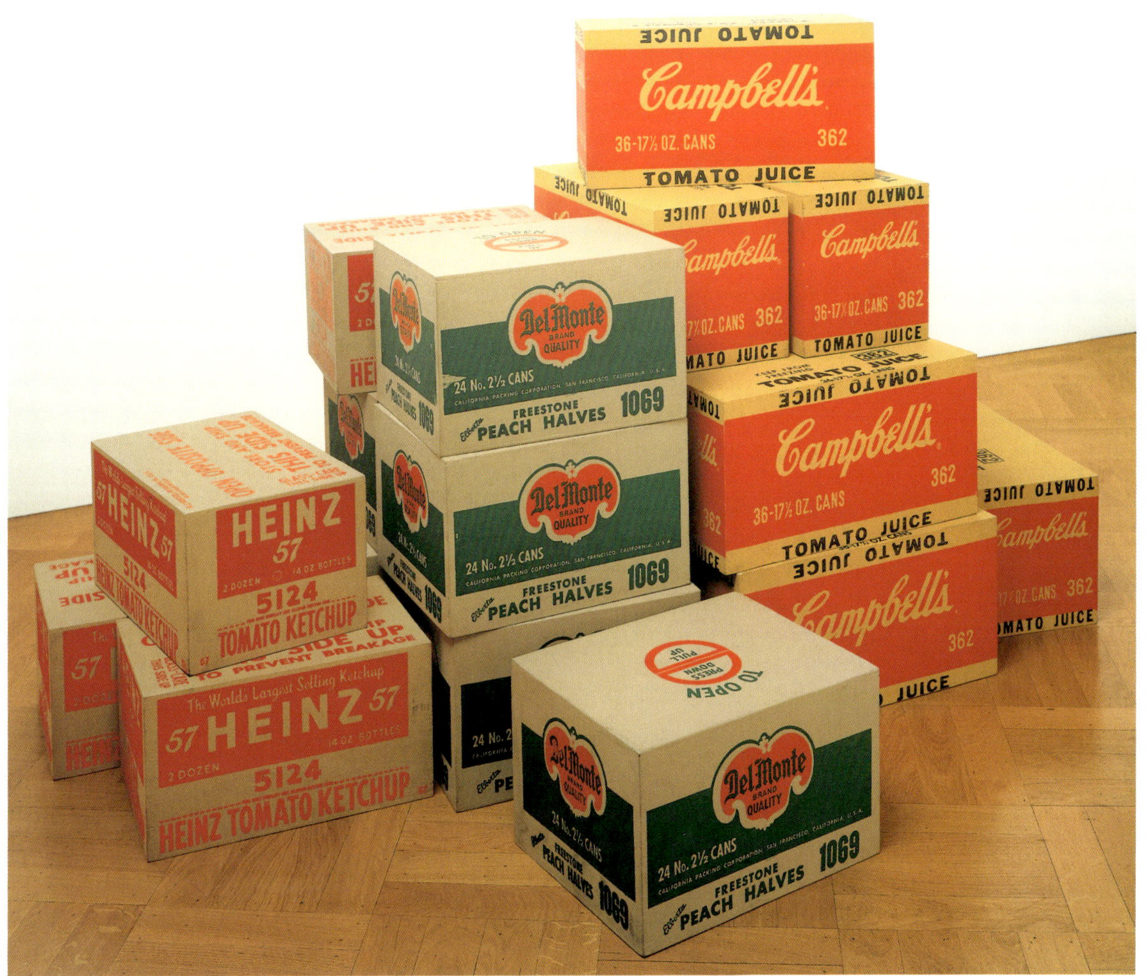

159 Campbell's Boxes (Tomato Juice) 1964
160 Del Monte Boxes (Peach Halves) 1964
161 Heinz Boxes (Tomato Ketchup) 1964
Courtesy Anthony d'Offay Gallery, London

162 **Brillo Boxes 1969**
(version of 1964 original)
Norton Simon Museum, Pasadena, CA
Gift of the Artist, 1969

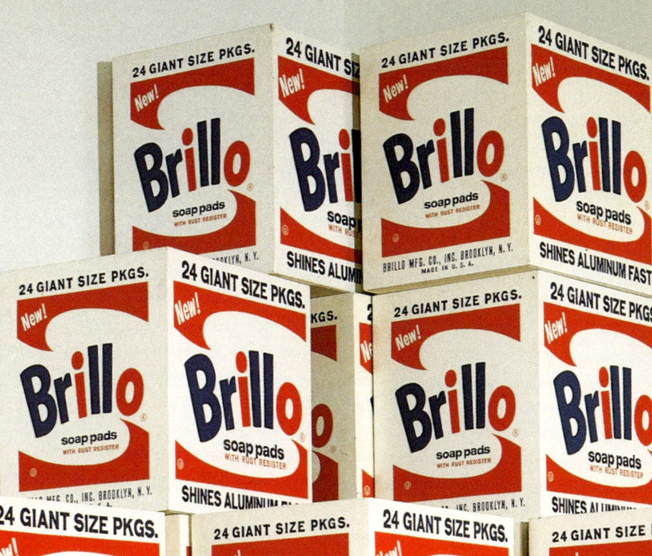
24 GIANT SIZE PKGS.
New!
Brillo
soap pads
SHINES ALUMINUM FAST
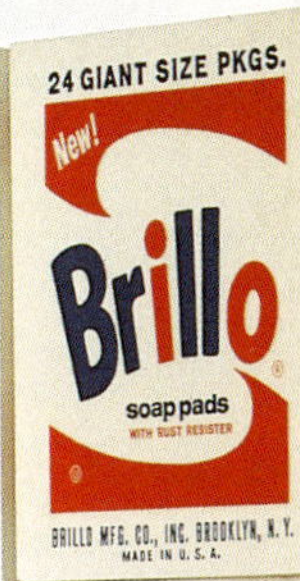
24 GIANT SIZE PKGS.
New!
Brillo
soap pads
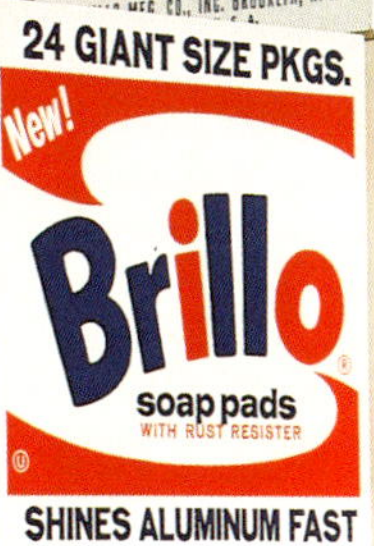
24 GIANT SIZE PKGS.
New!
Brillo
soap pads
SHINES ALUMINUM FAST
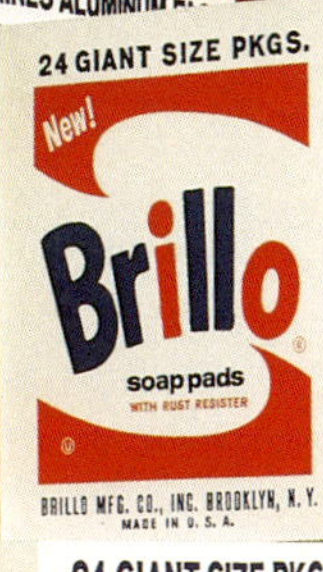
24 GIANT SIZE PKGS.
New!
Brillo
soap pads
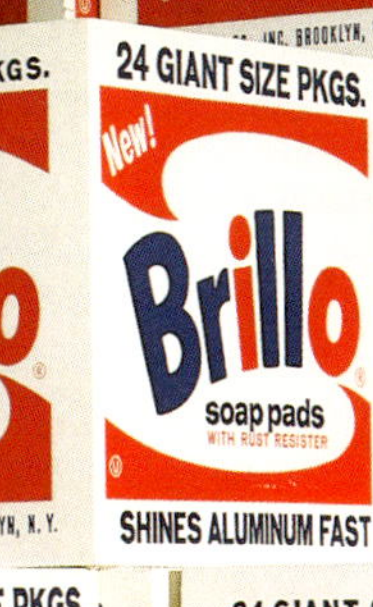
24 GIANT SIZE PKGS.
New!
Brillo
soap pads
SHINES ALUMINUM FAST
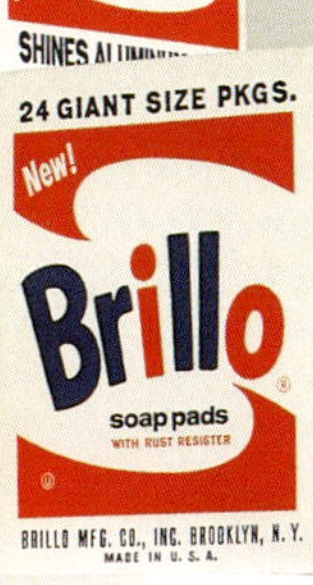
24 GIANT SIZE PKGS.
New!
Brillo
soap pads
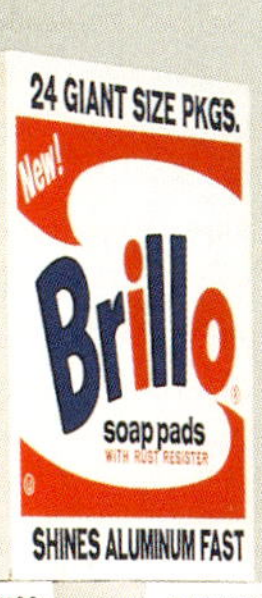
24 GIANT SIZE PKGS.
New!
Brillo
soap pads
SHINES ALUMINUM FAST
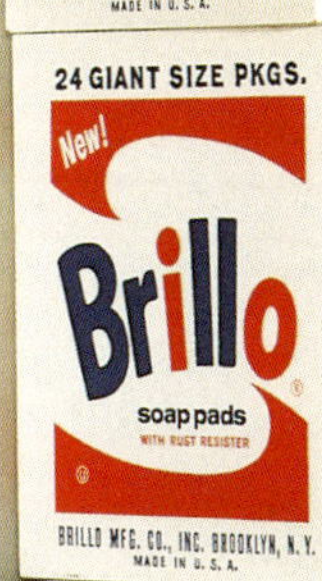
24 GIANT SIZE PKGS.
New!
Brillo
soap pads
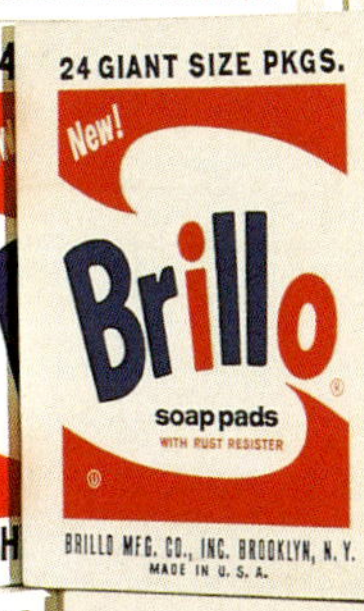
24 GIANT SIZE PKGS.
New!
Brillo
soap pads
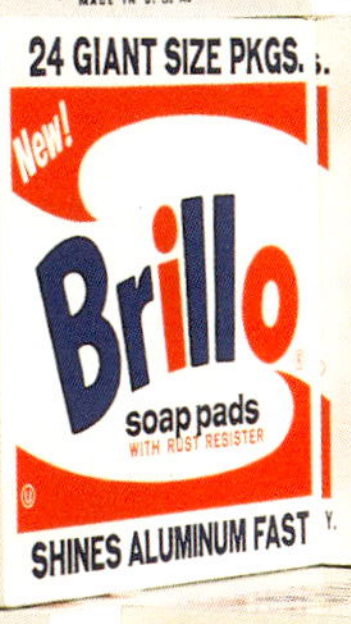
24 GIANT SIZE PKGS.
New!
Brillo
soap pads
SHINES ALUMINUM FAST
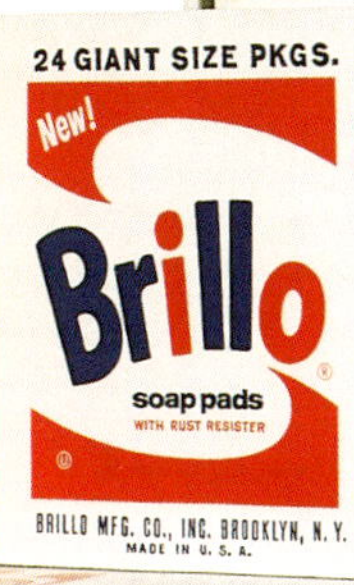
24 GIANT SIZE PKGS.
New!
Brillo
soap pads
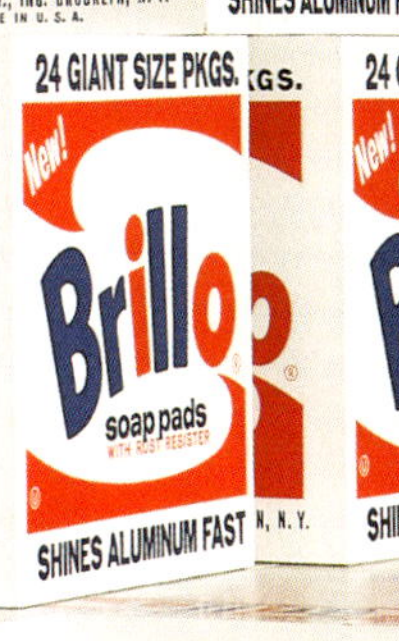
24 GIANT SIZE PKGS.
New!
Brillo
soap pads
SHINES ALUMINUM FAST
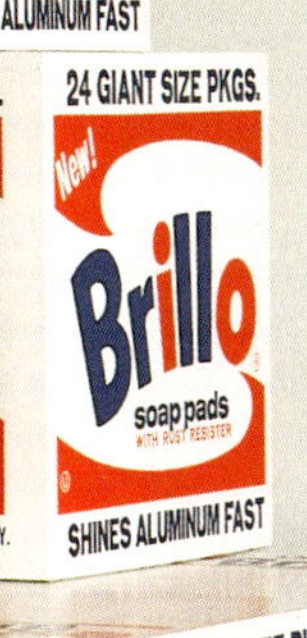
24 GIANT SIZE PKGS.
New!
Brillo
soap pads
SHINES ALUMINUM FAST
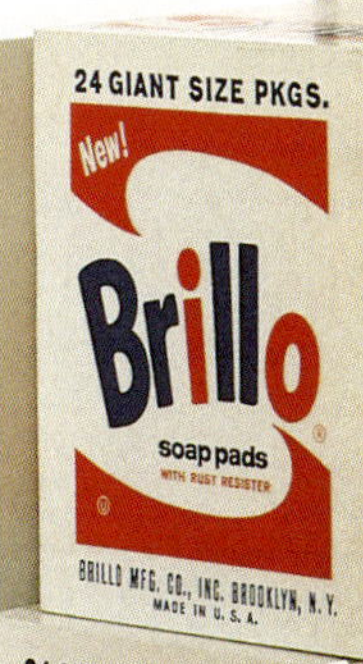
24 GIANT SIZE PKGS.
New!
Brillo
soap pads
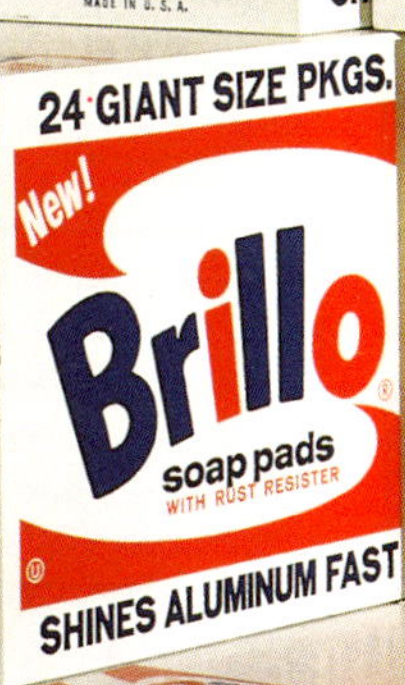
24 GIANT SIZE PKGS.
New!
Brillo
soap pads
WITH RUST RESISTER
SHINES ALUMINUM FAST
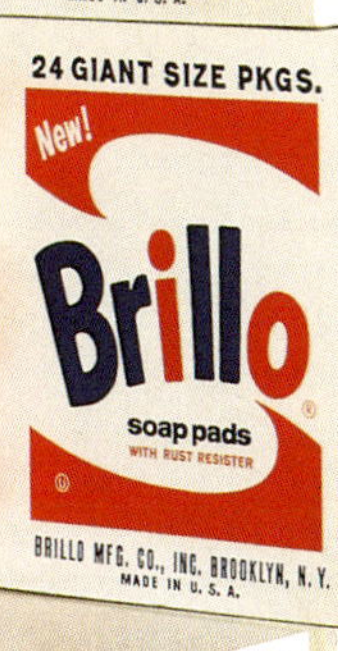
24 GIANT SIZE PKGS.
New!
Brillo
soap pads
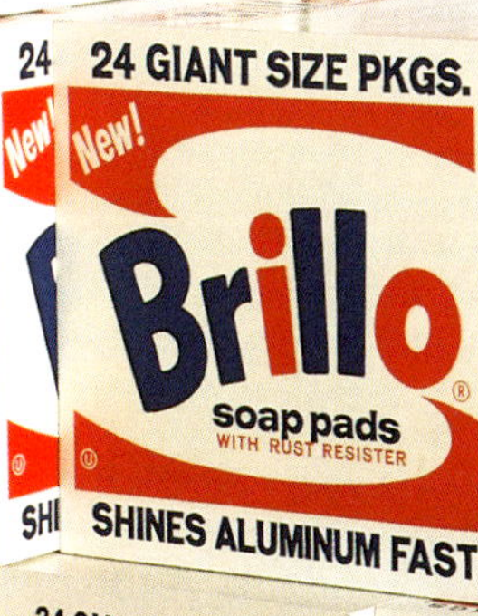
24 GIANT SIZE PKGS.
New!
Brillo
soap pads
WITH RUST RESISTER
SHINES ALUMINUM FAST
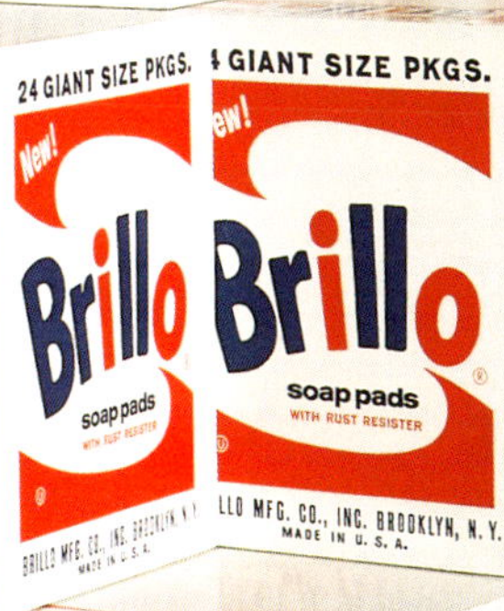
New!
Brillo
soap pads
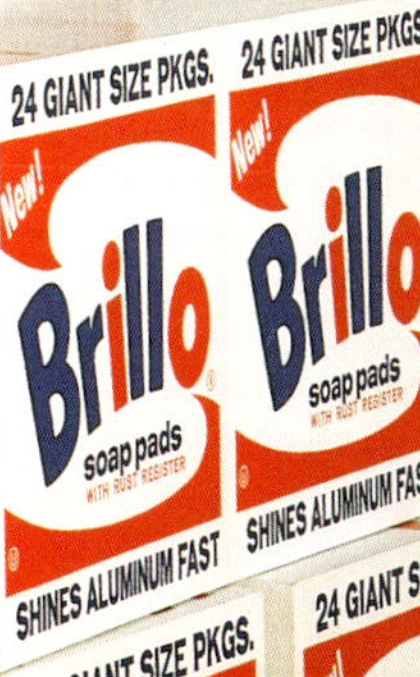
24 GIANT SIZE PKGS.
New!
Brillo
soap pads
SHINES ALUMINUM FAST
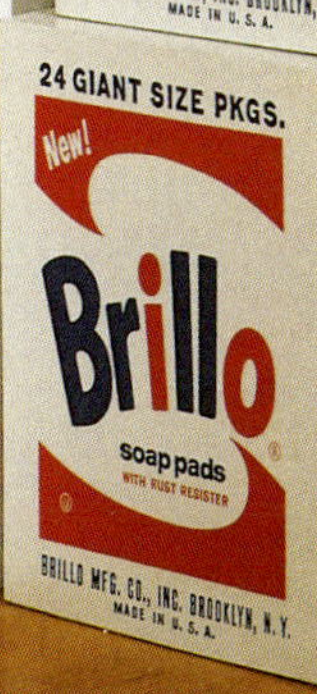
24 GIANT SIZE PKGS.
New!
Brillo
soap pads
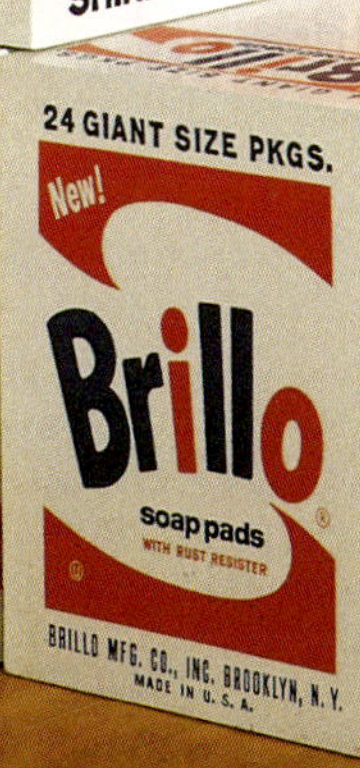
24 GIANT SIZE PKGS.
New!
Brillo
soap pads
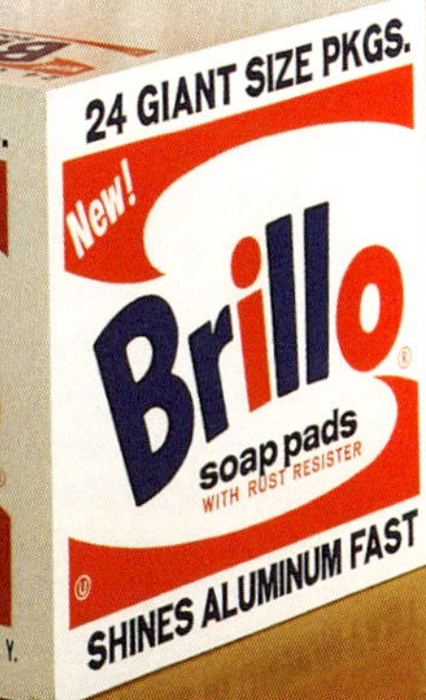
24 GIANT SIZE PKGS.
New!
Brillo
soap pads
WITH RUST RESISTER
SHINES ALUMINUM FAST
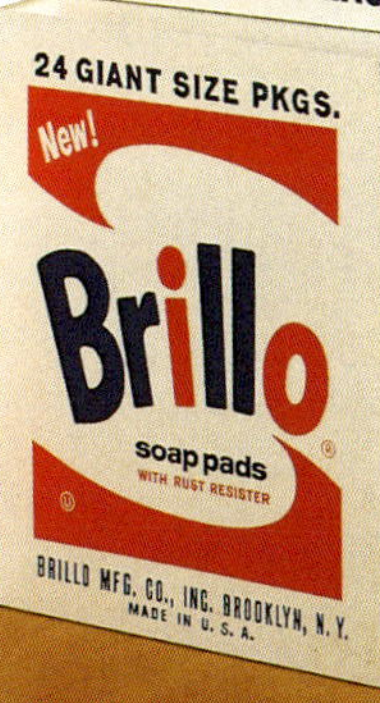
24 GIANT SIZE PKGS.
New!
Brillo
soap pads
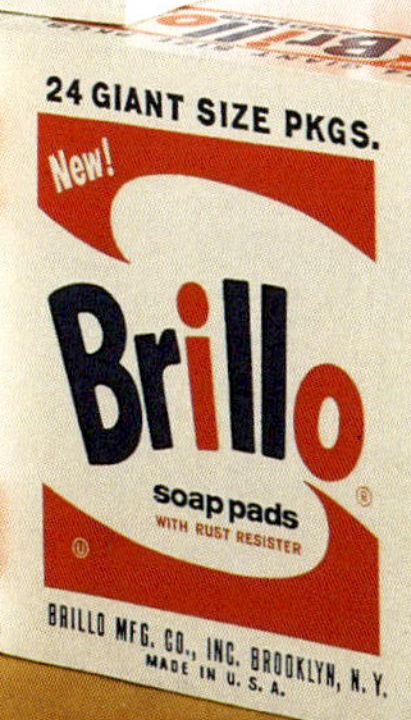
24 GIANT SIZE PKGS.
New!
Brillo
soap pads
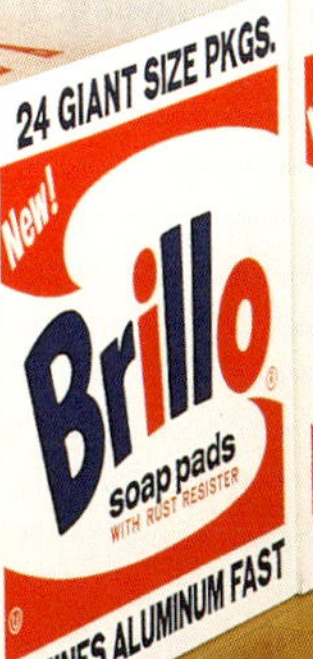
24 GIANT SIZE PKGS.
New!
Brillo
soap pads
SHINES ALUMINUM FAST
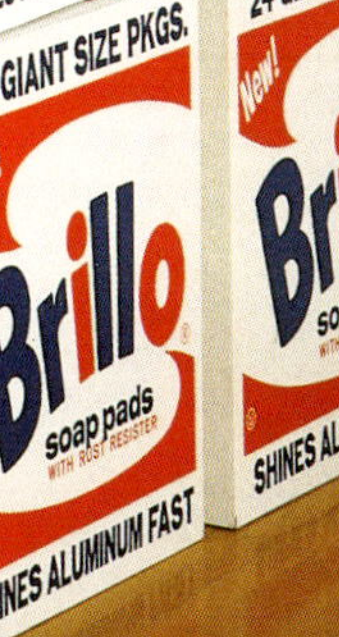
24 GIANT SIZE PKGS.
New!
Brillo
soap pads
SHINES ALUMINUM FAST

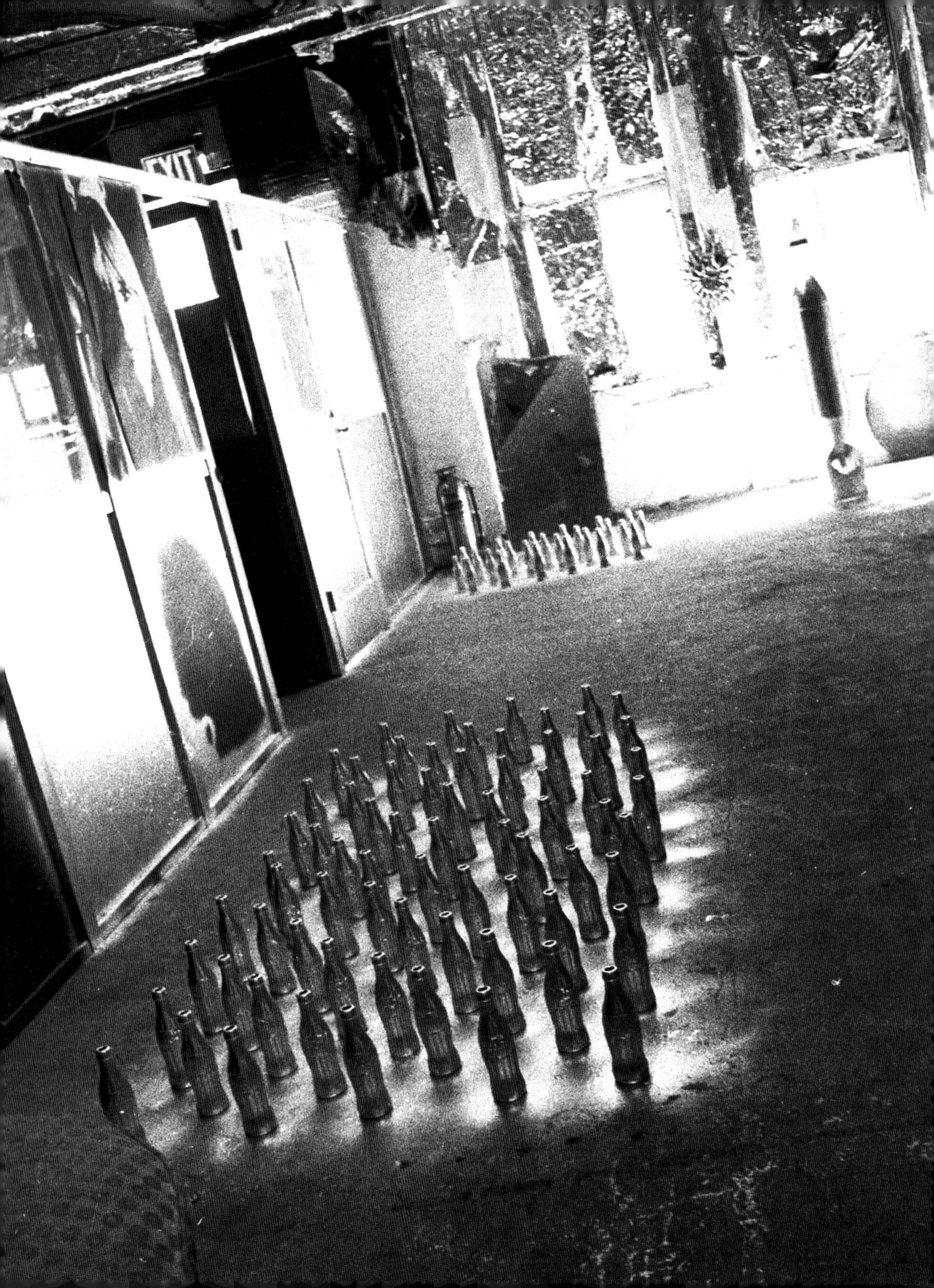
EXIT

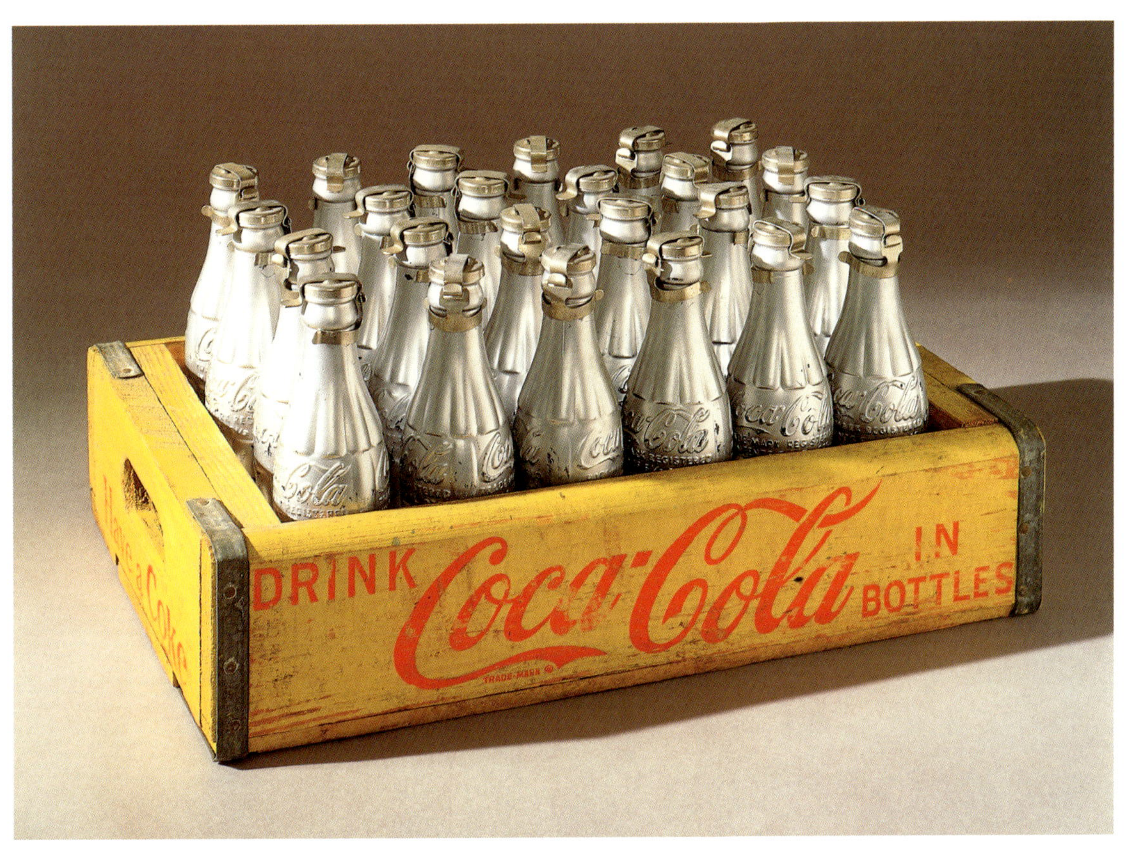

163 **Silver Coke Bottles 1967** Courtesy The Brant Foundation, Greenwich, CT

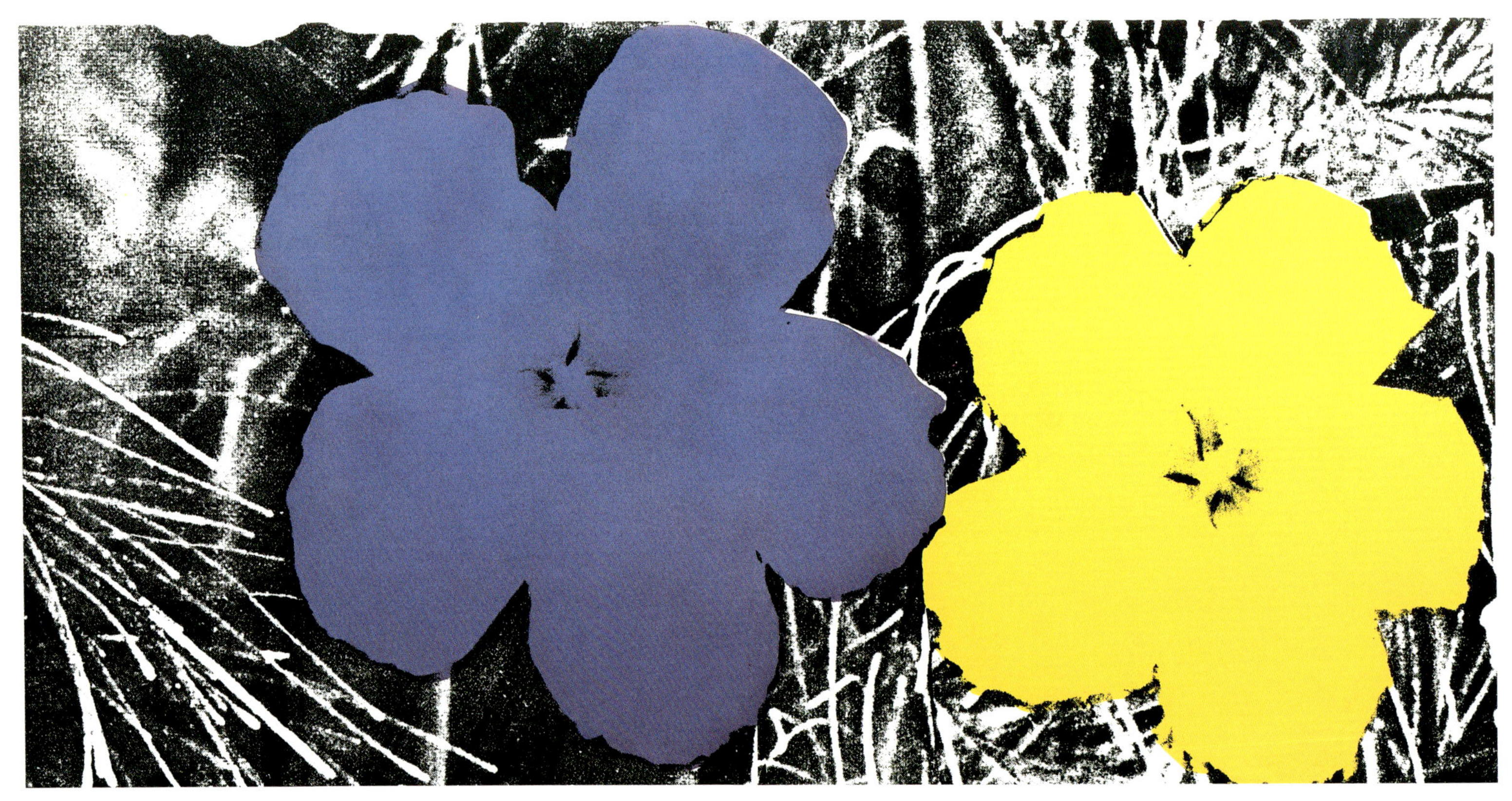

164 **Flowers** **1964** Stedelijk Museum, Amsterdam • Purchase through the Contribution of ›Vereniging Rembrandt‹

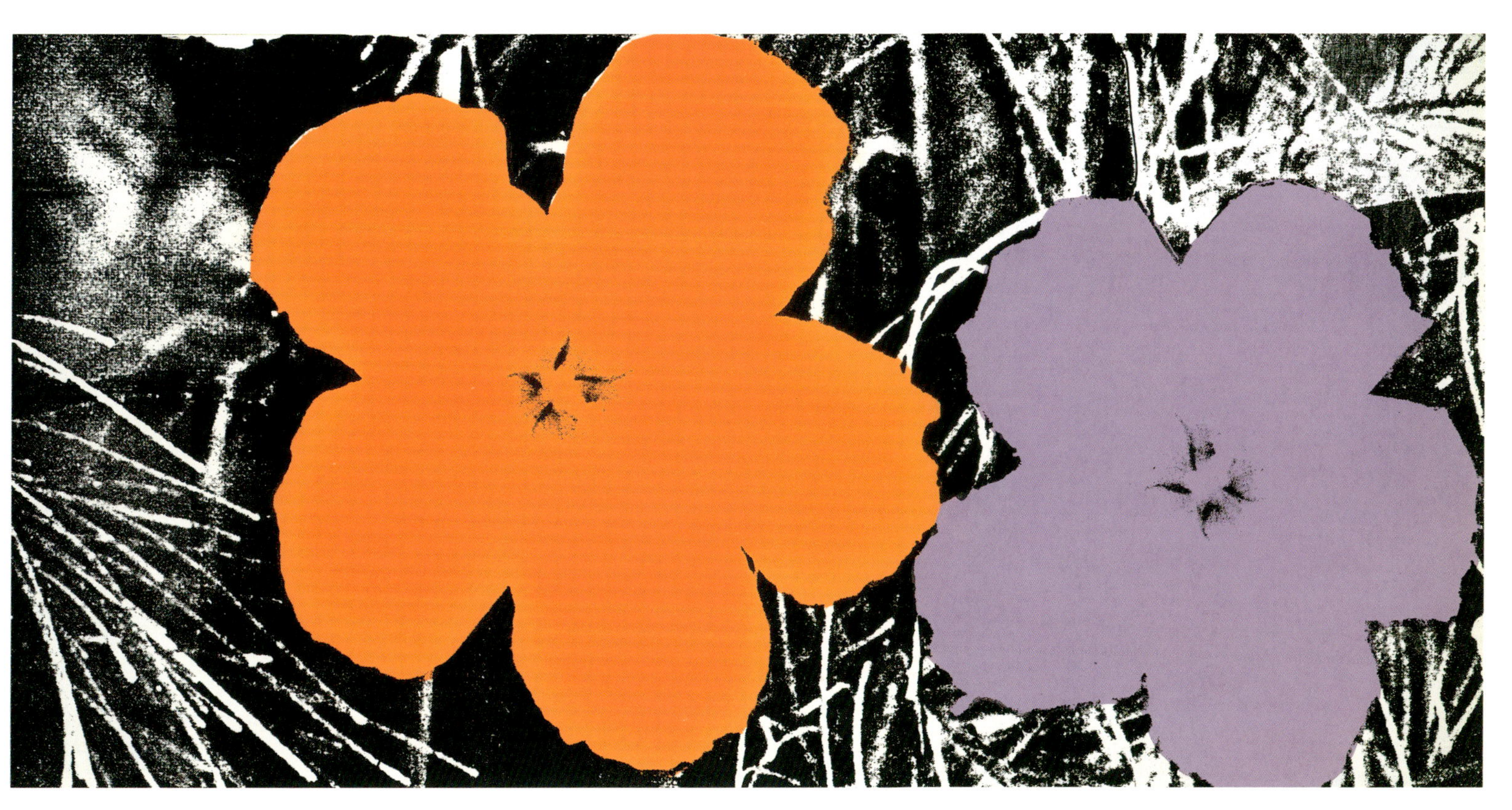

165 **Flowers** **1964** Courtesy The Brant Foundation, Greenwich, CT

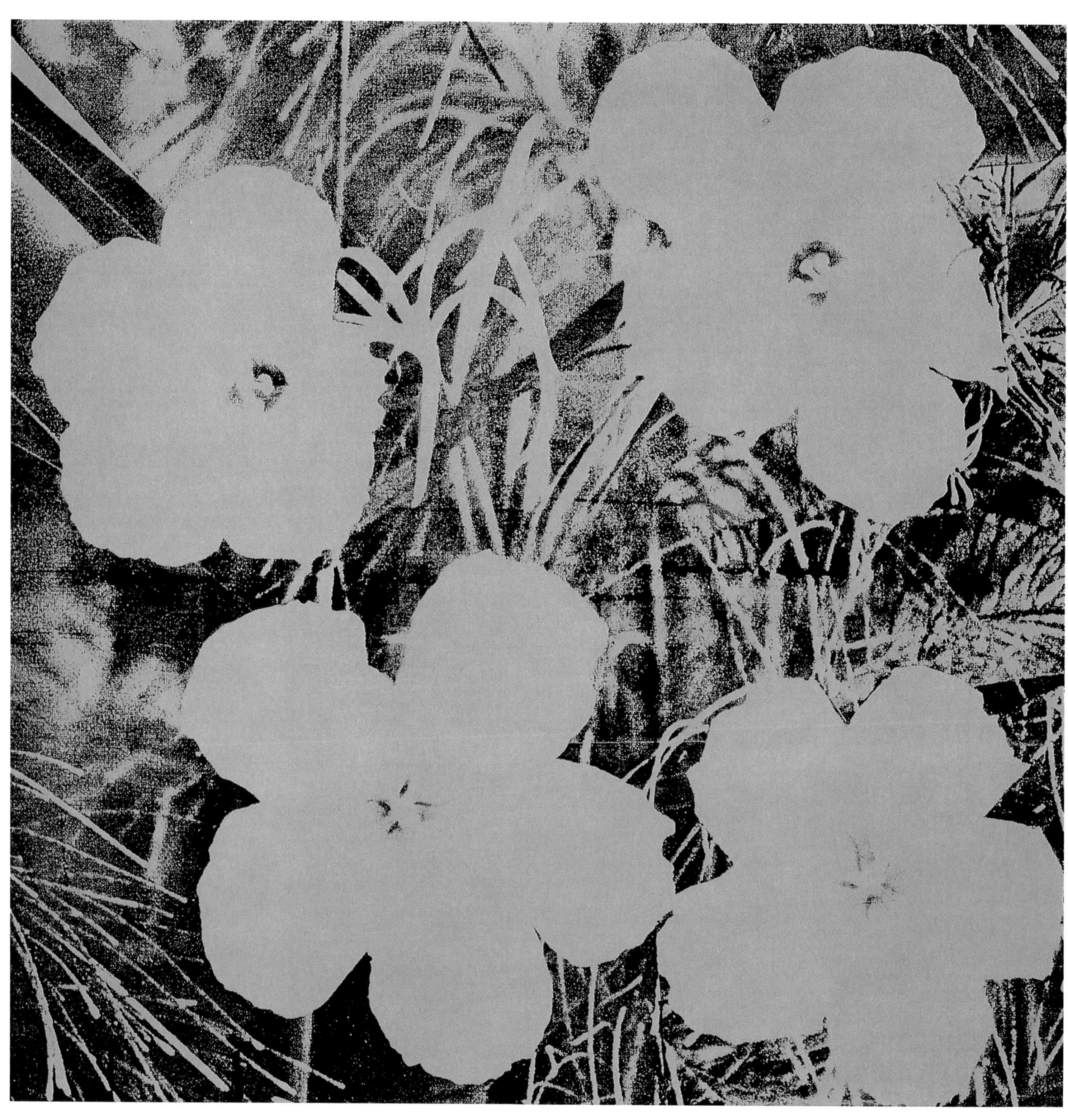

166 Ten-Foot Flowers 1967 Collection Museum of Contemporary Art, San Diego
Museum purchase with contributions from the Museum Art Council Fund

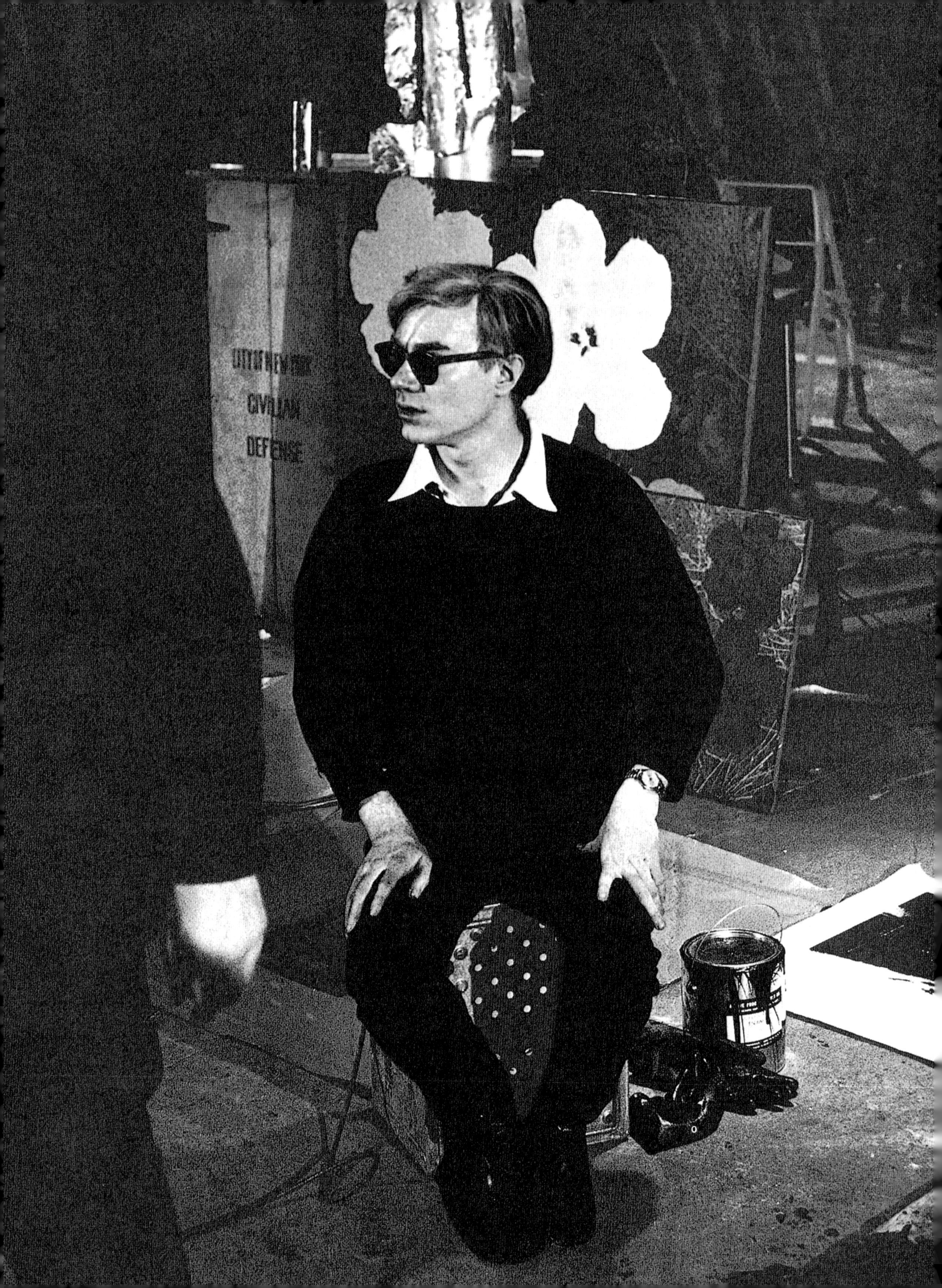
CIVILIAN
DEFENSE

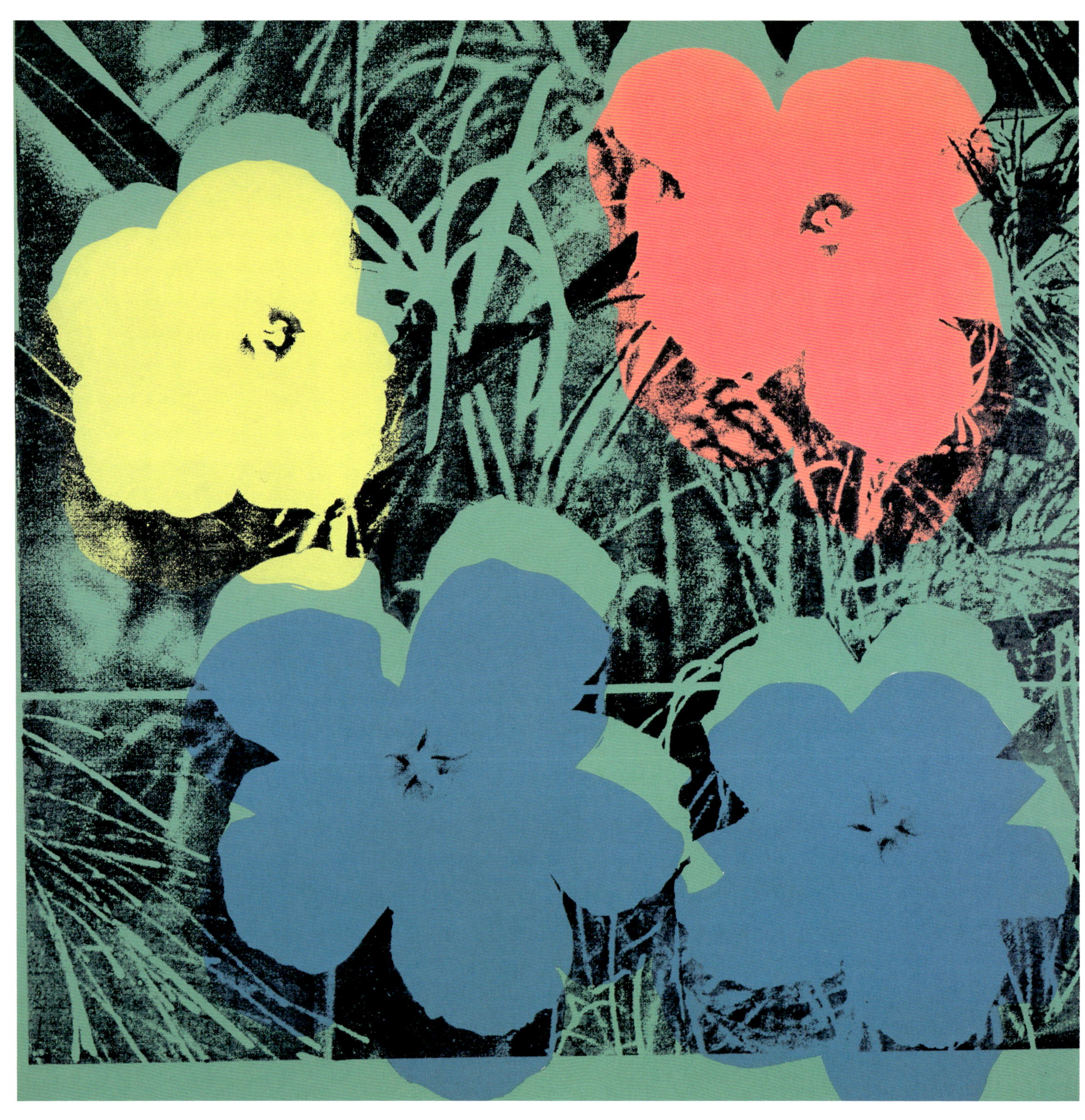

167 Ten-Foot Flowers 1967 Stiftung Sammlung Marx, Hamburger Bahnhof – Museum für Gegenwart, Berlin

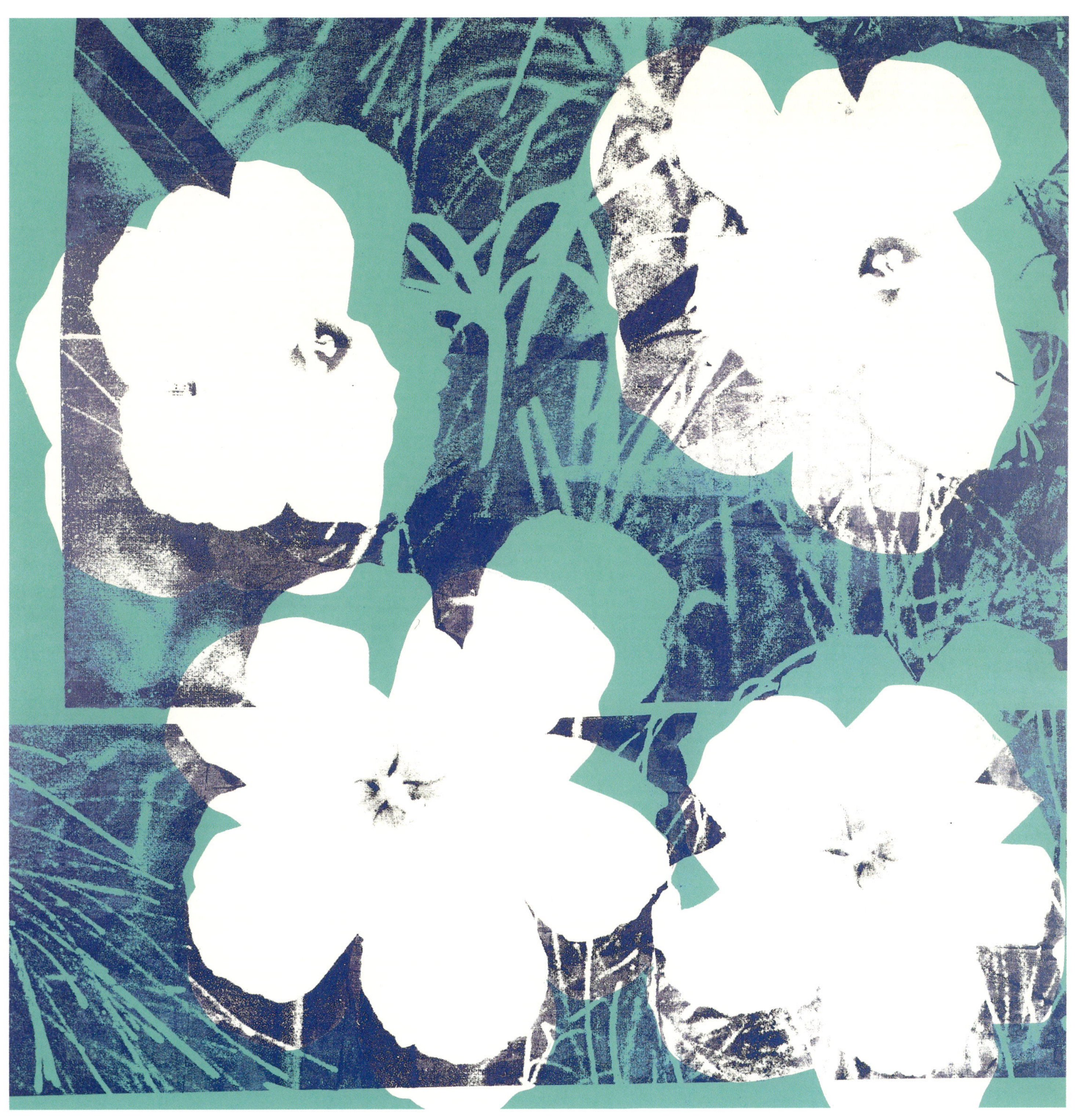

168 Ten-Foot Flowers 1967 Private collection

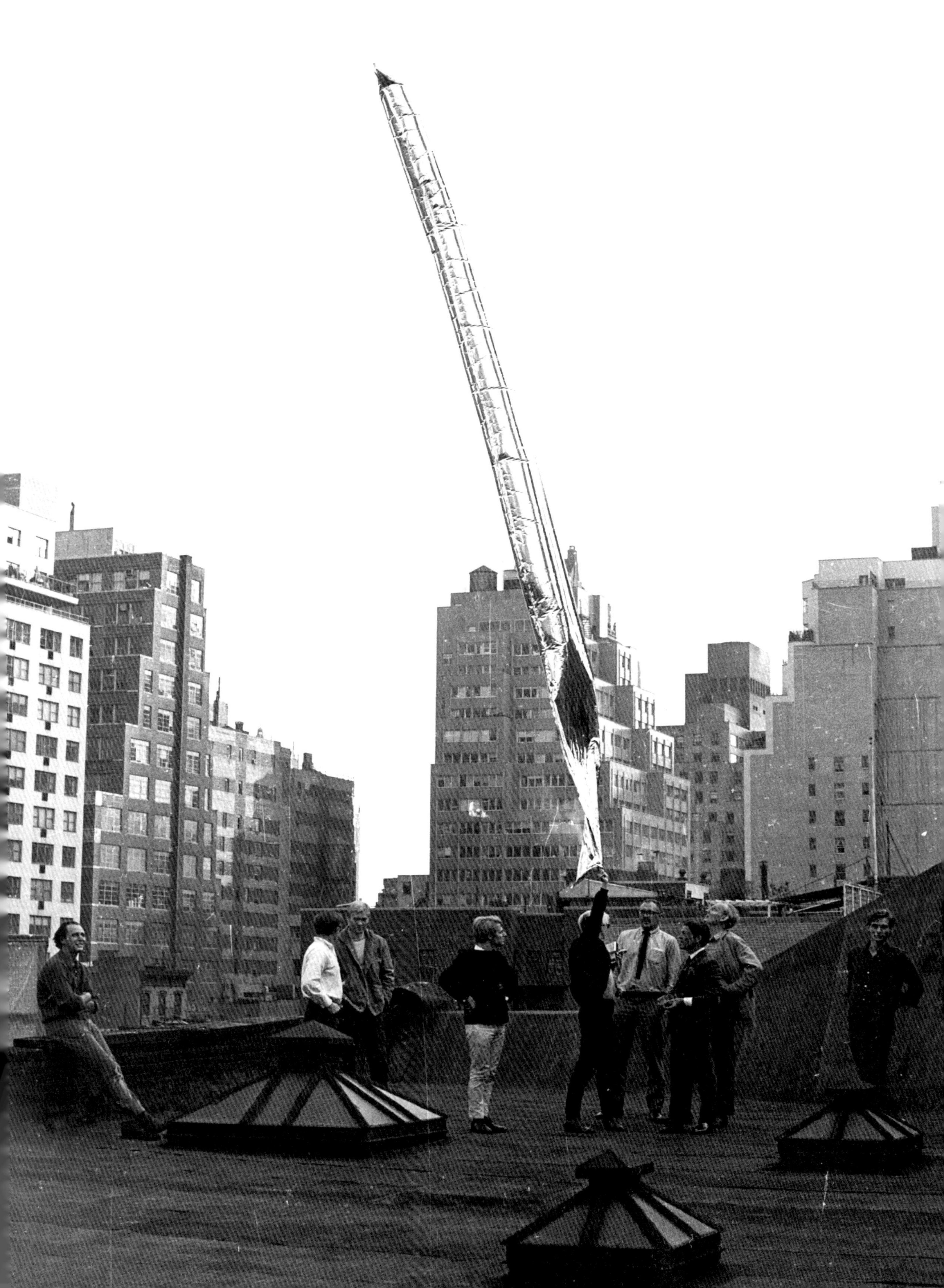

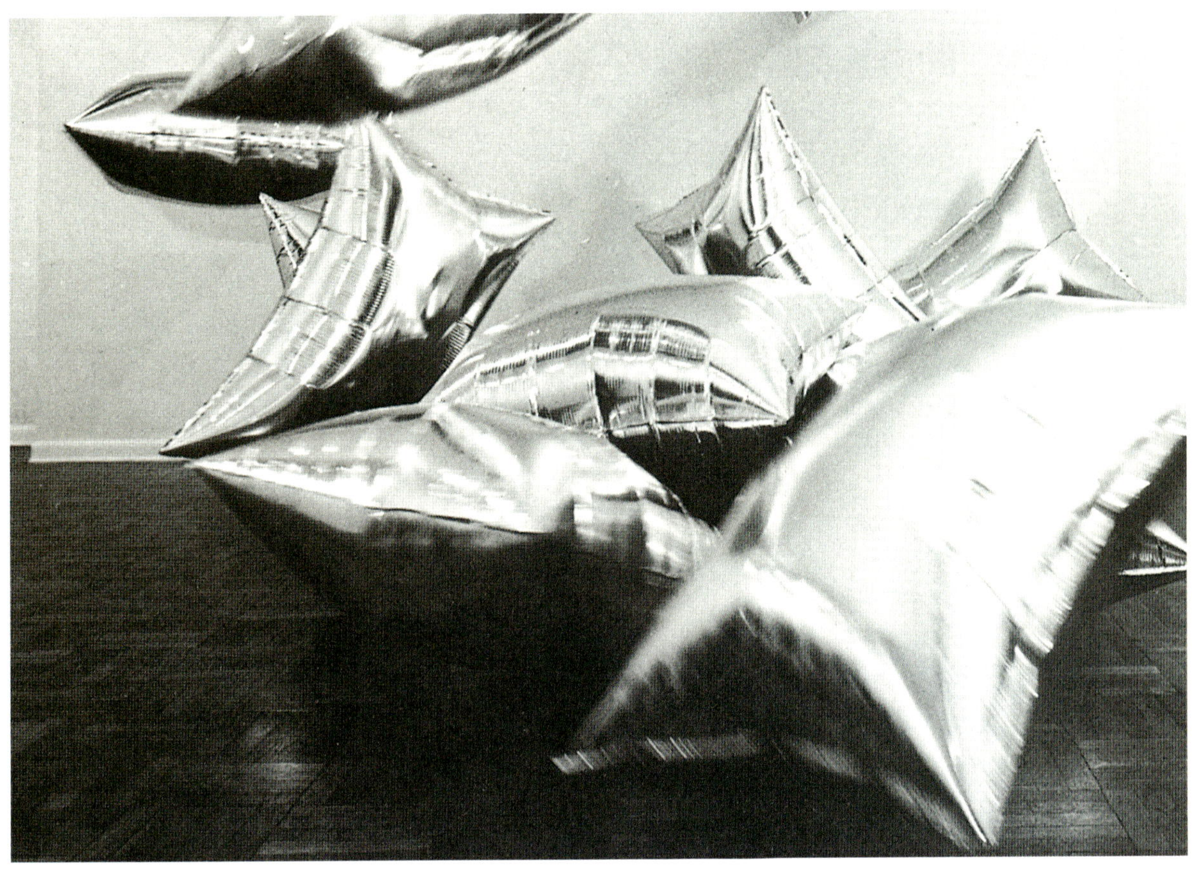

Exhibition of *Silver Clouds*, Leo Castelli Gallery, New York, April 1966

◂ Andy Warhol, Gerard Malanga, Pontus Hultén, Billy Klüver and friends on the roof of the Factory building, 1966

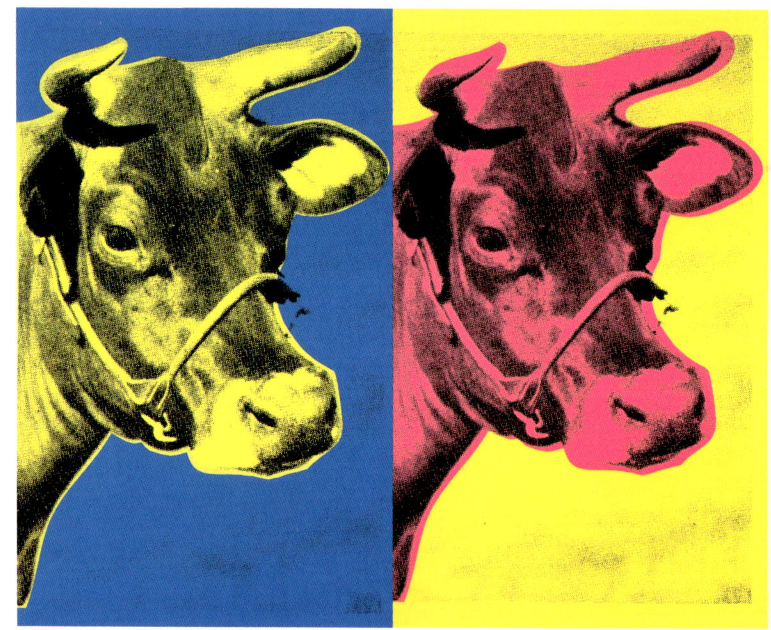

169 **Cow (Wallpaper)** 1966
Private collection

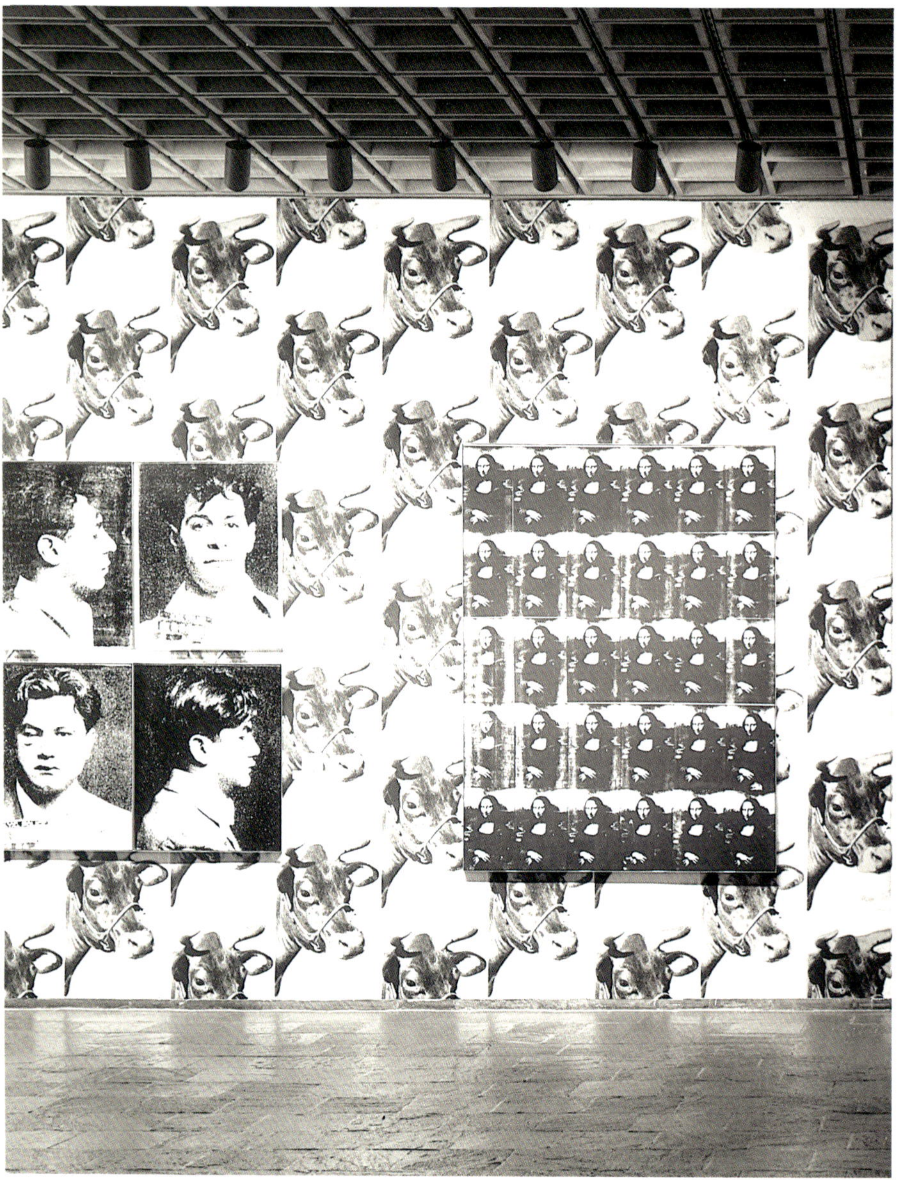

Andy Warhol exhibition, Whitney Museum of American Art, New York 1971

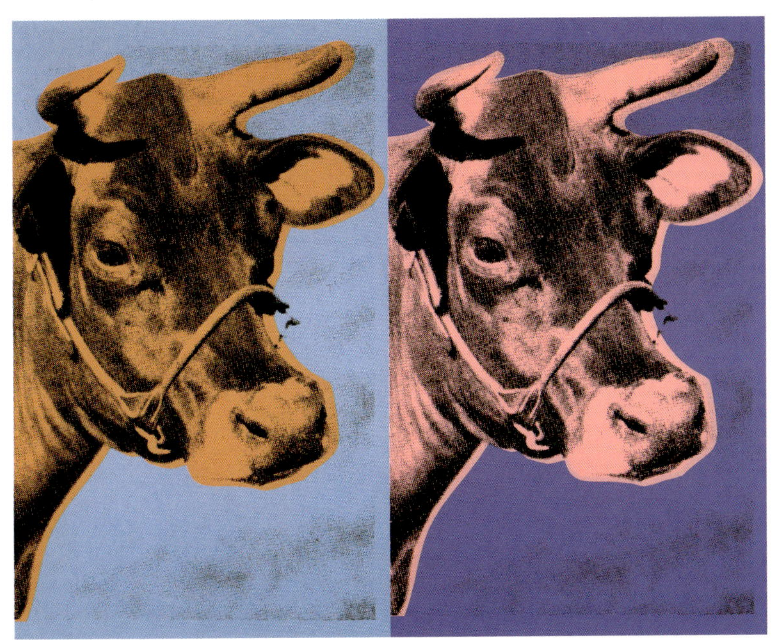

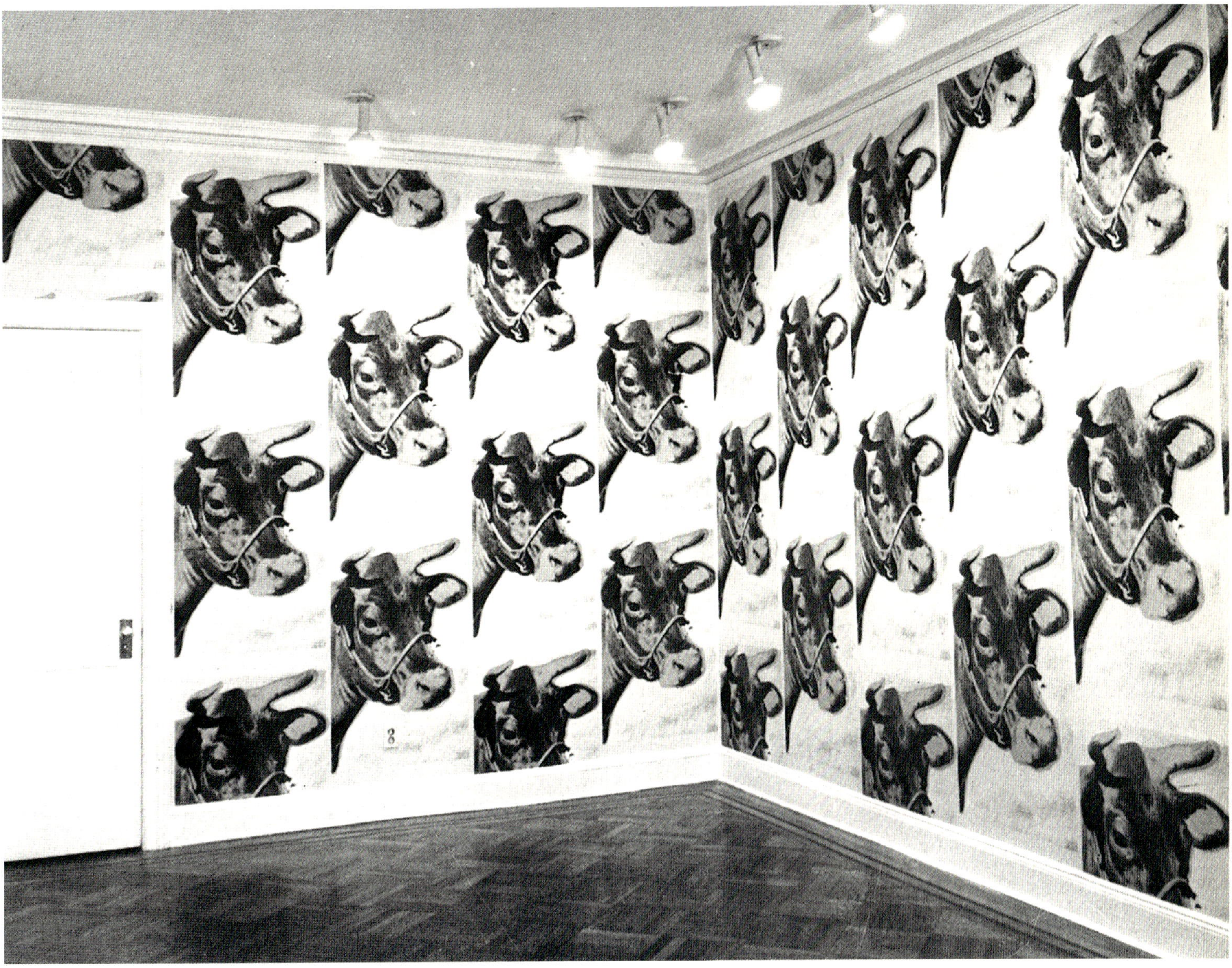

Exhibition of *Cow Wallpaper*, Leo Castelli Gallery, New York 1966

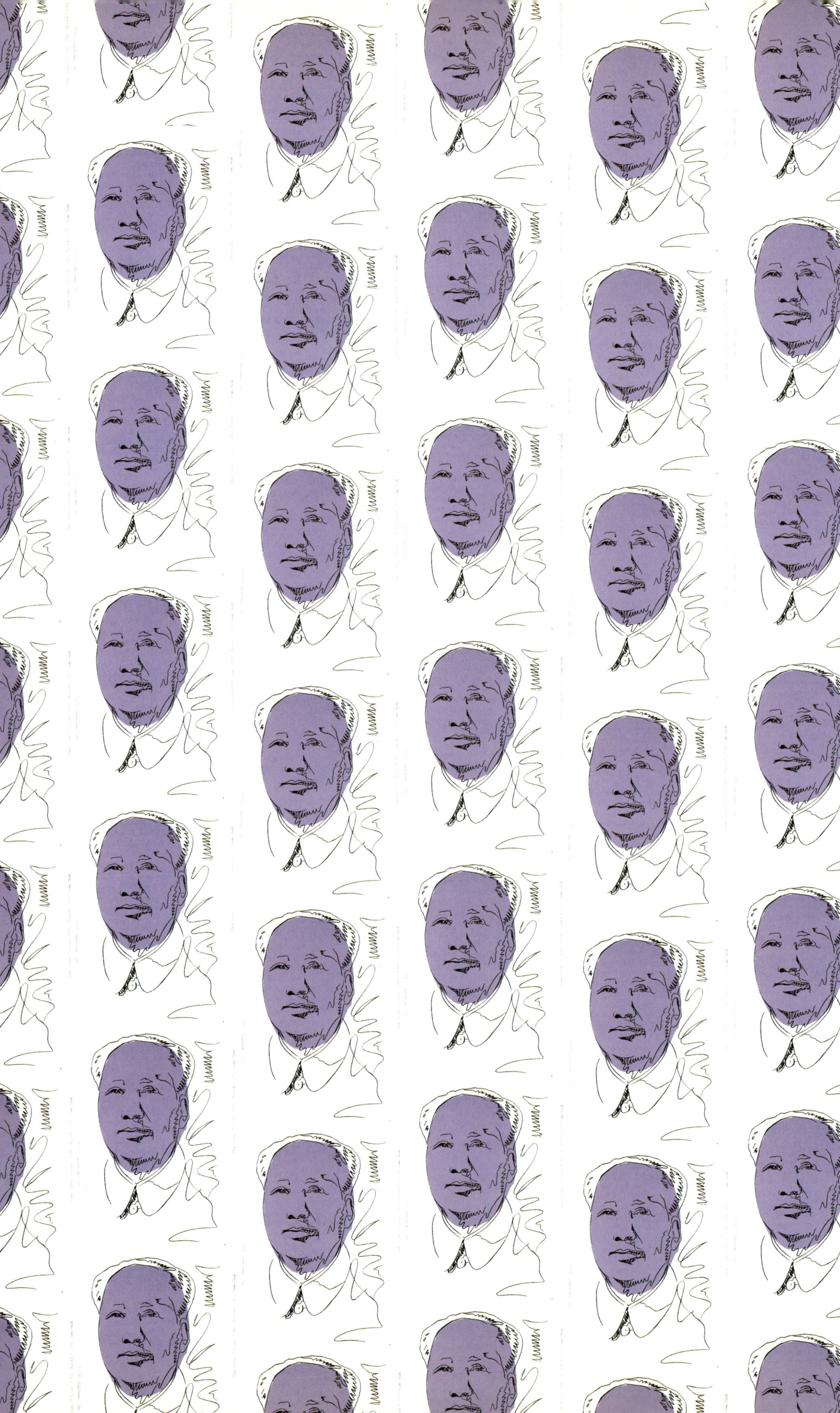

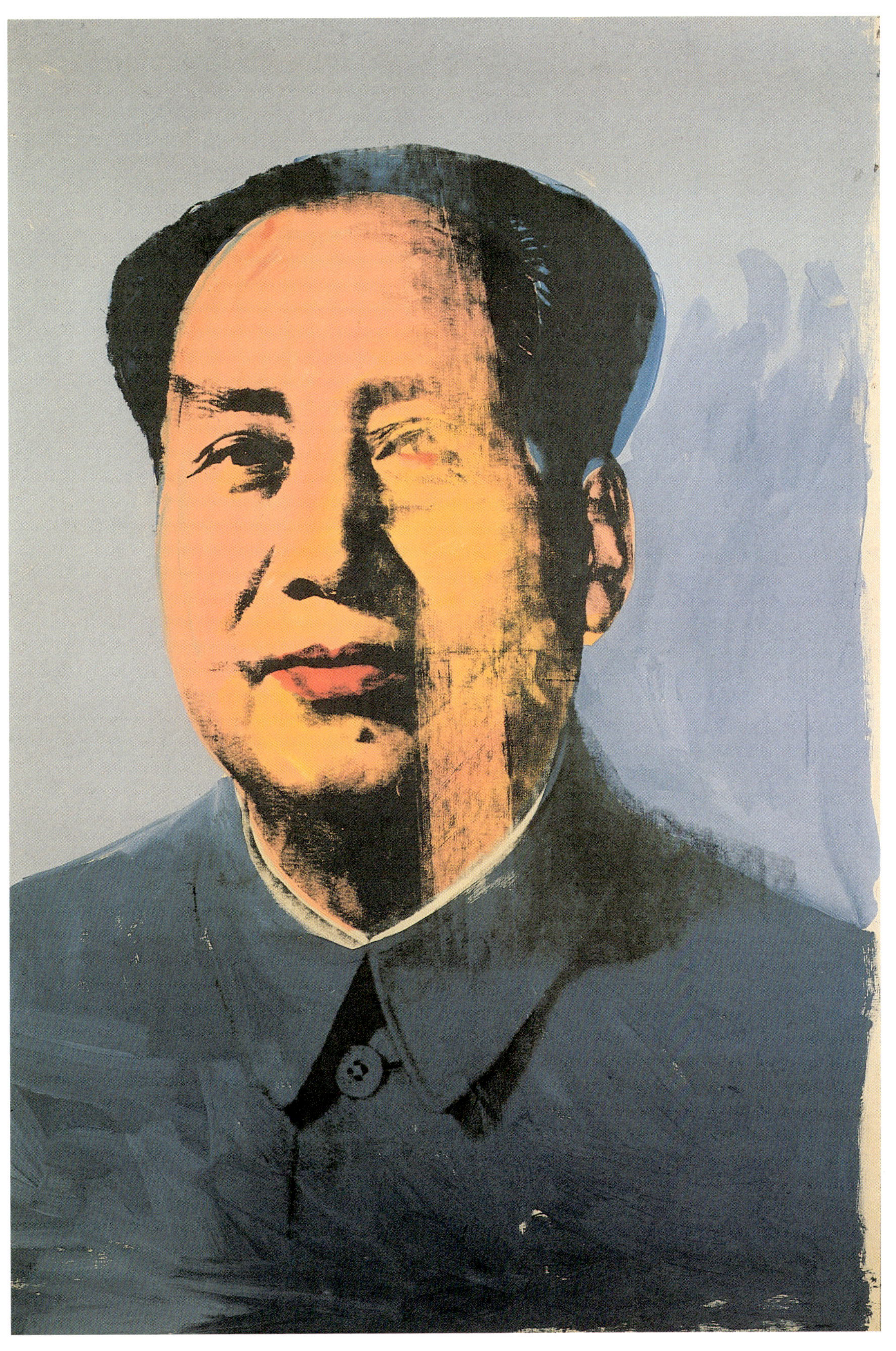

172 **Mao** **1972** Collection Froehlich, Stuttgart

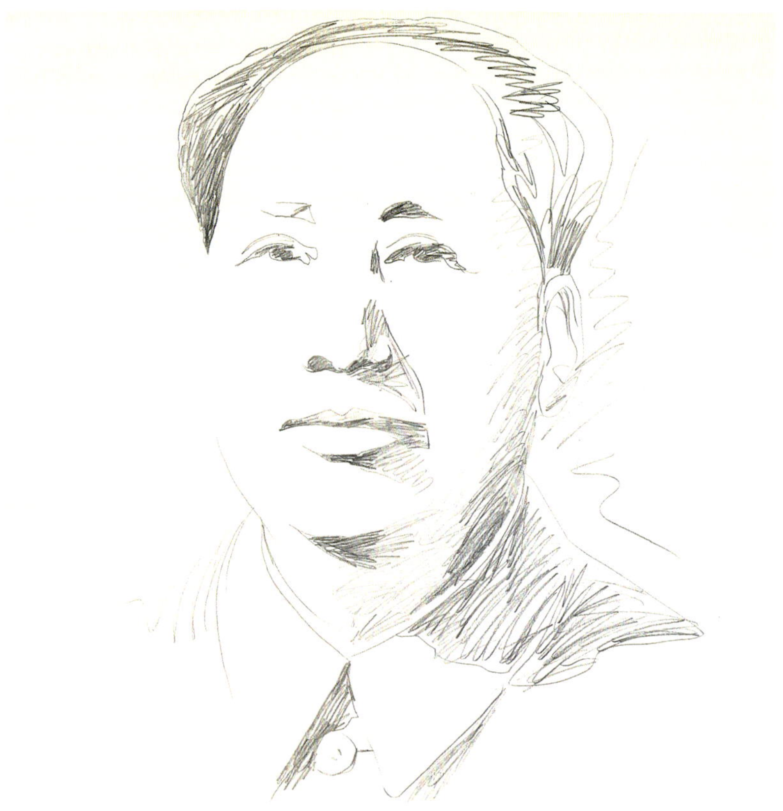

173 **Mao** **1973** Fondation H. Looser

174 **Mao** **1973**
Stiftung Sammlung Marx,
Hamburger Bahnhof –
Museum für Gegenwart, Berlin

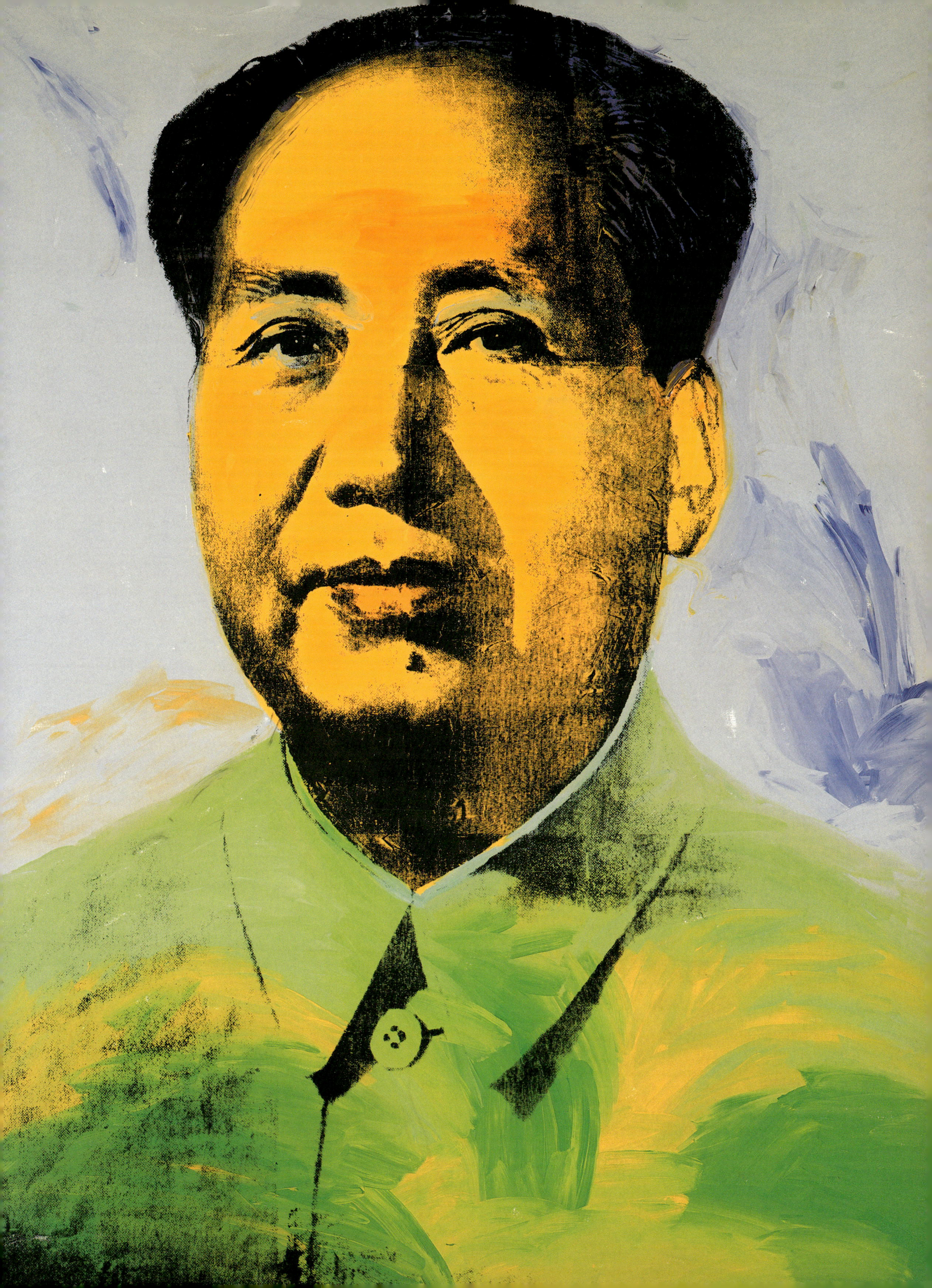

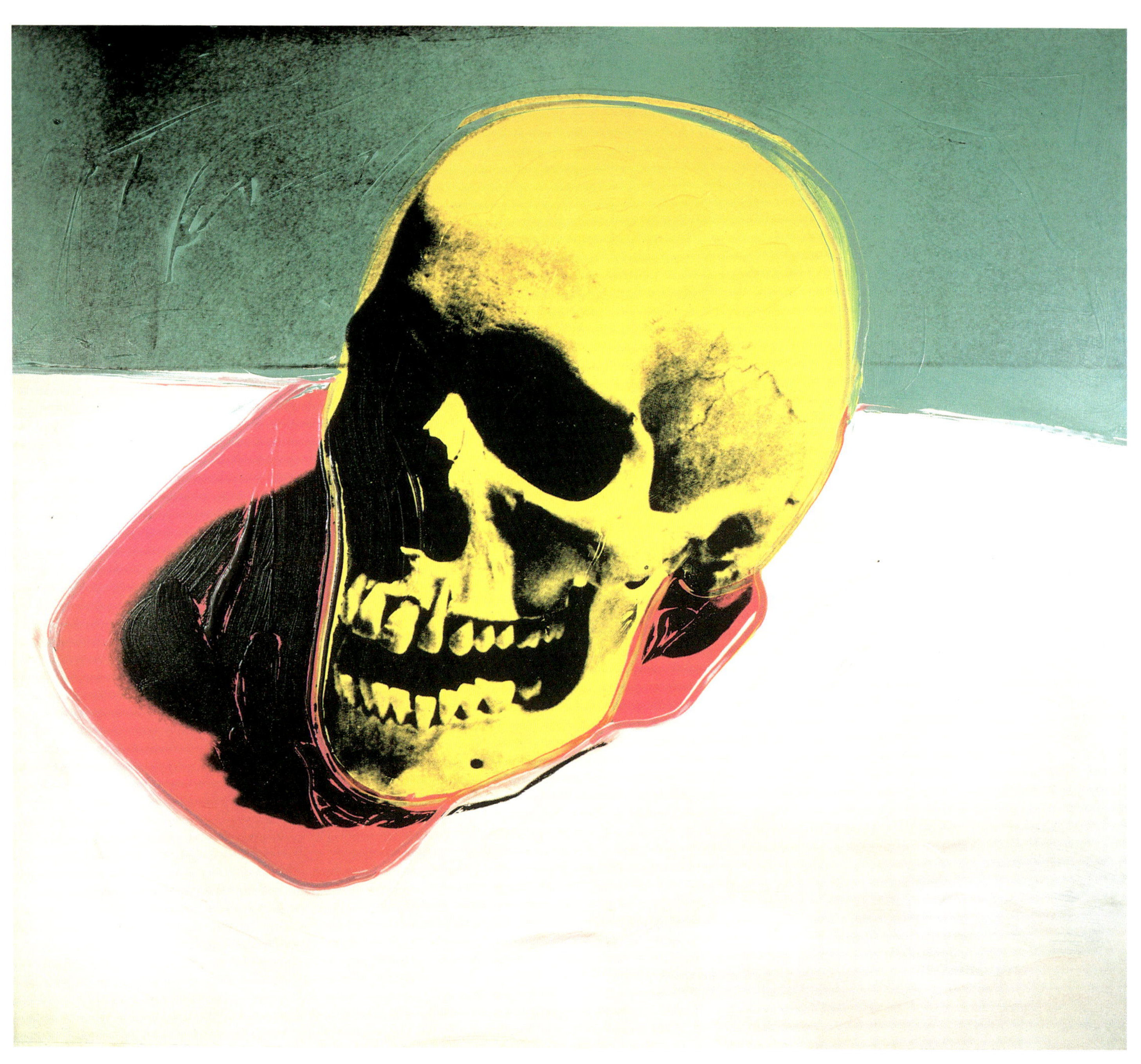

175 **Skull** **1976** Collection Froehlich, Stuttgart

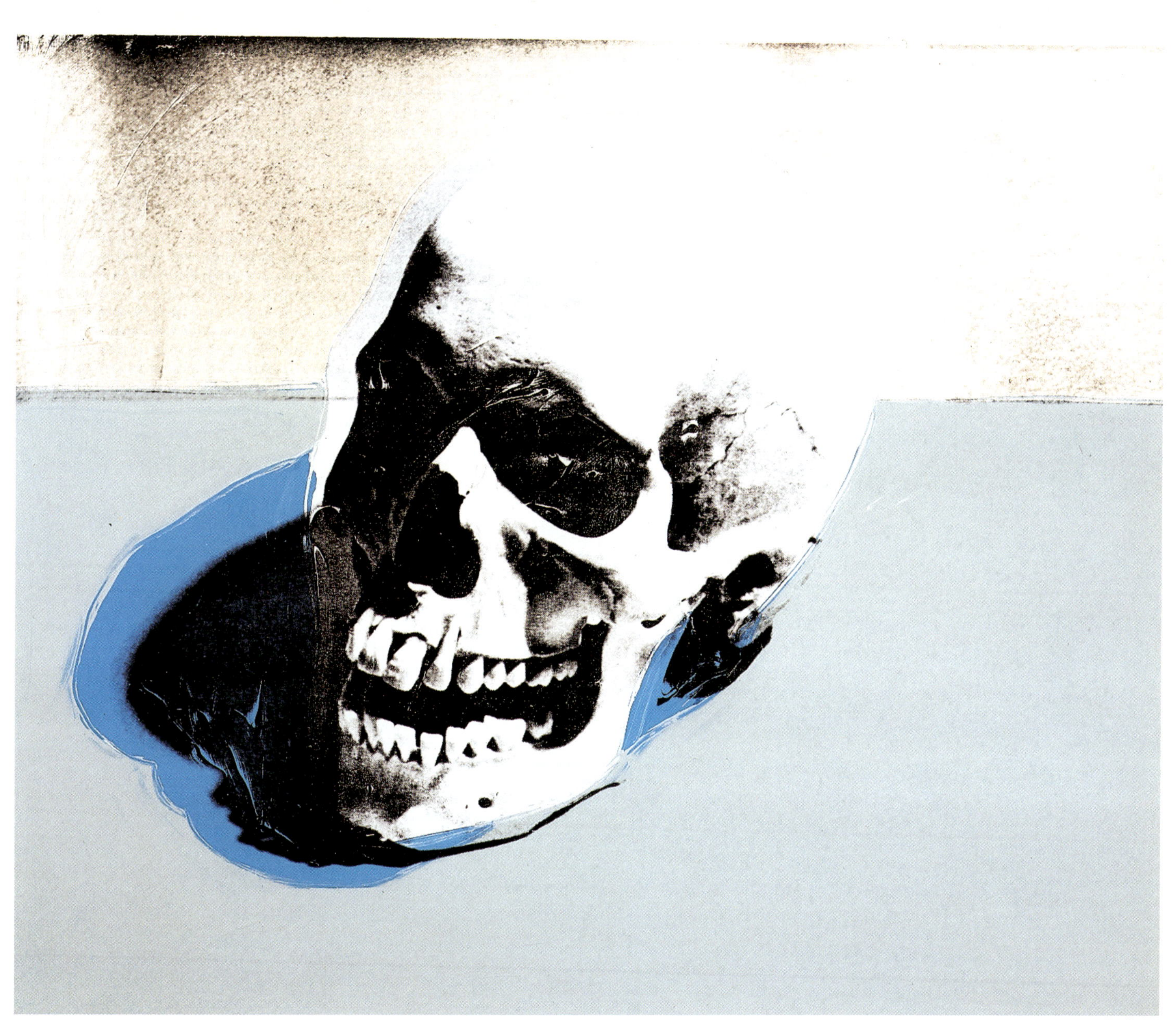

176 Skull 1976 The Andy Warhol Museum, Pittsburgh • Founding Collection, Contribution Dia Center for the Arts

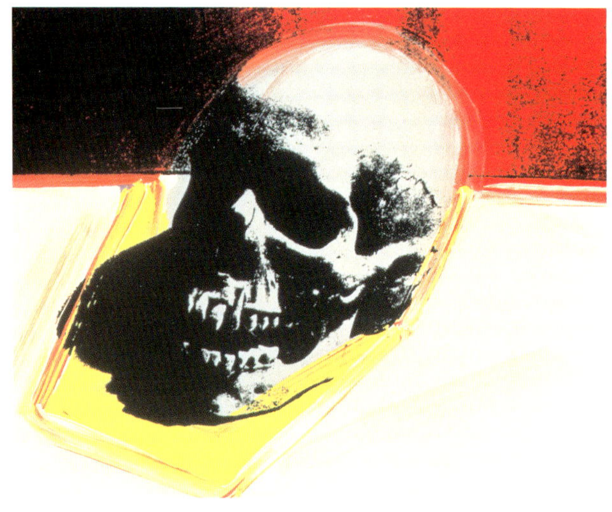

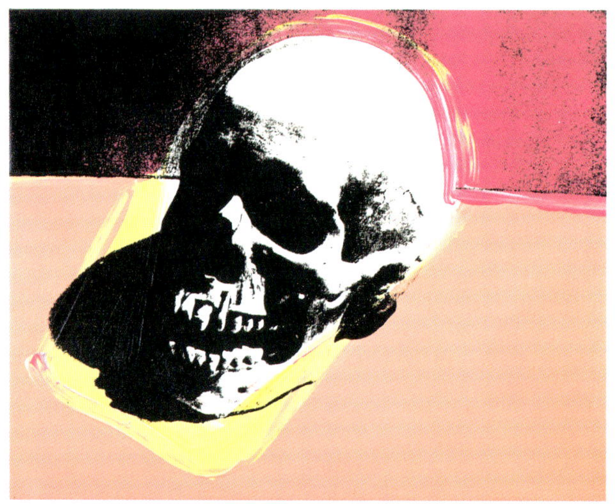

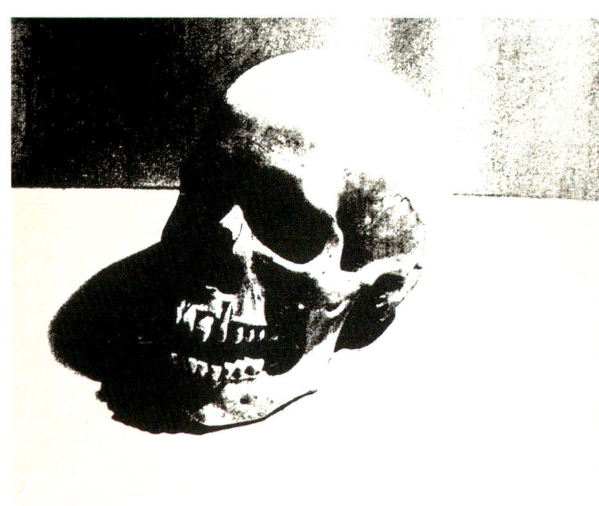

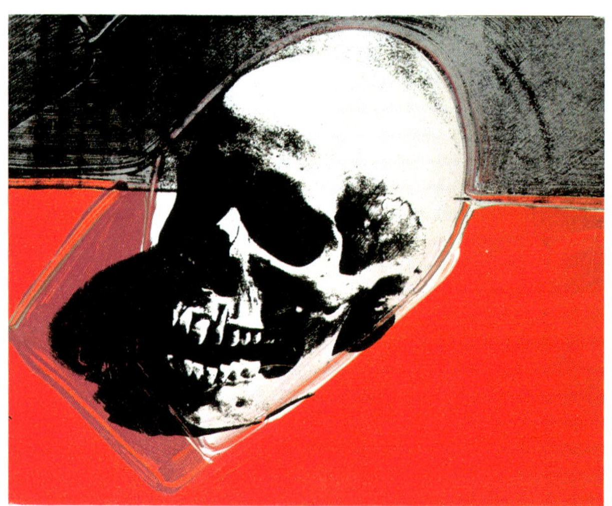

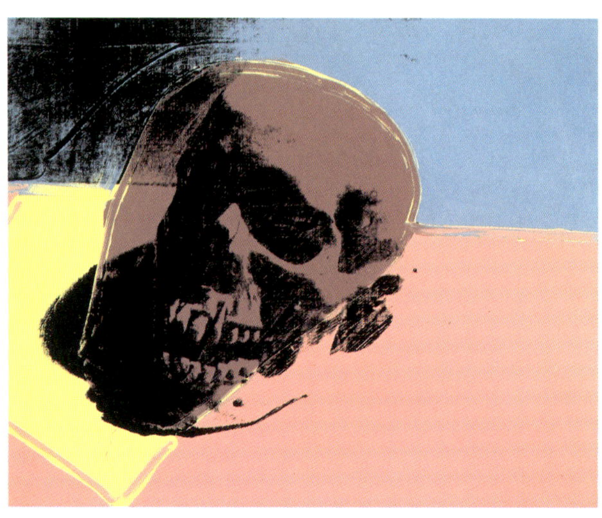

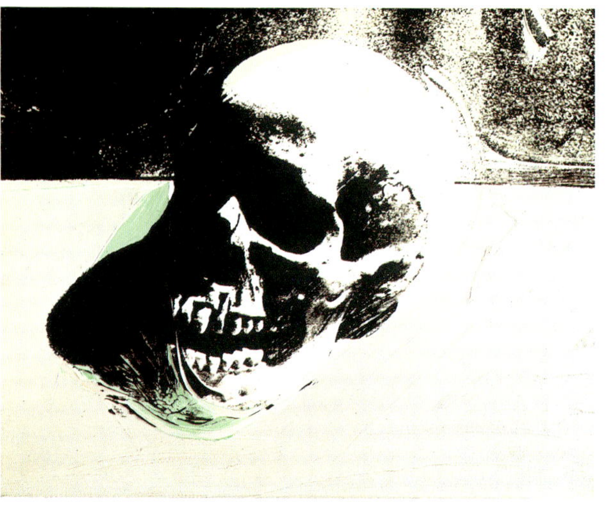

177 – 182 Skull 1976 Courtesy Anthony d'Offay Gallery, London

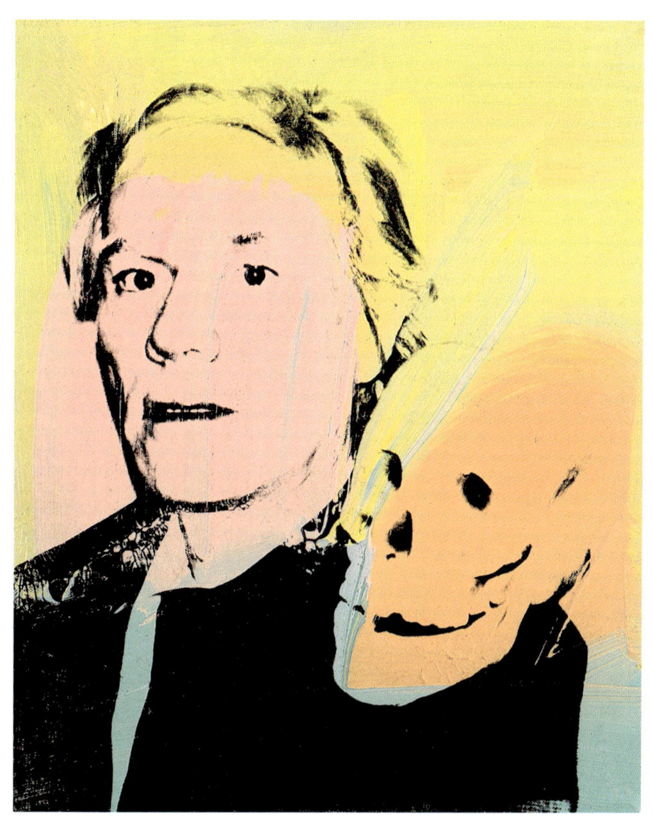

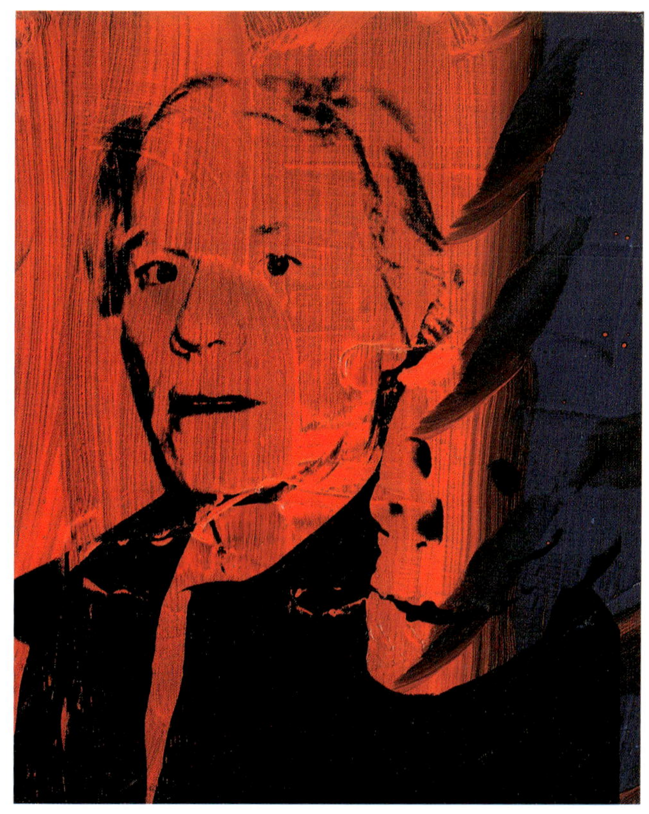

183 **Self-Portrait with Skull 1978**
Private collection

184 **Self-Portrait with Skull 1978**
Private collection

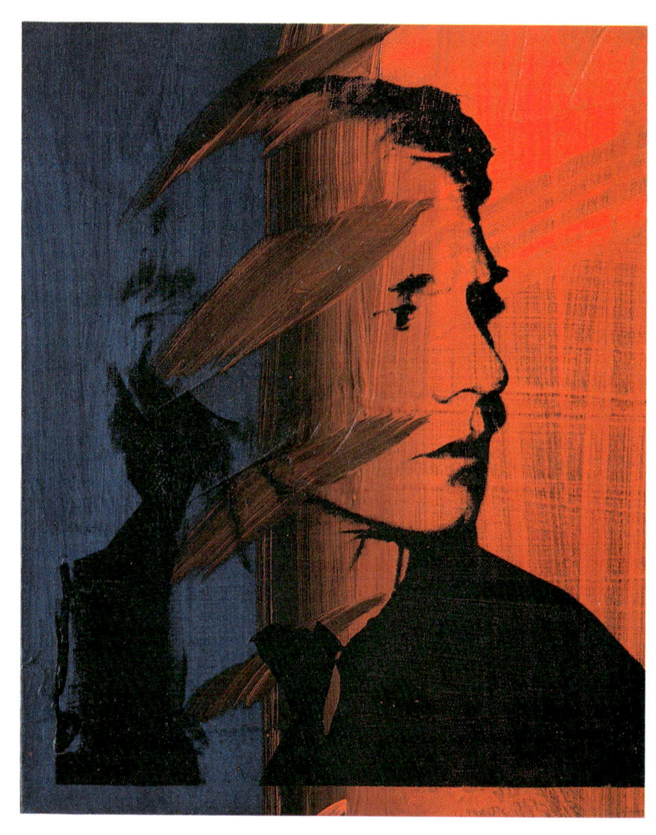

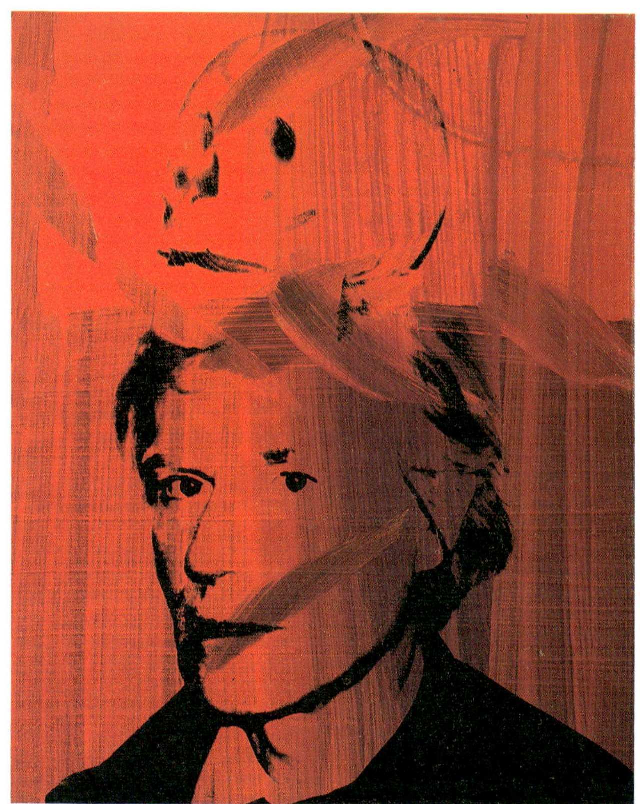

185 Self-Portrait 1978
Private collection

186 Self-Portrait with Skull 1978
Private collection

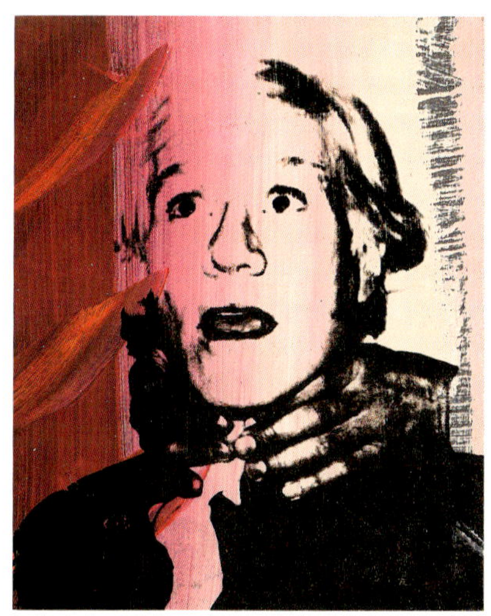
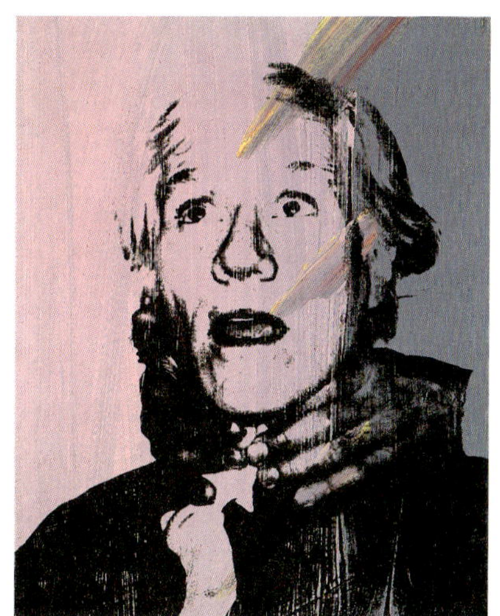
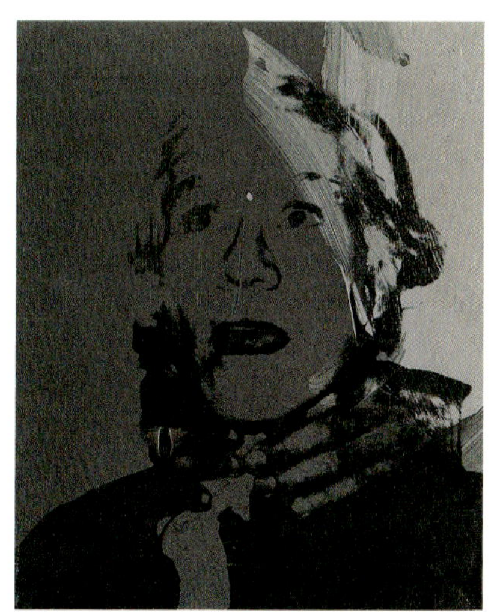
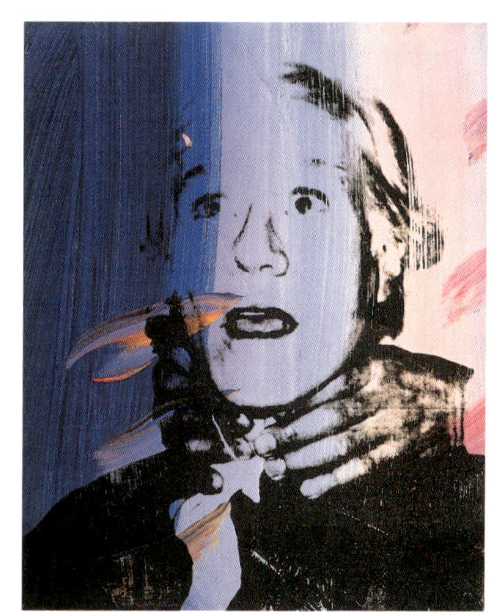
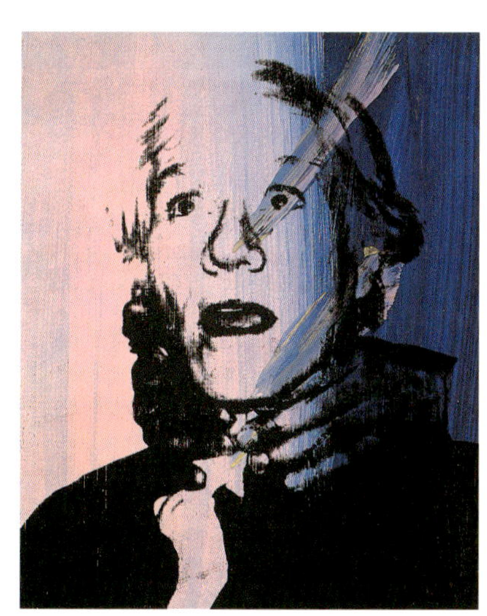
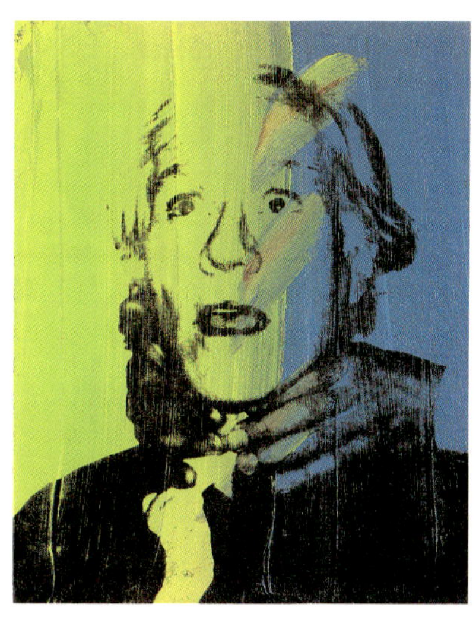

187 – 192 **Self-Portrait 1978** Courtesy Anthony d'Offay Gallery, London

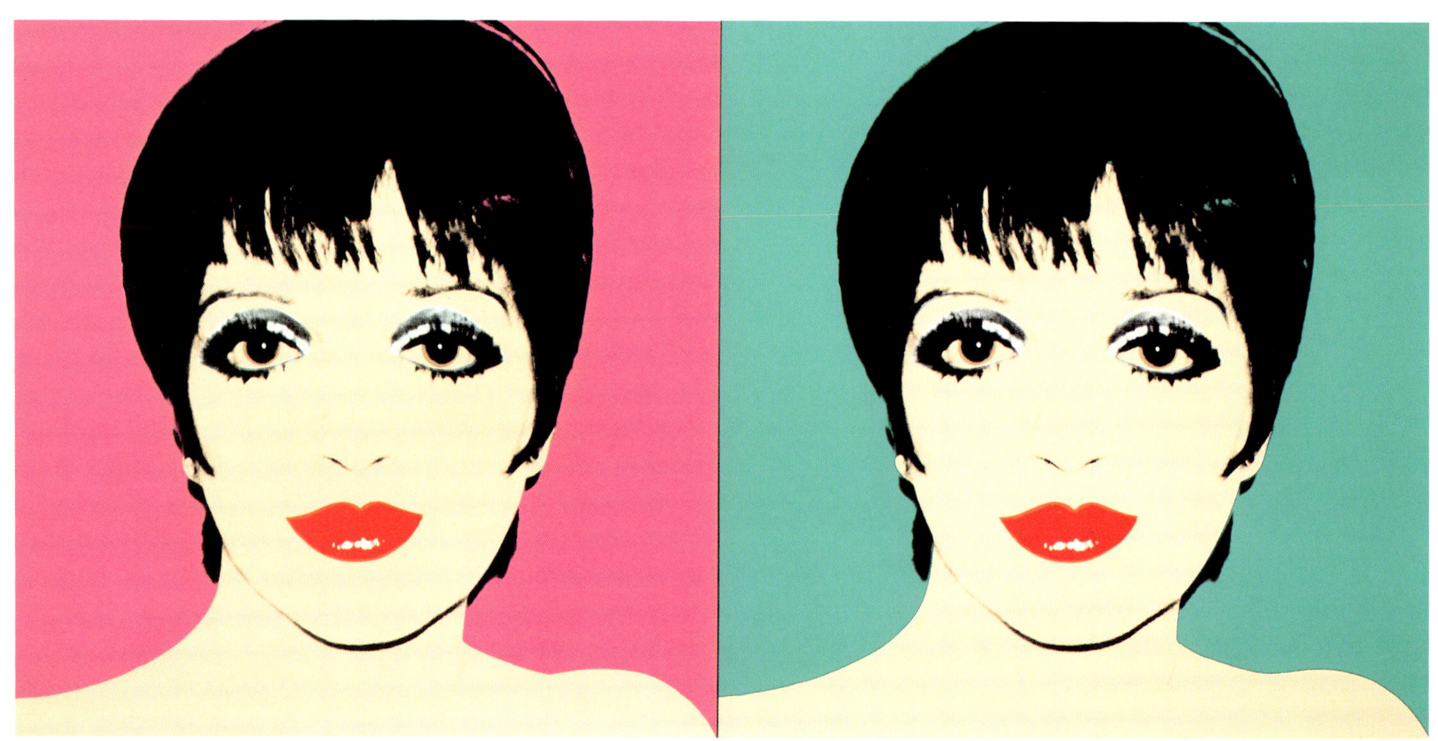

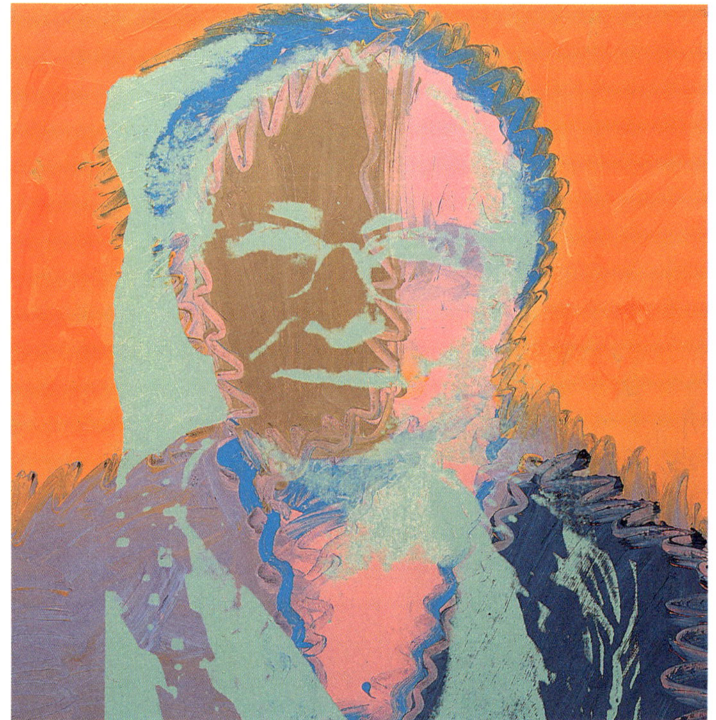

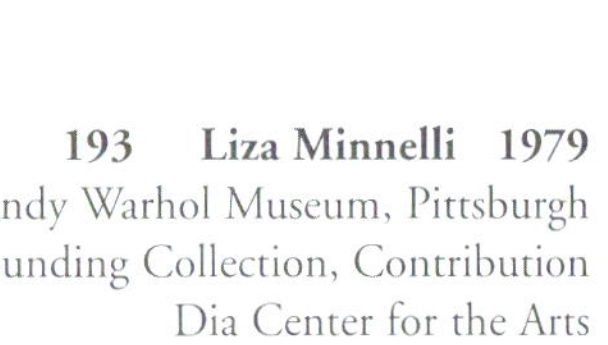

193 Liza Minnelli 1979
The Andy Warhol Museum, Pittsburgh
Founding Collection, Contribution
Dia Center for the Arts

194 Julia Warhola 1974
Private collection

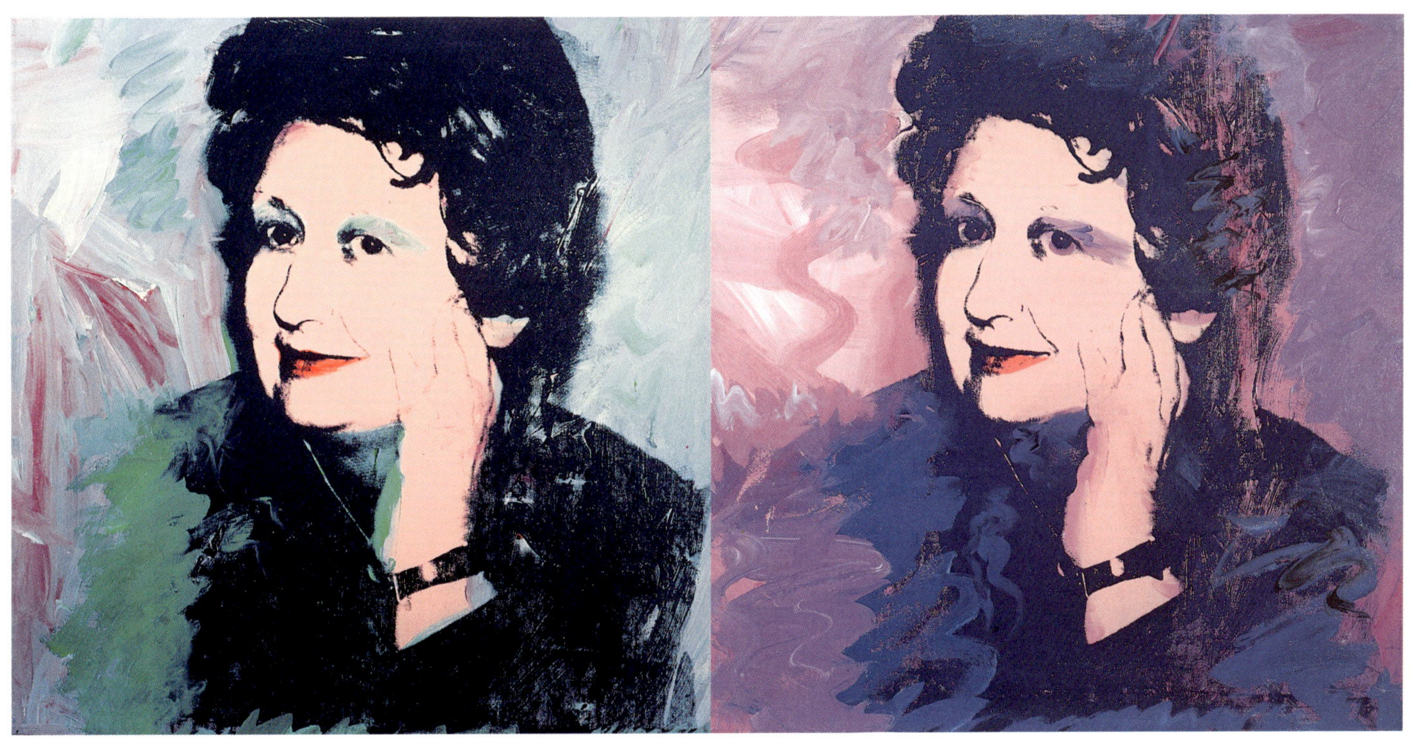

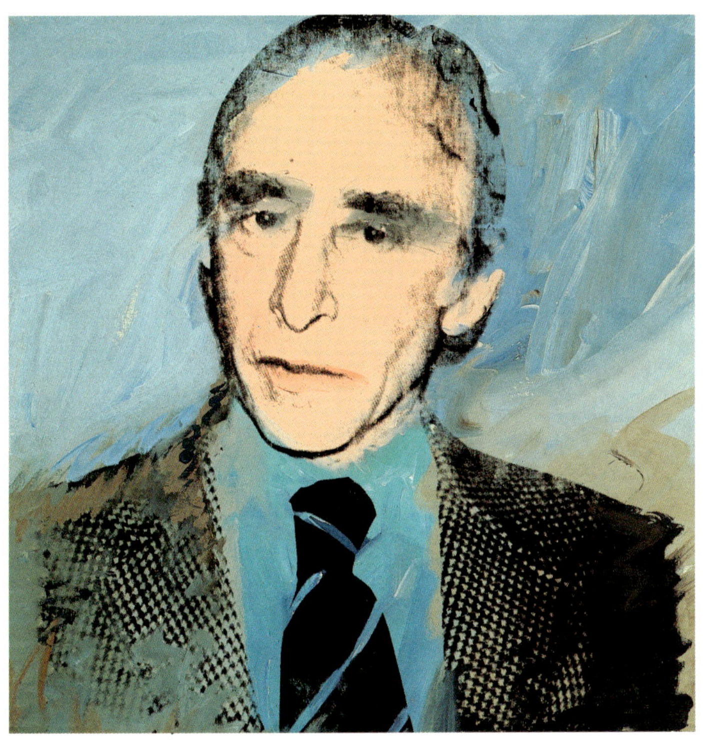

195 **Ileana Sonnabend**
Sonnabend Collection

196 **Portrait of Leo** 1973
Schroeder Collection

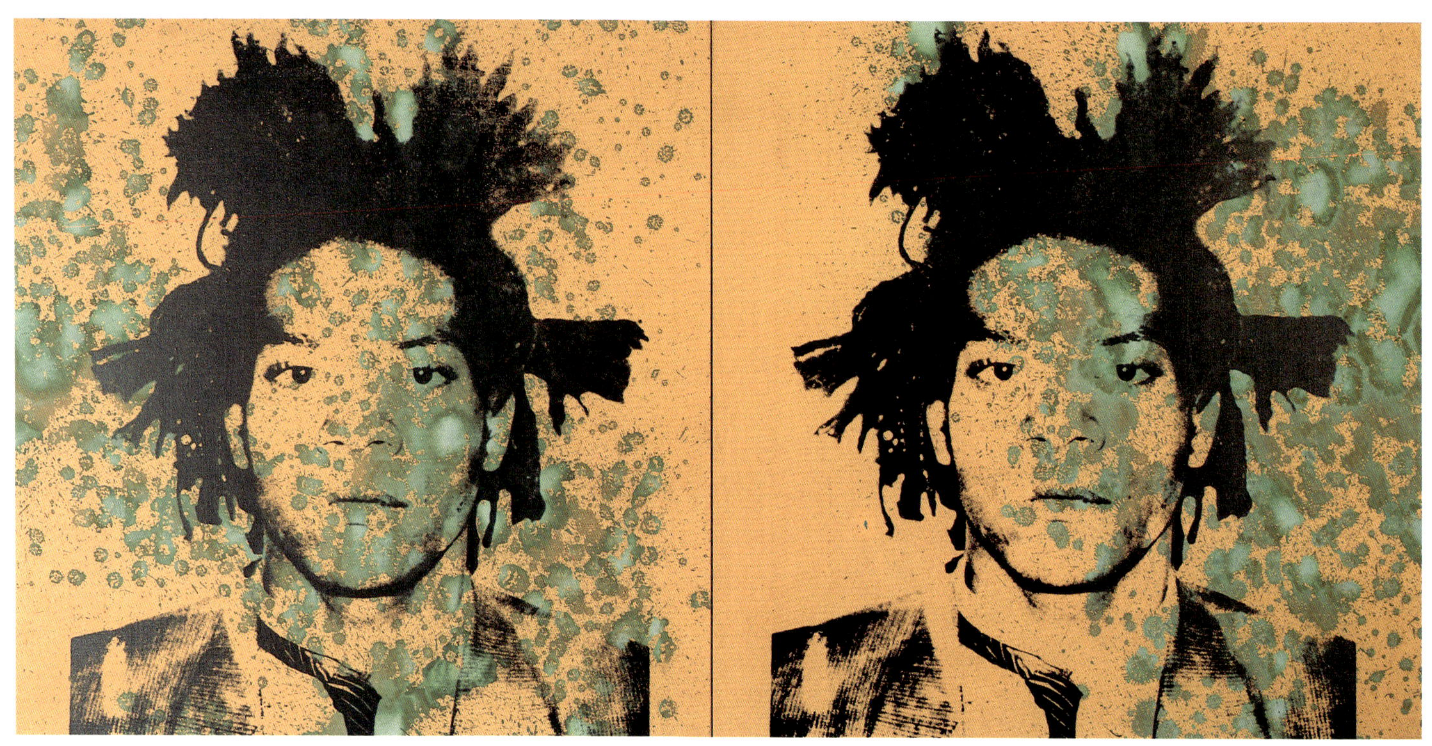

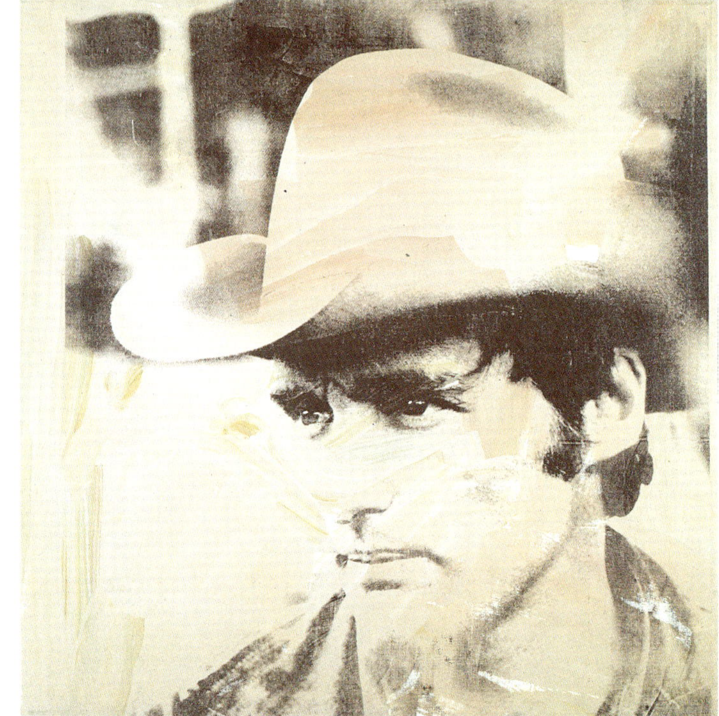

197 Jean-Michel Basquiat c. 1984
The Andy Warhol Museum, Pittsburgh
Founding Collection, Contribution
The Andy Warhol Foundation
for the Visual Arts, Inc.

198 Dennis Hopper 1971
Collection Froehlich, Stuttgart

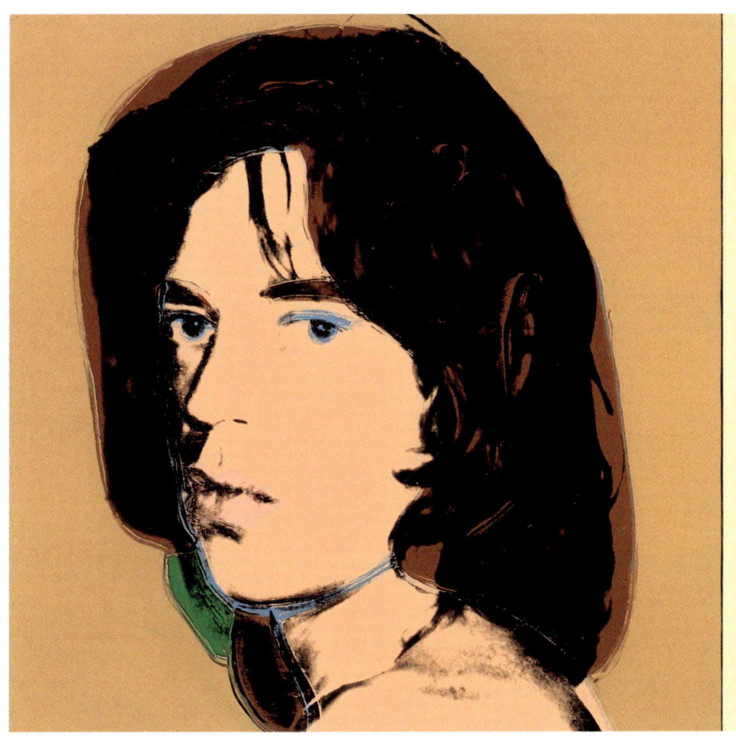

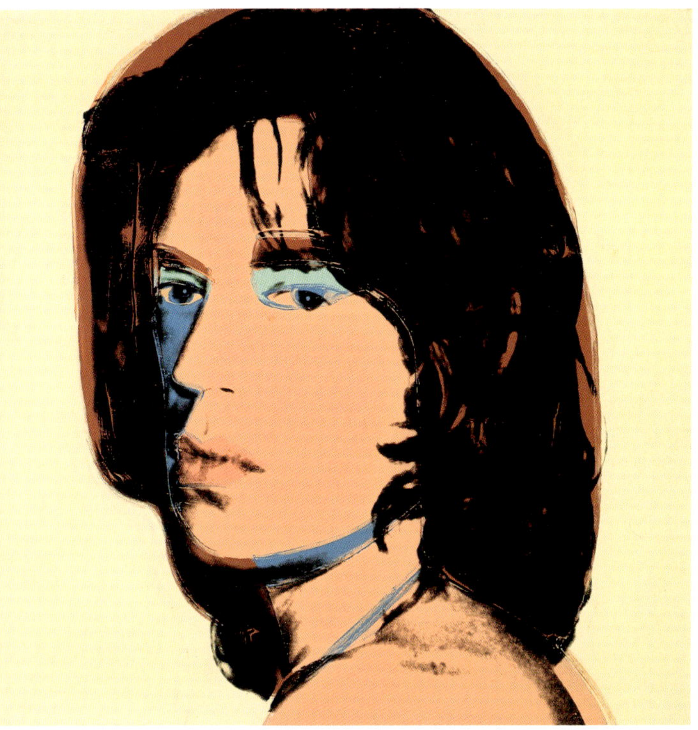

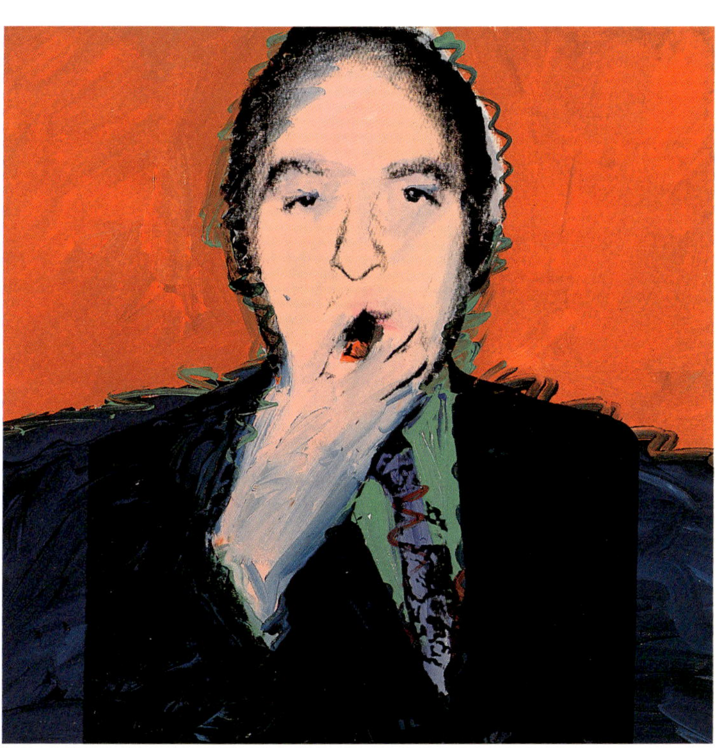

199 **Mick Jagger 1975**
The Andy Warhol Museum, Pittsburgh
Founding Collection, Contribution
Dia Center for the Arts

200 **Portrait Ivan C. Karp 1974**
Courtesy O.K. Harris Works of Art,
New York

201 **Portrait Thomas Ammann 1978** ▸
Private collection;
Courtesy Doris Ammann

202 **Portrait of Dominique 1969** ▸
The Menil Collection, Houston

203 **Portrait Erich Marx 1978** ▸
Stiftung Sammlung Marx, Hamburger Bahnhof –
Museum für Gegenwart, Berlin

204 **Portrait Peter Ludwig 1980** ▸
Ludwig Forum für Internationale Kunst,
Aachen – Collection Ludwig

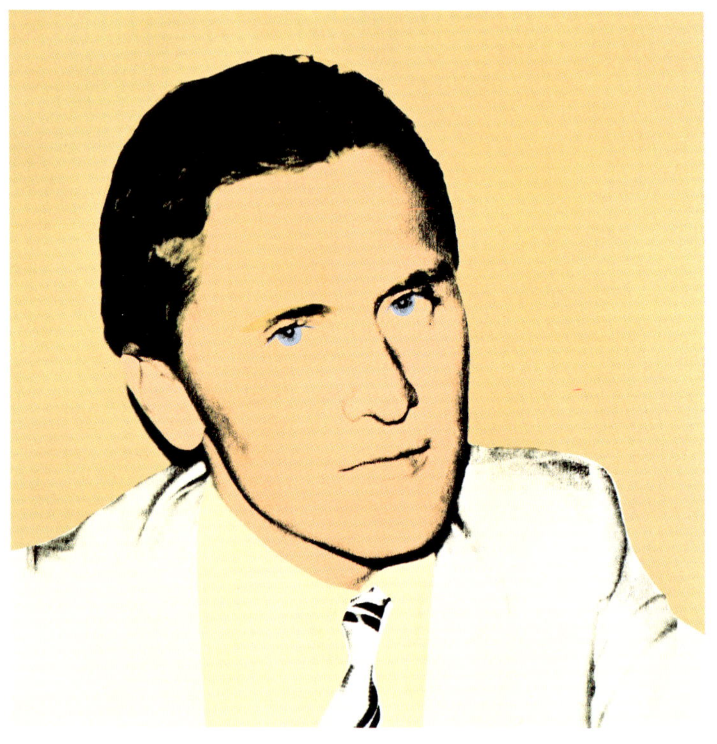
201 Portrait Thomas Ammann [Cat. Entry p. 249]

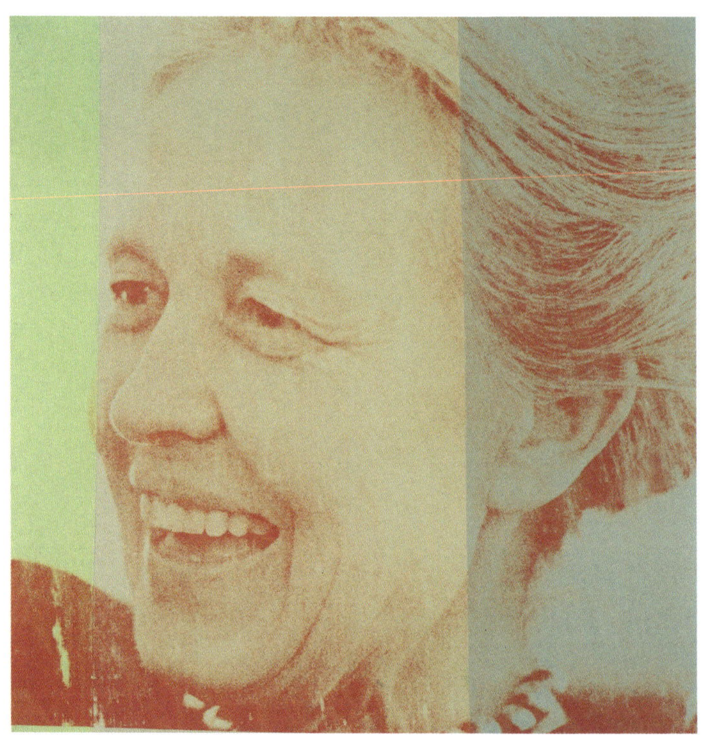
202 Portrait of Dominique [Cat. Entry p. 249]

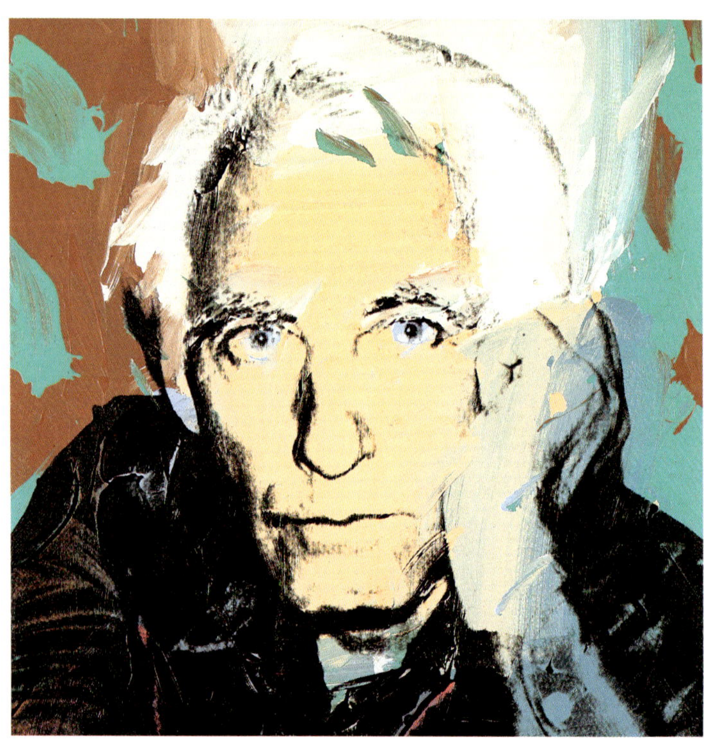
203 Portrait Erich Marx [Cat. Entry p. 249]

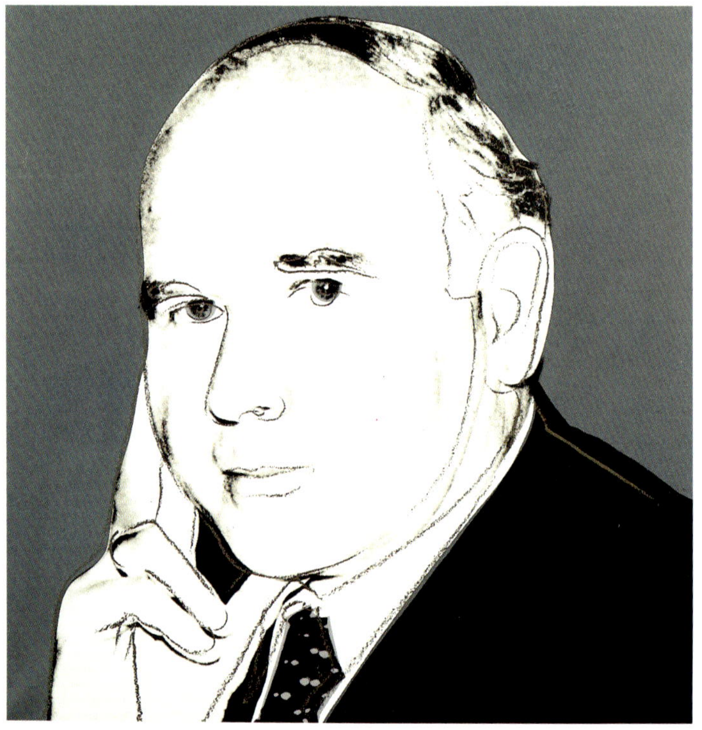
204 Portrait Peter Ludwig [Cat. Entry p. 249]

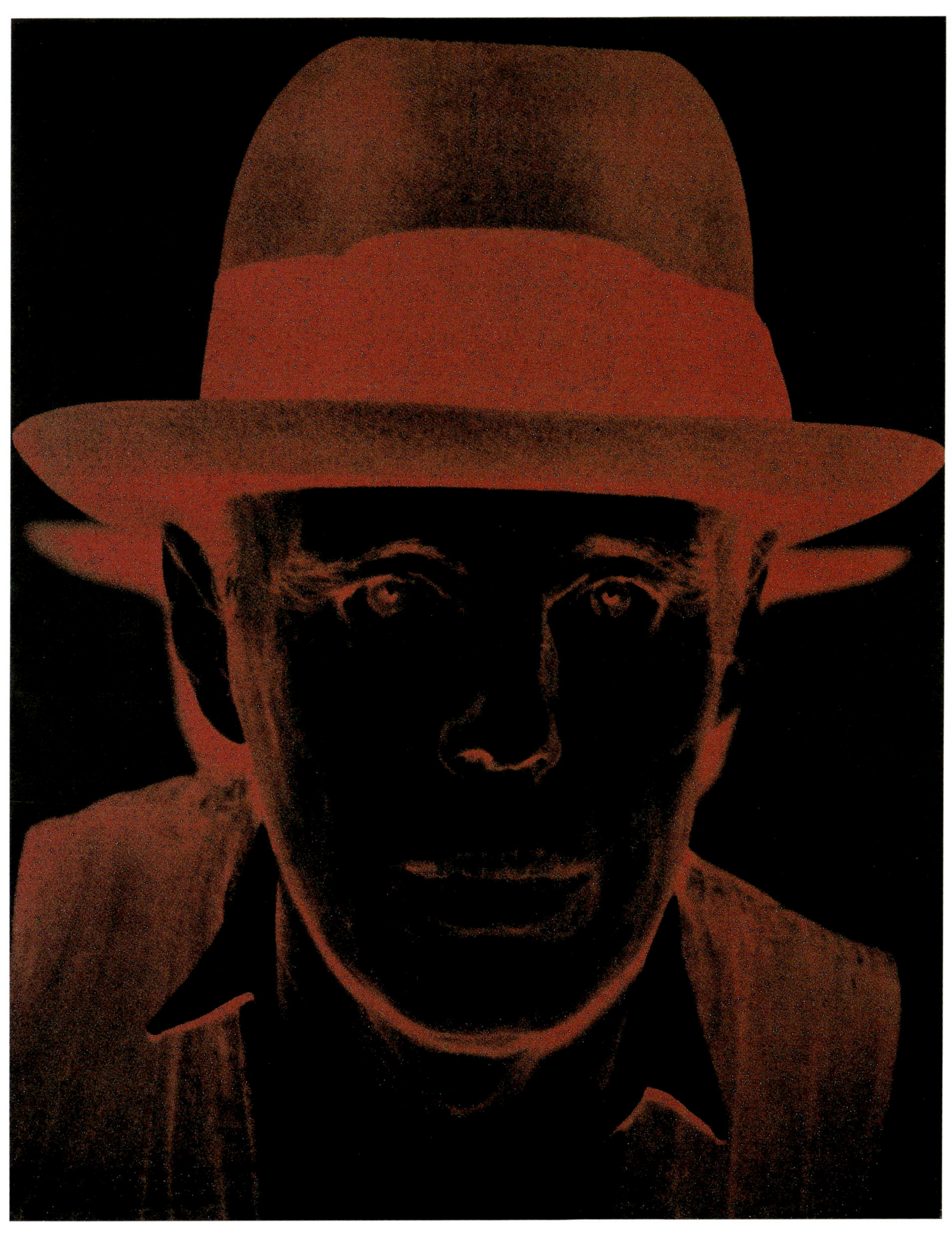

205 **Portrait Joseph Beuys** **1980** Stiftung Sammlung Marx, Hamburger Bahnhof – Museum für Gegenwart, Berlin

206 **Shadow Painting 1978** Courtesy The Brant Foundation, Greenwich, CT

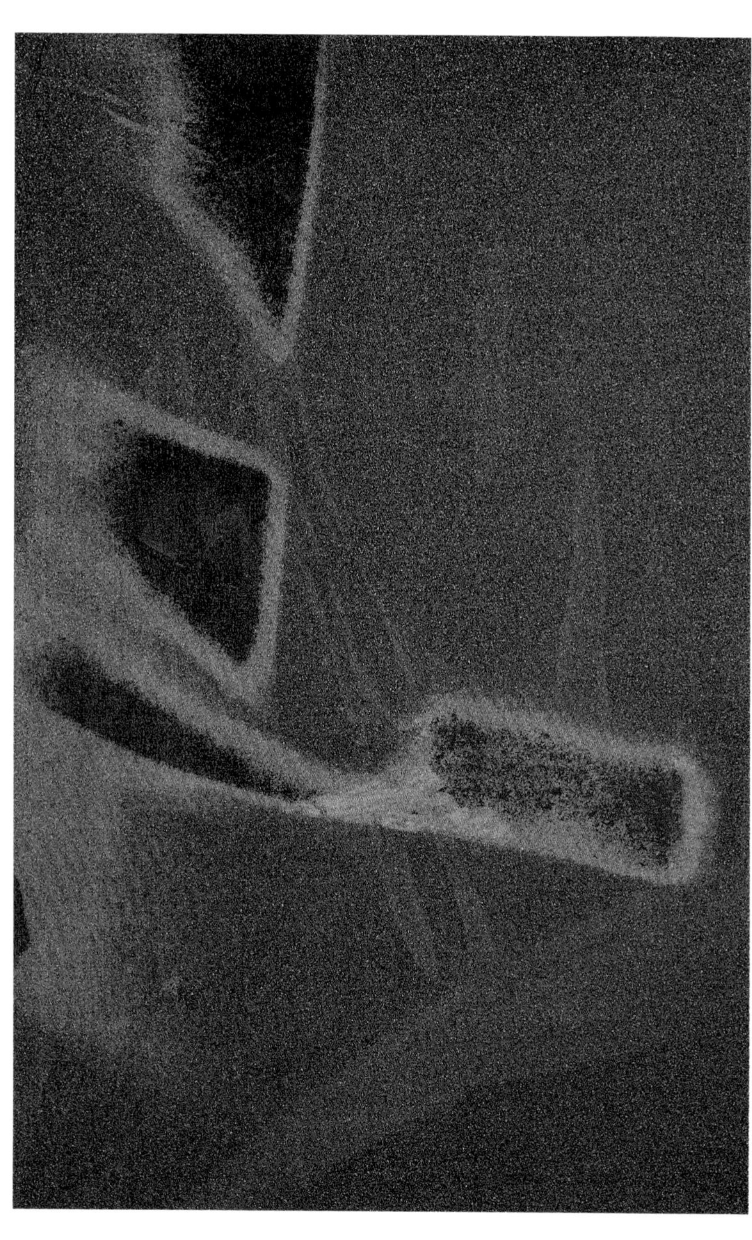

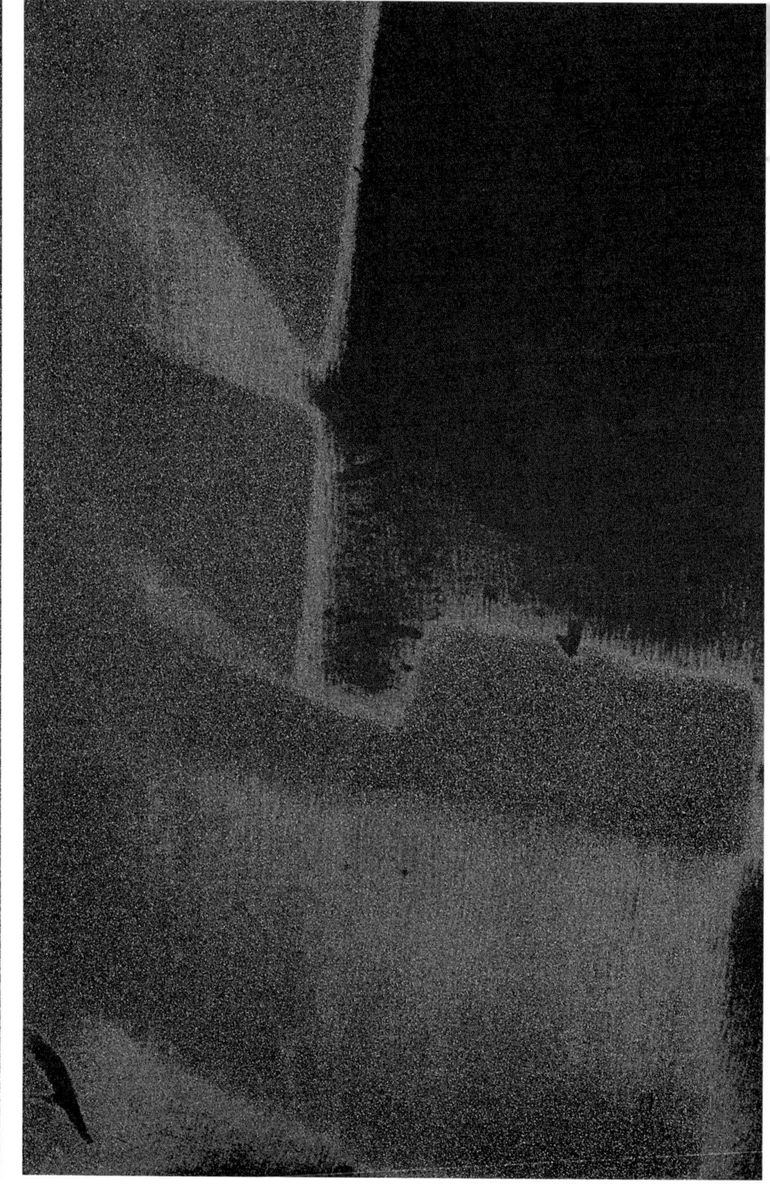

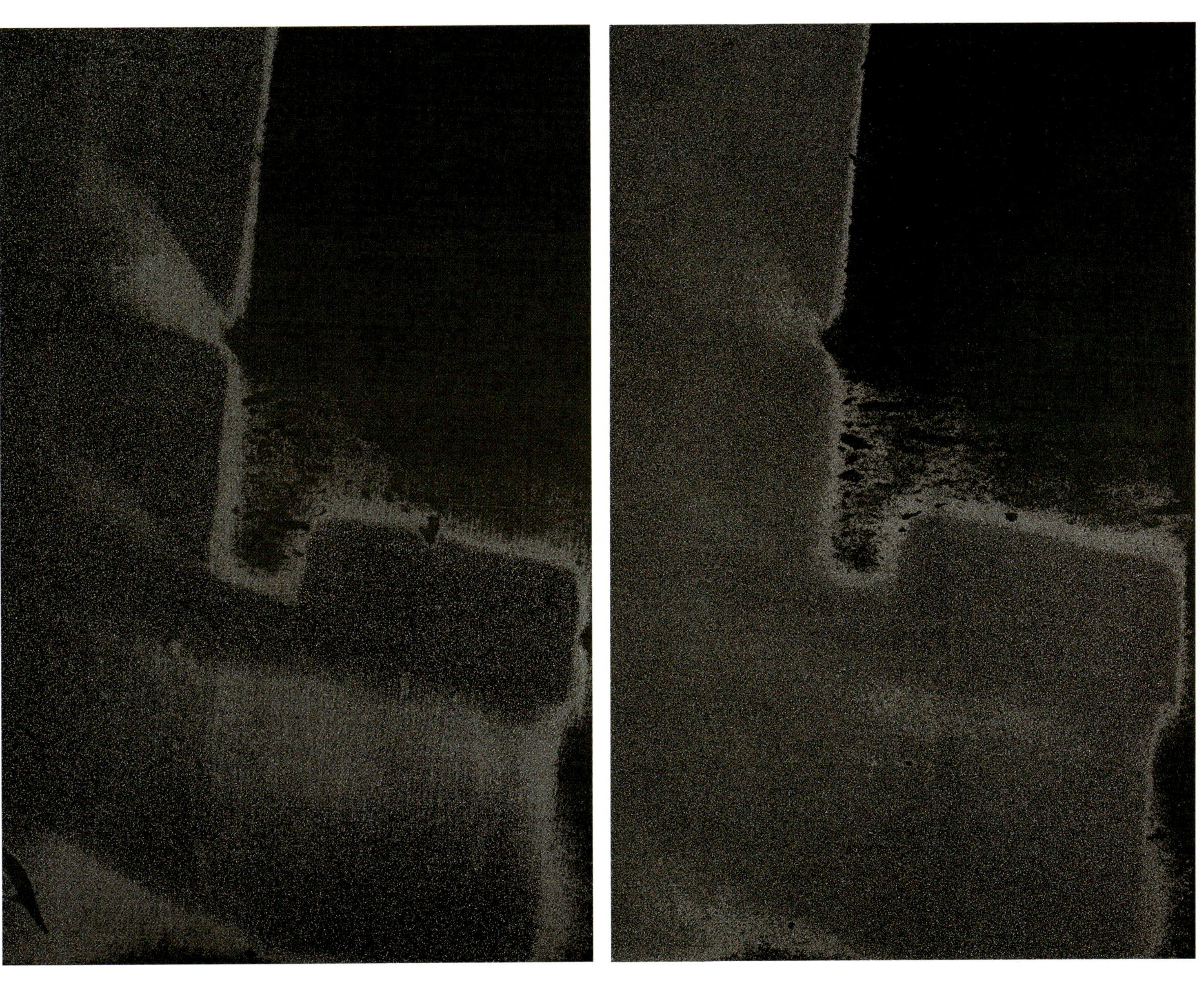

207 – 210 Diamond Dust Shadow c. 1979 Private collection

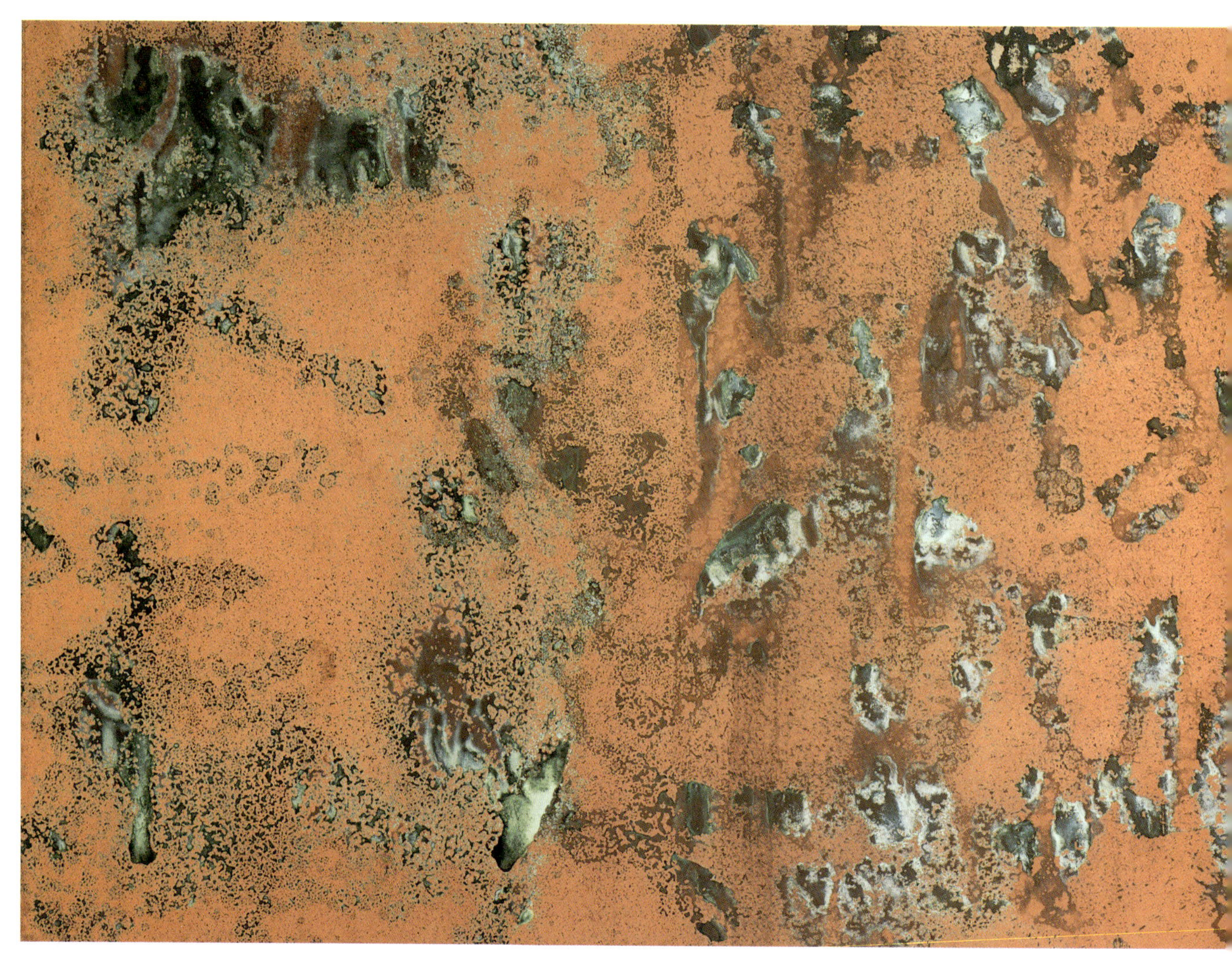

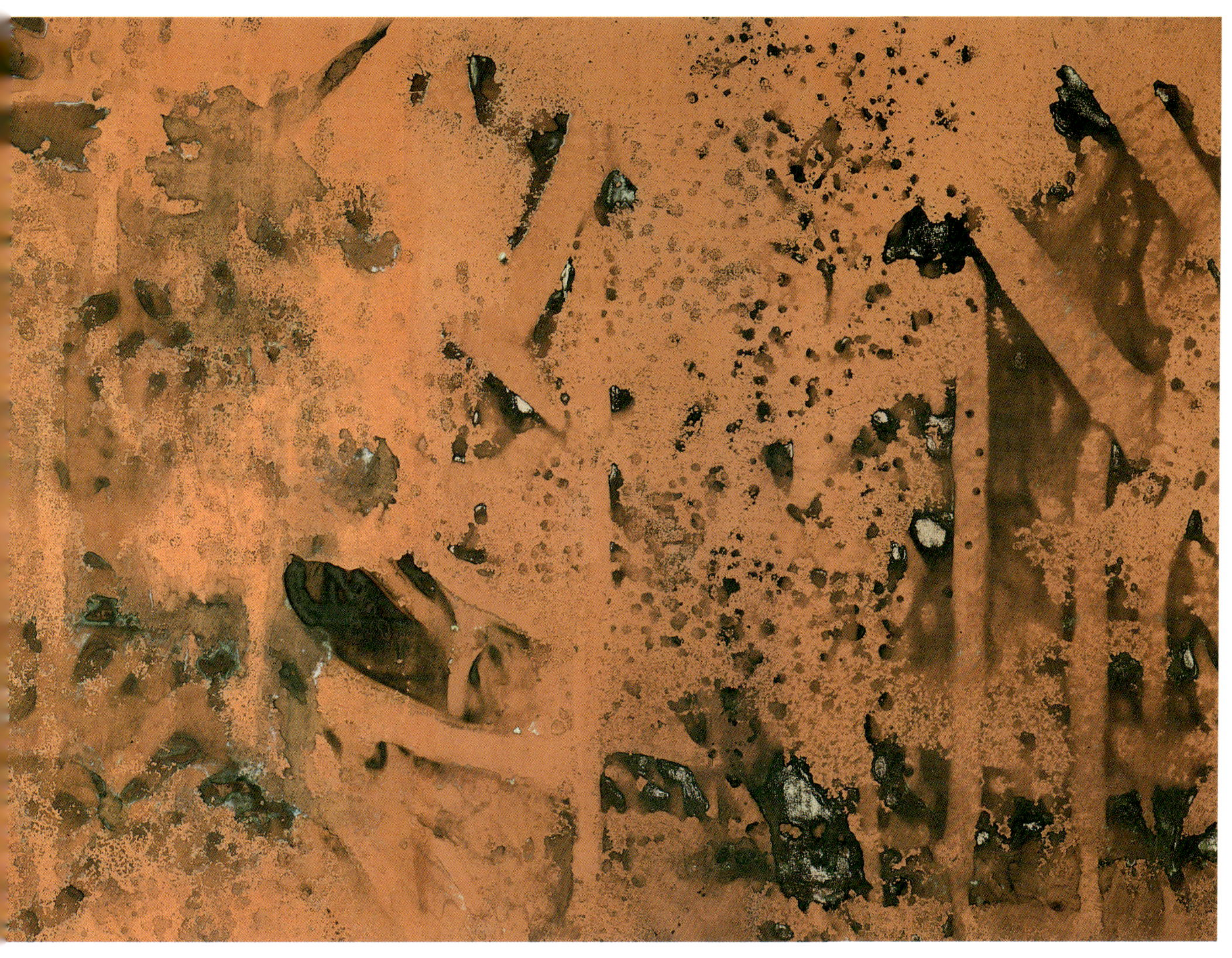

211 **Oxidation Painting** **1978** Courtesy The Brant Foundation, Greenwich, CT

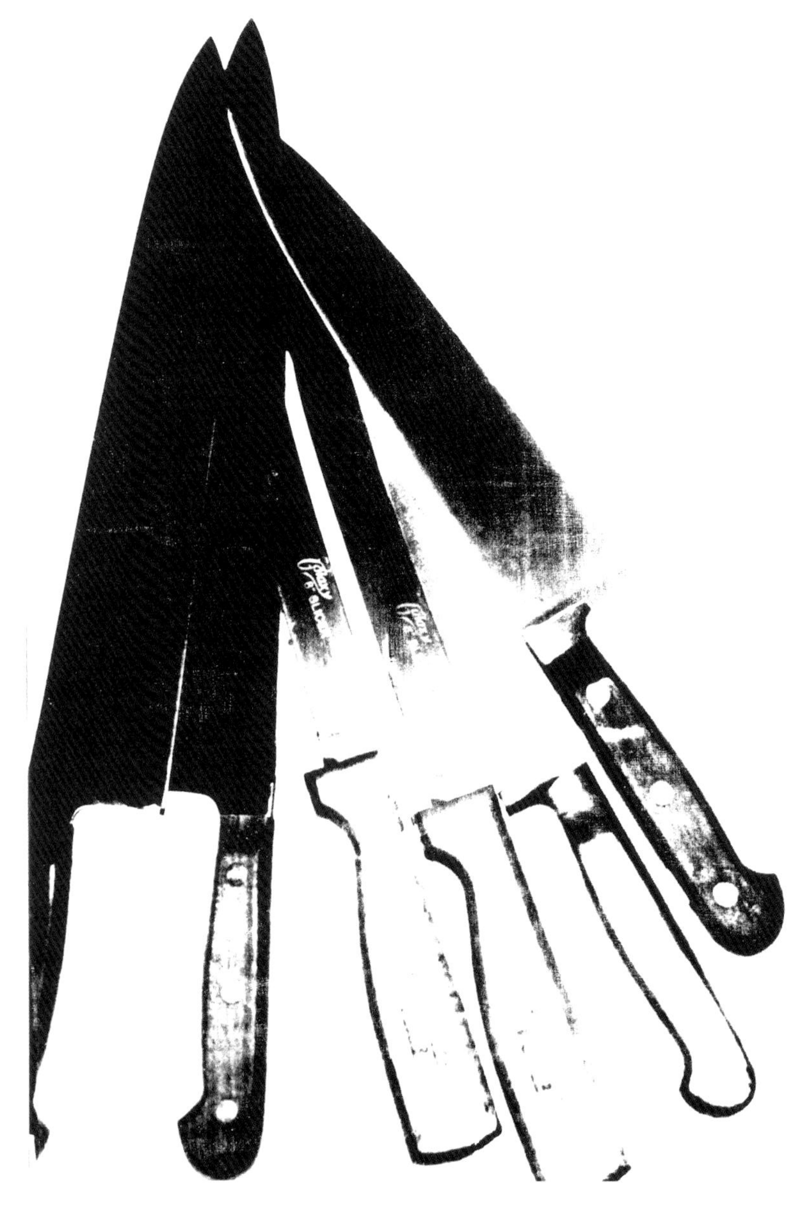

212 Knives c. 1981-82 Stiftung Sammlung Marx, Hamburger Bahnhof – Museum für Gegenwart, Berlin

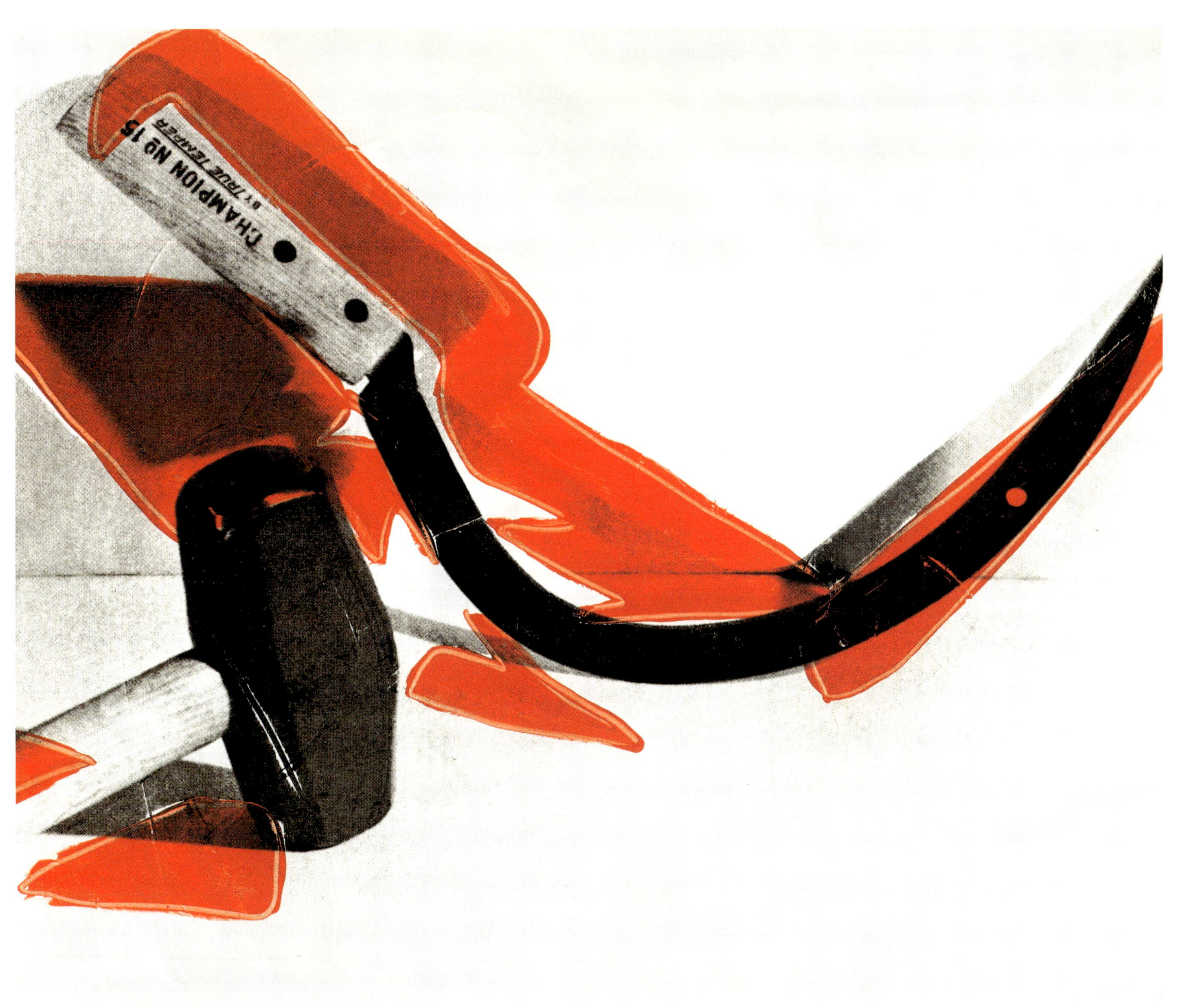

213 Hammer and Sickle 1976 Stiftung Sammlung Marx, Hamburger Bahnhof – Museum für Gegenwart, Berlin

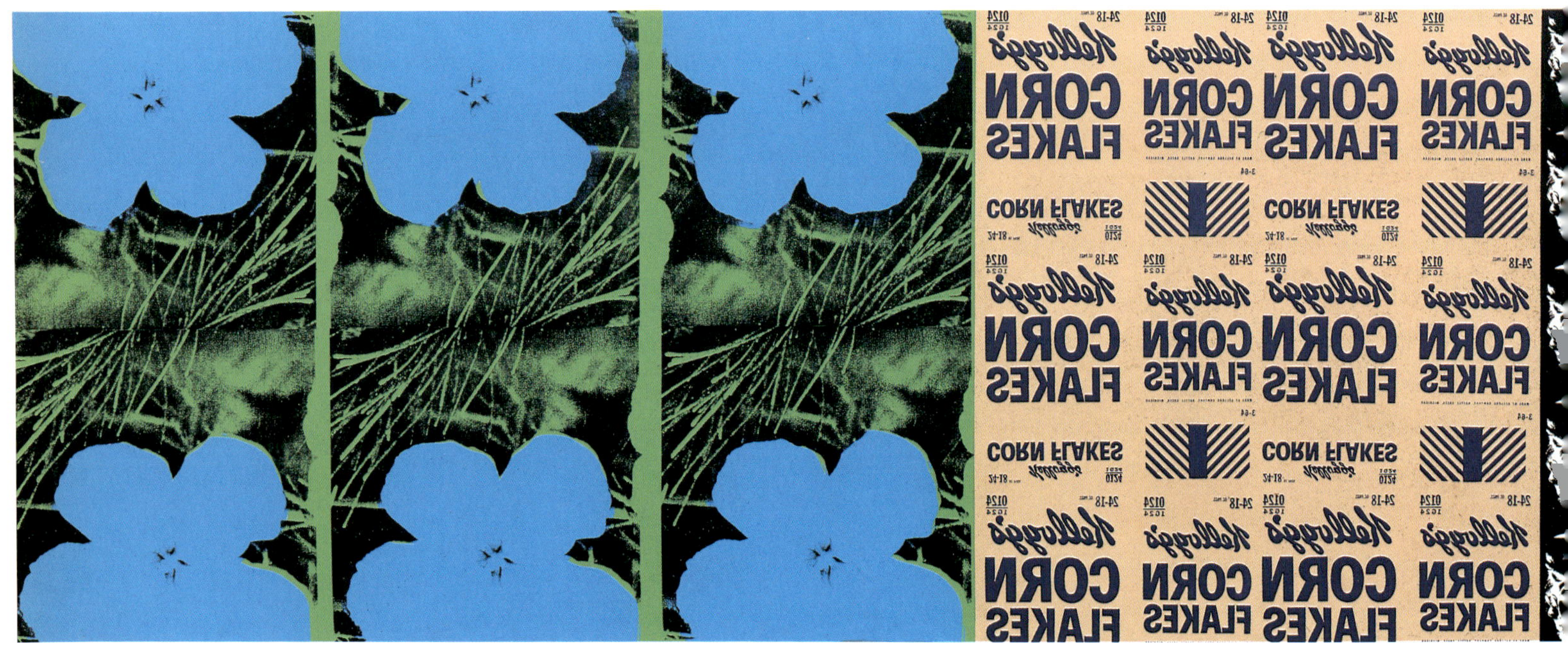
CORN FLAKES

214 Multicolored Marilyn 1979-1986
Stiftung Sammlung Marx, Hamburger Bahnhof –
Museum für Gegenwart, Berlin

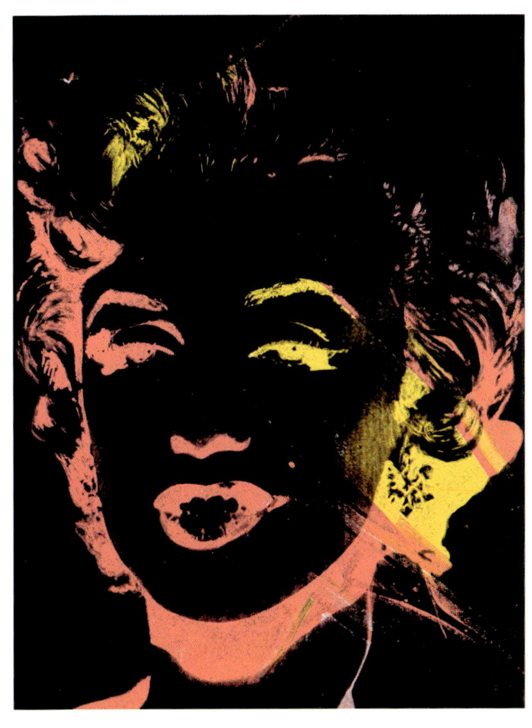

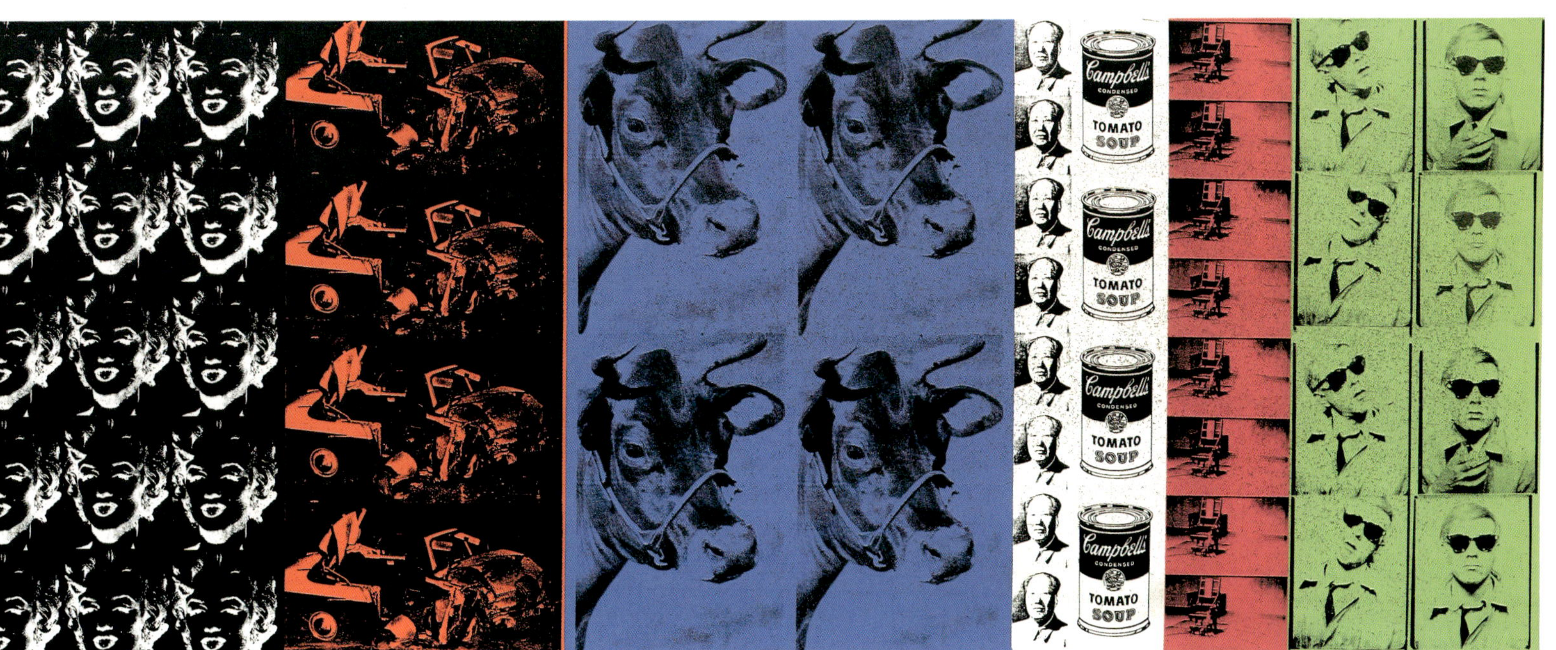

215 Big Retrospective 1979 Private collection, Courtesy Galerie Bruno Bischofberger, Zürich

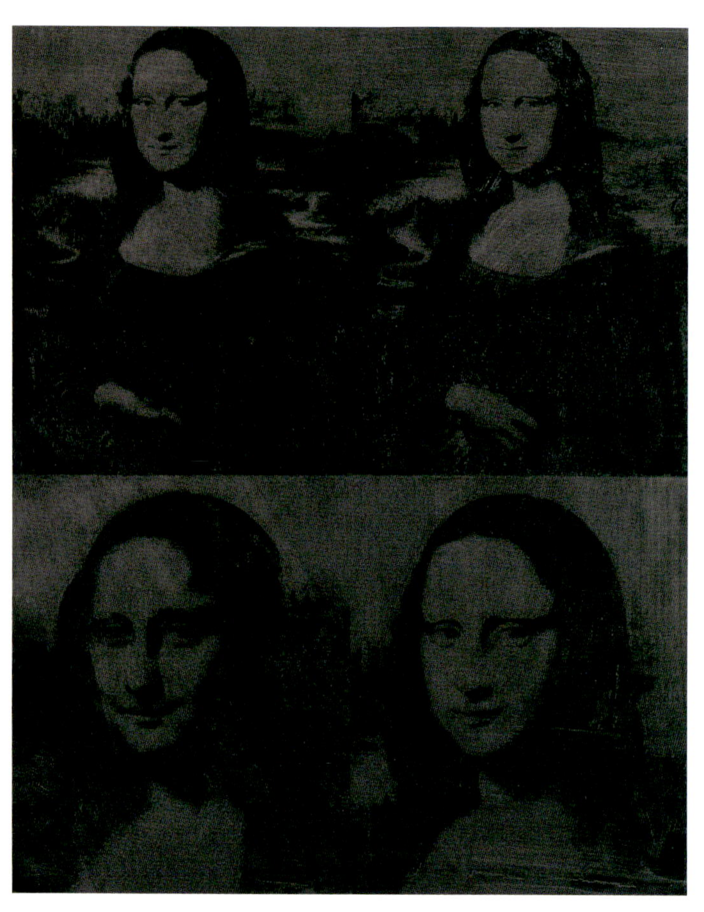

216 **Mona Lisa Four Times** 1973
Private collection, Germany

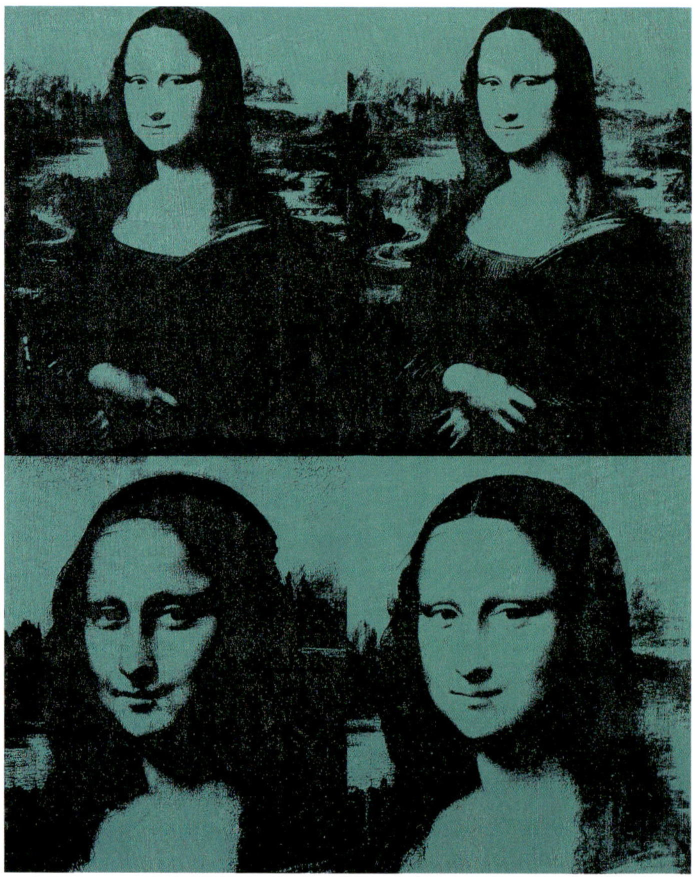

217 **Mona Lisa Four Times** 1978
Private collection, Germany

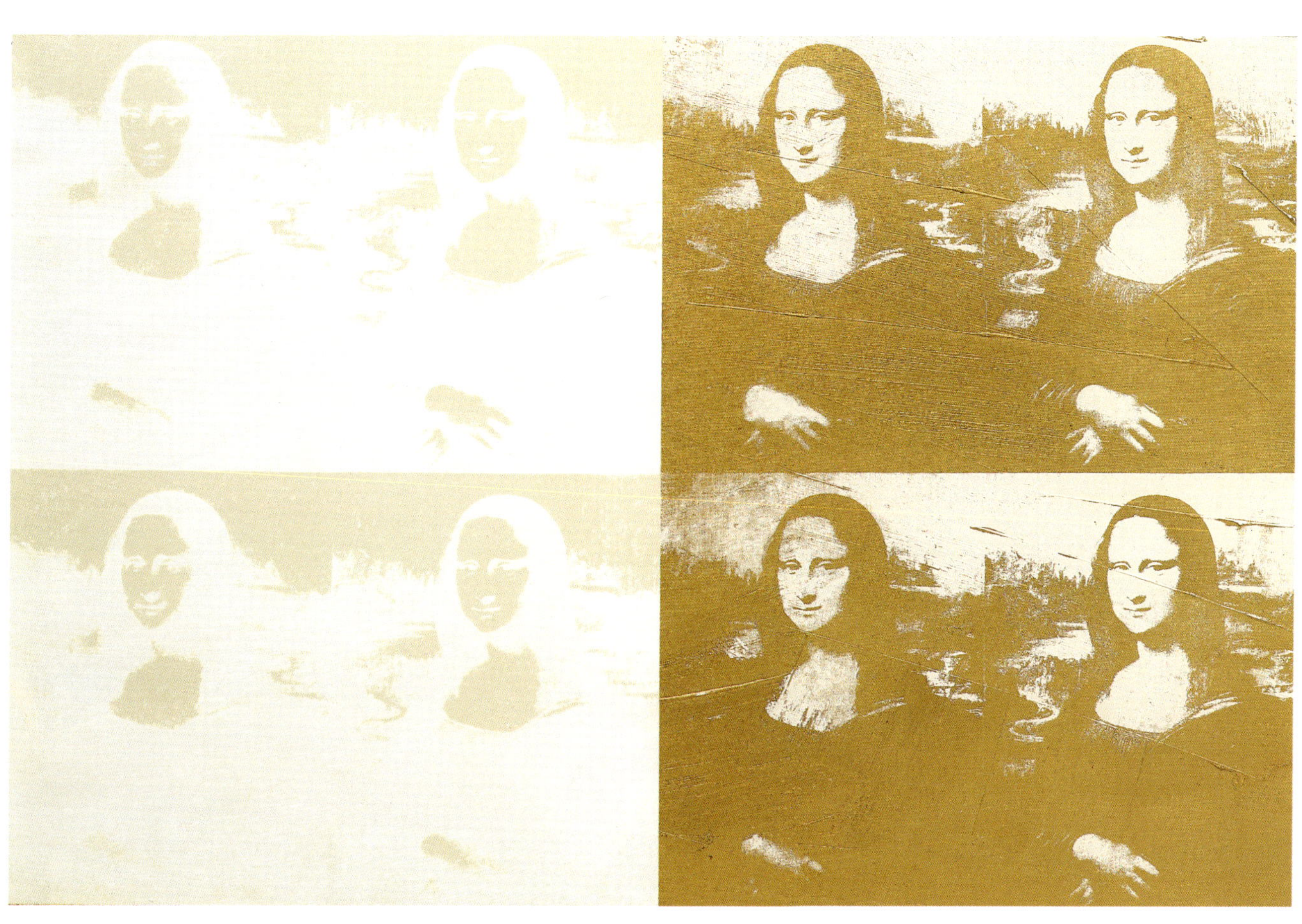

218 Four White On White And Four Gold On White Mona Lisas 1979 Collection Bruno Bischofberger, Zürich

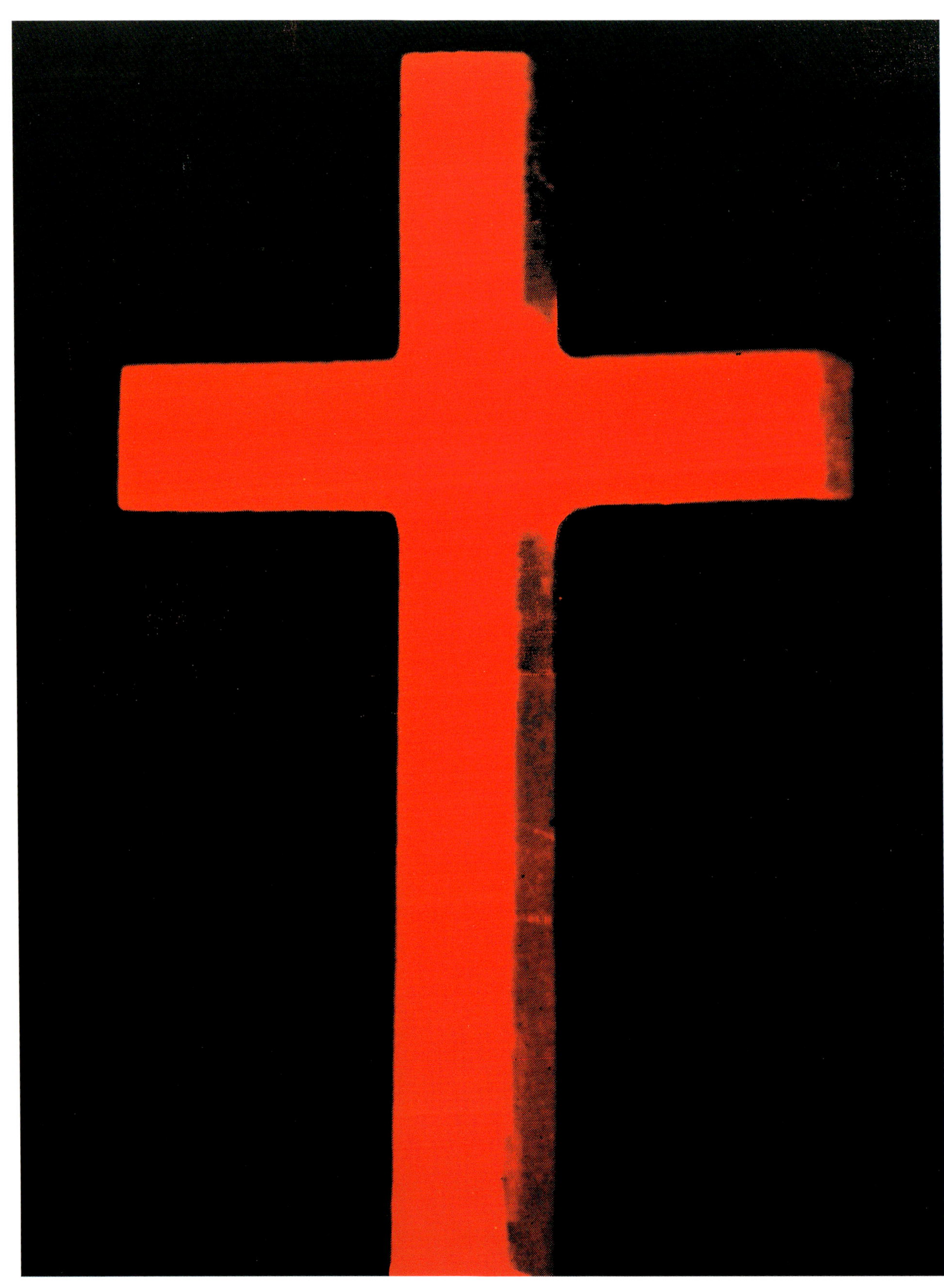

219 **Cross** **c. 1981-82** Erzbischöfliches Diözesanmuseum Köln

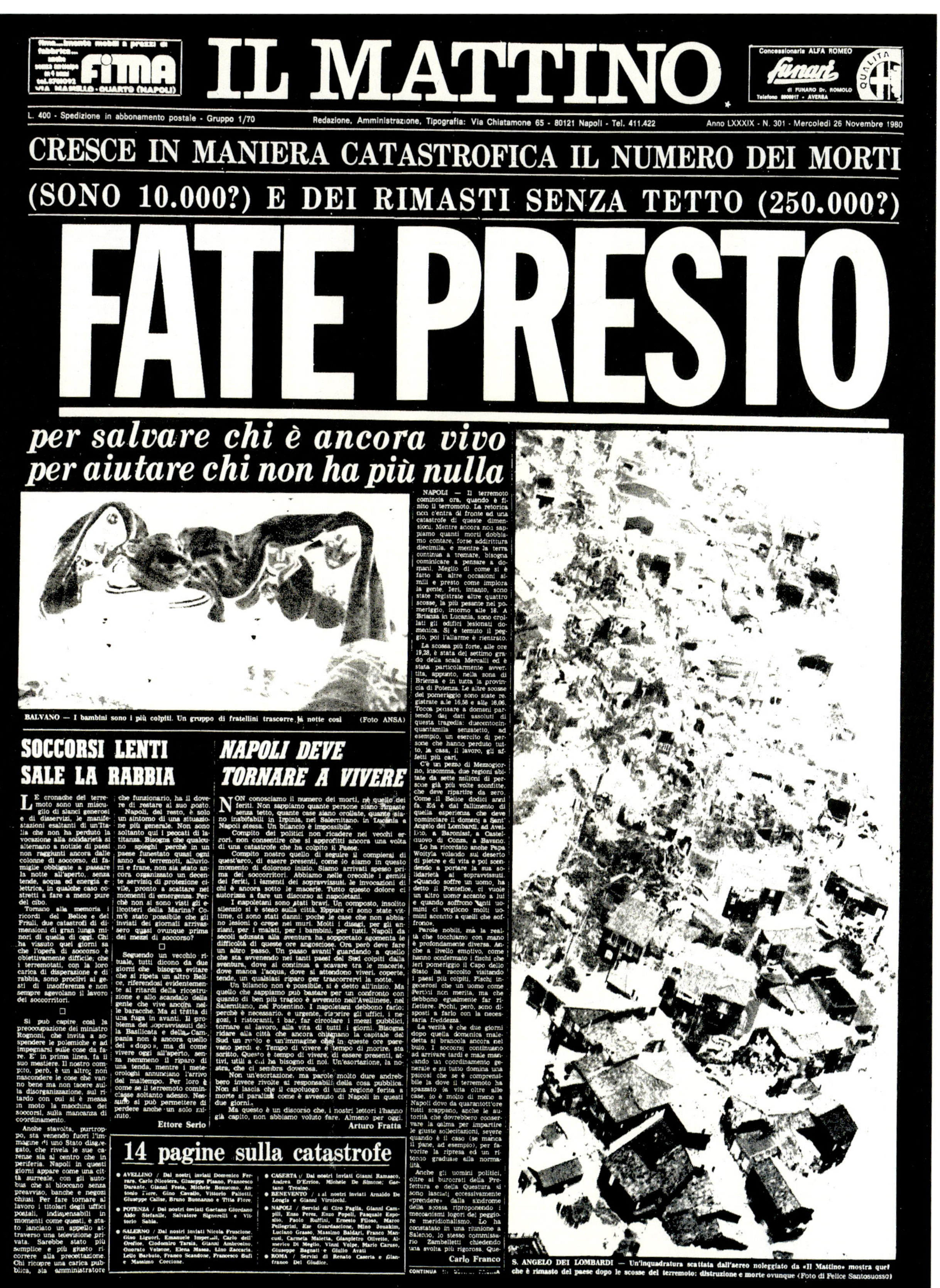

FIMA — mobili a prezzi di fabbrica — VIA MASULLO - QUARTO (NAPOLI)

IL MATTINO

Concessionaria ALFA ROMEO — Funari di FUNARO Dr. ROMOLO — AVERSA

L. 400 - Spedizione in abbonamento postale - Gruppo 1/70 — Redazione, Amministrazione, Tipografia: Via Chiatamone 65 - 80121 Napoli - Tel. 411.422 — Anno LXXXIX - N. 301 - Mercoledì 26 Novembre 1980

CRESCE IN MANIERA CATASTROFICA IL NUMERO DEI MORTI (SONO 10.000?) E DEI RIMASTI SENZA TETTO (250.000?)

FATE PRESTO

per salvare chi è ancora vivo per aiutare chi non ha più nulla

BALVANO — I bambini sono i più colpiti. Un gruppo di fratellini trascorre la notte così (Foto ANSA)

SOCCORSI LENTI SALE LA RABBIA

LE cronache del terremoto sono un miscuglio di slanci generosi e di disservizi, le manifestazioni esaltanti di un'Italia che non ha perduto la vocazione alla solidarietà si alternano a notizie di paesi non raggiunti ancora dalle colonne di soccorso, di famiglie obbligate a passare la notte all'aperto, senza tende, acqua ed energia elettrica, in qualche caso costretti a fare a meno pure del cibo.

Tornano alla memoria i ricordi del Belice e del Friuli, due catastrofi di dimensioni di gran lunga minori di quella di oggi. Chi ha vissuto quei giorni sa che l'opera di soccorso è obiettivamente difficile; che i terremotati, con la loro carica di disperazione e di rabbia, sono proclivi ai gesti di insofferenza e non sempre agevolano il lavoro dei soccorritori.

□

Si può capire così la preoccupazione del ministro Rognoni, che invita a sospendere le polemiche e ad impegnarsi sulle cose da fare. E' in prima linea, fa il suo mestiere. Il nostro compito, però, è un altro: non nascondere le cose che vanno bene ma non tacere sulla disorganizzazione, sul ritardo con cui si è messa in moto la macchina dei soccorsi, sulla mancanza di coordinamento.

Anche stavolta, purtroppo, sta venendo fuori l'immagine di uno Stato disgregato, che rivela le sue carenze sia al centro che in periferia. Napoli in questi giorni appare come una città surreale, con gli autobus che si bloccano senza preavviso, banche e negozi chiusi. Per fare tornare al lavoro i titolari degli uffici postali, indispensabili in momenti come questi, è stato lanciato un appello attraverso una televisione privata. Sarebbe stato più semplice e più giusto ricorrere alla precettazione. Chi ricopre una carica pubblica, sia amministratore che funzionario, ha il dovere di restare al suo posto.

Napoli, del resto, è solo un sintomo di una situazione più generale. Non sono soltanto qui i peccati di latitanza. Bisogna che qualcuno spieghi perchè in un paese funestato quasi ogni anno da terremoti, alluvioni e frane, non sia stato ancora organizzato un decente servizio di protezione civile, pronto a scattare nei momenti di emergenza. Perchè non si sono visti gli elicotteri della Marina? Com'è stato possibile che gli inviati dei giornali arrivassero quasi ovunque prima dei mezzi di soccorso?

□

Seguendo un vecchio rituale, tutti dicono da due giorni che bisogna evitare che si ripeta un altro Belice, riferendosi evidentemente ai ritardi della ricostruzione e allo scandalo della gente che vive ancora nelle baracche. Ma si tratta di una fuga in avanti. Il problema dei sopravvissuti della Basilicata e della Campania non è ancora quello del «dopo», ma di come vivere oggi all'aperto, senza nemmeno il riparo di una tenda, mentre i meteorologhi annunciano l'arrivo del maltempo. Per loro è come se il terremoto cominciasse soltanto adesso. Nessuno si può permettere di perdere anche un solo minuto.

Ettore Serio

NAPOLI DEVE TORNARE A VIVERE

NON conosciamo il numero dei morti, né quello dei feriti. Non sappiamo quante persone siano rimaste senza tetto, quante case siano crollate, quante stano inabitabili in Irpinia, nel Salernitano, in Lucania a Napoli stessa. Un bilancio è impossibile.

Compito dei politici non ricadere nei vecchi errori, non consentire che si approfitti ancora una volta di una catastrofe che ha colpito il Paese.

Compito nostro quello di seguire il compiersi di quest'arco, di essere presenti, come lo siamo in questo momento di doloroso inizio. Siamo arrivati spesso prima dei soccorritori. Abbiamo nelle orecchie i gemiti dei feriti, i lamenti dei sopravvissuti, le invocazioni di chi è ancora sotto le macerie. Tutto questo dolore ci autorizza a fare un discorso ai napoletani.

I napoletani sono stati bravi. Un composto, insolito silenzio si è steso sulla città. Eppure ci sono state vittime, ci sono stati danni: poche le case che non abbiano lesioni o crepe nei muri. Molti i disagi, per gli anziani, per i malati, per i bambini, per tutti. Napoli da secoli adusata alla sventura ha sopportato sgomenta le difficoltà di queste ore angosciose. Ora però deve fare un altro passo. Un passo avanti guardando a quello che sta avvenendo nei tanti paesi del Sud colpiti dalla sventura, dove si continua a scavare tra le macerie, dove manca l'acqua, dove si attendono viveri, coperte, tende, un qualsiasi riparo per trascorrervi la notte.

Un bilancio non è possibile, si è detto all'inizio. Ma quello che sappiamo può bastare per un confronto con quanto di ben più tragico è avvenuto nell'Avellinese, nel Salernitano, nel Potentino. I napoletani debbono farlo; perchè è necessario, e urgente, riaprire gli uffici, i negozi, i ristoranti, i bar, far circolare i mezzi pubblici, tornare al lavoro, alla vita di tutti i giorni. Bisogna ridare alla città che ancora chiamano la capitale del Sud un volto e un'immagine che in queste ore parevano perduti. Tempo di vivere e tempo di morire, sta scritto. Questo è tempo di vivere, di essere presenti, attivi, utili a chi ha bisogno di noi. Un'esortazione, la nostra, che ci sembra doverosa.

Non un'esortazione, ma parole molto dure andrebbero invece rivolte ai responsabili della cosa pubblica. Non si lascia che il capoluogo di una regione ferita a morte si paralizzi come è avvenuto di Napoli in questi due giorni.

Ma questo è un discorso che, i nostri lettori l'hanno già capito, non abbiamo voluto fare. Almeno per oggi.

Arturo Fratta

NAPOLI — Il terremoto comincia ora, quando è finito il terromoto. La retorica non c'entra di fronte ad una catastrofe di queste dimensioni. Mentre ancora non sappiamo quanti morti dobbiamo contare, forse addirittura diecimila, e mentre la terra continua a tremare, bisogna cominicare a pensare a domani. Meglio di come si è fatto in altre occasioni simili e presto come implora la gente. Ieri, intanto, sono state registrate altre quattro scosse, la più pesante nel pomeriggio, intorno alle 18. A Brianza in Lucania, sono crollati gli edifici lesionati domenica. Si è temuto il peggio, poi l'allarme è rientrato.

La scossa più forte, alle ore 19,28, è stata del settimo grado della scala Mercalli ed è stata particolarmente avvertita, appunto, nella zona di Brienza e in tutta la provincia di Potenza. Le altre scosse del pomeriggio sono state registrate alle 16,58 e alle 16,06. Tocca pensare a domani partendo dai dati assoluti di questa tragedia: duecentocinquantamila senzatetto, ad esempio, un esercito di persone che hanno perduto tutto, la casa, il lavoro, gli affetti più cari.

C'è un pezzo di Mezzogiorno, insomma, due regioni abitate da sette milioni di persone già più volte sconfitte, che deve ripartire da zero. Come il Belice dodici anni fa. Ed è dal fallimento di quella esperienza che deve cominciare il domani a Sant'Angelo dei Lombardi, ad Avellino, a Baronissi, a Castelnuovo di Conza, a Bavano.

Lo ha ricordato anche Papa Woityla volando sul deserto di pietre e di vita e poi scendendo a portare la sua solidarietà ai sopravvissuti. «Quando soffre un uomo, ha detto il Pontefice, ci vuole un altro uomo accanto a lui e quando soffrono tanti uomini ci vogliono molti uomini accanto a quelli che soffrono».

Parole nobili, ma la realtà che tocchiamo con mano è profondamente diversa. Anche a livello emotivo, come hanno confermato i fischi che ieri pomeriggio il Capo dello Stato ha raccolto visitando i paesi più colpiti. Fischi ingenerosi che un uomo come Pertini non merita, ma che debbono egualmente far riflettere. Pochi, però, sono disposti a farlo con la necessaria freddezza.

La verità è che due giorni dopo quella domenica maledetta si brancola ancora nel buio. I soccorsi continuano ad arrivare tardi e male mancando un coordinamento generale e su tutto domina una psicosi che se è comprensibile la dove il terremoto ha spazzato la vita oltre alle case, lo è molto di meno a Napoli dove da quarantott'ore tutti scappano, anche le autorità che dovrebbero conservare la calma per impartire le giuste sollecitazioni, severe quando è il caso (se manca il pane, ad esempio), per favorire la ripresa ed un ritorno graduale alla normalità.

Anche gli uomini politici, oltre ai burocrati della Prefettura e della Questura si sono lasciati eccessivamente «prendere» dalla sindrome della scossa riproponendo i meccanismi logori del peggiore meridionalismo. Lo ha constatato in una riunione a Salerno, lo stesso commissario Zambelletti chiedendo una svolta più rigorosa. Que-

Carlo Franco

CONTINUA

14 pagine sulla catastrofe

- AVELLINO / Dai nostri inviati Domenico Ferrara, Carlo Nicotera, Giuseppe Pisano, Francesco Durante, Gianni Festa, Michele Bonuomo, Antonio Fiore, Gino Cavallo, Vittorio Paliotti, Giuseppe Calise, Bruno Buonanno e Titta Fiore.
- POTENZA / Dai nostri inviati Gaetano Giordano Aldo Stefanile, Salvatore Signorelli e Vittorio Sabia.
- SALERNO / Dai nostri inviati Nicola Fruscione, Gino Liguori, Emanuele Imperiali, Carlo dell'Orefice, Clodomiro Tarsia, Gianni Ambrosino, Onorato Volzone, Elena Massa, Lino Zaccaria, Lello Barbuto, Franco Scandone, Francesco Bufi e Massimo Corcione.
- CASERTA / Dai nostri inviati Gianni Ramasco, Andrea D'Errico, Michele De Simone; Gaetano Trosino.
- BENEVENTO / Dai nostri inviati Arnaldo De Longis e Gianni Virnicchi.
- NAPOLI / Servizi di Ciro Paglia, Gianni Campili, Enzo Perez, Enzo Popoli, Pasquale Esposito, Paolo Ruffini, Ernesto Filoso, Marco Pellegrini, Ezz Guardascione, Mino Jouakim, Luciano Grasso, Massimo Baldari, Franco Mancusi, Carmela Maletta, Gianpietro Olivetto, Almerico Di Meglio, Vinni Volpe, Mario Caruso, Giuseppe Bagnati e Giulio Avati
- ROMA / Servizi di Renato Caserta e Gianfranco Del Giudice.

S. ANGELO DEI LOMBARDI — Un'inquadratura scattata dall'aereo noleggiato da «Il Mattino» mostra quel che è rimasto del paese dopo le scosse del terremoto: distruzione e morte ovunque (Foto di Felice Santosuosso)

220 Fate Presto 1981 Stiftung Sammlung Marx, Hamburger Bahnhof – Museum für Gegenwart, Berlin

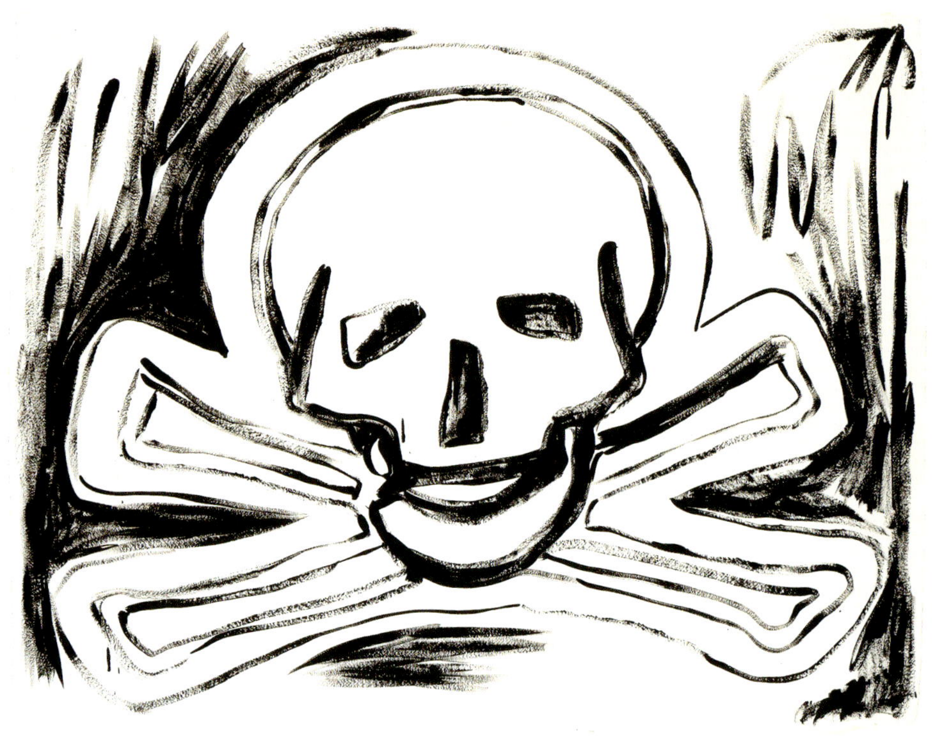

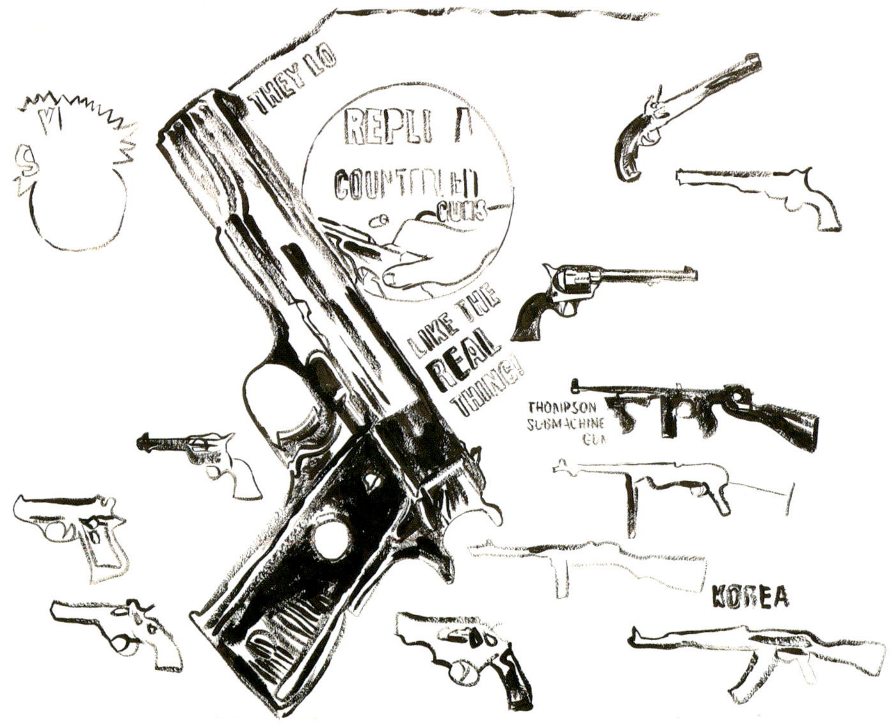

221 **Untitled (Skull and Crossbones) c. 1985-86** Private collection, Germany

222 **Replica Guns 1985-86** Courtesy The Brant Foundation, Greenwich, CT

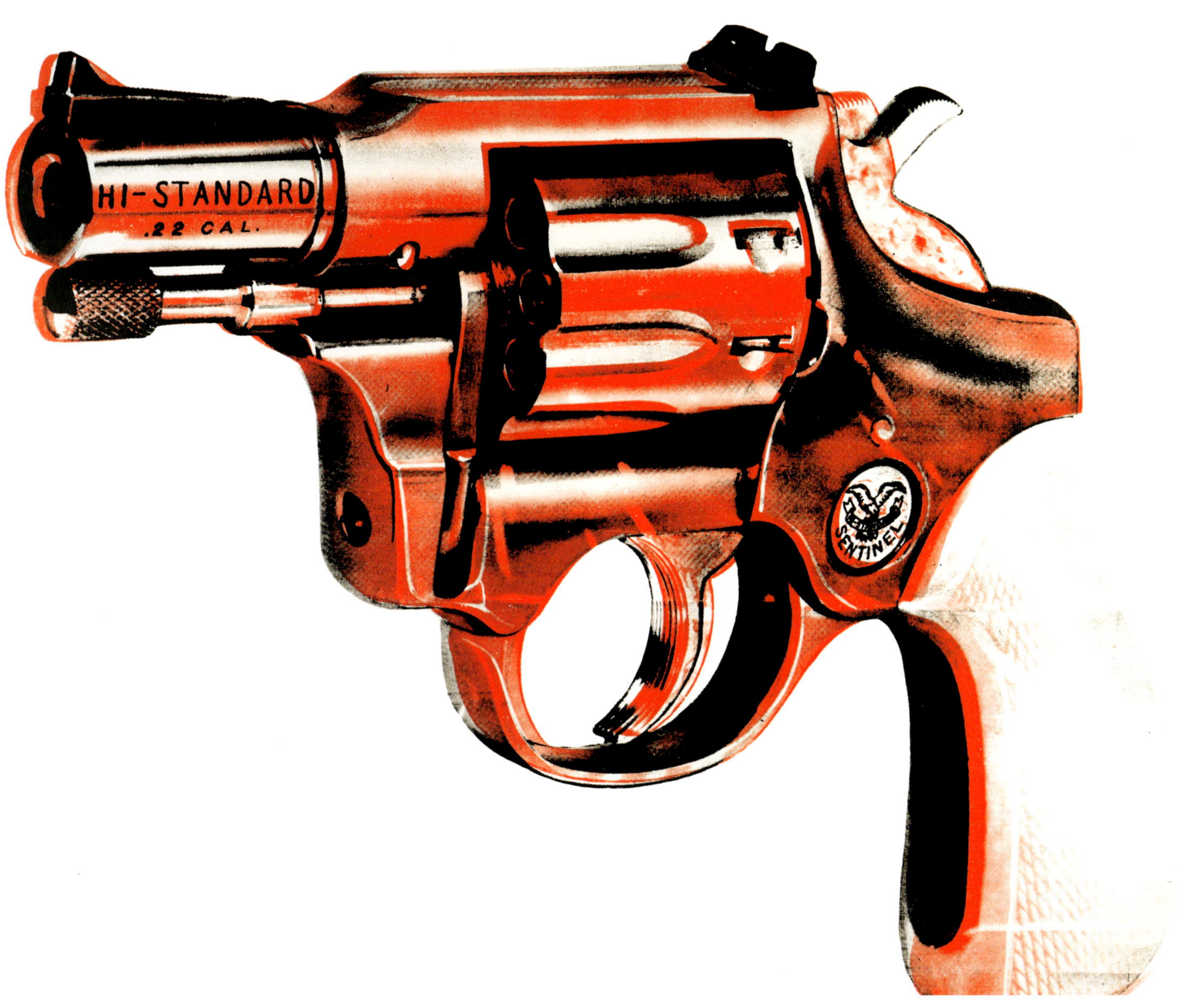

223 **Gun** **1981** Courtesy Anthony d'Offay Gallery, London

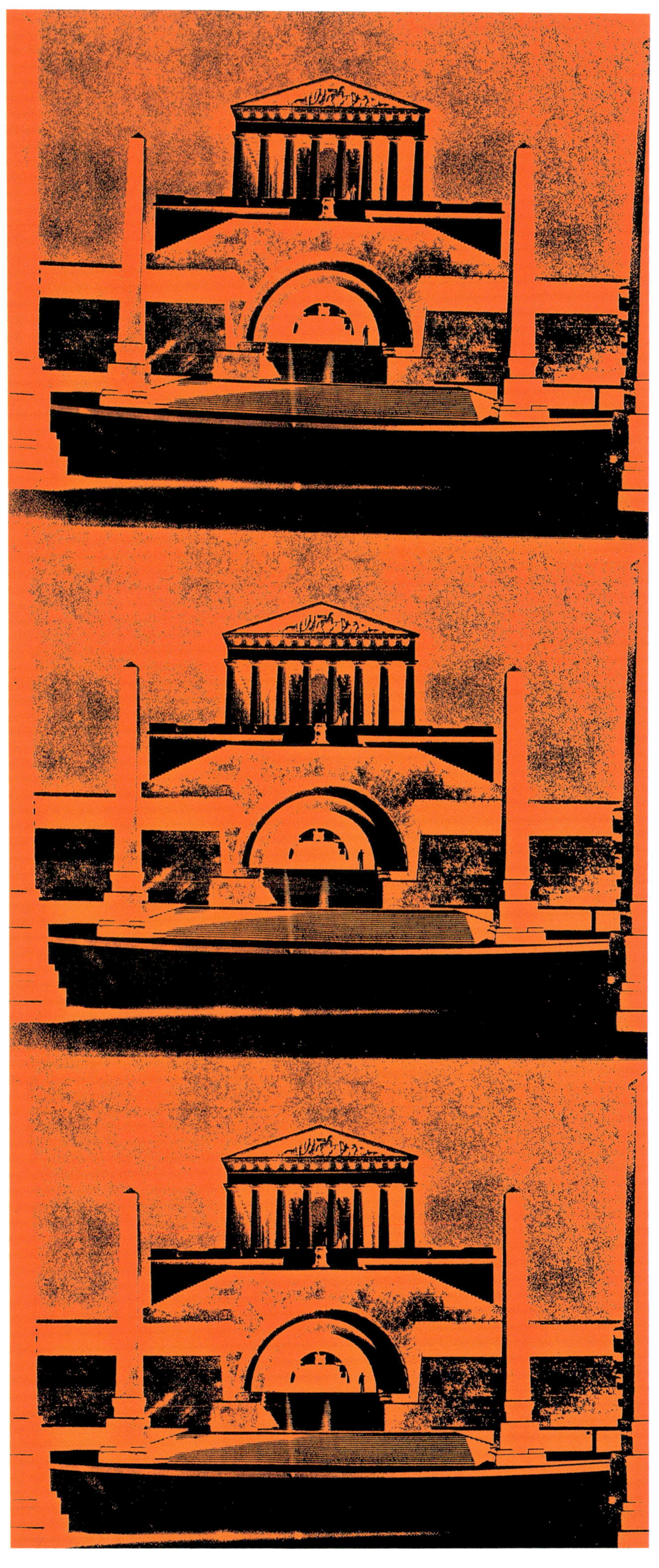

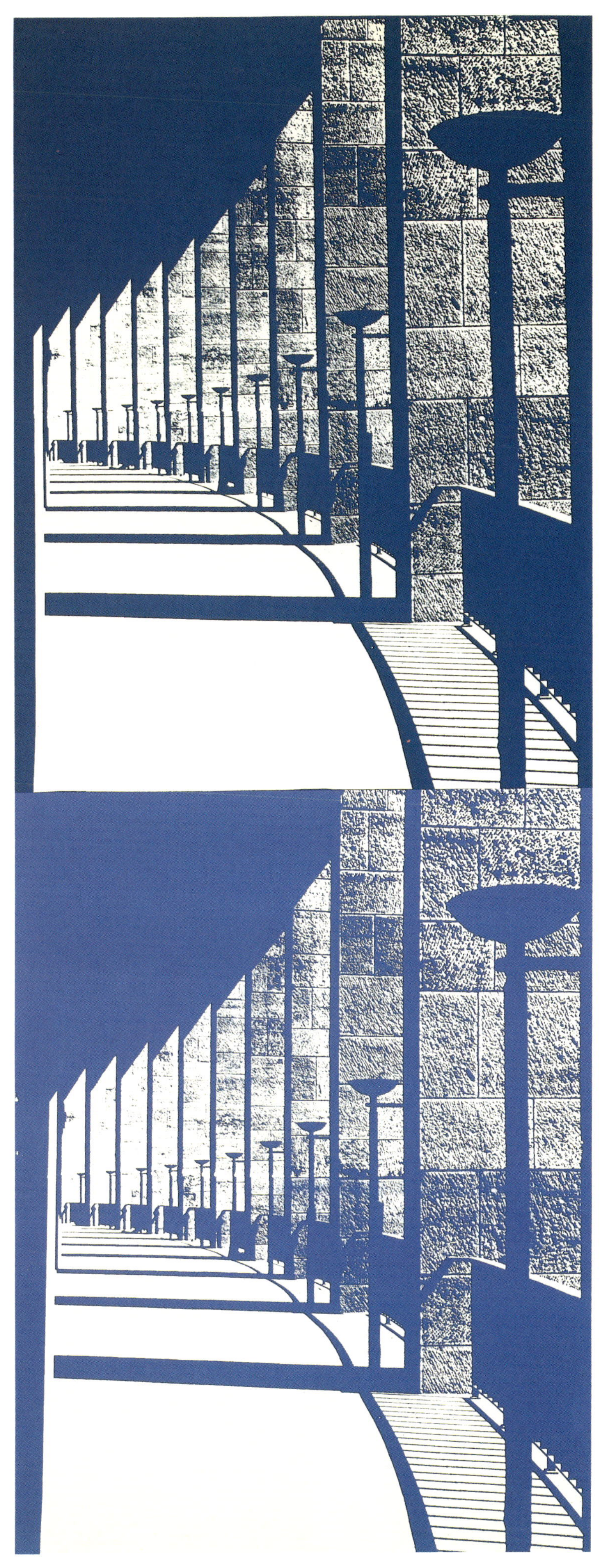

◂ 224 **The Berlin Friedrich Monument [Zeitgeist Series] 1982**
Stiftung Sammlung Marx, Hamburger Bahnhof – Museum für Gegenwart, Berlin

225 **Stadium [Zeitgeist Series] 1982**
Bruno Bischofberger, Zürich

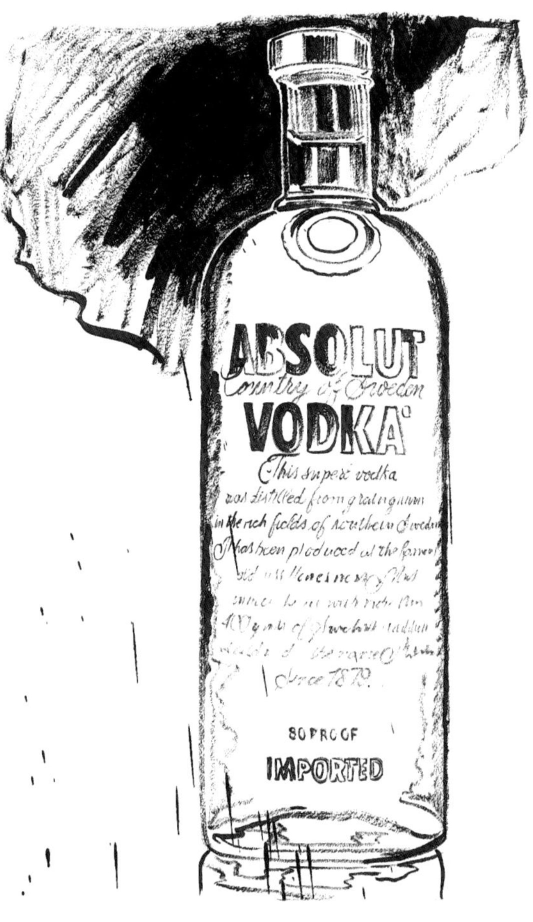

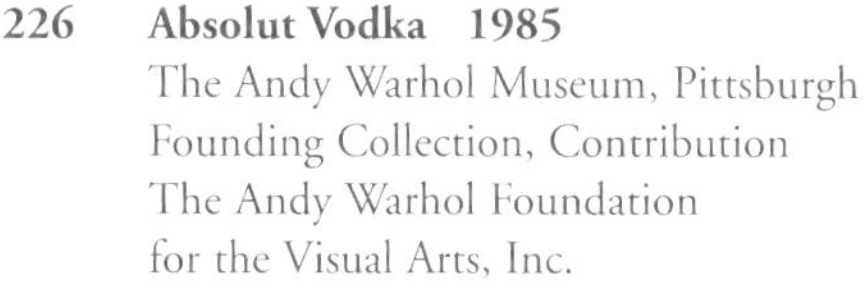

226 **Absolut Vodka 1985**
The Andy Warhol Museum, Pittsburgh
Founding Collection, Contribution
The Andy Warhol Foundation
for the Visual Arts, Inc.

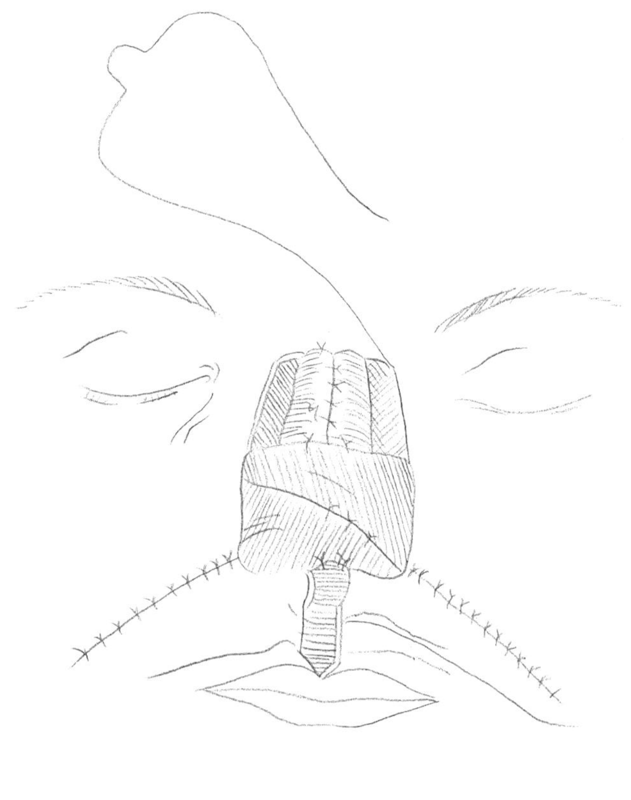

227 **Cosmetic Surgery c. 1985-86**
The Andy Warhol Museum, Pittsburgh
Founding Collection, Contribution
The Andy Warhol Foundation
for the Visual Arts, Inc.

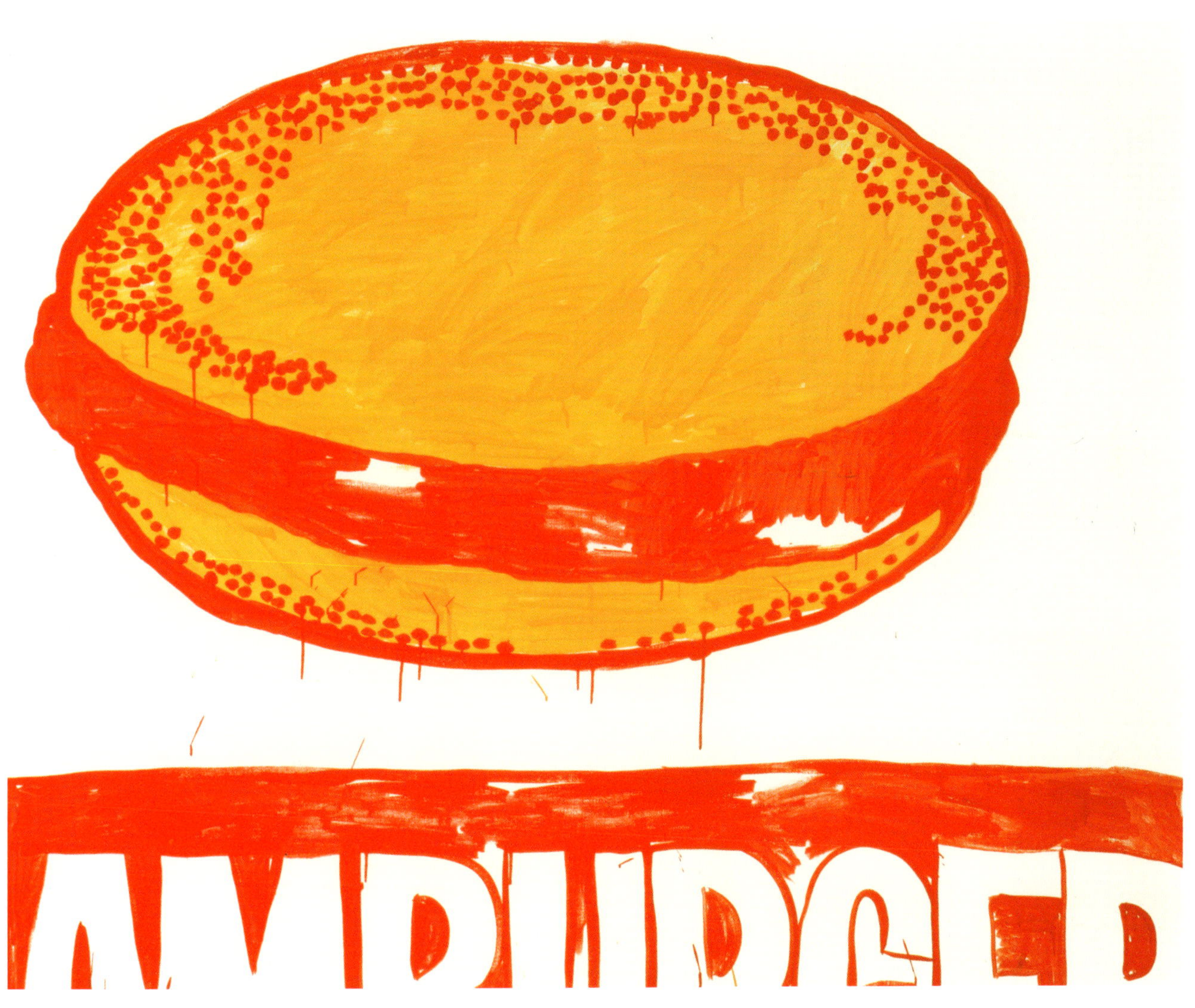

228 Hamburger 1985/86 Private collection, London

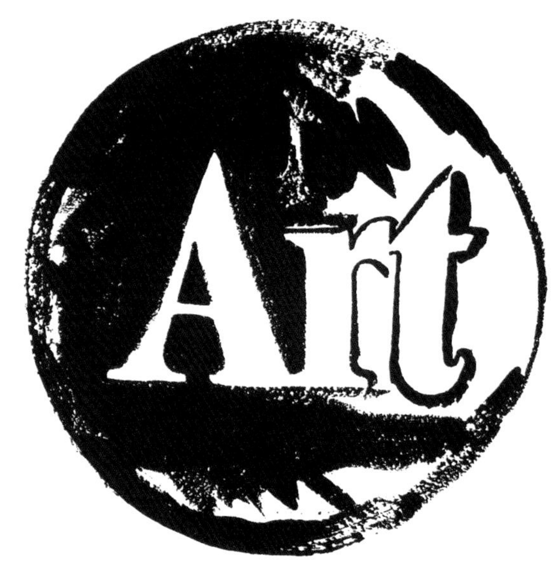

229 **Art** **1985** Private collection

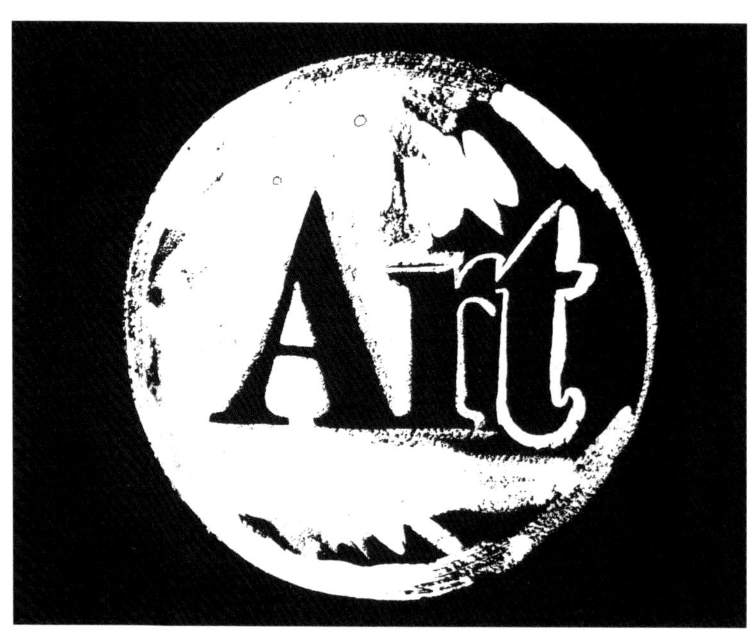

229a **Art** **1985** Private collection

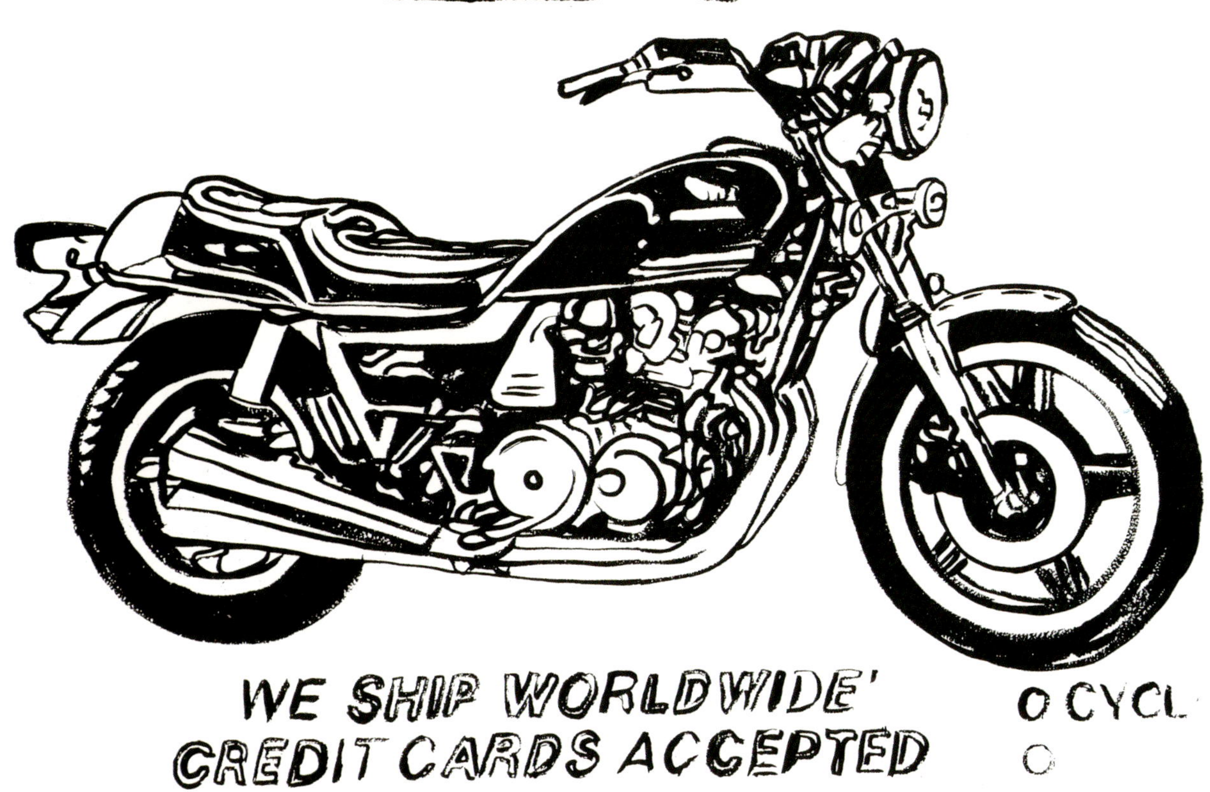

230 Mineola Motorcycle 1986 Private collection

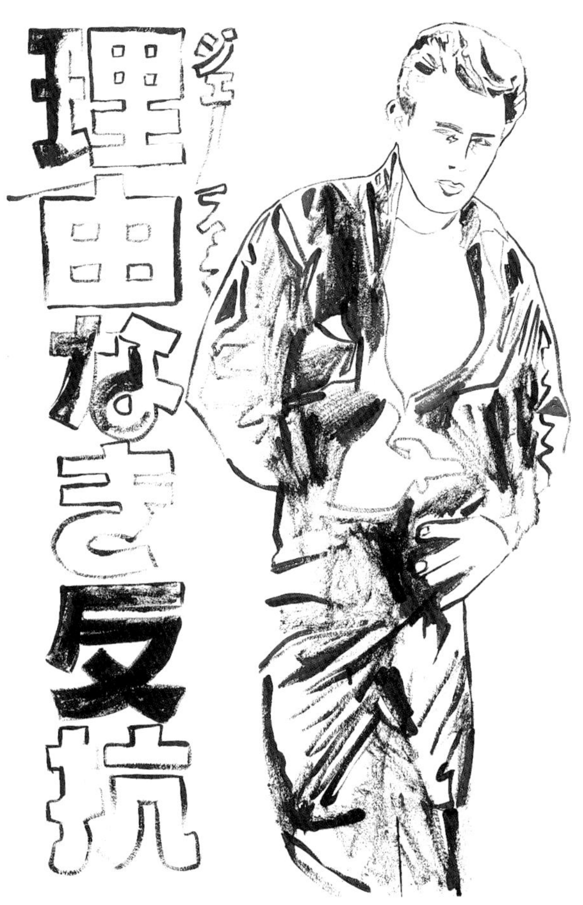

231 **Ads: Rebel Without a Cause (James Dean) c. 1985**
Courtesy Ronald Feldman Fine Arts, New York
The Andy Warhol Museum, Pittsburgh
Founding Collection, Contribution
The Andy Warhol Foundation
for the Visual Arts, Inc.

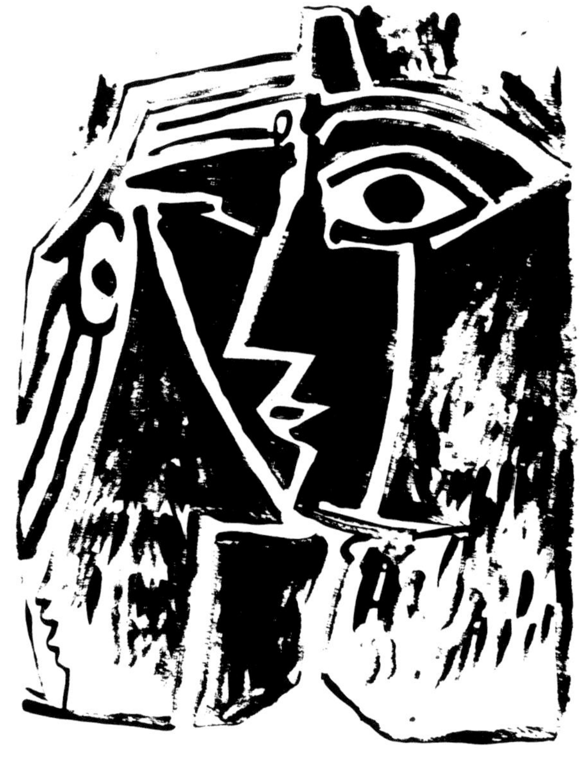

232 **Head (After Picasso) 1985**
Private collection, Saarbrücken

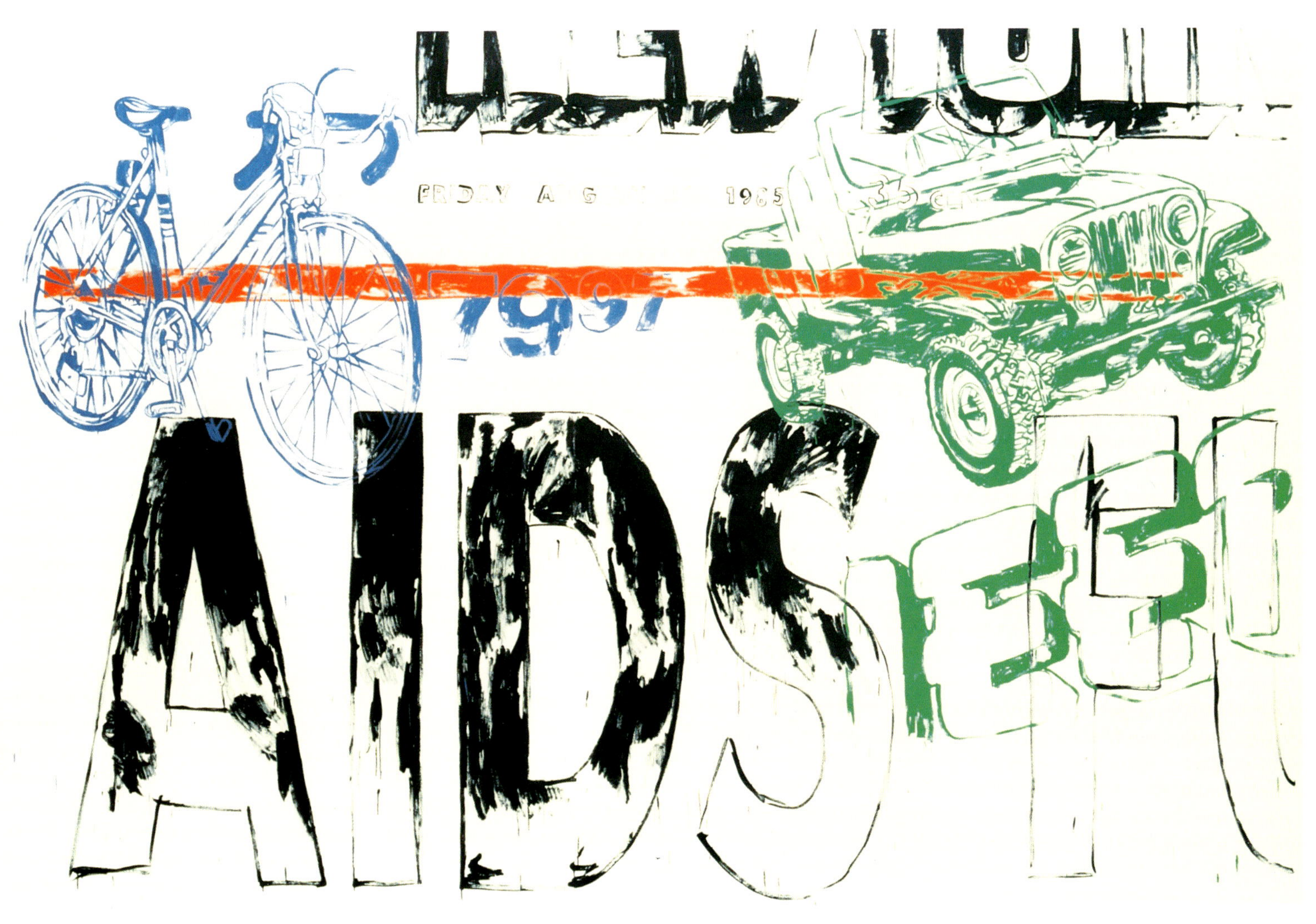

233 AIDS/Jeep/Bicycle c. 1985 Bayerische Staatsgemäldesammlungen, München

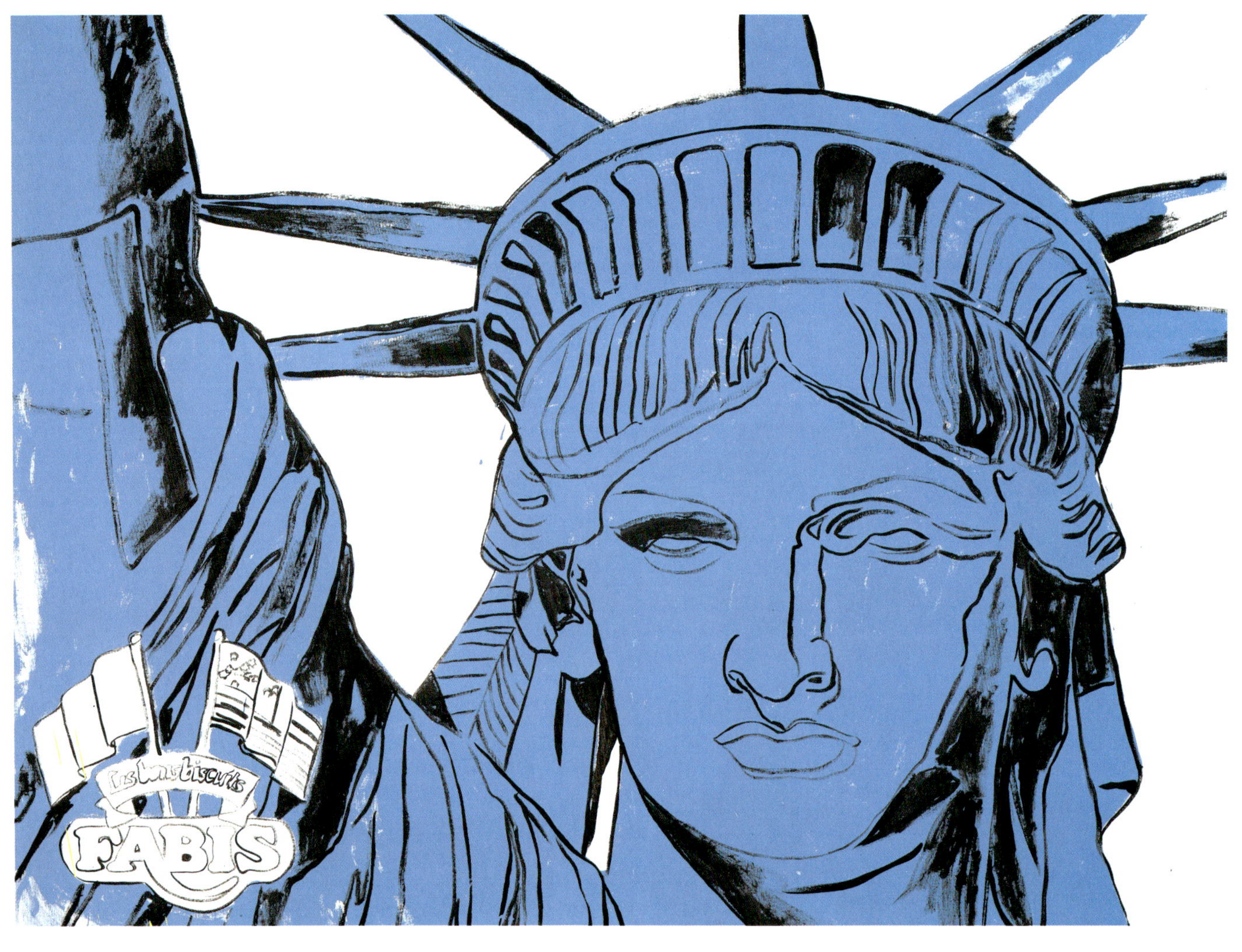

234 **Fabis Statue of Liberty** **1986** Stiftung Sammlung Marx, Hamburger Bahnhof – Museum für Gegenwart, Berlin

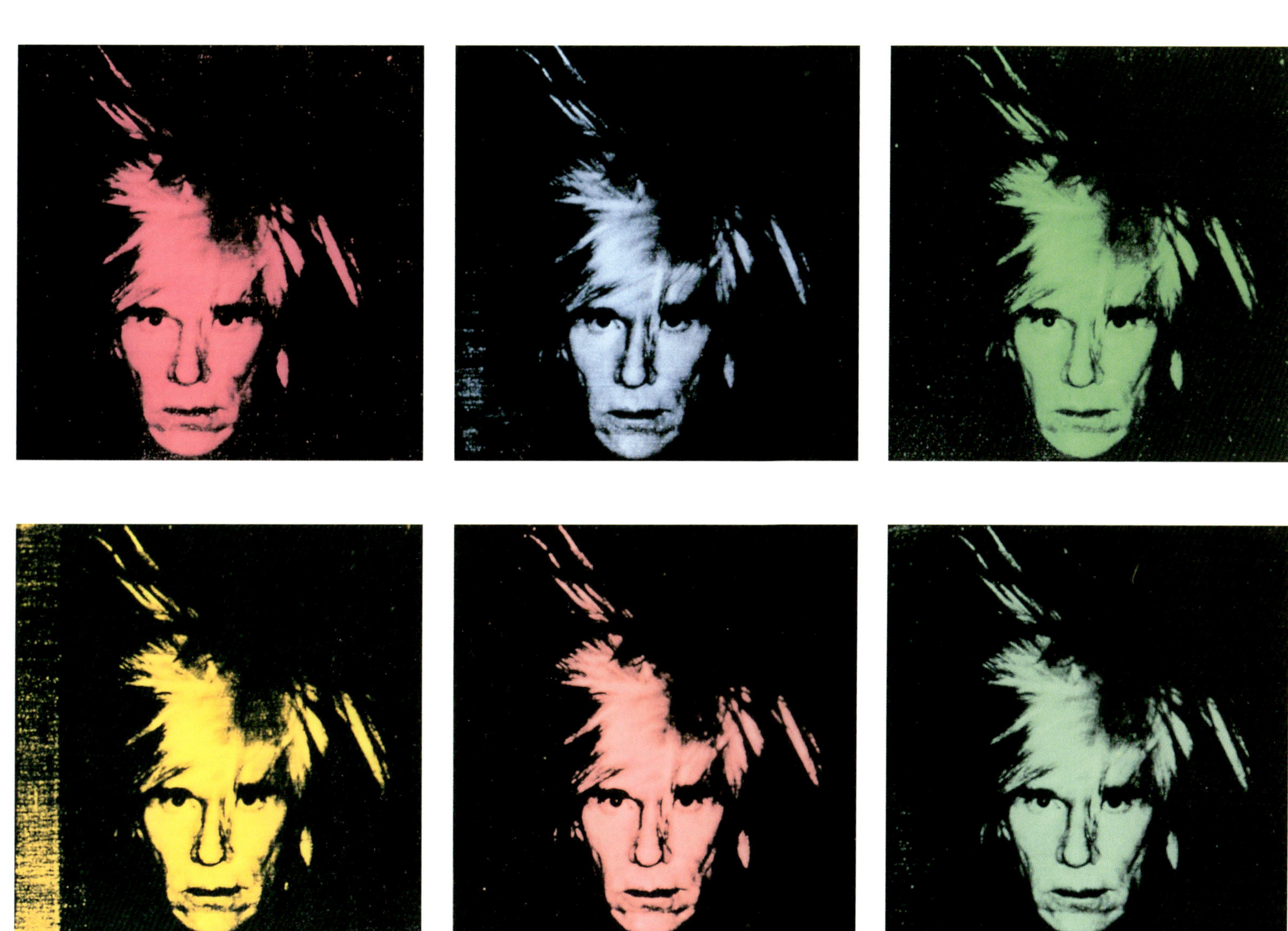

235 **Six Self-Portraits 1986** Collection Froehlich, Stuttgart

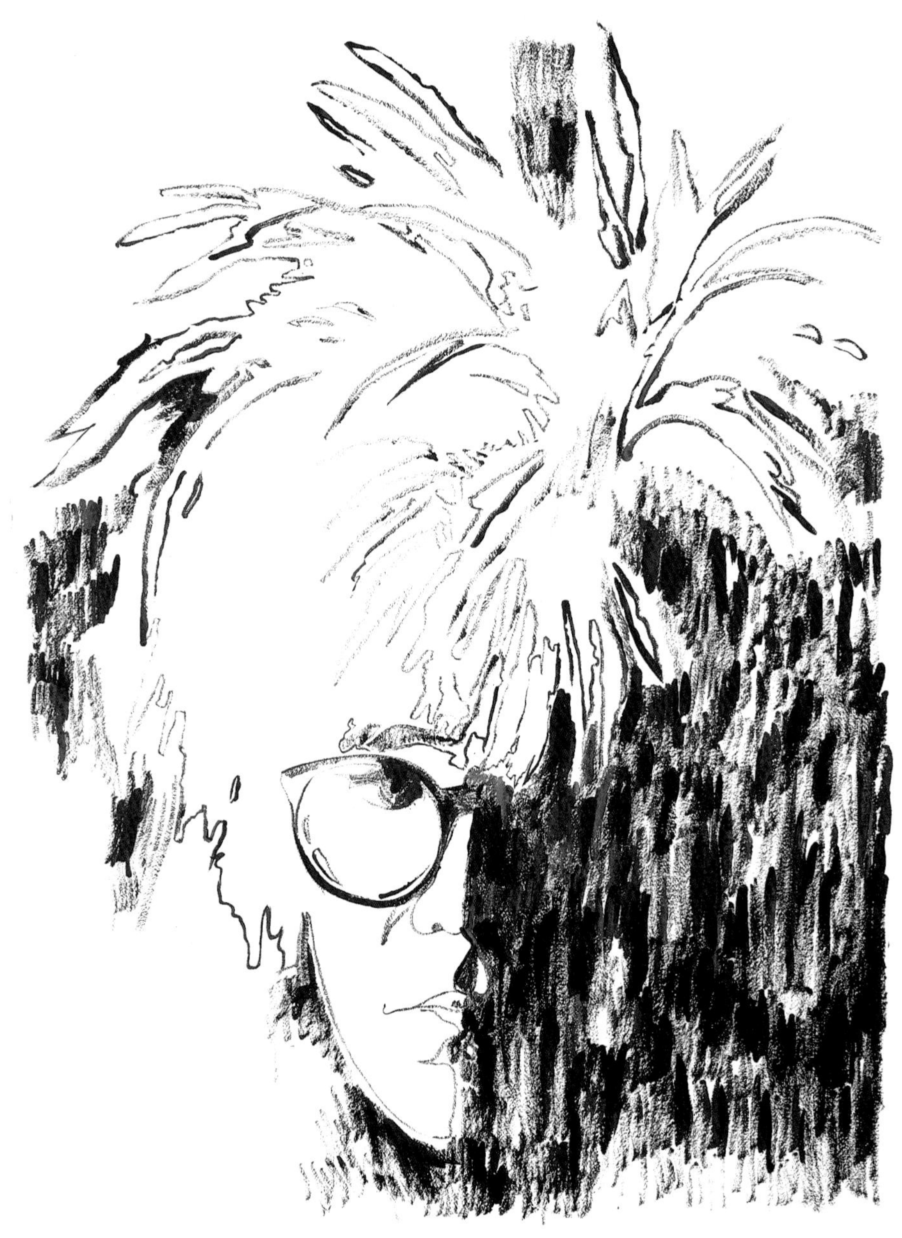

236 **Self-Portrait** **1986** The Andy Warhol Museum, Pittsburgh • Founding Collection, Contribution The Andy Warhol Foundation for the Visual Arts, Inc.

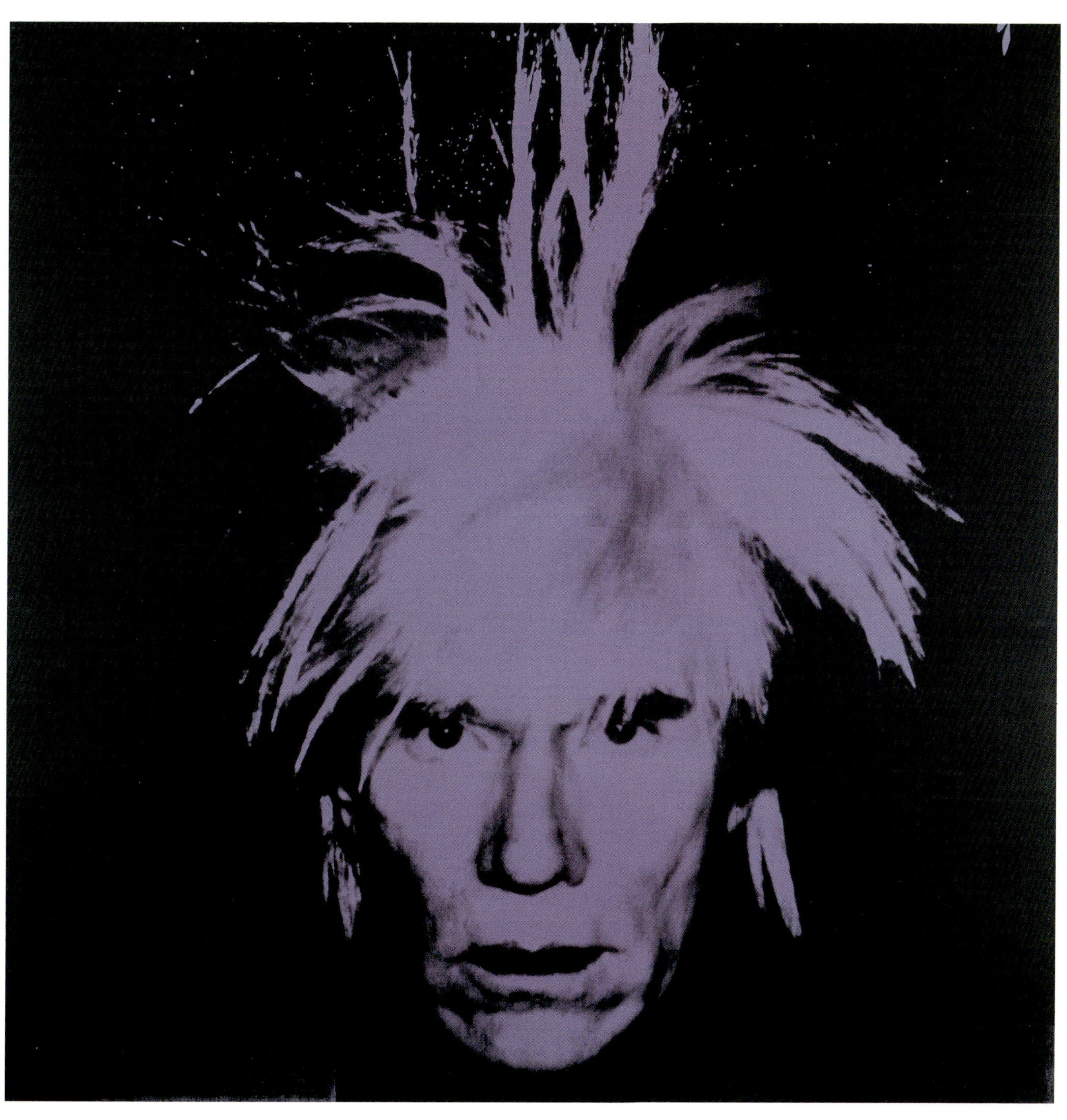

237 Self-Portrait 1986 Private collection

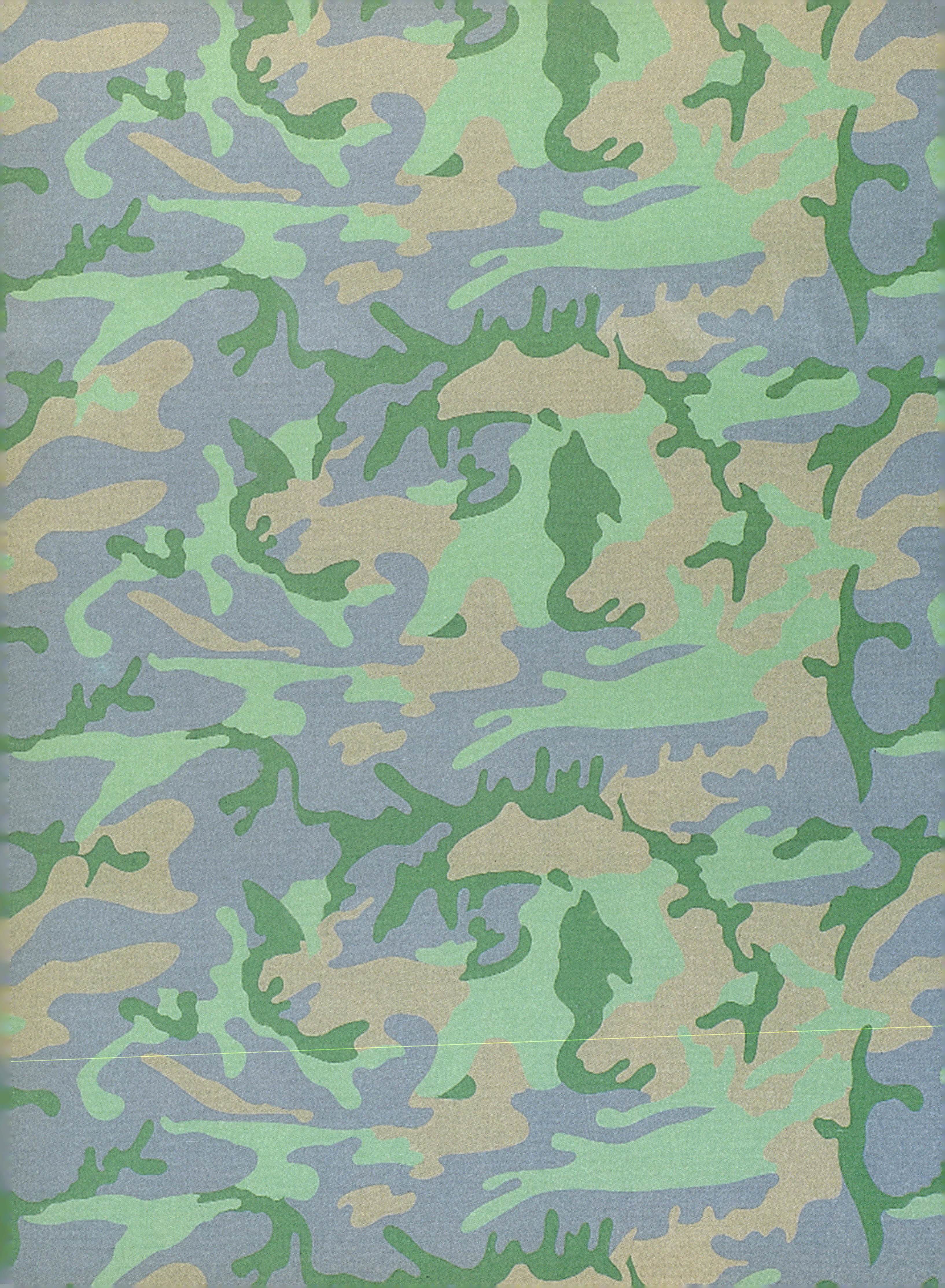

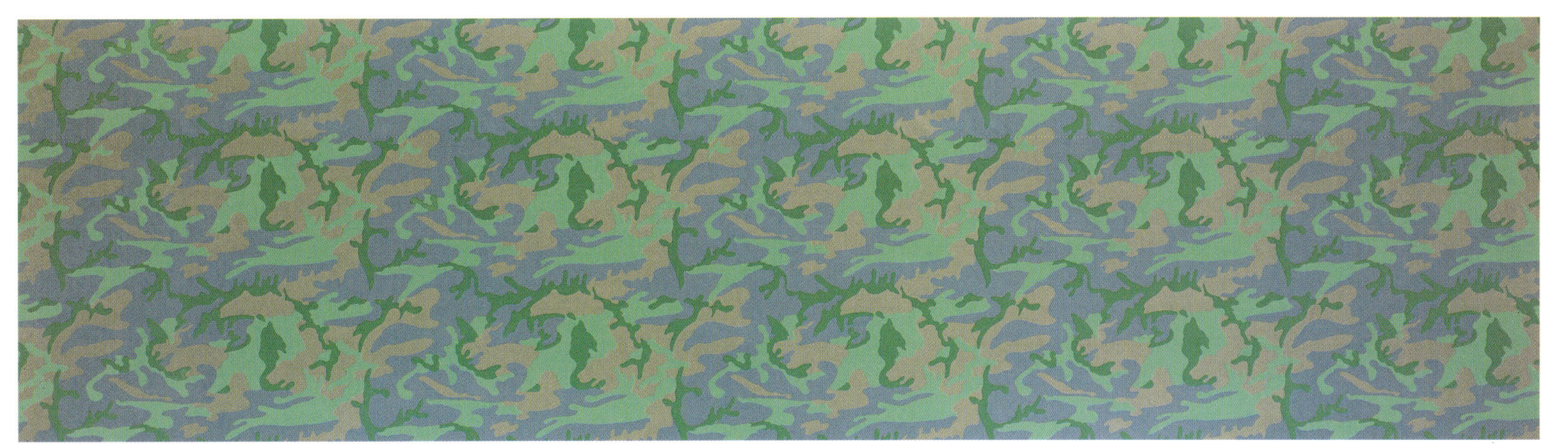

238 **Camouflage 1986** Stiftung Sammlung Marx, Hamburger Bahnhof – Museum für Gegenwart, Berlin

◂ [Enlarged detail of **Camouflage 1986**]

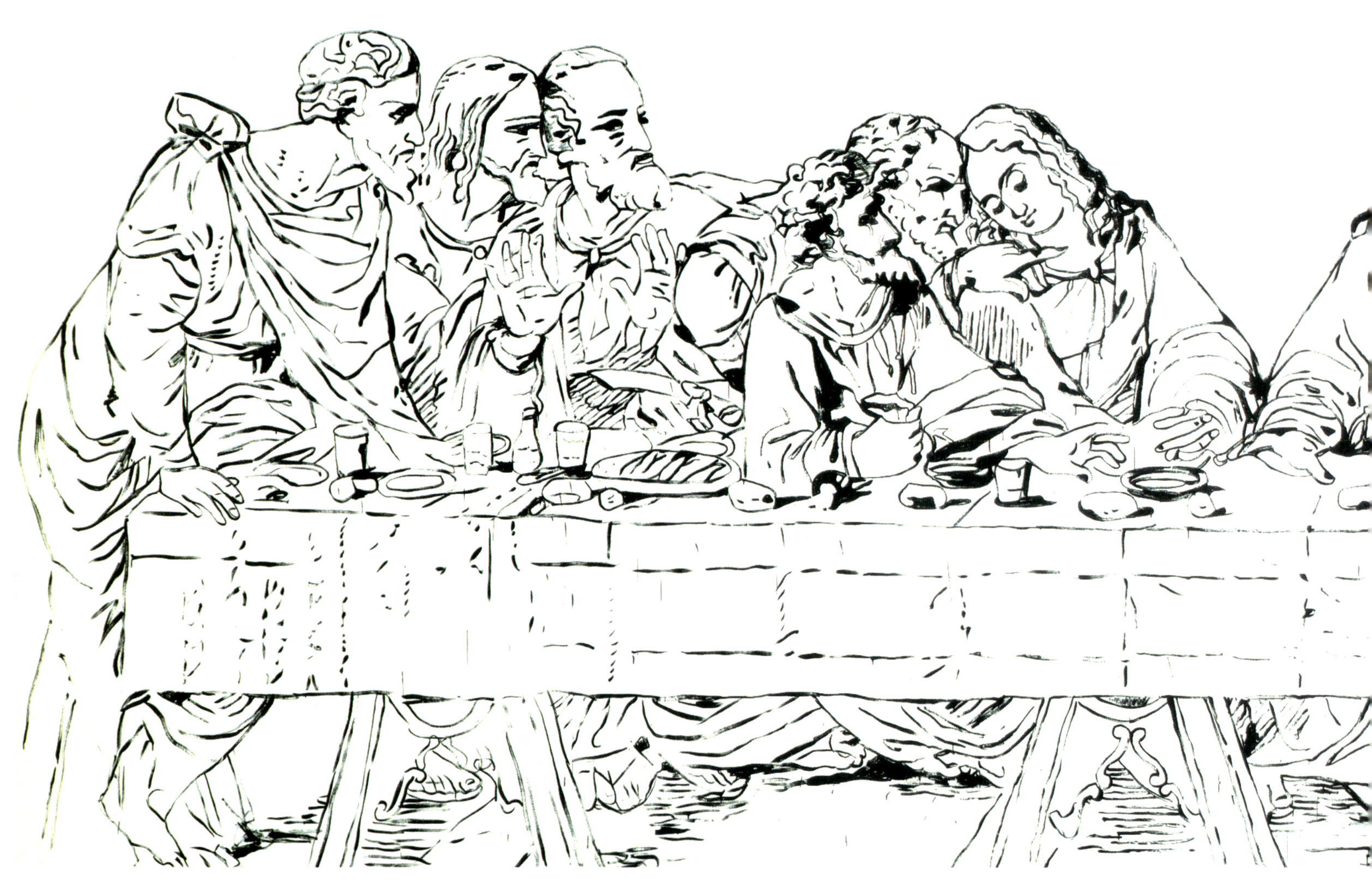

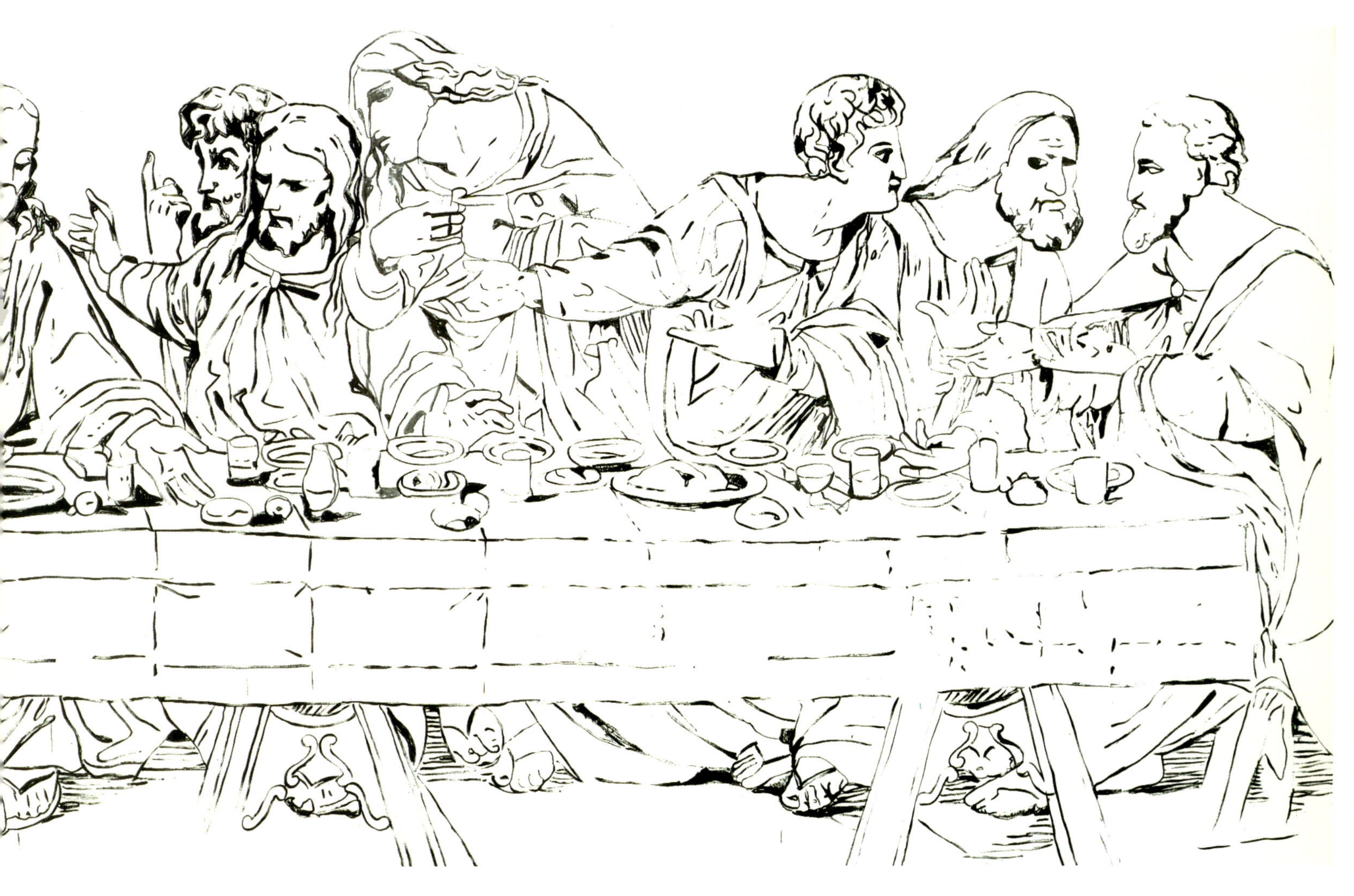

239 **The Last Supper** **1986** Courtesy The Brant Foundation, Greenwich, CT

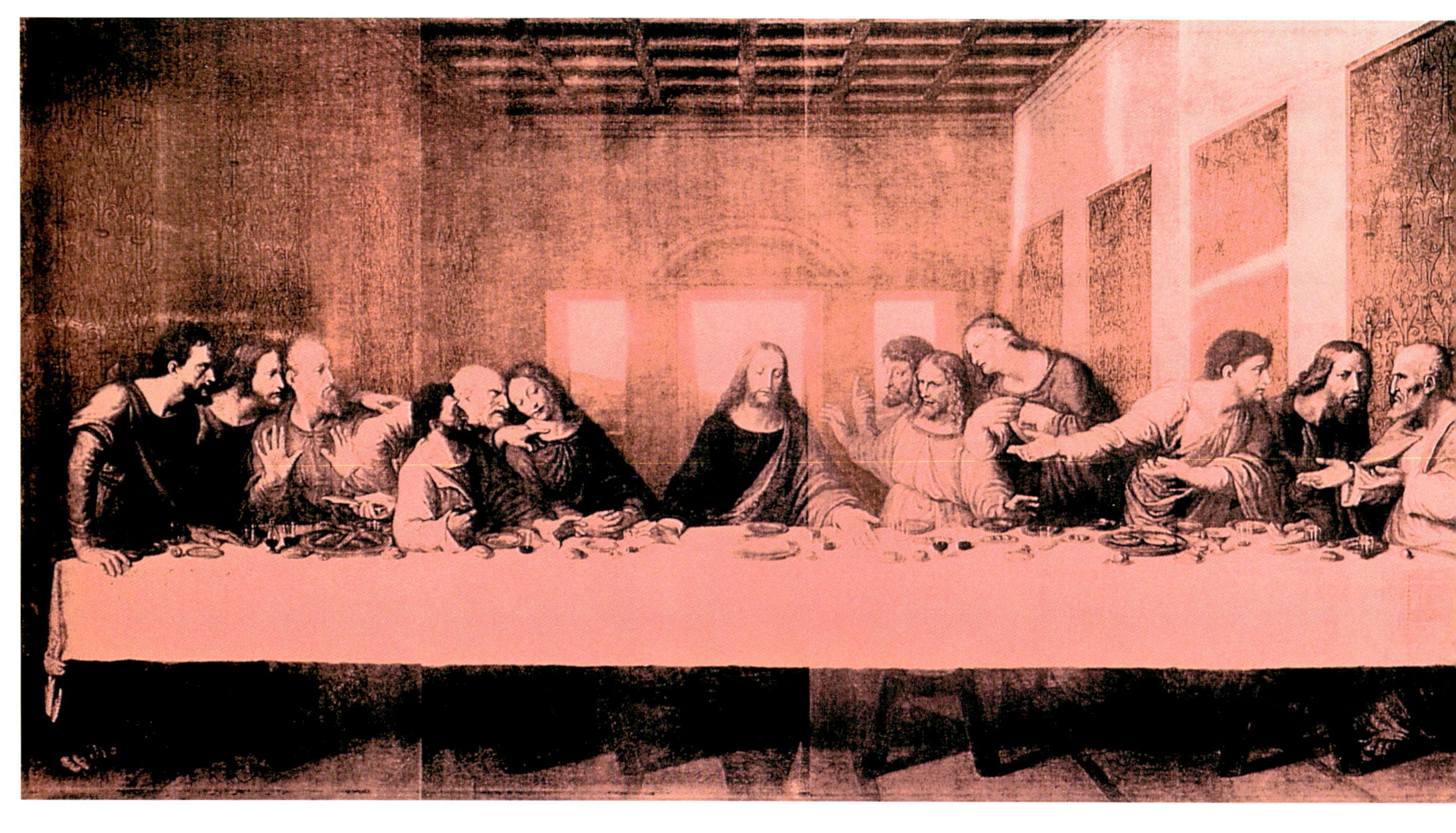

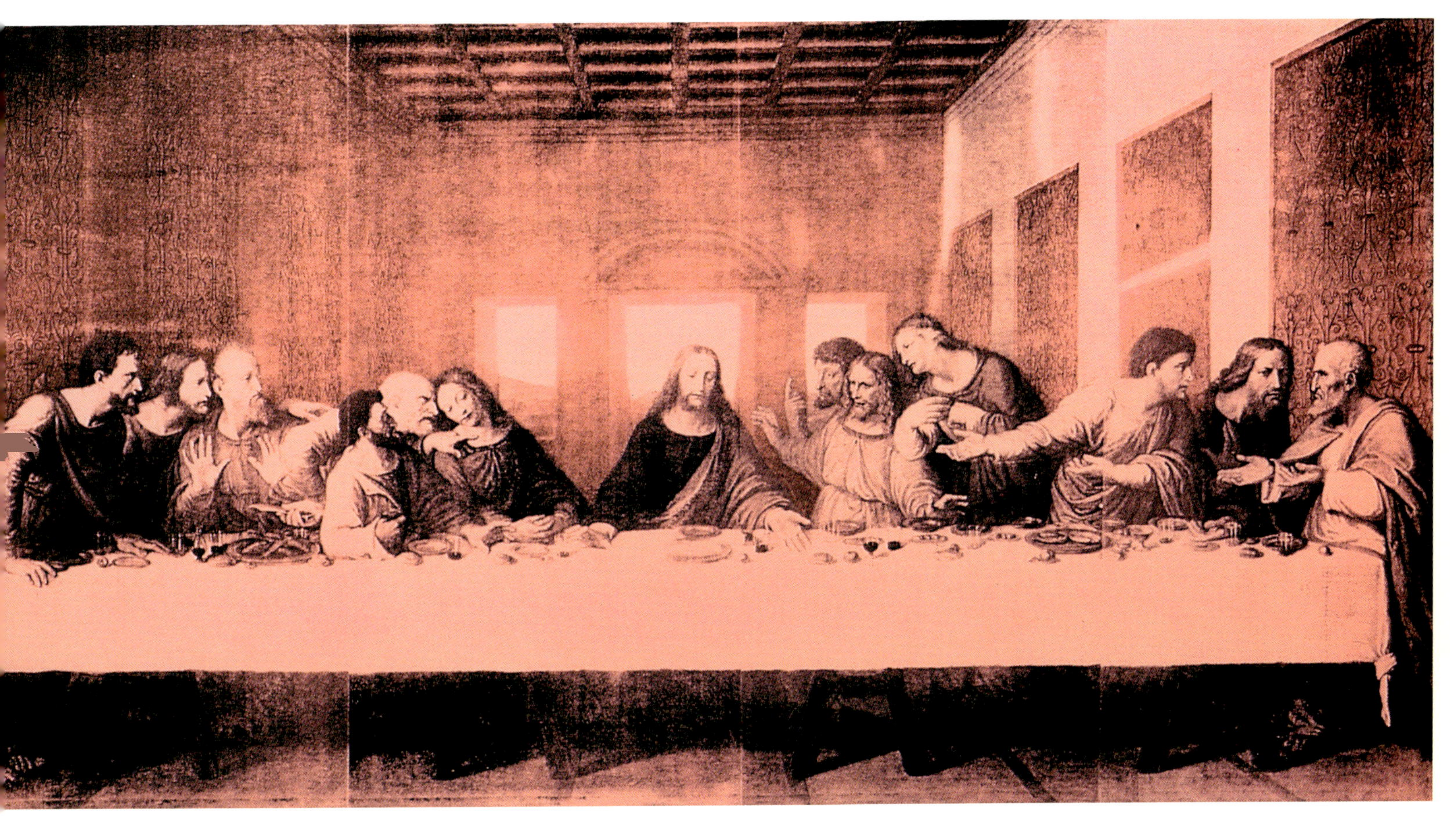

240 The Last Supper 1986 The Andy Warhol Museum, Pittsburgh • Founding Collection, Contribution The Andy Warhol Foundation for the Visual Arts, Inc.

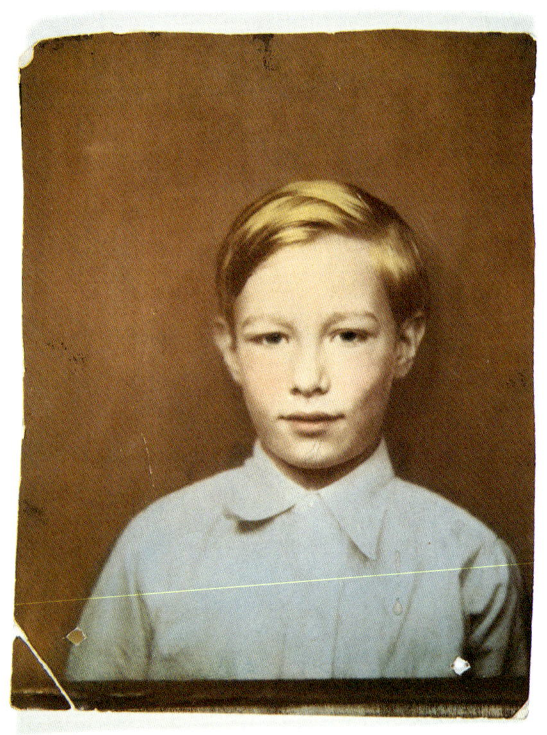

Andy Warhol, aged eight

ANDY WARHOL – A CHRONOLOGY IN AMERICA

Antje Dallmann

1928–1931 Andy Warhol is born on 6 August 1928. His parents are Julia and Andrej Warhola, who were married in Mikova, a village then on the border of the Austro-Hungarian Empire, now on the Slovakian border, with Ukraine. Both are members of the Ruthenian religious community, whose worship is close to that of the Russian Orthodox Church. The family's piety is a strong influence in Andrew's childhood and a constant, though little known, point of reference in his adult life. In 1913 Andrej Warhola emigrates to the United States and works in Pittsburgh, where he had lived for several years before his marriage. He promises to send for his wife as soon as he has a regular income and can raise the money for the crossing. It is a part of family lore that Andrej sent Julia the money five times over, but that it never arrived. In Europe, the civilian population suffers great privations during the First World War. Julia Warhola loses all her personal possessions. Finally in 1921, when Mikova is threatened by the advance of a devastating influenza epidemic, she borrows money from her priest and sets out for the United States – just before the embargo is imposed on immigration from Eastern Europe.

At first the Warholas live in the Soho section of Pittsburgh, a poor district dominated by Eastern European immigrants. Andy's elder brothers, Paul and John, are born in 1922 and 1925. The family is very much part of the local Ruthenian community. Among themselves the Ruthenians speak 'Po Nasemu', a mixture of Hungarian and Ukrainian. For a long time Julia Warhola refuses to learn English. Andy himself learns it only when he starts school.

In the 1920s Pittsburgh is the sixth largest city in the USA, a centre of the American coal and steel industry. The city is a Moloch, dirty, noisy and cramped, and Andy Warhol later calls it the most terrible place he has ever been in in his life. But Pittsburgh is also the almost proverbial 'melting pot', the model of the long sustained metaphor for the integration of cultural and ethnic minorities in the United States.

In 1928, at the start of the economic crisis, Andy's father loses his job with a construction firm and has to take casual work. The resourceful Julia Warhola takes various kinds of paid domestic work, and cuts up tin cans to make flowers which she sells from door to door. The three sons also try to contribute to the family income by casual work. The Warholas have to move into a smaller flat, but they are materially far better off than many other working-class families who lack even the basic necessities.

1932–1935 Andrej Warhola gets back his former assembly job with the construction firm. From now on he is rarely at home and is much missed by all the family. In the absence of his father, ten-year-old Paul, the eldest son, often has to act as head of the family. Julia Warhola, who has almost no command of English, cannot cope with the demands of everyday life. Paul, whose English is also poor and who consequently has severe problems at school, finds Andy, a very bright child, difficult to control and decides to register him for school at the age of four. After Andy comes home from his first day distraught and weeping, his schooling is put off for another two years.

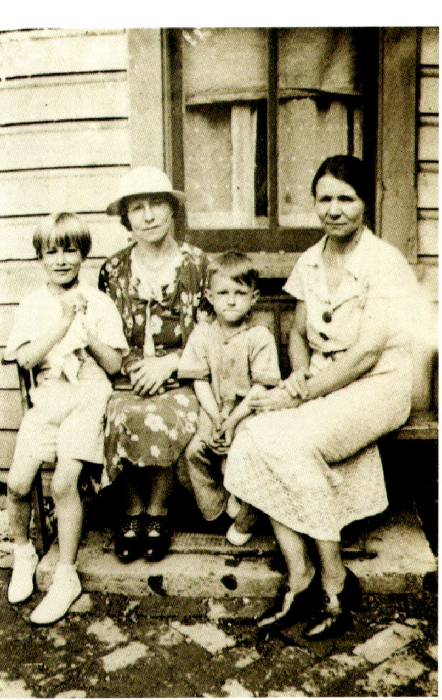

Andy (left) with his mother Julia Warhola, George Guke and Mary Preska, c. 1937

In 1933, with the end of the Depression, various restrictive laws are repealed: alcohol and Sunday gambling are no longer prohibited in the USA.

When Andrej Warhola's income rises in 1934 he is able to take out a loan and to move with his family to Dawson Street in Oakland, a considerably better district than Soho. There are a church and good schools close by.

Andy starts in second grade at Holmes Elementary School, his one day at the elementary school in Soho being counted as a whole year. His first year is successful, although to begin with Andy too speaks only broken English. At home Julia Warhola steadfastly continues to use 'Po Nasemu'. Although money is still short in the Warhola household, Andy's mother manages to save up and buy what her youngest son most desires – a film projector. From now on Andy watches the same short cartoons over and over again, and under the influence of those pictures begins to draw and paint a great deal himself. Aldous Huxley's *Brave New World* is published in London in 1932. On 10 May 1933 the first book burnings take place in Berlin. Thomas and Klaus Mann, Bertolt Brecht, Anna Seghers, Walter Benjamin and Lion Feuchtwanger emigrate; George Grosz goes to the United States. So, in 1937, does László Moholy-Nagy, who founds the 'New Bauhaus' (renamed the 'School of Design' in 1938) in Chicago.

1935 sees the setting up of the 'Works Progress Administration' (WPA), as part of the New Deal intended to improve conditions for the mass of Americans. One of its programmes is the 'Federal Art Project', which provides work for artists.

1936

In Washington the 'House Un-American Activities Committee' is formed.
In Frankfurt am Main the *Zeitschrift für Sozialforschung* publishes Walter Benjamin's essay "The Work of Art in the Age of Mechanical Reproduction".
The Warholas are concerned about the health of eight-year-old Andy. At school he often suffers from involuntary spasms which make him unable to write and cause him to be teased by other children. A doctor diagnoses chorea, a rheumatic illness. This disorder, popularly known as St Vitus' dance, is caused by poor diet and crowded, unhygienic living conditions. The doctor prescribes strict bed rest and intensive nursing. Andy spends the next eight weeks at home, being cared for by his mother and liberally provided with film magazines, comics and colouring books. He loves these and cuts out pictures from them. When Andy is better he returns to his other great passion: he spends almost every Saturday morning at the cinema. In the film *Poor Little Rich Girl* he sees Shirley Temple, who becomes his idol and role model. He writes letters to her – as he does to Mickey Rooney, Freddie Bartholomew and others – asking for photos and autographs.

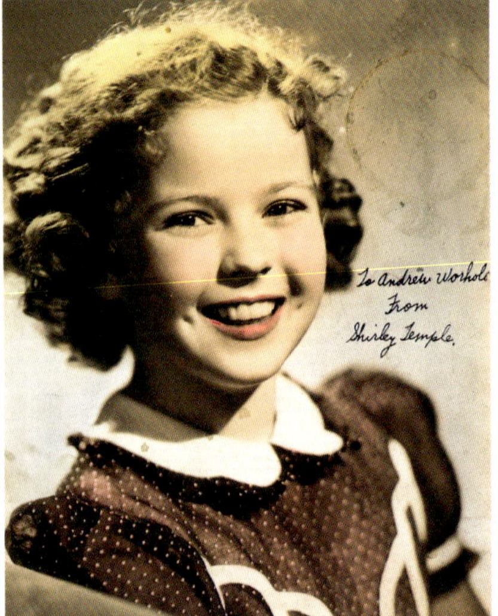

Autographed picture of Shirley Temple: "To Andrew Warhola from Shirley Temple"

1937–1940

On 30 June 1937 the National Socialists in Germany begin their purge of 'degenerate art': thousands of paintings, works of graphic art and sculptures from over a hundred German museums are confiscated. Ludwig Mies van der Rohe emigrates to the United States, where he heads the Department of Architecture at the Illinois Institute of Technology, Chicago, until 1958. On 30 October 1938 the broadcast of Orson Welles' radio play *Invasion from Mars*, based on the novel by H. G. Wells, causes widespread panic on the East Coast of the USA.
On 1 September 1939 the Second World War begins with Germany's invasion of Poland.

In 1937, Andy's art teacher at Holmes Elementary School recommends him for the highly-regarded free art course held on Saturday mornings at the Carnegie Museum. Andy attends these courses regularly until 1941. He is placed in the younger group of pupils, the 'Tam O'Shanters'. His teachers there, especially Joseph Fitzpatrick, are the first important artistic influences on him. In this year he skips the fifth grade.

1941–1944

Following the Japanese attack on Pearl Harbor on 7 December 1941, the USA enters the Second World War. Like many others of his age, Paul Warhola is called up.
In August 1942 Andrej Warhola dies after several years of serious illness. Andy feels this loss deeply. The family is left in a difficult financial situation. Only two years after her husband's death Julia Warhola contracts cancer and has to undergo an operation. In September 1941 Andy enters Schenley High School, which he attends until the spring of 1945.

In 1943 Dwight D. Eisenhower is appointed supreme commander of the Allied Forces in Europe. Robert J. Oppenheimer leads the 'Manhattan Project' at Los Alamos, which aims to develop a US nuclear bomb. Jean-Paul Sartre publishes the central text of existentialism, *L'Etre et le Néant*.
In 1944, Franklin D. Roosevelt becomes the first and last President in the history of the United States to be elected for a fourth term of office. The wartime food rationing comes to an end and the production of consumer goods is resumed.
Allied troops land in Normandy on D-Day. Paris and Brussels are liberated from German occupation. In the Civilian Public Service Camp for conscientious objectors in Waldport, Oregon, a large-scale art project is initiated. This is the origin of the 'San Francisco Renaissance'. At the Rockefeller Institute of Medical Research in New York scientists achieve the chemical analysis of DNA.

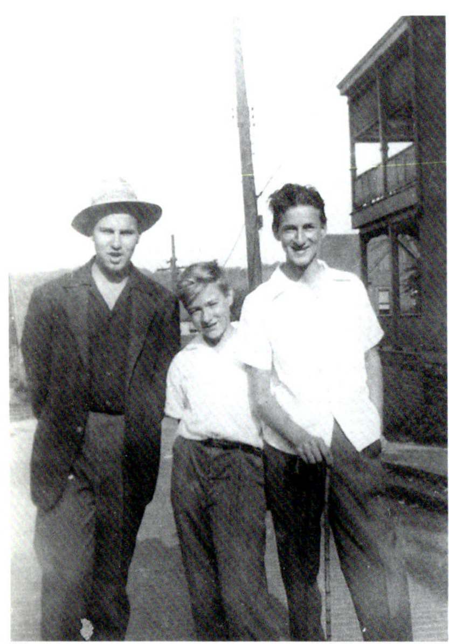

Andy (centre) with brothers Paul (left) and John (right), c. 1942

1945

After the death of Roosevelt in April, Harry S. Truman becomes President of the United States. On V.E. Day, 8 May, the victory of the Allies in Europe is proclaimed. At the end of the Second World War the USA is enjoying an economic boom, but also has 25 per cent inflation, and a wave of strikes spreads across the country. On 25 April the 'United Nations Conference on International Organization' meets in San Francisco and the United Nations charter is signed on 26 June. On 2 September, after the American Air Force drops nuclear bombs on Hiroshima and Nagasaki, Japan surrenders.

Andy graduates from Schenley High School. Under his name the yearbook reads, 'As genuine as a finger print'. In the autumn he embarks on his studies at the Carnegie Institute of Technology, now Carnegie Mellon University, majoring in pictorial design. He gets to know Philip Pearlstein. His teachers include Balcomb Greene, Robert Lepper, Samuel Rosenberg and Howard Worner. Andy becomes interested in the teachings of the Bauhaus and especially in the writings of László Moholy-Nagy.
Andy Warhol gives drawing lessons and during his summer vacations, this year and in the following years, works in the Joseph Horne department store in Pittsburgh. There he is taken on and supervised by Larry Vollmer, who becomes something of a role model.

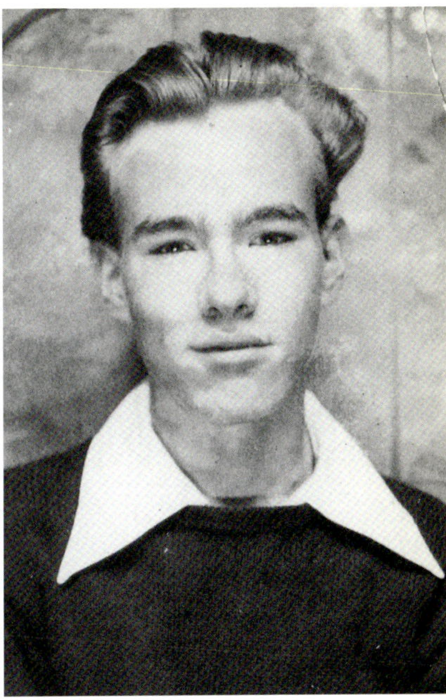

Andy at the start of his studies, photographed by his brother John, c. 1945

1946 With funding from John D. Rockefeller, the United Nations build a permanent headquarters in New York. The first Indo-Chinese War begins in Vietnam.
Winston Churchill coins the phrase, 'the Iron Curtain'.
For the first time black Americans take part in the Democratic Primary elections in the State of Mississippi.
The USA begins a series of atomic tests on Bikini Atoll in the South Pacific.
Andy is popular with his fellow-students, who call him André, no doubt with his approval. When he fails a course in perspective drawing his studies are in danger of coming to a premature end. However, an additional summer course enables him to achieve the necessary pass.

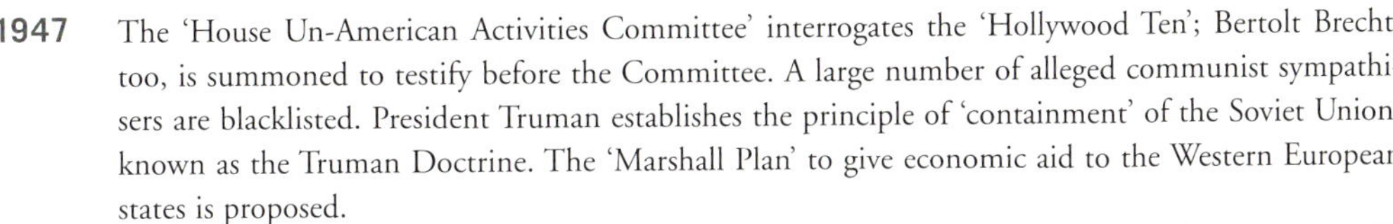

1947 The 'House Un-American Activities Committee' interrogates the 'Hollywood Ten'; Bertolt Brecht, too, is summoned to testify before the Committee. A large number of alleged communist sympathisers are blacklisted. President Truman establishes the principle of 'containment' of the Soviet Union, known as the Truman Doctrine. The 'Marshall Plan' to give economic aid to the Western European states is proposed.
1947 is Andy's 'junior year' at the university. He is awarded the John L. Porter Prize for Progress for some drawings done the previous year while he and his brother were selling fruit from a van.
In the summer he and fellow-students rent a barn which they use as a studio.

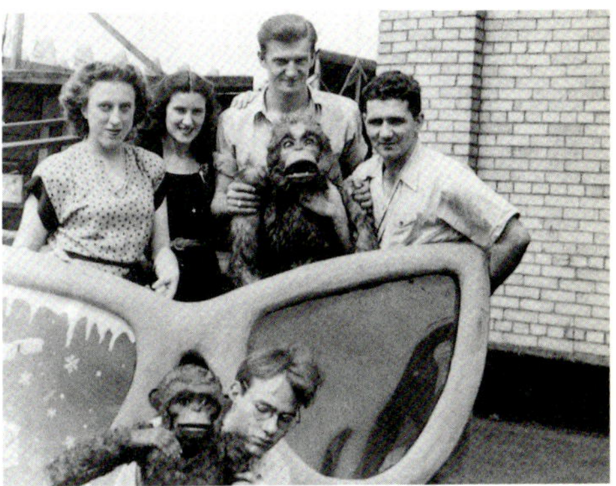

Andy (at the lower edge of the picture) with fellow-workers from the Joseph Horne department store in Pittsburgh, 1947

1948 The term 'Cold War', describing the relations between the powers of East and West, gains currency.
In the autumn Andy begins his 'senior year' at the Carnegie Institute. He works as picture editor for the student magazine *Cano*. In his designs for the magazine he is already using the 'blotted line', a monotype technique with an improvised look, which is to become the trademark in his commercial art.
Truman Capote publishes *Other Voices, Other Rooms*. The Kinsey Report appears.

1949 The North Atlantic Treaty Organization (NATO) is founded.
On 9 August an article appears in *Life* magazine hailing Jackson Pollock as the greatest living artist in America. Arthur Miller publishes *Death of a Salesman*. George Orwell's *1984* appears in Britain.
Andy submits *The Broad Gave Me My Face, But I Can Pick My Own Nose* for the Associated Artists of Pittsburgh annual exhibition. After intense debate the jury rejects the picture. George Grosz, a member of the jury, praises the work, which is finally shown in a second local exhibition and attracts favourable comment.
On 16 June Andy graduates as a Bachelor of Fine Arts.
That same summer he and Philip Pearlstein move to New York. To begin with they share an apartment on St Mark's Place. In September they move into a former factory building on West 21st Street as sub-tenants of the dance therapist Francesca Boas, daughter of the anthropologist Franz Boas.
Andy calls on the art directors of the major glossy magazines to show them examples of his work. The magazine *Glamour* gives him his first commission, which is to design illustrations for the article 'Success Is a Job in New York'. This is followed by many other commissions for, among others, *Vogue, Seventeen* and *Harper's Bazaar*. Alongside this Andy also works as a window dresser and book illustrator. He Americanises his name to 'Andy Warhol'.

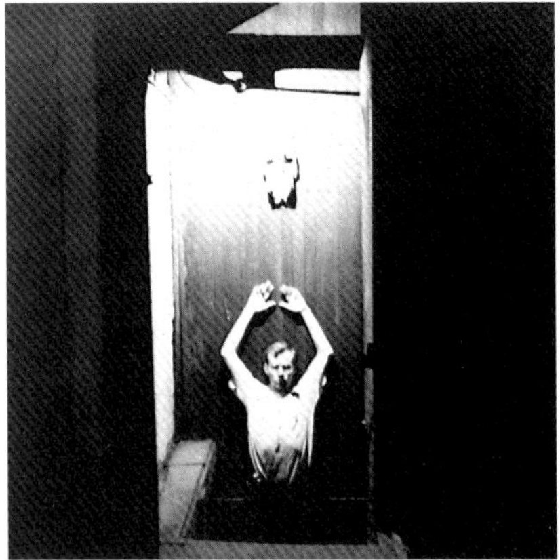

Andy Warhol as a student, c. 1946-9

Warhol develops an infatuation for Truman Capote after seeing his photograph on the dust jacket of *Other Voices, Other Rooms*. He writes letters to Capote and makes frequent telephone calls to him, but is only able to speak to Capote's mother, who asks him to stop.
Only much later a friendship grows up between Andy Warhol and Truman Capote which lasts until Capote's death in 1984.

1950

With the lack of military success in the Korean War, inflation rises steeply. All the same, the general level of affluence in the USA is higher than ever: 11 per cent of all American households already own a television set, and between 1947 and 1970 the real income of Americans rises by almost 80 per cent. Warhol, too, buys his first TV set.

With economic prosperity comes an increase in the rate of urbanisation and the growth of suburbs; the baby boom begins. The favourable economic situation is accompanied by an increasing fear of communist intrigue – Senator Joseph McCarthy claims to be in possession of a list of 205 signed-up members of the Communist Party within the State Department, and uses this to justify the hearings of the 'House Un-American Activities Committee'. Overriding Truman's veto, Congress passes the 'McCarran Act', which provides for the registration of communists and communist organisations. Among many others, the names of Gypsy Rose Lee, Arthur Miller, Pete Seeger and Orson Welles are placed on a blacklist. The term 'McCarthyism' begins to be used. Truman authorises the Atomic Energy Commission to produce the hydrogen bomb. In 1951 the USA carries out the first hydrogen bomb test.
Works by Willem de Kooning, Arshile Gorky and Jackson Pollock are shown in the American Pavilion at the Venice Biennale. The term 'action painting' is coined: Jackson Pollock creates *Lavender Mist*, one of his most important works.
Capote publishes *Breakfast at Tiffany's*, which marks his definitive breakthrough as a major contemporary American author.
Warhol moves into an apartment on West 103rd Street which he shares with dancers, actors and writers. Soon afterwards he is living on East 25th Street and finally on East 75th Street. The coffee house and boutique Serendipity, a haunt of young artists, becomes an important meeting-place.

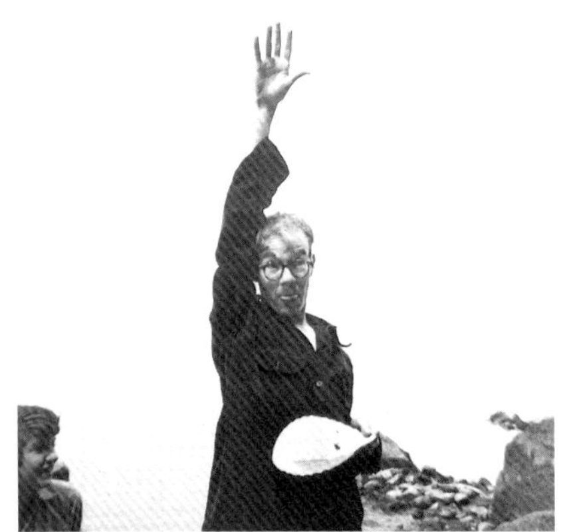

Picnic on 'Memorial Day', 1950

1951–1952

In 1951, Julius and Ethel Rosenberg are convicted of spying for the Soviet Union; they are sentenced to death and consequently executed in 1953.
Colour television is introduced in the USA, radically changing the world of advertising.
In the early 1950s Black Mountain College in North Carolina, founded in 1933, becomes increasingly important. What is taught there has a profound influence on artistic forms of expression in the whole of North America. Following Josef Albers, a Bauhaus artist who lives and teaches there from 1933 onwards, in the 1950s Franz Kline, Ben Shahn, Robert Motherwell and Jack Tworkov teach painting, John Cage teaches music and Merce Cunningham, dance. The *Black Mountain Review* is published under the editorship of Charles Olson, Robert Creeley and Robert Duncan.

The Betty Parsons Gallery in New York puts on the first one-man show of works by Robert Rauschenberg. Roy Lichtenstein's first one-man exhibition is held in the Carlsbach Gallery in New York. J.D. Salinger publishes *The Catcher in the Rye*. *Quo Vadis* is shown in the cinemas. *An American in Paris* wins the Oscar for best film.
Warhol designs newspaper publicity for the radio programme *The Nation's Nightmare*, which is aimed at combating drugs.
Charles Ginzburg discovers a way of magnetically recording images, creating the forerunner of the video recorder.

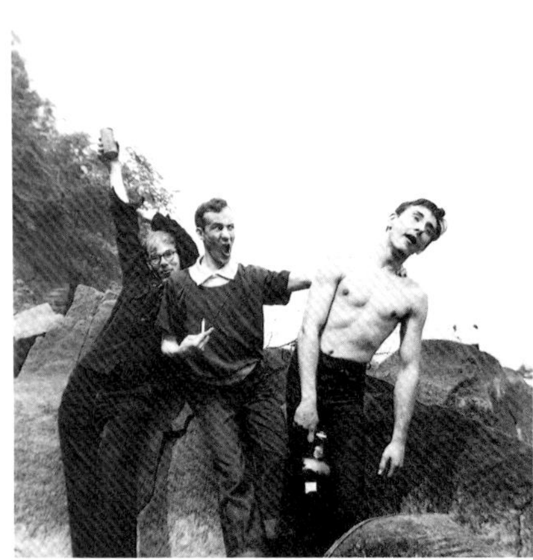

Andy with friends on 'Memorial Day', 1950

In 1952 the McCarthyite witch-hunt is at its height. General Dwight D. Eisenhower wins the presidential election. His Defense Secretary Charles E. Wilson coins the slogan, 'What's good for General Motors is good for America'.
Church membership in America reaches record levels. On 23 April a nuclear bomb test in the Nevada desert is transmitted live on American television.
Warhol is awarded the Art Directors Club Medal for various newspaper advertisements. Together with two other artists he illustrates *Amy Vanderbilt's Complete Book of Etiquette*. His first individual exhibi-

tion takes place from 16 June to 3 July in Alexandre Iolas's Hugo Gallery, New York: *Andy Warhol – Fifteen Drawings Based on the Writings of Truman Capote.*
Julia Warhola follows her son to New York. For the next twenty years they will live together, along with numerous cats. Now Julia Warhola often writes the texts for Andy's graphic works and signs them in her 'childlike' handwriting.

1953 The Korean War ends. After the death of Joseph Stalin there is a thaw in the relations between the USA and the Soviet Union. In Iran the nationalist regime is overthrown, with covert assistance from the CIA, and the rule of the Shah is restored; the nationalisation of the oil monopoly is reversed.
In San Francisco Peter D. Martin and Lawrence Ferlinghetti found City Lights, a publishing firm producing only paperbacks. It becomes the main publisher of the writers of the Beat Generation. Ace Books, which deals mainly in 'dime novels', brings out William Burroughs's *Junkie: Confessions of an Unredeemed Drug Addict* under the pseudonym of William Lee. Samuel Beckett's *Waiting for Godot* appears in an English translation. Tennessee Williams's *Cat on a Hot Tin Roof* is published. Ernest Hemingway receives the Nobel Prize for Literature.
Elvis Presley makes his first record.
Warhol joins the dramatic group 'Theatre 12', under the leadership of Dennis Vaughan. He becomes interested in Bertolt Brecht.
Together with 'Corkie' (Ralph Thomas Ward), Warhol publishes *Love is a Pink Cake, There Was Snow on the Street and Rain in the Sky* and *A Is an Alphabet*, promotional books sent as gifts to potential clients and to the art directors of major magazines.
During this year Warhol and his mother move to 242 Lexington Avenue.

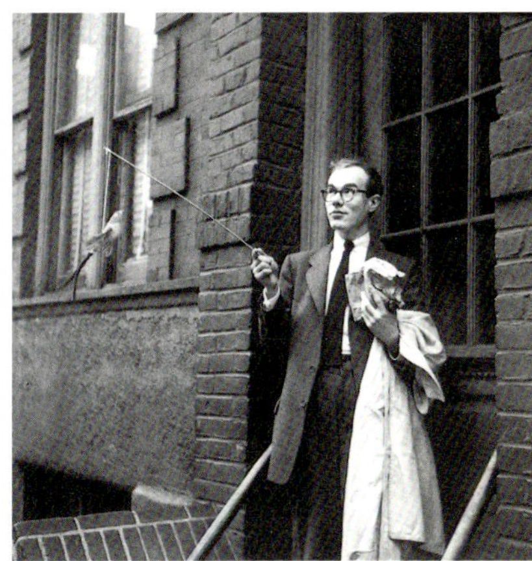

Andy Warhol on Jones Street, 1952

1954 After the defeat and withdrawal of its former colonial master, France, Vietnam is partitioned. The USA takes on the role of the protecting power of non-communist South Vietnam. McCarthy is discredited when he begins to extend his allegations to the army. A landmark judgment in favour of equal rights for black Americans comes in the unanimous decision of the Supreme Court in the case of Brown versus the Board of Education of Topeka, declaring racial segregation in schools to be unconstitutional.
Jasper Johns creates his first *Flag* and Robert Rauschenberg the 'combine-painting' *Charlene*. Ralph Ellison's *Invisible Man* appears. Ernest Hemingway publishes *The Old Man and the Sea*. The cinemas are showing *Singin' in the Rain*.
In 1954 Warhol receives a Certificate of Excellence from the American Institute of Graphic Arts for his commercial art. Together with Charles Lisanby who writes the texts, Warhol produces the book *25 Cats Name* [sic] *Sam and One Blue Pussy* as a promotional gift. He gets together with friends at Serendipity who help hand-colour the illustrations.

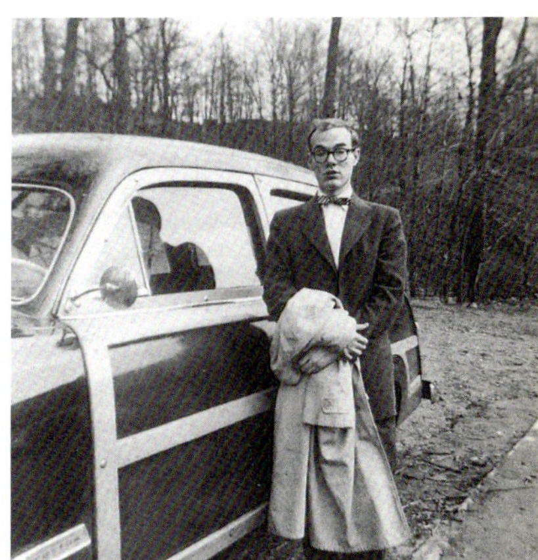

Andy Warhol, c. 1950-3

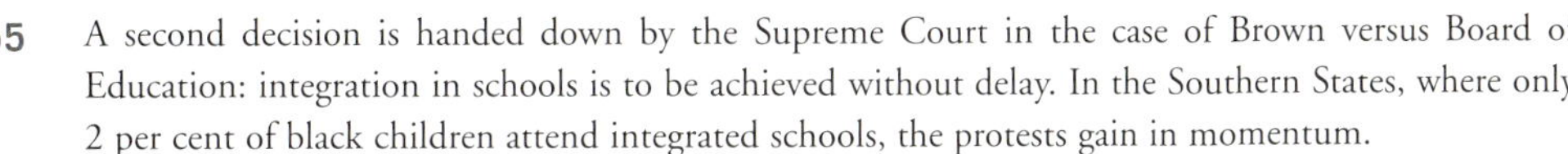

1955 A second decision is handed down by the Supreme Court in the case of Brown versus Board of Education: integration in schools is to be achieved without delay. In the Southern States, where only 2 per cent of black children attend integrated schools, the protests gain in momentum.
Intellectual debate in New York is led by three periodicals: the *Partisan Review*, which first appeared in 1934, plays a central role, alongside *Dissent*, founded in 1954, and *Commentary*, dating from 1945/6. The touring exhibition *The Family of Man*, consisting of photographs by Edward Steichen, selected by The Museum of Modern Art, New York, is seen by nine million people. Jasper Johns paints *Green Target*.
The 'San Francisco Poetry Renaissance' begins with a spectacular reading in the Six Gallery, with Allen Ginsberg, Kenneth Rexroth, Philip Lamantia, Michael McClure, Gary Snyder and Philip Whalen taking part. Ginsberg's reading from his still unpublished manuscript *Howl* is received with enthusiasm by the audience.
The cinemas are showing *Rebel without a Cause* and *The Blackboard Jungle*.
James Dean dies in an auto accident while on his way to a car race.
Warhol publishes *A la Recherche du Shoe Perdu*, with texts by Ralph Pomeroy. His highly-regarded designs advertising the shoe company I. Miller appear each week in the *New York Times*.
Warhol engages Vito Giallo and Nathan Gluck as his assistants.

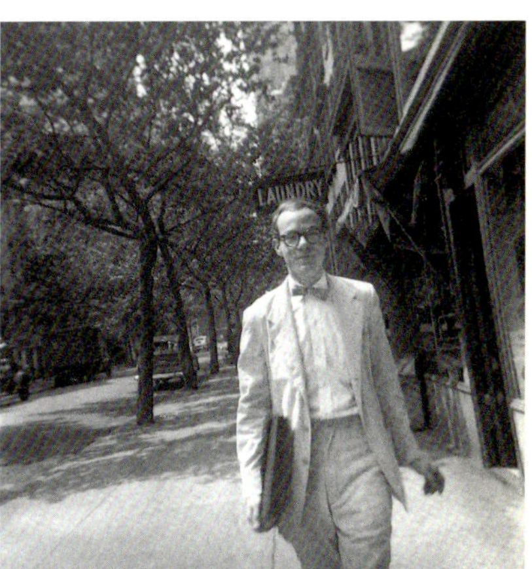

Andy Warhol 'doing the rounds': seeking commissions, New York, 1950

Eisenhower, using the slogan 'I like Ike', is re-elected as President. In Montgomery, Alabama, a bus boycott arising from an incident in which a black dressmaker refuses to give up her seat to a white man ends in success after 381 days. **1956**

In Britain a new art movement is beginning: it is Richard Hamilton's collage, *Just What Is It That Makes Today's Homes So Different, So Appealing?* that is to give Pop art its name. Under the title 'This Is Tomorrow', the Whitechapel Art Gallery in London puts on an exhibition of young British art. In New York the Leo Castelli Gallery opens. Saul Bellow publishes *Seize the Day*. Jackson Pollock is killed in a car crash.

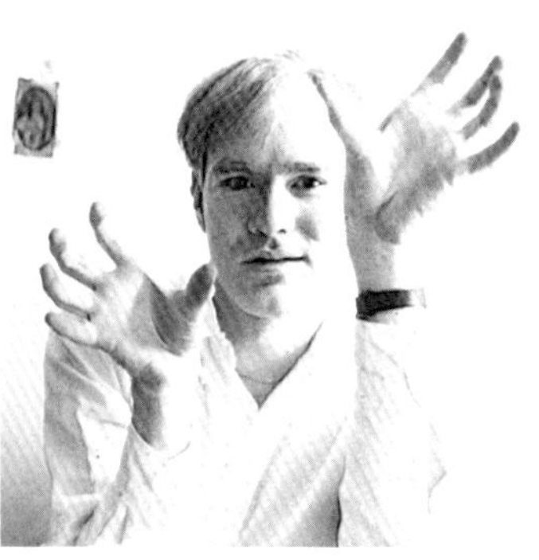

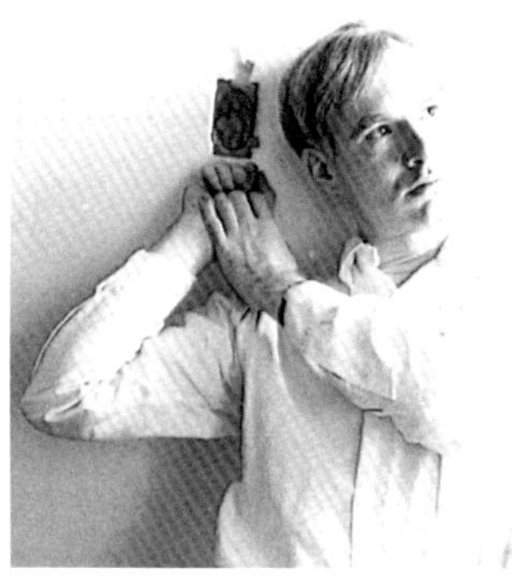

Andy Warhol, photographed by Duane Michals, 1958

Warhol receives the Art Directors Club's Award for Distinctive Merit for his shoe advertisements for I. Miller. From 14 February to 3 March the Bodley Gallery in New York shows *Drawings for a Boy-Book by Andy Warhol*, and in December *Andy Warhol: The Golden Slipper Show or Shoes Shoe in America. In the Bottom of My Garden* is published.

On 16 June Warhol and his friend Charles Lisanby set off on a world tour which will include Honolulu, Tokyo, Hong Kong, Manila, Bali, Singapore, Bangkok, Calcutta, Katmandu, New Delhi, Agra, Cairo, Luxor, Florence, Amsterdam and Rome. On 12 August they arrive back in New York, where a disappointed Warhol abruptly leaves Lisanby at the airport and makes his way home alone.

America is alarmed when the launching of Sputnik I and II appears to demonstrate Soviet superiority in space. In Little Rock, Arkansas, federal troops are deployed to ensure the access of black children to the High School. **1957**

In the autumn Jack Kerouac's *On the Road* appears. The book is a key work of the Beat Generation and also a huge commercial success. Bernard Malamud's *The Assistant* is published.

Warhol is by this time one of the most highly-regarded and best-paid commercial artists in the USA. He establishes 'Andy Warhol Enterprises, Inc.'. In *A Gold Book* he publishes 'blotted-line' drawings on gold paper. From 2 to 25 December the Bodley Gallery mounts *A Show of Golden Pictures by Andy Warhol. Life* magazine publishes a depreciatively critical report on the exhibition.

In the same year Warhol, unhappy with his appearance, undergoes corrective surgery on his nose but is dissatisfied with the result.

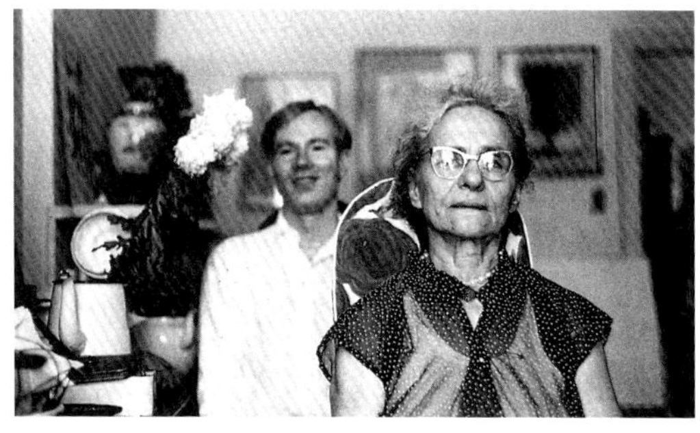

Andy Warhol with his mother Julia Warhola, photographed by Duane Michals, 1958

The USA launches the first American space satellite, Explorer I. The John Birch Society is founded. **1958**

Rauschenberg designs the sets and costumes for Cunningham's dance performance *Summerspace*. The term 'Pop art' appears for the first time in an essay by Lawrence Alloway. In January Johns's first one-man exhibition opens at the Leo Castelli Gallery, New York. In March Rauschenberg exhibits 'combine-paintings' in the same gallery. Warhol gradually realizes that he has no answer to this new direction in art, and begins to feel that working exclusively as a commercial artist is not enough.

The famous 'kitchen debate' between Nixon and Khrushchev is relayed live from a Moscow trade fair which Nixon is visiting. Martin Luther King publishes his programmatic book *Stride Toward Freedom*. In Manhattan the Solomon R. Guggenheim Museum, designed by Frank Lloyd Wright, is opened. Lawrence Ferlinghetti publishes his collection of poems, *A Coney Island of the Mind*. The new French films of the 'Nouvelle Vague' achieve international recognition and influence. *Cat on a Hot Tin Roof* and *Touch of Evil* are shown in American cinemas. **1959**

Allan Kaprow's performance *18 Happenings in 6 Parts*, put on at the Reuben Gallery in New York in October 1959, is the first public 'Happening' and is followed by many others in New York, Paris, Cologne and Stockholm. Warhol publishes a fanciful cookery book with Suzie Frankfurt, *Wild Raspberries*, which is his last promotional book. In December the drawings for this publication are exhibited by the Bodley Gallery.

1960 John F. Kennedy wins the election by the narrowest of margins, thereby becoming the youngest ever President of the United States.
In Greensboro, North Carolina, a sit-in movement develops when black students insist on being served in a cafeteria reserved for whites.
Timothy Leary and Allen Ginsberg talk about the 'psychedelic revolution'. Harper Lee's *To Kill a Mockingbird* and John Updike's *Rabbit, Run* are published. Charles Olson's *The Maximus Poems* appear. Alfred Hitchcock's *Psycho* has its cinema premiere.
Through Tina Fredericks, Warhol meets Emile de Antonio who is also a friend of Johns and Rauschenberg. Warhol produces his first hand-painted pictures based on comic-strip figures – Batman, Dick Tracy, Popeye and Superman. The most banal, everyday motifs from newspaper advertisements also become motifs for his pictures.
Warhol meets Billy Linich, later known as Billy Name, who is to be part of Warhol's circle for many years. (In 1996 Billy Name publishes photographs taken in the 'Factory': *Andy Warhol's Factory Photos.*)
Warhol purchases 1342 Lexington Avenue and he and his mother move in there.

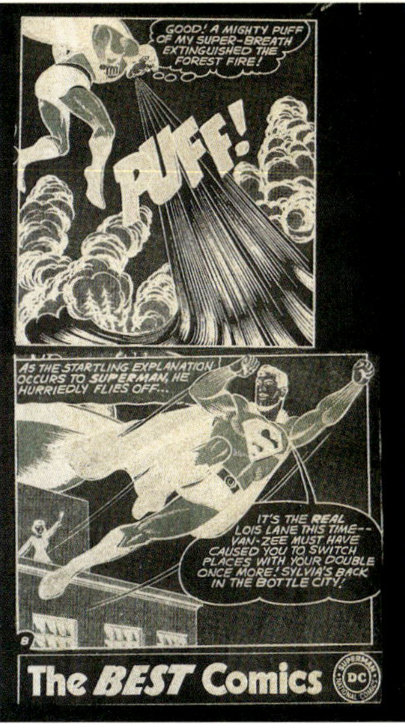

Andy Warhol's source image for *Superman*, 1960

1961 Tension between the superpowers is greater than ever. The Berlin Wall is built. A military force of Cuban exiles, trained by the CIA, lands in the Bay of Pigs in an attempt to overthrow Fidel Castro. The 'military-administrative complex' is the largest single provider of contracts to industry in the USA. In the Southern States black and white civil rights activists organize the 'freedom riders' campaign.
James Baldwin's *Nobody Knows My Name* is published. Joseph Heller's *Catch-22* and Ginsberg's *Kaddish and Other Poems* appear. *West Side Story* wins the Oscar for best feature film. On the Lower East Side in New York, Claes Oldenburg opens *Store*, an art exhibition conceived in the form of a supermarket.
At the Leo Castelli Gallery Warhol sees works by Roy Lichtenstein which, like his own recent pictures, use motifs from comic strips. Warhol invites Ivan Karp, Castelli's assistant, to his house to show him his own works. Castelli declines to represent Warhol as he fears that Warhol's works are too similar to those of Lichtenstein, whom he already represents. Warhol takes the logical step of abandoning the use of comic strips as sources for his pictures. In the same year Warhol meets Henry Geldzahler, curator of contemporary art at the Metropolitan Museum of Art. Irving Blum, who owns the Ferus Gallery in Los Angeles, visits Warhol's studio.
In April Warhol displays some early works – *Advertisement, Little King, Before and After, Superman* and *Saturday's Popeye* – in the window of the Bonwit Teller department store. Warhol asks friends what he should paint, and Muriel Latow tells him "to paint pictures of money … either that or … something you see every day that everyone would recognize. Something like a can of soup." Warhol starts on the series of thirty-two *Campbell's Soup Cans*. He is commissioned to produce illustrations for *Amy Vanderbilt's Complete Cookbook*, but pays Ted Carey to do them.
Warhol buys Johns' drawing *Light Bulb*.

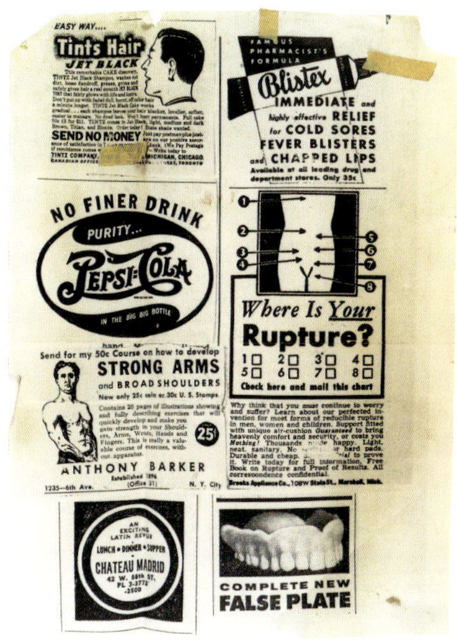

Seven newspaper advertisements, Warhol's sources for *Where Is Your Rupture?* and other pictures, 1960

1962 In September American reconnaissance planes discover Soviet nuclear missiles on Cuba: the Cuban missile crisis begins. On 22 October Kennedy imposes a naval blockade. A serious international situation has arisen, eased off only after the withdrawal of the soviet missiles. The USA builds up its presence in Vietnam, sending out 16,500 'military advisers'.
Edward Albee's play *Who's Afraid of Virginia Woolf?* is premiered on Broadway. Ken Kesey publishes *One Flew Over the Cuckoo's Nest*. John Steinbeck is awarded the Nobel Prize for Literature. The Oscar for best feature film goes to *Lawrence of Arabia*.
During the summer, and at about the same time as Rauschenberg, Warhol discovers the photo-silkscreen technique as a method of creating pictures. The first work that Warhol produces using this technique is *Baseball*, showing the famous baseball player Roger Maris. Warhol experiments with various kinds of stamps and stencils. Geldzahler advises Warhol to take less positive subjects for his pictures. Warhol accordingly paints *129 Die in Jet*, based on the front-page picture from the *New York Mirror* of 4 June 1962. This is followed by further *Disasters*, as well as matter-of-fact representations of Coca-Cola bottles. He also produces the five hand-painted *Do It Yourself* pictures, an ironical comment on neo-Dadaist programmes, and portraits of Elvis Presley and Marlon Brando.
On 4 August the exhibition of the thirty-two *Campbell's Soup Cans* opens at the Ferus Gallery, Los Angeles. After the exhibition, Irving Blum, owner of the Ferus Gallery, decides with Warhol's consent to keep the series together.

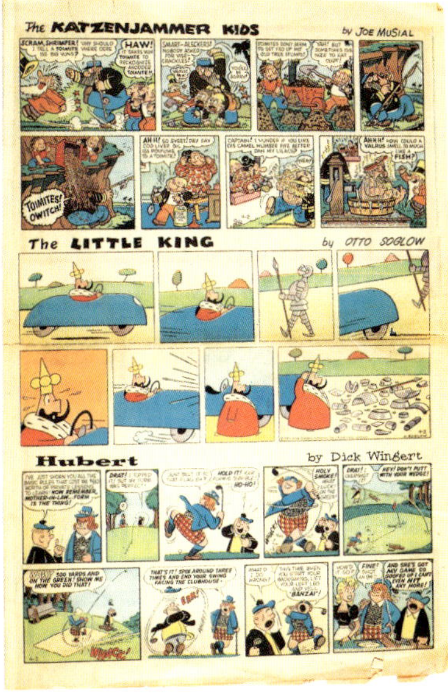

Comic-strip source for *Little King*, 1961

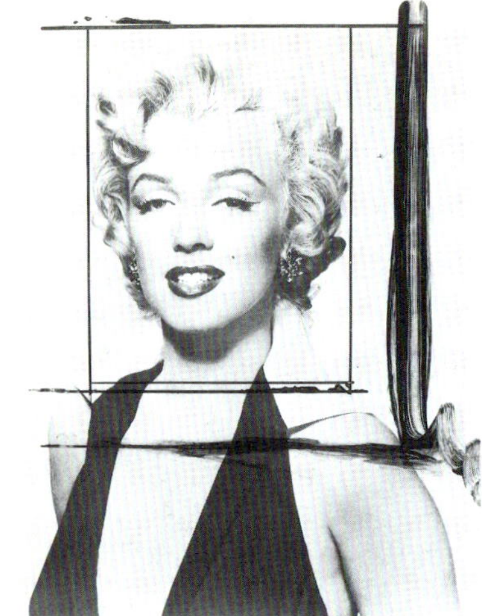

Marilyn Monroe, still from the film *Niagara*, 1953; Andy Warhol's source image for all the Marilyn portraits

Following the suicide of Marilyn Monroe on 5 August, Warhol produces a number of Marilyn portraits. They are based on a still from the film *Niagara*, 1953. Some weeks later he makes the silkscreen print *Suicide*.

On 31 October the group exhibition *The New Realists* opens at the Sidney Janis Gallery in New York. This show marks the appearance on the scene of a new generation of American artists. Warhol is included in this exhibition.

From 6 to 24 November Eleanor Ward's Stable Gallery in New York shows a selection of works by Warhol (Marilyn and Elvis portraits, *Close Cover Before Striking, Coca-Cola*, et al.). Philip Johnson buys a *Gold Marilyn* from this exhibition for The Museum of Modern Art.

Warhol finally gives up his commercial art, which has hitherto financed his artistic work.

1963

More than 250,000 black and white Americans demonstrate in Washington for equal rights for all citizens. At the centre of the movement is Martin Luther King, who declares in a historic speech, 'I have a dream'. The publication of Betty Friedan's *The Feminine Mystique* in this year is of great significance for the emerging feminist movement.

In January the *Mona Lisa* exhibition opens in the West Sculpture Hall of the National Gallery in Washington. The opening is a state ceremony, with speeches by André Malraux and John F. Kennedy. From February onwards the *Mona Lisa* is on show in the Metropolitan Museum in New York; altogether it is viewed by more than 1.7 million people.

Andy Warhol starts work on his remarkable versions of *Mona Lisa*, the most significant of which is *Thirty Are Better than One*.

Warhol works on his *Electric Chair* and *Race Riot* pictures. The *Race Riot* silkscreens are based on a photograph from the 17 May issue of *Life* magazine, showing a clash between civil rights demonstrators and police in Birmingham, Alabama.

He begins work on the *Tunafish Disaster* pictures after happening to see a report in the magazine *Newsweek* about a fatal food poisoning incident.

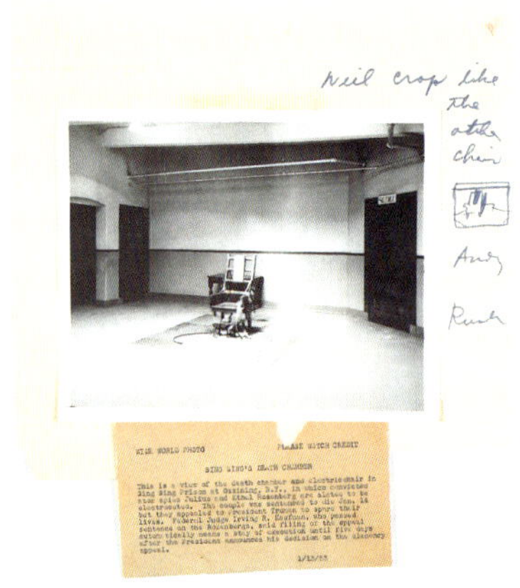

Source image for the *Electric Chair* pictures, 1964, 1967

On 22 November John F. Kennedy is assassinated during an electioneering visit to Dallas, Texas. Lee Harvey Oswald, the presumed murderer, is shot while being transferred from one prison to another. ABC, CBS and NBC broadcast live reports from just after the murder until Kennedy's funeral. Still on board the Air Force One, Lyndon B. Johnson is sworn in as President.

Warhol starts work on a number of portraits of Jacqueline Kennedy. For *The Week That Was*, he uses published photographs showing the grieving Jackie.

Warhol visits the Judson Memorial Church in Greenwich Village, where Rauschenberg and Johns are working with others including Cunningham. With Steve Paxton, Trisha Brown puts on *Lightfall*, a 'structured improvised' dance created in the avant-garde ambience of the Judson Memorial Church. Rauschenberg choreographs the dance performance *Pelican*.

Warhol buys a 16 mm camera and makes his first film, *Sleep*. This is followed by *Andy Warhol Films Jack Smith Filming 'Normal Love', Blow Job, Dance Movie, Eat, Haircut, Kiss, Salome and Delilah* and *Tarzan and Jane Regained ... Sort of.* These films are characterised by the use of a fixed camera and a lack of any editing or montage.

Warhol meets Jonas Mekas, director of the 'Filmmakers' Co-operative', which will give public screenings of Warhol's films. For the first time, Warhol uses photographs taken in a photograph booth for the portrait *Ethel Scull Thirty-Six Times*.

In November 1963 *ARTnews* publishes an interview between Gene R. Swenson and Warhol. Warhol mentions that he is working on a series which he is calling *Death in America*. 'I realized that everything I was doing must have been Death.' But he also says: '...the reason I'm painting this way is that I want to be a machine, and I feel that whatever I do and do machine-like is what I want to do.'

In June Warhol rents a studio with no telephone line, the first 'Factory', in a former fire station on East 87th Street.

The young writer Gerard Malanga, Warhol's assistant until 1970, Brigid Polk (Brigid Berlin), Ondine and 'Baby' Jane Holzer appear in his films. Together with Malanga, Warhol works on *Disaster* pictures (*Car Crash, Race Riot*) produced by the photo-silkscreen method. On 30 September Warhol travels to Los Angeles for the opening of his exhibition of Elvis portraits in the Ferus Gallery. On the following evening he meets Marcel Duchamp in Pasadena.

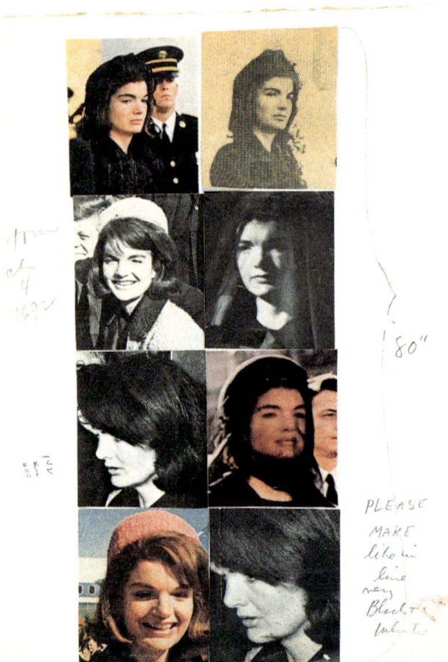

Press photographs used by Andy Warhol for *The Week That Was*, 1963, and other pictures

CBS television interv with Andy Warhol a Ivan Karp, New Yo 1964

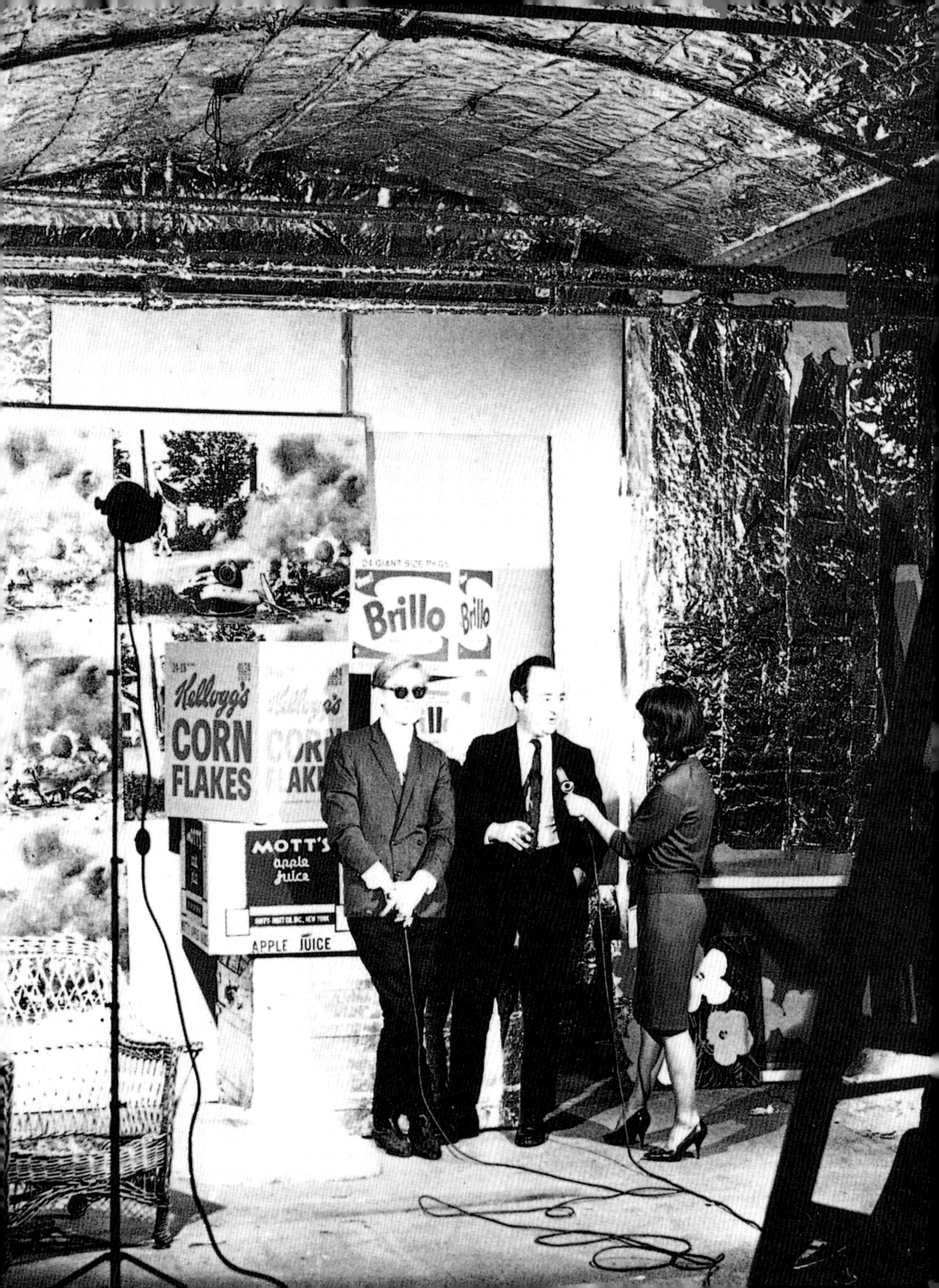
24 GIANT SIZE PKGS
Brillo
Brillo
Kellogg's
CORN
FLAKES
MOTT'S
apple
juice
APPLE JUICE

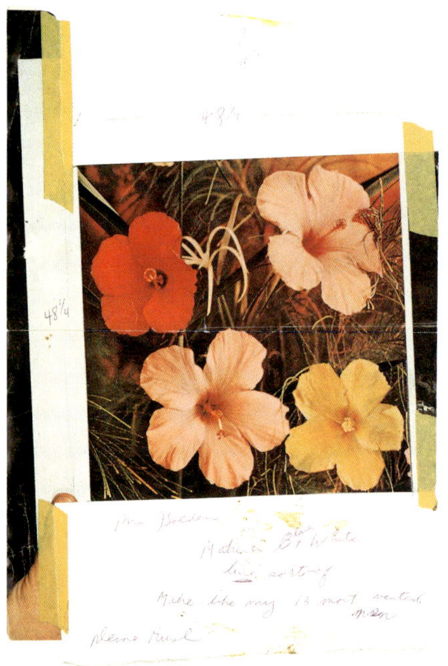

Patricia Caulfield's photograph used by Andy Warhol as his source for the *Flowers* silkscreens, 1964/7

In November the Factory moves to the loft of a building on East 47th Street. Billy Name covers the walls in aluminium foil and silver paint. In 1963 Sylvia Plath publishes *The Bell Jar*.
William Carlos Williams's *Pictures from Brueghel* appear. *The Birds* reaches the cinema screens.

1964

The Civil Rights legislation initiated by John F. Kennedy before his assassination represents an important legal breakthrough for black Americans. Lyndon B. Johnson is re-elected as President. On 10 August, after a deliberately engineered clash between US and North Vietnamese warships in the Gulf of Tonkin, Congress authorizes Johnson to engage in hostilities against Vietnam. The Vietnam War begins. At the Venice Biennale Rauschenberg, Johns and Oldenburg exhibit in the American Pavilion. Rauschenberg wins the Biennale Prize. The Jewish Museum in New York mounts a Johns retrospective. Stanley Kubrick's *Dr. Strangelove* is released. The Beatles' film *A Hard Day's Night (Yeah! Yeah! Yeah!)* has its first public screening. *Dutchman* by Amiri Baraka (the writer LeRoi Jones) receives its first performance. Hubert Selby publishes *Last Exit to Brooklyn*. Frank O'Hara's *Lunch Poems* appear. Herbert Marcuse's theoretical work *One-Dimensional Man* is published.
Warhol is commissioned by Philip Johnson to produce a mural for the façade of the New York State Pavilion at the New York World's Fair. He decides to make a work consisting of portraits of the *Thirteen Most Wanted Men*. The installation of the work, just a few days before the opening of the World's Fair, provokes controversy: it is deemed unacceptable for political reasons. In the end the portraits are sprayed over with silver paint.
In July the film *Empire* is shot from an office facing the Empire State Building. More films follow: *Batman, Dracula, Couch, Fifty Fantastics and Fifty Personalities, Harlot, Henry Geldzahler, Mario Banana, Shoulder, Soap Opera, Taylor Mead's Ass, The Thirteen Most Beautiful Girls* and *The Thirteen Most Beautiful Boys*.
Warhol receives the Independent Film Award from *Film Culture* magazine. In the Factory the first 'screen tests' are filmed – short films made with amateur actors.

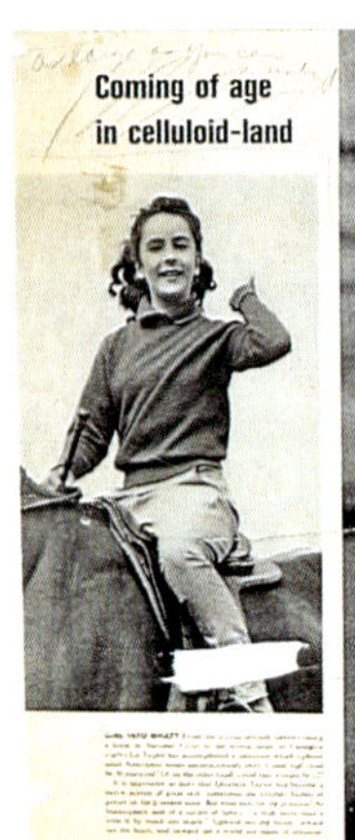

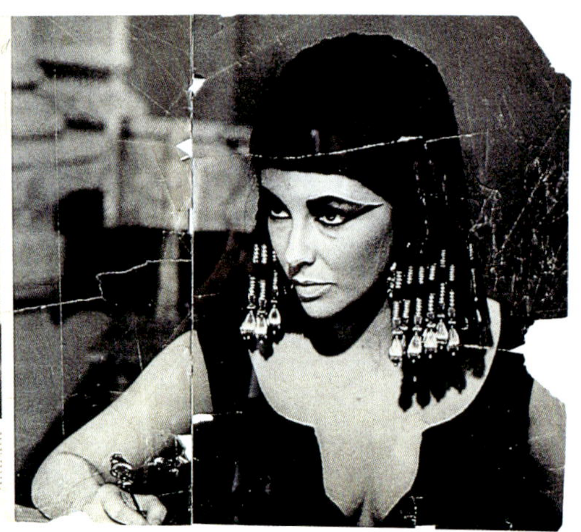

Source image for Andy Warhol's *National Velvet* and *Liz as Cleopatra*, from *Life* magazine, c. 1963

On 13 January the Galerie Ileana Sonnabend in Paris opens its exhibition of Warhol's *Disaster* pictures, which make a profound impression on the European critics. On 21 April the exhibition of *Brillo Boxes, Campbell's Soup Cans* and *Heinz Boxes* opens at the Stable Gallery in New York. The exhibition, together with the opening party in the Factory, enjoys a *succès de scandale*. The *Boxes*, based on an original by the Expressionist painter and commercial artist James Harey, prove almost impossible to sell. Warhol transfers to the Leo Castelli Gallery. In April he is advised by Geldzahler to put more positive life into his pictures now, and Warhol creates the first *Flowers* silkscreens, based on a picture of hibiscus blooms taken by the photographer Patricia Caulfield. Caulfield sues Warhol that same year, but the case is settled out of court. The *Flowers* are exhibited from 21 November to 17 December at the Leo Castelli Gallery, and are all sold.
Warhol acquires a tape recorder which he carries around with him, recording innumerable interviews and conversations.
The Factory is increasingly a rendezvous for young artists, dancers, drop-outs and admirers of Warhol. The 'amphetamine rapture group' – Orion de Winter, Diane di Prima and Dorothy Podber – are regular visitors.
Podber brings a gun to the Factory and fires a shot through a stack of four *Marilyn* portraits, after which Warhol calls these pictures *Shot Marilyns*.

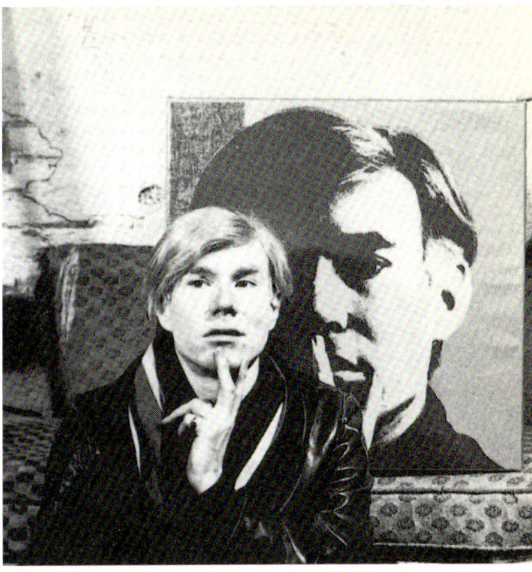

Andy with a *Self-Portrait*, 1967

1965 Malcolm X is murdered in Harlem; his autobiography urging a change in black Americans' self-perception appears in the same year. The first teach-in against the war in Vietnam is held at the University of Michigan. The 'Medicare' legislation guaranteeing the availability of medical care comes into force. Racial disturbances erupt in Watts, Los Angeles. In April the USA launches the first commercial communication satellite.

Warhol makes more films, including *Beauty # 2, Kitchen, My Hustler, Outer and Inner Space, Poor Little Rich Girl, Restaurant, Screen Test # 1, Space, Suicide, Vinyl.* He bases his silkscreens *Sleep* and *Kiss*, executed on Plexiglas, on film stills.

He produces more coloured silkscreens on canvas of his *Campbell's Soup Cans* and *Electric Chair.* Warhol's circle includes Ingrid Superstar, Ultra Violet (Isabelle Collin-Dufresne) and Edie Sedgwick. Warhol is introduced to Paul Morrissey, who will collaborate on all his films in future years. The members of the rock band Velvet Underground, Lou Reed, John Cale, Maureen Tucker and Sterling Morrison, frequent the Factory and appear in Warhol's films.

The second *Flowers* series is exhibited at the Paris Galerie Ileana Sonnabend in May. At the moment when he is being feted in Europe as the supreme exponent of Pop art, Warhol announces in Paris his intention to 'retire' from painting and concentrate exclusively on filmmaking.

A Warhol retrospective opens on 8 October at the Institute of Contemporary Art of the University of Pennsylvania, Philadelphia. Warhol is present, together with Sedgwick. Before the opening, at which many thousands of visitors are expected, Warhol's paintings are removed from the gallery walls for security reasons. Warhol exhibits in September at the Jerrold Morris International Gallery, Toronto, and at the Galleria Gian Enzo Sperone in Turin.

Lester Persky gives 'The Fifty Most Beautiful People' party at the Factory. The guests include William Burroughs, Montgomery Clift, Judy Garland, Allen Ginsberg, Rudolf Nureyev and Tennessee Williams.

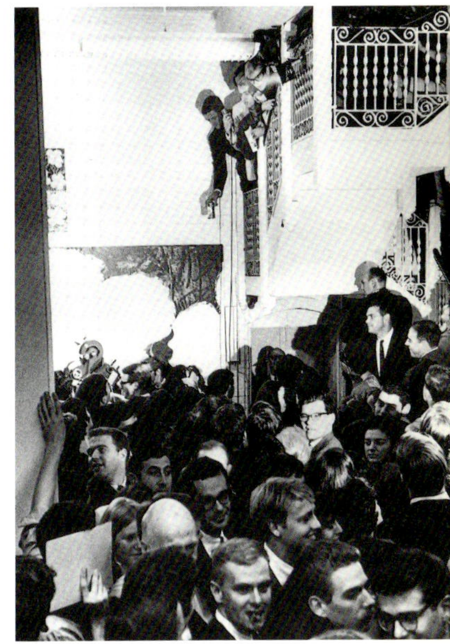

Opening of the Warhol exhibition at the ICA, Philadelphia, October 1965

1966 Capote's *In Cold Blood*, Thomas Pynchon's *The Crying of Lot 49* and Susan Sontag's *Against Interpretation* are published. *Blow Up* is on general release.

Warhol produces multi-media presentations – called 'The Erupting Plastic Inevitable', later changed to 'The Exploding Plastic Inevitable' – with the Velvet Underground band, which has now been joined by the singer Nico (Christa Päffgen). In the spring Warhol accompanies the band to performances at Rutgers University, New Jersey, in New Brunswick and at the University of Michigan. At the Leo Castelli Gallery Warhol exhibits his *Silver Clouds* – silver helium-filled pillows – while another room in the gallery is papered with his *Cow Wallpaper.*

Works by Warhol are exhibited in March and April at the Galleria Gian Enzo Sperone, Turin, and in May at the Contemporary Arts Center, Cincinnati, and the Ferus Gallery, Los Angeles. His exhibition at the Institute of Contemporary Art in Boston opens on 1 October with a concert by the Velvet Underground. In November Warhol accompanies the band to a performance at Detroit State Fairground Coliseum.

International Velvet (Susan Bottomly) and Eric Emerson join Warhol's entourage. Warhol makes the films *Bufferin (Gerard Malanga Reads Poetry), Eating Too Fast, **** (Four Stars)* and *The Velvet Underground and Nico.* His film *The Chelsea Girls*, intended to be projected on to two screens simultaneously, gains widespread recognition.

Morrissey increasingly takes over the direction of the films, with Warhol acting as producer.

Together with David Whitney, Warhol sets up 'Factory Additions' to handle the production and distribution of his prints.

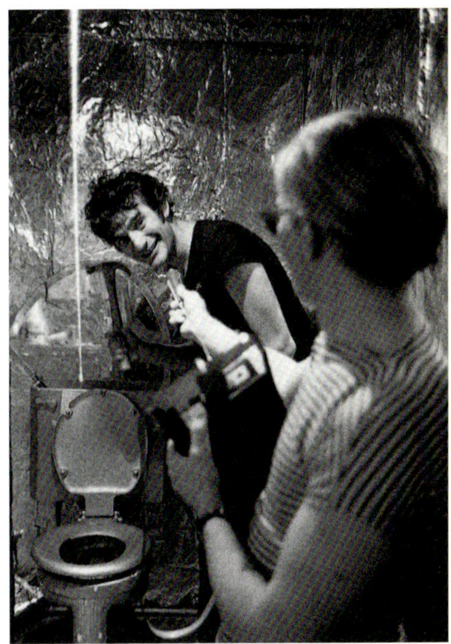

Warhol making taps recordings with Ondine for *A : A Novel*, Factory, c. 1967

1967 In Newark, New Jersey, and Detroit there are race riots and demonstrations, in the course of which people are killed. Tens of thousands take part in the peace march on Washington in the summer.

Stokely Carmichael's seminal work *Black Power!* and Marshall McLuhan's *The Medium Is the Message* are published. *Bonnie and Clyde* is released. The rock musical *Hair* has its New York premiere on 29 April.

Warhol creates a series of large-format *Electric Chair* pictures. He produces the Velvet Underground's first album. When the band performs a benefit concert on behalf of the Merce Cunningham Dance Company at Philip Johnson's Glass House in New Canaan, Warhol meets Frederick Hughes, who later becomes his manager.

Together with Morrissey, Malanga and others, Warhol travels to the Cannes Film Festival with the intention of showing *The Chelsea Girls*, but the film is not accepted by the organisers. In April, however, it receives its first screenings in Los Angeles and San Francisco, with Warhol present. In the same year he films *Bike Boy, I, a Man, Lonesome Cowboys, The Love of Ondine* and *Nude Restaurant*.
In October Warhol accepts the invitation of a number of colleges to undertake a lecture tour. After making several appearances, he engages the dancer and actor Allen Midgette to impersonate him; the impersonation is not immediately noticed.
At the Galerie Rudolf Zwirner in Cologne *Cows* and *Silver Clouds* are exhibited in January and February, and the series *Most Wanted Men* in October. The latter is also shown at the Galerie Ileana Sonnabend in Paris and the Neuendorf Galerie in Hamburg.
Andy Warhol's Index (Book) is published by Random House, and his *Screen Tests: A Diary*, produced in collaboration with Malanga, by Kulchur Press. Warhol creates *Marilyn*, a portfolio of ten silkscreens. He designs the poster for the New York Film Festival at the Lincoln Center. Important works of American art, among them outstanding works by Warhol, are brought together in the Ströher collection in Darmstadt and the Ludwig collection in Cologne.

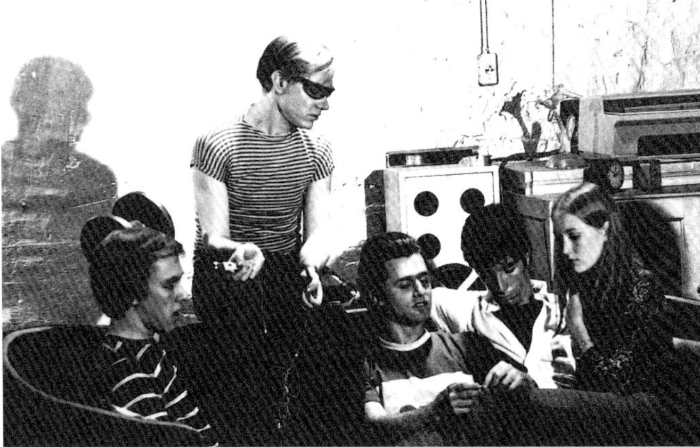

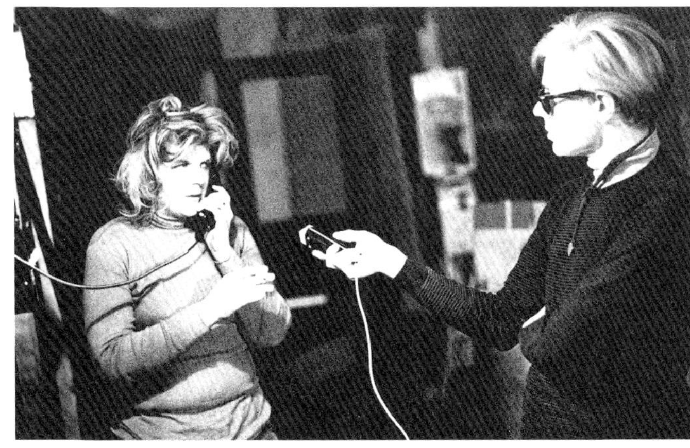

left: **Chuck Wein, Andy Warhol, Gerard Malanga, et al. at the Factory, 1965**
right: **Andy Warhol records Brigid Polk making a telephone call, 1967**

1968

US soldiers carry out the My Lai massacre of civilians in Vietnam. Martin Luther King is assassinated on 4 April. Robert Kennedy is shot on 5 June while on the election campaign trail in Los Angeles, and dies a day later.
Richard Nixon, the candidate of the 'silent majority', is elected President.
Merce Cunningham takes over the choreography of *Walk Around Time*, with a stage set inspired by Duchamp. Tom Wolfe publishes *The Electric Kool-Aid Acid Test. Rosemary's Baby, 2001: A Space Odyssey* and *Night of the Living Dead* reach the cinema screens.
In February the Factory moves to 33 Union Square West. Warhol meets Jed Johnson.
From 10 February to 17 March Stockholm's Moderna Museet mounts the first European retrospective of Warhol's work. The exhibition is then shown at the Stedelijk Museum, Amsterdam, the Kunsthalle, Berne, and the Kunstnernes Hus, Oslo. In March the Rowan Gallery in London exhibits the *Most Wanted Men* series and the *Marilyn* portraits.
Warhol takes part in the *documenta 4* in Kassel.
Following Soviet intervention he is awarded first prize in the Warsaw Poster Biennale – he is evidently judged to be anti-American.
Grove Press publish his *A: A Novel*. He makes the films *Blue Movie (Fuck)* and *Flesh*. The *Campbell's Soup* portfolio is issued by 'Factory Additions'.
In May Warhol embarks on another lecture tour of American colleges, accompanied by Viva and Paul Morrissey.
He designs more *Silver Clouds* for the set of Cunningham's dance *RainForest*.
On 3 June Valerie Solanas, who had appeared in one of Warhol's films and was also the founder of S.C.U.M. (Society for Cutting Up Men), comes into the Factory and fires a gun at Warhol and the art critic Mario Amaya. Warhol is seriously wounded. The attack is witnessed by Hughes, Jed Johnson and Morrissey. Warhol's life is saved by surgery lasting several hours, but he remains hospitalized for eight weeks and will never fully recover from his injuries. Solanas gives herself up to the police on the day of the attack.

Opposite: **Gerard Malanga, Andy Warhol and Buddy Wirtschafter during the filming of *Girls in Prison*, 1965**

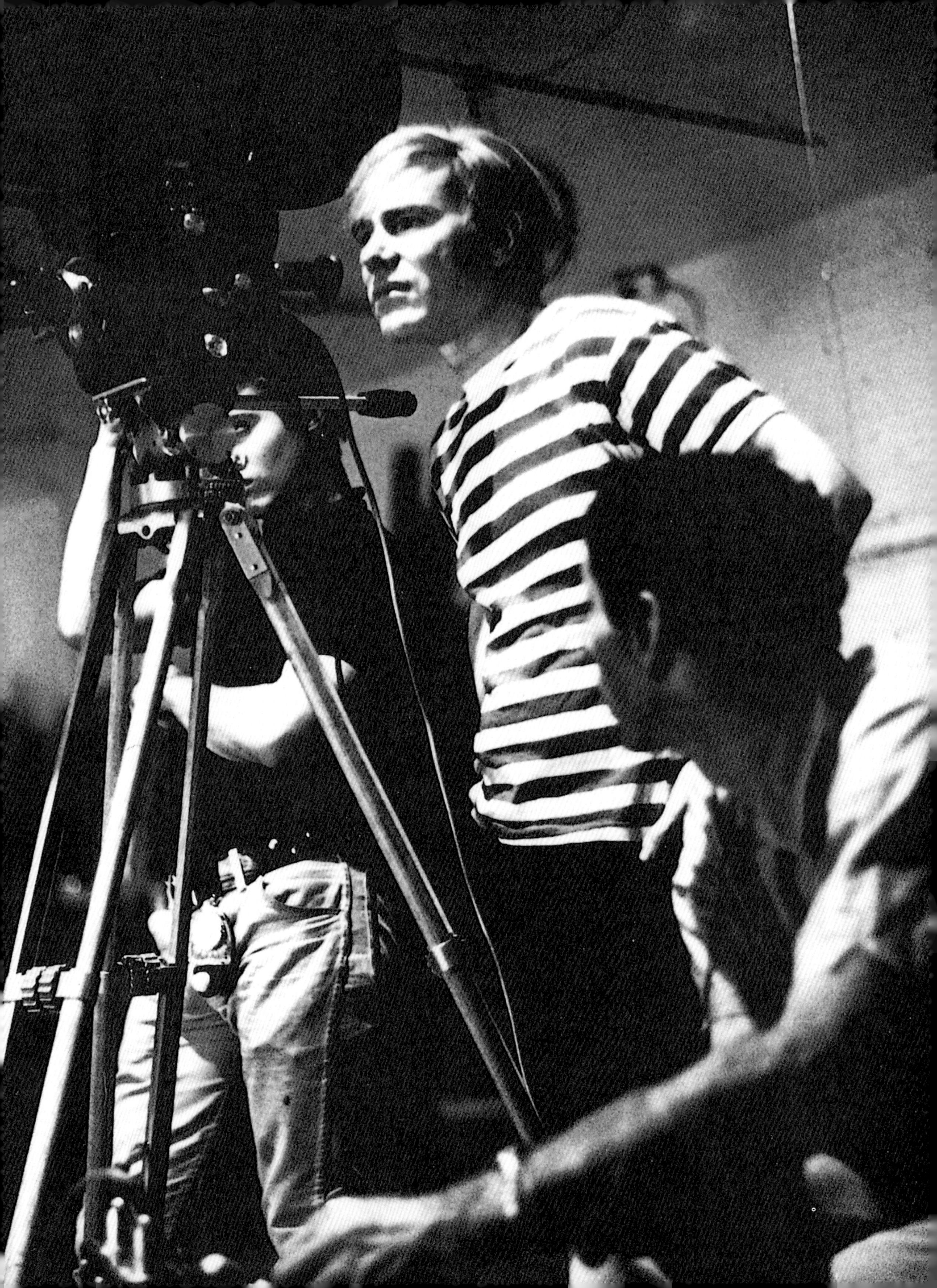

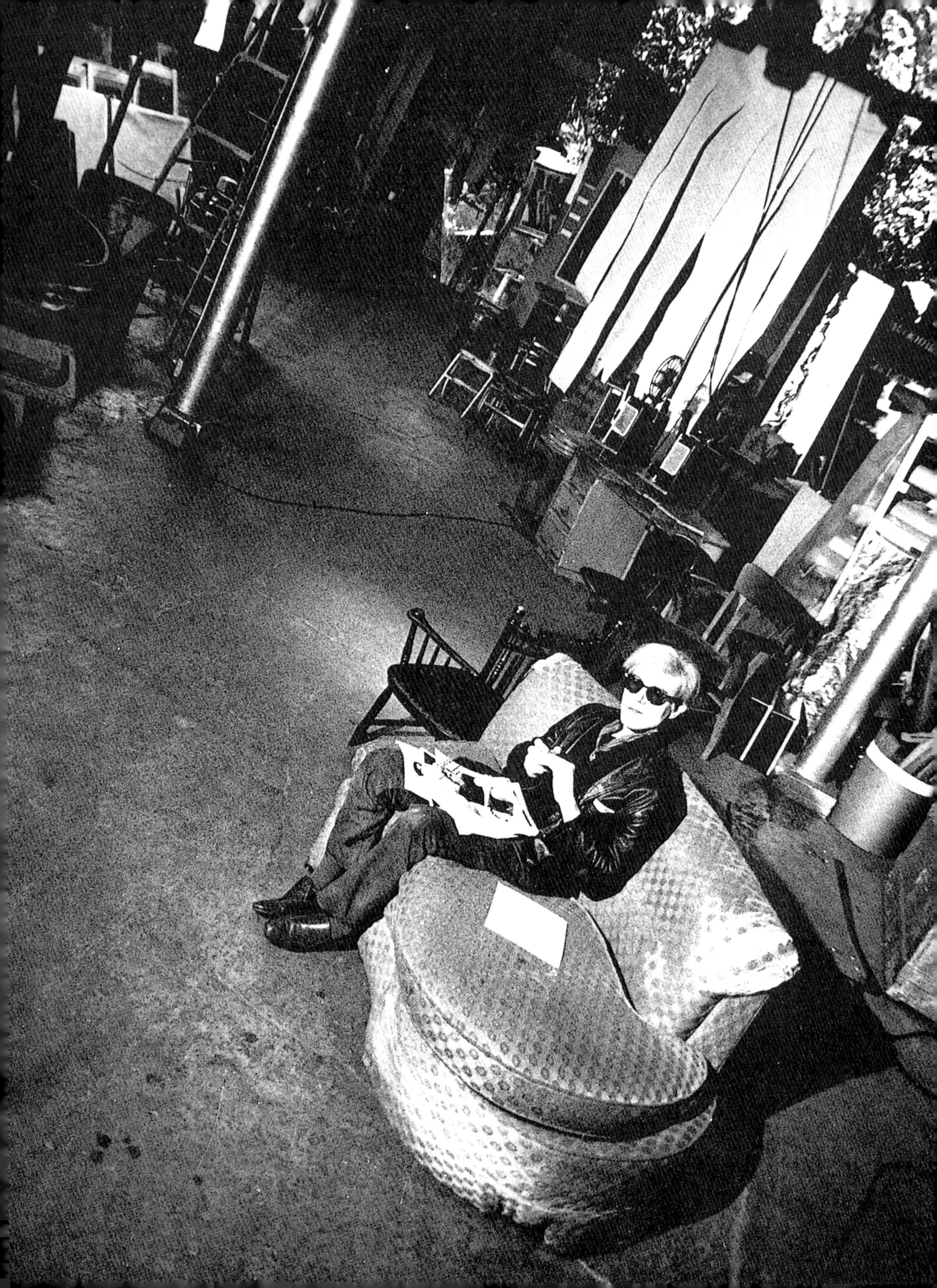

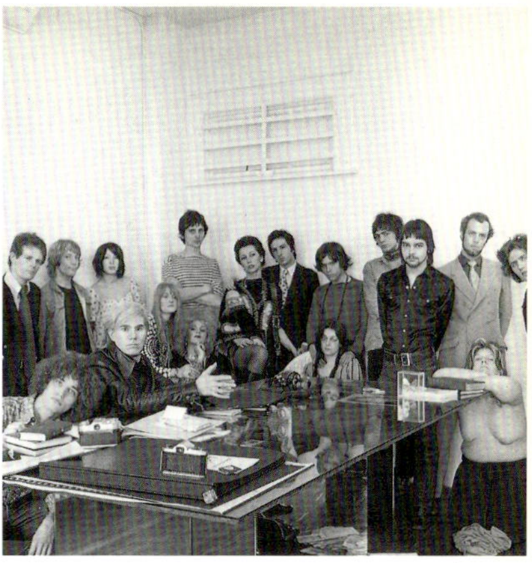

Factory... 1969

1969 On 21 July Neil Armstrong becomes the first man to set foot on the moon. In the USA protests against the Vietnam War intensify. 500,000 military conscripts burn their call-up papers or flee abroad.
In November the SALT negotiations begin, aimed at reducing the danger of escalation in the arms race between the USA and USSR.
Kurt Vonnegut's *Slaughterhouse-Five* is published. *Easy Rider*, directed by Dennis Hopper, who also co-stars in it, goes on general release and becomes a cult film.
A Warhol exhibition is mounted by the Nationalgalerie in Berlin from 1 March to 14 April. The first issue of the magazine *Interview* appears in March, with Warhol, Malanga, Morrissey and John Wilcock as its editors. Warhol makes the film *Trash*. For the first time his income as an artist exceeds his previous earnings from his commercial work.
At the suggestion of John and Dominique de Menil Warhol directs an exhibition of objects from the collection of the Rhode Island School of Design, Providence, under the title *Raid the Icebox I with Andy Warhol*. Warhol meets Vincent Fremont, who will later become one of his closest collaborators as manager of the Andy Warhol studio and vice-president of Andy Warhol Enterprises, Inc.

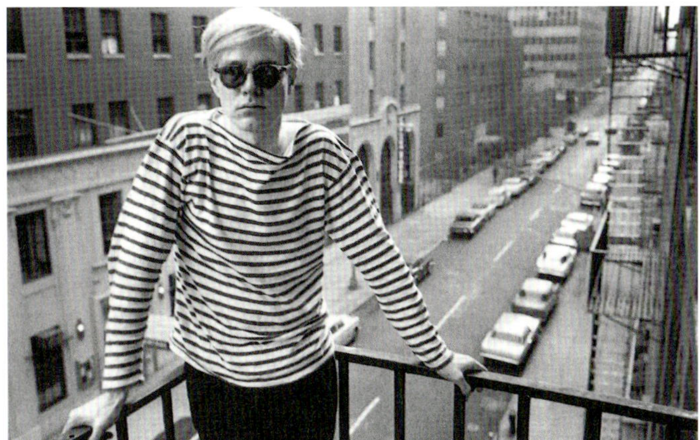

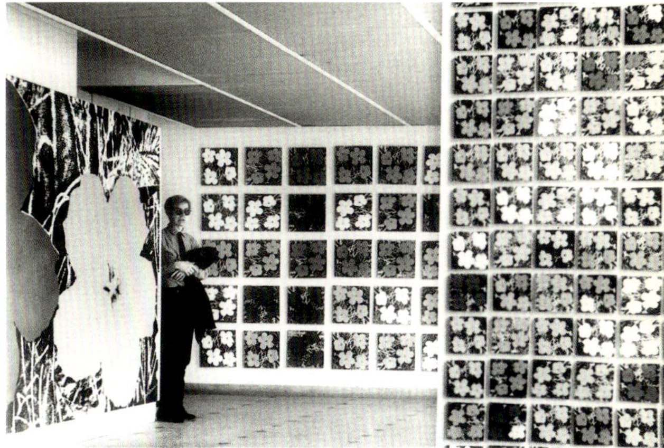

left: **Andy Warhol on the Factory fire escape, c. 1965**
right: **Andy Warhol during his *Flowers* exhibition at the Galerie Ileana Sonnabend, Paris, 1965**

1970 The Pasadena Art Museum opens an extensive retrospective of Warhol's works in May. This exhibition is subsequently shown at the Museum of Contemporary Art, Chicago; the Stedelijk Van Abbemuseum, Eindhoven; the Musée d'Art Moderne de la Ville de Paris; the Tate Gallery in London and the Whitney Museum of American Art, New York. For *Expo '70* in Osaka Warhol's *Rain Machine* is exhibited in the United States Pavilion.
The script of the film *Blue Movie* is published by Grove Press. Rainer Crone's first monograph on Warhol is published in Germany by Hatje Verlag; this remains the most reliable account on Warhol to date. The *Flowers* portfolio is issued by 'Factory Additions'. Toni Morrison's *The Bluest Eye* is published, as are Maya Angelou's *I Know Why the Caged Bird Sings* and Joyce Carol Oates's *Wheel of Love*. Stanley Kubrick's *Clockwork Orange* is released.

1971 Warhol's play *Pork* is performed by the LaMama Experimental Theater Club, New York, and at the Round House Theatre, London. Warhol designs the cover for the Rolling Stones album *Sticky Fingers*. The Gotham Book Mart Gallery, New York, puts drawings by Warhol from the 1950s on show for the first time. The Museum Haus Lange, Krefeld, exhibits graphic works by Warhol. Bruno Bischofberger is the publisher of the commissioned work *Electric Chair*, a portfolio of ten large-format silkscreens.
Together with Morrissey Warhol buys a plot of land with buildings in Montauk on Long Island.

1972 In February Nixon makes his first official visit to Peking.
Warhol produces a print in support of Senator McGovern, showing a portrait of Nixon with the slogan 'Vote McGovern'. His support for this candidate results in closer scrutiny of his income tax declarations from now until 1987. Warhol, like Norman Mailer, Terry Southern and Robert Rauschenberg, is regularly summoned to discuss his tax affairs with the Internal Revenue Service. He begins to dictate his diary to Pat Hackett, which will be published after Warhol's death. In the autumn presidential elections Nixon wins a second term.

◂ **Andy Warhol, Factory, 1967**

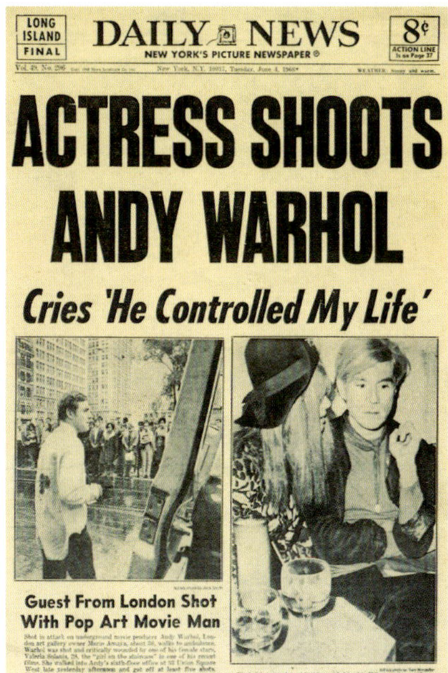

LONG ISLAND FINAL
DAILY NEWS
NEW YORK'S PICTURE NEWSPAPER
8¢
ACTRESS SHOOTS ANDY WARHOL
Cries 'He Controlled My Life'
Guest From London Shot With Pop Art Movie Man

New York Daily News, **4 June 1968**

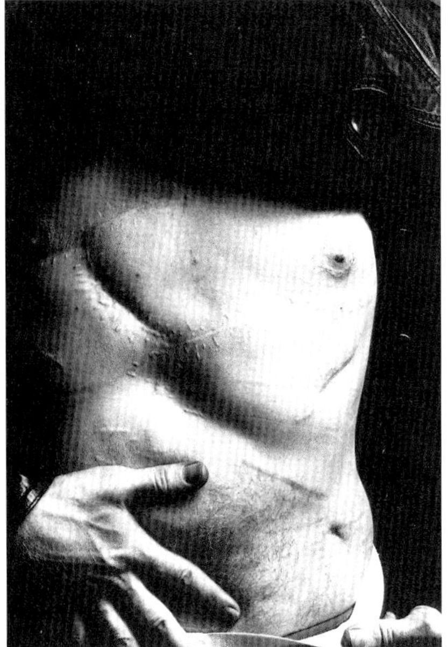

Richard Avedon: Andy Warhol, Artist, New York City, 20 August 1969

Warhol produces the first *Mao* portraits on a blue background, based on the cover photo of the publication *Quotations from Chairman Mao Tse-Tung*. In October the pictures are exhibited at the Kunstmuseum in Basel. The *Mao* motifs develop into one of Warhol's most extensive series, and at the same time constitute a first 'dialogue' between silkscreen technique and intensive 'painterly' treatment. Warhol produces portraits of Philip Johnson and Dennis Hopper. He makes the films *Heat* and *Women in Revolt*. Ronnie Cutrone becomes his studio assistant.
Warhol's mother, Julia Warhola, dies in Pittsburgh at the age of 80.

1973

A cease-fire in the Vietnam conflict is signed in Paris on 27 January. The USA commits itself to withdrawing its troops and recognizing Vietnamese sovereignty.
In the summer Warhol makes the film *Flesh for Frankenstein*. In Rome he has a small part in the movie *The Driver's Seat*, starring Elizabeth Taylor. He produces the film *L'Amour*.

1974

The Watergate Affair forces Nixon's resignation on 8 August. Gerald R. Ford is sworn in as President. One month after taking office he pardons Nixon.
In René Block's newly opened New York Gallery Joseph Beuys stages his 'action' *I Like America and America Likes Me*. Warhol creates a series of portraits of Julia Warhola, and works on portraits of Alexandre Iolas, Irving Blum, Ivan Karp, Ileana Sonnabend, Lita Hornick, and others. In February and March a large group of the *Mao* portraits is exhibited at the Musée Galliera in Paris.
Warhol makes the films *Andy Warhol's Frankenstein* and *Andy Warhol's Dracula*. He begins to assemble *Time Capsules*: assortments of everyday objects, documents, notes, letters, etc. are packed into cardboard boxes, labelled and stored away.
Andy Warhol buys a townhouse on East 66th Street. The Factory moves to 860 Broadway.

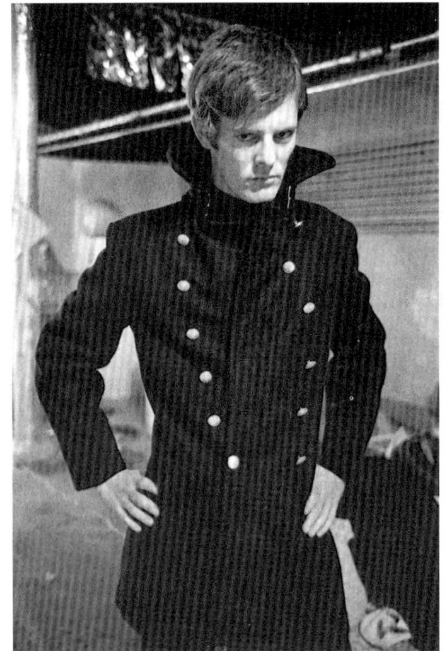

Paul Morrissey, filmmaker, c. 1969

1975

In April US scientists warn of the threat to the ozone layer from CFC gases.
The film *Taxi Driver* is in general release.
Warhol's *The Philosophy of Andy Warhol (From A to B and Back Again)*, written in collaboration with Pat Hackett, is published by Harcourt Brace Jovanovich.
Interview publishes a conversation with the President's son.
On 15 May Andy Warhol is invited to the White House for a banquet in honour of the Shah of Persia. From July to September the Baltimore Museum of Art holds a comprehensive exhibition of Warhol's works of the last thirteen years. Warhol works on *Ladies and Gentlemen,* a series depicting transvestites.

1976

Warhol starts work on a joint project with the painter Jamie Wyeth. He produces the *Skulls* series and the portrait of the revolutionary Native American leader Russell Means.
In March and April the Württembergischer Kunstverein in Stuttgart mounts the first comprehensive exhibition of Warhol's drawings with 224 exhibits, under the direction of Rainer Crone. The exhibition travels to museums in Düsseldorf, Bremen, Munich, Berlin, Vienna and Lucerne.

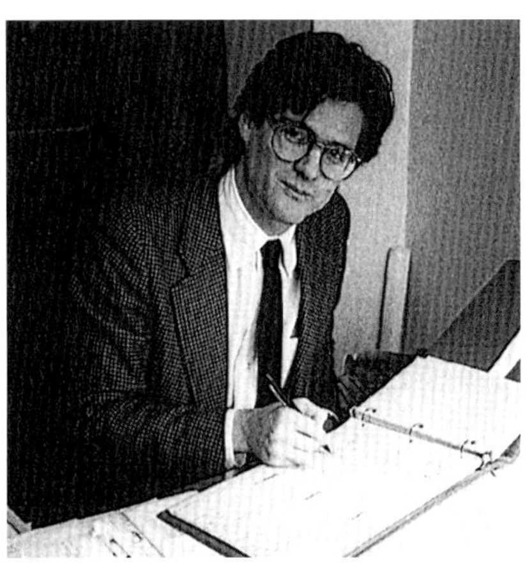

Vincent Fremont, c. 1975

1977

Punk rock is at its peak; many exponents of Punk see Warhol as one of its 'inventors'. In the spring the legendary Studio 54 opens in New York; Warhol becomes a regular visitor, together with Capote, the fashion designer Halston, Bianca Jagger, Liza Minnelli and Diane von Fürstenberg.
Elvis Presley dies in August.
The Museum of American Folk Art, New York, shows Warhol's folk-art collection in the exhibition *Andy Warhol's 'Folk and Funk'*.
Warhol produces his first *Hammer and Sickle* pictures. He works on a series of portraits of American athletes. In January the Pyramid Galleries, Washington, open their *Retrospective Exhibition of Paintings by Andy Warhol from 1962–1976*. Further exhibitions are held in the Galerie Daniel Templon, Paris; the Museum Folkwang, Essen; the Musée d'Art et d'Histoire, Geneva; the Coe Kerr Gallery, New York; the Sable-Castelli Gallery, Toronto; the Galerie Heiner Friedrich, Cologne; and the Leo Castelli Gallery, New York. Warhol, together with Fred Hughes and Jed Johnson, attends the opening of an exhibition in Kuwait.
Warhol makes the film *Andy Warhol's Bad*. Rupert Jasen Smith becomes his printer, whose first project is the portfolio of *Hammer and Sickle* silkscreens.

1978 Warhol produces portraits of Liza Minnelli, Muhammad Ali and Man Ray. He creates the *Oxidation* and *Shadow* pictures. The *Athletes* are exhibited at the Virginia Museum of Fine Arts in Richmond and the Institute of Contemporary Art in London. His *Portraits* are shown in the University Gallery of the Southern Methodist University, Dallas, and his *Torsos* at the Ace Gallery in Venice, California. An extensive retrospective of his work is held in the Kunsthaus, Zurich.

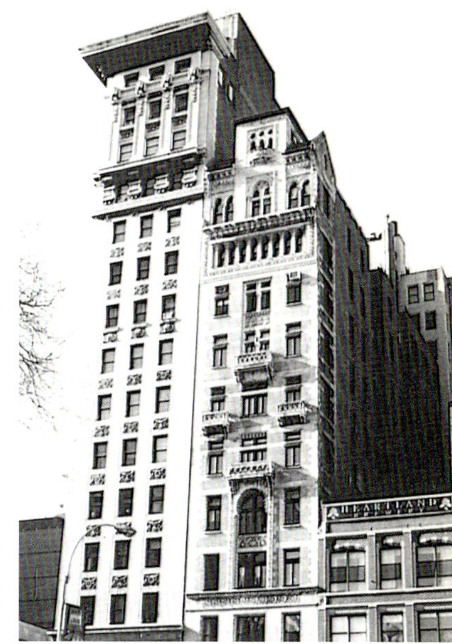

Factory, New York, 1968-74

1979 In Iran the Ayatollahs' fundamentalist revolution overthrows the Shah. The US embassy in Teheran is seized and occupied. The Soviet Union begins its invasion of Afghanistan.
Apocalypse Now is awarded the *Palme d'Or* at the Cannes Film Festival.
In November Warhol meets Joseph Beuys in New York on the occasion of the Beuys retrospective at the Guggenheim Museum; commissioned by Heiner Bastian, he takes polaroid photos on which the subsequent *Beuys* portraits will be based. He creates the *Retrospectives* and *Reversal* series. He publishes several portfolios of *Shadow* silkscreens. The *Shadow* pictures are shown in the Heiner Friedrich Gallery, New York. The *Skull* pictures are exhibited in the Galleria Massimo Valsecchi, Milan, and the *Torso* pictures in the Ace Gallery, Vancouver.
The Whitney Museum of American Art, New York, mounts the exhibition *Andy Warhol: Portraits of the 70s* from November 1979 to January 1980. The Wadsworth Atheneum, Hartford, Connecticut, holds a retrospective which then moves to the University Art Museum, University of California, Berkeley. *Andy Warhol's Exposures*, a book of photographs, is published.

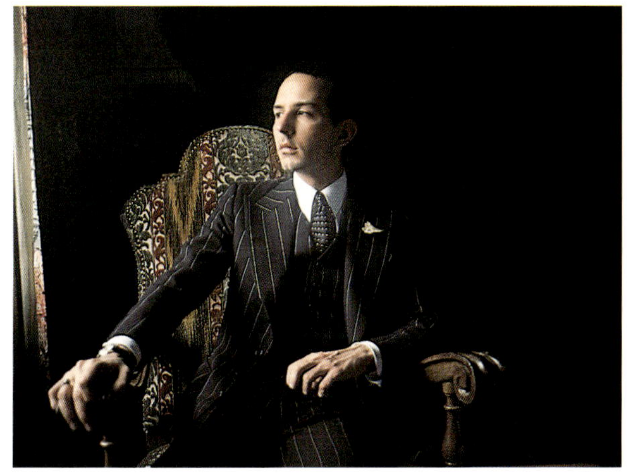

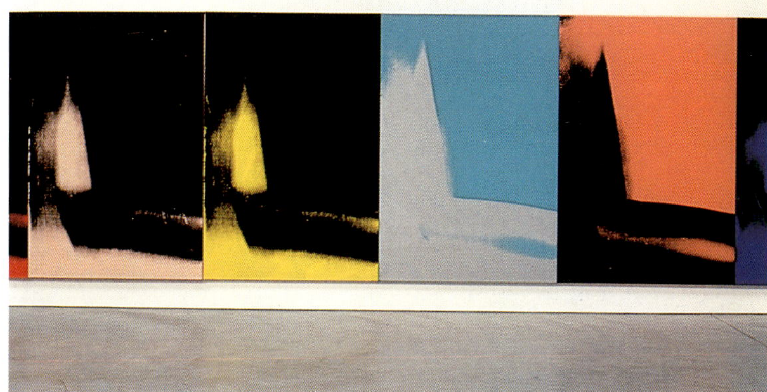

left: Frederick Hughes, photographed by David Hamilton, 1978/9
right: detail from an installation view of the *Shadows* exhibition, New York, 1979

1980 At the 'Global 2000' conference opened in July, a research study is presented predicting a population explosion and serious environmental problems in the near future.
In the autumn presidential contest Jimmy Carter is defeated by the 'great communicator', the almost 70-year-old Ronald Reagan.
John Lennon is shot dead in New York.
Warhol produces his first portraits of Beuys, as well as the portfolio *Ten Portraits of Jews of the Twentieth Century*. Exhibitions are mounted at the Galleria Lucio Amelio, Naples; the Centre d'Art Contemporain, Geneva; the Lowe Art Museum at the University of Miami, Coral Gables, Florida; the Lisson Gallery, London; the Jewish Museum, New York, and the Galerie Daniel Templon, Paris.
Warhol's *Reversals* are shown at the Galerie Bruno Bischofberger, Zurich, in May and June. His photographs are exhibited at the Museum Ludwig, Cologne, and the Stedelijk Museum, Amsterdam. He attends the opening of exhibitions in Düsseldorf and Paris.
POPism. The Warhol '60s (diary entries based on tape-recordings) by Warhol and Pat Hackett is published by Harcourt Brace Jovanovich.
'Andy Warhol's TV', a talk-show with guests, is shown on a cable channel and runs until 1982.
Warhol's friend Jed Johnson leaves him.
Warhol and Fred Hughes attend an audience with the Pope in the Vatican. Jay Shriver becomes Andy Warhol's studio assistant.

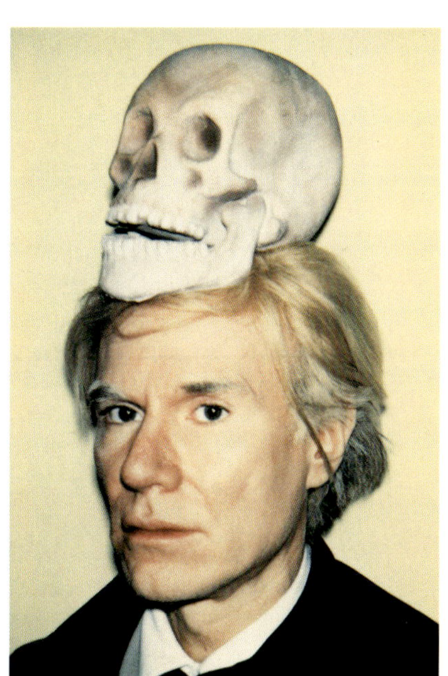

Andy Warhol, *Self-Portrait*, 1977

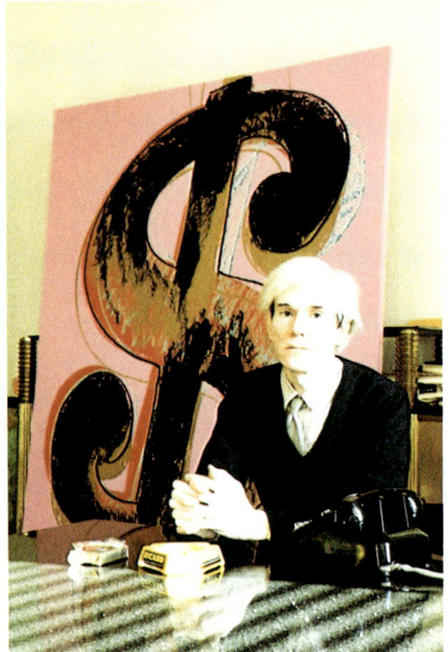

Andy Warhol, New York, 1979

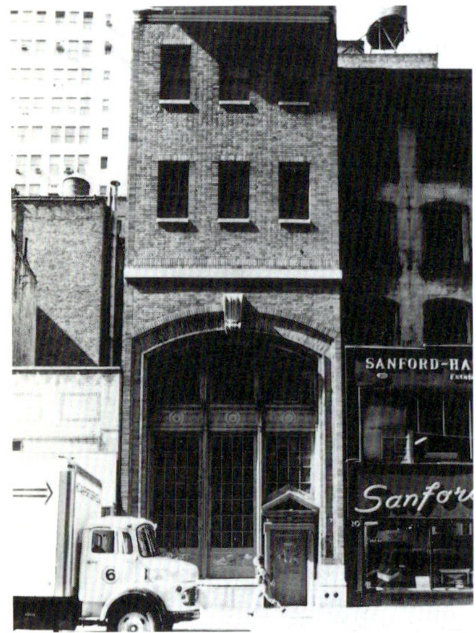

22 East 33rd Street, New York, Andy Warhol's last studio

After a devastating earthquake in the Naples region, Warhol produces the *Fate Presto* pictures, at the suggestion of Lucio Amelio. 1981
Warhol is engaged on several groups of works – *Crosses, Dollar Signs, Guns, Knives* – and a series based on American myths. He exhibits the *Shoe Portfolio* at the Watari Gallery in Tokyo. The *Reversal* pictures are displayed at the Museum Moderner Kunst, Vienna. The *Myths* series is exhibited by Ronald Feldman, New York. There are exhibitions at the Kestner-Gesellschaft, Hanover, and the Städtische Galerie im Lenbachhaus, Munich. Castelli Graphics, New York, mounts a retrospective of Warhol prints. *Andy Warhol: An Exhibition of Sports Paintings* opens at the Los Angeles Institute of Contemporary Art. Works by Warhol are among those shown at the *Westkunst* exhibition held in Cologne. Warhol travels to Bonn, Munich, Paris and Vienna.

The term 'Yuppie' (young urban professional) is coined. The freeze movement, demanding an immediate halt to nuclear arms acquisition, gains momentum. Under the presidency of the former actor Reagan, the USA becomes a 'mediacracy'. 1982
Warhol works on portraits of Goethe. For the Berlin *Zeitgeist* exhibition he creates pictures with motifs derived from Berlin: 'Gilly's Friedrich Monument', the 'Olympic Stadium' and the 'Lichtdom'. Warhol exhibits his *Reversals, Dollar Signs, Myths, Knives, Guns, Portraits* and *Crosses* at the Leo Castelli Gallery, New York; the Galerie Daniel Templon, Paris; the Kunstsammlung Thun and the Galeria Fernando Vijande, Madrid. His versions of works by de Chirico are shown in the Campidoglio, Rome. On 2 March the Marx Collection, with works by Warhol, Beuys, Rauschenberg and Twombly, is shown for the first time in the Nationalgalerie, Berlin. Warhol attends the opening. He meets Beuys and Rauschenberg, and visits Rainer Werner Fassbinder during the filming of *Querelle* in a Berlin studio. With Fred Hughes and the photographer Christopher Makos, Warhol travels to Paris and Zurich and to China, where he goes to see the Great Wall.
Warhol accepts more and more advertising commissions.

Reagan's plan for SDI (the 'Strategic Defense Initiative') is launched in March. The US economy is stimulated by falling interest rates and rising demand. 1983
Warhol and Jean-Michel Basquiat strike up a friendship and together produce so-called *Collaboration Works*. Warhol's works are exhibited at the Aldrich Museum of Contemporary Art, Ridgefield, Connecticut, and the Galerie Bruno Bischofberger, Zurich. For the exhibition in Zurich, which includes his *Paintings for Children*, he designs 'wallpaper' with fish motifs as background. He travels to Spain, Paris, Denver and St. Maarten. The exhibition *Warhol's Animals: Species at Risk* is shown at the American Museum of Natural History, New York, and then travels to a large number of natural history museums in the USA. Warhol designs the official poster for the celebrations marking the centenary of Brooklyn Bridge, New York.

Defeating Walter Mondale in the presidential elections, Reagan is elected for a second term. The AIDS virus HIV is identified by the biochemist Luc Mangagnier, and a test for AIDS is developed by the American research scientist Robert Gallo. 1984
Jay McInerney's *Bright Lights, Big City* is published.
The Museum of Modern Art, New York, mounts the exhibition *Primitivism in 20th Century Art*. Wim Wenders's film *Paris, Texas* is awarded the *Palme d'Or* at the Cannes Film Festival. *Terminator* is released.
With his *Renaissance* and *Munch* pictures Warhol returns to creating works based on models from art history. He creates the *Rorschach* paintings. With Basquiat and Francesco Clemente he produces further *Collaboration Works*. The Galerie Bruno Bischofberger, Zurich, mounts an exhibition of *Collaborations: Jean-Michel Basquiat, Francesco Clemente, Andy Warhol*. The Schellmann & Klüser Gallery, New York, shows *Andy Warhol: Details of Renaissance Paintings*.
Warhol purchases the Edison Building on East 33rd Street, New York. After conversion work it houses Warhol's studio, his office and the offices of the magazine *Interview*.

Warhol paints his *Ads* pictures, based on commonplace advertising motifs. Pictures from the *Collaboration* series are shown in the Tony Shafrazi Gallery, New York. The Art Gallery of Lehman College in the Bronx exhibits silkscreens produced by Warhol between 1962 and 1985. The Galerie Paul Maenz in Cologne shows a selection of paintings and early prints. 1985

At 'Area', a New York nightclub, Warhol creates an *Invisible Sculpture*: he first stands on a plinth, and then leaves it – the 'sculpture' remains in place, its presence indicated by a label. A selection of photographs by Warhol is published by Harper & Row under the title *America*.
Bret Easton Ellis's *Less Than Zero* appears.

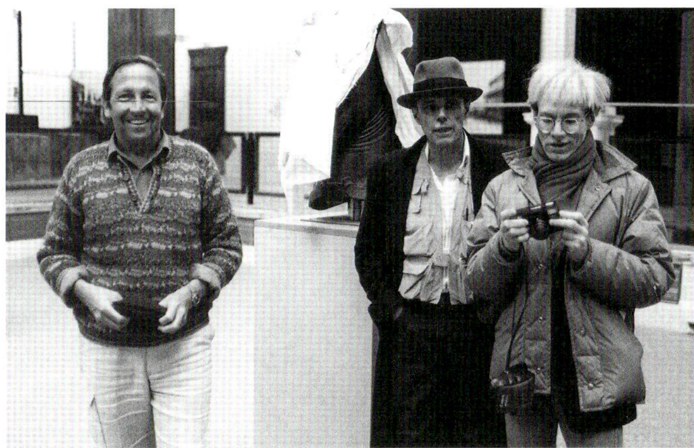

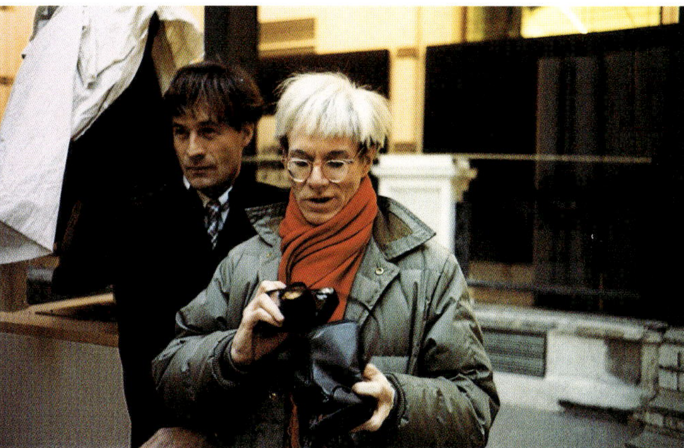

left: **Robert Rauschenberg, Joseph Beuys and Andy Warhol in the Martin-Gropius-Bau, Berlin, March 1982**
right: **Andy Warhol and Heiner Bastian in the Martin-Gropius-Bau, Berlin, March 1982**

1986 Warhol works on the *Cars* silkscreens, commissioned by Mercedes-Benz. He produces the *Camouflage* pictures, the *Lenin* portraits, a new series of *Campbell's Soup Boxes, Flowers, Self-Portraits* and portraits of Frederick the Great. For Alexandre Iolas he works on paintings which are paraphrases of Leonardo's *Last Supper*. The exhibition *Andy Warhol: Major Print* is shown at the Galerie Daniel Templon, and Warhol goes to Paris to attend the opening. The Dia Art Foundation, New York, mounts an exhibition surveying his work, which shows *Disaster* pictures from March to June and *Hand-Painted Images* from November until June 1987. The Anthony d'Offay Gallery in London holds an exhibition of Warhol's *Self-Portraits*, and he is present for the opening. His *Oxidation Paintings* are exhibited at the Larry Gagosian Gallery, New York. His television series is shown on MTV under the title 'Andy Warhol's Fifteen Minutes'.
Tarna Janowitz's *Slaves of New York* is published.

1987-1989 Warhol paints portraits of Beethoven and begins work on a series of prints, *The History of American TV*. He travels to Paris, and to Milan for the opening of an exhibition of his *Last Supper* pictures in the Palazzo delle Stelline.
The Robert Miller Gallery, New York, shows *Andy Warhol Photographs* from 6 to 31 January. On 22 February Warhol dies wholly unexpectedly in New York Hospital-Cornell Medical Center, following a gall bladder operation and complications arising from an allergic reaction to penicillin.
He is buried in Pittsburgh with only immediate family members and a small group of friends present. On 1 April a memorial service is held in St. Patrick's Cathedral in New York and is attended by more than two thousand mourners. Father Anthony Dalla Villa, who conducts the service, makes reference to the religious side of Warhol's personality and his close ties with the Catholic Church.
In the same year Frederick Hughes becomes president of the Andy Warhol Foundation for the Visual Arts, an institution established under the terms of Warhol's will to promote cultural aims. In 1988 Warhol's extensive personal collection of art, craft objects, jewellery and antiques is sold at record prices at two legendary auctions, with the proceeds going to the Foundation.

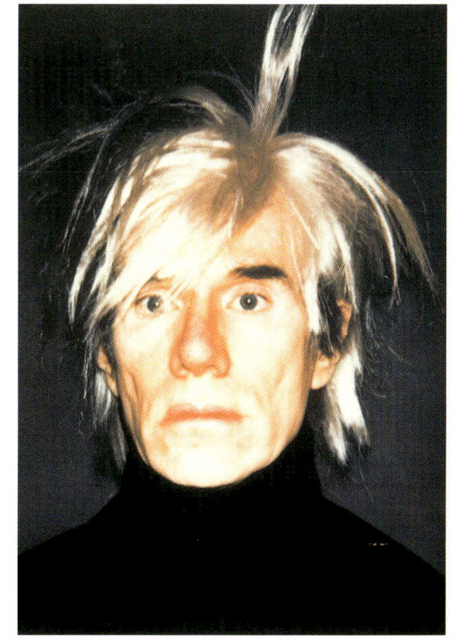

***Self-Portrait*, 1986**

In October 1987, 'Black Monday' on the Stock Exchange brings a decade of relative prosperity to an abrupt end: share prices fall to lower levels than in the Wall Street Crash of 1929.
In 1989 The Museum of Modern Art, New York, holds its large and representative retrospective of Andy Warhol's œuvre; the exhibition subsequently travels also to Chicago, and is later shown in a number of European cities: London, Cologne, Venice and Paris.

In 1994, The Andy Warhol Museum Pittsburgh opens to the public.
In the years that follow, a great number of thematic exhibitions devoted to individual groups of Warhol's works are held in Europe, Japan and the USA.

CATALOGUE

Céline Bastian

1 Self-Portrait **1942**
Pencil on paper
19 x $13^3/_8$ in. / 48.3 x 34 cm
Collection Mrs. John F. Steiner
On Loan to The Andy Warhol Museum, Pittsburgh

2 Boy Picking His Nose **1948/49**
Pencil on paper
11 x $8^1/_2$ in. / 27.9 x 21.6 cm
The Andy Warhol Museum, Pittsburgh
Founding Collection, Contribution
The Andy Warhol Foundation
for the Visual Arts, Inc.

3 The Broad Gave Me My Face, But I Can Pick My Own Nose **1948/49**
Tempera on masonite
37 x 18 in. / 94 x 45.7 cm
Collection Ethel and Leonard Kessler

4 Male Head **c. 1950**
Graphite on Bond paper
$10^7/_8$ x $8^5/_8$ in. / 27.6 x 21.9 cm
Private collection

5 Seated Aging Female **c. 1948**
Graphite on taped sheets of Bond paper
33 x 17 in. / 83.8 x 43.2 cm
Courtesy Anthony d'Offay Gallery, London

6 Untitled (Huey Long) **1948/49**
Pen, ink on paper
29 x 23 in. / 73.7 x 58.4 cm
Carnegie Museum of Art, Pittsburgh,
Gift of Russel G. Twiggs

7 Dead Stop **1954**
Ink on paper
21 x 23 in. / 53.3 x 58.4 cm
Private collection, New York

8 Communist Speaker **c. 1950**
Ink on paper
23 x 29 in. / 58.4 x 73.7 cm
The Andy Warhol Museum, Pittsburgh
Founding Collection, Contribution
The Andy Warhol Foundation
for the Visual Arts, Inc.

9 Grasping Figures With Tiger Head
Ink, tempera on coloured graphic arts paper **1956**
17 x $24^5/_8$ in. / 43.2 x 62.5 cm
Private collection, New York

10 Chess Player **1954**
Ink, Dr. Martin's Aniline Dye on Strathmore paper
$22^7/_8$ x $18^3/_4$ in. / 58.1 x 47.6 cm
Private collection

11 Untitled (»The Nation's Nightmare«)
Ink, graphite, acetate on Strathmore paper **1951**
$15^1/_2$ x $14^3/_8$ in. / 39.5 x 36.5 cm
Private collection, London

12 Male Seated at Automat Counter **1958**
Ink on Strathmore paper
$22^5/_8$ x $28^5/_8$ in. / 57.5 x 72.7 cm
Courtesy Anthony d'Offay Gallery, London

13 Truman Capote **c. 1954**
Ink on bookprinting paper
$16^7/_8$ x $13^7/_8$ in. / 42.9 x 35.2 cm
Stiftung Sammlung Marx, Hamburger Bahnhof – Museum für Gegenwart, Berlin

14 James Dean **1955**
Ball-point ink on tinted paper
$17^5/_8$ x $11^3/_4$ in. / 44.8 x 29.8 cm
Courtesy The Brant Foundation, Greenwich, CT

15 Untitled **c. 1955/57**
Ball-point ink on manila paper
$16^3/_4$ x $13^7/_8$ in. / 42.5 x 35.2 cm
Private collection

16 Untitled **c. 1957**
Ball-point ink on hand-laid paper
$16^7/_8$ x 14 in. / 42.9 x 35.6 cm
Stiftung Sammlung Marx, Hamburger Bahnhof – Museum für Gegenwart, Berlin

17 Untitled **1955**
Gold leaf, ink on Strathmore paper
$19^1/_2$ x $13^5/_8$ in. / 49.5 x 34.6 cm
Stiftung Sammlung Marx, Hamburger Bahnhof – Museum für Gegenwart, Berlin

18 Untitled (Golden Boy) **1957**
Gold leaf, ink, pencil on heavy cardboard
97 x $35^3/_4$ in. / 246.4 x 90.8 cm
Stiftung Sammlung Marx, Hamburger Bahnhof – Museum für Gegenwart, Berlin

19 Untitled **c. 1960**
Ball-point ink on paper
17 x $13^7/_8$ in. / 43.2 x 35.2 cm
Private collection

20 Golden Portrait with Cat **1957**
Gold leaf, ink on heavy paper
$21^1/_4$ x 16 in. / 54 x 40.6 cm
Stiftung Sammlung Marx, Hamburger Bahnhof – Museum für Gegenwart, Berlin

21 Angkor Wat, Cambodia **1956**
Ink, Dr. Martin's Aniline Dye on Strathmore paper
23 x $14^3/_4$ in. / 58.4 x 37.5 cm
Private collection

22 Angkor Wat, Cambodia **1956**
Ball-point ink on manila paper
17 x 14 in. / 43.2 x 35.6 cm
Private collection

23 Two Fencing Men **c. 1957**
Gold leaf, ink, Dr. Martin's Aniline Dye on Strathmore paper
$14^3/_4$ x 23 in. / 37.5 x 58.4 cm
Private collection

24 Still-Life (Flacon) **c. 1957**
Ball-point ink on manila paper
$16^3/_4$ x $13^7/_8$ in. / 42.5 x 35.2 cm
Private collection

25 Untitled **c. 1955**
Ball-point ink on bookprinting paper
$16^3/_4$ x $13^7/_8$ in. / 42.5 x 35.3 cm
Stiftung Sammlung Marx, Hamburger Bahnhof – Museum für Gegenwart, Berlin

26 Untitled **c. 1957**
Collage; 2 sheets:
gold leaf, ink on heavy paper;
ink on light cardboard
24 x 31 in. / 61 x 78.7 cm
Stiftung Sammlung Marx, Hamburger Bahnhof – Museum für Gegenwart, Berlin

27 Hats **c. 1958**
Ink, coloured ink wash on paper
23 x $17^1/_4$ in. / 58.4 x 43.8 cm
Private collection

28 Dancer **c. 1955**
Collage; ink, ink wash on paper
$16^3/_4$ x $13^3/_4$ in. / 42.5 x 35 cm
Private collection

29 Bullfighter **c. 1955**
Ink, coloured ink wash on paper
29 x 23 in. / 73.7 x 58.4 cm
Private collection

30 Elixir de Markoff (Royal Jelly) **c. 1960**
Ink on Strathmore paper
$14^3/_8$ x $11^1/_4$ in. / 36.5 x 28.6 cm
Courtesy Anthony d'Offay Gallery, London

31 **Jewelry (Necklace)** **c. 1960**
Ink, tempera on Strathmore paper, tissue paper
23 x $16^{1}/_{8}$ in. / 58.4 x 41 cm
Courtesy Anthony d'Offay Gallery, London

32 **Margaret Rutherford** **1957**
Gold leaf, ink on heavy cardboard
20 x 13 in. / 50.8 x 33 cm
Stiftung Sammlung Marx, Hamburger Bahnhof – Museum für Gegenwart, Berlin

33 **Golden Nude** **1957**
Gold leaf, China ink on paper
$17^{1}/_{2}$ x $11^{1}/_{2}$ in. / 44.4 x 29.2 cm
Collection Froehlich, Stuttgart

34 **Elvis Presley (Gold Boot)** **1956**
Ink, gold leaf, collage on paper
20 x 14 in. / 50.8 x 35.6 cm
Courtesy The Brant Foundation, Greenwich, CT

35 **Seated Male** **c. 1957**
Gold leaf, China ink on paper
20 x 15 in. / 50.8 x 38.1 cm
Collection Froehlich, Stuttgart

36 **(Stenciled) Violin and Bow** **c. 1958**
Tempera on Strathmore Seconds paper
$14^{1}/_{2}$ x $22^{7}/_{8}$ in. / 36.8 x 58.1cm
Private collection

37 **Abstract Stenciled Images** **c. 1958**
Sprayed paint on Strathmore paper
$14^{3}/_{4}$ x $14^{3}/_{4}$ in. / 37.5 x 37.5 cm
Private collection

38 **Bird on Branch of Leaves** **c. 1957**
Gold leaf, ink on Strathmore paper
$13^{7}/_{8}$ x $22^{3}/_{4}$ in. / 35.2 x 57.8 cm
Private collection

39 **Untitled (Baboon)** **c. 1957**
Gold leaf, ink on coloured graphic art paper
18 x 24 in. / 45.7 x 61 cm
Private collection

40 **Matches** **c. 1957**
Tempera on sketchbook paper
$24^{1}/_{4}$ x 18 in. / 61.6 x 45.7 cm
Stiftung Sammlung Marx, Hamburger Bahnhof – Museum für Gegenwart, Berlin

41 **Matchsticks** **c. 1962**
Tempera on sketchbook paper
$23^{3}/_{4}$ x 18 in. / 60.3 x 45.7 cm
Courtesy The Brant Foundation, Greenwich, CT

42 **Purse** **c. 1960**
Ink, tempera on Strathmore paper with acetate overlay
$14^{1}/_{4}$ x 11 in. / 36.2 x 27.9 cm
Courtesy Anthony d'Offay Gallery, London

43 **Shoe** **c. 1960**
Graphite, gouache on paper
24 x 18 in. / 61 x 45.7 cm
Courtesy Anthony d'Offay Gallery, London

44 **Strictly Personal** **1956**
Ball-point ink on paper
24 x 18 in. / 61 x 45.7 cm
Private collection, New York

45 **Journal American** **c. 1958/60**
Ball-point ink on paper
$23^{3}/_{4}$ x $17^{7}/_{8}$ in. / 60.3 x 45.4 cm
The Andy Warhol Museum, Pittsburgh
Founding Collection, Contribution Dia Center for the Arts

46 **Advertisement** **1960**
Casein, wax crayon on canvas
72 x 54 in. / 183 x 137.2 cm
Stiftung Sammlung Marx, Hamburger Bahnhof – Museum für Gegenwart, Berlin

47 **Little King** **1961**
Casein on canvas
54 x 40 in. / 137.2 x 101.6 cm
Private collection

48 **Superman** **1961**
Casein, wax crayon on canvas
67 x 52 in. / 170.2 x 132 cm
Collection Gunter Sachs

49 **Saturday's Popeye** **1961**
Casein on canvas
$42^{1}/_{2}$ x 39 in. / 108 x 99 cm
Ludwig Forum für Internationale Kunst, Aachen – Collection Ludwig

50 **Before and After [1]** **1961**
Casein on canvas
68 x 54 in. / 172.7 x 137.2 cm
The Metropolitan Museum of Art, New York · Gift of Halston, 1981

51 **Where Is Your Rupture?** **1960**
Casein on canvas
$69^{3}/_{4}$ x 54 in. / 177.2 x 137.2 cm
Private collection

52 **Batman** **1961**
Casein, wax crayon on canvas
$28^{3}/_{4}$ x $43^{3}/_{4}$ in. / 73 x 111.1 cm
Private collection

53 **Dick Tracy** **1961**
Casein, wax crayon on canvas
48 x $33^{3}/_{4}$ in. / 122 x 85.7 cm
Courtesy The Brant Foundation, Greenwich, CT

54 **Coca-Cola** **1960**
Casein, wax crayon, oil paint on canvas
52 x $40^{3}/_{4}$ in. / 132 x 103.5 cm
Private collection

55 **Coca-Cola** **1960**
Casein, wax crayon, oil paint on canvas
72 x 54 in. / 183 x 137.2 cm
The Andy Warhol Museum, Pittsburgh
Founding Collection, Contribution Dia Center for the Arts

56 **Peach Halves** **1962**
Oil paint, wax crayon on canvas
70 x 54 in. / 177.8 x 137.2 cm
Staatsgalerie Stuttgart*

57 **Icebox** **1960**
Oil paint, casein, wax crayon on canvas
67 x $53^{1}/_{8}$ in. / 170.2 x 134.9 cm
The Menil Collection, Houston

58 **Water Heater** **1960**
Casein on canvas
$44^{3}/_{4}$ x 40 in. / 113.7 x 101.6 cm
The Museum of Modern Art, New York
Gift of Roy Lichtenstein, 1971

59 **Drills 7.88** **1960**
Casein on canvas
$42^{5}/_{8}$ x $39^{3}/_{4}$ in. / 108.3 x 101 cm
Private collection

60 **Pipe** **1961**
Casein on canvas
30 x 40 in. / 76.2 x 101.6 cm
Private collection

61 **Crossword** **1960**
Casein on canvas
$44^{1}/_{4}$ x 63 in. / 112.4 x 160 cm
Private collection

62 **Imperial Car Detail** 1962
Graphite on paper
18 x 24 in. / 45.7 x 61 cm
Private collection

63 **Pontiac** c. 1961
Casein, pencil on canvas
25 x $30^{1}/_{8}$ in. / 63.5 x 76.5 cm
Private collection

64 **Telephone** 1961
Casein, pencil on canvas
$69^{3}/_{4}$ x 54 in. / 177.2 x 137.2 cm
The Museum of Contemporary Art, Los Angeles; Purchased with funds provided by an Anonymous Donor

65 **Close Cover Before Striking** 1962
Acrylic paint, Letraset, sandpaper on canvas
16 x 20 in. / 40.6 x 50.8 cm
The Andy Warhol Museum, Pittsburgh
Founding Collection, Contribution The Andy Warhol Foundation for the Visual Arts, Inc. Given in celebration of the first anniversary of the directorship of Thomas Sokolowski

66 **Food Kill** 1962
Graphite on purple paper
28 x 22 in. / 71.1 x 55.9 cm
Private collection

67 **Close Cover Before Striking** 1962
Acrylic paint on canvas
72 x 54 in. / 183 x 137.2 cm
Louisiana Museum of Modern Art, Humlebæk, Denmark

68 **Do It Yourself (Narcissus)** 1962
Pencil, wax crayon on paper
$23^{3}/_{4}$ x 18 in. / 60.3 x 45.7 cm
Öffentliche Kunstsammlung Basel, Kupferstichkabinett; Karl August Burckhardt-Koechlin-Fonds

69 **Do It Yourself (Landscape)** 1962
Acrylic paint, pencil, Letraset on canvas
70 x 54 in. / 177.8 x 137.2 cm
Museum Ludwig, Köln

70 **Do It Yourself (Seascape)** 1962
Acrylic paint, pencil, Letraset on canvas
$54^{3}/_{8}$ x 72 in. / 139 x 183 cm
Stiftung Sammlung Marx, Hamburger Bahnhof – Museum für Gegenwart, Berlin

71 **Do It Yourself (Sailboats)** 1962
Acrylic paint, pencil, Letraset on canvas
72 x 100 in. / 183 x 254 cm
Daros Collection, Switzerland

72 **Dance Diagram (Fox Trot)** 1962
Casein on canvas
72 x 54 in. / 183 x 137.2 cm
Collection Onnasch

73 **Dancestep (Two Feet)** 1962
Casein on canvas
$71^{1}/_{2}$ x 52 in. / 181.6 x 132 cm
Courtesy The Brant Foundation, Greenwich, CT

74 **One Dollar Bill with Lincoln's Portrait**
Graphite on paper 1962
$27^{1}/_{2}$ x $39^{3}/_{8}$ in. / 69.8 x 100 cm
Private collection

75 **Silver Certificate** 1962
Casein, silver paint, pencil on canvas
52 x 72 in. / 132 x 183 cm
Private collection, Switzerland

76 **Campbell's Soup Cans** 1962
Acrylic paint on canvas
32 works:
each 20 x 16 in. / 50.8 x 40.6 cm
The Museum of Modern Art, New York
Purchase and partial gift of Irving Blum, 1996

77 **Five Campbell's Soup Cans** 1962
Pencil, crayon on paper
18 x $23^{5}/_{8}$ in. / 45.7 x 60 cm
Courtesy Sonnabend Collection

78 **Big Coffee-Tin** 1962
Watercolour, crayon on paper
18 x $23^{3}/_{4}$ in. / 45.7 x 60.3 cm
Öffentliche Kunstsammlung Basel, Kupferstichkabinett; Karl August Burckhardt-Koechlin-Fonds

79 **Campbell's Soup Can (Cream of Chicken)** 1962
Synthetic polymer paint, pencil on canvas
$71^{3}/_{4}$ x $51^{1}/_{4}$ in. / 182.2 x 132.1 cm
Courtesy Gagosian Gallery

80 **Campbell's Soup Can (Chicken Noodle)** 1962
Pencil, tempera on paper
$23^{3}/_{4}$ x $17^{7}/_{8}$ in. / 60.3 x 45.4 cm
Courtesy Sonnabend Collection

81 **Campbell's Soup Cans (Black Bean Soup)** 1962
Crayon, pencil on paper
22 x 17 in. / 55.9 x 43.2 cm
Courtesy The Brant Foundation, Greenwich, CT

82 **100 Cans** 1962
Oil paint on canvas
72 x 52 in. / 183 x 132 cm
Albright-Knox Art Gallery, Buffalo, NY
Gift of Seymour H. Knox, Jr., 1963

83 **Handle with Care – Glass – Thank You** 1962
Silkscreen ink on canvas
82 x $66^{1}/_{8}$ in. / 208.3 x 168 cm
Daros Collection, Switzerland

84 **S & H Green Stamps** 1962
Silkscreen ink on canvas
$71^{3}/_{4}$ x $53^{3}/_{4}$ in. / 182.2 x 136.6 cm
The Museum of Modern Art, New York
Gift of Philip Johnson, 1998

85 **Untitled (Roll of Bills)** 1962
Watercolour, crayon, pencil on paper
40 x 30 in. / 101.6 x 76.2 cm
Courtesy The Brant Foundation, Greenwich, CT

86 **192 One Dollar Bills** 1962
Silkscreen ink, pencil, acrylic paint on canvas
98 x $74^{3}/_{8}$ in. / 249 x 189 cm
Stiftung Sammlung Marx, Hamburger Bahnhof – Museum für Gegenwart, Berlin

87 **Coca-Cola** 1962
Pencil, crayon on paper
$23^{3}/_{4}$ x 18 in. / 60.3 x 45.7 cm
Sonnabend Collection

88 **210 Coca-Cola Bottles** 1962
Silkscreen ink, acrylic paint on canvas
$81^{7}/_{8}$ x $105^{1}/_{8}$ in. / 208 x 267 cm
Daros Collection, Switzerland

89 **Liner Hijacked** 1961
Graphite on paper
29 x 23 in. / 73.7 x 58.4 cm
The Andy Warhol Museum, Pittsburgh
Founding Collection, Contribution The Andy Warhol Foundation for the Visual Arts, Inc.

90 **Daily News** 1962
Acrylic paint on canvas
$72^{1}/_{4}$ x 100 in. / 183.6 x 254 cm
Museum für Moderne Kunst, Frankfurt am Main [Former Ströher Collection]

91 **Gold Marilyn** 1962
Silkscreen ink, gold paint on canvas
2 tondi:
each $17^{7}/_{8}$ in. / 45.3 cm diameter
Collection Froehlich, Stuttgart

92 **Liquorice Marilyn** 1962
Silkscreen ink, acrylic paint on canvas
20 x 16 in. / 50.8 x 40.6 cm
Courtesy The Brant Foundation, Greenwich, CT

93 **Lavender Marilyn** 1962
Silkscreen ink, acrylic paint on canvas
20 x 15 7/8 in. / 50.8 x 40.3 cm
Collection Uli Knecht

94 **Marilyn Diptych** 1962
Silkscreen ink, acrylic paint on canvas
2 panels:
each 82 x 57 in. / 208.3 x 144.8 cm
overall 82 x 114 in. / 208.3 x 289.6 cm
The Trustees of the Tate Gallery

95 **Shot Blue Marilyn** 1964
Silkscreen ink, acrylic paint on canvas
40 x 40 in. / 101.6 x 101.6 cm
Courtesy The Brant Foundation, Greenwich, CT

96 **Shot Sage Blue Marilyn** 1964
Silkscreen ink, acrylic paint on canvas
40 x 40 in. / 101.6 x 101.6 cm
Private collection; Courtesy Doris Ammann

97 **Baseball** 1962
Silkscreen ink, oil paint on canvas
91 1/2 x 82 in. / 232.4 x 208.3 cm
Collection of The Nelson-Atkins Museum of Art, Kansas City, MO
Gift of the Guild of the Friends of Art and other Friends of the Museum

98 **Texan (Portrait Robert Rauschenberg)** 1963
Silkscreen ink on canvas
81 7/8 x 81 7/8 in. / 208 x 208 cm
Museum Ludwig, Köln

99 **Merce** 1963
Silkscreen ink, spray paint on linen
81 7/8 x 81 7/8 in. / 208 x 208 cm
Daros Collection, Switzerland

100 **Red Elvis** 1962
Silkscreen ink, acrylic paint on canvas
69 x 52 in. / 175 x 132 cm
Courtesy The Brant Foundation, Greenwich, CT

101 **Thirty Are Better Than One** 1963
Silkscreen ink, acrylic paint on canvas
110 x 94 1/2 in. / 279.4 x 240 cm
Courtesy The Brant Foundation, Greenwich, CT

102 **Liz** 1963
Silkscreen ink, acrylic paint, silver paint on canvas
40 x 40 in. / 101.6 x 101.6 cm
Collection Froehlich, Stuttgart

102a **Silver Liz** 1963
Silkscreen ink, acrylic paint, silver paint on canvas
40 x 40 in. / 101.6 x 101.6 cm
Courtesy The Brant Foundation, Greenwich, CT

103 **Blue Liz as Cleopatra** 1963
Silkscreen ink, acrylic paint on canvas
82 x 65 in. / 208.3 x 165.1 cm
Daros Collection, Switzerland

103a **Liz** 1963
Silkscreen ink, acrylic paint on canvas
40 x 40 in. / 101.6 x 101.6 cm
Mrs. and Mr. Irving Blum

103b **Liz** 1963
Silkscreen ink, acrylic paint on canvas
40 x 40 in. / 101.6 x 101.6 cm
Mrs. and Mr. Irving Blum

104 **Statue of Liberty** 1963
Silkscreen ink, acrylic paint on canvas
78 x 80 3/4 in. / 198 x 205 cm
Daros Collection, Switzerland

105 **Cagney** 1964
Silkscreen ink on paper, mounted on canvas
30 x 40 in. / 76.2 x 101.6 cm
Collection Froehlich, Stuttgart

106 **Cagney** 1962
Silkscreen ink, silver paint on canvas
204 3/4 x 81 7/8 in. / 520 x 208 cm
Stiftung Sammlung Marx, Hamburger Bahnhof – Museum für Gegenwart, Berlin

107 **Double Elvis** 1963
Silkscreen ink, silver paint on canvas
82 3/4 x 87 1/2 in. / 210.2 x 222.3 cm
Stiftung Sammlung Marx, Hamburger Bahnhof – Museum für Gegenwart, Berlin

108 **Elvis I and II** 1964
Silkscreen ink, acrylic paint, silver paint on canvas
2 panels:
each 82 x 82 in. / 208.3 x 208.3 cm
Art Gallery of Ontario, Toronto
Gift from the Women's Committee Fund, 1966

109 **129 Die in Jet (Plane Crash)** 1962
Acrylic paint on canvas
100 x 72 in. / 254 x 183 cm
Museum Ludwig, Köln

110 **Woman Suicide** 1963
Silkscreen ink on canvas
123 1/4 x 83 in. / 313 x 211 cm
Kunstsammlung Nordrhein-Westfalen, Düsseldorf

111 **Suicide (Silver Jumping Man)** 1963
Silkscreen ink, silver paint on canvas
141 3/4 x 79 3/4 in. / 360 x 202.5 cm
Daros Collection, Switzerland

112 **Bellevue II** 1963
Silkscreen ink on canvas
82 x 82 in. / 208.3 x 208.3 cm
Stedelijk Museum, Amsterdam

113 **Suicide (Fallen Body)** 1963
Silkscreen ink, silver paint on canvas
112 x 80 3/8 in. / 284.5 x 204.2 cm
Courtesy Doris Ammann

114 **Black and White Disaster** 1962
Silkscreen enamel, acrylic paint on canvas
96 x 72 in. / 243.8 x 183 cm
Los Angeles County Museum of Art
Gift of Castelli & Ferus galleries through the Contemporary Art Council

115 **White Burning Car III** 1963
Silkscreen ink, synthetic polymer paint on canvas
100 x 78 3/4 in. / 254 x 200 cm
The Andy Warhol Museum, Pittsburgh
Founding Collection, Contribution Dia Center for the Arts

116 **Green Disaster 10 Times** 1963
Silkscreen ink, acrylic paint on canvas
105 3/8 x 79 1/8 in. / 267.5 x 201 cm
Museum für Moderne Kunst, Frankfurt am Main [Former Ströher Collection]

117 **Orange Car Crash Fourteen Times** 1963
Silkscreen ink, acrylic paint on canvas
2 panels: overall 105 7/8 x 164 1/8 in. / 268.9 x 416.9 cm
The Museum of Modern Art, New York
Gift of Philip Johnson, 1991

118 **Foot and Tire** 1963
Silkscreen ink, acrylic paint on canvas
80 1/4 x 144 3/4 in. / 203.8 x 367.7 cm
The Andy Warhol Museum, Pittsburgh
Founding Collection, Contribution Dia Center for the Arts

119 **Ambulance Disaster** **1963**
Silkscreen ink, acrylic paint on canvas
124 x 80 in. / 315 x 203 cm
Stiftung Sammlung Marx, Hamburger Bahnhof – Museum für Gegenwart, Berlin

120 **Gangster Funeral** **1963**
Silkscreen ink, acrylic paint, pencil on canvas
105 x $73\frac{3}{4}$ in. / 266.7 x 187.3 cm
The Andy Warhol Museum, Pittsburgh
Founding Collection, Contribution Dia Center for the Arts

121 **Race Riot** **1963**
Silkscreen ink, acrylic paint on canvas
$120\frac{7}{8}$ x $82\frac{5}{8}$ in. / 307 x 210 cm
Daros Collection, Switzerland

122 **Tunafish Disaster** **1963**
Silkscreen ink, acrylic paint on canvas
$124\frac{3}{8}$ x 83 in. / 316 x 211 cm
Daros Collection, Switzerland

123 **Silver Disaster** **1964**
Silkscreen ink, acrylic paint on canvas
$79\frac{7}{8}$ x $83\frac{1}{2}$ in. / 203 x 212 cm
Collection Bruno Bischofberger, Zürich

124 **Twelve Electric Chairs** **1964/65**
Silkscreen ink, acrylic paint on canvas
12 panels:
each 22 x 28 in. / 55.9 x 71.1 cm
Courtesy The Brant Foundation, Greenwich, CT

125 **Red Disaster** **1963, 1985**
Silkscreen ink, acrylic paint on canvas
2 panels:
each 93 x $80\frac{1}{4}$ in. / 236.2 x 203.8 cm
[The artist added the monochrome panel in 1985]
Museum of Fine Arts, Boston
Charles H. Bayley Picture and Painting Fund, 1986

126 **Big Electric Chair** **1967**
Silkscreen ink, acrylic paint on canvas
54 x 73 in. / 137.2 x 185.4 cm
Collection Froehlich, Stuttgart

127 **Big Electric Chair** **1967**
Silkscreen ink, acrylic paint on canvas
$54\frac{1}{8}$ x 73 in. / 137.3 x 185.4 cm
Stiftung Sammlung Marx, Hamburger Bahnhof – Museum für Gegenwart, Berlin

128 **Atomic Bomb** **1965**
Silkscreen ink, acrylic paint on canvas
104 x $80\frac{1}{2}$ in. / 264.2 x 204.5cm
Daros Collection, Switzerland

129 **Most Wanted Men No. 1, John M.** **1964**
Silkscreen ink on canvas
2 panels:
each 48 x 40 in. / 122 x 101.6 cm
Kaiser Wilhelm Museum Krefeld

130 **Most Wanted Men No. 2, John Victor G.** **1964**
Silkscreen ink on canvas
2 panels: Front-view panel:
$48\frac{1}{2}$ x 37 in. / 123.2 x 94 cm
Side-view panel:
$48\frac{1}{2}$ x $38\frac{5}{8}$ in. / 123.2 x 98.1 cm
Daros Collection, Switzerland

131 **Most Wanted Men No. 3, Ellis Ruez B.** **1964**
Silkscreen ink on canvas
48 x 40 in. / 122 x 101.6 cm
Daros Collection, Switzerland

132 **Most Wanted Men No. 4, Redmond C.** **1964**
Silkscreen ink on canvas
48 x 40 in. / 122 x 101.6 cm
Private collection, San Francisco

133 **Most Wanted Men No. 5, Arthur Alvin M.** **1964**
Silkscreen ink on canvas
2 panels:
each 48 x 39 in. / 122 x 99 cm
Courtesy The Brant Foundation, Greenwich, CT

134 **Most Wanted Men No. 6, Thomas Francis C.** **1964**
[Front-view panel]
Silkscreen ink on canvas
$47\frac{5}{8}$ x $39\frac{1}{2}$ in. / 121 x 100.3 cm
The Eli and Edythe L. Broad Collection, Los Angeles

135 **Most Wanted Men No. 6, Thomas Francis C.** **1964**
[Side-view panel]
Silkscreen ink on canvas
48 x 39 in. / 122 x 99 cm
The Eli and Edythe L. Broad Collection, Los Angeles

136 **Most Wanted Men No. 7, Salvatore V.** **1964**
Silkscreen ink on canvas
2 panels: each $39\frac{1}{8}$ x 39 in. / 99.3 x 99 cm
Museum Ludwig, Köln

137 **Most Wanted Men No. 8, Andrew F.** **1964**
Silkscreen ink on canvas
48 x 40 in. / 122 x 101.6 cm
Daros Collection, Switzerland

138 **Most Wanted Men No. 9, John S.** **1964**
Silkscreen ink on canvas
48 x 40 in. / 122 x 101.6 cm
Daros Collection, Switzerland

139 **Most Wanted Men No. 10, Louis Joseph M.** **1964**
Silkscreen ink on canvas
2 panels:
each 48 x 40 in. / 122 x 101.6 cm
Städtisches Museum Abteiberg Mönchengladbach

140 **Most Wanted Men No. 11, John Joseph H.** **1964**
Silkscreen ink on canvas
2 panels:
each 48 x 40 in. / 122 x 101.6 cm
Museum für Moderne Kunst, Frankfurt am Main
[Former Ströher Collection]

141 **Most Wanted Men No. 12, Frank B.** **1964**
Silkscreen ink on canvas
2 panels:
each 48 x 39 in. / 122 x 99 cm
The Andy Warhol Museum, Pittsburgh
Founding Collection, Contribution The Andy Warhol Foundation for the Visual Arts, Inc.

142 **Most Wanted Men No. 13, Joseph F.** **1964**
Silkscreen ink on canvas
2 panels:
each 48 x $39\frac{3}{4}$ in. / 122 x 101 cm
Sonnabend Collection

143 **Profile of a Woman (Jackie Kennedy)** **1964**
Pencil, crayon, gouache on paper
29 x $22\frac{3}{4}$ in. / 73.7 x 57.8 cm
Courtesy The Brant Foundation, Greenwich, CT

144 **16 Jackies** **1964**
Silkscreen ink, acrylic paint on canvas
16 panels:
each 20 x 16 in. / 50.8 x 40.6 cm
Courtesy The Brant Foundation, Greenwich, CT

145 **Gold Jackie** **1964**
Silkscreen ink, gold paint on canvas
2 tondi:
each 17$^{3}/_{4}$ in. / 45.1 cm diameter
Collection Froehlich, Stuttgart

146 **Twenty Jackies** **1964**
Silkscreen ink on canvas
20 panels: each 20 x 16 in. /
50.8 x 40.6 cm / overall
80$^{1}/_{2}$ x 80$^{1}/_{2}$ in. / 204.5 x 204.5 cm
Stiftung Sammlung Marx, Hamburger
Bahnhof – Museum für Gegenwart,
Berlin

147 **Self-Portrait** **1964**
Silkscreen ink, acrylic paint on canvas
20 x 16 in. / 50.8 x 40.6 cm
Private collection

148 **Self-Portrait** **1964**
Silkscreen ink, acrylic paint on canvas
20 x 16 in. / 50.8 x 40.6 cm
Courtesy The Brant Foundation,
Greenwich, CT

149 **Self-Portrait** **1964**
Silkscreen ink, acrylic paint on canvas
20 x 16 in. / 50.8 x 40.6 cm
Courtesy The Brant Foundation,
Greenwich, CT

150 **Self-Portrait** **1964**
Silkscreen ink, acrylic paint on canvas
20 $^{3}/_{16}$ x 17$^{1}/_{8}$ in. / 51.3 x 43.5 cm
The Andy Warhol Museum, Pittsburgh
Founding Collection, Contribution
Dia Center for the Arts

151 **Self-Portrait** **1964**
Silkscreen ink, acrylic paint on canvas
20 x 16$^{1}/_{8}$ in. / 50.8 x 41 cm
Collection Froehlich, Stuttgart

152 **Self-Portraits** **1966/67**
Silkscreen ink, acrylic paint on canvas
2 panels:
each 22 x 22 in. / 55.9 x 55.9 cm
Courtesy The Brant Foundation,
Greenwich, CT

153 **Self-Portrait** **1967**
Silkscreen ink, acrylic paint on canvas
72 x 72 in. / 183 x 183 cm
Collection Froehlich, Stuttgart

154 **Green Self-Portrait** **1967**
Silkscreen ink, acrylic paint on canvas
8 x 8 in. / 20.3 x 20.3 cm
Private collection, Houston

155 **Self-Portrait** **1967**
Silkscreen ink, acrylic paint on canvas
22 x 20 in. / 55.9 x 50.8 cm
Aaron I. Fleischman

156 **Marlon** **1966**
Silkscreen ink on canvas
80$^{1}/_{4}$ x 59 in. / 204 x 150 cm
Westdeutsche Spielbanken, Münster

157 **Kiss** **1965**
Screenprint on perplex
63 x 42$^{5}/_{8}$ in. / 160 x 108.3 cm
The Andy Warhol Museum, Pittsburgh
Founding Collection, Contribution
The Andy Warhol Foundation
for the Visual Arts, Inc.

158 **The Kiss (Bela Lugosi)** **1964**
Monotype on paper
30$^{1}/_{8}$ x 40 in. / 76.5 x 101.6 cm
Collection Sylvio Perlstein, Antwerp

159 **Campbell's Boxes (Tomato Juice)** **1964**
Silkscreen ink on plywood
10 boxes: each 10 x 18 x 9$^{1}/_{2}$ in. /
25.4 x 45.7 x 24 cm [H x W x D]
Courtesy Anthony d'Offay Gallery,
London

160 **Del Monte Boxes (Peach Halves)** **1964**
Silkscreen ink on plywood
6 boxes: each 9$^{1}/_{2}$ x 15$^{1}/_{2}$ x 12 in. /
24 x 39.4 x 30.5 cm [H x W x D]
Courtesy Anthony d'Offay Gallery,
London

161 **Heinz Boxes (Tomato Ketchup)** **1964**
Silkscreen ink on plywood
4 boxes: each 8$^{1}/_{2}$ x 15$^{1}/_{2}$ x 12 in. /
21.6 x 39.4 x 30.5 cm [H x W x D]
Courtesy Anthony d'Offay Gallery,
London

162 **Brillo Boxes** **1969**
Silkscreen ink on plywood
45 boxes: each 20 x 20 x 17 in. /
50.8 x 50.8 x 43.2 cm [H x W x D]
[Version of 1964 original]
Norton Simon Museum, Pasadena, CA
Gift of the Artist, 1969

163 **Silver Coke Bottles** **1967**
Silver paint on Coca-Cola bottles in
wooden crate
8$^{1}/_{4}$ x 18$^{1}/_{4}$ x 11$^{5}/_{8}$ in. /
21 x 46.4 x 30 cm [H x W x D]
Courtesy The Brant Foundation,
Greenwich, CT

164 **Flowers** **1964**
Silkscreen ink, acrylic paint on canvas
84 x 145$^{3}/_{8}$ in. / 213.4 x 369.3 cm
Stedelijk Museum, Amsterdam
Purchase through the Contribution of
›Vereniging Rembrandt‹

165 **Flowers** **1964**
Silkscreen ink, acrylic paint on canvas
70 x 140$^{1}/_{8}$ in. / 177.8 x 356 cm
Courtesy The Brant Foundation,
Greenwich, CT

166 **Ten-Foot Flowers** **1967**
Silkscreen ink, synthetic polymer paint
on canvas
115$^{1}/_{2}$ x 115$^{1}/_{2}$ in. / 293.7 x 293.7 cm
Collection Museum of Contemporary
Art, San Diego, Museum purchase
with contributions from the Museum
Art Council Fund

167 **Ten-Foot Flowers** **1967**
Silkscreen ink, acrylic paint on canvas
120 x 120 in. / 304.8 x 304.8 cm
Stiftung Sammlung Marx, Hamburger
Bahnhof – Museum für Gegenwart,
Berlin

168 **Ten-Foot Flowers** **1967**
Silkscreen ink, acrylic paint on canvas
120 x 120 in. / 304.8 x 304.8 cm
Private collection

169 **Cow (Wallpaper)** **1966**
Silkscreen ink on wallpaper
4 works:
each 45$^{1}/_{2}$ x 29$^{3}/_{4}$ in. / 115.6 x 75.6 cm
Private collection

170 **Mao** **1973**
Silkscreen ink, acrylic paint on canvas
50 x 42 in. / 127 x 106.6 cm
Private collection

171 **Vote McGovern** **1973**
Collage, screenprint on acetate,
acrylic paint on manila paper
42$^{1}/_{4}$ x 42$^{1}/_{4}$ in. / 107.3 x 107.3 cm
Courtesy The Brant Foundation,
Greenwich, CT

172 **Mao** **1972**
Silkscreen ink, acrylic paint,
pencil on canvas
81$^{3}/_{4}$ x 55$^{3}/_{4}$ in. / 207.6 x 141.6 cm
Collection Froehlich, Stuttgart

173 **Mao** **1973**
Pencil, crayon on paper
36$^{1}/_{4}$ x 36$^{1}/_{2}$ in. / 92.1 x 92.7 cm
Fondation H. Looser

174 **Mao** **1973**
Silkscreen ink, acrylic paint on canvas
176 1/2 x 136 1/4 in. / 448.3 x 346.1 cm
Stiftung Sammlung Marx, Hamburger Bahnhof – Museum für Gegenwart, Berlin

175 **Skull** **1976**
Silkscreen ink, acrylic paint on canvas
72 1/4 x 80 1/4 in. / 184.2 x 203.8 cm
Collection Froehlich, Stuttgart

176 **Skull** **1976**
Silkscreen ink, acrylic paint on canvas
72 1/8 x 80 1/2 in. / 183.2 x 204.5 cm
The Andy Warhol Museum, Pittsburgh
Founding Collection, Contribution
Dia Center for the Arts

177–182 **Skull** **1976**
6 panels
Silkscreen ink, acrylic paint on canvas
each 15 x 18 3/4 in. / 38.1 x 47.6 cm
Courtesy Anthony d'Offay Gallery, London

183 **Self-Portrait with Skull** **1978**
Silkscreen ink, acrylic paint on canvas
16 x 13 in. / 40.6 x 33 cm
Private collection

184 **Self-Portrait with Skull** **1978**
Silkscreen ink, acrylic paint on canvas
16 x 13 in. / 40.6 x 33 cm
Private collection

185 **Self-Portrait** **1978**
Silkscreen ink, acrylic paint on canvas
16 x 13 in. / 40.6 x 33 cm
Private collection

186 **Self-Portrait with Skull** **1978**
Silkscreen ink, acrylic paint on canvas
16 x 13 in. / 40.6 x 33 cm
Private collection

187–192 **Self-Portrait** **1978**
Silkscreen ink, acrylic paint on canvas
6 panels: each 16 x 13 in. / 40.6 x 33 cm
Courtesy Anthony d'Offay Gallery, London

193 **Liza Minnelli** **1979**
Silkscreen ink, acrylic paint on canvas
2 panels:
each 40 x 40 in. / 101.6 x 101.6 cm
The Andy Warhol Museum, Pittsburgh
Founding Collection, Contribution
Dia Center for the Arts

194 **Julia Warhola** **1974**
Silkscreen ink, acrylic paint on canvas
40 x 40 in. / 101.6 x 101.6 cm
Private collection

195 **Ileana Sonnabend** **1973**
Silkscreen ink, acrylic paint on canvas
2 panels:
each 40 x 40 in. / 101.6 x 101.6 cm
Sonnabend Collection

196 **Portrait of Leo** **1973**
Silkscreen ink, acrylic paint on canvas
40 x 40 in. / 101.6 x 101.6 cm
Schroeder Collection

197 **Jean-Michel Basquiat** **c. 1984**
Silkscreen ink, copper metallic paint on canvas
2 panels:
each 40 x 40 in. / 101.6 x 101.6 cm
The Andy Warhol Museum, Pittsburgh
Founding Collection, Contribution
The Andy Warhol Foundation for the Visual Arts, Inc.

198 **Dennis Hopper** **1971**
Silkscreen ink, acrylic paint on canvas
40 x 40 1/8 in. / 101.6 x 102 cm
Collection Froehlich, Stuttgart

199 **Mick Jagger** **1975**
Silkscreen ink, acrylic paint on canvas
2 panels:
each 40 x 40 in. / 101.6 x 101.6 cm
The Andy Warhol Museum, Pittsburgh
Founding Collection, Contribution
Dia Center for the Arts

200 **Portrait Ivan C. Karp** **1974**
Silkscreen ink, acrylic paint on canvas
40 x 40 in. / 101.6 x 101.6 cm
Courtesy O.K. Harris Works of Art, New York

201 **Portrait Thomas Ammann** **1978**
Silkscreen ink, acrylic paint on canvas
47 1/4 x 45 1/4 in. / 120 x 115 cm
Private collection; Courtesy Doris Ammann

202 **Portrait of Dominique** **1969**
Silkscreen enamel, acrylic paint on canvas
40 x 40 in. / 101.6 x 101.6 cm
The Menil Collection, Houston

203 **Portrait Erich Marx** **1978**
Silkscreen ink, acrylic paint on canvas
40 x 40 in. / 101.6 x 101.6 cm
Stiftung Sammlung Marx, Hamburger Bahnhof – Museum für Gegenwart, Berlin

204 **Portrait Peter Ludwig** **1980**
Silkscreen ink, acrylic paint on canvas
41 1/2 x 41 1/2 in. / 105.4 x 105.4 cm
Ludwig Forum für Internationale Kunst, Aachen – Collection Ludwig

205 **Portrait Joseph Beuys** **1980**
Silkscreen ink, acrylic paint, diamond dust on canvas
100 x 80 in. / 254 x 203.2 cm
Stiftung Sammlung Marx, Hamburger Bahnhof – Museum für Gegenwart, Berlin

206 **Shadow Painting** **1978**
Silkscreen ink, acrylic paint on canvas
76 3/4 x 161 3/8 in. / 195 x 410.5 cm
Courtesy The Brant Foundation, Greenwich, CT

207–210 **Diamond Dust Shadow** **c. 1979**
Silkscreen ink, acrylic paint, diamond dust on canvas
4 panels: each 78 x 50 in. / 198 x 127 cm
Private collection

211 **Oxidation Painting** **1978**
Mixed media, copper metallic paint on canvas
78 3/8 x 218 1/8 in. / 199 x 554 cm
Courtesy The Brant Foundation, Greenwich, CT

212 **Knives** **c. 1981-82**
Silkscreen ink, acrylic paint on canvas
90 x 70 in. / 228.5 x 177.8 cm
Stiftung Sammlung Marx, Hamburger Bahnhof – Museum für Gegenwart, Berlin

213 **Hammer and Sickle** **1976**
Silkscreen ink, acrylic paint on canvas
72 x 86 in. / 183 x 218.4 cm
Stiftung Sammlung Marx, Hamburger Bahnhof – Museum für Gegenwart, Berlin

214 **Multicolored Marilyn** **1979-1986**
Silkscreen ink, acrylic paint on canvas
18 1/8 x 13 3/4 in. / 46 x 34.9 cm
Stiftung Sammlung Marx, Hamburger Bahnhof – Museum für Gegenwart, Berlin

215 **Big Retrospective** 1979
Silkscreen ink, acrylic paint on canvas
81 1/2 x 425 in. / 207 x 1080 cm
Private collection; Courtesy Galerie Bruno Bischofberger, Zürich

216 **Mona Lisa Four Times** 1973
Silkscreen ink, acrylic paint on canvas
50 x 40 1/2 in. / 127 x 102.8 cm
Private collection, Germany

217 **Mona Lisa Four Times** 1978
Silkscreen ink, acrylic paint on canvas
50 x 40 1/2 in. / 127 x 102.8 cm
Private collection, Germany

218 **Four White On White And Four Gold On White Mona Lisas** 1979
Silkscreen ink, acrylic paint on canvas
52 3/4 x 80 1/4 in. / 134 x 204 cm
Collection Bruno Bischofberger, Zürich

219 **Cross** c. 1981-82
Silkscreen ink, acrylic paint on canvas
89 3/4 x 70 in. / 228 x 177.8 cm
Erzbischöfliches Diözesanmuseum Köln

220 **Fate Presto** 1981
Silkscreen ink, acrylic paint on canvas
106 1/4 x 78 3/4 in. / 270 x 200 cm
Stiftung Sammlung Marx, Hamburger Bahnhof – Museum für Gegenwart, Berlin

221 **Untitled (Skull and Crossbones)** c. 1985-86
Acrylic paint on paper
30 x 40 in. / 76.2 x 101.6 cm
Private collection, Germany

222 **Replica Guns** 1985-86
Acrylic paint on paper
30 5/8 x 40 1/4 in. / 77.8 x 102.2 cm
Courtesy The Brant Foundation, Greenwich, CT

223 **Gun** 1981
Silkscreen ink, acrylic paint on canvas
70 x 90 in. / 177.8 x 228.6 cm
Courtesy Anthony d'Offay Gallery, London

224 **The Berlin Friedrich Monument [Zeitgeist Series]** 1982
Silkscreen ink, acrylic paint on canvas
165 1/8 x 69 7/8 in. / 419.5 x 177.5
Stiftung Sammlung Marx, Hamburger Bahnhof – Museum für Gegenwart, Berlin

225 **Stadium [Zeitgeist Series]** 1982
Silkscreen ink, acrylic paint on canvas
180 x 70 in. / 457.2 x 177.8 cm
Bruno Bischofberger, Zürich

226 **Absolut Vodka** 1985
Acrylic paint on paper
31 3/4 x 24 in. / 80.6 x 61 cm
The Andy Warhol Museum, Pittsburgh Founding Collection, Contribution The Andy Warhol Foundation for the Visual Arts, Inc.

227 **Cosmetic Surgery** c. 1985/86
Pencil on paper
31 7/8 x 23 1/2 in. / 81 x 59.7 cm
The Andy Warhol Museum, Pittsburgh Founding Collection, Contribution The Andy Warhol Foundation for the Visual Arts, Inc.

228 **Hamburger** 1985/86
Acrylic paint on canvas
50 x 62 in. / 127 x 157.5 cm
Private collection, London

229 **Art** 1985
Silkscreen ink, synthetic polymer paint on canvas; 16 x 20 in. / 40.6 x 50.8 cm
Private collection

229a **Art** 1985
Silkscreen ink, synthetic polymer paint on canvas; 16 x 20 in. / 40.6 x 50.8 cm
Private collection

230 **Mineola Motorcycle** 1986
Silkscreen ink, synthetic polymer paint on canvas
72 x 80 in. / 182.8 x 203.2 cm
Private collection

231 **Ads: Rebel Without a Cause (James Dean)** c. 1985
Acrylic paint on paper
40 1/4 x 30 1/8 in. / 102.2 x 76.5 cm
The Andy Warhol Museum, Pittsburgh Founding Collection, Contribution The Andy Warhol Foundation for the Visual Arts, Inc.

232 **Head (After Picasso)** 1985
Acrylic paint on paper
31 7/8 x 24 in. / 81 x 61 cm
Private collection, Saarbrücken

233 **AIDS/Jeep/Bicycle** c. 1985
Acrylic paint on canvas
116 x 180 in. / 294.6 x 457.2 cm
Bayerische Staatsgemäldesammlungen, München

234 **Fabis Statue of Liberty** 1986
Silkscreen ink, acrylic paint on canvas
50 x 68 in. / 127x 172.7 cm
Stiftung Sammlung Marx, Hamburger Bahnhof – Museum für Gegenwart, Berlin

235 **Six Self-Portraits** 1986
Silkscreen ink, acrylic paint on canvas
6 panels:
each 22 x 22 in. / 55.9 x 55.9 cm
Collection Froehlich, Stuttgart

236 **Self-Portrait** 1986
Acrylic paint on paper
40 1/8 x 30 1/4 in. / 101.9 x 76.8 cm
The Andy Warhol Museum, Pittsburgh Founding Collection, Contribution The Andy Warhol Foundation for the Visual Arts, Inc.

237 **Self-Portrait** 1986
Silkscreen ink, acrylic paint on canvas
80 x 80 in. / 203.2 x 203.2 cm
Private collection

238 **Camouflage** 1986
Silkscreen ink, acrylic paint on canvas
116 x 426 in. / 294.6 x 1082 cm
Stiftung Sammlung Marx, Hamburger Bahnhof – Museum für Gegenwart, Berlin

239 **The Last Supper** 1986
Synthetic polymer paint on canvas
116 x 396 in. / 294.6 x 1005.8 cm
Courtesy The Brant Foundation, Greenwich, CT

240 **The Last Supper** 1986
Synthetic polymer paint, silkscreen ink on canvas
78 x 306 in. / 198.1 x 777.2 cm
The Andy Warhol Museum, Pittsburgh Founding Collection, Contribution The Andy Warhol Foundation for the Visual Arts, Inc.

Editorial remarks:

The information concerning the titles, the technique and measurements of works given in the available literature still varies greatly. The present catalogue entries therefore rely on the lenders' indications. Height precedes width and depth.
This checklist comprises works presented in Berlin and London, and does not reflect all changes made for the Los Angeles presentation.

SELECTED INDIVIDUAL EXHIBITIONS

Harriet Häußler

1952 New York, Hugo Gallery, *Andy Warhol: Fifteen Drawings Based on the Writings of Truman Capote.*

1954 New York, Loft Gallery, *Warhol.*

1956 New York, Bodley Gallery, *Drawings for a Boy-Book by Andy Warhol.*
New York, Bodley Gallery, *Andy Warhol: The Golden Slipper Show or Shoes Shoe in America.*

1957 New York, Bodley Gallery, *A Show of Golden Pictures by Andy Warhol.*

1959 New York, Bodley Gallery, *Andy Warhol: Wild Raspberries.*

1961 New York, Bonwit Teller, window display.

1962 Los Angeles, Ferus Gallery, *Andy Warhol. Campbell's Soup Cans.*
New York, Stable Gallery, *Andy Warhol* (Cat.).

1963 Los Angeles, Ferus Gallery, *Andy Warhol [Elvis Portraits].*

1964 Paris, Galerie Ileana Sonnabend, *Warhol* (Cat.).
New York, Stable Gallery, *Warhol [Brillo-Campbell's-Heinz-Boxes].*
New York, Leo Castelli Gallery, *Andy Warhol: Flowers* (Cat.).

1965 Paris, Galerie Ileana Sonnabend, *Andy Warhol: Flowers* (Cat.).
Buenos Aires, Galeria Rubbers, *Andy Warhol* (Cat.).
Philadelphia, University of Pennsylvania, Institute of Contemporary Art, *Andy Warhol* (Cat.).
Toronto, Jerrold Morris International Gallery, *Andy Warhol.*
Turin, Gian Enzo Sperone Arte Moderna, *Warhol* (Cat.).

1966 New York, Leo Castelli Gallery, *Andy Warhol: Wallpaper and Silver Clouds.*
Turin, Gian Enzo Sperone Arte Moderna, *Warhol.*
Cincinnati, Contemporary Arts Center, *Andy Warhol. Holy Cow! Silver Clouds!! Holy Cow!*
Los Angeles, Ferus Gallery, *Andy Warhol.*
Boston, The Institute of Contemporary Art, *Andy Warhol* (Cat.).

1967 Cologne, Galerie Rudolf Zwirner, *Kühe und schwebende Kissen von Andy Warhol.*
Paris, Galerie Ileana Sonnabend, *Andy Warhol: The Thirteen Most Wanted Men* (Cat.).
Hamburg, Galerie Hans Neuendorf, *Andy Warhol: The Thirteen Most Wanted Men.*
Cologne, Galerie Rudolf Zwirner, *Andy Warhol: Most Wanted.*

1968 Stockholm, Moderna Museet, *Andy Warhol* (Cat.); exh. travelled to: Amsterdam, Stedelijk Museum / Bern, Kunsthalle / Oslo, Kunstnernes Hus (Cat.).
London, Rowan Gallery, *Andy Warhol: Most Wanted Men.*

1969 Berlin, Nationalgalerie, *Andy Warhol* (Cat.).
New York, Castelli/Whitney Graphics, *Andy Warhol.*

1970 Pasadena, Pasadena Art Museum, *Andy Warhol* (Cat.); exh. travelled to: Chicago, Museum of Contemporary Art / Eindhoven, Stedelijk Van Abbemuseum / Paris, Musée d'Art Moderne de la Ville de Paris (Cat.) / London, The Tate Gallery (Cat.) / New York, Whitney Museum of American Art.

1971 Milan, Cenobio-Visualita, *Andy Warhol.*
New York, Gotham Book Mart Gallery, *Andy Warhol: His Early Works 1947-1959* (Cat.).
Krefeld, Museum Haus Lange, *Andy Warhol: Graphik, 1964 bis 1970.*

1972 Basel, Kunstmuseum, *Warhol Maos. Zehn Bildnisse von Mao Tse-tung* (Cat.).
Naples, Modern Art Agency, *Andy Warhol.*
Turin, Galleria Galatea, *Andy Warhol* (Cat.).
Minneapolis, MN, Walker Art Center, *Andy Warhol* [*Films*].
New York, Leo Castelli Gallery, *Andy Warhol: Mao Prints.*

1973 Los Angeles, Irving Blum Gallery, *Andy Warhol.*
Cleveland, New Gallery, *Andy Warhol.*
San Francisco, John Berggruen Gallery, *Andy Warhol.*

1974 Paris, Musée Galliera, *Andy Warhol: Mao.*
Milwaukee, Art Museum, *Warhol.*
Milan, Galleria Il Fauno, *Andy Warhol* (Cat.).
Washington, D. C., Max Protetch Gallery, *Andy Warhol: Old Paintings, New Prints.*
Paris, Galerie Ileana Sonnabend, *Andy Warhol.*
London, Mayor Gallery, *Andy Warhol.*
Bogotá, Museo de Arte Moderno, *Andy Warhol* (Cat.).
Toronto, Jared Sable Gallery, *Andy Warhol.*

1975 Baltimore, The Baltimore Museum of Art, *Andy Warhol: Paintings 1962-1975.*
Los Angeles, Margo Leavin Gallery, *Andy Warhol: Paintings.*
Minneapolis, Locksley Shea Gallery, *Andy Warhol.*
New York, Leo Castelli Gallery, *Andy Warhol: Hand-Colored Flowers.*
Washington, D. C., Max Protetch Gallery, *Andy Warhol.*

1976 Stuttgart, Württembergischer Kunstverein, *Andy Warhol: Das zeichnerische Werk 1942-1975* (Cat.); exh. travelled to: Düsseldorf, Städtische Kunsthalle / Bremen, Kunsthalle / Munich, Städtische Galerie im Lenbachhaus / Berlin, Haus am Waldsee / Vienna, Museum Moderner Kunst, Museum des 20. Jahrhunderts / Lucerne, Kunstmuseum.
London, Mayor Gallery, *Cats and Dogs by Andy Warhol.*
New York, Arno Schefler, *Andy Warhol: Animals.*
Boissano, Centro Internazionale di Sperimentazioni Artistiche Marie-Louise Jeanneret, *Andy Warhol: 1974-1976* (Cat.).

1977 Washington, D. C., Pyramid Galleries, *Retrospective Exhibition of Paintings by Andy Warhol from 1962-1976.*
Paris, Galerie Daniel Templon, *Andy Warhol: Hammer and Sickle.*
Essen, Museum Folkwang, *Andy Warhol Flash, Electric Chair, Campbell's Soup Serigraphien.*
Geneva, Musée d'Art et d'Histoire, *Andy Warhol: The American Indian* (Cat.).
New York, Coe Kerr Gallery, *Athletes by Andy Warhol.*
Toronto, Sable-Castelli Gallery, *Andy Warhol.*
Cologne, Galerie Heiner Friedrich, *Andy Warhol.*
New York, Leo Castelli Gallery, *Andy Warhol.*

1978 Dallas, University Gallery, Southern Methodist University, *Andy Warhol: Portraits.*
Richmond, Virginia Museum of Fine Arts: *Athletes by Andy Warhol.*
Zurich, Kunsthaus, *Andy Warhol* (Cat.); exh. travelled to:
– Humlebæk, Louisiana Museum of Modern Art (Cat.).
London, Institute of Contemporary Arts, *Andy Warhol: Athletes.*
Venice, CA, Ace Gallery, *Andy Warhol: Torsos.*
New York, Blum Helman Gallery, *Andy Warhol: Early Paintings.*

1979 New York, Heiner Friedrich Gallery, *Andy Warhol: Shadows.*
Milan, Massimo Valsecchi, *Andy Warhol: Skulls.*
Vancouver, Ace Gallery, *Andy Warhol: Torsos.*
Hartford, Wadsworth Atheneum, *Andy Warhol* (Cat.); exh. travelled to: Berkeley, University Art Museum.
Baltimore, Arts Gallery, *Andy Warhol: Multiple Images – Landscapes, City Spaces, Country Places.*
New York, Whitney Museum of American Art, *Andy Warhol: Portraits of the 70s.* (Cat.).

1980 Naples, Galleria Lucio Amelio, *Joseph Beuys by Andy Warhol.*
Zurich, Galerie Bruno Bischofberger, *Andy Warhol: Reversals* (Cat.).
Cologne, Museum Ludwig, *Andy Warhol: Fotografien.*
Amsterdam, Stedelijk Museum, *Andy Warhol: Exposures.*
Geneva, Centre d'Art Contemporain, *Joseph Beuys by Andy Warhol.*
Portland, OR, Portland Center for the Visual Arts, *Andy Warhol: Paintings and Prints.*
Coral Gables, FL, University of Miami, Lowe Art Museum, *Andy Warhol: Ten Portraits of Jews of the Twentieth Century* (Cat.).
London, Lisson Gallery, *Andy Warhol: Photographs.*
Paris, Galerie Daniel Templon, *Andy Warhol: Œuvres récentes, Reversal.*

Munich, Schellmann & Klüser, *Beuys by Warhol.*
New York, The Jewish Museum, *Andy Warhol: Portraits of Jews of the Twentieth Century*; exh. travelled to: Akron, Akron Art Museum, OH.

1981 Vienna, Museum Moderner Kunst, Museum des 20. Jahrhunderts, *Warhol '80: Reversal Serie* (Cat.).
New York, Ronald Feldman Fine Arts, *Andy Warhol: Myths* (Cat.).
Boston, Thomas Segal Gallery, *Andy Warhol: Myths 1981.*
Tokyo, Watari Gallery, *Andy Warhol: The Shoe Portfolio.*
New York, Castelli Graphics, *Andy Warhol: A Print Retrospective.*
Fort Collins, Colorado State University, *Andy Warhol at Colorado State University* (Cat.).
Hanover, Kestner-Gesellschaft, *Andy Warhol: Bilder 1961 bis 1981* (Cat.); exh. travelled to: Munich, Städtische Galerie im Lenbachhaus.

1982 New York, Leo Castelli Gallery, *Andy Warhol Reversals.*
New York, Leo Castelli Gallery, *Andy Warhol: Dollar Signs.*
Chicago, Marianne Deson Gallery, *Andy Warhol: Myths.*
Thun, Kunstsammlung Thun, *Andy Warhol: Schweizer Portraits* (Cat.).
Paris, Galerie Daniel Templon, *Andy Warhol: Dollar Signs.*
San Francisco, Modernism, *Andy Warhol: Myths.*
Nice, Galerie des Ponchettes, *Warhol au plus juste* (Cat.).
East Hampton, NY, Castelli-Goodman, *Andy Warhol: Dollar Signs/Knives/Guns.*
Dover, Dover Museum, *Andy Warhol: Portrait Screenprints 1965-80*; exh. travelled to: Ashington, Wansbeck Square Gallery / Lincoln, Usher Gallery / Aberystwyth, Arts Center.
Rome, Campidoglio, *Warhol verso de Chirico* (Cat.).
Madrid, Galeria Fernando Vijande, *Andy Warhol: Guns, Knives, Crosses* (Cat.).

1983 New York, American Museum of Natural History, *Warhol's Animals: Species at Risk* (Cat.).
Ridgefield, CT, Aldrich Museum of Contemporary Art, *Andy Warhol in the 1980's* (Cat.); exh. travelled to: Aspen, CO, Aspen Center for the Visual Arts.
San Francisco, Fraenkel Gallery, *Andy Warhol's Electric Chairs.*
Zurich, Galerie Bruno Bischofberger, *Andy Warhol: Paintings for Children* (Cat.).

1984 Zurich, Galerie Bruno Bischofberger, *Collaborations: Jean-Michel Basquiat, Francesco Clemente, Andy Warhol* (Cat.).
Malmö, Galerie Börjeson, *Portraits of Ingrid Bergman by Andy Warhol* (Cat.).
London, Waddington Graphics, *Andy Warhol: Renaissance Paintings.*
New York, Schellmann & Klüser Gallery, *Andy Warhol: Details of Renaissance Paintings.*

1985 New York, Leo Castelli Gallery, *Andy Warhol: Reigning Queens 1985.*
New York, Amelie A. Wallace Gallery, State University of New York at Old Westbury, *Ads.*
New York, Tony Shafrazi Gallery, *Warhol, Basquiat Paintings.*
New York, Lehman College, Art Gallery, *The Silkscreens of Andy Warhol: 1962-1985.*
Cologne, Paul Maenz Gallery, *Andy Warhol: Paintings 1962-1985 & Early Prints.*
Naples, Museo di Capodimonte, *Vesuvius by Warhol* (Cat.).

1986 New York, Dia Art Foundation, *Andy Warhol: Disaster Paintings 1963.*
Paris, Galerie Daniel Templon, *Andy Warhol: Major Prints.*
London, Anthony d'Offay Gallery, *Andy Warhol. Self-Portraits.*
New York, Robert Miller Gallery, *Andy Warhol: Photographs* (Cat.).
New York, Dia Art Foundation, *Hand-Painted Images: Andy Warhol 1960-1962.*
New York, Larry Gagosian Gallery, *Andy Warhol: Oxidation Paintings.*

1987 Milan, Refettorio delle Stelline, *Andy Warhol: Il Cenacolo* (Cat.).
Houston, The Menil Collection, Richmond Hall, *Warhol Shadows* (Cat.).
Hamburg, Kunstverein in Hamburg, *Andy Warhol : "Ich erkannte, daß alles, was ich tue, mit dem Tod zusammenhängt"* (Cat.).
Tokyo, Watari Gallery, *Remembering Andy: Warhol's Recent Works* (Cat.).
Munich, Galerie Bernd Klüser, *Lenin by Warhol* (Cat.).
New York, Leo Castelli Gallery, *Andy Warhol: Recent Work.*
Bridgehampton, Dia Art Foundation, *Andy Warhol: A Memorial* (Cat.).
New York, Dia Art Foundation, *Andy Warhol: Skulls 1976.*
Salzburg, Galerie Thaddaeus Ropac, *Andy Warhol: Arbeiten / Works 1962-1986* (Cat.).

1988 Houston, The Menil Collection, *Andy Warhol: Death and Disasters* (Cat.).
New York, Whitney Museum of American Art, *The Films of Andy Warhol* (Cat.).
New York, Larry Gagosian Gallery, *Andy Warhol: Most Wanted Men.*
Bogotá, Galeria Fernando Quintana, *Andy Warhol* (Cat.).
Munich, Edition Schellmann, *Andy Warhol: Working Proofs and Unique Prints 1972-1987.*
Tübingen, Kunsthalle, *Andy Warhol. Cars: Die letzten Bilder* (Cat.); exh. travelled to: Bern, Kunstmuseum / New York, The Solomon R. Guggenheim Museum.

1989 New York, Grey Art Gallery, *Success is a Job in New York.... The Early Art and Business of Andy Warhol* (Cat.); exh. travelled to: Pittsburgh, The Carnegie Museum of Art / Philadelphia, University of Pennsylvania, Institute of Contemporary Art / London, Serpentine Gallery / Newport Beach, Newport Harbor Art Museum / Turin, Lingotto / Jouy-en-Josas, Fondation Cartier pour l'Art Contemporain.
London, Anthony d'Offay Gallery, *Andy Warhol: Self-Portraits 1964 to 1986* (Cat.).
New York, Larry Gagosian Gallery, *Andy Warhol: Shadow Paintings* (Cat.).
Detroit, Institute of Arts, *Andy Warhol: Fifteen Minutes of Fame* (Cat.).
Reggio Emilia, Teatro Municipale 'Romolo Valli', *Le cento immagine di Andy Warhol* (Cat.); exh. travelled to: Genoa, Museo d'Arte Contemporanea Villa Croce / Bolzano, Castel Mareccio / Milan, Società per la Bella Arte / Salerno, Pinacoteca Provinciale / Lyon, Espace Lyonnais Art Contemporaine.
New York, The Museum of Modern Art, *Andy Warhol: A Retrospective* (Cat.); exh. travelled to: Chicago, The Art Institute of Chicago / London, Hayward Gallery / Cologne, Museum Ludwig / Venice, Palazzo Grassi / Paris, Musée national d'art moderne, Centre Georges Pompidou.

1990 Humlebæk, Louisiana Museum of Modern Art, *Andy Warhol* (Cat.).
Jouy-en-Josas, Fondation Cartier pour l'Art Contemporain, *The Prints of Andy Warhol* (Cat.).
New York, Jason McCoy Inc., *Andy Warhol: Self-Portraits* (Cat.).

1991 Tokyo, Isetan Museum, *Andy Warhol 1982-1987* (Cat.); exh. travelled to: Vienna, KunstHausWien / Athens, Ethniki Pinakothiki Museum Alexander Soytsos / Orlando, Museum of Modern Art / Fort Lauderdale, FL, Museum of Art.

1992 New York, Larry Gagosian Gallery, *Andy Warhol: Heaven and Hell Are Just One Breath Away! Late Paintings and Related Works, 1984-1986* (Cat.).
Bridgehampton, NY, Dia Art Foundation, *Andy Warhol: Oxidation Paintings.*
Augsburg, Zeughaus, *Pop goes Art: Warhol & Velvet Underground.*
Zurich, Galerie Bruno Bischofberger, *Andy Warhol: Works of the Sixties.*

1993 Vienna, KunstHausWien, *Andy Warhol: 1928-1987* (Cat.).
Basel, Kunsthalle, *Andy Warhol: abstrakt* (Cat.); exh. travelled to: Vienna, Museum für Angewandte Kunst / Rotterdam, Kunsthal / Malmö, Rooseum / Valencia, I.V.A.M., Centro Julio Gónzales.
Sydney, Museum of Contemporary Art, *Andy Warhol: Portraits of the Seventies and Eighties* (Cat.); exh. travelled to: London, Anthony d'Offay Gallery.
Hamburg, Deichtorhallen, *Andy Warhol: Retrospektiv* (Cat.); exh. travelled to: Stuttgart, Württembergischer Kunstverein.
Houston, The Menil Collection, *Andy Warhol: Abstract Paintings*.

1994 Cologne, Edition Schellmann, *Andy Warhol: Art from Art. Unique Screenprints, Drawings and Collages* (Cat.).
Seoul, The Ho-Am Art Gallery, *Andy Warhol: The Last Supper Paintings*.
Oslo, The Henie-Onstad Art Center, *Andy Warhol*.
New York, Dia Center for the Arts, *Andy Warhol: The Last Supper Paintings* (Cat.).

1995 New York, Robert Miller Gallery, *Andy Warhol Nudes*.
Lucerne, Kunstmuseum, *Andy Warhol: Paintings 1960-1986* (Cat.).
London, Anthony d'Offay Gallery, *Andy Warhol: Vanitas: Skulls and Self-Portraits 1976-1986* (Cat.).

1996 Tokyo, Museum of Contemporary Art, *Andy Warhol: 1956-86. Mirror of His Time* (Cat.); exh. travelled to: Fukuoka, Art Museum/ Kobe, Hyogo Prefectural Museum of Modern Art.
New York, Gagosian Gallery, *Andy Warhol: Rorschach Paintings* (Cat.).

1997 Cologne, Jablonka Galerie, *Eggs by Andy Warhol* (Cat.).
New York, Tony Shafrazi Gallery, *Andy Warhol: Thirty Are Better Than One* (Cat.).
Paris, Galerie Thaddaeus Ropac, *Andy Warhol: Heads (After Picasso)* (Cat.).
London, Anthony d'Offay Gallery, *Andy Warhol: Gun Paintings*.
Beverly Hills, CA, Gagosian Gallery, *Andy Warhol: $* (Cat.).
Tokyo, Parco Gallery, *"F" Andy Warhol's Factory Photos. Foto by Billy Name* (Cat.).
Dublin, The Irish Museum of Modern Art, *After the Party. Andy Warhol Works 1957-1986* (Cat.).

1998 Cologne, Jablonka Galerie, *Andy Warhol: Knives* (Cat.).
Basel, Kunstmuseum, *Andy Warhol: Zeichnungen 1942-1987* (Cat.); exh. travelled to: Kleve, Museum Schloß Moyland / Tübingen, Kunsthalle / Linz, Neue Galerie der Stadt Linz / Minneapolis, Walker Art Center / Pittsburgh, The Andy Warhol Museum.
Munich, Staatsgalerie moderner Kunst, *Andy Warhol: The Last Supper* (Cat.); exh. travelled to: New York, Guggenheim Museum SoHo.
Wolfsburg, Kunstmuseum, *Andy Warhol: A Factory* (Cat.); exh. travelled to: Vienna, Kunsthalle / Brussels, Palais des Beaux-Arts / Bilbao, Guggenheim Museum.
New York, Gagosian Gallery, *Andy Warhol: Camouflage* (Cat.).
New York, Dia Center for the Arts, *Andy Warhol: Shadows* (Cat.).

1999 London, Anthony d'Offay Gallery, *Andy Warhol: Paintings and Sculpture*.
Cologne, Diözesanmuseum, *Andy Warhol: Crosses* (Cat.).
Paris, Galerie Thaddaeus Ropac, *Andy Warhol: The Statue of Liberty* (Cat.).
Hamburg, Kunsthalle, *Andy Warhol: Photography* (Cat.); exh. travelled to: Pittsburgh, The Andy Warhol Museum / New York, International Center of Photography.
New York, Gagosian Gallery, *Andy Warhol: Philip's Skull* (Cat.).
Zurich, Thomas Ammann Fine Art, *Andy Warhol: Hammer and Sickle* (Cat.).
New York, Gagosian Gallery, *Andy Warhol: Diamond Dust Shoes* (Cat.).
Hartford, CT, Wadsworth Atheneum, *About Face: Andy Warhol Portraits* (Cat.); exh. travelled to: Miami, Art Museum.

2000 New York, C & M Arts, *Women of Andy Warhol: Marilyn, Liz & Jackie* (Cat.).
Humlebæk, Louisiana Museum of Modern Art, *Andy Warhol and his World* (Cat.).
New York, Gagosian Gallery, *Andy Warhol: Diamond Dust Shadow Paintings* (Cat.).
Paris, Galerie Thaddaeus Ropac, *Andy Warhol: Campbell's Soup Boxes* (Cat.).
Basel, Fondation Beyeler, *Andy Warhol: Series and Singles* (Cat.).

2001 Zurich, Galerie Bruno Bischofberger, *Andy Warhol: Visual Memory* (Cat.).
New York, Stellan Holm Gallery, *Andy Warhol: Little Electric Chair Paintings* (Cat.).

SELECTED CATALOGUES

1962 *Andy Warhol*. New York, Stable Gallery.

1964 *Warhol*. Paris, Galerie Ileana Sonnabend.
Andy Warhol: Flowers. New York, Leo Castelli Gallery.

1965 Otto Hahn, *Andy Warhol*. Paris, Galerie Ileana Sonnabend.
Jorge Romero Brest, *Andy Warhol*. Buenos Aires, Galeria Rubbers.
Samuel Adams Green, *Andy Warhol*. Philadelphia, Institute of Contemporary Art, University of Pennsylvania.
Luigi Carluccio, *Warhol*. Turin, Gian Enzo Sperone Arte Moderna.

1966 Alan Solomon, *Andy Warhol*. Boston, Institute of Contemporary Art.

1967 *Andy Warhol – The Thirteen Most Wanted Men*. Paris, Galerie Ileana Sonnabend.

1968 Pontus Hultén, Kaspar König, Olle Granath, *Andy Warhol*. Stockholm, Moderna Museet.
Morten Krohg, *Andy Warhol*. Oslo, Kunstnernes Hus.

1969 *Andy Warhol*. Berlin, Nationalgalerie und Deutsche Gesellschaft für Bildende Kunst.

1970 John Coplans, *Andy Warhol*. Pasadena, Pasadena Art Museum.

1971 Richard Morphet, *Andy Warhol*. London, The Tate Gallery.
Alfred Pacquement, Gilbert Brownstone, *Andy Warhol*. Paris, Musée d'Art Moderne de la Ville de Paris.
Andreas Brown, *Andy Warhol: His Early Works, 1947-1959*. New York, Gotham Book Mart Gallery.

1972 *Warhol Maos: Zehn Bildnisse von Mao Tse-tung*. Basel, Kunstmuseum.
Maria Chiaretti, *Andy Warhol*. Turin, Galleria Galatea.

1974 *Warhol*. Milan, Galleria Il Fauno.
Eduardo Serrano, *Andy Warhol*. Bogotá, Museo de Arte Moderno.

1976 Rainer Crone, *Andy Warhol: Das zeichnerische Werk 1942-1962*. Stuttgart, Württembergischer Kunstverein.
Marcello Levi, *Andy Warhol: 1974-1976*. Boissano, Centro Internazionale di Sperimentazioni Artistiche Marie-Louise Jeanneret.

1977 Rainer Michael Mason, *The American Indian: Une série de six dessins et onze peintures d'Andy Warhol*. Geneva, Musée d'Art et d'Histoire.

1978 Erika Billeter, *Andy Warhol: Ein Buch zur Ausstellung im Kunsthaus Zürich*. Zurich, Kunsthaus.
Andy Warhol. Humlebæk, Louisiana Museum of Modern Art.

1979 John Paoletti, *Andy Warhol*. Hartford, Wadsworth Atheneum.
David Whitney (ed.), *Andy Warhol: Portraits of the 70s*. New York, Whitney Museum of American Art.

1980 *Andy Warhol: Reversals*. Zurich, Galerie Bruno Bischofberger.
Ira Licht, *Andy Warhol: Ten Portraits of Jews of the Twentieth Century*. Coral Gables, FL / Lowe Art Museum, University of Miami.

1981 Dieter Schrage, *Warhol '80. Reversal Serie*. Vienna, Museum Moderner Kunst, Museum des 20. Jahrhunderts.

Andy Warhol: Myths. New York, Ronald Feldman Fine Arts.
Andy Warhol at Colorado State University. Fort Collins, Colorado State University.
Carl Haenlein, *Andy Warhol: Bilder 1961 bis 1981*. Hanover, Kestner-Gesellschaft.
1982 Georg J. Dolezal, *Andy Warhol: Schweizer Portraits*. Thun, Kunstsammlung Thun.
Claude Fournet, *Warhol au plus juste*. Nice, Galerie des Ponchettes.
Achille Bonito Oliva, *Warhol verso de Chirico*. Rome, Campidoglio.
Rodrigo Vijande, *Andy Warhol: Guns, Knives, Crosses*. Madrid, Galeria Fernando Vijande.
1983 *Warhol's Animals: Species at Risk*. New York, American Museum of Natural History.
Andy Warhol in the 1980's. Ridgefield, CT, Aldrich Museum of Contemporary Art.
Andy Warhol: Paintings for Children. Zurich, Edition Galerie Bruno Bischofberger.
1984 *Collaborations. Jean-Michel Basquiat, Francesco Clemente, Andy Warhol*. Zurich, Edition Galerie Bruno Bischofberger.
Per-Olov Börjeson, *Portraits of Ingrid Bergman by Andy Warhol*, Malmö, Galerie Börjeson.
1985 Michele Bonuomo, Angela Tecce, *Vesuvius by Warhol*. Naples, Museo di Capodimonte.
1986 Stephen Koch, *Andy Warhol Photographs*. New York, Robert Miller Gallery.
1987 Alexandre Iolas, *Warhol: Il Cenacolo*. Milan, Refettorio delle Stelline.
Warhol Shadows. Houston, The Menil Collection.
Karl-Egon Vester (ed.), *Andy Warhol: "Ich erkannte, daß alles, was ich tue, mit dem Tod zusammenhängt"*. Hamburg, Kunstverein in Hamburg.
Remembering Andy: Warhol's Recent Works. Tokyo, Watari Gallery.
Lenin by Warhol. Munich, Galerie Bernd Klüser.
Henry Geldzahler, *Andy Warhol: A Memorial*. Bridgehampton, NY, Dia Art Foundation.
Andy Warhol: Arbeiten/Works, 1962-1986. Salzburg, Galerie Thaddaeus Ropac.
1988 Walter Hopps, *Andy Warhol: Death and Disasters*. Houston, The Menil Collection.
The Films of Andy Warhol. New York, Whitney Museum of American Art.
Henry Geldzahler, *Andy Warhol*. Bogotá, Galeria Fernando Quintana.
Werner Spies, *Andy Warhol. Cars: Die letzten Bilder*. Tübingen, Kunsthalle.
1989 Donna De Salvo, *"Success is a Job in New York.... The Early Art and Business of Andy Warhol"*. New York, Grey Art Gallery.
Andy Warhol: *Self-Portraits 1964 to 1986*. London, Anthony d'Offay Gallery.
Andy Warhol: Shadow Paintings. New York, Gagosian Gallery.
Andy Warhol: Fifteen Minutes of Fame. Detroit, Detroit Institute of Arts.
Attilio Codognato, *Le Cento Immagini di Andy Warhol: opere grafiche*. Reggio Emilia, Teatro Municipale 'Romolo Valli'.
Kynaston McShine (ed.), *Andy Warhol: A Retrospective*. New York, The Museum of Modern Art.
1990 *Andy Warhol: A Retrospective*. Humlebæk, Louisiana Museum of Modern Art.
The Prints of Andy Warhol. Jouy-en-Josas, Fondation Cartier pour l'Art Contemporain.
Andy Warhol: Self-Portraits. New York, Jason McCoy.
1991 *Andy Warhol 1982-1987*. Tokyo, Isetan Museum.
1992 *Andy Warhol: Heaven and Hell Are Just One Breath Away! Late Paintings and Related Works, 1984-1986*. New York, Gagosian Gallery.
1993 Thomas Kellein, *Andy Warhol: abstrakt*. Basel, Kunsthalle.
Jacob Baal-Teshuva, *Andy Warhol 1928-1987*. Vienna, KunstHausWien.
Andy Warhol: Portraits of the Seventies and Eighties. London, Anthony d'Offay Gallery.
Felix Zdenek, *Andy Warhol: Retrospektiv*. Hamburg, Deichtorhallen.
1994 Jörg Schellmann (ed.), *Andy Warhol: Art from Art*. Cologne, Edition Schellmann.
Andy Warhol: The Last Supper Paintings. New York, Dia Center for the Arts.
1995 *Andy Warhol: Vanitas: Skulls and Self-Portraits 1976-1986*. London, Anthony d'Offay Gallery.
Martin Schwander (ed.), *Andy Warhol: Paintings 1960-1986*. Lucerne, Kunstmuseum.
1996 *Andy Warhol: 1956-86: Mirror of His Time*. Tokyo, Museum of Contemporary Art.
Andy Warhol: Rorschach Paintings. New York, Gagosian Gallery.
1997 *Eggs by Andy Warhol*. Cologne, Jablonka Galerie.
Andy Warhol: Thirty Are Better Than One. New York, Tony Shafrazi Gallery.
Andy Warhol: Heads (After Picasso). Paris, Galerie Thaddaeus Ropac.
Andy Warhol: $. Beverly Hills, CA, Gagosian Gallery.
"F" Andy Warhol's Factory Photos. Factory Foto by Billy Name. Tokyo, Parco Gallery.
After the Party: Andy Warhol Works 1956-1986. Dublin, The Irish Museum of Modern Art.
1998 *Andy Warhol: Knives*. Cologne, Jablonka Galerie.
Mark Francis, Dieter Koepplin, *Andy Warhol: Zeichnungen 1942-1987*. Pittsburgh, The Andy Warhol Museum / Basel, Kunstmuseum.
Carla Schulz-Hoffmann, *Andy Warhol. The Last Supper*. Munich, Staatsgalerie Moderner Kunst.
Andy Warhol: A Factory. New York, Solomon R. Guggenheim Museum / Wolfsburg, Kunstmuseum.
Ealan Wingate (ed.), *Andy Warhol: Camouflage*. New York, Gagosian Gallery.
Andy Warhol: Shadows. New York, Dia Center for the Arts.
1999 *Andy Warhol: Crosses*. Cologne, Diözesanmuseum.
Andy Warhol: The Statue of Liberty. Paris, Galerie Thaddaeus Ropac.
Andy Warhol: Philip's Skull. New York, Gagosian Gallery.
Andy Warhol: Photography. Hamburg, Hamburger Kunsthalle / Pittsburgh, The Andy Warhol Museum.
Georg Frei (ed.), *Andy Warhol: Hammer and Sickle*. Zurich, Thomas Ammann Fine Art.
Andy Warhol: Diamond Dust Shoes. New York, Gagosian Gallery.
Nicholas Baume (ed.), *About Face: Andy Warhol Portraits*. Hartford, Wadsworth Atheneum, CT.
2000 Robert Pincus-Witten, *Women of Warhol: Marilyn, Liz & Jackie*. New York, C & M Arts.
Andy Warhol and His World. Humlebæk, Louisiana Museum of Modern Art.
Andy Warhol: Diamond Dust Shadow Paintings. New York, Gagosian Gallery.
Andy Warhol: Series and Singles. Basel, Fondation Beyeler.
Andy Warhol: Campbell's Soup Boxes. Paris/Salzburg, Galerie Thaddaeus Ropac.
2001 Bruno Bischofberger, *Andy Warhol's Visual Memory*. Zurich, Galerie Bruno Bischofberger.
Andy Warhol: Little Electric Chair Paintings. New York, Stellan Holm Gallery.
Heiner Bastian, *Andy Warhol Retrospektive*, Berlin, Neue Nationalgalerie / London, Tate Modern.

SELECTED BOOKS

1970 Rainer Crone, *Andy Warhol.* Stuttgart: Verlag Gert Hatje.

1972 *Andy Warhol: Transcript of David Bailey's ATV Documentary.* London: Bailey Litchfield / Matthews Miller Dunbar Ltd.

Rainer Crone, Winfried Wiegand, *Die revolutionäre Ästhetik Andy Warhols.* Darmstadt: Melzer Verlag.

1976 Rainer Crone, *Das bildnerische Werk Andy Warhols.* Berlin: Kommisionsvertrieb Wasmuth.

1981 *Andy Warhol: Portrait Screenprints, 1965-1980.* London: Arts Council of Great Britain.

1983 Carter Ratcliff, *Andy Warhol.* New York: Abbeville Press.

1985 Stephen Koch, *Stargazer: Andy Warhol's World and His Films.* 2nd ed., New York: Marion Boyars [1st ed., New York: Praeger, 1973].

1986 Patrick S. Smith, *Andy Warhol's Art and Films.* Ann Arbor, MI: UMI Research Press.

Jesse Kornbluth, *Pre-Pop Warhol.* New York: Random House.

Christopher Makos, *Warhol: A Personal Photographic Memoir.* London: W. H. Allen.

Patrick S. Smith, *Warhol: Conversations About the Artist.* Ann Arbor, MI: UMI Research Press.

1989 Victor Bockris, *Warhol: The Biography.* London: Frederick Muller.

David Bourdon, *Warhol.* New York: Harry N. Abrams.

Gary Garrels (ed.), *The Work of Andy Warhol.* New York: Dia Art Foundation / Seattle: Bay Press.

Pat Hackett (ed.), *The Andy Warhol Diaries,* New York: Warner Books.

Nat Finkelstein, *Andy Warhol: "Oh this is fabulous." The Silver Age at the Factory 1964-1967.* Rotterdam: Bébert Editions.

1990 Heiner Bastian (ed.), *Silkscreens from the Sixties.* Munich: Schirmer / Mosel.

Bob Colacello, *Holy Terror: Andy Warhol Close Up.* New York: Harper Collins Publishers.

1991 Eric Shanes, *Warhol: The Masterworks.* London: Studio Editions.

Mike Wrenn, *Andy Warhol in his own words.* London / New York / Sydney: Omnibus Press.

1992 Gudrun Inboden, *Andy Warhol: White Disaster I, 1963.* Stuttgart: Edition Cantz.

Stefana Sabin, *Andy Warhol: Mit Selbstzeugnissen und Bilddokumenten.* Reinbek: Rowohlt.

1993 Lothar Romain, *Andy Warhol.* Munich: Bruckmann.

John Yau, *In the Realm of Appearances: The Art of Andy Warhol.* Hopewell, N.J.: The Ecco Press.

Mamoru Yonekura, *Andy Warhol.* Tokyo: Kodansha Ltd.

1994 The Andy Warhol Museum, Pittsburgh (ed.), *The Andy Warhol Museum.* New York: Distributed Art Publishers.

1995 Michael Lüthy, *Andy Warhol: Thirty Are Better Than One.* Frankfurt a. M.: Insel Verlag.

Lynne Tillman, Stephen Shore, *The Velvet Years: Warhol's Factory 1965-67.* London: Pavilion Books.

1996 Heiner Bastian, *Andy Warhol: Frühe Zeichnungen. Sammlung Marx. Hamburger Bahnhof, Museum für Gegenwart, Berlin.* Munich: Schirmer / Mosel.

1997 Philippe Trétiack, *Warhol's America.* London: Thames & Hudson.

Frayda Feldman, Jörg Schellmann, Claudia Defendi, *Andy Warhol Prints: A Catalogue Raisonné. 1962-1987.* 3rd revised ed., New York: Ronald Feldmann Fine Arts et al. [1st ed., Frayda Feldman, Jörg Schellmann, 1985].

Matthew Slotover (ed.), *All Tomorrow's Parties. Billy Name's Photographs of Andy Warhol's Factory.* London: frieze.

1998 Jane Dagget Dillenberger, *The Religious Art of Andy Warhol.* New York: Continuum.

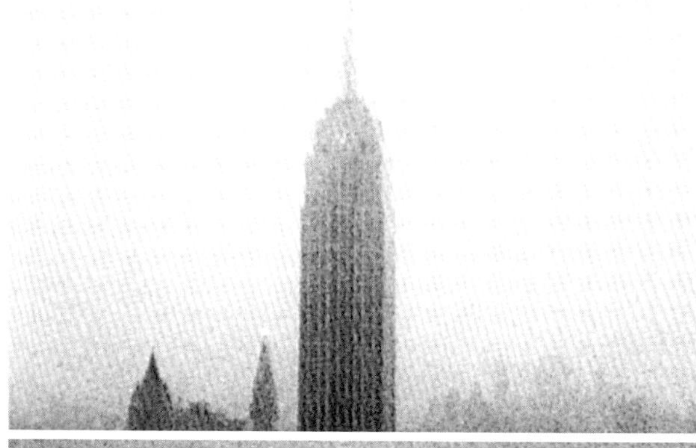
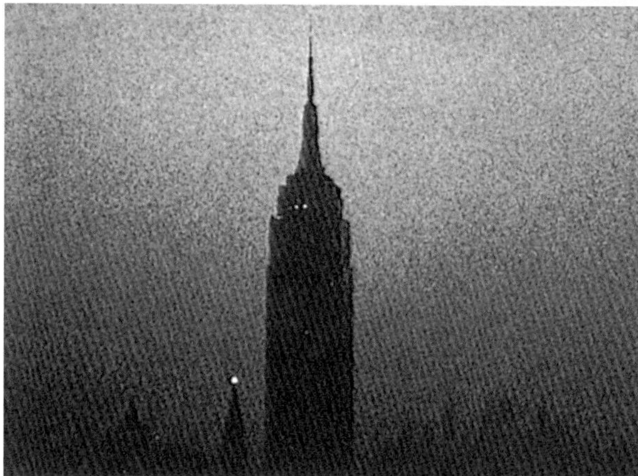
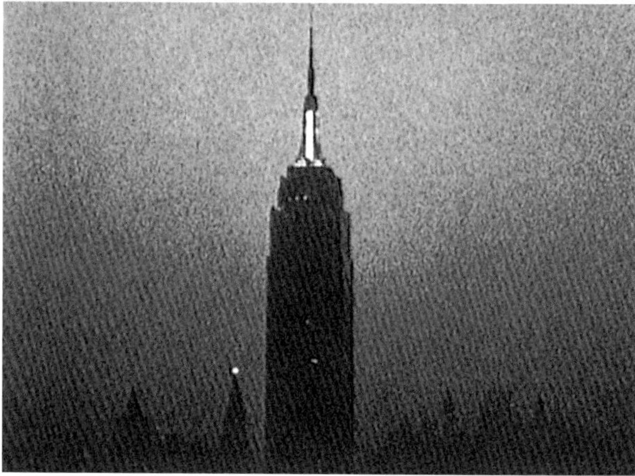
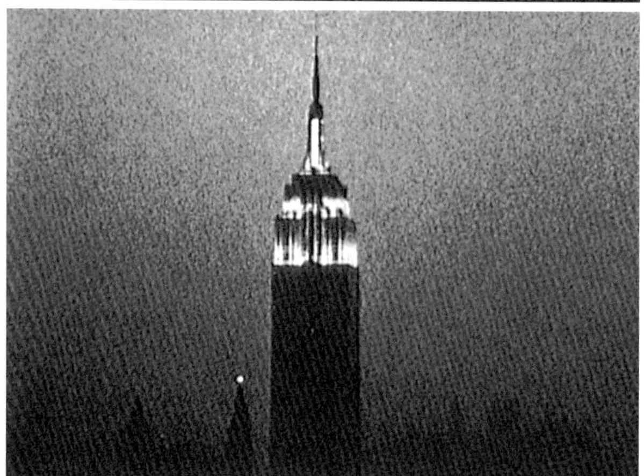
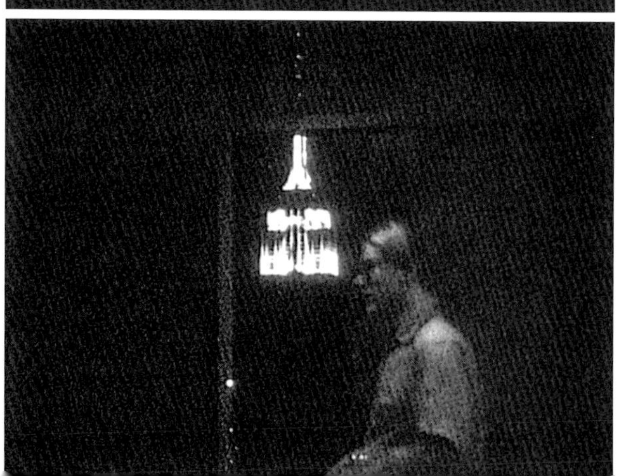

Frames from Andy Warhol's film "Empire", 1964 ▸

PHOTOGRAPH CREDITS

Jan Abbot, courtesy Dia Center for the Arts, New York: p. 303 centre right;
Courtesy Albright-Knox Art Gallery, Buffalo, New York: p. 131;
Courtesy Thomas Ammann Fine Art, Zurich: pp. 145, 168, 250 top left;
The Archives of The Andy Warhol Museum, Pittsburgh, Founding Collection, Contribution The Andy Warhol Foundation for the Visual Arts, Inc.: pp. 39, 176, 232/233 top, 287, 288 top, bottom, 289 top, bottom, 290 bottom, 291 centre and bottom, 293 centre, 294 centre, bottom, 296 top, bottom, 297 centre, 304 bottom, (Richard Stoner: pp. 170, 290 top, 291 centre, 293 top, 294 top, 301 bottom), (Robert Ruschak: pp. 191, 286, 293 bottom), (Courtesy of Leila Davies Singeles: pp. 290 top, 291 centre);
Courtesy The Andy Warhol Museum, Pittsburgh, Founding Collection, Contribution The Andy Warhol Foundation for the Visual Arts, Inc.: pp. 61, 62 left, 66, 67, 93, 138, 178, 201, 210, 216, 246 top, 249 top, 270, 274 left, 278, (Richard Stoner: pp. 105, 114 top, 174/175, 241, 246 top, 248 top), (Kevin Ryan: p. 97);
Richard Avedon, Courtesy F. C. Gundlach, Hamburg: p. 302 top;
Céline Bastian, Berlin: p. 305 top right;
Heiner Bastian, Berlin: p. 304 top;
Courtesy Bayerische Staatsgemäldesammlungen, Munich: p. 275;
Cecil Beaton, Courtesy of Sotheby's, London: p. 301 top;
Irving Blum, Los Angeles: pp. 125, 154, 158;
Courtesy The Brant Foundation, Greenwich, CT: pp. 71, 85 left, 89, 103, 121, 130 bottom, 134, 141 left, 144, 149, 151, 152 bottom, 183, 195, 204, 205, 209, 212, 223, 225, 236, 266 bottom, 282/283;
Courtesy Leo Castelli Gallery, New York: pp. 231, 233 bottom;
Martin Bühler, Basel: p. 128 bottom;
Courtesy Carnegie Museum of Art, Pittsburgh: p. 65;
Geoffrey Clements, Courtesy Whitney Museum of American Art, New York: p. 232 bottom;
Courtesy Rainer Crone, Berlin: pp. 95, 203;
D. James Dee, New York: pp. 213, 249 bottom;
Courtesy Daros Collection, Zurich: pp. 119, 132, 137, 148, 153, 193, 194 left, 198;
Courtesy Anthony d'Offay Gallery, London: pp. 219, 242-245, 267, 305 bottom;
Courtesy Aaron I. Fleischman: p. 214 bottom;
Courtesy Collection Froehlich, Stuttgart: pp. 84 right, 85 right, 140, 152 top, 206, 211, 237, 240, 248 bottom, 277;
Courtesy Galerie Bruno Bischofberger, Zurich: pp. 102, 104, 182, 260/261, 263, 269;
Courtesy Galerie Thaddaeus Ropac, Salzburg: p. 274 right;
Courtesy Art Gallery of Ontario, Toronto: pp. 160/161;
Anne Gold, Aachen: pp. 99, 250 bottom right;
Paula Goldman: p. 113;
David Hamilton: p. 303 centre left;
Robert Häusser, Mannheim: p. 200;
David Heald: pp. 109, 111, 246 bottom;
Paul Hester (painting facsimiles), Courtesy Dia Art Foundation, New York: p. 49;
Hickey-Robertson, Houston: pp. 107, 250 top right;
Ruth Kaiser, Viersen: p. 199;
Courtesy Kaiser Wilhelm Museum Krefeld: p. 192;
Courtesy James Kelly Contemporary, Inc., Santa Fe, New Mexico: p. 279;
Courtesy Collection Ethel and Leonard Kessler: p. 62 right;
Walter Klein, Düsseldorf: p. 165;
Courtesy Collection Uli Knecht, Stuttgart: p. 141 right;
Kunstsammlung Nordrhein-Westfalen, Düsseldorf: p. 165;
Jochen Littkemann, Berlin: pp. 63, 64, 68-70, 72-83, 84 left, 86-88, 90, 91, 96, 101, 110, 112 bottom, 118, 135, 155, 157, 159, 166; 177, 179, 181, 187, 189, 207, 228, 229, 235, 239, 250 bottom left, 251-255, 258, 259, 261 top, 262, 265, 266 top, 268, 276, 281;
Courtesy Fondation H. Looser, Zurich: p. 238;
Courtesy Louisiana Museum of Modern Art, Humlebæk: p. 115;
Horst Luedeking, Berlin: p. 305 top left;
©Christopher Makos: p. 302 bottom;
©Fred W. McDarrah, New York: p. 218;
Robert Mckeever: p. 129;
©2002 The Metropolitan Museum of Art, New York, all rights reserved: p. 100;
Duane Michals, Courtesy Pace/MacGill Gallery, New York: p. 292 top and bottom;
Courtesy Mitchell-Innes & Nash, New York: p. 114 bottom;
©2002 Museum Associates, Los Angeles County Museum of Art, all rights reserved: p. 169;
Courtesy Museum of Contemporary Art, San Diego: p. 226;
©2002 Museum of Fine Arts, Boston, all rights reserved: pp. 184/185;
©2002 The Museum of Modern Art, New York, all rights reserved: pp. 108, 126/127, 133, 172/173;
Billy Name / SLP Stock, New York: pp. 2, 12, 46, 59, 222, 227, 230, 295, 297 top, 298 centre left and right, 299, 300;
Courtesy The Nelson-Atkins Museum of Art, Kansas City, MO: p. 146;
Courtesy Neue Nationalgalerie, Berlin: p. 214 top;
Courtesy Norton Simon Museum, Pasadena, CA: p. 221;
Courtesy Öffentliche Kunstsammlung Basel, Kupferstichkabinett: p. 116;
Douglas M. Parker Studio: p. 196 right;
Courtesy Sylvio Perlstein, Antwerp: p. 217;
Eric Pollitzer: p. 190;
©Rheinisches Bildarchiv, Cologne: pp. 117, 147, 163, 197;
Paul Rocheleau: p. 284;
Friedrich Rosenstiel: p. 120;
Kevin Ryan, Courtesy Gagosian Gallery, New York: pp. 271, 272, 273;
Courtesy Collection Gunter Sachs, Pully: p. 98;
Axel Schneider, Frankfurt/Main: pp. 139, 171;
Lothar Schnepf, Cologne: p. 264;
Courtesy Schroeder Collection, London: p. 247 bottom;
©Stephen Shore, Tivoli, NY: pp. 297 bottom, 301 centre left, 302 centre;
©Harry Shunk, Courtesy The Andy Warhol Museum, Pittsburgh: p. 301 centre right;
Uwe H. Seyl, Stuttgart: pp. 156, 186;
Courtesy Sonnabend Collection, New York: pp. 128 top, 130 top, 136, 202, 247 top;
Courtesy Staatsgalerie Stuttgart: p. 106;
Courtesy Stedelijk Museum, Amsterdam: pp. 167, 224;
Courtesy The Tate Modern, London: pp. 142/143;
James Trainor, New York: p. 303 top;
Elke Walford, Courtesy F.C. Gundlach, Hamburg: p. 303 bottom;
Courtesy Westdeutsche Spielbanken, Münster: p. 215;
Courtesy Thea Westreich Art Advisory Services: pp. 256/257.